Adam Sposato
A Grammar of Xong

Mouton Grammar Library

Edited by
Georg Bossong
Bernard Comrie
Patience L. Epps
Irina Nikolaeva

Volume 84

Adam Sposato

A Grammar of Xong

DE GRUYTER
MOUTON

ISBN 978-3-11-108762-7
ISSN 0933-7636

Library of Congress Control Number: 2020942948

Bibliographic information published by the Deutsche Nationalbibliothek
The Deutsche Nationalbibliothek lists this publication in the Deutsche Nationalbibliografie; detailed bibliographic data are available on the Internet at http://dnb.dnb.de.

© 2022 Walter de Gruyter GmbH, Berlin/Boston
This volume is text- and page-identical with the hardback published in 2021.
Typesetting: Integra Software Services Pvt. Ltd.
Printing and binding: CPI books GmbH, Leck

www.degruyter.com

Acknowledgments

This grammar began its existence as my doctoral dissertation, and so the fieldwork necessary to complete it was partially funded by a Doctoral Dissertation Research Improvement Grant from the National Science Foundation (award number BCS-1251564), by a Dissertation Fellowship from the College of Arts and Sciences at the University at Buffalo, and by Summer Research Funds from the Linguistics Department at the University at Buffalo. I thank each of these organizations for their assistance.

The description of Xong contained in this grammar would have been entirely impossible without the help of my Xong-speaking consultants, especially Mrs. Chenghua Long, Mrs. Haili Shi, Mr. Xingyu Shi, Mrs. Lijun Wu, Mrs. Shixiang Wu, and Mrs. Xiaohui Wu. This is particularly true for Mrs. Chenghua Long, Mrs. Haili Shi, and Mrs. Shixiang Wu, who endured the lion's share of my questions and elicitation requests while I was in the field. One of the most rewarding aspects of my fieldwork was watching Chenghua, Haili, and Shixiang develop not only as linguistic consultants but also as properly inquisitive linguists in their own right. I wish all of my consultants and their families nothing but the best in the future.

I would also like to thank Mrs. Yan Long and her husband, Mr. Haixing Shi, for taking me into their home and allowing me to experience Miao hospitality firsthand. I am grateful to Mrs. Long's mother, Mrs. Qiumei Wu, and to Mr. Shi's father, Mr. Deshan Shi, for their unfailing kindness. I am equally grateful to Yan and Haixing's daughter and son, Jing Shi and Bo Shi, and to Mrs. Chenghua Long's daughter, Ziyu Long, for providing brief moments of cheer during many otherwise dreary days. I received much valuable advice from Mr. Hemin Long, the chief of Yankan Village and a good friend. Finally, I owe a very great debt to Mrs. Tingting Fan and Mr. Linwei Hu, two fellow outsiders who well understood the challenges and frustrations that come with spending months living and working alone in La'ershan.

All three members of my advising committee – Drs. Jeff Good, Matthew Dryer, and Tsan Huang – have had a profound influence on my development as a linguist. After learning so much from these scholars and friends over so many years, any expression of gratitude here would seem trite at best, and so I can only hope that this grammar itself can in some small measure stand in as a token of my respect and appreciation for them. This is especially true for Dr. Huang, who is deeply missed. I will be forever grateful to Drs. Nerida Jarkey, Yunbing Li, Martha Ratliff, Defu Shi, Yoshihisa Taguchi, and Zaibiao Yang for everything they have taught me about the Miao-Yao family and its many fascinating member languages. Dr. Bernard Comrie deserves an equal measure of my thanks, since without his generous and very timely editorial assistance this description would never have made the transition from dissertation to proper book. Drs. Jesse Lovegren, Hiroto Uchihara, Jenny Wilson, and my other fellow doctoral students may have had minimal direct influence on this grammar, but I still look back fondly on the time we were able to spend together. Finally, my parents, Dr. and Mrs. Mark and Kathleen Sposato, provided me with a great deal of emotional (and no small amount of financial) support throughout my graduate career, although I like to think they already realize how grateful I am.

I thank my wife, Mrs. Xueqing Zhao, for absolutely everything.

Table of contents

List of figures

List of tables

List of glossing abbreviations

???	unidentified morpheme
1PL	the first-person plural pronoun *boub* (see Section 7.1.1)
1SG	the first-person singular pronoun *wel* (see Section 7.1.1)
2PL	the second-person plural pronoun *manx* (see Section 7.1.1)
2SG	the second-person singular pronoun *monx/mx* (see Section 7.1.1)
3	the third-person pronoun *beul* (see Section 7.1.1)
3PL	the third-person plural pronoun *miant* (see Section 7.1.1)
ABIL	the abilitative marker *niaons* (see Section 12.3.3)
AN	the "animal" nominal prefix *daob-* (see Section 5.4.2.2)
ASSOC	the associative marker *naond* (see Section 9.2.3.2)
AT	the locative morpheme *manx* (see Section 5.5.2.8)
AUG	the augmentative nominal prefix *minl-* (see Section 5.4.2.4)
BCKG	the particle *meh* (see Section 9.2.1.2)
BUG	the "bug" nominal prefix *baod-* (see Section 5.4.2.6)
CLF	the most semantically general classifier *leb* (see Section 6.1.4.1)
CLF:PL	the classifier *hant*, meaning roughly 'some' or 'a few' (see Section 6.1.4.1)
CLF:X	classifier for 'X' (so 'CLF:person' means 'classifier for people') (see Section 6.1)
COP	the copular verb *nins*
COUT	the ideophone root *-cout* (see Section 11.1.2)
DAOD	the syllable *-daod* in the [VERB-*lib*-VERB-*daod*] construction (see Section 10.5.3)
DID	the verbal prefix *(d)id-* (see Sections 10.5.1 and 10.5.2)
DIM	the diminutive marker/quantifier *deb* (see Sections 5.4.2.3, 6.1.3.4, and 9.2.3.3)
$DSMY_1$	the "dismay" interjection *ih* (see Section 11.3.4)
$DSMY_2$	the "dismay" interjection *aos.il* (see Section 11.3.4)
DU	the dual suffix *-leb* (see Section 7.1.2.1)
EMPH	the emphatic particle *ih* (see Section 9.2.1.3)
FAM	the familiar "quasi-prefix" *leud-/lod-* (see Section 5.4.2.10)
FM	the female nominal prefix *nek-* (see Section 5.4.2.8)
FRT	the "fruit" nominal prefix *bid-* (see Section 5.4.2.5)
IDEO	the second syllable of a template C ideophone (see Section 11.1.2)
IDEO:X:Y	ideophone in template 'X' whose root means 'Y' (see Section 11.1)
INTJ	infrequent interjection or interjection with unclear meaning (see Section 11.3)
KIN	the kinship "quasi-prefix" *aod-* (see Section 5.4.2.10)
LEH	the particle *leh* (see Section 9.2.1.1)
LIB	the syllable *-lib-*, which occurs in certain morphologically complex verbal constructions (see Sections 10.5.2 and 10.5.3)
LOC	the locative nominal prefix *dib-/ib-/jeub-/jil-* (see Section 5.4.2.9)
ML	the male nominal prefix *baod-* (see Section 5.4.2.7)
NEG_1	the negative marker *(j)ix* (see Section 9.2.2.1)
NEG_2	the negative marker *jud* (see Section 9.2.2.2)
NEG.IMP	the negative imperative marker *ghad(.maons)/ghaod(.maons)* (see Section 9.3.1)
NEX	the "semi-pronominal" form *nex/ninx* (see Section 7.1.4)

NOM	the most semantically general nominal prefix *ghaob-/ob-/aob-* (see Section 5.4.2.1)
ONOM:X	onomatopoeic form referring to a sound like 'X' (see Section 11.2)
ORD	the ordinal prefix *dib-* (see Section 6.2.3)
or.INT	the interrogative disjunctive marker *haf.shib/hes.shib/hel.shib* (see Section 12.6.4)
or.STND	the standard disjunctive marker *huel.zex* (see Section 12.6.4)
PART	infrequent particle or particle with unclear meaning (see Section 9.2.1)
PL	the plural suffix *-god/-gud* (see Section 7.1.2.1)
PN	personal name (see Section 4.4.3)
PRF	the perfect-marking particle *lah* (see Section 9.2.1.4)
QP.NTRL	the neutral question particle *yoh/yah* (see Section 9.3.2.3)
QUOT	the complementation marker *deux* (see Section 12.4.3)
RED	reduplicated (usually nominal) morpheme (see Section 5.6)
REFL	the reflexive morpheme *daut/dauk* (see Section 7.1.3)
REL	the relative clause marker *manx* (see Section 8.1.4)
SAT	the quantifier/intensifier *(s)at* (see Section 9.2.3.1)
SIMUL	the simultaneous action markers *biank* and *deit* (see Section 12.6.1)
SPRS	the "surprise" interjection *it* (see Section 11.3.3)

1 Introduction

This work is a descriptive grammar of Xong (ISO 639-3 code *mmr*), a language belonging to the Miao branch of the Miao-Yao (or Hmong-Mien) family. Xong (or, segmentally, /ɕõ/) is spoken by approximately 900,000 people, with the vast majority of these speakers living in mountainous parts of western Hunan Province and eastern Guizhou Province in south-central China. In particular, this grammar concentrates on several fully mutually intelligible Xong varieties spoken in Fenghuang County, located in the far west of Hunan Province. In producing this grammar, the author primarily relied on the fieldwork data he collected over a period of ten (non-consecutive) months in Fenghuang County, although in the following chapters reference is also made to many of the previously published Chinese-language descriptions of Xong. To the best of the author's knowledge, this work is the first full-length English-language grammar of any Miao language, and it is only the second such grammar of any Miao-Yao language (with the first being Court's 1985 grammar of the Yao language Iu Mien).

The remainder of this chapter is divided into four sections. The first of these presents a brief phonological and grammatical overview of the Xong language as a whole, while the second discusses certain aspects of the language which may be of particular theoretical interest. The third section then describes the author's collected Xong corpus and the texts that it contains. Finally, the fourth section discusses some potentially fruitful avenues for future research on Xong.

1.1 Language overview

In gross phonological and grammatical terms Xong is a fairly typical member of the Miao-Yao family, in that it is a highly isolating, highly tonal language with a simple syllable structure, a large consonant inventory, a robust system of classifiers, several high-frequency nominal prefixes, predominantly SVO constituent order, and extensive multiverbal constructions. This section presents a very basic overview of some of the most salient phonological and grammatical properties of the language, though naturally each of the properties discussed below is covered much more thoroughly in subsequent chapters of this grammar.

Phonologically, Xong is characterized by a very large consonant inventory, a fairly large vowel inventory, pervasive syllable-level tones, and very strict restrictions on syllable structure. Most varieties of Fenghuang Xong arguably have 65 consonants (though see Sections 1.2.1 and 3.7 for some caveats), the most typologically unusual of which are perhaps their breathy nasals (/m^{ɦ}/ and /n^{ɦ}/, discussed in Section 3.2.2.2) and breathy laterals (/l^{ɦ}/ and /lj^{ɦ}/, discussed in Section 3.2.3). They also feature seven oral monophthongal vowels, four nasal monophthongal vowels, and four diphthongal vowels, one of which is nasalized (see Section 3.3). With the exception of a few toneless forms (Section 3.6), every monosyllabic Fenghuang Xong form produced in isolation will bear one of eight lexically specified tones, and phonologically triggered tone sandhi is not uncommon (Section 3.5). Like many tone languages, Xong appears to feature an additional phrase-level intonational system (Section 3.6) superimposed upon its tone system, though much more research will be needed before this intonational system can be described in any detail. Finally, the only allowable syllable structure in Xong is (C)V^{T}, with each syllable consisting of an optional initial consonant, an obligatory vowel (or, in a handful of cases, a syllabic bilabial nasal; see Section 3.3.4), and an obligatory tone (though, again, a few toneless forms do occur).

Xong is overall a highly isolating language, in the sense that most morphemes display a high degree of combinatorial freedom and the boundaries between adjacent morphemes are easily identified (incidentally, the vast majority of Xong morphemes are monosyllabic). The only morphological processes that play any significant role in Xong grammar are compounding (see, e.g., Section 5.3), reduplication (see Sections 5.6, 6.1.3.2, and 10.5.4), and some degree of affixation, especially prefixation (see Sections 5.4 and 10.5.1). Ideophones (Section 11.1) could be argued to display some degree of nonconcatenative morphology, but they are much fewer in number than Xong's other major lexical categories (i.e. nouns, classifiers, and verbs) and occur much less frequently in naturalistic speech.

Ignoring relative clauses for the moment (see further below in this section), a maximal Xong noun phrase will have the following basic structure:

[POSSESSOR NUMERAL-CLASSIFIER NOUN DEMONSTRATIVE]

Examples of Xong noun phrases displaying the full structure shown in the schema above are given in (1.1) and (1.2) below.

(1.1) [*boub naond*] [*aod-ndaut*] [*aub*] [*neind*]
[1PL ASSOC]$_{\text{POSS}}$ [one-CLF:river]$_{\text{NUM-CLF}}$ [water]$_{\text{NOUN}}$ [this]$_{\text{DEM}}$
'this river of ours' (Qiusheng Long, in *Ngel.kanx*)

(1.2) [*manx*] [*oub-zheinb*] [*beub*] [*dox*]
[2PL]$_{\text{POSS}}$ [two-CLF:tool]$_{\text{NUM-CLF}}$ [quilt]$_{\text{NOUN}}$ [that]$_{\text{DEM}}$
'those two quilts of yours (pl.)' (Shixiang Wu, fieldnotes)

A possessor (see Section 8.2) may – but need not – occur with an overt possessive marker, but in either case it will invariably occur in noun-phrase–initial position. Many noun phrases will also contain either a numeral-classifier phrase, which consists of a numeral and a following classifier, or a bare classifier, which occurs without a preceding numeral (see Chapter 6 for information on classifiers, numerals, and numeral-classifier phrases). These constituents will occur following the noun phrase's possessor. If the noun phrase contains a noun (Chapter 5), that noun will occur after the noun phrase's numeral-classifier phrase or bare classifier. Nouns in Xong can be monomorphemic forms, but the language also features several types of noun compound (Section 5.3) and a number of nominal prefixes (Section 5.4). The set of demonstratives (Section 7.2) is fairly small, and such forms always occur noun-phrase–finally. Xong also has a wide variety of distinct relative clause constructions (Section 8.1) that can occur in a number of positions relative to their head noun, although due to these various positioning possibilities such constructions are not represented in the schema above. Note that all of the noun-phrase–internal constituents mentioned so far are optional in any given noun phrase, and furthermore any of them can constitute an independent noun phrase in its own right.

Three other types of noun-phrase–internal constituents are not represented in the schema above but still deserve some mention here. The first of these are locative nouns, which are a closed subset of nouns that serve to express various spatial concepts like 'inside', 'edge', 'top', and 'right (side)' (see Section 5.5). The second are pronouns, which are another closed subset of nouns with inherently deictic reference, such as *wel* '1SG' or *manx* '2PL' (Section 7.1). Xong pronouns are much more similar to Sinitic pronouns than to those of certain major Southeast Asian languages (e.g. Lao or Vietnamese) in that they are relatively few in number and make few if any distinctions in terms of formality or politeness. The third and final type are ignoratives, which are forms that can serve as either interrogative or indefinite pro-forms depending on the discourse context (Section 7.3).

Aside from verbs (see further below in this section), the most important constituents of Xong clauses are arguments, grammatical operators, and clause-final forms.[1] Any given argument in a univerbal clause will occur in one of five grammaticalized syntactic roles: (i) SUBJECT (representing the sole argument of a semantically intransitive verb), (ii) AGENT (representing the more agent-like argument of a semantically transitive verb or the most agent-like argument of a semantically ditransitive verb), (iii) PATIENT (representing the more patient-like argument of a semantically transitive verb), (iv) RECIPIENT (representing the most recipient-like argument of a semantically ditransitive verb), or (v) THEME (representing the most theme-like argument of a semantically ditransitive verb). In a pragmatically neutral univerbal clause, a SUBJECT can occur on either side of its verb, an AGENT will occur in preverbal position, and PATIENTS, RECIPIENTS, and THEMES will all occur in postverbal position, with the RECIPIENT preceding the THEME when the two co-occur in a single clause. See Section 9.1.1 for further discussion of each of these grammaticalized syntactic roles as well as of semantically intransitive, transitive, and ditransitive verbs.

1 Note that the description in this section is restricted to major constituents of Xong clauses, and so it does not discuss certain minor clausal constituent types like temporal phrases or degree markers.

Grammatical operators occur in immediate preverbal position. High-frequency examples of such forms include negative markers (see Section 9.2.2), certain quantifiers (Section 9.2.3.1), and a variety of forms with temporal meanings like 'then', 'still', 'not until, only then', 'also', or 'again' (see the introduction to Section 9.2). Multiple grammatical operators can and often do co-occur within a single clause. Clause-final forms include particles (Section 9.2.1), which are toneless, and a handful of other non-particle, tone-bearing forms (Section 9.3.2.3). Both particles and non-particle clause-final forms tend to express relatively abstract grammatical or discourse-pragmatic notions. Unlike grammatical operators, it appears that only a single clause-final form can occur in any given clause.

Taking all of the above into account, Xong's basic clausal structure can be represented with the three schemas given in (1.3), (1.6), and (1.8) below. In particular, the schema in (1.3) represents a clause featuring a semantically intransitive verb and its single argument, the one in (1.6) represents a clause featuring a semantically transitive verb and its two arguments, and the one in (1.8) represents a clause featuring a semantically ditransitive verb and its three arguments. The Xong sentences in (1.4), (1.5), (1.7), and (1.9) then each provide a representative example of the preceding clause type, with (1.4) and (1.5) showing two equally acceptable orders for a single clause. Note that in these examples each argument has been enclosed within brackets and marked with a following subscript letter indicating its syntactic role (<$_{S}$> for SUBJECT, <$_{A}$> for AGENT, etc.). Each grammatical operator and clause-final form has also been enclosed within brackets; in addition, each grammatical operator has been marked with a following subscript <$_{GO}$> and each clause-final form has been marked with a following subscript <$_{CFF}$>. Finally, each clause's verb has been bolded.

(1.3) SUBJECT GO VERB CFF /
GO VERB SUBJECT CFF (two possible orders)

(1.4) [*Aub*] ***xub*** [*lah*].
[water]$_{S}$ **small** [PRF]$_{CFF}$
'The water pressure's dropped.' (Qiumei Wu, fieldnotes)

(1.5) ***Xub*** [*aub*] [*lah*].
small [water]$_{S}$ [PRF]$_{CFF}$
'The water pressure's dropped.' (Qiumei Wu, fieldnotes) (same as (1.4) above)

(1.6) AGENT GO VERB PATIENT CFF

(1.7) [*Oub-meinl*] [*doub*] ***ndax*** [*beul*]...
[two-CLF:person]$_{A}$ [then$_{1}$]$_{GO}$ **lift.up** [3]$_{P}$
'The two of them lifted (the cage) up...' (Xingyu Shi, in *Oub Meinl Yaos Geud*)

(1.8) AGENT GO VERB RECIPIENT THEME CFF

(1.9) *Nieux-hnef* [*wel*] [*chad*] ***beb*** [*monx*] [*oub-shauk*]
yester-CLF:day [1SG]$_{A}$ [not.until]$_{GO}$ **share** [2SG]$_{R}$ [two-CLF:yuan]$_{T}$
[*ih*]*!*
[EMPH]$_{CFF}$
'I just gave you two *yuan* (unit of currency) yesterday!' (Haili Shi, fieldnotes)

It is important to note that the schemas given in (1.3), (1.6), and (1.8) above only represent pragmatically neutral, univerbal clauses in which all arguments are overtly expressed, although clauses of this sort are in fact quite uncommon in naturalistic Xong speech. See Section 9.2.2 for information on argument ellipsis, Sections 9.2.3 and 9.4 for information on less pragmatically neutral clauses, and Chapter 12 for information on multiverbal constructions.

Verbs in Xong (see Chapter 10) are never marked for any grammatical categories like tense, aspect, mode, person, number, or finiteness, although they often occur with a prefix *(d)id-* 'DID' that can serve as a purposive marker, durative marker, or reciprocal marker depending on context (Section 10.5.1). Xong does not possess a distinct lexical category of "adjectives"; instead, property-denoting forms (i.e. semantic adjectives) are fully canonical members of the verb class (Section 10.3). Verbs can co-occur with ideophones (Section 11.1), which convey a wide variety of adverbial notions and display a number of unusual phonological (and, arguably, morphological) properties. However, as was noted earlier in this section, ideophones occur only very infrequently in naturalistic Xong speech.

Finally, multiverbal constructions (again, see Chapter 12) are extremely common, carry a very high functional load, and display a great deal of structural variety in Xong. Examples of such constructions are given in (1.10) and (1.11) below, where each constituent verb has been bolded.

(1.10) *Aod-ngonl* *naus* ***beux*** ***daos*** ***geud*** ***giab*** ***nonx.***
one-CLF:animate bird **hit** **die** **hold** **stir.fry** **eat**
'(I) killed the bird and cooked it (to eat).' (Xingyu Shi, in *Oub Meinl Yaos Geud*)

(1.11) *Beul* *dad.kit* ***monl*** ***ncot*** ***nqif*** ***meb*** ***shok***
3 not.until **go** **wash.clothing** **clean** **take** **dry.in.sun**
zhel.
sun
'She took (the shoes), washed (them) clean, and put (them outside) to dry in the sun.' (Xingyu Shi, in *Oub Meinl Yaos Geud*)

1.2 Some issues of potential theoretical interest

1.2.1 Xong's consonant inventory and syllable structure

By crosslinguistic standards (see, e.g., Maddieson 2013a), all varieties of Fenghuang Xong with which the author is familiar have very large consonant inventories.[2] For instance, the variety of Xong spoken in Yankan Village arguably has 65 consonants (see Section 3.2), and other varieties spoken by the author's primary consultants have similarly large inventories. These counts are not very different from those that have been reported for other varieties of Xong spoken outside of Fenghuang County: Jiwei Xong is reported to have 67 consonants (Xiang 1999: 7), Daxing Xong is also reported to have 67 consonants (Chen 2009: 8), and Aizhai Xong is reported to have 59 consonants (Yu 2011: 20). These large consonant inventories are especially noteworthy given the recent attention devoted to phoneme inventory size in the linguistic literature (see Hay and Bauer 2007, Atkinson 2011, and Trudgill 2011, among many others). Note, though, that these consonant inventories are in fact only slightly larger than average for the Miao-Yao family (Niederer 1998: 210, 211).

However, all of the consonant counts mentioned so far assume a simple (C)V segmental syllable structure, one in which palatalized consonants (e.g. /pj/ or /tj/) and labialized consonants (e.g. /qw/ or /ŋw/) are considered unitary phonemes rather than /Cj/ or /Cw/ clusters. If palatalized and labialized consonants were analyzed as polyphonemic clusters rather than as unitary phonemes, the consonant inventory of (for instance) Yankan Xong would drop from 65 to 44 (which would admittedly still be quite large by crosslinguistic standards), and the consonant inventories of other varieties of Fenghuang Xong would undergo similar reductions. Analyzing affricate consonants (e.g. /ts/ or /tɕ/) as stop–fricative clusters rather than as unitary phonemes would reduce the size of the consonant inventories in question even further, as would analyzing prenasalized consonants (e.g. /^{n}p/ or /^{n}q/) as nasal–plosive clusters. Thus, different analyses of Xong's segmental syllable structure have major consequences for the overall size of Xong's consonant inventory.

As is discussed in much more detail in Section 3.7, though, there does not appear to be any compelling evidence one way or the other. The paucity of obvious (segmental) phonological and morphophonological processes in Xong means that the choice among these analyses is a rather arbitrary one. The author would argue that analyzing

2 All varieties of Fenghuang Xong with which the author is familiar also have relatively large vowel and tone inventories. Yankan Xong, for example, has fifteen vowels and eight tones. However, this Section 1.2.1 focuses solely on consonants for two reasons. First, while the vowel and tone inventories of the varieties in question are indeed rather large by crosslinguistic standards, they are not quite as strikingly large as their consonant inventories. Second, the size of Xong's consonant inventory varies depending on the particular phonological analysis adopted, as is discussed further below in this section. This is not true for Xong's vowel and tone inventories, which are much more straightforward.

Xong's segmental syllable structure as (C)V (as indeed is done in Chapter 3 of this grammar) is no more or less defensible than analyzing it as (C)(j/w)V, with palatalized and labialized consonants considered to be polyphonemic sequences, or even as (N)(C)(C)(j/w)V, with prenasalized consonants, affricate consonants, palatalized consonants, and labialized consonants all considered to be polyphonemic sequences. In truth, the author suspects that this may well be an artificial dilemma, one that arises from the fact that Western phonological theories tend to emphasize the consonant–vowel distinction. It may be that a more natural analysis would involve a division of Xong syllables not into consonants and vowels, but rather into "initials" (essentially onsets) and "finals" (essentially rhymes). This latter type of analysis is in fact standard practice for phonological studies of Miao-Yao languages done within the framework of traditional Chinese linguistic theory (see Section 2.5.1).

Finally, while the large consonant inventories of most Xong varieties are certainly crosslinguistically rare, it should be noted that most reconstructions of Proto-Miao-Yao involve very large consonant inventories themselves; see Purnell (1970: 168), Wang and Mao (1995: 41–54), and Ratliff (2010: 31, 32). Given what these Miao-Yao specialists have claimed about Proto-Miao-Yao, the author suspects that the appropriate question to ask is not why most Xong varieties have such large consonant inventories, but rather why certain other Miao-Yao varieties have such small ones.

1.2.2 The nature of Xong lexical categories

"Zero derivation" (i.e. the appearance of a form ostensibly belonging to one lexical category in a grammatical position or function more canonically associated with another lexical category without any overt marker of derivation) is quite common in Xong, to the point that it raises certain questions about the nature of lexical categories in the language. For instance, a great number of nouns have been attested serving as classifiers (e.g. *bioud* 'home; CLF:home', *ndeind* 'knife; CLF:knife', *zhet* 'bowl; CLF:bowl'; see Sections 6.1.1 and 6.1.4), as have a somewhat smaller number of verbs (e.g. *zhox* 'kick; CLF:kick', *giud* 'pinch; CLF:pinch', *qonf* 'shove; CLF:shove'; see Sections 6.1.1 and 6.1.4.9). In fact, the author suspects that any noun or verb could do so given an appropriate enough discourse context, though for some nouns and verbs, like *aub* 'water' or *daos* 'to die', it is difficult to imagine what an appropriate enough context might be. The author has also encountered a handful of forms which can serve equally readily as verbs or as nouns, including *ghot* 'old; old person', *mb* 'to hurt (intrans.), to be sick; illness', *nbut* 'to be named; name', *gied/giand* 'icy, to freeze; ice', and *ntiot* 'smoky; smoke'.

It may be that all of these facts are simply idiosyncratic ones, with little relevance for Xong grammar as a whole. However, it is also possible that they are in fact evidence that Xong lexical items (or at least certain Xong lexical items) are not inherently, or "underlyingly", specified for any lexical category, and that they are only assigned a category like "noun", "verb", or "classifier" when they appear in certain constructions. In other words, it may be that notions like "noun", "verb", and "classifier" can be more meaningfully defined in Xong as sets of syntactic positions that display similar properties than as sets of lexical items that display similar properties (of course, this would mean that, strictly speaking, notions like "noun", "verb", and "classifier" would not be *lexical* categories in Xong, since they would not be associated with particular sets of lexical items). Unfortunately, more detailed work on this topic will have to wait until a larger Xong corpus, with more relevant naturalistic examples, can be collected.

Finally, the reader may have noticed that this discussion has concerned itself solely with three of Xong's four major lexical categories, namely nouns (see Chapter 5), classifiers (Section 6.1), and verbs (Chapter 10). This is not accidental, as Xong's fourth major lexical category, ideophones (Section 11.1), displays essentially no overlap with any of the other three.

1.3 The author's Xong corpus

Xong is one of the most thoroughly described members of the Miao-Yao family, with many dozens of articles, several book-length studies, and even a handful of text collections already having been published on the language, nearly all of which have been written in Chinese (see Section 2.5 for an overview). Nevertheless, while reference is made to many of these previous publications in the following chapters, the author has relied solely on his own elicited Xong texts and example sentences for primary linguistic data. Most of these texts and example sentences were collected in the Xong-speaking town of La'ershan, located in Fenghuang County in the far west of China's Hunan Province (see Sections 2.6.2 and 2.7 for further information).

Many example sentences have been taken from two texts in particular, each of which has been included in its entirety at the end of this grammar. The first of these, *Oub Meinl Yaos Geud*, is a 25-minute folktale narrated by Mr. Xingyu Shi of Yankan Village. The story itself concerns a virtuous younger sister, her cruel older sister, and their interactions over the years. The second, *Tooth Conversation*, is a 6-minute, three-participant conversation among Mrs. Chenghua Long of Shanjiang Town, Mrs. Haili Shi of Yankan Village, and Mrs. Shixiang Wu of Zhuigaolai Village. The main topic of the conversation was Mrs. Shi's recent toothache.

The author's ten other recorded Xong texts have not been included in this grammar, but many other example sentences have still been taken from them. Each of these texts has been listed (in no particular order) and described below. For information about the authors of certain of these texts and their hometowns, see Sections 2.6.2 and 2.7.

1. *Qiusheng Long's Life History*, by Mr. Qiusheng Long of Yankan Village. This is a 16-minute autobiographical narrative, primarily focusing on Mr. Long's childhood. Mr. Long is quite elderly (though his exact age is unknown), and he is well known in La'ershan Town and nearby areas for his oratorical abilities in Xong.

2. *Ngel.kanx* ('Yankan'), by Mr. Qiusheng Long of Yankan Village. This is a 17-minute narrative by Mr. Long, primarily focusing on his hometown of Yankan (or, in Xong, *Ngel.kanx*) Village and the changes it has undergone over the course of his life.
3. *Conversation in La'ershan*, by Mrs. Chenghua Long, Mrs. Haili Shi, Mrs. Shixiang Wu, and Mrs. Xiaohui Wu. This is a four-participant conversation recorded in La'ershan Town. The conversation lasts 45 minutes, but the author has so far only glossed and translated perhaps a third of it. All four participants are primary school teachers in La'ershan Town, and all four have been close friends for many years. The conversation itself covers a variety of topics, but most of the example sentences in this grammar that were taken from it concern the recent death of the local school principal's mother.
4. *Conversation in Yankan*, by Mrs. Qiumei Wu of Shanjiang Town and another Xong-speaking woman of unknown background. This is a two-participant conversation recorded in Yankan Village, with the conversation itself encompassing a variety of topics related to daily life. The conversation lasts 60 minutes, but the author has so far only glossed and translated perhaps a quarter of it. Both speakers are quite elderly (though their exact ages are unknown), and they have been close friends for several decades.
5. *Xaub Honl Mob* ('Little Red Hat'), by Mrs. Haili Shi of Yankan Village. The title of this text is literally [little red hat], with all three of the title's morphemes being the Xong pronunciations of the equivalent Sinitic forms rather than "native" Xong forms. This is a 5-minute retelling of the Little Red Riding Hood folktale. Mrs. Shi was consulting a written Chinese-language version of the folktale while narrating the story to the author. This was hardly ideal practice, especially given the relatively high degree of typological similarity between the languages involved. Nevertheless, a comparison of the written Chinese-language version of the story used by Mrs. Shi and the Xong text that she produced herself clearly showed that Mrs. Shi was in fact retelling the story in Xong, not simply doing a morpheme-by-morpheme translation.
6. *Guef Waonl Hauk Nggaob* ('The King Takes His Medicine'), by Mrs. Haili Shi of Yankan Village. The title of this text is literally [country-king drink medicine], with the first two morphemes of the title being the Xong pronunciations of the equivalent Sinitic forms and the last two being more "native" Xong forms (though they may in fact simply be older, less transparent borrowings from Sinitic).[3] This is a 3-minute retelling of a Chinese-language folktale, one taken from the same

3 The reader will note that a hyphen appears in the morphemic analysis of the title of this text (i.e. [country-king drink medicine]), though it does not appear in the title itself (i.e. *Guef Waonl Hauk Nggaob*). The same is true of two other texts described in this section, namely *Deb Guk Ronf* and *Oub Leb Naob Geud*. Hyphens are used in the morphemic analyses of these texts' titles to indicate relatively "tight" grammatical bonds between adjacent morphemes, but they are not used in the titles themselves purely for aesthetic reasons.

collection of tales as the text *Xaub Honl Mob*. All of the comments above regarding the text *Xaub Honl Mob* apply to this text as well.

7. *Deb Guk Ronf* ('The Little Dragon-Frog'), by Mr. Xingyu Shi of Yankan Village. The title of this text is literally [DIM-frog-dragon], and the text itself is a 14-minute folktale about the adventures of a frog who can shapeshift into a human.
8. *Frog, Where Are You?*, by Mrs. Chenghua Long of Shanjiang Town. This is a 6-minute narration of the eponymous wordless picture book (Mayer 1981), which depicts a boy and his dog searching for the boy's lost pet frog.
9. *Pear Story*, by Mrs. Lijun Wu of Suode Village. This is a 3-minute narration of the events shown in the 6-minute silent film titled *The Pear Film*, developed by Wallace Chafe at the University of California, Berkeley, in 1975 (see Chafe 1980). As of the time of writing, the film could be downloaded for free at http://www.linguistics.ucsb.edu/faculty/chafe/pearfilm.htm.
10. *Oub Leb Naob Geud* ('The Two Brothers'), by Mrs. Chunman Tang of Songtao County in Guizhou Province. The title of this text is literally [two-CLF older.brother-younger.sibling], and the text itself is a 2-minute folktale about a misunderstanding between two brothers that results in the murder of the elder by the younger.

1.4 Directions for future research

While this description contains as much phonological and grammatical analysis of Xong as the author was able to perform in the time available to him, it is still far from complete. Any chapter in this grammar could be further expanded using additional fieldwork data, but it appears to the author that there are three aspects of Xong phonology and grammar which particularly merit further investigation.

First, Xong appears to possess at least two distinct suprasegmental systems: a syllable-level system of lexically specified tones, many of which involve distinctive phonation types in addition to distinctive pitch heights and contours (see Section 3.5), and a phrase-level system of intonation contours overlaid on those tones (Section 3.6). The author has investigated the former system in some depth for three of his primary consultants, but there appears to be a significant degree of tonal phonetic variation among Fenghuang Xong speakers. This is certainly worthy of further research, especially because this phonetic variation does not appear to hinder mutual intelligibility in any way. In addition, Xong's intonational system has barely been described at all, and any future description of this system itself or of its interactions with the language's tone system would be a significant contribution to the study of Xong phonology.

Second, this grammar primarily concentrates on the Xong variety spoken in Yankan Village when it comes to phonetics and phonology, with lesser attention paid to the sound systems of certain other Xong varieties spoken by some of the author's other primary consultants (see Chapter 3 in general, and Section 3.1 in particular). All of these varieties are spoken within Fenghuang County in Hunan Province (Section 2.7). However, there is a great deal of phonetic variation among Xong speakers in Fenghuang County (Section 3.8), especially when it comes to suprasegmental phenomena (Sections 3.5 and 3.6). There appears to be significantly less phonological variation among the Fenghuang Xong speakers with whom the author has worked, but this may simply be due to the fact that the author was primarily working with a relatively small number of consultants. Phonetic and phonological variation among mutually intelligible varieties of Xong (or, indeed, among mutually intelligible varieties of any Miao-Yao language spoken in China) appears to be underreported in most Chinese-language descriptions, but it would constitute an excellent topic for future research in the area.

Third, multiverbal constructions in Xong are extremely common, show a great deal of structural variety, and carry a very high functional load. The author's description of these constructions in Chapter 12 of this grammar is really just a sketch, one which merely attempts to give the reader some idea of the structural variety that they display and the grammatical and semantic functions that they serve. A comprehensive classification and description of Xong's multiverbal constructions would require a great deal more fieldwork, and it would likely double the overall length of this grammar. Still, in the author's opinion, no other grammatical phenomenon in Xong is currently in greater need of further investigation.

2 Background

2.1 Introduction

Since the topics covered in this chapter form less of a conceptually cohesive whole than is the case in subsequent chapters, a brief initial outline may be helpful here. The first section below, Section 2.2, discusses Xong in relation to the other languages of the Xiangxi Miao sub-branch of the Miao-Yao family. In addition to providing information on the speaker populations, geographic extents, internal subdivisions, and mutual intelligibility of the Xiangxi Miao languages (including Xong), this section also covers some important terminological issues.

Section 2.3 then presents a brief overview of the Miao-Yao family as a whole and discusses Xong's position within it, an issue on which there is still no widespread agreement. Section 2.4 examines Xong's status within China with respect to linguistic classification schemes, official recognition, and governmental policies. It also provides information on the "standard" Xong variety spoken in Jiwei Township, and it discusses the meaning of the Chinese linguistic terms *yuyan* and *fangyan*, an understanding of which is crucial for making sense of the vast Chinese literature on Xong and other Miao-Yao languages.[4]

Section 2.5 then reviews previous studies of Xong, nearly all of which have been published in Chinese, while Section 2.6 discusses the author's theoretical framework and research methodology. Finally, Section 2.7 presents a geographic, demographic, and sociolinguistic overview of Fenghuang County, from which all of the author's Xong-speaking consultants hail and in which all of the author's fieldsites are located. This final section also discusses precisely which Xong varieties are actually described in this grammar, as well as how applicable the phonological and grammatical claims made in the grammar are to other varieties of Xong.

2.2 The Xiangxi Miao languages

2.2.1 "Xong" vs. "Xiangxi Miao"

Although they have sometimes been conflated in the literature, the terms "Xong" and "Xiangxi Miao" are used to refer to different concepts in this grammar. The term "Xong" is used to refer to a set of very closely related Miao varieties spoken primarily

4 In this grammar, the written form of Modern Standard Chinese is simply referred to as "Chinese". Spoken Sinitic varieties are always referred to using more specific terms, such as "Standard Mandarin" for the official language of the PRC or "Fenghuang Chinese" for the Gan variety spoken in Fenghuang County.

in western Hunan and eastern Guizhou Provinces in southern China.[5] The collective ISO 639-3 code for these varieties is *mmr* (Eberhard et al. 2019), and they are collectively referred to as "Western Xiangxi Miao" (*Xiāngxī Miáoyǔ Xībù Cìfāngyán* 湘西苗语西部次方言) in Yang's 2004 survey of Xiangxi Miao. This means that the term "Xong" as used by this author and the term "Western Xiangxi Miao" as used by Yang are synonymous. In the interest of clarity, though, from this point on only the term "Xong" will be used in this grammar.

Yang (2004: 42) reports that all varieties of Xong are mostly mutually intelligible, although the author's own consultants and other Xong-speaking contacts have disputed this (see Section 2.2.2). Still, despite the fact that it may well contain several mutually unintelligible (or at best marginally mutually intelligible) speech varieties, Xong is referred to as a single "language" in this grammar. Regional subdivisions of Xong – for example, the Xong spoken in a particular village, or town, or county – are simply referred to as "varieties" regardless of their size.

"Xiangxi Miao", in contrast, refers to a larger set of Miao varieties, some of which are completely mutually unintelligible. It encompasses all of Xong along with three other Miao varieties that have much smaller speaker populations. These latter three varieties together constitute "Eastern Xiangxi Miao" (*Xiāngxī Miáoyǔ Dōngbù Cìfāngyán* 湘西苗语东部次方言), which is discussed in more detail in Section 2.2.4. Since Yang (2004: 42) and the author's own consultants all report that these three other varieties are largely or entirely mutually unintelligible with Xong (and Yang reports that they are almost entirely mutually unintelligible with each other as well), they are referred to as independent "languages" here.

The term "Xiangxi" (*Xiāngxī* 湘西) itself literally means "West Hunan" in Chinese, and indeed Xiangxi Miao has been referred to as "West Hunan Miao" in some English-language publications.[6] Chinese-language sources often use the term "Eastern Miao" (*Miáoyǔ Dōngbù Fāngyán* 苗语东部方言) to refer to Xiangxi Miao, but, confusingly, English-language sources use the term "Northern Miao" (or "Northern Hmongic") instead. For clarity's sake, neither "Eastern Miao" nor "Northern Miao" will be used in this grammar.

Figure 2.1 shows the basic classificatory scheme for Xiangxi Miao and its constituent varieties as presented in Yang (2004: 42). (For information on where Xiangxi Miao

5 The term "Xong" is simply the Latinized form of the Xong autonym /ɕõ1/. It is derived from the word *Xongb* used in the standard Xong orthography, minus the final tone letter *-b* (see Section 4.3.2). The Xong autonym is reported to be cognate with the autonyms used in a number of other Miao languages, including Hmu, Hmong, and Ahmao (Shi 2004; Ratliff 2010: 40). For discussion of alternate terms for the Xong language, see Section 2.2.3.

6 Note that the term "Xiangxi" is often used in isolation as a shorthand for the Xiangxi Tujia and Miao Autonomous Prefecture (*Xiāngxī Tǔjiāzú Miáozú Zìzhìzhōu* 湘西土家族苗族自治州), which is located in the far western part of Hunan Province along the border with Guizhou (see Figure 2.5 in Section 2.7.1 below) and in which a majority of China's Xiangxi Miao-speaking population is found.

1. Xong (i.e. Western Xiangxi Miao)
    1.1. *Tuyu* 1
    1.2. *Tuyu* 2
    1.3. *Tuyu* 3
2. Eastern Xiangxi Miao
    2.1. *Tuyu* 4 (i.e. Suang)
    2.2. *Tuyu* 5 (i.e. Seu)
    2.3. *Tuyu* 6 (i.e. San)

Figure 2.1: The internal structure of Xiangxi Miao according to Yang (2004).

fits into the Miao-Yao family as a whole, see Section 2.3.4.) Note that Yang divides Xong into three first-order subdivisions, and he uniformly uses the Chinese term *tuyu* (*tǔyǔ* 土语) to refer both to these three subdivisions (which he claims are mutually intelligible) and to the three Eastern Xiangxi Miao languages (which he claims are mutually unintelligible). The term *tuyu* has no exact equivalent in English, but it is perhaps closest in meaning to "variety" (see Section 2.4).

To the best of the author's knowledge, the following passage from Yang (2004) is the only published description of mutual intelligibility within Xiangxi Miao as a whole. It should be kept in mind, though, that the author's own Xong-speaking consultants have disagreed with Yang's judgment on certain points; see Section 2.2.2 for discussion.

> Impressionistically, there is rather less variation within Xong [than there is within Eastern Xiangxi Miao]. Speakers of *tuyu* 1, 2, and 3 can understand most of each other's speech. Of these, *tuyu* 1 and 2 are especially close, so that speakers of these two *tuyu* can basically understand each other.
>
> There is rather more variation within Eastern Xiangxi Miao. Speakers of *tuyu* 4 and 5 cannot understand each other, although if speakers of these two *tuyu* live together for a week, they will be able to understand most of each other's speech. Speakers of *tuyu* 6 and 4 cannot understand each other, and speakers of *tuyu* 6 and 5 can understand a small portion of each other's speech. But phonologically and lexically, *tuyu* 4, 5, and 6 display a number of similar features.
>
> Speakers of Xong and *tuyu* 4 cannot understand each other. Speakers of Xong and *tuyu* 5 can understand a small portion of each other's speech, and speakers of Xong and *tuyu* 6 can understand about half of each other's speech. (Yang [2004: 42]; author's translation)

2.2.2 General background on the Xong language

Xong is reported to have slightly over 900,000 speakers, nearly all of whom are ethnically Miao (Yang 2004: 44, 45). This makes it one of the largest Miao-Yao languages in the world in terms of speaker population, surpassed only by the two Miao languages Hmong and Hmu (Lemoine 2005; Niederer 1998: 51–54; Eberhard et al. 2019). Virtually all Xong speakers live in southern China, with most of them being found in the mountainous region straddling the Hunan–Guizhou border.[7] Much of this region is administratively part of Xiangxi Prefecture (see Sections 2.2.1 and 2.7.1). As of 2006, approximately 33% of Xiangxi's 2.7 million inhabitants were reported to be ethnically Miao, fewer than the Tujia (42%) but more numerous than the (national) majority Han (25%).[8] In any case, Xong speakers can be found in most of Xiangxi Prefecture's constituent counties, including Fenghuang (*Fènghuáng Xiàn* 凤凰县), Huayuan (*Huāyuán Xiàn* 花垣县), Guzhang (*Gǔzhàng Xiàn* 古丈县), Baojing (*Bǎojìng Xiàn* 保靖县), and the county-level city of Jishou (*Jíshǒu Shì* 吉首市). Many are also found in Songtao County (*Sōngtáo Xiàn* 松桃县) in eastern Guizhou Province (Yang 2004: 44, 45).

Smaller Xong-speaking populations can be found scattered throughout the prefecture-level city of Huaihua (*Huáihuà Shì* 怀化市) in western Hunan Province and the counties of Rongjiang (*Róngjiāng Xiàn* 榕江县) and Ziyun (*Zǐyún Xiàn* 紫云县) in eastern Guizhou Province. Outside of Hunan and Guizhou, a handful of Xong-speaking villages are found in Xuan'en County (*Xuān'ēn Xiàn* 宣恩县) in Hubei Province (see also Section 4.4.1), in Nandan County (*Nándān Xiàn* 南丹县) and in the Du'an Yao Autonomous County (*Dū'ān Yáozú Zìzhìxiàn* 都安瑶族自治县) in the Guangxi Zhuang Autonomous Region, and in the Xiushan Tujia and Miao Autonomous County (*Xiùshān Tǔjiāzú Miáozú Zìzhìxiàn* 秀山土家族苗族自治县) in Sichuan Province (Yang 2004: 44, 45).

Much work remains to be done on Xong dialectology, but Yang (2004) is by far the most comprehensive study published on the topic to date (see Section 2.5.2.3 for more on Yang's work). On the basis of certain phonological and lexical differences, Yang (2004: 45–73) divides Xong into three *tuyu* (see Section 2.2.1 for more on this term), with *tuyu* 1 being by far the largest of the three in terms of number of speakers and geographic extent. Yang (2004: 44) reports that *tuyu* 1 has about 770,000 speakers, which is nearly 85% of the total Xong-speaking population. Speakers of *tuyu* 1 can be found in nearly all of the Xong-speaking areas listed earlier in this section; the only exceptions are Guzhang County in Hunan Province and Xuan'en County in Hubei Province, where only speakers of *tuyu* 2 are found, and Baojing County in Hunan

7 Regrettably, no map showing the geographic extents of Xong, its constituent *tuyu*, and the three Eastern Xiangxi Miao languages (i.e. Suang, Seu, and San) has been included in this grammar. The only such maps known to the author are the two found near the beginning of Yang (2004), but those two maps are somewhat blurry and not particularly detailed, to the point that the author is reluctant to attempt to reproduce them here. However, a map showing the extent of the Xiangxi Miao languages as a whole is given in Figure 2.2 in Section 2.3.2, another map showing the location of Xiangxi Prefecture within China is given in Figure 2.5 in Section 2.7.1, and a third map showing various locations within Fenghuang County (where the target variety of this grammar is spoken) is given in Figure 2.6 in Section 2.7.1.

8 These population figures were obtained from the official government website of the Xiangxi Tujia and Miao Autonomous Prefecture (at http://www.xxz.gov.cn/tzxx/tzhj/201109/t20110909_18737.html) on 2014-1-23. See Section 2.7.1 of this grammar for more information on the Tujia and their language.

Province, where only speakers of *tuyu* 2 and 3 are found (Yang 2004: 44, 45). The target variety of this grammar, Fenghuang Xong, belongs to *tuyu* 1 itself.

The governmentally recognized “standard” variety of Xong (see Section 2.4) on which the official Xong orthography is based (see Section 4.3) belongs to *tuyu* 1, and so virtually all Xong-language publications (such as text collections) produced to date have transcribed varieties of this *tuyu*. Most academic publications on Xong, including this grammar, have also focused on varieties of this *tuyu*, although Yu (2011) is a notable exception (see Section 2.5.1).

Tuyu 2 is reported to have 120,000 speakers, far fewer than *tuyu* 1. Still, *tuyu* 2 has a fairly wide geographic distribution. Speakers are found in most Xong-speaking county-level subdivisions of Xiangxi Prefecture, including Huayuan, Guzhang, Baojing, and Jishou. Speakers of *tuyu* 2 are also found in the village of Baren (*Bārén Cūn* 叭仁村) in Fenghuang County (see Figure 2.6 in Section 2.7.1), and the sole Xong-speaking community in Hubei Province belongs to this *tuyu* as well (Yang [2004: 44]; see also Section 4.4.1 of this grammar). While the author is not aware of any text collections or other Xong-language publications for this *tuyu*, it has been described in several academic studies. These include much of Jinzhi Yu’s work, most notably her 2011 grammar of Aizhai Xong (again, see Section 2.5.1).

Finally, Xong’s *tuyu* 3 is by far the smallest one, with only about 30,000 speakers spread across several towns and villages in Huayuan and Baojing Counties in Xiangxi Prefecture (Yang 2004: 45). The author is not aware of any publications (academic or otherwise) devoted specifically to this *tuyu*.

Although Yang (2004: 42) reports that all Xong varieties are mostly mutually intelligible (see Section 2.2.1 above), the amount of internal variation within Xong should not be underestimated. For example, the author’s consultants, all of whom hail from Fenghuang County and speak varieties of *tuyu* 1, report that Aizhai Xong (a variety of *tuyu* 2) is completely unintelligible when spoken at normal speed, and only partially intelligible when spoken very slowly. These consultants also report that even Jiwei Xong (spoken in Huayuan County in Hunan Province) and Songtao Xong (spoken in Songtao County in Guizhou Province) are only partially intelligible when spoken at normal speed (though they are mostly intelligible when spoken slowly), despite the fact that Fenghuang, Jiwei, and Songtao Xong are all varieties of *tuyu* 1. Furthermore, when the author visited Mibei (*Mǐbèi Xiāng* 米贝乡), a predominantly Xong-speaking township in the prefecture-level city of Huaihua (which, like Xiangxi Prefecture, is located in western Hunan Province), the inhabitants there reported that Fenghuang Xong is completely unintelligible to them when spoken at any speed, despite the fact that Fenghuang Xong and Mibei Xong are both listed as varieties of *tuyu* 1 in Yang (2004: 44) The author suspects that if one were to delimit languages strictly on the basis of mutual intelligibility, Xong itself would likely have to be divided up into at least five separate languages, and possibly even more. Regrettably, though, temporal and financial constraints did not allow for extensive investigation into mutual intelligibility while the author was in the field, and so for convenience Xong will still be referred to as a single “language” in this grammar.

2.2.3 Alternate terms for the Xong language

In addition to the terms already discussed in Section 2.2.1 above (including "Xiangxi Miao", "Eastern Miao", "Northern Miao", and "West Hunan Miao"), a handful of other terms have also been used to refer to Xong in the literature. The most frequently encountered is probably "Qo-Xong", along with variants like "Qo-Xiong", "Qoxung", "Ghaob-Xong", and "Ghaob-Xiong". These are simply variant spellings of the Xong term *ghaob-Xonb*, which is composed of the nominal prefix *ghaob-* 'NOM' (see Section 5.4.2.1) and the Xong term for 'Miao' (*Xonb*).[9] However, in Xong the term *ghaob-Xonb* can only be used to refer to native speakers of a Miao language (who in Xiangxi Prefecture, at least, are almost always ethnically Miao) or to the Miao ethnicity as a whole. It is never used to refer to the Xong language, which is simply called *Xonb*.[10] Using the term "Qo-Xong" to refer to the Xong language is thus just as inappropriate as (for example) using the term "Frenchman" to refer to the French language or "Spaniard" to refer to Spanish.

Even more inappropriate is the term "Red Miao", though thankfully it is rarely seen in more recent publications. Diamond (1995) argues that colorful terms like "Red Miao", "Black Miao", "Flowery Miao", and "Short-Skirt Miao" were not originally based on any emically relevant cultural, ethnic, or linguistic categories recognized by speakers of the Miao languages themselves. They were instead invented by non-Miao authors and artists in the Ming (1368–1644 C.E.) and Qing (1644–1912 C.E.) dynasties on the basis of relatively superficial differences in material culture among the Miao communities of southern China, particularly those related to clothing. The following passage describes the popular "Miao albums" of late imperial China in which these supposed ethnic subdivisions would be illustrated and described, often with considerable embellishment:

9 In this grammar, the term *Xonb* is glossed and translated as 'Xong' when it is used specifically to refer to language, but it is glossed and translated as 'Miao' when used to refer to ethnicity or to (non-linguistic) culture.

10 For Xong speakers, the term *Xonb* 'Miao' stands in contrast to the term *zhaol* 'non-Miao', and the precise meaning of that latter form also deserves some comment here. While *zhaol* is glossed as 'Han' (*Hàn* [汉], the majority ethnic group in the People's Republic of China) in every Chinese-language publication on Xong with which the author is familiar, the author's Xong-speaking consultants unanimously agree that the form in fact means merely 'not Miao'. When preceded by the nominal prefix *ghaob-* 'NOM' (see Section 5.4.2.1), the form *zhaol* can be used to refer to anyone who is not a native speaker of a Miao language, including ethnic Han, members of China's other (i.e. non-Miao) ethnic minorities, ethnic Miao who do not speak a Miao language natively, and even non-Chinese foreigners (but *not* foreigners who speak a Miao language natively, e.g. Hmong speakers from Laos or Thailand). The form can also be used alone as a noun meaning 'non-Miao language', although in practice this almost always refers to either Standard Mandarin or Fenghuang Chinese, as these are the only other languages widely spoken in Fenghuang County (see Section 2.7.2).

> The odd ways of the peoples of Guizhou and Yunnan became a focus of a genre of books that Western scholars refer to as 'Miao albums' since the term Miao appears in most of the titles. These began to appear in the early eighteenth century and continued on into the mid-twentieth century. The format is a collection of paintings or block prints, each with a descriptive text that derives primarily from the Guizhou gazetteer materials, sometimes shortened and sometimes elaborated. The artist may have added a short poem. Each depicts a different group, as defined by the gazetteer classification. It is questionable whether most of the artists had ever traveled extensively through the Yunnan and Guizhou frontier areas, let alone spent any time in the Miao communities. At best they may have seen some of these peoples in towns, markets, or along the roads and then, relying on available texts and/or access to other 'Miao albums,' let their imaginations take over to highlight a special marker discussed in the text. (Diamond 1995: 101)

Most of the author's own Xong-speaking consultants have reacted with nothing but puzzlement when presented with terms like "Red/Black/Flowery Miao", and the few who were familiar with them have given conflicting responses. For instance, one consultant from Yankan Village told the author with no small degree of certainty that all Xong speakers in Fenghuang County were Black Miao, another consultant from the same village asserted they were all Red Miao, and a third consultant from the nearby town of La'ershan was positive that they were all in fact Green Miao.

2.2.4 The other Xiangxi Miao languages

Aside from Xong itself, at least three other Xiangxi Miao languages have been described in the literature: Suang, Seu, and San. The best source of information for all three languages is Yang (2004), which is a book-length survey of Xiangxi Miao as a whole. Of course, Yang himself refers to these languages only as *tuyu* of Xiangxi Miao (see Sections 2.2.1 and 2.4), not as distinct languages. Thus Suang is described only as "*tuyu* 4" in Yang's work, Seu is described only as "*tuyu* 5", and San is described only as "*tuyu* 6".[11] Still, Yang does clearly state that all three languages are largely mutually unintelligible with each other and with Xong (Yang [2004: 42]; see also Section 2.2.1 above). All three languages – Suang, Seu, and San – are subsumed under a single ISO 639-3 code (*muq*) in the Ethnologue (Eberhard et al. 2019).

Yang groups Suang, Seu, and San together as Eastern Xiangxi Miao, and indeed these three languages do share a number of features that set them apart from Xong. These include phonological characteristics (Yang 2004: 74, 75, 89–124) as well as grammatical and lexical ones (Yang 2004: 124–127, 161–165). Yang convincingly argues that many of the differences between Eastern Xiangxi Miao and Xong are due

11 Yang never refers to the three languages in question as "Suang", "Seu", or "San", either. Since the author felt it might be confusing to continue referring to these languages merely as "*tuyu* 4", "*tuyu* 5", and "*tuyu* 6", he derived the terms "Suang", "Seu", and "San" from the autonyms given in Yang (2004: 74): "Suang" from /suɑŋ^{53}/, "Seu" from /sɤ^{53}/ (since /ɤ/ is represented with <eu> in the standard Xong orthography), and "San" from /sã^{44}/.

to unequal levels of Sinitic influence. The Eastern Xiangxi Miao languages, with their smaller, more scattered speaker populations (see below in this section), have been much more heavily influenced by Sinitic varieties than Xong has. This has resulted in the Eastern Xiangxi Miao languages having on the whole smaller consonant inventories, larger rhyme inventories, more Sinitic loanwords, and more Sinitic-like constituent order than Xong.

Of course, the fact that most of these phonological, grammatical, and lexical differences appear to be largely due to language contact raises the question of whether Eastern Xiangxi Miao and Xong are genetic units or simply areal ones. Yang himself never explicitly states which hypothesis he favors in his 2004 book, and to the best of the author's knowledge the issue has not been addressed anywhere else in the literature.

The remainder of this section will be devoted to brief summaries of the available information on Suang, Seu, and San. Note that all cities, counties, towns, townships, and villages listed below are located within Xiangxi Prefecture, since none of the three Eastern Xiangxi Miao languages are reported to have any speakers outside of Xiangxi.

The Suang language is spoken by approximately 6,000 people in Luxi County (*Lúxī Xiàn* 泸溪县), specifically in certain villages belonging to Xiaozhang Township (*Xiǎozhāng Xiāng* 小章乡), Jiefangyan Township (*Jiěfàngyán Xiāng* 解放岩乡), and Baiyangxi Township (*Báiyángxī Xiāng* 白羊溪乡) (Yang 2011: 121). To the best of the author's knowledge, Suang has so far been described in only three publications: Yang (2004), Yang (2011), and Long and Yang (2012). Most of the information on Suang given in Yang (2011) is simply repeated from Yang (2004), with the principal differences between the two being that Yang (2004) contains a much more extensive Chinese–Suang wordlist than Yang (2011), and that Yang (2011) contains a small amount of Suang syntactic data not found in Yang (2004). Suang is discussed on pages 119–180 of Yang (2011), but the discussion of the language in Yang (2004) is more scattered, with preliminary phoneme and tone inventories given on pages 85 and 86, a four-page Suang text with interlinear glosses and free translations in Chinese given on pages 223–228, and a Chinese–Suang wordlist with approximately 2,500 entries given on pages 243–371. In contrast, Long and Yang (2012) is simply a brief phonetic study of the Suang tone system.

The Seu language is spoken in a number of towns and villages in Luxi County (*Lúxī Xiàn* 泸溪县), Guzhang County (*Gǔzhàng Xiàn* 古丈县), and Jishou City (*Jíshǒu Shì* 吉首市). It is by far the most widely spoken of the Eastern Xiangxi Miao languages, with a reported speaker population of approximately 48,000. Seu was first described in Yang (2004), which includes the geographic and demographic information just given (Yang 2004: 45), preliminary phoneme and tone inventories (2004: 86, 87), a five-page Seu text with interlinear glosses and free translations in Chinese (2004: 228–234), and a Chinese–Seu wordlist with approximately 2,500 entries (2004: 243–371). Dai, Yu, and Yang (2005) contains additional information on the phonology, grammar, and lexicon of Seu, while Dai, Yang, and Yu (2005) discusses some of the effects that intense contact with local Sinitic varieties has had on the language.

The San language has speakers in a handful of villages in Longshan County (*Lóngshān Xiàn* 龙山县) and Yongshun County (*Yǒngshùn Xiàn* 永顺县), although apparently no villages remain in which San is spoken by a majority of the village's inhabitants. The language is likely critically endangered, with only about 300 speakers reported to remain. The only publication to describe San is Yang (2004), which includes the geographic and demographic information just given (Yang 2004: 45), preliminary phoneme and tone inventories for the language (2004: 87–89), a seven-page San text with interlinear glosses and free translations in Chinese (2004: 234–242), and a Chinese–San wordlist with approximately 2,500 entries (2004: 243–371).

2.3 The Miao-Yao language family

2.3.1 The size of the Miao-Yao family

Xong is universally agreed to belong to the Miao branch of the Miao-Yao (or Hmong-Mien) family, one of the major language families of southern China and mainland Southeast Asia.[12] For good overviews of the family as a whole, see Niederer (1998) (in French), Ratliff (2010) (in English), and Chen (2013) (in Chinese). Estimates about the number of mutually unintelligible Miao-Yao languages have varied widely over the years, with recent claims ranging from thirty-nine (Eberhard et al. 2019) to more than one hundred (Gerner and Bisang 2010: 620).

While the issue is far from settled, a number of factors suggest that Gerner and Bisang's 2010 figure of one-hundred-plus mutually unintelligible Miao-Yao languages is likely the most accurate one. Although most studies of the Miao-Yao family and its member languages fail to discuss mutual intelligibility at all, instead focusing on the varieties spoken in one or more "representative" towns or villages and ignoring any intermediate varieties, those few publications that do discuss mutual intelligibility within Miao-Yao often underestimate it. For instance,

12 Only the term "Miao-Yao" (*Miáo-Yáo* 苗瑶) is used in the Chinese-language literature on the family, while both "Miao-Yao" and "Hmong-Mien" are used in the English-language literature. The term "Hmong-Mien" is derived from the names of the most widely spoken member languages in each branch of the family (i.e. the Miao language Hmong and the Yao language Iu Mien) – which, incidentally, also happen to be the two Miao-Yao languages most widely spoken outside of China, and thus most readily accessible to Western scholars. Although he would not go so far as to advise against the use of "Hmong-Mien", the author himself prefers the term "Miao-Yao", since (i) all of his Xong-speaking and Suang-speaking consultants self-identify as ethnically Miao (not Hmong) and refer to their language as "Miao" (not "Hmong") when speaking a Sinitic variety, (ii) nearly all published work on Xong (and indeed on many Miao-Yao languages other than Hmong and Iu Mien) has been written in Chinese, where only the term "Miao-Yao" is used, and (iii) unlike "Hmong-Mien", the term "Miao-Yao" does not give the appearance of favoring any particular languages within the family.

the Xiangxi sub-branch of Miao has been reported to contain from two (Eberhard et al. 2019) to four (Yang 2004: 42) mutually unintelligible speech varieties, but the author's own fieldwork in western Hunan leads him to suspect that even the latter figure may be far too low (see Sections 2.2.1 and 2.2.2 above).[13] Furthermore, Chinese-to-English mistranslations can unintendedly give a false impression of linguistic homogeneity within Miao-Yao to scholars not literate in Chinese, as is explained in more detail in Section 2.4. When these factors are considered together along with the widely scattered geographic distribution of the Miao-Yao languages, the relative isolation of many Miao-Yao–speaking communities, and the extent to which linguistic diversity in China has consistently been underreported (see Bradley 2006), the author cannot help but feel that Gerner and Bisang's 2010 figure is, if anything, a conservative one.

2.3.2 Geographic distribution of the Miao-Yao languages

Regardless of the exact number of Miao-Yao languages currently in existence, it is clear that the modern heartland of the family lies in southern China. The Miao-Yao languages spoken there have larger speaker populations (Eberhard et al. 2019) and display a far greater degree of typological and genetic diversity than those spoken outside of China (i.e. in mainland Southeast Asia or in certain Western nations).

The Miao-Yao family as a whole currently forms a sort of linguistic "archipelago" extending across much of southern China, with many scattered Miao-Yao–speaking communities surrounded by a "sea" of Sinitic and other languages. This unusual geographic distribution can be seen in Figure 2.2, which is adapted from Li, Xiong, and Zhang (1987) and which shows the locations of the Miao-Yao languages in southern China as of the mid 1980s.

In Figure 2.2, the orange areas represent the Xiangxi, Qiandong, and Chuanqiandian Miao languages, the purple areas represent the Bahengic, Bunuic, and Jiongnai languages, the red areas represent the She language, and the green areas represent the Yao languages.[14] A black ellipse has been added by the author around the Xiangxi Miao languages. The cream-colored areas represent non–Miao-Yao languages spoken within

13 Yang's 2004 figure of four mutually unintelligible Xiangxi Miao varieties is presumably based on his extensive fieldwork in areas where these varieties are spoken. The evidence for Eberhard et al.'s (i.e. the Ethnologue's) 2019 figure of two mutually unintelligible varieties is unclear, since the source cited for the Xiangxi Miao data included in the Ethnologue (Wang and Mao 1995) makes no mention of mutual intelligibility.

14 Li, Xiong, and Zhang's grouping together of the Xiangxi, Qiandong, and Chuanqiandian Miao languages reflects the received view of Miao-Yao's internal divisions among Chinese linguists in the 1980s, as does their grouping together of the Bahengic, Bunuic, and Jiongnai languages (Mao and Li 1997: 238, 239). See Sections 2.3.4 and 2.4 for further discussion.

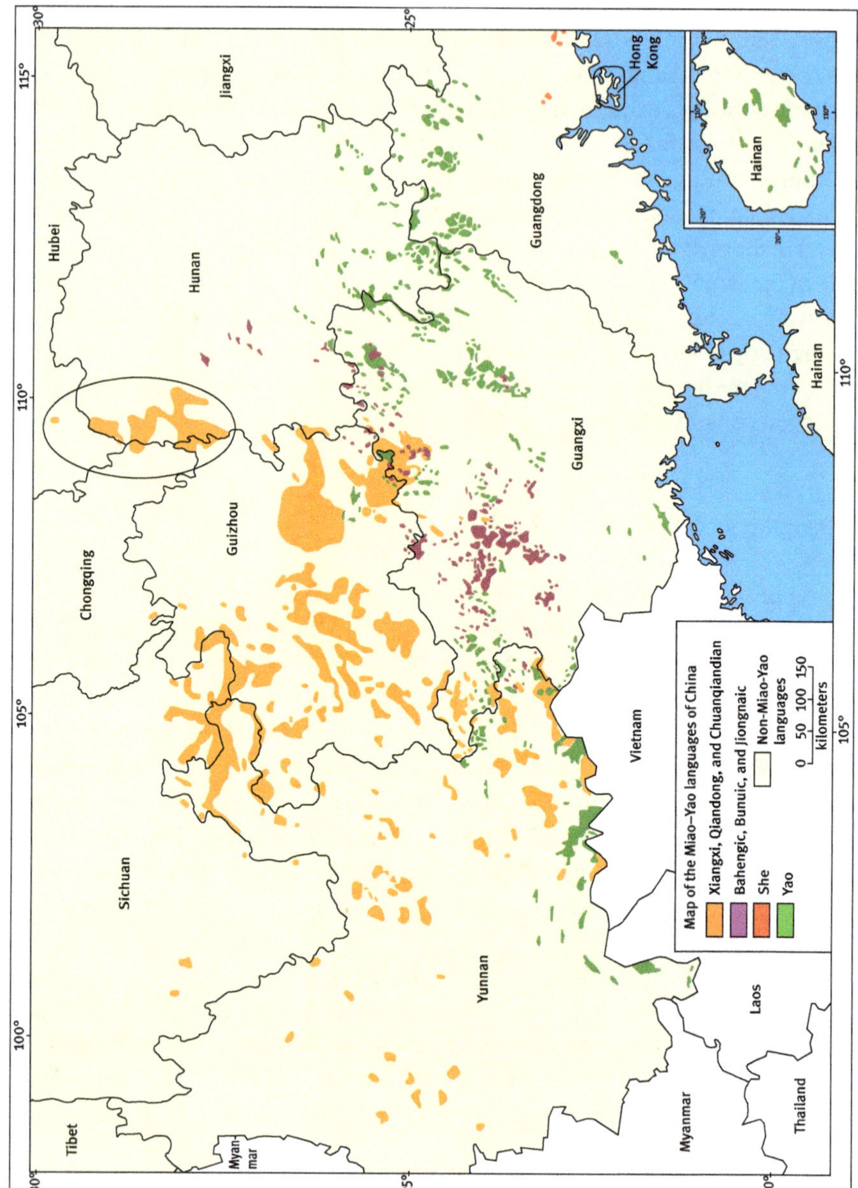

Figure 2.2: Map of the Miao-Yao languages of China.

China, and the white areas represent territory outside China. Of course, Figure 2.2 does not necessarily reflect the current distribution of the Miao-Yao languages, since many of these languages have lost territory to other (primarily Sinitic) languages during the three decades since the map was published. This is certainly the case for Xiangxi Miao, as is detailed in Yang (2004: 6–8). Furthermore, the geographic distribution shown in Figure 2.2 almost certainly does not represent the original location of the Miao-Yao family. Ratliff (2010: 240, 241) argues convincingly on the basis of family-wide cognate terms for certain plant and animal species that the Miao-Yao Urheimat must have been further to the north, along the central and lower reaches of the Yangtze River.[15]

Although not shown in Figure 2.2, a number of Miao-Yao–speaking communities are found outside of China as well. Some of these are quite large, with hundreds of thousands of speakers. For instance, the Ethnologue (Eberhard et al. 2019) reports that more speakers of the Miao variety Mong Njua are found outside of China – in Laos (100,000 speakers), Thailand (60,000), and Myanmar (10,000) – than are found in China itself (40,000).[16] The same is true of the Yao language Iu Mien, which the Ethnologue reports has 383,000 speakers in China, but 350,000 speakers in Vietnam, 21,200 in Thailand, and 32,400 in Laos. Other Miao-Yao languages (or varieties) with significant speaker populations in mainland Southeast Asian nations include Kim Mun (Yao), Baheng (Miao), and Hmong Daw (Miao). However, the author is not aware of any Xiangxi Miao-speaking communities outside of mainland China.

Still, despite their large speaker populations, the Miao-Yao languages of mainland Southeast Asia represent only a small portion of the linguistic diversity found within the family. This is presumably due to the fact that Miao-Yao speakers are relatively recent arrivals in the area. These speakers did not begin to migrate from southern China to mainland Southeast Asia in large numbers until the late eighteenth century,

15 Many Chinese-language publications assert that the ancestors of the modern Miao-Yao speakers lived on the Central Plains of northern China and only began migrating south in the third millennium B.C.E. after their mythic leader, Chiyou (*Chīyóu* 蚩尤), was defeated in battle by the mythic leader of the Han, the Yellow Emperor (*Huángdì* 黄帝). This not only assumes that Chiyou and the Yellow Emperor did indeed exist and did indeed war with each other, it also assumes direct ethnic and linguistic connections between the populations referred to as "Miao" in ancient Chinese documents (many of which predate the Common Era) and the modern Miao. The former assumption is questionable, and the latter one is almost certainly unjustified. First, although the same Chinese character (i.e. 苗, pronounced *Miáo*) is used to refer both to the modern Miao and to certain populations that inhabited the Central Plains of ancient China, it is likely that the character in question did not originally indicate a specific ethnic group, but instead meant something closer to "(generic) southern barbarian" (Diamond 1995: 99, 100; Culas and Michaud 1997: 213–215). Second, the character in question disappears from the historical record for several centuries between the Han (206 B.C.E.–220 C.E.) and Song (960–1279 C.E.) dynasties, making any purported connections between the character's ancient and modern referents even more tenuous (Culas and Michaud 1997: 215).

16 Of course, many of these population figures are likely out of date by now, but they do at least give some idea of the *relative* speaker populations found inside and outside of China for the Miao-Yao languages in question.

when demographic pressures, armed conflict with the Chinese state, and new economic opportunities outside of China began to make such migration more appealing (Michaud 1997).

An even smaller subset of the Miao-Yao languages is also spoken in Western nations like the United States, France, and Australia, with speaker communities in these countries generally having their origins in refugee populations that fled mainland Southeast Asia during and after the Vietnam War of 1955–1975 (Ratliff 2010: 1). It is of course no coincidence that the vast majority of research on the Miao-Yao family published in languages other than Chinese has so far focused on Miao-Yao languages spoken outside of China, especially those spoken in these Western nations. This includes Court's 1985 grammar of the Yao language Iu Mien, which is the sole English-language reference grammar of a Miao-Yao language to precede this Xong grammar.[17]

2.3.3 Typological characteristics of Miao-Yao

Although an in-depth discussion of the Miao-Yao family in a typological context lies well outside the scope of this grammar, a few brief notes on the topic may help put later Xong material into better perspective. In most respects the Miao-Yao languages are fairly "typical" members of the greater mainland Southeast Asian linguistic area, which encompasses Vietnam, Laos, Cambodia, Thailand, and Myanmar as well as much of southern China (Enfield 2005: 182). Even by mainland Southeast Asian standards, most Miao-Yao languages have very large consonant, vowel, and tone inventories (see Niederer [1998: 210–213]), although the exact number of phonemes (and in particular consonants) in a given Miao-Yao language can sometimes vary dramatically depending on differing analytical assumptions (for some discussion of this issue in Xong, see Sections 1.2.1 and 3.7 of this grammar). In general, the Miao languages tend to have larger consonant inventories (or at least larger inventories of possible syllable onsets), while the Yao languages tend to have larger vowel inventories (or at least larger inventories of possible syllable rhymes) (Ratliff 2010: 10, 11). Morphologically the Miao-Yao languages are all highly isolating, although certain morphological phenomena – like noun compounding (see Section 5.3) and nominal prefixes (Section 5.4) – are still found in many members of the family. Relatively little work has been done on comparative Miao-Yao syntax, but all Miao-Yao languages known to the author feature well developed systems of numeral classifiers (Section 6.1), widespread multiverbal constructions (Chapter 12), and predominantly SVO, VO, and SV constituent orders (Li 2008: 157–189; Sposato 2014).

17 Despite its title, Lyman's 1979 *Grammar of Mong Njua (Green Miao)* is really no more than a grammatical sketch, and a rather idiosyncratic one at that.

2.3.4 External and internal relations of the Miao-Yao languages

Miao-Yao is regarded as an independent language family by nearly all linguists outside of China, including every non-Chinese Miao-Yao specialist with whose work the author is familiar. These scholars attribute the many lexical, phonological, and grammatical similarities between Miao-Yao and other nearby language families (especially Sino-Tibetan) to extensive, long-term language contact (see, e.g., Ratliff [2010: 1, 2, 224–238]). Within the last two decades or so, a small but growing number of Chinese linguists have also begun to argue that Miao-Yao is most likely an independent language family (Luo 2002, Hu 2009, Defu Shi p.c. 2009).

However, the received view within China continues to be that Miao-Yao constitutes one of the first-order branches of the Sino-Tibetan language family (as indeed, in this received view, does Tai-Kadai). This view is even held by many prominent Miao-Yao specialists publishing in Chinese, including Fushi Wang (1985: 2), Yunbing Li (2008: 2, 3), and Qiguang Chen (2013: 14). These scholars assume that the lexical, phonological, and grammatical similarities between Miao-Yao and "other" Sino-Tibetan languages are largely the result of descent from a common ancestor, although they do not rule out the possibility of more recent (i.e. post-Proto-Sino-Tibetan) contact among these languages as well.

Although the issue is largely irrelevant for the purposes of this grammar, the author finds the theory that Miao-Yao is an independent language family to be the more convincing one, at least on the basis of currently available evidence. First, it should be kept in mind that nearly every logically possible combination of the five major language families of greater mainland Southeast Asia – i.e. Miao-Yao, Sino-Tibetan, Tai-Kadai, Austroasiatic, and Austronesian – has been suggested as a valid language family at one point or another (see van Driem 2005 and Sagart, Blench, and Sanchez-Mazas 2005 for historical overviews of these proposals). The multiplicity of these proposed families is presumably due – at least in part – to the intense nature of language contact in the greater mainland Southeast Asian linguistic area, which can make it extremely difficult to determine whether shared linguistic features are due to contact or to inheritance from a common ancestor. Furthermore, the relative lack of morphology and the predominance of monosyllabic morphemes in many Southeast Asian languages makes the determination of genetic relationships among them even harder than in many other areas of the world. Second, many Chinese-language publications rely heavily on relatively superficial phonological and syntactic similarities (rather than, for example, regular sound correspondences) as evidence for genetic relationships among the languages of East and Southeast Asia. However, it has long been known that intense language contact can result in dramatic phonological and syntactic convergence (see, for example, Gumperz and Wilson 1971, Bradley 1980, and Ross 1996, 2001, and 2007), making such evidence rather unconvincing. Third and finally, although a massive number of Sino-Tibetan (especially Sinitic) loanwords

1. Yao (including Iu Mien, Mun, Biao Min, and Zao Min)
2. Miao
    2.1. Bahengic (including Baheng and Mnai)
    2.2. Non-Bahengic
        2.2.1. Xiangxi Miao (including **Xong**, Suang, Seu, and San)
        2.2.2. Jiongnaic (including Jiongnai, She, and Bana)
        2.2.3. Qiandong–Bunuic–Chuanqiandian
            2.2.3.1. Qiandong Miao (including Hmu)
            2.2.3.2. Bunuic–Chuanqiandian
                2.2.3.2.1. Bunuic
                2.2.3.2.2. Chuanqiandian Miao (including Hmong, Ahmao, and Hmyo)

Figure 2.3: The Miao-Yao family tree according to Taguchi (2015).

can be found in virtually every Miao-Yao language, these languages still share a unique set of basic vocabulary not present in Sino-Tibetan (Ratliff 2010: 2).

The internal relations of the Miao-Yao family are also a matter of some controversy, perhaps to an even greater extent than the family's external relations. Nevertheless, a tentative family tree for Miao-Yao has been given in Figure 2.3 above. This tree is largely based on the one found in Taguchi (2015), though it should be noted that the terms used to refer to certain subgroups of the family in Figure 2.3 differ from those used in Taguchi's work.[18] It should also be noted that the tree given above is not exhaustive, in the sense that the individual languages listed in it (e.g. Iu Mien, Xong, Hmong, etc.) constitute only a small portion of the likely hundred-plus Miao-Yao languages in existence (Gerner and Bisang 2010: 620).

There is at least universal agreement that Miao-Yao consists of two first-order subdivisions, Miao (sometimes referred to as "Hmongic" in the English-language literature) and Yao (sometimes referred to as "Mienic").[19] It has often been claimed that the Yao branch contains much less internal diversity than the Miao one (see, e.g.,

18 These terminological adjustments were generally made for one of two reasons. First, some of the subgroups in Taguchi (2015) are referred to using cardinal directions (e.g. "Northern Hmongic", "Eastern Hmongic", etc.). This could potentially lead to confusion, since in some cases the same subgroup is referred to using different cardinal directions in English and Chinese (see Section 2.2.1). The author has replaced these directional terms with what he hopes are less ambiguous ones. Second, Taguchi occasionally recognizes the existence of a particular subgroup without providing a specific term for it. The author has coined a new, maximally compositional term for each such subgroup himself, such as "Non-Bahengic" (referring to the subgroup that consists of all Miao languages outside of Bahengic) or "Qiandong–Bunuic–Chuanqiandian" (referring to the subgroup that consists of the Qiandong Miao, Bunuic, and Chuanqiandian Miao languages). Still, the author wishes to stress that the overall structure of Taguchi's 2015 tree has been faithfully maintained here; only the terminology has changed.
19 The She language was formerly considered a third first-order subdivision of the family, but it has since been conclusively demonstrated to belong to Miao (Ratliff 1998).

Ratliff [2010: 3]), although Yoshihisa Taguchi has suggested to the author that internal diversity within Yao may in fact be much greater than what is commonly reported (p.c. 2012). In any case, the internal structure of the Yao branch is not represented in Figure 2.3, with the author instead simply listing the four most frequently cited subdivisions within the branch: Iu Mien, Mun, Biao Min, and Zao Min (see, e.g., Mao [2004: 10] or Ratliff [2010: 3]).

The larger first-order subdivision of the family, Miao, is here divided into two second-order subdivisions: Bahengic and Non-Bahengic. The Non-Bahengic group is then further divided into three third-order subdivisions: Xiangxi Miao (which includes Xong), Jiongnaic, and Qiandong–Bunuic–Chuanqiandian. This trinary division of the Non-Bahengic languages follows Taguchi (2015), but it is Figure 2.3's most drastic departure from the trees given in many previous studies, including Purnell (1970: 40), Wang and Mao (1995: 2), and Ratliff (2010: 3). Although the details may differ from scholar to scholar, the received view among both Chinese and non-Chinese linguists has long been that (contra Figure 2.3) Xiangxi Miao is quite closely related to Qiandong Miao and Chuanqiandian Miao – certainly, at least, much more closely related to them than either Jiongnaic or Bahengic is.

However, a number of scholars have recently begun to argue that Xiangxi Miao actually split off from the main Miao stock fairly early on, and that it is thus not particularly closely related to either Qiandong Miao or Chuanqiandian Miao. These scholars have so far based their arguments on lexicostatistical evidence (Wang and Deng 2003), on certain unusually conservative reflexes of Proto-Miao rhymes in the Xiangxi Miao languages (Ratliff 2010: 20, 21, 24, 25, 122, 130, 147), or on both (Taguchi 2012b, 2013, 2015). The position of Xiangxi Miao in Figure 2.3 thus reflects what appears to the author to be a growing consensus about Miao-Yao phylogeny.

Still, the author wishes to make it clear that his Figure 2.3 should not be considered an authoritative representation of the historical relationships among the various members of the Miao-Yao family. As mentioned above, the figure includes only a small portion of all extant Miao-Yao languages, and many details relating to the internal structure of certain subdivisions have yet to be confirmed. In any case, since the primary goal of this grammar is synchronic phonological and grammatical description, these genealogical issues will not be addressed again. However, they do serve to highlight the potential importance that Xong has to Miao-Yao studies in general. As Ratliff (2010: 24) states, "[t]he archaism of Qo Xiong [i.e. Xong] suggests that the structure of the Hmong-Mien [i.e. Miao-Yao] family tree needs to be re-calculated from the beginning, with no preconceptions about Hmongic [i.e. Miao] language sub-grouping."

2.4 Xong's status within China

The bulk of this section concerns itself with Xong's status within China, including its place in Chinese linguistic classification schemes, its degree of recognition by the

Chinese government, and those governmental policies that have affected it. Popular attitudes toward Xong will not be discussed here; since the author only has firsthand knowledge of popular attitudes toward Xong within Fenghuang County, these attitudes are discussed in Section 2.7.2 instead. Before moving on to Xong in particular, though, it is necessary to first explain the meanings of two Chinese linguistic terms, *yuyan* and *fangyan*. Understanding the precise meanings of *yuyan* and *fangyan* is critical for understanding Chinese linguistic publications and language policies. This is true even for those publications and policies which have already been translated into English, since imprecise translations of *yuyan* and *fangyan* have sometimes resulted in confusion between Chinese- and English-speaking scholars.

The first term, *yuyan* (*yǔyán* 语言), is often translated as "language" in English-language discussions and translations of Chinese-language linguistic publications. However, the meanings of *yuyan* and "language" differ in at least two important ways. First, *yuyan* does not imply any degree of mutual intelligibility whatsoever. This is in contrast to the English term "language", which is often (though not always) used specifically to refer to a mutually intelligible set of linguistic varieties. Thus, for many decades all Sinitic varieties were considered to belong to a single Han (i.e. Sinitic) *yuyan*, although Chinese linguists of course were and are aware that there exist dozens, if not hundreds, of mutually unintelligible Sinitic varieties.[20] Even today, the received view in China is that all varieties of Xiangxi Miao, Qiandong Miao, and Chuanqiandian Miao belong to a single Miao *yuyan*, despite the fact that these three sub-branches likely do not even form a valid genetic grouping within Miao-Yao (see Section 2.3.4 above) and may contain dozens of mutually unintelligible speech varieties. Second, *yuyan* have often been defined in China on ethnic, cultural, and political grounds as much as on the basis of purely linguistic criteria, making *yuyan* as much an anthropological or sociological notion as it is a linguistic one. In fact, official policy in China from the late 1950s to the late 1970s was that there were exactly 54 *yuyan* spoken in the country: one Han (i.e. Sinitic) *yuyan*, plus one additional *yuyan* each for 53 of the country's 54 officially recognized minority ethnicities. (One such ethnicity, the Hui, was said to lack a *yuyan* of its own.) A 55th *yuyan* was added only in 1979, when the Jinuo were recognized as an official minority ethnicity, although many more *yuyan* have been recognized in the decades since then (Bradley 2005).

The second term, *fangyan* (*fāngyán* 方言), is often translated as "dialect" in English-language sources. But this too is problematic: the English term "dialect" is notoriously ambiguous (see, e.g., Groves [2008: 6–35]), and the Chinese term *fangyan* no less so. Historically, the term *fangyan* simply referred to the speech of a particular area, regardless of whether that area was as small as a single village or as large as an

20 Beginning in the 1980s, some Chinese linguists began suggesting that the Han *yuyan* be divided up into several smaller *yuyan*, and at least ten such smaller *yuyan* have been proposed so far (see, e.g., Li, Xiong, and Zhang 1987). Nevertheless, each of these new, smaller *yuyan* still contains many mutually unintelligible speech varieties.

entire province – or even several provinces (Mair 1991). The term is still used in much this way by many Chinese-speaking laypeople. Among Chinese linguists, though, *fangyan* is more often used to refer to a first-order subdivision of a *yuyan*, although such subdivisions can of course vary greatly in size. The term *cifangyan* (*cìfāngyán* 次方言), literally meaning "sub-*fangyan*", is then used to refer to a first-order subdivision of a *fangyan*, and the term *tuyu* (*tǔyǔ* 土语) is used to refer to a first-order subdivision of a *cifangyan* (see also Section 2.2.1).

In this grammar, the term *yuyan* is not translated at all. The term has little linguistic validity and is rarely used outside of this Section 2.4, but when necessary it will simply be transliterated in italics as has been done so far in this section. The term *fangyan* will not be translated either when it is used in its more technical sense (i.e. when used to refer to a first-order subdivision of a *yuyan*), instead simply being transliterated in italics. But when used to refer to the speech of a particular area, *fangyan* will be translated as "variety", regardless of the size of the area in question.[21]

Returning now to Xong, the current received view in China is that all of Xiangxi Miao (including Xong, Suang, Seu, and San) together constitutes one of the three *fangyan* of the Miao *yuyan*. This view has been espoused in virtually every relevant governmental and academic Chinese-language publication the author has encountered. Xong and Eastern Xiangxi Miao (i.e. Suang, Seu, and San) are then each considered a *cifangyan*, or "sub-*fangyan*", of the Xiangxi Miao *fangyan*, and each is further divided into three *tuyu*, although many of these *tuyu* would likely be considered distinct languages by linguists outside of China (see Section 2.2 for more information on Xong and Eastern Xiangxi Miao and their internal subdivisions). Xiangxi Miao varieties smaller than a *tuyu* – for instance, the speech of a particular village, or town, or even an entire county – are simply referred to as "the Miao of [place]" in Chinese-language sources.

In this received view, the Miao *yuyan* is said to contain two other *fangyan* besides Xiangxi Miao, namely Qiandong Miao (*Qiándōng Miáoyǔ* 黔东苗语), which includes the language Hmu and likely several other languages (or at least mutually unintelligible speech varieties), and Chuanqiandian Miao (*Chuānqiándiān Miáoyǔ* 川黔滇苗语), which includes Hmong, Ahmao, and a great many other languages (or mutually unintelligible speech varieties). The Miao-Yao family as a whole is then typically said to contain six other *yuyan* in addition to the Miao one.[22] Mao and Li (2007: 233) provide a visual representation of this classificatory scheme, which has been adapted in Figure 2.4 below.

---

21 However, *yuyan* is indeed translated as "language" and *fangyan* as "dialect" in the titles of Chinese-language sources cited in this grammar. While this is admittedly inconsistent, the author felt that not doing so might result in confusion for any readers who consulted the list of references in this grammar without first reading this Section 2.4.

22 An eighth Miao-Yao *yuyan*, Bana (*Bānàyǔ* 巴那语), has been described in two publications by Qiguang Chen (2001; 2013: 24, 341–348). Chen argues that Bana belongs to the Miao branch of the family, and that it is most closely related to She. However, Bana is not mentioned in Mao and Li (2007),

1. Miao branch
    1.1. Miao *yuyan*
        1.1.1. Xiangxi *fangyan*
        1.1.2. Qiandong *fangyan*
        1.1.3. Chuanqiandian *fangyan*
    1.2. Bunu *yuyan*
    1.3. Baheng *yuyan*
    1.4. Younuo *yuyan*
    1.5. Jiongnai *yuyan*
    1.6. She *yuyan*
2. Yao branch
    2.1. Mian *yuyan*

Figure 2.4: The Miao-Yao family tree according to Mao and Li (2007).

Note that while Mao and Li (2007) do not include the three *fangyan* of the Miao *yuyan* in their tree, these three *fangyan* have been included in Figure 2.4 for clarity. Note also that in this received classification scheme the term "Miao" is used for both a first-order subdivision of the Miao-Yao family (i.e. the Miao branch) and a second-order subdivision of the family (i.e. the Miao *yuyan*, one of the constituent *yuyan* of the Miao branch).

The scheme represented in Figure 2.4 is admittedly a marked improvement over earlier ones favored by the Chinese government. In the early 1950s, for instance, Miao-Yao was said to contain only two *yuyan* – Miao and Yao – since nearly all speakers of Miao-Yao languages in China were classified as belonging to either the Miao or the Yao ethnicities (Chen 1998: 151).[23] Nevertheless, this scheme is still seriously flawed. Perhaps most problematically, it groups the Xiangxi, Qiandong, and Chuanqiandian Miao languages together into a singular Miao *yuyan*, but in recent years more and

and it is unclear to what extent Bana has come to be accepted as a distinct *yuyan* in Chinese linguistic circles.

23 The process by which these and others of China's officially recognized ethnic minority groups were decided upon is an interesting one. In the years immediately following the founding of the PRC, the Chinese government largely adopted a Stalinist view of ethnicity. This meant that the political recognition of any given group as a legitimate ethnicity was, at least in theory and in official discourse, to be based on "common language, common territory, common economic life, and a typical cast of mind manifested in a common culture" (Stalin [1913: 307], quoted in Kaup [2002: 880]). Accordingly, although more than four hundred groups submitted applications for recognition as official ethnic minorities in the 1950s, only 54 of these groups (in addition to the majority Han) were granted such recognition, ostensibly because they met these four criteria (Kaup 2002: 880). In some cases, however, political concerns – especially the fear of agitation for increased political autonomy – trumped one or more of Stalin's criteria, as happened with the Zhuang ethnicity (Kaup 2002). In other cases, all four of Stalin's criteria appear to have been ignored entirely, as was the case with the Miao ethnicity (Diamond 1995).

more evidence that these three sub-branches do not form a valid genetic unit has been accumulating. The closest relatives of Chuanqiandian Miao may in fact be the Bunuic languages, while Xiangxi Miao may be no more closely related to Chuanqiandian and Qiandong Miao than Jiongnai and She are (see Section 2.3.4).

These issues are not merely academic, as the classificatory status of any particular non-Sinitic linguistic variety spoken in China can have a significant impact on the degree of official support accorded to that variety. For each of the three *fangyan* of the Miao *yuyan* (i.e. the Xiangxi, Qiandong, and Chuanqiandian *fangyan*), the local speech of a single town or village was selected in the 1950s to serve as the "standard" variety of that *fangyan*. The large speaker population and geographic extent of Xong made it all but certain that a Xong variety (rather than a Suang or Seu or San variety) would be selected as the Xiangxi Miao standard, and indeed the Xong variety spoken in Jiwei Township (*Jíwèi Xiāng* 吉卫乡) in Xiangxi Prefecture's Huayuan County was eventually chosen.

Since its selection as the "standard" variety of Xiangxi Miao, Jiwei Xong has received a relatively large amount of governmental support. A Latin-based (or, more precisely, *pinyin*-based) practical orthography was developed for the variety in the 1950s (see Section 4.3), and a number of dictionaries (including Xiang 1992 and Shi 1997), textbooks, and text collections have been produced using this orthography. Some bilingual Xong–Chinese primary education programs have also been formally instituted, and these are generally taught using the Jiwei-based Xong orthography, even in areas outside of Jiwei (note, though, that official and popular enthusiasm for these programs has varied significantly over the past half-century).

In contrast, the "non-standard" varieties of Xiangxi Miao – which include all varieties of Xong spoken outside of Jiwei as well as the languages Suang, Seu, and San – have received no official recognition and thus generally no support. In most cases these varieties are not even named, with native speakers and academic linguists alike referring to them simply as "the Miao of [place]". While many (though by no means all) of these varieties have received some measure of phonological and/or grammatical description, there is usually little or no support for them in terms of practical orthographies, text collections, textbooks, and the like. It is perhaps also worth pointing out here that popular awareness of Jiwei Xong's status as the "standard" variety of Xiangxi Miao seems to be largely restricted to Jiwei itself and areas immediately nearby. None of the author's Xong-speaking consultants in Fenghuang County or Suang-speaking consultants in Luxi County have even been aware that Xiangxi Miao has a "standard" variety, much less which variety that might be.

2.5 Previous descriptions of Xong

There is a vast body of linguistic literature on Xong, nearly all of which has been written in Chinese (but see Section 2.5.4). Attested transcriptions of Xong by non-native speakers date back at least several hundred years (for discussion of early transcriptions of Xong by native speakers, see Section 4.2). For example, the *Miao Fangbei Lan* [*On Repelling the Miao*], Ruyu Yan's 1820 volume of suggested policies for "securing" the Miao frontier of present-day Xiangxi, contains a Chinese–Xong wordlist with over two hundred entries. Yang (2004: 8) reports that an even earlier Chinese–Xong wordlist is found in the *Qianzhou Zhi* [*Qianzhou Gazetteer*], a geographic, political, economic, and cultural almanac of the Xong-speaking region compiled by Wei Wang and published in 1739, although the author of this grammar has not had the opportunity to consult this work himself. Note, though, that the Xong "transcriptions" in these early works were written using Chinese characters whose pronunciation only very roughly approximated that of the Xong forms in question.

The first linguistic publication on Xong to be couched in any sort of modern analytical framework was Ling and Rui's *Xiangxi Miaozu Diaocha Baogao* [*An Ethnographic Report on the Miao People in the Xiangxi Area*], completed in 1937 but not published until 1947 (and then reprinted in 2003). This was followed by Qigui Shi's *Xiangxi Miaozu Shidi Diaocha Baogao* [*Report on a Field Survey of the Miao People of Xiangxi*], completed in 1940 but not published until 1986 (and then reprinted in 2002). Both books are lengthy ethnographic accounts of the Xong-speaking inhabitants of the Xiangxi region, covering a multitude of topics like economic pursuits, daily life, government, and religion.

Both also contain substantial sections on the Xong language. Much of Ling and Rui's discussion of Xong (1947: 416–467) deals with Fenghuang Xong in particular, and so it is reviewed in more detail in Section 2.5.3.2 below. However, the equivalent section in Shi (2002: 526–611) does not contain any data on Fenghuang Xong, and furthermore it uses only Chinese characters to record Xong material rather than any sort of phonemic transcription system.[24] Just as with the earlier *Miao Fangbei Lan* and *Qianzhou Zhi*, these characters only very roughly approximate the pronunciation of the Xong forms they are intended to represent. For these reasons, Shi's work will not be discussed further in this chapter (though see Section 4.1).

Relatively few publications on Xong were produced during the 1950s, 1960s, and 1970s. The 1980s, though, saw the appearance of over a dozen articles on Xong as well as several Xong text collections, and each subsequent decade has seen significant increases in the number and sophistication of such publications. At this point, the great number of existing publications on Xong means that providing a completely exhaustive literature review would increase the size of this chapter several times over. Furthermore, the quality of work done on Xong over the past few decades has been rather uneven, and not every publication is necessarily equally deserving of comment.

24 When Shi's book was finally published in 1986, the book's editors used a modified version of IPA to add phonemic transcriptions for the Xong forms which Shi himself had originally transcribed using Chinese characters. While helpful to the reader, the fact that these phonemic transcriptions were added nearly half a century after the book's completion means that they have rather limited historical value.

Thus, the author has divided this section into four subsections, each of which deals with a separate category of publication that is of particular relevance to this grammar (of course, other Xong-related publications are cited in subsequent sections and chapters wherever appropriate). Section 2.5.1 presents a critical review of Yu's 2011 grammar of Aizhai Xong. This devotion of an entire section to a single publication is justified in that Yu's grammar is the single most comprehensive grammatical description of any Xong variety published prior to this grammar. Section 2.5.2 then discusses several other major studies of Xong, including Xiang's 1999 description of Jiwei Xong, Luo's 1990 and 2005 descriptions of Songtao Xong, Yang's 2004 historical and dialectal survey of Xiangxi Miao as a whole, and Chen's 2009 description of Daxing Xong. Section 2.5.3 reviews those publications which (like this grammar itself) concentrate on varieties of Xong spoken within Fenghuang County. Finally, Section 2.5.4 lists the few publications in languages other than Chinese that have contained some Xong data.[25]

2.5.1 Yu (2011)

Yu's 2011 grammar of Aizhai Xong is by far the most comprehensive grammatical description of any Xong variety to precede this grammar, and indeed it remains one of the most comprehensive descriptions of any Miao language known to the author. Yu (2011) is a slightly revised version of Yu's 2010 dissertation, and it contains nearly 350 pages of fairly dense text along with another 150 pages of appendices. All examples and texts are given in a modified version of IPA rather than in a practical orthography. Yu's grammar and dissertation are both written in Chinese, and both are couched in an unusual theoretical framework that blends basic linguistic theory with traditional Chinese linguistic theory (for information on the former, see Section 2.6.1 below).[26]

25 The reader may observe that this literature review is rather longer and more detailed than is typical for a descriptive grammar. This is because the vast majority of the material to be reviewed here is (as was noted above) written in Chinese and is thus inaccessible to most linguists outside of China.

26 By "traditional Chinese linguistic theory" the author means the common set of theoretical assumptions and the common organizational framework found in nearly every Chinese-language publication on China's minority languages produced within the past few decades – or at least in nearly every such publication the author has encountered. Common traits (at least for book-length works written within this theoretical framework) include (i) a rather perfunctory phonology section, usually with little evidence given for the author's phonological analysis, (ii) a substantial section devoted to lexical categories, usually with the same lexical categories assumed for every language (generally these are nouns, pronouns, numerals, classifiers, verbs, adjectives, ideophones, adverbs, prepositions, conjunctions, particles, and interjections), (iii) a shorter section on various phrase types (e.g. modifier phrases, complement phrases, etc.), although the specific types of phrases discussed in any given work do tend to vary more among authors than lexical categories do, (iv) another relatively short section on syntactic constituents, which are rarely given rigorous definitions and which, like

While the rest of this section will focus solely on Yu's grammar, not her dissertation, the two works are similar enough that nearly all of the comments below apply equally to both. Furthermore, while several of Yu's numerous earlier publications have also examined certain aspects of Aizhai Xong, virtually all of the data found in those publications is also found in Yu (2011), and so there is no need to discuss them separately.

Aizhai Xong is the variety of Xong spoken in Aizhai Town (*Ǎizhài Zhèn* 矮寨镇), which is administratively part of Jishou City (*Jíshǒu Shì* 吉首市), the capital of Xiangxi Prefecture (see Figure 2.6 in Section 2.7.1 below). This author's own consultants (all of whom hail from Fenghuang County, immediately to the southwest of Jishou) uniformly report that Aizhai Xong is completely unintelligible to them when spoken at normal speeds, and only partially intelligible when spoken very slowly. While the author has no reason to doubt his consultants' intelligibility judgments, it is perhaps worth mentioning that these claims of theirs are at odds with certain claims in Yang's 2004 study of Xiangxi Miao (see Section 2.2.1 above). Yang explicitly states that all varieties of Xiangxi Miao's *tuyu* 1 (including Fenghuang Xong) and *tuyu* 2 (including Aizhai Xong) are "basically" mutually intelligible (2004: 42, 44). Grammatically, though, the differences between Aizhai Xong and any particular variety of Fenghuang Xong appear to be only slightly larger than the differences between any two varieties of Fenghuang Xong. In any case, it is reported in Yu (2011: 4, 6–8) that the vast majority of Aizhai's approximately 15,000 inhabitants are ethnically Miao, and that nearly all of them are bilingual in "Chinese" (no particular Sinitic variety is specified) and Xong.

Chapter 1 of Yu's grammar briefly discusses several background issues, including the Miao-Yao family as a whole (2011: 1–4), Aizhai Town and its sociolinguistic

---

lexical categories, vary little from language to language (a typical list would include subject, object, predicate, complement, modifier, and adverbial), (v) a few short sections on various sentence-related issues, such as simple vs. complex sentences and sentence modality, (vi) the common organizational scheme suggested by traits (i) to (v) above, with the section on phonology preceding the one on lexical categories, which in turn precedes the one on phrase types, and so on, and (vii) a lengthy section devoted to phonological, morphological, and semantic characteristics of borrowings from Sinitic. The author has not been able to find any metatheoretical discussion of this framework in either the Chinese- or the English-language literature, and so it is simply referred to as "traditional Chinese linguistic theory" in this grammar.

In a rather superficial sense this framework is somewhat akin to basic linguistic theory (see Section 2.6.1), as both frameworks make very little use of formalist devices and are typically used by fieldworkers studying underdescribed languages rather than major, widely spoken ones (e.g. English, Standard Mandarin). At a more fundamental level, though, the two frameworks are almost diametrically opposed. One of the primary goals of basic linguistic theory is the avoidance of Anglocentric analyses when working on languages other than English, or, more generally, the avoidance of Eurocentric analyses when working on non-European languages (see, e.g., Dryer [2006: 211]). Traditional Chinese linguistic theory, in contrast, is almost invariably Sinocentric (see Chappell 2006), in the sense that it takes the phonology and grammar of Standard Mandarin as its analytical and organizational point of departure regardless of how much the language under analysis differs from Mandarin in typological terms.

setting (4–8), and the research methodology and theoretical assumptions used in the book (8–10). Chapter 2 provides a fairly comprehensive review of previous Chinese-language publications on the Miao languages (11–19). However, the reader should be aware that this literature review, like many similar reviews in other Chinese-language studies of Xong, freely mixes citations of (i) studies of Xong in particular, (ii) studies of other Miao languages like Hmu and Hmong, and (iii) studies of the Miao-Yao family (or at least its Miao branch) as a whole, all with roughly equal frequency. Since these publications' titles rarely make clear which particular Miao language(s) they describe, and since this information is rarely provided in Yu (2011) itself, this section of Yu's grammar could potentially be confusing for non-specialists.

Chapter 3 gives a very brief overview of Aizhai Xong phonology (2011: 20–27). There is relatively little to say about this chapter, as it essentially consists of just a phoneme and tone inventory, some minimal pairs, a list of possible syllable structures, and some lexically specified tone sandhi rules.

The entirety of Chapter 4, over 150 pages in length, is devoted to lexical categories (2011: 28–180). Many of these lexical categories are covered in much more detail here in Yu's grammar than in any previous study of Xong. For example, a full eight pages (38–45) are devoted to locative nouns (cf. Section 5.5 of this grammar), another eight pages (84–92) to the verbal prefix /tɕi^{44}/ (cf. Section 10.5.1), and seven pages (170–177) to clause-final particles (cf. Section 9.2.1). Chapter 4 also discusses several topics that have never been examined in any previous publications, including Xong personal names (32, 33) and verbal aspect (92–96).

Unfortunately, parts of this chapter give the reader the distinct impression that Yu's grammar is being organized more on the basis of grammatical concepts found in Standard Mandarin than on any Xong-internal ones. For instance, the forms listed in the section on "prepositions" (2011: 159–162) seem to share very little in terms of their grammatical properties, and no definitional criteria are given to explain why these particular forms have been grouped together *as* prepositions. In fact, the only thing these forms seem to have in common is that their translation equivalents in Standard Mandarin are all prepositions (or "coverbs").[27] One could even argue that this Sinocentric theoretical framework is the single largest problem with Yu (2011), as many of the other problems mentioned below might ultimately stem from it (for more on Sinocentrism in general, see Chappell 2006). Still, in the interest of fairness, it must be pointed out that this issue is hardly unique to Yu's work. Many of the other publications discussed in Sections 2.5.2 and 2.5.3 below also suffer from Sinocentrism, often to an even greater degree than Yu (2011).

27 This author would argue that Xong does not in fact feature "prepositions" as a distinct lexical category, with the closest translation equivalents in the language (including the forms discussed in Yu [2011: 159–162]) instead being fully canonical members of the verb class. See, for instance, examples (12.99–12.102) and the accompanying discussion in Section 12.5 of this grammar.

Chapter 5 deals with an assortment of phrase types, including modifier phrases, complement phrases, and numeral-classifier phrases. Just as in Chapter 4, the mismatch between the organizational scheme used in Yu's book and the grammatical structure of the Xong language is difficult to overlook here, as the nine phrase types discussed in this chapter seem to have very little in common with each other. Furthermore, in this chapter it starts to become apparent that the division of Yu's grammar into chapters on lexical categories, phrases, syntactic constituents, and so on means that information on any particular grammatical topic will usually be scattered across several chapters. This latter problem is further compounded by the fact that the book contains only a handful of cross-references and completely lacks an index.

A particularly striking example is Yu's coverage of relative clauses. Discussion of these clauses is scattered throughout various sections of Chapters 4, 5, and 6. For instance, relative clauses marked with /naŋ^{44}/ (the cognate form in Fenghuang Xong is *naond* 'ASSOC'; see Section 8.1.2 of this grammar) are discussed in Chapter 4 on pages 167 and 168, in Chapter 5 on pages 188 and 189, and in Chapter 6 on pages 240 to 243. Similarly, relative clauses marked with /ma^{31}/ (the cognate form in Fenghuang Xong is *manx* 'REL'; see Section 8.1.4 of this grammar) are discussed in Chapter 4 on pages 102, 103, 123, 124, 168, and 169, in Chapter 5 on pages 186 and 187, and in Chapter 6 on pages 240 to 243. None of these pages cross-references any of the others and, again, the book lacks an index.

Chapter 6 focuses on syntactic constituents, including subjects, objects, complements, and predicates. Unfortunately, many of these constituent types are defined through vague combinations of syntactic and semantic criteria, and the results are sometimes difficult to make sense of. Another problem is that argument ellipsis is not factored into any of the analyses presented in this chapter. Instead, it seems to be implicitly assumed that every argument must be overtly expressed and, conversely, that arguments which are not overtly expressed are irrelevant to a sentence's analysis (cf. Section 9.1.2 of this grammar).

Chapter 7 discusses various types of Xong sentences (e.g. simple sentences, comparative sentences, topic-comment sentences, etc.), and the analyses here range from impressive to frustrating. The section on comparative sentences (2011: 286–296), for instance, is remarkably thorough and leaves the reader with very few unanswered questions. In contrast, the analysis of Aizhai Xong's so-called "passive" construction (277–286) is rather shallow, and in fact it seems to be disproved by the very example sentences provided. However, since fairly extensive data is needed to argue against the analysis of the "passive" construction given in Yu (2011), this issue will be set aside for now and taken up again in detail in Section 9.3.4 of this grammar.

While Chapter 8 is a relatively straightforward overview of sentential moods (i.e. declarative, imperative, interrogative, and exclamatory), Chapter 9 and the appendices following it constitute some of the strongest sections of Yu's grammar. The comprehensive and well organized discussion of tetrasyllabic expressions on pages 325 to 338 (cf. Sections 5.3.3 and 12.2.2 of this grammar) is especially useful. The appendices at the end of Yu's book include transcribed texts from a variety of genres, including folktales (2011: 350–403), conversations (404–408), songs (409–413), and riddles (414–424), all with interlinear glosses and free translations in Chinese. These appendices also contain a long list of tetrasyllabic expressions arranged by the initial consonant of each expression's first syllable (425–455), as well as a Chinese–Xong wordlist with over 3,000 entries arranged by semantic field (456–500).

Despite the various criticisms that have been leveled at it in this section, Yu's grammar remains one of the most thorough descriptions of any Miao language published to date. While this author disagrees with many of the conclusions reached in it, it still deserves credit for greatly surpassing most previous studies of Xong, both in the amount of linguistic data provided and in the depth of argumentation applied to that data. However, it is clear that the publication of Yu (2011) has not obviated the need for a comprehensive, typologically informed, and above all non-Sinocentric phonological and grammatical description of Xong written within the framework of basic linguistic theory.

2.5.2 Other major Chinese publications on Xong

This section briefly reviews five of the most significant studies of Xong produced prior to Yu (2011): Xiang (1999), Luo (1990) and (2005), Yang (2004), and Chen (2009).[28] While Xiang (1999) was of course published after Luo (1990), it is discussed first in this section due to the many similarities it shares with Yu's 2011 grammar (see Section 2.5.1 above).

2.5.2.1 Xiang (1999)

Xiang (1999) is essentially a grammatical sketch of the "standard" variety of Xong spoken in Jiwei Township (*Jíwèi Xiāng* 吉卫乡), located in Xiangxi Prefecture's Huayuan County (*Huāyuán Xiàn* 花垣县) (see Section 2.4 for discussion of what that "standard" status entails, and see Figure 2.6 in Section 2.7.1 for a map showing Jiwei Township's location within Huayuan County). This author's own consultants, all of whom hail from Fenghuang County (see Section 2.7), report that Jiwei Xong is mostly intelligible when spoken slowly but only partially intelligible when spoken at normal conversational speed. It is thus more intelligible to these consultants than Aizhai Xong is (see Section 2.5.1), but still less intelligible to them than other Xong varieties spoken within Fenghuang are.

Xiang's book opens with an introduction written by Fushi Wang, which outlines the division of the Miao *yuyan* into the Chuanqiandian, Qiandong, and Xiangxi

28 Note, though, that any studies which focus specifically on Xong varieties spoken within Fenghuang County are discussed in Section 2.5.3 below rather than here.

fangyan (see Section 2.4 of this grammar) as well as the division of Xiangxi Miao into Xong and Eastern Xiangxi Miao (see Section 2.2.1). The main body of the book is then divided into four chapters, focusing in turn on phonology, morphology and loanwords, grammar, and orthography. Four appendices, all quite useful, are included as well. While Xiang discusses the standard Xong orthography at several points throughout the book, all Xong utterances and texts in it are transcribed using a modified version of IPA alone.

Xiang's phonology chapter (1999: 7–15) is roughly the same length as the one in Yu (2011). It provides phoneme and tone inventories as well as some notes on allophonic variation, syllable structure, and lexically specified tone sandhi. This chapter is slightly more comprehensive than the equivalent chapter in Yu (2011) in that it includes a short phonetic description of each phoneme and tone, but overall the phonological portion of Xiang (1999) is still quite brief.

The following chapter is divided into two main sections. The first is devoted to morphological phenomena (1999: 16–29), including compounding, reduplication, nominal prefixes, and tetrasyllabic expressions. The second focuses on borrowings from Sinitic (29–34), and it includes discussion of some factors that determine the tones on borrowed forms along with a list of semantic fields in which borrowings are particularly common.

At nearly ninety pages in length, Xiang's chapter on Jiwei Xong grammar (1999: 35–122) is by far the longest one in the book. In terms of its organization and analyses, this chapter is nearly an archetypical example of traditional Chinese linguistic theory (see Section 2.5.1 above). Like most studies written within this theoretical framework, the chapter consists of an initial section on lexical categories (nouns, pronouns, classifiers, etc.), then a section on phrase types (modifier phrases, complement phrases, serial verb phrases, etc.), then a section on syntactic constituents (subjects, objects, complements, etc.), and then finally a series of short sections on miscellaneous sentence-level issues, including simple vs. complex sentences and sentential mood (declarative, interrogative, etc.).

Many of the criticisms directed at the grammatical analyses in Yu (2011) also apply to those found in Xiang (1999), including a certain degree of Sinocentrism and the use of vague definitions (or no definitions at all) for many important grammatical concepts. On the whole, though, the analyses in Xiang (1999) tend to be shallower than the ones in Yu (2011), with several sections consisting of nothing more than a handful of examples of the grammatical category or construction in question.

The final chapter of Xiang's book (1999: 123–127) gives a straightforward overview of the standard Xong orthography, and the first appendix (128–131) provides the actual text of the official Xong orthography guide released in 1959. The remaining three appendices consist of a series of tables listing all attested syllables in Jiwei Xong (132–171), a set of three Jiwei Xong folktales with interlinear glosses and free translations in Chinese (172–218), and a Chinese–Jiwei Xong wordlist (219–257).

In conclusion, Xiang (1999) is certainly the most complete grammatical description available for the Jiwei variety of Xong, and it should be of interest to all Xong scholars for the extensive glossed texts it contains. But in terms of breadth of grammatical coverage or depth of grammatical analysis, Xiang's book offers little to recommend it over Yu (2011) or Luo (1990) and (2005).

2.5.2.2 Luo (1990) and (2005)

Luo (1990) and (2005) are both primarily grammatical descriptions of Xong, although the latter publication also includes a substantial Xong–Chinese dictionary. Oddly, it is never explicitly stated which particular Xong variety is being described in either book. In Luo's 2005 study it is only mentioned that the Xong variety being described is spoken within Songtao County (*Sōngtáo Xiàn* 松桃县) in eastern Guizhou Province (see Figure 2.6 in Section 2.7.1 below), and in his 1990 study the Xong variety being described is not identfied in any way. However, many of Luo's previous publications on Xong grammar focused on the variety spoken in Xiunao Village (*Xiùnǎo Zhài* 臭脑寨) in Songtao County (Niederer 1998: 300), and so it is quite possible that the Xong varieties described in Luo (1990) and (2005) are in fact Xiunao Xong as well.

While this author's own consultants from Fenghuang County were not familiar with Xiunao Xong in particular, they did report that most Songtao Xong varieties are largely intelligible to them when spoken slowly, but only partially intelligible when spoken at normal speed. In other words, Songtao Xong is roughly as intelligible to Fenghuang Xong speakers as Jiwei Xong is (see Section 2.5.2.1), and it is significantly more intelligible to them than Aizhai Xong is (see Section 2.5.1).

The overall organizational structures in Luo (1990) and Luo (2005) are nearly identical. The latter book is simply an expanded version of the former, with a few new sections added in and a few original sections enlarged. Because of this, most comments in this section apply to both books equally, although occasional differences between the books will be mentioned where relevant. Note that Luo (1990) transcribes Xong forms and utterances using a practical orthography very similar to the standard Jiwei-based one (see Section 4.3 of this grammar), while Luo (2005) uses a modified version of IPA instead.

While Luo (1990) contains no phonological information whatsoever, a simple phoneme and tone inventory for the Xong variety under description is given in Luo (2005: 3–7). This is accompanied by a short phonetic description of each phoneme and tone, along with a suggested practical orthography. Each book also contains a section that describes the theoretical framework and major analytical assumptions used in it ([1990: 1–10], [2005: 8–34]).

The two books then move through several chapters devoted to lexical categories, covering in turn (i) nouns, (ii) numerals, (iii) classifiers, (iv) demonstratives and pronouns, (v) adjectives and ideophones, (vi) verbs, prepositions, and adverbs,

(vii) conjunctions, particles, and interjections, and finally (viii) "articles".[29] All these chapters together occupy slightly less than a hundred pages in each book ([1990: 11–106], [2005: 35–132]). There is little information in these chapters that will be new to readers who are already familiar with Xiang (1999) and Yu (2011), although of course Luo (1990) was published before either of those works. On the whole, these sections of Luo (1990) and (2005) are more comprehensive than the equivalent sections of Xiang (1999) but less so than those of Yu (2011).

These chapters on lexical categories are followed by chapters on phrase types ([1990: 107–130], [2005: 133–156]), which are followed in turn by chapters on syntactic constituents ([1990: 131–157], [2005: 157–186]) and miscellaneous sentence-related issues ([1990: 158–170], [2005: 197–219]). Most of these chapters are broadly similar to the equivalent ones in Xiang (1999) and Yu (2011), and they thus require little comment here.

Finally, the most significant difference between Luo (1990) and Luo (2005) is the inclusion of a substantial Xong–Chinese dictionary in the latter. This dictionary takes up nearly two hundred pages (2005: 223–414) and includes nearly nine hundred Xong lexical items. Note that this is a true dictionary, not just a wordlist, as it includes semantic and grammatical notes as well as example sentences (or at least example phrases) for most Xong forms listed in it.

Overall, Luo (1990) and Luo (2005) were each the most complete grammatical description available for any Xong variety at the time of their respective publications. Even though Yu's 2011 grammar is much more comprehensive than Luo's books, the analyses in it are not always more insightful or better supported by the relevant data. Still, it must be said that both of Luo's books would have been significantly improved by the addition of more (or, in the case of Luo 1990, any) information on the phonological and sociolinguistic aspects of the varieties they describe, as well as by the addition of some Xong texts.

2.5.2.3 Yang (2004)

Yang (2004) is quite unlike the other works reviewed in this section. Rather than concentrating on a single Xong variety, Yang's book is a phonological and lexical survey of the entire Xiangxi Miao sub-branch of Miao-Yao. Much of the book focuses on six representative Xiangxi Miao varieties, but Yang also provides a great deal of background information on the history of Xiangxi Miao in general. Yang (2004) is also notable for including the most comprehensive and well supported scheme for internal

29 Four "articles" (*guàncí* 冠词) are discussed in each of Luo's books ([1990: 85–106], [2005: 115–132]). Two of these forms are cognate with Fenghuang Xong's nominal prefixes *ghaob-* 'NOM' and *daob-* 'AN' (see Sections 5.4.2.1 and 5.4.2.2 of this grammar), one is cognate with Fenghuang Xong's relative clause marker *manx* 'REL' (see Section 8.1.4), and one is cognate with Fenghuang Xong's verbal prefix *(d)id-* 'DID' (see Section 10.5.1).

divisions within Xiangxi Miao proposed so far (see Section 2.2.1 of this grammar for details). All Xiangxi Miao forms in the book are presented in a modified version of IPA rather than in a practical orthography.

The book is divided into six chapters and a single lengthy appendix. Chapter 1 covers a variety of topics, beginning with the modern and historical speaker population sizes and geographic distributions of Xiangxi Miao (2004: 1–8). This is followed by a literature review (8–12, 31–37) and an extremely thorough discussion of the various Sinitic- and Latin-derived orthographies that have been used to transcribe the Xiangxi Miao languages (12–20, 22–31).

Chapter 2 presents Yang's suggested scheme for internal divisions within Xiangxi Miao. After reviewing and rejecting earlier such schemes proposed by other scholars (2004: 38–42), Yang describes how his own scheme divides Xiangxi Miao into six *tuyu* (see Sections 2.2.1 and 2.4 for more on this term). Three of these *tuyu* are grouped together as Xong, and the other three (comprising the languages Suang, Seu, and San) are grouped together as Eastern Xiangxi Miao. Yang then compares his six proposed *tuyu* in terms of geographic extent and number of speakers (43–45), phonological characteristics (45–50), and lexical characteristics (50–73). Finally, he concludes the chapter by explaining why he groups *tuyu* 1, 2, and 3 together as Xong and *tuyu* 4, 5, and 6 together as Eastern Xiangxi Miao (74–79).

Chapter 3 deals with Xiangxi Miao phonology. In the chapter's first section (2004: 80–89), Yang provides a phoneme inventory, a tone inventory, and a few notes on allophonic variation for each of the six specific Xiangxi Miao varieties discussed in his book (one from each of his six proposed *tuyu*). The second, much longer section of the chapter (89–123) then outlines the phonological development of these six Xiangxi Miao varieties from a common ancestor.

Chapter 4 is similarly divided into two parts. The first of these (2004: 124–138) covers various morphological phenomena in Xiangxi Miao, focusing in particular on nominal and verbal prefixes, noun compounds, and tetrasyllabic expressions. Of particular interest here is Yang's discussion of variation in prefix systems across the six Xiangxi Miao varieties examined in his book (124–126). The second part of the chapter (138–160) then provides a thorough discussion of Sinitic borrowings in the Xiangxi Miao languages.

Chapter 5 is devoted to grammar. The chapter begins with a brief discussion of grammatical variation within Xiangxi Miao, especially variation concerning nominal prefixes and constituent ordering in lexical compounds (2004: 161–166). The bulk of the chapter is then taken up by a grammatical sketch of the Xong variety spoken in Yangmeng Village (*Yángmèng Cūn* 阳孟村) (167–199). Yangmeng is a subsidiary village of Aizhai Town (see Section 2.5.1 above), and like Aizhai Xong, Yangmeng Xong belongs to Yang's *tuyu* 2. Unfortunately, the grammatical sketch that Yang gives here is firmly situated within the framework of traditional Chinese linguistic theory (again, see Section 2.5.1), and there is little information in it that will be new to readers already familiar with Luo (1990), Xiang (1999), Luo (2005), or Yu (2011).

Chapter 6 consists of six short texts, one for each of the six specific Xiangxi Miao varieties described in the book (2004: 200–242). Each text is a different folktale ranging from four to eight pages in length, with interlinear glosses and free translations in Chinese. The appendix following this chapter contains an extensive wordlist with approximately 2,500 entries organized by semantic field (243–371). For each entry, Yang provides seven forms: an initial gloss in Chinese, and then the equivalent form in each of those same six Xiangxi Miao varieties.

In summary, Yang (2004) not only provides a wealth of data on the history of Xiangxi Miao studies and on the history of the Xiangxi Miao languages themselves, it also provides a great deal of synchronic information on several severely underdescribed Xiangxi Miao varieties. While the grammatical sketch it contains obviously cannot compare to Yu's 2011 grammar, Yang's book still remains one of the most important publications on Xiangxi Miao to date.

2.5.2.4 Chen (2009)

Chen (2009) is a doctoral dissertation that examines a number of phonetic, phonological, grammatical, and historical aspects of the Xong variety spoken in Daxing Town (*Dàxīng Zhèn* 大兴镇), located in Songtao County in Guizhou Province (see also Section 2.5.2.2 above). The dissertation is divided into seven chapters, all of which use only a modified version of IPA (never a practical orthography) to transcribe Xong forms.

Chapter 1 (2009: 1–5) contains a brief literature review and a discussion of the author's research methodology. Chapter 2 then provides information on a range of topics, including some background on Daxing Town itself (6, 7), a brief phonological description of Daxing Xong (8–13), and a sketch of Daxing Xong grammar (14–31). The phonological description in this chapter is similar in length to those in Xiang (1999) and Yu (2011). It includes phoneme and tone inventories, an example syllable for each phoneme and tone (but no minimal pairs), a pitch plot for each tone, and some notes on tone sandhi. Unfortunately, the following grammatical sketch is heavily Sinocentric and even shorter than the one in Yang (2004).

Chapter 3 is devoted to Daxing Xong morphology. The chapter focuses on three morphological phenomena in particular, namely nominal prefixes, reduplication, and fossilized sub-syllabic morphology. Chen's thorough discussion of nominal prefixes is probably the strongest section of the chapter (2009: 37–52). Especially noteworthy is the observation that it is sometimes impossible to draw a clear line between nominal prefixes and noun roots, since the former arise from grammaticalization of the latter (40). The following section on reduplication is somewhat less impressive, as it consists merely of a handful of examples of reduplicated forms from various lexical categories (53–55). Finally, the section on fossilized sub-syllabic morphology presents several dozen pairs of monosyllabic morphemes whose members show some phonological and semantic similarities and which Chen suggests might be the result of derivational processes no longer operational in modern Xong (55–58). Some of the proposed pairs in this section do indeed seem to suggest some sort of historical relationship between their members (e.g. /tɑ5/ 'to kill' vs. /tɑ6/ 'to die'), but many others show only vague phonological and semantic resemblances which could easily be due to chance (e.g. /pj^{h}ɔ1/ 'to blow' vs. /p^{h}u3/ 'to speak'). This section is also weakened by the fact that none of the modern Xong forms in question are compared with their reconstructed etymological sources in Proto-Miao or Proto-Miao-Yao (or in Middle or Old Chinese, for those forms borrowed from Sinitic).

Chapter 4 covers several phonetic and phonological topics, including tone sandhi (2009: 60–63), prenasalized consonants (63–69), syllabic nasals (69, 70), nasal spreading (70, 71), and age- and gender-based phonetic variation (73–80). Not all of the arguments advanced in this chapter seem to be supported by the data provided. For example, no phonological (as opposed to phonetic) evidence whatsoever is given for the argument that syllables with prenasalized initial consonants consist of three moras while other syllables consist of only two (64–69). Still, on the whole this chapter constitutes one of the most thorough studies of Xong phonetics published so far. Unfortunately, the following Chapter 5 is rather less interesting, as it merely compares the phoneme and tone inventories of Daxing Xong with those of Jiwei Xong, with little actual analysis involved (81–90).

Chapter 6, the longest in the dissertation, focuses on Sinitic loanwords in Daxing Xong (2009: 91–158). These are divided into three historical levels: those borrowed in the modern era, those borrowed from the Middle Chinese (*Zhōnggǔ Hànyǔ* 中古汉语) of the mid first millenium C.E., and those borrowed from the Old Chinese (*Shànggǔ Hànyǔ* 上古汉语) of the first millennium B.C.E. The very brief Chapter 7 summarizes some of Chen's findings (159–161), and the dissertation then ends with a Chinese–Daxing Xong wordlist roughly organized by semantic field (169–196).

Overall, Chen's dissertation covers quite an eclectic range of topics. Some of these (such as the grammatical sketch in Chapter 2 or the entirety of Chapter 5) could have been left out without much loss, while others (such as the discussion of tone sandhi in Chapter 4) could have been covered in slightly greater depth. Nevertheless, while particular analyses in Chen (2009) may not always be entirely convincing, on the whole the dissertation is still certainly worth consulting, especially for its valuable phonetic and phonological information on a relatively understudied Xong variety.

2.5.3 Chinese publications on Fenghuang Xong

This section discusses all Chinese-language publications known to the author which – like this grammar itself – examine Xong varieties spoken within Fenghuang County. Sections 2.5.3.1 and 2.5.3.2 each discuss one of the two book-length works published on Fenghuang Xong, while Section 2.5.3.3 discusses several shorter studies. Note that Sposato (2012), an English-language publication dealing with relative clauses in Fenghuang Xong, is discussed in Section 2.5.4 further below.

2.5.3.1 He (2009)

He (2009) is primarily a phonological study of the Sinitic variety spoken across Fenghuang County (hereafter referred to as "Fenghuang Chinese") and the Xong variety spoken in Gouliang Village (*Gōuliáng Cūn* 勾良村), a subsidiary village of Fenghuang's Luochaojing Township (*Luòcháojǐng Xiāng* 落潮井乡) (see Figure 2.6 in Section 2.7.1). Note that Gouliang Xong is also described in Wu (2007), Wu (2011), and Zhenghai Long (2011), all of which are discussed in Section 2.5.3.3 below.

He's first chapter surveys previous studies of Fenghuang Chinese and Fenghuang Xong (2009: 2–7), discusses the author's research methodology (9, 10), and provides background information on Fenghuang County in general (11). His second chapter focuses on Fenghuang Chinese, which He argues is a variety of Gan Chinese that has been heavily influenced by Southwestern Mandarin (31–34). He gives phoneme and tone inventories (12–14), discusses some of the variety's noteworthy phonological characteristics (14–17, 27–30) and its historical development (30–34), and provides lists of attested syllables (17–26) and homophones (34–54). The largest section of the chapter is a Standard Mandarin–Fenghuang Chinese wordlist organized by semantic category (54–91), which is followed by notes on a handful of grammatical forms (pronouns, aspectual markers, etc.) at the end of the chapter (91–94).

Chapter 3, by far the longest one in the book (2009: 95–216), deals exclusively with Fenghuang Xong (primarily the variety spoken in Gouliang Village, although He does include a handful of forms from other Fenghuang Xong varieties on pages 99–102). The chapter is divided into four sections. The first of these gives phoneme and tone inventories for Gouliang Xong, along with a few phonetic notes (95–98). The second section discusses a variety of phonological and phonetic issues related to Gouliang Xong, including comparisons between the segmental inventories of Gouliang Xong and Jiwei Xong, prensasalized consonants, and the relationship between tones and breathy voicing (98–107). The third section provides tables of all attested syllables in Gouliang Xong (107–178), and the fourth provides a Chinese–Gouliang Xong wordlist organized by semantic category (179–216).

Most of the phonological distinctions recorded in Chapter 3 of He (2009) match up with those encountered by this author in the speech of his own consultants from Fenghuang County. There are a number of phonetic differences between Gouliang Xong as described in He's book and the Xong varieties described in Chapter 3 of this grammar (especially in terms of phonetic realization of vowels), but little that exceeds the degree of interspeaker variation found among this author's own consultants. However, there do appear to be some major differences between the tone system of Gouliang Xong and the tone systems described in Section 3.5 of this grammar, as a comparison of He (2009: 97, 98, 103–107) with that section will show.

Finally, Chapters 4 and 5 are both devoted to various aspects of Sinitic loanwords in Fenghuang Xong. Chapter 4 (2009: 217–237) classifies these loanwords into three historical layers, while Chapter 5 (238–250) focuses specifically on loanwords borrowed from Sinitic varieties spoken primarily in Hunan Province (as opposed to those borrowed from less geographically constrained varieties, such as Old Chinese or Standard Mandarin).

Overall, He (2009) contains one of the most thorough phonological studies of any Xong variety to precede this grammar, and the information contained in He's book has proven invaluable to the author in the course of his own fieldwork in Fenghuang County.

2.5.3.2 Ling and Rui ([1947] 2003)

Ling and Rui ([1947] 2003) is primarily an ethnographic study of the Xong-speaking inhabitants of the Xiangxi region. It covers a wealth of topics, including the geography and climate of Xiangxi and the economic pursuits, family life, and religion of the region's Xong speakers. The book also includes a sizable collection of Xong folktales and other texts, though unfortunately only free translations in Chinese are provided for these, not the original Xong.

Of course, the section of Ling and Rui's work most relevant to this grammar is the chapter on the Xong language (1947: 416–467) (note that all page numbers cited here from Ling and Rui's work refer to the original 1947 version rather than the 2003 reprint, since the author of this grammar only had access to the former). Ling and Rui's two primary Xong-speaking consultants both hailed from Fenghuang County, although the exact locations of their home villages are unclear – Ling and Rui merely state that one consultant's village was located approximately twenty kilometers from the county seat, while the other's was approximately forty kilometers from the county seat (1947: 419).

There are significant differences between the phonological system described in Ling and Rui (1947: 421–432) and the one described in Chapter 3 of this grammar. For instance, Ling and Rui's book lists only a single series of sibilant affricates (retroflex, in this case), although all varieties of Fenghuang Xong known to this author have three contrastive series of sibilant affricates (see Sections 3.2.1.6 through 3.2.1.8). The book also describes Fenghuang Xong as contrasting (i) unaspirated, non-prenasalized plosives, (ii) aspirated, non-prenasalized plosives, and (iii) aspirated, prenasalized plosives, but not (iv) unaspirated, prenasalized plosives (cf. Section 3.2.1.1). Ling and Rui's claim that only five tones are distinguished in their consultants' speech (1947: 431) is also somewhat surprising, since all varieties of Fenghuang Xong encountered by this author (see Section 3.5) or described by other scholars (see Sections 2.5.3.1 and 2.5.3.3) distinguish at least seven. It is unclear, though, which differences between the phonological system described in Ling and Rui's work and those described in this grammar and in other studies are due to actual dialectal and/or diachronic variation, and which are due to simple errors of analysis.

Ling and Rui's book also features a brief grammatical sketch of Fenghuang Xong (1947: 432–451) and a Chinese–Xong wordlist organized by semantic field (451–466). The wordlist is uncontroversial, but unfortunately the grammatical sketch is written firmly within the framework of traditional Chinese linguistic theory (see

Section 2.5.1 above) and concentrates almost entirely on vaguely defined lexical categories. It is thus likely to be of only limited use to modern scholars.

2.5.3.3 Other publications on Fenghuang Xong

The author is aware of two master's theses that focus on the Xong variety spoken in Gouliang Village in Fenghuang County (see also Section 2.5.3.1 above). The first such thesis, Wu (2007), is purportedly a study of the relative morphological productivity of various morphemes in Gouliang Xong (or, in other words, the relative potential of these morphemes to occur in a large number of distinct lexemes). The main argument of Wu (2007) is that, due to the productivity of these morphemes, there should be a one-to-one correspondence between *ci* (*cí* 词) and orthographic words in texts that use Latin-derived Xong orthographies (including the standard Xong orthography described in Section 4.3 of this grammar), rather than a one-to-one correspondence between syllables and orthographic words. That is, orthographic spaces should be used to separate adjacent *ci* in Xong publications rather than being used to separate adjacent syllables (for similar arguments applied to Songtao Xong, see Peng 2007). The term *ci* has no exact equivalent in English, as it encompasses free morphemes and lexical compounds as well as certain idioms and proverbs. However, a reasonable translation in the context of Wu (2007) might be "linguistic word", in contrast to the orthographic words that Wu also discusses.

Unfortunately, the term *ci* is never actually defined in Wu (2007), with the author apparently relying solely on intuition to determine what counts as a *ci* and what does not. Furthermore, there does not appear to be any logical relationship between the data presented in Wu's thesis and the conclusion eventually reached in it. Aside from a brief introduction (2007: 1–8) and conclusion (72, 73), the thesis consists of just three sections. The first of these contains tables that list all attested Gouliang Xong morphemes (8–32), the second contains a Gouliang Xong–Chinese wordlist (32–51), and the third contains a short Gouliang Xong–Chinese dictionary (51–72). This dictionary is organized by lexical category (nouns, verbs, etc.), and a few example compounds and phrases are provided for each of its entries. It is not clear how the data in any of these three sections is intended to support the thesis' main argument, nor is it clear what connection any of these sections has to orthographic considerations.

In contrast, Wu (2011) – the second master's thesis to focus on Gouliang Xong – is a very competent study of Xong relative clauses. Wu is a native speaker of Gouliang Xong, and she bases her study on a corpus consisting of thirty hours of recorded speech plus several text collections compiled by other authors (Wu 2011: 7, 8). Wu's thesis provides thorough discussion and plentiful examples of all the relative clause types discussed in Sposato (2012) (see Section 2.5.4 below), as well as several others. It also displays significantly more familiarity with contemporary typological literature and analytic techniques than any other work on Xong known to the author. While the author does not necessarily agree with all of the conclusions reached in Wu

(2011), overall the study is one of the more impressive ones to be published on Xong in recent years. Note that since Wu's thesis concerns itself solely with relative clauses, it is discussed in more detail in Section 8.1.1 of this grammar.

Finally, at least three short articles have also been published on varieties of Fenghuang Xong. The first of these, Mingchun Long (2011), is essentially just a proposed list of phonemes and tones for the Xong variety spoken in Yangguang Village (*Yángguāng Cūn* 阳光村), located near Sangongqiao Township (*Sāngǒngqiáo Xiāng* 三拱桥乡) in Fenghuang County (see Figure 2.6 in Section 2.7.1 below). The second article, Zhenghai Long (2011), is a fairly straightforward survey of Sinitic loanwords in Gouliang Xong. The third article, Liang (2012), uses purely phonetic data in an attempt to determine the number of tones in the Xong variety spoken in Bandanghe Village (*Bǎndānghé Cūn* 板当禾村), located near Shanjiang Town (*Shānjiāng Zhèn* 山江镇) (again, see Figure 2.6 in Section 2.7.1 below). Unfortunately, certain methodological aspects of Liang (2012) are rather questionable. For instance, fewer than two dozen Xong syllables (types, not tokens) were examined, and non-modal phonation types were completely ignored.

2.5.4 Publications on Xong in languages other than Chinese

The author is aware of only a single publication in a language other than Chinese that is devoted exclusively to Xong, this being the author's own 2012 paper on Xong relative clauses. Much of the data in Sposato (2012) was collected by the author during his preliminary fieldwork in Yankan Village (*Yánkǎn Cūn* 岩坎村) in Fenghuang County (see Section 2.7), though the article also incorporates some data from Xiang (1999), Yang (2004), and Luo (2005). However, since at the time Sposato (2012) was published the author had performed only a few weeks of fieldwork on Xong and had only a limited understanding of Yankan Xong phonology, several Xong forms in the article were mistranscribed. For example, *jeud* 'alcohol' was mistranscribed as **jud*, *nins* 'COP' as **nis*, and *manx* 'REL' as **max*. Furthermore, it was claimed in Sposato (2012: 50, fn. 4) that Yankan Xong has only seven tones, when in fact it has eight (see Section 3.5.2). Naturally, the description of Xong relative clauses in Section 8.1 of this grammar supersedes the one in Sposato (2012).

While Sposato (2012) is the only non-Chinese publication that focuses on Xong in particular, there are a number of publications in English (as well as at least one in French, namely Niederer 1998) that present some Xong data in the context of a family-wide survey of Miao-Yao. In nearly all cases known to the author, this Xong data is taken from previously published Chinese-language studies rather than being collected through the authors' own fieldwork (but see the following paragraph for one exception). Examples include (i) a phonological sketch of Jiwei Xong and some notes on the development of that variety from Proto-Miao in Purnell's dissertation on Proto-Miao, Proto-Yao, and Proto-Miao-Yao (1970: 20, 21, 91–95), (ii) another phonological sketch of Jiwei Xong in Niederer's survey of the Miao-Yao family (1998: 66–71), (iii) lexical data from Jiwei Xong scattered throughout Ratliff's 2010 book on the history of Miao-Yao, and (iv) word order information and example sentences (the latter taken from Yu 2011) from Aizhai Xong in Sposato's 2014 study of word order in Miao-Yao. A discussion of ordering constraints in Aizhai Xong noun compounds (based on data taken from Yu 2004) can also be found in Mortensen (2006: 261–268).

Finally, Gerner's 2009 survey of Miao demonstratives and Gerner and Bisang's 2010 study of Miao classifiers both include some data from Jiwei Xong, which is referred to in both papers as "Huayuan Qoxung" (Huayuan being the county in which Jiwei Township is located; see Figure 2.6 in Section 2.7.1 below). Gerner (2009) in particular is noteworthy in that – to the best of this author's knowledge – it is the only previous publication (aside from Sposato 2012) in a language other than Chinese that includes primary Xong data elicited from a native speaker, rather than merely including data taken from previous Chinese-language publications.

2.6 Theoretical framework and research methodology

2.6.1 Theoretical framework

This grammar is written within the framework of basic linguistic theory, which is essentially a typologically informed, non-Eurocentric version of traditional Western grammar. This framework has been used (though often only implicitly) in a number of highly regarded descriptive grammars published over the past several decades, including Matisoff's 1973 grammar of Lahu, Haspelmath's 1993 grammar of Lezgian, Evans' 1995 grammar of Kayardild, Kruspe's 2004 grammar of Semelai, and Enfield's 2007 grammar of Lao, among many others. Useful overviews of the theory itself can be found in Dryer (2006) and Dixon (2010a, 2010b, 2012).

In contrast to other popular theoretical frameworks, basic linguistic theory was not proposed in any single publication by any one linguist or group of linguists. Instead, it developed gradually out of traditional Western grammar (which itself had its origins in the work of the Greek and Roman grammarians of antiquity), although it has absorbed influences from structuralism, linguistic typology, and early generative approaches as well (Dryer 2006: 211). These idiosyncratic origins are responsible for a number of major differences between basic linguistic theory and other theoretical frameworks.

Perhaps the most salient such difference is that analyses in basic linguistic theory are presented with a minimum of formalist devices. For better or worse, many theoretical frameworks are characterized not only by the general philosophical and analytical assumptions underlying each framework, but also by the particular presentational devices favored by the framework's practitioners. Examples include the binary-branching tree diagrams used to present analyses in Minimalism (see, e.g.,

Boeckx 2003), the nested attribute value matrices used in Head-Driven Phrase Structure Grammar (Pollard and Sag 1994), and the tables of eye-catching punctuation marks and dingbats (e.g. <!>, <*>, <☞>) used in Optimality Theory (Prince and Smolensky 2004). In contrast to these, analyses in basic linguistic theory are typically presented using comparatively non-technical English (or whatever the metalanguage of description is), with straightforward tables and charts (often no more complex than those found in a typical pedagogical grammar) used in a supplementary fashion.

A less obvious (though even more important) difference is basic linguistic theory's emphasis on language-specific criteria for positing and defining grammatical concepts. Basic linguistic theory does not presume the universal existence of any grammatical categories (like "determiner phrase", "subject", or even "noun"), features (like "number" or "gender"), or constructions (like "serial verb" or "passive"), though it freely admits that some of these concepts are present in the great majority of attested languages, and some may even be present in every attested language. Instead, an analysis of a particular language done in basic linguistic theory will posit only those grammatical concepts necessary to describe the observed facts of that language, with no regard for other languages (including prestigious European languages like English) or for universal conceptions of grammar. For example, Xong lacks anything that could profitably be described as grammatical gender, and so the concept of grammatical gender simply plays no part in the analyses presented in this grammar. Even when a widely attested grammatical concept (like "noun phrase" or "verb") is postulated for a particular language, an analysis done in basic linguistic theory will define that concept solely on language-internal criteria.

For these reasons, presenting a grammatical description within the framework of basic linguistic theory should help to minimize any Anglocentric or Eurocentric analytical biases. At the same time, it also ensures that the description will be maximally accessible both synchronically and diachronically: synchronically in the sense that the author's analyses will be comprehensible to linguists of all theoretical persuasions, and diachronically in the sense that the analyses should remain comprehensible to a majority of linguists for a relatively long period of time – longer, at least, than the average shelf-life of more formalist theories.

2.6.2 Research methodology

The author's research methodology involved relatively standard linguistic fieldwork techniques (see, e.g., Mosel 2006 and Bowern 2008). The author first made two short fieldwork trips, one in 2009 and one in 2010, to various Xong-speaking communities in Fenghuang County to meet possible consultants and collect some preliminary recordings. Each of these early fieldwork trips lasted about a month, and during both of them (just as during all subsequent trips) the author was traveling and working alone.

The author then made three subsequent fieldwork trips that lasted approximately eight months in total. The first was a four-month trip made in late 2012, the second a three-month trip made in late 2013, and the third a one-month trip made in mid 2014. The great majority of these eight months were spent in La'ershan Town (*Là'ěrshān Zhèn* 腊尔山镇; see Section 2.7.1), although the author did make periodic trips to nearby villages to collect recordings from older monolingual (or nearly so) speakers. The author stayed with a Xong-speaking family while in La'ershan, which afforded him the opportunity to collect examples of casual conversation among family members in addition to more formal elicited texts. Most of the author's elicitation sessions were done either in his host family's home or at the primary school in La'ershan, where a majority of his primary consultants lived and worked. All such sessions were conducted in Standard Mandarin and recorded on the author's Marantz PMD 661 portable SD recorder.

While the author ended up collecting texts from over a dozen Xong speakers (as well as occasional utterances from a much greater number), only six of his consultants actually participated in phonological and grammatical elicitations or text glossing and translation. All six were native speakers of Xong, although all six were also fluent in Fenghuang Chinese (see Section 2.7.2) and Standard Mandarin. Four of these consultants were female teachers working at the primary school in La'ershan, one was a female farmer, and one was a male farmer and part-time taxi driver. All six were in their twenties or thirties. Some basic biographical information about these primary consultants is given (with each consultant's permission) in Table 2.1 below.

Table 2.1: Biographical information for the author's primary consultants.

NAME (XONG)	NAME (CHINESE PINYIN)	NAME (CHINESE CHARACTERS)	GENDER	YEAR OF BIRTH	HOMETOWN	PROFESSION
Lonl Cheinf Huaok	Lóng Chénghuā	龙成花	F	1980	Shanjiang Town (山江镇)	Primary school teacher
Shif Hex Lib	Shí Hǎilì	石海丽	F	1980	Yankan Village (岩坎村)	Primary school teacher
Shif Xink Ib	Shí Xīngyù	石星玉	M	Early 1980s	Yankan Village (岩坎村)	Farmer/taxi driver
Ul Lib Jink	Wú Lìjūn	吴丽君	F	1985	Suode Village (所德村)	Farmer
Ul Shib Xaonk	Wú Shìxiāng	吴世香	F	1976	Zhuigaolai Village (追高来村)	Primary school teacher
Ul Xox Hueib	Wú Xiǎohuì	吴晓慧	F	1978	Hangka Village (夯卡村)	Primary school teacher

Two aspects of Table 2.1 deserve some additional comment. First, note that the Xong name of each consultant is essentially just the Xong pronunciation of the consultant's Chinese name, as indeed was the case for every Xong speaker the author met in Fenghuang County. Second, for a detailed representation of the relative locations of the consultants' hometowns, the reader is encouraged to consult Figure 2.6 in Section 2.7.1 below.

Ideally, at least some of the author's primary consultants would have been monolingual Xong speakers, so that their Xong could be compared with that of the author's multilingual consultants. While such monolingual speakers are not difficult to find in the Xong-speaking villages of Fenghuang County, it became clear to the author very early on that enlisting them as primary consultants would be impractical. Aside from the obvious fact that communicating with such speakers would require an interpreter, the author found that monolingual Xong adults (who were almost always quite elderly) had difficulty adjusting to the demands of a typical elicitation session, including making judgments about semantic entailments, identifying the tones on particular syllables, and so on. In the end, the author decided to record Xong texts from both older monolingual and younger multilingual speakers, and then analyze the texts with the help of his younger multilingual consultants alone.[30] Elicitations on specific phonological and grammatical topics were also done only with these younger consultants.

Still, it must be emphasized that the primary consultants listed in Table 2.1 are fully native speakers of Xong. Each of them grew up in a Xong-speaking household, and each of them learned Fenghuang Chinese and Standard Mandarin only after beginning formal schooling. They each use Xong for most daily speech tasks, including communicating with family, friends, and coworkers, and none of them ever had any difficulty understanding the speech of older monolingual Xong speakers. Furthermore, it should be kept in mind that multilingualism in Xong and one or more Sinitic varieties is in no way merely a recent phenomenon. The extensive phonological, grammatical, and lexical convergence between Xong and nearby Sinitic varieties is clear evidence of a long history of linguistic contact and the multilingualism that presumably accompanied it; see, for instance, Yang (2004: 144–160), Chen (2009: 91–158), or Ratliff (2010: 1, 2, 224–238). Thus, the author did not see any reason to try to hide or downplay the effects that multilingualism in Sinitic languages has had on Xong. After all, even the speech of the very oldest, most strictly monolingual Xong speakers is still riddled with borrowings from Sinitic; it is simply that the great age of these borrowings often serves to conceal their Sinitic origins from casual observers, including most Xong speakers themselves.

30 Unless otherwise noted, all Xong example forms and sentences in this grammar have been taken from the author's own Xong corpus, which is described in detail in Section 1.3.

2.7 Fenghuang County

2.7.1 General information

Fenghuang County (*Fènghuáng Xiàn* 凤凰县) is one of the first-order administrative subdivisions of the Xiangxi Tujia and Miao Autonomous Prefecture (*Xiāngxī Tǔjiāzú Miáozú Zìzhìzhōu* 湘西土家族苗族自治州), which is itself one of the first-order administrative subdivisions of China's Hunan Province. The map in Figure 2.5 shows the locations of Xiangxi Prefecture and Hunan Province in south-central China, with Xiangxi in orange (and also indicated by a black arrow) and the remainder of Hunan in light green.[31]

Fenghuang County lies at the very southern end of Xiangxi Prefecture, where it is bordered by Huayuan County (*Huāyuán Xiàn* 花垣县) and Jishou City (*Jíshǒu Shì* 吉首市) to the north, by Luxi County (*Lúxī Xiàn* 泸溪县) and the prefecture-level city of Huaihua (*Huáihuà Shì* 怀化市) to the east and south, and by Songtao County (*Sōngtáo Xiàn* 松桃县) and Tongren City (*Tóngrén Shì* 铜仁市) in Guizhou Province to the west. All this can be seen in the map in Figure 2.6, which also shows the locations of all towns and townships within Fenghuang County (though in most cases only the former are labeled), as well as six villages within the county that feature prominently in this grammar. Due to space constraints, those six villages have been labeled only with numbers in the map, and these should be interpreted as follows: 1 = Baren Village (*Bārén Cūn* 叭仁村), 2 = Yankan Village (*Yánkǎn Cūn* 岩坎村), 3 = Zhuigaolai Village (*Zhuīgāolái Cūn* 追高来村), 4 = Suode Village (*Suǒdé Cūn* 所德村), 5 = Hangka Village (*Hāngkǎ Cūn* 夯卡村), and 6 = Gouliang Village (*Gōuliáng Cūn* 勾良村). Two prominent Xong-speaking locales outside Fenghuang County are also shown, namely Jiwei Township (*Jíwèi Xiāng* 吉卫乡) and Aizhai Town (*Ǎizhài Zhèn* 矮寨镇).[32]

Fenghuang County's total permanent population was reported to be approximately 375,000 in 2004 (Feng 2008: 36). However, the actual resident population is usually lower, since many of Fenghuang's inhabitants spend much of each year doing migrant work outside the county. Fenghuang's population is mainly divided up among three ethnic groups, with about 55% of the county's inhabitants being ethnically Miao, 25% being ethnically Han, and 20% being ethnically Tujia (Feng 2008: 35).[33]

31 The base map for the one given in Figure 2.5 was created by Seth Underhill, using data from the SEDAC/CIESIN China Dimensions collection and from Global Mapping International, and was retrieved from http://sumgis.blogspot.com/2011/07/gmi-chinas-provinces-prefectures-and.html on 2013-1-21. The only changes the author made to the base map were coloring Xiangxi Prefecture in orange and adding an arrow indicating its location.

32 The base map used for Figure 2.6 was the excellent one found in Feng (2008: 37), although Feng's original map has here been very heavily modified.

33 Although Tujia (Tibeto-Burman; ISO 639-3 codes *tji* and *tjs*) was reported in the Ethnologue (Eberhard et al. 2019) to still have 70,000 speakers as of 2005, there appear to be few if any such speakers in Fenghuang County, with ethnic Tujia in Fenghuang instead (at least in the author's experience) mostly speaking Sinitic varieties.

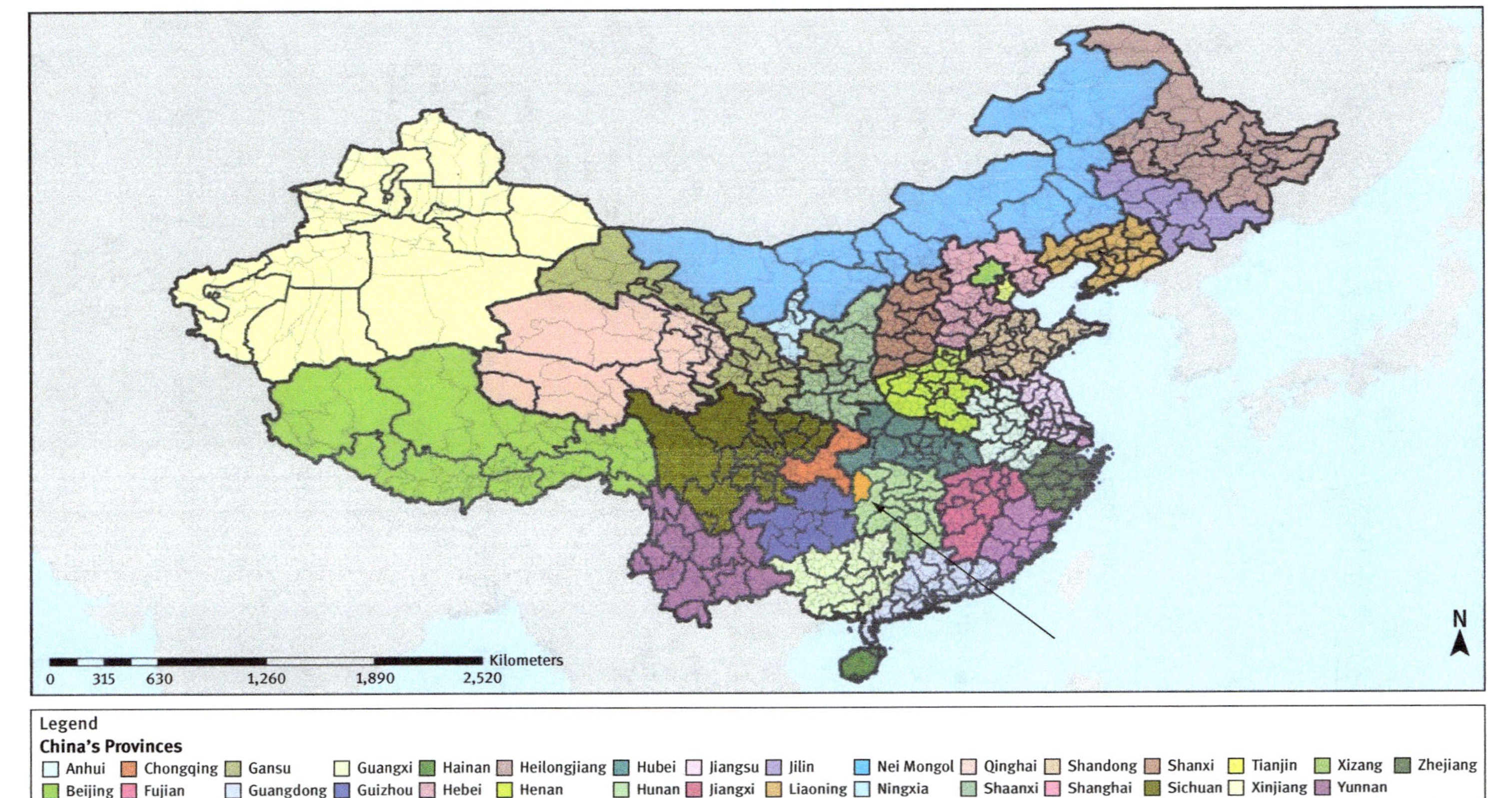

Figure 2.5: Map of China showing the location of Xiangxi Prefecture.

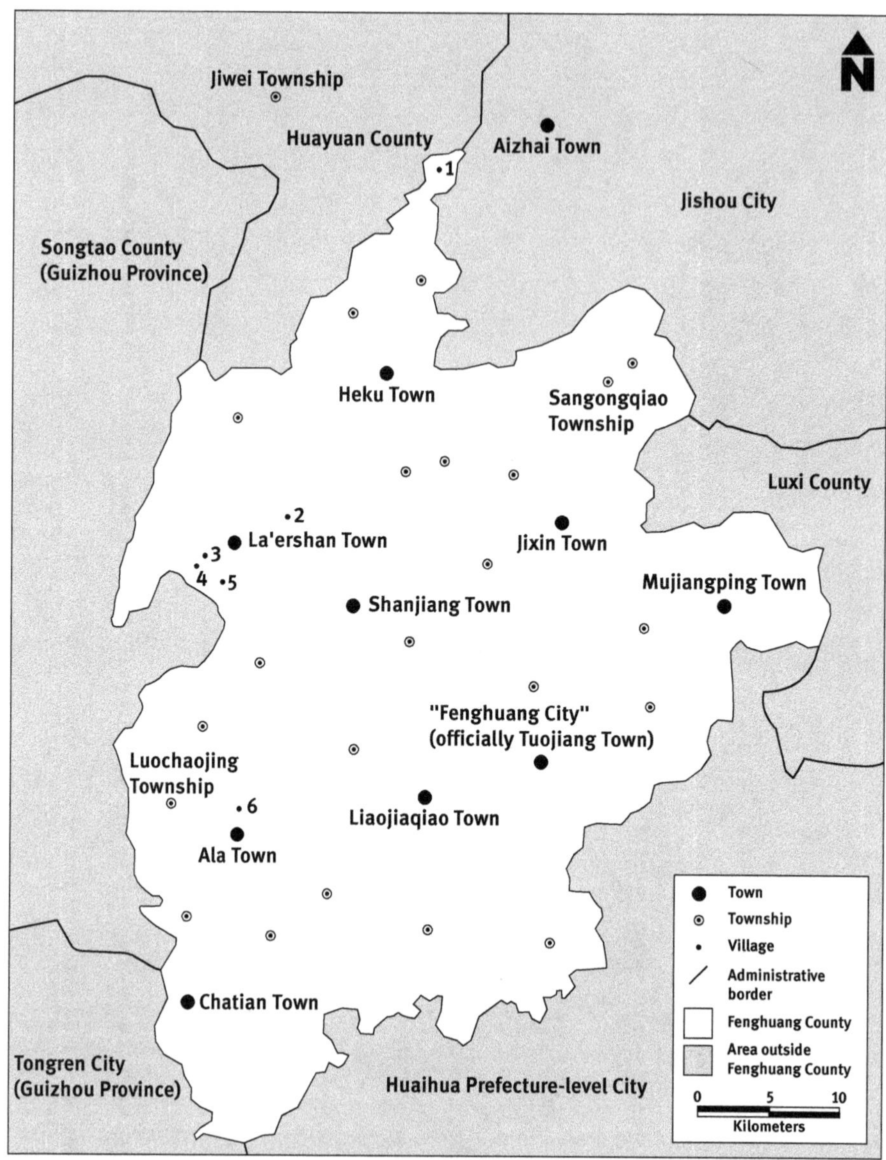

Figure 2.6: Map of Fenghuang County.

Administratively, Fenghuang County is divided into nine towns (*zhèn* 镇), one of which is the county seat, and nearly two dozen smaller townships (*xiāng* 乡) (Feng 2008: 38).[34] Each of these towns and townships has anywhere from four to twenty subsidiary villages (*cūn* 村).[35] Aside from the county seat, which has a population of over 40,000, most of Fenghuang County's towns have between 10,000 and 20,000 inhabitants. The town of La'ershan (*Là'ěrshān Zhèn* 腊尔山镇), which served as the author's primary fieldsite, is among the largest of these, with a population of over 17,000. Fenghuang's townships then range in size from 2,000 to 10,000 inhabitants, and its villages are naturally smaller still. The ethnic makeup of individual towns, townships, and villages in Fenghuang can vary widely. For example, La'ershan is nearly 98% ethnically Miao, but the county seat is roughly 45% Han, 35% Miao, and 20% Tujia (Feng 2008: 38).

Fenghuang County is heavily mountainous, and most communities in Fenghuang are located in narrow mountain valleys. Crops are grown on the valley floor and lower mountain slopes, while wild plants, mushrooms, and firewood are gathered on the more heavily forested upper mountain slopes. The region has a subtropical climate, with hot, humid summers and 925 mm of average precipitation per year (Feng 2008: 40). Due to Fenghuang's overall elevation, though, winters are bitterly cold, and accumulated ice and snow make certain roads impassable for several months out of each year.

Due in large part to these challenging geographic conditions, Fenghuang County is quite poor. In the early 1980s Fenghuang was ranked as the least economically developed of Hunan Province's 108 counties, and even in 2005 the county's per capita GDP was only 29.42% of China's national average (Feng 2008: 47). Most of the county's population is engaged in small-scale agriculture, with rice, corn, and tobacco as the major crops. As mentioned above, however, many rural inhabitants of Fenghuang County spend much of each year doing migrant work in China's wealthier eastern provinces, leaving the very young and very old to tend the family fields.

In recent decades cultural tourism has become one of the most important industries in Fenghuang. Fenghuang's tourism industry caters almost entirely to the Chinese domestic market, with countless independent tour guides and larger organizations offering tour packages that focus on the county's "exotic" Miao culture. The economic benefits from this increasing tourism have so far been distributed very unevenly, and tourists remain a rare sight in much of Fenghuang County, including the

34 The county seat (*xiànchéng* 县城) of Fenghuang County is officially called "Tuojiang Town" (*Tuójiāng Zhèn* 沱江镇), although in the author's experience this name is never used by Fenghuang's actual inhabitants. Instead, they refer to the county seat as either "Fenghuang" (*Fènghuáng* 凤凰) or simply "the county seat" (*xiànchéng* 县城) when speaking Standard Mandarin, and as "Fenghuang" (*Dib-Zhes*) when speaking Xong.

35 Note that in China the terms "town", "township", and "village" are used to refer both to a geographic subdivision of a larger administrative unit and to the relatively compact settlement at the center (more or less) of such a subdivision.

author's own primary fieldsite of La'ershan. (For a much more thorough discussion of Fenghuang County's economic situation in the early 21st century, with a particular focus on the tourism industry, the reader is encouraged to consult Feng 2008.)

2.7.2 Language use and language attitudes

There are three main languages spoken in Fenghuang County: Xong, Fenghuang Chinese, and Standard Mandarin. By this point neither Xong nor Standard Mandarin needs any introduction, but Fenghuang Chinese may well be unfamiliar to many readers of this grammar. The most detailed description of this Sinitic variety known to the author is found in He (2009: 12–94), although this description concentrates almost entirely on phonological, lexical, and historical issues rather than grammatical ones (see Section 2.5.3.1). He (2009: 30–34) argues that Fenghuang Chinese is a member of the Gan branch of Sinitic, albeit one that has been heavily influenced by Southwestern Mandarin.[36]

In phonological, grammatical, and lexical terms Fenghuang Chinese is much more similar to other Sinitic varieties than to Xong, and this grammar will not discuss it in any detail. Still, it should be kept in mind that Fenghuang Chinese is the second language of all of the author's Xong-speaking consultants in terms of age of acquisition (with Standard Mandarin then being their third), and it is Fenghuang Chinese – not Standard Mandarin – that is the primary source of recent Sinitic loanwords in Fenghuang Xong.

Multilingualism is the norm in Fenghuang County, although the particular languages a given inhabitant of Fenghuang is able (or willing) to speak often varies based on age, location, ethnicity, and personal language attitudes. For instance, in most villages (or at least most villages whose inhabitants are predominantly ethnically Miao), it is still easy to find monolingual Xong speakers, especially among young children and the elderly. Most children in Fenghuang's villages still learn Xong as their first language, and it is used by most villagers in almost every social sphere. Still, the vast majority of Xong-speaking villagers that the author met in Fenghuang were also fluent in Fenghuang Chinese, and most spoke some amount of Standard Mandarin as well. Proficiency in Standard Mandarin is especially common among older children and younger adults, who are more likely to be exposed to the language through formal schooling, popular media, and (for the adults) migrant work in areas outside Fenghuang County. Many villages have a small primary school of their own, and classes in these are generally conducted mostly in Standard Mandarin by the second or third year of schooling. Outside the classroom, though, Sinitic varieties are

36 Although the author of this grammar is fluent in Standard Mandarin, he found Fenghuang Chinese almost completely unintelligible upon his initial arrival in Fenghuang County. He was, however, able to understand most of it after his first two or three months of fieldwork.

usually only used in Fenghuang's majority-Miao villages when the village inhabitants need to communicate with non–Xong-speakers. Most marriages among Xong speakers in Fenghuang are ethnically endogamous, though the author has heard of a handful of ethnic Han women (usually from outside Hunan Province) who have married into Xong-speaking villages in Fenghuang. These women typically acquire fluency in Xong within a few years, and their children grow up speaking Xong as a first language.

Similarly, most inhabitants of Fenghuang's majority-Miao towns and townships are also fluent in Fenghuang Chinese, and most also speak Standard Mandarin to at least some degree. Just as in the villages, Xong is still the primary language used by most adults and older teenagers in most social spheres, except when talking to outsiders. However, some younger children in these towns and townships can neither speak nor understand Xong, instead using Fenghuang Chinese to communicate with other inhabitants of Fenghuang County and Standard Mandarin to communicate with visitors from further away. This is even true for some children whose parents are Xong speakers themselves. Many more children in these towns and townships can understand Xong and are able to speak it when called upon to do so, but almost never use it voluntarily amongst themselves. For instance, in La'ershan Town, it was quite common – perhaps even the norm – for ethnically Miao adults to use Xong to communicate with each other and with children, while ethnically Miao children would use Fenghuang Chinese to communicate with each other and with adults.

Still, there are several caveats about these sociolinguistic observations that should be mentioned here. The author's very presence in Fenghuang County may have resulted in some degree of observational bias, since, as an obvious outsider, those locals who were proficient in Standard Mandarin and/or Fenghuang Chinese would presumably be more likely to speak or otherwise interact with him than those who were not. This may well have given the author the false impression that Sinitic varieties are more widely used in Fenghuang's towns and townships than they actually are. There is also a considerable degree of fluidity between town (or township) and village in Fenghuang County. Many villagers visit the nearest town every five days for market day, often spending a night or two with town-dwelling relatives when they do so, and many town-dwellers make periodic returns to their home village to visit relatives and to tend their family's crops.

On the whole, Xong speakers in Fenghuang County have a very positive view of their language. Most Xong speakers with whom the author has discussed the issue have expressed pride in their ability to speak Xong, in particular because Xong is seen by these speakers as being much more difficult to learn than either Fenghuang Chinese or Standard Mandarin. These speakers are also quite confident that Xong is not in any immediate danger of extinction, a view with which the author is inclined to agree (see below). At the same time, many Xong speakers have told the author that fluency in Xong is of little practical use these days. These speakers see proficiency in a widely spoken Sinitic variety (especially Standard Mandarin) as a prerequisite for any sort of socioeconomic mobility in modern China, and many of them are prouder of their children's ability to speak Standard Mandarin than of their ability to speak Xong. Literacy in the standard Xong orthography (see Section 4.3) in particular is seen as thoroughly useless by nearly every Xong speaker who is aware of the orthography's existence – or, at least, by every such speaker the author has met.

Incidentally, it is worth pointing out here that none of the Xong speakers the author met in Fenghuang County had any conception of speaking a distinct "Xong" or "Xiangxi Miao" language – instead, they universally thought of themselves as merely speaking the local variety of the Miao *yuyan* (see Section 2.4). These speakers referred to the Xong varieties spoken in particular villages, towns, or counties as "the Miao of [place]", and they referred to all other (non-Xong) Miao varieties the same way. For instance, the author's consultants would refer to the Xong variety spoken in the town of Heku (*Hékù Zhèn* 禾库镇) in Fenghuang County as simply "Heku Miao", and they would also refer to the various Hmu varieties spoken in Guizhou Province as simply "Guizhou Miao", despite the fact that all consultants agreed that the latter varieties were completely unintelligible to them.[37]

Finally, just like most non-Sinitic languages in mainland China, Xong is under some degree of demographic pressure from Sinitic varieties, especially Standard Mandarin. But given the language's large speaker population (see Section 2.2.2), its use in a wide variety of social spheres, and the fact that it is still being learned as a first language by many children, Xong is not likely to be in danger of extinction or even moribundity for at least several decades, and possibly much longer. Of course, the author is here speaking only of the language as a whole; the future prospects of particular varieties of Xong may in some cases be much less hopeful.

2.7.3 The target variety of this grammar

This grammar is primarily a phonological and grammatical description of certain Xong varieties spoken in Fenghuang County. All of the author's fieldwork for this grammar was performed in Fenghuang, and all of his primary consultants were born and raised there. Most consultants were either from La'ershan Town or from one of its surrounding villages, although one consultant was from Shanjiang Town (*Shānjiāng Zhèn* 山江镇), located less than an hour's drive from La'ershan (see Table 2.1 in Section 2.6.2 above). The author has encountered only a few subtle grammatical differences among the Xong varieties spoken by his various consultants, and in many cases it is not entirely clear whether these differences are dialectal or merely idiolectal. In

37 This is somewhat parallel to the way that Xong speakers in Fenghuang County (who almost universally identify as ethnically Miao and who are almost universally classified as such by the Chinese government) quite clearly saw themselves as merely a local manifestation of a unitary Miao ethnicity, even though they understood that other Miao communities might often differ from their own in customs, material culture, and nationality (e.g. Chinese vs. Thai vs. American) as well as in speech.

any case, a systematic study of grammatical variation within Fenghuang Xong lies outside the scope of this grammar, but those differences which the author has so far observed will be mentioned where relevant in subsequent chapters.

Lexical differences among the Xong varieties spoken by the author's consultants are somewhat more pronounced, though still never enough to hinder comprehension. Lexical variation will not be discussed in any great detail in this grammar, although idiolectally or dialectally variant forms of certain grammatical morphemes will also be noted where appropriate in subsequent chapters.

The degree of phonological and, especially, phonetic variation present in Fenghuang Xong is greater still. Most of Chapter 3, which is devoted to phonology, describes in particular the phonological and phonetic characteristics of the Xong variety spoken in Yankan Village (*Yánkǎn Cūn* 岩坎村), a subsidiary village of La'ershan Town (see Figure 2.6 in Section 2.7.1 above). Yankan Xong was chosen as the phonological and phonetic "target" of Chapter 3 for several reasons; see Section 3.1 for discussion. However, to a much greater extent than is the case in later chapters, Chapter 3 also discusses phonological and phonetic variation among the Xong varieties spoken by the author's primary consultants.

Lexical and phonological differences between Fenghuang Xong and the Xong varieties spoken in other counties are much sharper, often to the point of significantly hindering comprehension, and so any lexical or phonological claims made in this grammar should not be assumed to apply to Xong varieties spoken outside of Fenghuang. Impressionistically, grammatical differences between Fenghuang Xong and other Xong varieties spoken outside the county are much less pronounced. Still, this is not to say that no such differences exist, and the grammatical claims made in this grammar cannot necessarily be assumed to apply to all Xong varieties.

3 Phonology

3.1 Introduction

As is typical for the Miao-Yao family (and indeed, for much of the greater mainland Southeast Asian linguistic area in general), the syllable is the most important unit of analysis in Xong phonology. The syllable is the only tone-bearing unit in Xong, nearly all Xong morphemes consist of exactly one syllable, and speakers typically pause after each syllable (rather than, for example, after each word or phrase) when asked to repeat an utterance slowly. Xong syllables have a rigid phonotactic structure: with only a handful of exceptions (see Sections 3.3.4 and 3.6), each syllable is composed of an optional initial consonant, an obligatory vowel, and an obligatory tone.

However, Xong's lack of phonotactic complexity is more than made up for by the size of its phonological inventory. The Xong varieties discussed in this chapter each have 65 consonants, seven oral monophthongal vowels, eight diphthongal and/or nasal vowels, and (at least in monosyllabic forms produced in isolation) eight tones. In addition to their sheer size, the segmental inventories of these varieties are also noteworthy for some of the typologically unusual phonemes they contain, most particularly their breathy nasals and laterals (discussed in Sections 3.2.2.2 and 3.2.3).

While Xong's tonal inventory is not unusually large for a member of the Miao-Yao family, several aspects of the language's tone system (discussed in Section 3.5) are still somewhat remarkable, including a high degree of phonetic similarity among several tones and a high level of intervarietal variation in tonal phonetics.

Sections 3.1 to 3.7, which constitute the bulk of this chapter, focus primarily on the sound system of the Xong variety spoken in Yankan Village (*Yánkǎn Cūn* 岩坎村), located about a two hours' walk away from La'ershan Town (*Là'ěrshān Zhèn* 腊尔山镇) in western Hunan's Fenghuang County (*Fènghuáng Xiàn* 凤凰县). Yankan Xong was chosen as the target variety of this chapter for two main reasons. First, the selection of Yankan Xong represents a compromise of sorts between two of the largest predominantly Xong-speaking towns in Fenghuang County. Yankan was originally settled by Xong speakers from near Shanjiang Town (*Shānjiāng Zhèn* 山江镇), but geographically and economically Yankan is much closer to La'ershan Town. Second, a plurality of the author's primary consultants hail from Yankan Village, as do most members of the family with whom the author lived while performing fieldwork in La'ershan (see Section 2.6.2). The author thus unavoidably ended up with more phonological data from Yankan Xong than from any other Xong variety.

Still, it should be kept in mind that there is a significant amount of low-level phonetic variation among the Xong varieties spoken in Fenghuang County, along with a much smaller amount of phonological variation.[38] Although the phonetic and phonological differences among Yankan Xong and other Fenghuang Xong varieties have yet to be comprehensively documented, some points of variation that the author has observed among his consultants' idiolects will be discussed where relevant throughout the remaining portions of this chapter (see especially Section 3.8, and also Section 2.7.3). Particular attention is devoted to tonal variation across different varieties of Fenghuang Xong in Section 3.5. Aside from those who come from Yankan Village, all of the author's primary consultants hail from Shanjiang Town, La'ershan Town, or one of several villages near La'ershan (aside from Yankan Village, these also include Zhuigaolai Village [*Zhuīgāolái Cūn* 追高来村], which is discussed in some detail in Section 3.5.3.2). Naturally, then, most phonetic and phonological comparisons made in this chapter will involve one or more of these varieties. The reader is encouraged to consult Section 2.7 of this grammar for more information on Yankan Village, Shanjiang Town, La'ershan Town, and other Xong-speaking communities in Fenghuang County.

The complete phoneme inventory of Yankan Xong is presented below in Tables 3.1 to 3.4 and the accompanying commentary (for the complete tone inventory of Yankan Xong, see Table 3.5 and the accompanying commentary in Section 3.5.2.1). In Tables 3.1 to 3.4, the most common IPA value of each phoneme is given on the left and the corresponding orthographic symbol in the author's practical orthography (see Section 4.4) is given in italics on the right. In Tables 3.1 and 3.2, manners of articulation are listed across the top of each table, and places of articulation (including secondary articulations like labialization and palatalization) are given along the left side. Solely for convenience, prenasalization, aspiration, and breathy voicing are represented with superscript symbols in the IPA transcription of each phoneme, while labialization, palatalization, and the fricative portions of affricate consonants are represented with ordinary (i.e. non-superscript) symbols. In many cases this means that a single phoneme will be represented with a digraph, e.g. /ts/ or /kj/. Note that the terms used to refer to manners and places of articulation in Tables 3.1 and 3.2 have in many cases been simplified for convenience; see Section 3.2 for more detailed articulatory information.

38 In contrast to the various forms of Xong spoken within Fenghuang County, Xong varieties spoken outside Fenghuang often depart much more significantly from the sound system described in this chapter. See, for example, the phonological description of Songtao Xong in Chen (2009: 8–13), the phonological description of Aizhai Xong in Yu (2011: 20–27), or the phonological descriptions of three Xong varieties in Yang (2004: 80–84).

Table 3.1: Plosive consonants of Yankan Xong.

	UNASPIRATED, NON-PRENASALIZED		ASPIRATED, NON-PRENASALIZED		UNASPIRATED, PRENASALIZED		ASPIRATED, PRENASALIZED	
PLAIN BILABIAL	p	*b*	p^{h}	*p*	^{n}p	*nb*	^{n}p^{h}	*np*
PALATALIZED BILABIAL	pj	*bi*	pj^{h}	*pi*			^{n}pj^{h}	*npi*
PLAIN ALVEOLAR	t	*d*	t^{h}	*t*	^{n}t	*nd*	^{n}t^{h}	*nt*
PALATALIZED ALVEOLAR	tj	*di*	tj^{h}	*ti*	^{n}tj	*ndi*	^{n}tj^{h}	*nti*
ALVEOLAR AFFRICATE	ts	*z*	ts^{h}	*c*	^{n}ts	*nz*	^{n}ts^{h}	*nc*
ALVEOLO-PALATAL	tɕ	*j*	tɕ^{h}	*q*	^{n}tɕ	*nj*	^{n}tɕ^{h}	*nq*
APICAL–POST-ALV.	ṭṣ	*zh*	ṭṣ^{h}	*ch*	^{n}ṭṣ	*nzh*	^{n}ṭṣ^{h}	*nch*
PLAIN VELAR	k	*g*	k^{h}	*k*	^{n}k	*ngg*	^{n}k^{h}	*nk*
PALATALIZED VELAR	kj	*gi*	kj^{h}	*ki*	^{n}kj	*ngi*	^{n}kj^{h}	*nki*
PLAIN UVULAR	q	*gh*	q^{h}	*kh*	^{n}q	*ngh*	^{n}q^{h}	*nkh*
LABIALIZED UVULAR	qw	*gu*	qw^{h}	*ku*	^{n}qw	*nggu*	^{n}qw^{h}	*nku*

Table 3.2: Non-plosive consonants of Yankan Xong.

	MODAL NASAL		BREATHY NASAL		MODAL LATERAL		BREATHY LATERAL		VOICELESS FRICATIVE		VOICED APPROXIMANT	
PLAIN BILABIAL	m	*m*	m^{ɦ}	*hm*								
PALATALIZED BILABIAL	mj	*mi*										
LABIODENTAL									f	*f*	ʋ	*w*
PLAIN ALVEOLAR	n	*n*	n^{ɦ}	*hn*	l	*l*	l^{ɦ}	*hl*				
PALATALIZED ALVEOLAR	nj	*ni*			lj	*li*	lj^{ɦ}	*hli*				
ALVEOLAR SIBILANT									s	*s*		
(ALVEOLO-) PALATAL									ɕ	*x*	j	*y*
APICAL–POST-ALV.	ṇ	*nh*							ṣ	*sh*	ẓ	*r*
PLAIN VELAR	ŋ	*ng*										

Table 3.2 (continued)

	MODAL NASAL	BREATHY NASAL	MODAL LATERAL	BREATHY LATERAL	VOICELESS FRICATIVE	VOICED APPROXIMANT
LABIALIZED VELAR	ŋw *ngu*					
GLOTTAL					h *h*	
LABIALIZED GLOTTAL					hw *hu*	

The seven oral monophthongs of Yankan Xong are given in Table 3.3. In addition, Yankan Xong also has four nasal monophthongs: /ĩ/ (orthographically <in>), /ã/ (<an>), /ɑ̃/ (<aon>), and /õ/ (<on>).

Table 3.3: Oral monophthongs of Yankan Xong.

	FRONT (UNROUNDED)	CENTRAL (UNROUNDED)	UNROUNDED BACK	ROUNDED BACK
HIGH	i *i*			u *u*
MID	ɛ *e*		ɤ *eu*	o *o*
LOW		a *a*	ɑ *ao*	

The three oral diphthongs of Yankan Xong are given in Table 3.4. These have been arranged according to the more prominent nucleus of each diphthong rather than the subsequent offglide. Yankan Xong also has a single nasal diphthong /ɤ̃j/ (orthographically <ein>).

Table 3.4: Oral diphthongs of Yankan Xong.

	FRONT	CENTRAL	BACK
HIGH			
MID	ɛɰ *ou*		ɤj *ei*
LOW		aw *au*	

Beyond the vowels listed above, Yankan Xong also features a single syllabic nasal /m̩/. For more information on the vowels (both monophthongal and diphthongal) of Yankan Xong and on this syllabic nasal, see Section 3.3.

In addition to any segmental material, nearly every monosyllabic form produced in isolation in Yankan Xong will bear one of eight lexically specified tones. Note that the term "tone", as used in this grammar, does not simply refer to the relative pitch of a syllable. Rather, it is a complex combination of pitch height, pitch contour, and phonation type. Tone in general is discussed in Section 3.5 below, with tone in Yankan Xong in particular being discussed in Section 3.5.2.

Before moving on to a description of Yankan Xong's consonant phonemes, there are a few general issues which the reader should keep in mind throughout the following sections of this chapter. First, unlike in subsequent chapters (with the exception of Chapter 4), in this chapter all transcriptions of Xong material given in the author's practical orthography (see Section 4.4) will be enclosed within angle brackets < >, while transcriptions of material given in IPA will be enclosed within slashes / / or square brackets [ ]. In Chapter 5 and all subsequent chapters, transcriptions of any Xong material given in a practical orthography will simply be italicized.

Second, as is the case with most Miao-Yao languages (see Ratliff [2010: 225–234]), a massive portion of the Xong lexicon is composed of borrowings from Sinitic. These borrowings can be divided into a number of historical layers, some of which appear to date as far back as the first millennium B.C.E. (see, e.g., He [2009: 217–237]). This process of borrowing from Sinitic varieties into Xong is still very much ongoing in the Xong-speaking communities of Fenghuang County today. In fact, such borrowing has if anything accelerated over the past several decades due to increased public schooling (almost always conducted in Standard Mandarin), the rapid proliferation of Standard Mandarin popular media, and increasing migrant work by younger Xong speakers in Sinitic-speaking regions outside of Fenghuang County. See Section 2.7.2 for further discussion of these and other issues related to language contact.

However, the phonological description in this chapter differs from those found in many other publications on Xong in that it devotes essentially no attention to loanword phonology.[39] This is partially because the topic has already been studied so thoroughly in other publications (see Section 2.5), and partially because borrowings from Sinitic display a very large amount of intervarietal and even inter-idiolectal variation in Fenghuang Xong, to the point that the author feels a significant amount of additional fieldwork would be necessary before a proper description of the topic could be given.

Finally, note that the phonetic descriptions in this chapter are based primarily on the author's own impressionistic observations in the field and spectrographic analysis of recorded Xong speech in Praat, along with some additional observations from some of the author's more phonetically minded consultants.

39 However, the author would at least like to point out that borrowings from Sinitic into Fenghuang Xong are almost always adapted to Xong's phonological system, meaning that they are (at least in phonological terms) largely indistinguishable from "native" Xong forms.

3.2 Consonants

While the bulk of this section is devoted to particular consonant phonemes, there are a few general aspects of the Fenghuang Xong consonantal system that merit some discussion here. First, certain consonants are extremely uncommon in the Xong lexicon. In fact, several of them have only been attested occurring in one or two morphemes each, though these morphemes may in some cases be relatively high-frequency forms. Specifically, (i) the prenasalized, unaspirated, palatalized velar stop /^{n}kj/ occurs only in /^{n}kjɛ1/ <ngieb> 'gold' and /^{n}kjɛ5/ <ngiet> 'to hiccup' (or /^{n}kjã5/ <ngiant> for speakers not from Yankan Village; see Section 3.2.1.10), (ii) the prenasalized, aspirated, labialized uvular stop /^{n}qw^{h}/ occurs only in /^{n}qw^{h}ɛɰ5/ <nkuout> 'to insert one's foot (e.g. into a boot or hole)' and the onomatopoeic form /^{n}qw^{h}ɑ̃5.^{n}qw^{h}ɑ̃5/ <nkuaont.nkuaont> 'ONOM:nkuaon.nkuaon' (see Section 3.2.1.12), and (iii) the breathy bilabial nasal /m^{ɦ}/ occurs only in /m^{ɦ}ɑ̃5/ <hmaont> 'evening' (see Section 3.2.2.2).

Naturally, the rarity of these consonants sometimes makes it impossible to find perfect minimal pairs proving that they are distinct phonemes. (It is much less difficult to find perfect minimal pairs for Xong's vowels and tones, though, as the relatively small size of Xong's vowel and tone inventories – relative, that is, to the size of Xong's consonant inventory – means that each such vowel and tone appears in a relatively large number of distinct lexical items.) Despite this, the consonants in question still appear to be phonemically distinct, since there is no other way to explain why they differ phonetically from the more well attested consonants, and since the places of articulation, manners of articulation, and voicing qualities of these consonants are shared by at least some of Xong's other, more well attested consonants. For example, given that four plosive phonemes – namely (i) unaspirated, non-prenasalized, (ii) aspirated, non-prenasalized, (iii) unaspirated, prenasalized, and (iv) aspirated, prenasalized – occur at most places of articulation in Fenghuang Xong, the existence of the plosive phonemes /^{n}kj/ and /^{n}qw^{h}/ is to be expected, and their absence would leave unexplained (and likely merely accidental) "gaps" in the variety's consonant inventory (and indeed one such gap does occur, as the consonant */^{n}pj/ is not attested in Fenghuang Xong; see Section 3.2.1.3 for details). The well-attestedness of the breathy alveolar nasal /n^{ɦ}/ means that the same is true (though to a lesser degree) for the breathy bilabial nasal /m^{ɦ}/. The author would be much more hesitant to argue for the existence of a consonant phoneme that occurred in only one or two morphemes if that consonant featured a place of articulation, manner of articulation, or voicing quality that was not shared by any of Xong's other consonants (for example, a hypothetical ejective velar stop */k'/ or voiced interdental fricative */ð/), but fortunately no such consonants have been encountered.

Due to these difficulties, the minimal and near-minimal pairs given for the consonants in Sections 3.2.1.2 to 3.2.5 disregard tones to a much greater extent than do the minimal and near-minimal pairs given for the vowels in Section 3.3. For both consonants and vowels, though, the author attempted as much as possible to give minimal pairs and example words that do not involve obvious, recent borrowings from any Sinitic varieties. Furthermore, for the sake of clarity, the author also attempted as much as possible to provide monomorphemic example forms in Sections 3.2.1.2 through 3.2.5 and Section 3.3, even if the forms in question would typically occur with a nominal prefix (see Section 5.4) when produced in isolation. Finally, note that periods have been added between adjacent syllables of monomorphemic polysyllabic forms (as indeed is done in general throughout this grammar), and the relevant syllable of each such form (which varies depending on the particular phonological distinction under discussion in each section) has been bolded.

A second general issue is that most of the consonants described in Sections 3.2.1.2 to 3.2.5 have few if any notable allophonic variants, certainly much fewer than many of the vowels described in Section 3.3 have. This is likely due – at least in part – to Xong's significant phonotactic restrictions. Leaving aside the syllabic nasals discussed in Section 3.3.4 and the alternate syllable structure analyses discussed in Section 3.7, every Xong consonant only ever occurs as the onset of a CV syllable. Each such syllable is typically a complete morpheme, and it is always preceded and followed by either a pause or by another (C)V syllable-morpheme. In comparison to many other languages (including, for example, most European languages), this does not afford the possibility of many environmentally conditioned allophones. In addition, though this is only speculation, it seems to the author that Xong's relative lack of consonantal allophony may also in some way be connected to the large number of distinct consonant phonemes in the language (see Section 1.2.1), which might result in there being relatively little articulatory "space" left over for significant allophonic variation.

Finally, some brief notes on consonant-related terminology may be helpful here. The term "plosive" is used in this grammar to refer to obstruent consonants involving a complete closure of the oral tract. It thus includes /p, pj, t, tj, ts, tɕ, tʂ, k, kj, q, qw/ but not /m, n, ŋ/. The term "stop" is used to refer to the non-affricate plosives, including /p, pj, t, tj, k, kj, q, qw/ but not /ts, tɕ, tʂ/ or /m, n, ŋ/. The term "plain stop" is used to refer to those stops that do not involve any secondary articulation like labialization or palatalization. It thus includes consonants like /p, t, k, q/, but not /pj, tj, kj, qw/. Finally, when used with respect to consonants, the term "nasal" refers to sonorant consonants involving nasal airflow. It thus includes /m, n, ŋ, $m^ɦ$, $n^ɦ$/, but not prenasalized plosives like /^{n}p, ^{n}t, ^{n}k, ^{n}q/.

3.2.1 Plosives

3.2.1.1 Aspiration and prenasalization among plosives

At nearly all places of articulation – including those distinguished by secondary articulations like labialization and palatalization – every variety of Fenghuang Xong has four contrastive plosive phonemes (the palatalized bilabial stops constitute the only exception, as only three such stops have been attested; see Section 3.2.1.3). This four-way contrast is based on two binary oppositions: aspiration vs. non-aspiration, and prenasalization vs. non-prenasalization. In other words, at each place of articulation there occurs an unaspirated, non-prenasalized plosive (e.g. /p, t, k, q/), an aspirated, non-prenasalized plosive (e.g. /p^h, t^h, k^h, q^h/), an unaspirated, prenasalized plosive (e.g. /^np, ^nt, ^nk, ^nq/), and an aspirated, prenasalized plosive (e.g. /$^np^h$, $^nt^h$, $^nk^h$, $^nq^h$/). Impressionistically, aspirated consonants are much less frequent in the Xong lexicon than unaspirated ones, and prenasalized consonants are somewhat less frequent than non-prenasalized ones.[40]

In all varieties of Fenghuang Xong known to the author, the initial nasal portions of prenasalized plosives are extremely salient. Syllables beginning with prenasalized plosives are noticeably longer than syllables beginning with other consonants, almost to the point of being sesquisyllabic (at least when produced carefully in isolation). The initial nasal portion of a prenasalized plosive is always homorganic with the following stop portion. Thus, for example, the aspirated, prenasalized plosives /$^np^h$, $^nt^h$, $^nk^h$, $^nq^h$/ are phonetically [$^mp^h$, $^nt^h$, $^{ŋ}k^h$, $^{\text{N}}q^h$]. Furthermore, spectrographic analysis clearly shows that the initial nasal portions of these consonants are always voiced, regardless of whether the following stop (or affricate) portion is aspirated, voiced, or neither.

There is relatively little interspeaker variation among the author's primary consultants with respect to the unaspirated, non-prenasalized plosives, the aspirated, non-prenasalized plosives, and the aspirated, prenasalized plosives. For all consultants, these plosives are realized just as their phonological descriptions would suggest: /p, t, k, q/ are thus [p, t, k, q], /p^h, t^h, k^h, q^h/ are [p^h, t^h, k^h, q^h], and /$^np^h$, $^nt^h$, $^nk^h$, $^nq^h$/ are [$^mp^h$, $^nt^h$, $^{ŋ}k^h$, $^{\text{N}}q^h$]. Note in particular that in the case of the aspirated, prenasalized plosives, the stop (or affricate) portion of the plosive is clearly voiceless, despite the presence of the preceding nasal portion.

There is, however, some degree of interspeaker (or perhaps intervarietal) variation among the author's consultants with respect to the unaspirated, prenasalized plosives. For the majority of consultants, these are phonetically realized as voiced, prenasalized, unaspirated plosives, so that /^np, ^nt, ^nk, ^nq/ are [^mb, nd, ^{ŋ}g, $^{\text{N}}ɢ$]. This is true for all of the author's consultants from Yankan Village and Shanjiang Town, as well as for several consultants from La'ershan Town and some of its surrounding villages. But for Mrs. Shixiang Wu, one of the author's consultants from Zhuigaolai Village (near La'ershan), the prenasalized, unaspirated plosives are realized exactly as their phonological description implies, with /^np, ^nt, ^nk, ^nq/ being phonetically [^mp, ^nt, ^{ŋ}k, $^{\text{N}}q$]. In other words, for this consultant, these plosives consist phonetically of

40 Furthermore, it is interesting to note that most small, closed lexical categories in Xong do not contain any morphemes beginning with aspirated and/or prenasalized plosives, though they often include several morphemes beginning with unaspirated, non-prenasalized ones. Such lexical categories include nominal prefixes (see Section 5.4), numerals with the sole exception of /ts^hã8/ <canf> 'thousand' (Section 6.2), personal pronouns (Section 7.1), demonstratives (Section 7.2), and particles (Section 9.2.1).

an initial voiced nasal portion followed by a voiceless unaspirated stop (or affricate) portion. Finally, for Mrs. Xiaohui Wu, a consultant from Hangka Village (also near La'ershan), these plosives vary freely between these two possibilities (i.e. between [^{m}b, ^{n}d, ^{ŋ}g, ^{N}ɢ] and [^{m}p, ^{n}t, ^{ŋ}k, ^{N}q]) with no obvious conditioning factors.

Further research is needed to determine whether these varying phonetic details reflect true dialectal differences or merely idiolectal variation. In any case, the phonetic transcriptions of unaspirated, prenasalized plosives in the remainder of this chapter will always reflect their most common realization as voiced, prenasalized, unaspirated sounds.

3.2.1.2 The plain bilabial stops /p/, /p^h/, /^{n}p/, and /^{n}p^h/

These consonants are straightforward bilabial stops, and there is relatively little to be said about them. They are typically realized as [p], [p^h], [^{m}b], and [^{m}p^h], and they are represented in the practical orthography used in this grammar with <b>, <p>, <nb>, and <np>.

Examples of syllables containing plain bilabial stops in Yankan Xong include /pi1/ <bib> 'hair', /pɤ̃j2/ <beinx> 'flower', /p^{h}ɛɰ8/ <pouf> 'paternal grandfather', /p^{h}u7/ <puk> 'to speak', /^{n}pã2/ <nbanx> 'to think', /^{n}pu5/ <nbut> 'to be named; name', /^{n}p^{h}ɑ7/ <npaok> 'woman', and /^{n}p^{h}ã3/ <npand> 'ant'. Some minimal and near-minimal pairs involving plain bilabial stops are given below.

/p/ vs. /p^h/:	/pu7/ <buk> 'fart' vs. /p^{h}u7/ <puk> 'to speak'
/^{n}p/ vs. /^{n}p^h/:	/^{n}pã2/ <nbanx> 'to think' vs. /^{n}p^{h}ã3/ <npand> 'ant'
/p/ vs. /^{n}p/:	/pã1/ <banb> 'CLF:half; CLF:some' vs. /^{n}pã2/ <nbanx> 'to think'
/p/ vs. /pj/:	/pɛɰ1/ <boub> '1PL' vs. /pjɛɰ3/ <bioud> 'home, family'
/p/ vs. /m/:	/pɤ̃j2/ <beinx> 'flower' vs. /mɤ̃j4/ <meinl> 'CLF:person'
/^{n}p/ vs. /m/:	/^{n}pã2/ <nbanx> 'to think' vs. /mã2/ <manx> '2PL'
/p/ vs. /f/:	/pɤ̃j2/ <beinx> 'flower' vs. /fɤ̃j5/ <feint> 'manure'

3.2.1.3 The palatalized bilabial stops /pj/, /pj^h/, and /^{n}pj^h/

Yankan Xong also possesses a series of palatalized bilabial stops, typically realized as [pj], [pj^h], and [^{m}pj^h]. They are represented in the practical orthography with <bi>, <pi>, and <npi>. Many other varieties of Xong (including Jiwei Xong and Aizhai Xong) have three series of bilabial stops, contrasting plain bilabials, palatalized bilabials, and rhotacized bilabials (e.g. /pɹ/, /^{n}pɹ/, etc.). However, the rhotacized bilabial stops have completely merged with the palatalized ones in all varieties of Fenghuang Xong that the author has encountered, leaving only a contrast between plain and palatalized bilabials.[41]

41 Interestingly, Chen (2009: 74, 75) reports that the Daxing variety of Xong spoken in neighboring Songtao County (see Section 2.5.2.4) is currently in the process of undergoing just such a merger. In this variety, older (especially older female) speakers still have two distinct series of rhotacized and

The series of palatalized bilabial stops in all varieties of Fenghuang Xong spoken by the author's primary consultants are "defective", in a sense, as no prenasalized, unaspirated stop (i.e. */^{n}pj/, orthographically *<nbi>) has been attested in any of them. However, given that prenasalized, unaspirated plosives occur at all other places of articulation in these varieties, there is no reason to believe that the absence of a prenasalized, unaspirated, palatalized bilabial stop in them is anything other than accidental.

Examples of syllables containing palatalized bilabial stops in Yankan Xong include /pjɛɰ3/ <bioud> 'home, family', /pjɑ1/ <biaob> 'five', /pj^{h}a8/ <piaf> 'to blow (said of wind)', /pj^{h}ɤ5/ <pieut> 'to stroke', /^{n}pj^{h}a8/ <npiaf> 'to measure', and /^{n}pj^{h}ɤ5/ <npieut> 'to shout'. Some minimal and near-minimal pairs involving palatalized bilabial stops are given below.

/pj/ vs. /pj^{h}/:	/pja5/ <biat> 'cliff' vs. /pj^{h}a8/ <piaf> 'to blow (said of wind)'
/pj^{h}/ vs. /^{n}pj^{h}/:	/pj^{h}ɤ5/ <pieut> 'to stroke' vs. /^{n}pj^{h}ɤ5/ <npieut> 'to shout'
/pj/ vs. /p/:	/pjɛɰ3/ <bioud> 'home, family' vs. /pɛɰ1/ <boub> '1PL'
/pj/ vs. /p/:	/qɑ3.**pju7**/ <ghaod.**biuk**> 'buttocks' vs. /pu7/ <buk> 'fart'
/pj^{h}/ vs. /p^{h}/:	/pj^{h}ɤ5/ <pieut> 'to stroke' vs. /p^{h}ɤ8/ <peuf> 'to dig'
/pj/ vs. /mj/:	/pjaw7/ <biauk> 'dark' vs. /mjaw2/ <miaux> 'leaf'

3.2.1.4 The plain alveolar stops /t/, /t^{h}/, /^{n}t/, and /^{n}t^{h}/

These stops are typically realized as [t], [t^{h}], [^{n}d], and [^{n}t^{h}], and they are represented orthographically with <d>, <t>, <nd>, and <nt>. The author's consultants all report that the production of these stops involves simultaneous laminal-alveolar and apical-dental contact, although these same consultants accept purely laminal-alveolar, purely apical-dental, and simultaneous laminal-alveolar/apical-dental articulations as equally "good" when produced by the author. However, since the corresponding alveolar affricates (see Section 3.2.1.6) and, at least for some consultants, palatalized alveolar stops (see Section 3.2.1.5) involve only laminal-alveolar contact, it seems simplest to describe these "plain alveolar stops" as phonologically laminal-alveolar, with incidental apical-dental contact usually accompanying them.

Examples of syllables containing plain alveolar stops in Yankan Xong include /taw5/ <daut> 'speech', /tɑ7/ <daok> 'maternal grandmother', /t^{h}ɤ8/ <teuf> 'to scoop', /t^{h}i8/ <tif> 'stomach', /ntã1/ <ndanb> 'to jump', /^{n}taw5/ <ndaut> 'tree', /^{n}t^{h}ɑ3/ <ntaod> 'to take off', and /^{n}t^{h}õ3/ <ntond> 'CLF:wall'. Some minimal and near-minimal pairs involving plain alveolar stops are given below.

---

palatalized bilabial consonants, while younger (especially younger male) speakers have only a single series of palatalized bilabial consonants.

/t/ vs. /t^{h}/: /ti1/ <dib> 'which' vs. /t^{h}i8/ <tif> 'stomach'

/t/ vs. /^{n}t/: /taw5/ <daut> 'speech' vs. /^{n}taw5/ <ndaut> 'tree'

/t/ vs. /tj/: /tõ5/ <dont> 'to listen' vs. /tjõ1/ <dionb> 'to lead'

/^{n}t^{h}/ vs. /^{n}ts^{h}/: /^{n}t^{h}ɑ3/ <ntaod> 'to take off' vs. /^{n}ts^{h}ɑ6/ <ncaos> 'to be done'

/t/ vs. /ʈ͡ʂ/: /tɑ4/ <daol> 'to step on' vs. /ʈ͡ʂɑ4/ <zhaol> 'non-Miao'

/t/ vs. /n/: /taw5/ <daut> 'speech' vs. /naw6/ <naus> 'bird'

3.2.1.5 The palatalized alveolar stops /tj/, /tj^{h}/, /^{n}tj/, and /^{n}tj^{h}/

Yankan Xong also has a series of palatalized alveolar stops, typically realized as [tj], [tj^{h}], [^{n}dj], and [^{n}tj^{h}]. These are represented in the orthography with <di>, <ti>, <ndi>, and <nti>. The precise place of articulation for these stops shows some variation among the author's consultants, in some cases even among those who hail from a single village. Some consultants (including some from Yankan Village) report that these stops involve simultaneous laminal-alveolar and apical-dental contact, just as was the case with the plain alveolar stops described in Section 3.2.1.4 above. Other consultants (again including some from Yankan Village) report that these stops are purely laminal-alveolar (though obviously with a palatal release), with no contact between the teeth and tongue occurring. For all consultants, though, these palatalized stops are always realized as stops, never as affricates.

Examples of syllables containing palatalized alveolar stops in Yankan Xong include /tju4/ <diul> 'to complete', /tjõ1/ <dionb> 'to lead', /tj^{h}ɛ2/ <tiex> 'diaper', /tj^{h}u5/ <tiut> 'to press down', /^{n}tjo5/ <ndiot> 'to recognize', /^{n}tju7/ <ndiuk> 'to peck', /^{n}tj^{h}o5/ <ntiot> 'smoky; smoke', and /^{n}tj^{h}ɛ1/ <ntieb> 'to weigh'. Some minimal and near-minimal pairs involving palatalized alveolar stops are given below.

/tj/ vs. /tj^{h}/: /tju4/ <diul> 'to complete' vs. /tj^{h}u5/ <tiut> 'to press down'

/tj/ vs. /^{n}tj/: /tju4/ <diul> 'to complete' vs. /^{n}tju7/ <ndiuk> 'to peck'

/^{n}tj/ vs. /^{n}tj^{h}/: /^{n}tjo5/ <ndiot> 'to recognize' vs. /^{n}tj^{h}o5/ <ntiot> 'smoky; smoke'

/tj/ vs. /t/: /tjõ1/ <dionb> 'to lead' vs. /tõ5/ <dont> 'to listen'

/^{n}tj^{h}/ vs. /^{n}ts^{h}/: /^{n}tj^{h}o5/ <ntiot> 'smoky; smoke' vs. /^{n}ts^{h}o5/ <ncot> 'to wash (clothing)'

/tj/ vs. /tɕ/: /tjõ1/ <dionb> 'to lead' vs. /tɕõ6/ <jons> 'seven'

/^{n}kj^{h}/ vs. /^{n}tj^{h}/: /^{n}kj^{h}o1/ <nkiob> 'magic, sorcery' vs. /^{n}tj^{h}o5/ <ntiot> 'smoky; smoke'

3.2.1.6 The alveolar affricates /ts/, /ts^{h}/, /^{n}ts/, and /^{n}ts^{h}/

These affricates are generally realized as [ts], [ts^{h}], [^{n}dz], and [^{n}ts^{h}], and they are represented orthographically with <z>, <c>, <nz>, and <nc>. These alveolar affricates are purely laminal-alveolar for all of the author's primary consultants, typically being produced without any contact between the tongue and the teeth.

Examples of syllables containing alveolar affricates in Yankan Xong include /tsã4/ <zanl> 'cold (said of water)', /tsɤ̃j5/ <zeint> 'ceramic jar', /ts^{h}ɑ̃5/ <caont> 'to meet', /tsʰɛɰ8/ <couf> 'vinegar', /^{n}tsɤj5/ <nzeit> 'skinny', /^{n}tso3/ <nzod> 'early', /^{n}tsʰo5/ <ncot> 'to wash (clothing)', and /^{n}tsʰɑ6/ <ncaos> 'to be done'. Some minimal and near-minimal pairs involving alveolar affricates are given below.

/ts/ vs. /tsʰ/: /tsã4/ <zanl> 'cold (said of water)' vs. /kõ1.**tsʰã2**/ <Gonb.**canx**> 'Communist (Party)'
/^{n}ts/ vs. /^{n}tsʰ/: /^{n}tso5/ <nzot> 'uncooked rice' vs. /^{n}tsʰo5/ <ncot> 'to wash (clothing)'
/^{n}tsʰ/ vs. /^{n}tʰ/: /^{n}tsʰɑ6/ <ncaos> 'to be done' vs. /^{n}tʰɑ3/ <ntaod> 'to take off'
/^{n}tsʰ/ vs. /^{n}tjʰ/: /^{n}tsʰo5/ <ncot> 'to wash (clothing)' vs. /^{n}tjʰo5/ <ntiot> 'smoky; smoke'
/^{n}ts/ vs. /^{n}tɕ/: /^{n}tsɑ7/ <nzaok> 'to kiss, to suck' vs. /^{n}tɕɑ3/ <njaod> 'CLF:piece'
/^{n}ts/ vs. /^{n}ʈʂ/: /^{n}tsɑ7/ <nzaok> 'to kiss, to suck' vs. /^{n}ʈʂɑ7/ <nzhaok> 'to open one's mouth'
/ts/ vs. /s/: /tsɤ̃j5/ <zeint> 'ceramic jar' vs. /**sɤ̃j7**.ʈʂʰɤ̃j8/ <**seink**.cheinf> 'naturally'

3.2.1.7 The alveolo-palatal affricates /tɕ/, /tɕʰ/, /^{n}tɕ/, and /^{n}tɕʰ/

The alveolo-palatal affricates are realized as [tɕ], [tɕʰ], [^{n}dʑ], and [^{n}tɕʰ], and they are represented orthographically with <j>, <q>, <nj>, and <nq>. As their IPA representations suggest, the stop portion of each of these consonants is laminal-alveolar, and the subsequent fricative portion is alveolo-palatal (and, of course, sibilant).

Examples of syllables containing alveolo-palatal affricates in Yankan Xong include /tɕõ5/ <jont> 'to sit', /tɕɤ3/ <jeud> 'alcohol', /tɕʰo3/ <qod> 'to grab', /tɕʰõ8/ <qonf> 'to shove', /^{n}tɕɤ3/ <njeud> 'salt', /^{n}tɕɑ3/ <njaod> 'CLF:piece', /^{n}tɕʰĩ5/ <nqint> 'red', and /^{n}tɕʰa5/ <nqat> 'to fear'. Some minimal and near-minimal pairs involving alveolo-palatal affricates are given below.

/tɕ/ vs. /tɕʰ/: /tɕo2/ <jox> 'nine' vs. /tɕʰo3/ <qod> 'to grab'
/tɕ/ vs. /^{n}tɕ/: /tɕɤ3/ <jeud> 'alcohol' vs. /^{n}tɕɤ3/ <njeud> 'salt'
/tɕ/ vs. /tj/: /tɕõ6/ <jons> 'seven' vs. /tjõ1/ <dionb> 'to lead'
/^{n}tɕ/ vs. /^{n}ts/: /^{n}tɕɑ3/ <njaod> 'CLF:piece' vs. /^{n}tsɑ7/ <nzaok> 'to kiss, to suck'
/^{n}tɕ/ vs. /^{n}ʈʂ/: /^{n}tɕɑ3/ <njaod> 'CLF:piece' vs. /^{n}ʈʂɑ3/ <nzhaod> 'to return'
/tɕ/ vs. /k/: /tɕi2/ <jix> 'NEG$_1$' vs. /ki5/ <git> 'wind'
/tɕʰ/ vs. /kjʰ/: /tɕʰo3/ <qod> 'to grab' vs. /kjʰo5/ <kiot> 'strange, sneaky, crafty; trick'
/tɕ/ vs. /ɕ/: /tɕõ6/ <jons> 'seven' vs. /ɕõ1/ <Xonb> 'Miao'

3.2.1.8 The apical–post-alveolar affricates /ʈʂ/, /ʈʂʰ/, /^{n}ʈʂ/, and /^{n}ʈʂʰ/

Yankan Xong's apical–post-alveolar affricates are typically realized as [ʈʂ], [ʈʂʰ], [^{n}ɖʐ], and [^{n}ʈʂʰ], and they are represented in the orthography with <zh>, <ch>, <nzh>, and <nch>. These consonants have uniformly been represented with retroflex symbols in previous publications on Xong. This is true even of those publications that focus on varieties of Xong spoken within Fenghuang County, such as He (2009). However, they are clearly apical–post-alveolar in all varieties of Fenghuang Xong encountered by the author so far. They are produced with the tip (*not* the underside) of the tongue raised up into contact with the post-alveolar region.

The apical–post-alveolar affricates show more intervarietal and interspeaker phonetic variation than perhaps any other Xong consonants, and they do so mainly with respect to the amount of frication involved in their articulation. Speakers from Yankan Village and Shanjiang Town tend to produce these sounds with relatively heavy frication (though impressionistically still rather less than typically occurs in the apical–post-alveolar affricates of Standard Mandarin, as in *chē* [车] 'vehicle' or *zhàn* [站] 'to stand'). In contrast, speakers from La'ershan Town and many of its surrounding villages (not including Yankan) tend to produce them with much less frication, sometimes even to the point of realizing them as mere apical–post-alveolar stops (e.g. [ṭ], [ṭʰ]) rather than affricates.

Examples of syllables containing apical–post-alveolar affricates in Yankan Xong include /ṭṣo7/ <zhok> 'to smile, to laugh', /ṭṣɑ4/ <zhaol> 'non-Miao' (see Section 2.2.3 for more on the precise meaning of this form), /ṭṣʰaw7/ <chauk> 'to do', / ṣʰo5/ <chot> 'to take', /^{n}ṭṣa3/ <nzhad> 'to split open', /^{n}ṭṣɑ3/ <nzhaod> 'to return', /^{n}ṭṣʰo5/ <nchot> 'tight', and /^{n}ṭṣʰɑ7/ <nchaok> 'to roll up (one's sleeves)'. Some minimal and near-minimal pairs involving apical–post-alveolar affricates are given below.

/ṭṣʰ/ vs. /^{n}ṭṣʰ/: /ṭṣʰo5/ <chot> 'to take' vs. /^{n}ṭṣʰo5/ <nchot> 'tight'
/^{n}ṭṣ/ vs. /^{n}ṭṣʰ/: /^{n}ṭṣɤ1/ <nzheub> 'to knock' vs. /^{n}ṭṣʰɤ5/ <ncheut> 'full (from eating)'
/ṭṣ/ vs. /t/: /ṭṣɑ4/ <zhaol> 'non-Miao' vs. /tɑ4/ <daol> 'to step on'
/^{n}ṭṣ/ vs. /^{n}ts/: /^{n}ṭṣɑ7/ <nzhaok> 'to open one's mouth' vs. /^{n}tsɑ7/ <nzaok> 'to kiss, to suck'
/^{n}ṭṣ/ vs. /^{n}tɕ/: /^{n}ṭṣɑ3/ <nzhaod> 'to return' vs. /^{n}tɕɑ3/ <njaod> 'CLF:piece'
/ṭṣ/ vs. /ṣ/: /ṭṣɑ̃6/ <zhaons> 'fat' vs. /ṣɑ̃5/ <shaont> 'fast'

3.2.1.9 The plain velar stops /k/, /kʰ/, /^{n}k/, and /^{n}kʰ/

These are straightforward dorsal-velar stops. They are generally realized as [k], [kʰ], [^{n}g], and [^{n}kʰ], and they are represented orthographically with <g>, <k>, <ngg>, and <nk>.

Examples of syllables containing plain velar stops in Yankan Xong include /ku7/ <guk> 'conical bamboo hat', /kɑ̃6/ <gaons> 'to give', /kʰo3/ <kod> 'poor (not wealthy)', /kʰi8/ <kif> 'angry', /^{n}kɤ1/ <nggeub> 'mushroom', /^{n}kɑ1/ <nggaob> 'medicine', /^{n}kʰu7/ <nkuk> 'curved, bent', and /^{n}kʰɑ3/ <nkaod> 'to bow with hands clasped in front'. Some minimal and near-minimal pairs involving plain velar stops are given below.

/k/ vs. /k^h/: /ki5/ <git> 'wind' vs. /k^{h}i8/ <kif> 'angry'
/^{n}k/ vs. /^{n}k^h/: /^{n}kɑ1/ <nggaob> 'medicine' vs. /^{n}k^{h}ɑ3/ <nkaod> 'to bow with hands clasped in front'
/k/ vs. /tɕ/: /ki5/ <git> 'wind' vs. /tɕi2/ <jix> 'NEG$_1$'
/k^h/ vs. /kj^h/: /k^{h}o3/ <kod> 'poor (not wealthy)' vs. /kj^{h}o5/ <kiot> 'strange, sneaky, crafty; trick'
/k/ vs. /q/: /kɤ3/ <geud> 'to hold' vs. /qɤ4/ <gheul> 'village'
/^{n}k/ vs. /^{n}q/: /^{n}kɤ1/ <nggeub> 'mushroom' vs. /^{n}qɤ1/ <ngheub> 'to sing'
/k/ vs. /qw/: /kɤ3/ <geud> 'to hold' vs. /qwɤ1/ <gueub> 'white'
/^{n}k/ vs. /ŋ/: /^{n}kɑ1/ <nggaob> 'medicine' vs. /ŋɑ3/ <ngaod> 'short (not tall)'

3.2.1.10 The palatalized velar stops /kj/, /kj^h/, /^{n}kj/, and /^{n}kj^h/

Nearly all previous descriptions of Xong phonology have included a series of palatal stops (/c/, /c^h/, etc.). A corresponding series of stops is found in Yankan Xong and all other varieties of Fenghuang Xong known to the author, but it is not clear – at least in articulatory phonetic terms – whether they should be considered purely palatal consonants (or, more precisely, dorsal-palatal consonants) or palatalized dorsal-velar consonants. The author's consultants accept both dorsal-palatal articulations (i.e. [c], [c^h], [^{n}ɟ], and [^{n}c^h]) and palatalized dorsal-velar articulations (i.e. [kj], [kj^h], [^{n}gj], and [^{n}kj^h]) as equally "good", and attempts to have consultants distinguish which articulations they use in their own production of these segments have met with little success. However, since all varieties of Fenghuang Xong known to the author have a clear series of palatalized bilabial stops (see Section 3.2.1.3) and a clear series of palatalized alveolar stops (Section 3.2.1.5), the stops under discussion in this section are analyzed as palatalized dorsal-velar stops purely in the interest of symmetry. (And in any case, from a purely phonological point of view the decision is largely irrelevant; the only relevant point is that there is clearly no contrast between dorsal-palatal and palatalized dorsal-velar consonants in the speech of any of the author's consultants.)

While /kj/, /kj^h/, and /^{n}kj^h/ are all relatively well attested in the Xong varieties spoken by the author's consultants, only two syllables beginning with /^{n}kj/ have been found so far. These are the term for 'gold', which is /^{n}kjɛ1/ <ngieb> for all consultants, and the term for 'to hiccup', which is /^{n}kjɛ5/ <ngiet> for speakers from Yankan Village and /^{n}kjã5/ <ngiant> for all other speakers (see also Section 3.3.2.2 below).

Other examples of syllables containing palatalized velar stops in Yankan Xong include /kja1/ <giab> 'to stir-fry', /kjɛ1/ <gieb> 'burnt', /kj^{h}a7/ <kiak> 'to open', /kj^{h}o5/ <kiot> 'strange, sneaky, crafty; trick', /^{n}kj^{h}o1/ <nkiob> 'magic, sorcery', and /^{n}kj^{h}ɛ3/ <nkied> 'to stand on tiptoe'. Some minimal and near-minimal pairs involving palatalized velar stops are given below.

/kj/ vs. /kj^h/: /kja1/ <giab> 'to stir-fry' vs. /kj^{h}a7/ <kiak> 'to open'
/kj/ vs. /^{n}kj/: /kjɛ1/ <gieb> 'burnt' vs. /^{n}kjɛ1/ <ngieb> 'gold'

/kj^{h}/ vs. /^{n}kj^{h}/: /kj^{h}o5/ <kiot> 'strange, sneaky, crafty; trick' vs. /^{n}kj^{h}o1/ <nkiob> 'magic, sorcery'
/^{n}kj/ vs. /^{n}kj^{h}/: /^{n}kjɛ1/ <ngieb> 'gold' vs. /^{n}kj^{h}ɛ3/ <nkied> 'to stand on tiptoe'
/^{n}kj^{h}/ vs. /^{n}tj^{h}/: /^{n}kj^{h}o1/ <nkiob> 'magic, sorcery' vs. /^{n}tj^{h}o5/ <ntiot> 'smoky; smoke'
/kj^{h}/ vs. /tɕ^{h}/: /kj^{h}o5/ <kiot> 'strange, sneaky, crafty; trick' vs. /tɕ^{h}o3/ <qod> 'to grab'
/kj^{h}/ vs. /k^{h}/: /kj^{h}o5/ <kiot> 'strange, sneaky, crafty; trick' vs. /k^{h}o3/ <kod> 'poor (not wealthy)'

3.2.1.11 The plain uvular stops /q/, /q^{h}/, /^{n}q/, and /^{n}q^{h}/

These dorsal-uvular stops are most often realized as [q], [q^{h}], [^{N}ɢ], and [^{N}q^{h}], although they are occasionally realized as uvular affricates (i.e. [qχ], [qχ^{h}], [^{N}ɢʁ], and [^{N}qχ^{h}]) in emphatic speech. Impressionistically, these affricated allophones seem to occur rather more often with the aspirated uvular stops than with the unaspirated ones. Regardless of their precise phonetic realization, these four consonants are represented orthographically with <gh>, <kh>, <ngh>, and <nkh>.

Examples of syllables containing plain uvular stops in Yankan Xong include /qɑ3/ <ghaod> 'feces', /qo5/ <ghot> 'old; old person', /q^{h}a3/ <khad> 'dry', /q^{h}aw7/ <khauk> 'hole', /^{n}qɤ1/ <ngheub> 'to sing', /^{n}qɤ̃j5/ <ngheint> 'to carry on a shoulder-pole', / ^{n}q^{h}ɛ3/ <nkhed> 'to look', and /^{n}q^{h}ɛɰ3/ <nkhoud> 'to fall out'. Some minimal and near-minimal pairs involving plain uvular stops are given below.

/q/ vs. /q^{h}/: /**qa3**.mɑ̃6/ <**ghad**.maons> 'NEG.IMP' vs. /q^{h}a3/ <khad> 'dry'
/q/ vs. /^{n}q/: /qɤ4/ <gheul> 'village' vs. /^{n}qɤ1/ <ngheub> 'to sing'
/q/ vs. /k/: /qɤ4/ <gheul> 'village' vs. /kɤ3/ <geud> 'to hold'
/^{n}q/ vs. /^{n}k/: /^{n}qɤ1/ <ngheub> 'to sing' vs. /^{n}kɤ1/ <nggeub> 'mushroom'
/q/ vs. /qw/: /qɤ4/ <gheul> 'village' vs. /qwɤ1/ <gueub> 'white'
/q^{h}/ vs. /qw^{h}/: /q^{h}a3/ <khad> 'dry' vs. /qw^{h}a3/ <kuad> 'to stir'

3.2.1.12 The labialized uvular stops /qw/, /qw^{h}/, /^{n}qw/, and /^{n}qw^{h}/

All varieties of Fenghuang Xong known to the author possess a single series of labialized dorsal stops. These stops are much more often produced with a dorsal-uvular articulation than a dorsal-velar one, being typically realized as [qw], [qw^{h}], [^{N}ɢw], and [^{N}qw^{h}]. They are represented in the author's practical orthography with <gu>, <ku>, <nggu>, and <nku>. Just as with the plain uvular stops discussed in Section 3.2.1.11 above, the labialized uvular stops (especially the aspirated ones) are sometimes realized as affricates in emphatic speech, yielding [qχw], [qχw^{h}], [^{N}ɢʁw], and [^{N}qχw^{h}].

It is worth pointing out that every Xong variety spoken outside of Fenghuang County (or at least every such variety the author has seen described in the literature) has contrastive labialized velar and labialized uvular stops. The merger of these labialized velar and labialized uvular stops is thus one of the major distinguishing features of Fenghuang Xong as a whole.

None of the consonants /qw/, /qw^{h}/, and /^{n}qw/ are particularly rare in the Fenghuang Xong lexicon, but the author has only encountered two syllables containing /^{n}qw^{h}/. The first of these is /^{n}qw^{h}ɛɰ5/ <nkuout>, meaning 'to insert one's foot (e.g. into a boot or hole)'. This form is found in the idiolects of all the author's consultants from La'ershan Town and its surrounding villages (including Yankan Village), but the corresponding form for the author's consultant from Shanjiang Town (Mrs. Chenghua Long) is instead /qw^{h}ɛɰ5/ <kuout>. The second such syllable occurs twice in an obligatorily disyllabic onomatopoeic form /^{n}qw^{h}ɑ̃5.^{n}qw^{h}ɑ̃5/ <nkuaont.nkuaont> 'ONOM:nkuaon. nkuaon', which represents the sound of a dog barking (see Section 11.2 for more on onomatopoeic forms in general).

Other examples of syllables containing labialized uvular stops in Yankan Xong include /qwɛ1/ <gueb> 'black', /qwɤ1/ <gueub> 'white', /qw^{h}a3/ <kuad> 'to stir', /qw^{h}ɛ4/ <kuel> 'to trip', /^{n}qwɑ5/ <ngguaot> 'to collapse', and /^{n}qwɤj5/ <nggueit> 'naughty, mischievous'. Some minimal and near-minimal pairs involving labialized uvular stops are given below.

/qw/ vs. /^{n}qw/:	/qwɑ5/ <guaot> 'to pass' vs. /^{n}qwɑ5/ <ngguaot> 'to collapse'
/^{n}qw/ vs. /^{n}qw^{h}/:	/^{n}qwɛɰ5/ <ngguout> 'to lose one's hair' vs. /^{n}qw^{h}ɛɰ5/ <nkuout> 'to insert one's foot'
/qw/ vs. /k/:	/qwɤ1/ <gueub> 'white' vs. /kɤ3/ <geud> 'to hold'
/qw/ vs. /q/:	/qwɤ1/ <gueub> 'white' vs. /qɤ4/ <gheul> 'village'
/qw^{h}/ vs. /q^{h}/:	/qw^{h}a3/ <kuad> 'to stir' vs. /q^{h}a3/ <khad> 'dry'
/qw/ vs. /ŋw/:	/qwɤ1/ <gueub> 'white' vs. /ŋwɤ4/ <ngueul> 'to flow'

3.2.2 Nasals

3.2.2.1 The modal nasals /m/, /mj/, /n/, /nj/, /ṇ/, /ŋ/, and /ŋw/

All varieties of Fenghuang Xong known to the author have seven distinct nasal phonemes that involve modally voiced phonation: (i) the plain bilabial /m/, typically realized as [m] and represented orthographically with <m>, (ii) the palatalized bilabial /mj/, realized as [mj] and represented with <mi>, (iii) the plain alveolar /n/, realized as [n] and represented with <n>, (iv) the palatalized alveolar /nj/, realized as [nj] and represented with <ni>, (v) the apical–post-alveolar /ṇ/, realized as [ṇ] and represented with <nh>, (vi) the plain velar /ŋ/, realized as [ŋ] and represented with <ng>, and (vii) the labialized velar /ŋw/, realized as [ŋw] and represented with <ngu>.

Most of Xong's modal nasals are fairly straightforward and require little comment, with a few exceptions. First, while many Xong varieties spoken outside of Fenghuang County have contrastive plain bilabial, palatalized bilabial, and rhotacized bilabial (/mɹ/) nasals, the latter two have merged in all Fenghuang Xong varieties known to the author, leaving only a contrast between /m/ and /mj/ (see also Section 3.2.1.3 above).

Second, the alveolar nasal /n/ is like the alveolar stops described in Section 3.2.1.4 in that it typically involves simultaneous laminal-alveolar and apical-dental contact. However, the palatalized alveolar nasal /nj/ is unlike the palatalized alveolar stops described in Section 3.2.1.5 in that the author's consultants all report that it typically involves only laminal-alveolar contact, not apical-dental contact.

Finally, note that the velar articulation of /ŋw/ lends a degree of articulatory asymmetry to Yankan Xong's consonant inventory (and indeed to the consonant inventories of all Fenghuang Xong varieties with which the author is familiar), since the only labialized nasal in the inventory is dorsal-velar while the only labialized stops are dorsal-uvular.

Examples of syllables containing modal nasals in Yankan Xong include /mo1/ <mos> 'tired', /mɛ6/ <mes> 'to sell', /mjɤj4/ <mieil> 'spicy', /mjɛɰ4/ <mioul> 'fish', /nɑ̃3/ <naond> 'ASSOC', /nɛ6/ <nes> 'to ask', /nja2/ <niax> 'meat', /njɤ6/ <nieus> 'to buy', /ṇo1/ <nhob> 'to walk', /ṇaw1/ <nhaub> 'seed', /ŋõ4/ <ngonl> 'CLF:animate', /ŋɑ3/ <ngaod> 'short (not tall)', /ŋwɤj8/ <ngueif> 'unmarried woman', and /ŋwɤ4/ <ngueul> 'to flow'. Some minimal and near-minimal pairs involving modal nasals are given below.

/m/ vs. /mj/: /mɤj4/ <meil> 'coal' vs. /mjɤj4/ <mieil> 'spicy'
/m/ vs. /n/: /mɛ6/ <mes> 'to sell' vs. /nɛ6/ <nes> 'to ask'
/n/ vs. /nj/: /nɛ6/ <nes> 'to ask' vs. /njɛ6/ <nies> 'to steal'
/n/ vs. /ṇ/: /no6/ <nos> 'hemp' vs. /ṇo1/ <nhob> 'to walk'
/n/ vs. /ŋ/: /nɑ̃3/ <naond> 'ASSOC' vs. /ŋɑ̃2/ <ngaonx> 'boat'
/ŋ/ vs. /ŋw/: /ŋɤ4/ <ngeul> 'smooth, slippery' vs. /ŋwɤ4/ <ngueul> 'to flow'
/m/ vs. /p/: /mɤ̃j4/ <meinl> 'CLF:person' vs. /pɤ̃j2/ <beinx> 'flower'
/m/ vs. /^{n}p/: /mã2/ <manx> '2PL' vs. /^{n}pã2/ <nbanx> 'to think'
/mj/ vs. /pj/: /mjaw2/ <miaux> 'leaf' vs. /pjaw7/ <biauk> 'dark'
/n/ vs. /t/: /naw6/ <naus> 'bird' vs. /taw5/ <daut> 'speech'
/n/ vs. /l/: /nɛ6/ <nes> 'to ask' vs. /lɛ1/ <leb> 'CLF'
/ŋ/ vs. /^{n}k/: /ŋɑ3/ <ngaod> 'short (not tall)' vs. /^{n}kɑ1/ <nggaob> 'medicine'

3.2.2.2 The breathy nasals /mʱ/ and /nʱ/

In published descriptions of other Xong varieties, these nasal consonants are typically described as either voiceless and unaspirated (Chen 2009: 8–10; Yu 2011: 20, 21) or voiceless and aspirated (Xiang 1999: 9, 10; Yang 2004: 80; He 2009: 95, 96). Thus, in all these previous descriptions, these consonants are implied to begin with an initial voiceless nasal. Xiang (1999), Yang (2004), and He (2009) further imply that this initial nasal is followed by a short period of continued voicelessness after its release and before the onset of voicing in the following vowel, while Chen (2009) and Yu (2011) imply that no such intervening voicelessness occurs.

However, spectrographic analysis shows that in the speech of the author's consultants, these phonemes are in fact quite clearly breathy voiced. They consist of an initial modally voiced (*not* voiceless) nasal, which is then followed by a short period of breathy voicing (*not* voicelessness) after the release of that nasal and before the onset of modal voicing in the following vowel. Phonetically, then, the breathy bilabial nasal is [m^{ɦ}] (represented orthographically with <hm>), and the breathy alveolar nasal is [n^{ɦ}] (orthographically <hn>). They are thus broadly similar to the breathy nasal consonants found in Hindi and Tsonga, as described in Ladefoged and Maddieson (1996: 107, 108). It is unclear whether the description of these Xong consonants as voiceless (un)aspirated in Xiang (1999), Yang (2004), Chen (2009), He (2009), and Yu (2011) reflects true dialectal variation or is simply an artifact of impressionistic analysis.

The breathy bilabial nasal /m^{ɦ}/ has so far been attested in only a single morpheme. This is /m^{ɦ}ɑ̃5/ <hmaont>, meaning roughly 'evening'.[42] The breathy alveolar nasal /n^{ɦ}/ is rather more common, occurring in at least six morphemes: /n^{ɦ}ã8/ <hnanf> 'CLF:clothing', /n^{ɦ}ã5/ <hnant> 'to call', /n^{ɦ}ã5/ <hnant> 'CLF:li (unit of length equivalent to 500 meters)', /n^{ɦ}ɛ8/ <hnef> 'day; CLF:day', /n^{ɦ}ɑ̃3/ <hnaond> 'to sense, to hear', and /n^{ɦ}ɤ̃j3/ <hneind> 'to wear'. These claims apply to all varieties of Fenghuang Xong spoken by the author's primary consultants, though for some consultants not from Yankan Village the form meaning 'CLF:clothing' is pronounced /n^{ɦ}ã1/ <hnanb> and/or the form meaning 'day; CLF:day' is pronounced /n^{ɦ}ɛ1/ <hneb>.

Some minimal and near-minimal pairs involving breathy nasals are given below.

/m^{ɦ}/ vs. /m/: /m^{ɦ}ɑ̃5/ <hmaont> 'evening' vs. /mɑ̃3/ <maond> 'late'
/n^{ɦ}/ vs. /n/: /n^{ɦ}ɤ̃j3/ <hneind> 'to wear' vs. /nɤ̃j3/ <neind> 'this'
/n^{ɦ}/ vs. /n/: /n^{ɦ}ɛ8/ <hnef> 'day; CLF:day' vs. /nɛ6/ <nes> 'to ask'
/m^{ɦ}/ vs. /n^{ɦ}/: /m^{ɦ}ɑ̃5/ <hmaont> 'evening' vs. /n^{ɦ}ɑ̃3/ <hnaond> 'to sense, to hear'

3.2.3 The laterals /l/, /lj/, /l^{ɦ}/, and /lj^{ɦ}/

The so-called plain alveolar lateral /l/ is a modally voiced lateral approximant whose articulation involves both laminal-alveolar and apical-dental contact. It is thus

42 Although /m^{ɦ}ɑ̃5/ <hmaont> and /mɑ̃3/ <maond> are respectively glossed as 'evening' and 'late' in this section, their actual meanings are slightly more specific. The form /m^{ɦ}ɑ̃5/ <hmaont> can be used (i) as a verb meaning 'late (in the day, at night)', (ii) as a classifier for evenings, and (iii) as the first syllable of the disyllabic form /m^{ɦ}ɑ̃5-tju6/ <hmaont-dius> [evening-???] 'evening'. The form /mɑ̃3/ <maond> is a verb meaning 'late (for some event)'.

realized as [l] and represented orthographically with <l>. The palatalized alveolar lateral /lj/ is also a modally voiced lateral approximant for all consultants, although for some consultants it involves only laminal-alveolar contact and for others it involves simultaneous laminal-alveolar and apical-dental contact. In all cases it is realized with a palatal release, making it phonetically [lj] (orthographically <li>). Still, for simplicity's sake /l/ and /lj/ can both be analyzed as phonologically laminal-alveolar, just as was done with the plain and palatalized alveolar stops discussed in Sections 3.2.1.4 and 3.2.1.5.

All varieties of Fenghuang Xong known to the author also include two breathy laterals /lʱ/ and /ljʱ/.[43] Most of what was said about Fenghuang Xong's breathy nasals in Section 3.2.2.2 also applies to these consonants. Other scholars of Xong typically describe them as either voiceless and unaspirated (Chen 2009: 8–10; Yu 2011: 20, 21) or voiceless and aspirated (Xiang 1999: 9, 10; Yang 2004: 80; He 2009: 95, 96). In the case of the author's consultants, though, spectrographic analysis shows quite clearly that these consonants are produced with breathy voicing. Phonetically, they consist of an initial modally voiced lateral approximant, followed by a short period of breathy voicing, which is then in turn followed by the onset of modal voicing in the following vowel. The breathy plain alveolar lateral can be transcribed phonetically with [lʱ] (orthographically <hl>), and the breathy palatalized alveolar lateral with [ljʱ] (orthographically <hli>). As was the case with Xong's breathy nasals, it is unclear whether the description of these consonants as voiceless (un)aspirated in Xiang (1999), Yang (2004), Chen (2009), He (2009), and Yu (2011) reflects dialectal variation or is an artifact of impressionistic analysis.

Examples of syllables containing laterals in Yankan Xong include /lo4/ <lol> 'to come', /lɛ1/ <leb> 'CLF', /lja2/ <liax> 'to resemble', /ljo2/ <liox> 'big', /lʱi5/ <hlit> 'cooked rice', /lʱɤ̃j5/ <hleint> 'sweat', /ljʱa5/ <hliat> 'tin', and /ljʱɑ7/ <hliaok> 'to drag'. Some minimal and near-minimal pairs involving laterals are given below.

/l/ vs. /lj/: /lɤ5/ <leut> 'top' vs. /ljɤ6/ <lieus> 'to guard'
/l/ vs. /lj/: /lo4/ <lol> 'to come' vs. /ljo2/ <liox> 'big'
/l/ vs. /lʱ/: /lo4/ <lol> 'to come' vs. /lʱo3/ <hlod> 'bamboo'
/l/ vs. /lʱ/: /lɑ2/ <laox> 'slow' vs. /lʱɑ5/ <hlaot> 'moon; CLF:month'
/lj/ vs. /ljʱ/: /ljo2/ <liox> 'big' vs. /ljʱo8/ <hliof> 'many'
/lj/ vs. /ljʱ/: /lja2/ <liax> 'to resemble' vs. /ljʱa5/ <hliat> 'tin'
/lʱ/ vs. /ljʱ/: /lʱɑ5/ <hlaot> 'moon; CLF:month' vs. /ljʱɑ7/ <hliaok> 'to drag'
/l/ vs. /n/: /lɛ1/ <leb> 'CLF' vs. /nɛ6/ <nes> 'to ask'
/lj/ vs. /nj/: /lja2/ <liax> 'to resemble' vs. /nja2/ <niax> 'meat'

43 While breathy lateral consonants such as these are hardly common among the languages of the world, they are also attested in several languages belonging to the Indo-Aryan branch of Indo-European and the Wu and Yue branches of Sinitic (Ladefoged and Maddieson 1996: 201, 202).

3.2.4 The voiceless fricatives /f/, /s/, /ɕ/, /ʂ/, /h/, and /hw/

The consonant /f/ is a straightforward voiceless labiodental fricative, realized as [f] and represented orthographically with <f>. In addition, all varieties of Fenghuang Xong that the author has encountered distinguish three voiceless sibilant fricatives. The first of these is a laminal-alveolar (not apical-dental or simultaneous laminal-alveolar/apical-dental) fricative /s/ (orthographic <s>), the second is an alveolo-palatal fricative /ɕ/ (orthographic <x>), and the third is an apical–post-alveolar fricative /ʂ/ (orthographic <sh>).

In phonetic terms, the so-called "glottal fricatives" /h/ and /hw/ (orthographic <h> and <hu>) are not actually fricatives at all for any of the author's consultants. Instead, as in many of the world's languages, they simply represent a period of initial voicelessness on the following vowel (with /hw/ involving lip rounding as well). However, /h/ and /hw/ do pattern with Fenghuang Xong's other consonants in at least two respects: they only appear in syllable-onset position, and, like Xong's uvular stops and velar nasals, they display a phonemic distinction between labialization and non-labialization. Furthermore, /hw/ is in mostly free variation with another voiceless fricative, namely /f/ (see discussion below). Thus, it seems clear that /h/ and /hw/ are phonologically voiceless fricative consonants, if not phonetically so, and they have been grouped with the other voiceless fricatives here and in Table 3.2.

The consonants /f/ and /hw/ are usually in free variation with each other, to the point that the distinction between them appears to be only minimally phonemic. Both consonants generally only appear in recent, obvious borrowings from Sinitic varieties, most of which can be produced in Xong with either consonant without any change in meaning.[44] Thus, for example, 'chemistry' can be produced as either /**fɑ7**.ɕo1/ <**faok**.xob> or /**hwɑ7**.ɕo1/ <**huaok**.xob>, 'airplane' can be produced as either /**fɤj7**.tɕi7/ <**feik**.jik> or /**hwɤj7**.tɕi7/ <**hueik**.jik>, and 'sneaky, cunning' can be produced as either /tɕo2.**fɑ1**/ <jox.**faob**> or /tɕo2.**hwɑ1**/ <jox.**huaob**>. There are no obvious conditioning factors that determine whether /f/ or /hw/ appears in these forms, including phonological, dialectal, or even idiolectal ones. All of the author's consultants, regardless of which particular variety of Fenghuang Xong they speak, will often produce the same lexical item sometimes with /f/ and sometimes with /hw/, and they accept both pronunciations as equally valid.[45]

44 There is of course a clear distinction between initial /f/ and /xw/ in Standard Mandarin, as in *fēi* (飞) 'to fly' vs. *huī* (灰) 'ashes'. He (2009: 49, 50) implies that Fenghuang Chinese (see Section 2.7.2 of this grammar) makes a similar distinction, as in /fã^{53}/ 'to spin (cloth)' vs. /xwã^{53}/ 'to lie, a lie'. In both of these Sinitic varieties, /xw/ is the closest phonetic equivalent to Fenghuang Xong's /hw/.

45 The author has also found a single lexical item in which /f/ alternates with /h/ rather than with /hw/. This is the term for 'peanut', which the author's consultants report can be freely pronounced as either /pi3-**fɑ7**.sɤ̃j3/ <bid-**faok**.seind> or /pi3-**hɑ7**.sɤ̃j3/ <bid-**haok**.seind> (morphemically [FRT-peanut] in either case).

However, five forms have been found in which only /f/ can be used, not /hw/, and there may well be other such forms which the author has not yet encountered. The five such forms attested so far are /**fɤ̃j7**.ʈʂõ7/ <**feink**.zhonk> 'CLF:minute', /fɤ̃j7/ <feink> 'CLF:currency.fen (unit of currency)', /fu1/ <fub> 'CLF:pair', /**fu2**.ɕɑ̃1/ <**fux**.xaonb> 'Buddhist monk', and /**fu8**.nɑ̃8/ <**Fuf**.nanf> 'Hunan (Province)'. None of the author's consultants have ever produced these forms with an initial /hw/ instead, and they do not accept such alternate pronunciations when produced by the author. The existence of these five non-alternating forms proves that the distinction between /f/ and /hw/ is at least minimally phonemic in the Fenghuang Xong varieties spoken by the author's consultants. Interestingly, no forms have yet been attested in which only /hw/ can be used, and not /f/.

Examples of syllables containing voiceless fricatives in Yankan Xong include /fɤ̃j7/ <feink> 'CLF:currency.fen (unit of currency)', /fɤ̃j2/ <feinx> or /hwɤ̃j2/ <hueinx> 'rice noodles', /fɑ1/ <faob> or /hwɑ1/ <huaob> 'to draw, to paint; drawing, painting', /sɑ5/ <saot> 'to beg', /sa3/ <sad> 'blade', /ɕu1/ <xub> 'small', /ɕõ1/ <Xonb> 'Miao', /ʂɑ̃5/ <shaont> 'fast', /ʂɤj5/ <sheit> 'to write', /haw7/ <hauk> 'to drink', and /hɤ̃j3/ <heind> 'heavy'. Some minimal and near-minimal pairs involving voiceless fricatives are given below.

/f/ vs. /p/:	/fɤ̃j2/ <feinx> 'rice noodles' vs. /pɤ̃j2/ <beinx> 'flower'
/f/ vs. /ʋ/:	/tɕo2.**fɑ1**/ <jox.**faob**> 'sneaky, cunning' vs. /ʋɑ1/ <waob> 'cherry'
/s/ vs. /ts/:	/tsʰo8.**sɤ̃j1**/ <cof.**seinb**> 'to worry' vs. /tsɤ̃j5/ <zeint> 'ceramic jar'
/s/ vs. /ɕ/:	/sɑ̃1/ <saonb> 'to carve' vs. /ɕɑ̃3/ <xaond> 'not yet'
/ɕ/ vs. /tɕ/:	/ɕõ1/ <Xonb> 'Miao' vs. /tɕõ6/ <jons> 'seven'
/ɕ/ vs. /ʂ/:	/ɕɑ̃3/ <xaond> 'not yet' vs. /ʂɑ̃5/ <shaont> 'fast'
/ʂ/ vs. /ʈʂ/:	/ʂɑ̃5/ <shaont> 'fast' vs. /ʈʂɑ̃6/ <zhaons> 'fat'
/s/ vs. /ʂ/:	/sɑ̃1/ <saonb> 'to carve' vs. /ʂɑ̃5/ <shaont> 'fast'
/ʂ/ vs. /h/:	/ʂaw7/ <shauk> 'CLF:yuan (unit of currency)' vs. /haw7/ <hauk> 'to drink'
/h/ vs. /hw/:	/hɤj7/ <heik> 'chair' vs. /**hwɤj7**.tɕi7/ <**hueik**.jik> 'airplane'
/hw/ vs. /ʋ/:	/hwɑ1/ <huaob> 'to draw, to paint; drawing, painting' vs. /ʋɑ1/ <waob> 'cherry'

3.2.5 The voiced approximants /ʋ/, /j/, and /ʐ/

In addition to the lateral approximants discussed in Section 3.2.3 above, all varieties of Fenghuang Xong known to the author feature three additional non-lateral voiced approximant consonants. The first of these is represented orthographically with <w>. For all of the author's consultants, this consonant has two allophones which occur in free variation: a voiced bilabial approximant [β] and a voiced labiodental approximant [ʋ]. Since Fenghuang Xong has a corresponding voiceless labiodental fricative /f/ (see Section 3.2.4) but no corresponding voiceless bilabial continuant, the approximant in question is represented in phonological transcriptions with /ʋ/ and is listed in the LABIODENTAL row of Table 3.2 in Section 3.1.

All varieties of Fenghuang Xong also feature a voiced palatal approximant /j/, which is phonetically [j] and is represented orthographically with <y>. The corresponding consonant is transcribed in most published descriptions of other Xong varieties as a voiced alveolo-palatal fricative /ʑ/, but in all varieties of Xong spoken by the author's consultants the sound in question is quite clearly an approximant, not a fricative. There is, however, some phonological evidence that this sound should in fact be analyzed as a voiced alveolo-palatal approximant /ʑ̞/ in the variety of Xong spoken in Shanjiang Town; see Section 3.3.1.6 for details. But since the phonological evidence in question does not apply to Yankan Xong, and since the author has no phonetic evidence from any variety of Fenghuang Xong that the approximant under discussion is alveolo-palatal rather than simply palatal, this approximant is still analyzed – and referred to – as a palatal approximant /j/ in this grammar.

The final consonant discussed in this section is represented orthographically with <r>. Due to typographic considerations, this consonant is always represented in phonological transcriptions with the symbol for a voiced apical–post-alveolar fricative (i.e. /ẓ/), but phonetically it varies between a voiced apical–post-alveolar fricative and a voiced apical–post-alveolar approximant. These two allophones seem to be in completely free variation for all of the author's primary consultants, although for most of them the approximant allophone is noticeably more frequent. Since this approximant allophone is more frequent, and since Yankan Xong has several other voiced approximants but no other voiced fricatives, the phoneme in question is analyzed – and referred to – as an approximant in this grammar.

Examples of syllables containing these consonants in Yankan Xong include /ʋɛ4/ <wel> '1SG', /ʋã4/ <wanl> 'pot', /ʋɑ1/ <waob> 'cherry', /ju4/ <yul> 'cow', /ja1/ <yab> 'also', /jɤj4/ <yeil> 'to rinse', /ẓɑ4/ <raol> 'urine', /ẓo6/ <ros> 'strength', and /ẓɛɰ5/ <rout> 'far'. Some minimal and near-minimal pairs involving these consonants are given below.

/ʋ/ vs. /f/: /ʋɑ1/ <waob> 'cherry' vs. /tɕo2.**fɑ1**/ <jox.**faob**> 'sneaky, cunning'
/ʋ/ vs. /m/: /ʋɛ4/ <wel> '1SG' vs. /mɛ4/ <mel> 'horse'
/j/ vs. /ɕ/: /ju4/ <yul> 'cow' vs. /ɕu1/ <xub> 'small'
/j/ vs. /nj/: /ja1/ <yab> 'also' vs. /nja2/ <niax> 'meat'
/ẓ/ vs. /ṣ/: /ẓɑ̃5/ <raont> 'young' vs. /ṣɑ̃5/ <shaont> 'fast'
/ẓ/ vs. /ṇ/: /ẓaw5/ <raut> 'good' vs. /ṇaw1/ <nhaub> 'seed'

3.2.6 The "empty" initial /Ø/

Some Xong syllables do not begin with any phonemic initial consonant, phonologically consisting solely of a vocalic nucleus and an accompanying tone. (Other phonologically onset-less syllables consist solely of a syllabic nasal and an accompanying tone; see Section 3.3.4 for discussion of these.) These syllables can be realized either with an initial glottal stop [ʔ] or with no phonetic onset at all; the two are in completely free variation. For instance, /aw1/ <aub> 'water' can be realized as either [ʔaw1] or [aw1] in all environments.

Examples of syllables with no initial consonant in Yankan Xong include /ɑ3/ <aod> 'one', /ɤ3/ <eud> 'clothing', /o1/ <ob> 'to burn', /ã1/ <anb> 'bitter', /ɛɰ1/ <oub> 'two', /aw1/ <aub> 'water', and /ɤ̃j5/ <eint> 'to fly'.

3.3 Vowels

Like most varieties of Fenghuang Xong, Yankan Xong features seven oral monophthongs, four nasal monophthongs, three oral diphthongs, and one nasal diphthong (see Tables 3.3 and 3.4 in Section 3.1 above). While slightly larger than the worldwide average in some respects (see Maddieson 2013b), this vowel system is not particularly large when compared to those found in other Miao-Yao languages (Niederer 1998: 211, 212) or those found in other mainland Southeast Asian languages generally (Enfield 2005: 186).

Unlike those of many other mainland Southeast Asian languages, though, Yankan Xong's vowel system is not a particularly "balanced" one. There are four back vowels, but only two front vowels and a single central vowel. Only four of Yankan Xong's seven oral monophthongs have nasal counterparts, and rounding is only contrastive for the two mid back oral vowels (i.e. /o/ and /ɤ/).

Yankan Xong also has a surprisingly restricted inventory of diphthongs given its relatively large number of monophthongs. Furthermore, one of these diphthongs, /ɛɰ/, is particularly interesting in that its offglide [ɰ] does not occur as a syllable onset */ɰ/ or (in fully vocalic form) as a monophthongal vowel */ɯ/. This restricted diphthongal inventory is in fact one of the major motivations for analyzing the sounds in question as unitary phonemes rather than as sequences of two phonemes, as is discussed in more detail in Section 3.7.

Finally, note that Yankan Xong, like most varieties of Fenghuang Xong, has a single syllabic nasal /m̩/. In phonetic terms this sound is of course a consonant, not a vowel. Nevertheless, it is discussed in Section 3.3.4 below because it shares a number of phonological properties with Xong's vowels, including its ability to bear tone and its ability to serve as a syllable nucleus.[46]

46 All varieties of Fenghuang Xong which the author has encountered (including Yankan Xong) also feature a handful of syllables that are represented orthographically with <erX> in this grammar, where <X> is any tone letter. The phonetic realization of these syllables varies widely from consultant to consultant, even among consultants from the same village, but it often involves some sort of low central to mid central unrounded vowel produced with some degree of apical–post-alveolar articulation.

3.3.1 Oral monophthongs

3.3.1.1 The high front unrounded vowel /i/

This is a high front unrounded vowel, most often realized as [i] and represented orthographically with <i>. It has two noteworthy allophones. First, it is realized as a syllabic voiced alveolar fricative [z̩] after alveolar sibilant consonants, including the affricates /ts/, /ts^h/, /^{n}ts/, and /^{n}ts^h/ and the voiceless fricative /s/. Second, it is realized as a syllabic voiced apical–post-alveolar fricative [ẓ̩] after apical–post-alveolar sibilant consonants, including the affricates /ṭṣ/, /ṭṣ^h/, /^{n}ṭṣ/, and /^{n}ṭṣ^h/, the voiceless fricative /ṣ/, and the voiced approximant /ẓ/. Thus /ts^{h}i8/ <cif> 'CLF:occurrence' is realized as [ts^{h}z̩8], /ṭṣi2/ <zhix> 'to cure' as [ṭṣẓ̩2], and /ẓi1.tsi1/ <rib.zib> 'day' as [ẓẓ̩1.tsz̩1]. Note that the vowel /i/ only occurs in these environments (i.e. after alveolar sibilant consonants and apical–post-alveolar sibilant consonants) in recent borrowings from Sinitic varieties, such as the three example lexical items just given.

Examples of syllables containing /i/ in Yankan Xong include /tɕi2/ <jix> 'NEG$_1$', /pi3/ <bid-> 'FRT', /ki3/ <gid> 'to run', /l^{ɦ}i5/ <hlit> 'cooked rice', /ti3/ <did-> 'DID', and /ɕi1/ <xib> 'hungry'. Some minimal and near-minimal pairs involving /i/ are given below.

/i/ vs. /ɛ/: /mi2/ <mix > 'CLF:meter' vs. /mɛ2/ <mex> 'to exist'
/i/ vs. /ɛ/: /tɕi2/ <jix> 'NEG$_1$' vs. /tɕɛ3/ <jed> 'older sister'
/i/ vs. /ɤ/: /ki3/ <gid> 'to run' vs. /kɤ3/ <geud> 'to hold'
/i/ vs. /u/: /pi1/ <bib> 'hair' vs. /pu1/ <bub> 'three'
/i/ vs. /ĩ/: /mi2/ <mix > 'CLF:meter' vs. /mĩ2/ <minx> 'to understand'
/i/ vs. /ɤj/: /ti3/ <did-> 'DID' vs. /tɤj3/ <deid> 'bean'

3.3.1.2 The mid front unrounded vowel /ɛ/

For Xong speakers from Yankan Village and Shanjiang Town, this is a mid front unrounded vowel, most often realized as [ɛ] and represented orthographically with <e>. However, for most speakers from La'ershan and nearby villages other than Yankan (such as Zhuigaolai), this vowel is noticeably lower, closer to [æ] than [ɛ]. For all speakers, this vowel has one noteworthy allophone: it is realized as [e] after all consonants that involve a palatal articulation, including all palatalized bilabial, palatalized alveolar, palatalized velar, and alveolo-palatal consonants, as well as the palatal approximant /j/.[47]

Such syllables never occur with an initial consonant, and they only occur in recent borrowings from Sinitic varieties, such as <erk> 'two', <guk.**erf**> 'orphan', and <ngeux.**erx**> 'occasionally'. Note that no phonological representation of these syllables is given here due to their marginal status in Fenghuang Xong and the wide variety of interspeaker variation that they display.

47 In theory, the sound [e] under discussion here could be analyzed as an allophone of /i/ rather than of /ɛ/, since in the environment in question (i.e. after consonants involving a palatal articulation) neither [i] nor [ɛ] occurs, only [e]. The author has no (e.g.) morphophonological evidence to support

Thus /tjɛ2/ <diex> 'to finish' is realized as [tje2], /tɕɛ3/ <jed> 'older sister' is realized as [tɕe3], and /jɛ6.ʋɛ1/ <**yes**.web> 'landlord' is realized as [**je6**.ʋɛ1].

Examples of syllables containing /ɛ/ in Yankan Xong include /tɛ1/ <deb> 'child', /lɛ1/ <leb> 'CLF', /mɛ2/ <mex> 'to exist', /ʋɛ4/ <wel> '1SG', /^{n}q^{h}ɛ3/ <ṇkhed> 'to look', and /^{n}pɛ5/ <nbet> 'snow'. Some minimal and near-minimal pairs involving /ɛ/ are given below.

/ɛ/ vs. /i/: /tɕɛ3/ <jed> 'older sister' vs. /tɕi2/ <jix> 'NEG$_{1}$'
/ɛ/ vs. /i/: /mɛ2/ <mex> 'to exist' vs. /mi2/ <mix > 'CLF:meter'
/ɛ/ vs. /a/: /mɛ2/ <mex> 'to exist' vs. /ma2/ <max> 'to slap'
/ɛ/ vs. /o/: /^{n}tj^{h}ɛ1/ <ntieb> 'to weigh' vs. /^{n}tj^{h}o5/ <ntiot> 'smoky; smoke'
/ɛ/ vs. /ɤ/: /qwɛ1/ <gueb> 'black' vs. /qwɤ1/ <gueub> 'white'
/ɛ/ vs. /ɛɰ/: /tɛ1/ <deb> 'child' vs. /tɛɰ1/ <doub> 'to answer'
/ɛ/ vs. /ɤj/: /mɛ4/ <mel> 'horse' vs. /mɤj4/ <meil> 'coal'

3.3.1.3 The low central unrounded vowel /a/

The low central unrounded vowel /a/ is generally realized as [a], and it is represented in the orthography with <a>. It has no other noteworthy allophones.

Examples of syllables containing /a/ in Yankan Xong include /kja1/ <giab> 'to stir-fry', /nja2/ <niax> 'meat', /ta5/ <dat> 'CLF:morning', /lja2/ <liax> 'to resemble', /qa1/ <ghab> 'to bite', and /ja1/ <yab> 'also'. Some minimal and near-minimal pairs involving /a/ are given below.

/a/ vs. /ɛ/: /ma2/ <max> 'to slap' vs. /mɛ2/ <mex> 'to exist'
/a/ vs. /ɑ/: /ta5/ <dat> 'CLF:morning' vs. /tɑ5/ <daot> 'to kill'
/a/ vs. /ɑ/: /nja2/ <niax> 'meat' vs. /njɑ2/ <niaox> 'paternal grandmother'
/a/ vs. /ɤ/: /nja2/ <niax> 'meat' vs. /njɤ6/ <nieus> 'to buy'
/a/ vs. /ã/: /qa1/ <ghab> 'to bite' vs. /qã6/ <ghans> 'to see'
/a/ vs. /ã/: /^{n}pa5/ <nbat> 'pig' vs. /^{n}pã2/ <nbanx> 'to think'

3.3.1.4 The low back unrounded vowel /ɑ/

This is a low back unrounded vowel, most often realized as [ɑ] and represented orthographically with <ao>. Like /a/, the vowel /ɑ/ has no other noteworthy allophones.

Examples of syllables containing /ɑ/ in Yankan Xong include /pɑ2/ <baox> 'father', /qɑ1/ <ghaob-> 'NOM', /ṭṣɑ4/ <zhaol> 'non-Miao', /^{n}ts^{h}ɑ6/ <ncaos> 'to be

---

his analysis of [e] as an allophone of /ɛ/ rather than of /i/, but note that the [e] allophone in question is (to both the author's ears and his consultants') impressionistically much closer to [ɛ] in phonetic terms than it is to [i], and his consultants greatly prefer that this [e] allophone be represented with <e> in the author's practical orthography rather than with <i>.

done', /lɑ2/ <laox> 'slow', and /qwɑ5/ <guaot> 'to pass'. Some minimal and near-minimal pairs involving /ɑ/ are given below.

/ɑ/ vs. /a/: /tɑ5/ <daot> 'to kill' vs. /ta5/ <dat> 'CLF:morning'
/ɑ/ vs. /a/: /njɑ2/ <niaox> 'paternal grandmother' vs. /nja2/ <niax> 'meat'
/ɑ/ vs. /o/: /mɑ4/ <maol> 'blister, boil' vs. /mo6/ <mos> 'tired'
/ɑ/ vs. /ɤ/: /tɑ3/ <daod> 'older brother' vs. /tɤ3/ <deud> 'skin'
/ɑ/ vs. /ɑ̃/: /mɑ4/ <maol> 'blister, boil' vs. /mɑ̃4/ <maonl> 'small flying insect'
/ɑ/ vs. /ɑ̃/: /ŋɑ2/ <ngaox> 'sprout, seedling' vs. /ŋɑ̃2/ <ngaonx> 'boat'
/ɑ/ vs. /ɛɰ/: /mjɑ4/ <miaol> 'tongue' vs. /mjɛɰ4/ <mioul> 'fish'

3.3.1.5 The mid back rounded vowel /o/

This is a mid back rounded vowel, generally realized as [o] and represented in the orthography with <o>. It has no other noteworthy allophones.

Examples of syllables containing /o/ in Yankan Xong include /to2/ <dox> 'that', /ljo2/ <liox> 'big', /^{n}tj^{h}o5/ <ntiot> 'smoky; smoke', /ɕo1/ <xob> 'sour', /ʂo2/ <shox> 'sweet potato', and /n̥o1/ <nhob> 'to walk'. Some minimal and near-minimal pairs involving /o/ are given below.

/o/ vs. /ɛ/: /^{n}tj^{h}o5/ <ntiot> 'smoky; smoke' vs. /^{n}tj^{h}ɛ1/ <ntieb> 'to weigh'
/o/ vs. /ɑ/: /mo6/ <mos> 'tired' vs. /mɑ4/ <maol> 'blister, boil'
/o/ vs. /ɤ/: /ɕo1/ <xob> 'sour' vs. /ɕɤ1/ <xeub> 'CLF:body'
/o/ vs. /u/: /ɕo1/ <xob> 'sour' vs. /ɕu1/ <xub> 'small'
/o/ vs. /õ/: /tɕo2/ <jox> 'nine' vs. /tɕõ6 / <jons> 'seven'
/o/ vs. /õ/: /no6/ <nos> 'hemp' vs. /nõ6/ <nons> 'rain'

3.3.1.6 The mid back unrounded vowel /ɤ/

The mid back unrounded vowel /ɤ/ is typically realized as [ɤ], and it is represented orthographically with <eu>. This vowel has no other noteworthy allophones in Yankan Xong, being realized as [ɤ] in all environments.

However, /ɤ/ does have one significant allophone in Shanjiang Xong. In this variety, /ɤ/ is realized as a high back unrounded vowel [ɯ] after the alveolo-palatal affricates /tɕ/, /tɕ^{h}/, /^{n}tɕ/, and /^{n}tɕ^{h}/, after the voiceless alveolo-palatal fricative /ɕ/, and after the palatal approximant /j/. It is realized as [ɤ] elsewhere, including after the palatalized bilabial, palatalized alveolar, and palatalized velar consonants. This could be taken as evidence that the so-called palatal approximant /j/ should in fact be analyzed as an *alveolo*-palatal approximant /ʑ̞/ in Shanjiang Xong. Obviously, though, this evidence would not be applicable to Yankan Xong, where /ɤ/ is always realized as [ɤ]. See Section 3.2.5 for further discussion.

Examples of syllables containing /ɤ/ in Yankan Xong include /pɤ4/ <beul> '3', /^{n}kɤ1/ <nggeub> 'mushroom', /ɕɤ1/ <xeub> 'CLF:body', /tjɤ3/ <dieud> 'CLF:time$_2$',

/^{n}ṭṣ^{h}ɤ5/ <ncheut> 'full (from eating)', and /qwɤ1/ <gueub> 'white'. Some minimal and near-minimal pairs involving /ɤ/ are given below.

/ɤ/ vs. /i/: /kɤ3/ <geud> 'to hold' vs. /ki3/ <gid> 'to run'
/ɤ/ vs. /ɛ/: /qwɤ1/ <gueub> 'white' vs. /qwɛ1/ <gueb> 'black'
/ɤ/ vs. /a/: /njɤ6/ <nieus> 'to buy' vs. /nja2/ <niax> 'meat'
/ɤ/ vs. /ɑ/: /tɤ3/ <deud> 'skin' vs. /tɑ3/ <daod> 'older brother'
/ɤ/ vs. /o/: /ɕɤ1/ <xeub> 'CLF:body' vs. /ɕo1/ <xob> 'sour'
/ɤ/ vs. /u/: /ɕɤ1/ <xeub> 'CLF:body' vs. /ɕu1/ <xub> 'small'
/ɤ/ vs. /ɛɰ/: /tɤ3/ <deud> 'skin' vs. /tɛɰ3/ <doud> 'to skin'
/ɤ/ vs. /ɤj/: /tɤ3/ <deud> 'skin' vs. /tɤj3/ <deid> 'bean'

3.3.1.7 The high back rounded vowel /u/

Like all other varieties of Fenghuang Xong the author has encountered, Yankan Xong has a single high back vowel, which (unsurprisingly) is a rounded vowel /u/. This is typically realized as [u], and it is represented in the orthography with <u>. This vowel has no other significant allophones in Yankan Xong.

Many phonological descriptions of other Xong varieties also include a high back unrounded vowel phoneme /ɯ/. No such vowel occurs phonemically in any variety of Fenghuang Xong with which the author is familiar, although it does occur as an allophone of /ɤ/ for some speakers (see Section 3.3.1.6 immediately above). The cognates of forms transcribed with /ɯ/ in other sources generally contain either /ɛɰ/ or /ɤ/ instead in most varieties of Fenghuang Xong.[48]

Examples of syllables containing /u/ in Yankan Xong include /p^{h}u7/ <puk> 'to speak', /qɑ3.**pju7**/ <ghaod.**biuk**> 'buttocks', /ɕu1/ <xub> 'small', /tju4/ <diul> 'to complete', /ku7/ <guk> 'frog', and /tɕu1/ <jub> 'needle'. Some minimal and near-minimal pairs involving /u/ are given below.

/u/ vs. /i/: /pu1/ <bub> 'three' vs. /pi1/ <bib> 'hair'
/u/ vs. /o/: /ɕu1/ <xub> 'small' vs. /ɕo1/ <xob> 'sour'
/u/ vs. /ɤ/: /ɕu1/ <xub> 'small' vs. /ɕɤ1/ <xeub> 'CLF:body'
/u/ vs. /ɤ/: /ku4/ <gul> 'ten' vs. /kɤ3/ <geud> 'to hold'
/u/ vs. /ɛɰ/: /pu1/ <bub> 'three' vs. /pɛɰ1/ <boub> '1PL'
/u/ vs. /aw/: /qɑ3.**pju7**/ <ghaod.**biuk**> 'buttocks' vs. /pjaw7/ <biauk> 'dark'

48 Interestingly, the vowel /ɯ/ is even listed in the Gouliang Xong phoneme inventory included in He (2009: 97), although Gouliang Xong is spoken within Fenghuang County (see Sections 2.5.3.1 and 2.5.3.3). The author has not had the opportunity to work with speakers of Gouliang Xong himself, and so he is unable to verify He's description.

3.3.2 Nasal monophthongs

3.3.2.1 The high front unrounded nasal vowel /ĩ/

This is the nasalized counterpart of the high front unrounded oral vowel /i/. It is typically realized as [ĩ], and it is represented in the orthography with <in>. Unlike its oral counterpart /i/, the nasal vowel /ĩ/ does not display any noteworthy allophonic variation. While the oral vowel /i/ is realized as a syllabic voiced sibilant fricative after alveolar sibilant and apical–post-alveolar sibilant consonants (see Section 3.3.1.1 above), the nasal vowel /ĩ/ never occurs after these consonants at all.

Examples of syllables containing /ĩ/ in Yankan Xong include /kĩ1/ <ginb> 'bug', /mĩ2/ <minx> 'to understand', /mĩ4/ <minl> 'mother', /^{n}tɕ^{h}ĩ5/ <nqint> 'red', /nĩ6/ <nins> 'COP', and /p^{h}ĩ8/ <pinf> 'bottle'. Some minimal and near-minimal pairs involving /ĩ/ are given below.

/ĩ/ vs. /i/: /mĩ2/ <minx> 'to understand' vs. /mi2/ <mix> 'CLF:meter'
/ĩ/ vs. /i/: /kĩ1/ <ginb> 'bug' vs. /ki3/ <gid> 'to run'
/ĩ/ vs. /ɛ/: /mĩ2/ <minx> 'to understand' vs. /mɛ2/ <mex> 'to exist'
/ĩ/ vs. /ã/: /mĩ4/ <minl> 'mother' vs. /mã4/ <manl> 'vellus hair'
/ĩ/ vs. /ɣ̃j/: /nĩ6/ <nins> 'COP' vs. /nɣ̃j3/ <neind> 'this'
/ĩ/ vs. /ɣ̃j/: /mĩ2/ <minx> 'to understand' vs. /mɣ̃j4/ <meinl> 'CLF:person'

3.3.2.2 The low central unrounded nasal vowel /ã/

The low central unrounded nasal vowel /ã/ is most often realized as [ã], and it is represented orthographically with <an>. For many of the speakers the author has worked with, including those from Shanjiang Town, those from La'ershan Town, and those from villages near La'ershan Town (with the notable exception of Yankan Village), this vowel has one particularly noteworthy allophone: it is realized as a nasalized mid front vowel [ɛ̃] after consonants involving a palatal articulation, which includes the palatalized bilabial, palatalized alveolar, palatalized velar, and alveolo-palatal consonants as well as the palatal approximant /j/. (Note that this is the same environment that triggers the /ɛ/ → [e] rule described in Section 3.3.1.2 above.) Thus, for these speakers, /mjã1/ <mianb> 'noodles' is realized as [mjɛ̃1], and /ɕã1/ <xanb> 'oil' is realized as [ɕɛ̃1].

However, for speakers from Yankan Village, /ã/ has merged with /ɛ/ in all post-[+palatal] environments. For these speakers, 'noodles' is simply /mjɛ1/ <mieb> (realized as [mje1] due to the application of the /ɛ/ → [e] rule described in Section 3.3.1.2), not */mjã1/, and 'oil' is /ɕɛ1/ <xeb> (realized as [ɕe1] due to the application of the same rule), not */ɕã1/.[49]

49 Even clearer evidence of this merger is provided by the terms for 'happy' and 'to stand on tiptoe'. For Shanjiang and La'ershan speakers, 'happy' is /^{n}kj^{h}ã3/ <nkiand> (realized as [^{n}kj^{h}ɛ̃3]) and 'to stand

Examples of syllables containing /ã/ in Yankan Xong include /mã2/ <manx> '2PL', /ʂã1/ <shanb> 'tall', /n^{ɦ}ã8/ <hnanf> 'CLF:clothing', /mã4/ <manl> 'vellus hair', /tã3/ <dand> 'to arrive', and /pã1/ <banb> 'CLF:half; CLF:some'. Some minimal and near-minimal pairs involving /ã/ are given below.

/ã/ vs. /a/: /^{n}pã2/ <nbanx> 'to think' vs. /^{n}pa5/ <nbat> 'pig'
/ã/ vs. /a/: /qã6/ <ghans> 'to see' vs. /qa1/ <ghab> 'to bite'
/ã/ vs. /ɑ̃/: /mã4/ <manl> 'vellus hair' vs. /mɑ̃4/ <maonl> 'small flying insect'
/ã/ vs. /ɑ̃/: /pã1/ <banb> 'CLF:half; CLF:some' vs. /pɑ̃3/ <baond> 'to shoot'
/ã/ vs. /õ/: /mã4/ <manl> 'vellus hair' vs. /mõ4/ <monl> 'to go'
/ã/ vs. /ɤ̃j/: /mã4/ <manl> 'vellus hair' vs. /mɤ̃j4/ <meinl> 'CLF:person'

3.3.2.3 The low back unrounded nasal vowel /ɑ̃/

Yankan Xong's low back unrounded nasal vowel is realized as [ɑ̃] and represented orthographically with <aon>. It does not have any other notable allophones.

Examples of syllables containing /ɑ̃/ in Yankan Xong include /pɑ̃3/ <baond> 'to shoot', /mɑ̃4/ <maonl> 'small flying insect', /tɑ̃5/ <daont> 'money', /qɑ̃5/ <ghaont> 'eggplant; purple', /ŋɑ̃2/ <ngaonx> 'boat', and /m^{ɦ}ɑ̃5/ <hmaont> 'evening'. Some minimal and near-minimal pairs involving /ɑ̃/ are given below.

/ɑ̃/ vs. /ɑ/: /mɑ̃4/ <maonl> 'small flying insect' vs. /mɑ4/ <maol> 'blister, boil'
/ɑ̃/ vs. /ɑ/: /ŋɑ̃2/ <ngaonx> 'boat' vs. /ŋɑ2/ <ngaox> 'sprout, seedling'
/ɑ̃/ vs. /ã/: /mɑ̃4/ <maonl> 'small flying insect' vs. /mã4/ <manl> 'vellus hair'
/ɑ̃/ vs. /ã/: /pɑ̃3/ <baond> 'to shoot' vs. /pã1/ <banb> 'CLF:half; CLF:some'
/ɑ̃/ vs. /õ/: /tɑ̃5/ <daont> 'money' vs. /tõ5/ <dont> 'to listen'
/ɑ̃/ vs. /õ/: /mɑ̃4/ <maonl> 'small flying insect' vs. /mõ4/ <monl> 'to go'

3.3.2.4 The mid back rounded nasal vowel /õ/

This nasal counterpart of the mid back rounded vowel /o/ is represented in the practical orthography with <on>, and it is realized as [õ] in most environments – in particular, after all non-nasal consonants (including after all prenasalized plosives) and after the alveolar nasal /n/. Thus, for instance, /tõ5/ <dont> 'to listen' is realized as [tõ5], and /nõ6/ <nons> 'rain' is realized as [nõ6].

However, /õ/ has one very striking allophone, [ɤ̃] (or perhaps even [ə̃]), which occurs after the bilabial nasal /m/ and the velar nasal /ŋ/. For example, /mõ2/ <monx> '2SG' is realized as [mɤ̃2], and /ŋõ4/ <ngonl> 'CLF:animate' is realized as [ŋɤ̃4]. There are no attested instances of /õ/ occurring after any other nasal consonants in Yankan

on tiptoe' is /^{n}kj^{h}ɛ3/ <nkied> (realized as [^{n}kj^{h}e3]). However, for Yankan speakers, the two forms are completely homophonous: both are simply /^{n}kj^{h}ɛ3/ <nkied> (realized as [^{n}kj^{h}e3]).

Xong (that is, aside from /m, n, ŋ/), including the modal nasals /mj, nj, ṇ, ŋw/ and the breathy nasals /m^{ɦ}, n^{ɦ}/.

One could take this phonological rule as evidence that /m/ and /ŋ/ should be grouped together as "peripheral" nasals in Yankan Xong, but there does not appear to be any further evidence for such a grouping aside from the rule under discussion itself. Note also that /õ/ is uniformly realized as [õ] after non-nasal bilabial, velar, and uvular (i.e. "peripheral") consonants: /põ1/ <bonb> 'apricot' is realized as [põ1], /**kõ1**.ts^{h}ã2/ <**Gonb**.canx> 'Communist (Party)' is realized as [**kõ1**.ts^{h}ã2], and /sõ3-**qõ3**/ <sond-**ghond**> [bone-**neck**] 'neck' is realized as [sõ3-**qõ3**].

Examples of syllables containing /õ/ in Yankan Xong include /nõ2/ <nonx> 'to eat', /tɕõ6/ <jons> 'seven', /pjõ4/ <bionl> 'to exit', /nõ6/ <nons> 'rain', /ŋõ2/ <ngonx> 'silver', and /mõ4/ <monl> 'to go'. Some minimal and near-minimal pairs involving /õ/ are given below.

/õ/ vs. /o/: /tɕõ6/ <jons> 'seven' vs. /tɕo2/ <jox> 'nine'
/õ/ vs. /o/: /nõ6/ <nons> 'rain' vs. /no6/ <nos> 'hemp'
/õ/ vs. /o/: /ŋõ2/ <ngonx> 'silver' vs. /ŋo2/ <ngox> 'fierce'
/õ/ vs. /ã/: /mõ4/ <monl> 'to go' vs. /mã4/ <manl> 'vellus hair'
/õ/ vs. /ɑ̃/: /tõ5/ <dont> 'to listen' vs. /tɑ̃5/ <daont> 'money'
/õ/ vs. /ɑ̃/: /mõ4/ <monl> 'to go' vs. /mɑ̃4/ <maonl> 'small flying insect'

3.3.3 Diphthongs

3.3.3.1 The diphthong /ɛɰ/

This vowel is realized as [ɛɰ] – that is, as a diphthong with a mid front unrounded nucleus and a high back unrounded offglide – and represented orthographically with <ou>. It has no other noteworthy allophones. As was mentioned in the introduction to Section 3.3, this diphthong differs from all others found in Yankan Xong (or in any other varieties of Fenghuang Xong, for that matter) in that its offglide does not occur as an independent vowel */ɯ/ or as a syllable onset */ɰ/.

Examples of syllables containing /ɛɰ/ in Yankan Xong include /pɛɰ1/ <boub> '1PL', /p^{h}ɛɰ8/ <pouf> 'paternal grandfather', /tɛɰ5/ <dout> 'frost', /ẓɛɰ5/ <rout> 'far', /mjɛɰ4/ <mioul> 'fish', and /qwɛɰ3/ <guoud> 'dog'. Some minimal and near-minimal pairs involving /ɛɰ/ are given below.

/ɛɰ/ vs. /ɛ/: /tɛɰ1/ <doub> 'to answer' vs. /tɛ1/ <deb> 'child'
/ɛɰ/ vs. /ɑ/: /mjɛɰ4/ <mioul> 'fish' vs. /mjɑ4/ <miaol> 'tongue'
/ɛɰ/ vs. /ɤ/: /tɛɰ3/ <doud> 'to skin' vs. /tɤ3/ <deud> 'skin'
/ɛɰ/ vs. /u/: /pɛɰ1/ <boub> '1PL' vs. /pu1/ <bub> 'three'
/ɛɰ/ vs. /aw/: /ẓɛɰ5/ <rout> 'far' vs. /ẓaw5/ <raut> 'good'
/ɛɰ/ vs. /aw/: /tɛɰ5/ <dout> 'frost' vs. /taw5/ <daut> 'speech'

3.3.3.2 The diphthong /aw/

This vowel is realized as [aw] and is represented in the orthography with <au>. It thus has a low central unrounded nucleus and a high back rounded offglide. This vowel has no other notable allophonic variants.

Unlike the case with the offglide [ɯ̯] discussed in Section 3.3.3.1 above, the offglide [w] does have a fully vocalic monophthongal counterpart /u/ (as in /pu1/ <bub> 'three'). While strictly speaking no labial-velar syllable-onset counterpart */w/ is found in Yankan Xong, a phonetically similar bilabial/labiodental approximant /ʋ/ does indeed occur (see Section 3.2.5). However, there are still good reasons for analyzing /aw/ and all other diphthongs in Yankan Xong as unitary phonemes rather than as clusters; see Section 3.7 for discussion.

Examples of syllables containing /aw/ in Yankan Xong include /ṭṣ^{h}aw7/ <chauk> 'to do', /aw1/ <aub> 'water', /ẓaw5/ <raut> 'good', /taw5/ <daut> 'speech', /haw7/ <hauk> 'to drink', and /pjaw7/ <biauk> 'dark'. Some minimal and near-minimal pairs involving /aw/ are given below.

/aw/ vs. /a/: /q^{h}aw7/ <khauk> 'hole' vs. /q^{h}a3/ <khad> 'dry'
/aw/ vs. /ɑ/: /^{n}taw5/ <ndaut> 'tree' vs. /^{n}tɑ5/ <ndaot> 'to curse'
/aw/ vs. /o/: /aw1/ <aub> 'water' vs. /o1/ <ob> 'to burn'
/aw/ vs. /u/: /pjaw7/ <biauk> 'dark' vs. /qɑ3.**pju7**/ <ghaod.**biuk**> 'buttocks'
/aw/ vs. /ɛɯ̯/: /ẓaw5/ <raut> 'good' vs. /ẓɛɯ̯5/ <rout> 'far'
/aw/ vs. /ɛɯ̯/: /taw5/ <daut> 'speech' vs. /tɛɯ̯5/ <dout> 'frost'

3.3.3.3 The diphthong /ɤj/

This vowel is realized as [ɤj] and represented in the orthography with <ei>. It thus has a mid back unrounded nucleus and a high front unrounded offglide. Like /ɛɯ̯/ and /aw/ (see Sections 3.3.3.1 and 3.3.3.2), the vowel /ɤj/ has no other noteworthy allophones.

The offglide component of this diphthong, [j], has a fully vocalic monophthongal counterpart /i/ (as in /tɕi2/ <jix> 'NEG$_1$') and a syllable-onset counterpart /j/ (as in /ja1/ <yab> 'also'). However, just as with Yankan Xong's other diphthongs, there is evidence that /ɤj/ should be analyzed as a single, unitary phoneme rather than as a cluster. See Section 3.7 for discussion.

Examples of syllables containing /ɤj/ in Yankan Xong include /ṣɤj5/ <sheit> 'to write', /tɤj5/ <deit> 'still', /mɤj4/ <meil> 'coal', /mjɤj4/ <mieil> 'spicy', /ẓɤj1/ <reib> 'vegetable', and /pɤj7/ <beik> 'to carry on one's back'. Some minimal and near-minimal pairs involving /ɤj/ are given below.

/ɤj/ vs. /i/: /tɤj3/ <deid> 'bean' vs. /ti3/ <did-> 'DID'
/ɤj/ vs. /ɛ/: /mɤj4/ <meil> 'coal' vs. /mɛ4/ <mel> 'horse'

/ɤj/ vs. /a/: /tɤj5/ <deit> 'still' vs. /ta5/ <dat> 'CLF:morning'
/ɤj/ vs. /ɤ/: /tɤj3/ <deid> 'bean' vs. /tɤ3/ <deud> 'skin'
/ɤj/ vs. /ɤ̃j/: /mɤj4/ <meil> 'coal' vs. /mɤ̃j4/ <meinl> 'CLF:person'
/ɤj/ vs. /ɤ̃j/: /pɤj7/ <beik> 'to carry on one's back' vs. /pɤ̃j2/ <beinx> 'flower'

3.3.3.4 The diphthong /ɤ̃j/

This is simply a nasalized version of the diphthong /ɤj/ that was discussed in Section 3.3.3.3 immediately above. It is Yankan Xong's only nasal diphthong. Like the other diphthongs found in this variety, though, /ɤ̃j/ has no other significant allophones.

The diphthong /ɤ̃j/ is realized as [ɤ̃j̃] (that is, with a nasalized mid back unrounded nucleus and a nasalized high front unrounded offglide), and it is represented in the orthography with <ein>. Note that while both the nucleus and offglide of /ɤ̃j/ are nasalized, nasalization is only marked on the symbol for the nucleus due to typographic considerations.

Examples of syllables containing /ɤ̃j/ in Yankan Xong include /qwɤ̃j2/ <gueinx> 'yellow', /pɤ̃j2/ <beinx> 'flower', /nɤ̃j3/ <neind> 'this', /hɤ̃j3/ <heind> 'heavy', /n^{ɦ}ɤ̃j3/ <hneind> 'to wear', and /^{n}qɤ̃j5/ <ngheint> 'to carry on a shoulder-pole'. Some minimal and near-minimal pairs involving /ɤ̃j/ are given below.

/ɤ̃j/ vs. /ĩ/: /mɤ̃j4/ <meinl> 'CLF:person' vs. /mĩ2/ <minx> 'to understand'
/ɤ̃j/ vs. /ĩ/: /nɤ̃j3/ <neind> 'this' vs. /nĩ6/ <nins> 'COP'
/ɤ̃j/ vs. /ã/: /mɤ̃j4/ <meinl> 'CLF:person' vs. /mã4/ <manl> 'vellus hair'
/ɤ̃j/ vs. /õ/: /mɤ̃j4/ <meinl> 'CLF:person' vs. /mõ4/ <monl> 'to go'
/ɤ̃j/ vs. /ɤj/: /mɤ̃j4/ <meinl> 'CLF:person' vs. /mɤj4/ <meil> 'coal'
/ɤ̃j/ vs. /ɤj/: /pɤ̃j2/ <beinx> 'flower' vs. /pɤj7/ <beik> 'to carry on one's back'

3.3.4 The syllabic bilabial nasal /m̩/

Like most varieties of Xong spoken in Fenghuang County which the author has encountered, Yankan Xong has a single syllabic nasal /m̩/. This syllabic nasal is always realized as [m̩] (i.e. it is always bilabial, modally voiced, and unaspirated, with the lips remaining completely closed throughout the production of the sound), and it is represented orthographically with <m>. Like Yankan Xong's vowel phonemes, the syllabic nasal /m̩/ is tone-bearing. Unlike those vowels, however, /m̩/ is never preceded by an initial consonant. Thus, syllables containing /m̩/ will always consist of /m̩/ itself and an accompanying tone, but no other segmental material.

Only five morphemes featuring a syllabic bilabial nasal have so far been attested in Yankan Xong. The first four of these are /m̩1/ <mb> 'to hurt (intrans.), to be sick; illness', /qɛɰ3.**m̩2**/ <ghoud.**mx**> 'heart', /m̩6/ <ms> 'kiwifruit', and /m̩6/ <ms>

'aunty'.[50] A fifth apparent morpheme /m̩2/ <mx> also occurs in the forms /pɑ3-**m̩2**-tɤ4/ <baod-**mx**-deul> 'firefly' (morphemically [BUG-**???**-fire]) and /pɑ3-**m̩2**-ku7/ <baod-**mx**-guk> 'tadpole' (morphemically [BUG-**???**-frog]), though its meaning is still opaque at present.

There is some degree of free variation in Yankan Xong between monosyllabic morphemes consisting solely of the syllabic nasal /m̩/ and monosyllabic morphemes consisting of /m/ followed by /õ/. Only two examples of the latter type of morpheme have been found so far – /mõ2/ <monx> '2SG' and /mõ4/ <monl> 'to go' – and both can alternately be realized as syllabic bilabial nasals, especially in fast or casual speech. Thus, when spoken quickly, '2SG' can also be realized as [m̩2], and 'to go' can also be realized as [m̩4]. In careful speech, though, these forms are always realized as [mɤ̃2] and [mɤ̃4] (see Section 3.3.2.4 for discussion of the allophone [ɤ̃], which occurs when /õ/ is preceded by /m/ or /ŋ/).

However, this free variation is strictly unidirectional. While morphemes that underlyingly consist of /m/ followed by /õ/ (such as '2SG' and 'to go') can be realized as syllabic nasals in casual speech, morphemes that are underlyingly syllabic nasals are always realized as such. Thus /m̩1/ <mb> 'to hurt (intrans.), to be sick; illness' is always realized as [m̩1], never as *[mɤ̃1], and /m̩6/ <ms> 'aunty' is always realized as [m̩6], never as *[mɤ̃6].

Keeping this free variation in mind, some minimal and near-minimal pairs involving /m̩/ are given below.

/m̩/ vs. /mɑ/: /m̩6/ <ms> 'aunty' vs. /mɑ4/ <maol> 'blister, boil'
/m̩/ vs. /mo/: /m̩6/ <ms> 'aunty' vs. /mo6/ <mos> 'tired'
/m̩/ vs. /mɑ̃/: /m̩6/ <ms> 'aunty' vs. /qa3.**mɑ̃6**/ <ghad.**maons**> 'NEG.IMP'
/m̩/ vs. /mõ/: /qɛɰ3.**m̩2**/ <ghoud.**mx**> 'heart' vs. /qɛɰ3 **mõ2**/ <ghoud **monx**> 'to stare at you' (morphemically [stare **2SG**])

3.4 A note on intersyllabic segmental phonological processes

While a number of syllable-internal phonological processes have been described in Sections 3.2 and 3.3 above, the author has not yet observed any segmental phonological processes that operate across syllable boundaries (including, for example, assimilation, dissimilation, epenthesis, or any sort of vowel or consonant harmony). While Yankan Xong consonants and vowels can have significant effects on each other within

50 Note that the morpheme /m̩6/ <ms> 'kiwifruit' will typically occur preceded by the nominal prefix /pi3/ <bid-> 'FRT' (see Section 5.4.2.5). Note also that the morpheme /m̩6/ <ms> 'aunty' can actually be used to refer to any affinal female relative of the same generation as one's parents, including one's mother-in-law, one's mother's brother's wife, one's father's brother's wife, one's father-in-law's brother's wife, and so on.

a single syllable, they appear to have relatively little effect on the phonetic realization of segments in the preceding and following syllables. Of course, the author is here speaking only of segmental phonological processes, as the underlying tone of a given syllable is often responsible for dramatic changes in the surface suprasegmental characteristics of the preceding and/or following syllables; see Section 3.5 below for details.

Note that it is not being claimed here that intersyllabic segmental phonological processes do not exist in Yankan Xong, but rather merely that none have yet been observed. It is quite possible (and in fact the author rather suspects it is the case) that some such processes do occur in relatively fast or casual speech, and that they have simply escaped notice so far due to their subtlety.

3.5 Tones and tone sandhi

3.5.1 Overview

In all varieties of Fenghuang Xong, tone is primarily a syllable-level phenomenon. With only a few exceptions (see Section 3.6), each syllable produced in isolation in any variety of Fenghuang Xong will be accompanied by one of eight lexically specified tones. These tones are not simply specified pitch heights or contours; rather, they are each a complex "bundle" consisting of a specified pitch height, a specified pitch contour, and a specified phonation type (i.e. modal, breathy, or creaky). These three elements – pitch height, pitch contour, and phonation type – determine the basic suprasegmental characteristics associated with each tone, and thus the basic suprasegmental characteristics of each syllable that carries a particular tone.

However, while the basic suprasegmental characteristics of each syllable are largely determined by the syllable's tone, there appears to be an additional intonational system which is overlaid upon the Xong tone system. This additional system is not tonal (in the sense that it is not a paradigmatic system of contrastive suprasegmental categories), and its functions in Xong phonology are quite different from those of tone. Much work still remains to be done on Xong's intonational system, and only some initial notes are provided in Section 3.6 below. Neverthless, intonation has important effects on the suprasegmental characteristics of every Xong syllable in every utterance. This is true even of monosyllabic forms produced in isolation, since each such form constitutes a full utterance and is thus subject to utterance-level prosodic factors (e.g. an utterance-final fall). Thoroughly understanding these non-tonal prosodic factors will thus eventually be necessary for anyone seeking to produce a comprehensive description of Xong's entire suprasegmental system.

The author has not yet encountered tone being used for any grammatical purposes, such as distinguishing case, number, tense, or modality. The function of tone in Fenghuang Xong seems to largely be limited to distinguishing lexical items, e.g. /tɑ2/ <daox>

'to precipitate' vs. /tɑ5/ <daot> 'to kill' vs. /tɑ7/ <daok> 'maternal grandmother'. Most lexical items are realized with the same phonological tone in all varieties of Fenghuang Xong, although the phonetic details of each tone can vary significantly from one variety to another. For example, the form meaning 'to speak' (/pʰu7/ <puk>) bears tone *-k* for all of the author's Xong-speaking consultants, although tone *-k* is a mid-low level tone for speakers from Yankan Village, a mid-low to mid rising tone for speakers from Shanjiang Town, and a mid-high level tone for speakers from Zhuigaolai Village. There are some exceptions to this generalization, though, especially in the case of recent borrowings from Sinitic varieties, which often bear different tones in different varieties of Fenghuang Xong.

The tone systems of all varieties of Fenghuang Xong investigated by the author so far appear to be significantly more complex than the tone system of the "standard" Xong variety spoken in Jiwei Township (see Sections 2.4 and 4.3). That latter variety is generally reported to have only six distinct tones appearing on monosyllabic forms produced in isolation, as well as very little tone sandhi (see, e.g., Xiang [1999: 14, 15]). However, the Fenghuang Xong tone systems described in the following sections are (impressionistically) more or less average for the Miao-Yao family in terms of both the size of their tonal inventories (Niederer 1998: 213) and the degree of tone sandhi present.

As was discussed in Section 3.1, Yankan Xong is the primary subject of this chapter, and the entirety of Section 3.5.2 is devoted to a description of this variety's tone system. However, there is noticeably more variation among the tone systems of the author's primary consultants than among their consonant or vowel systems. To give the reader a better sense of the extent of this variation, Section 3.5.3 presents information on the tone systems of Shanjiang Xong and Zhuigaolai Xong, two other varieties of Xong spoken within Fenghuang County. While there are a number of reasons for choosing Yankan Xong as the primary focus of Section 3.5 (again, see Section 3.1), the author's decision to present tonal information on Shanjiang and Zhuigaolai Xong (rather than on any other two Xong varieties) was largely due to convenience: these two varieties just happened to be the ones spoken by the author's most experienced, most phonetically and phonologically sensitive, and most readily available non-Yankan consultants. The author has no reason to expect that the degree of tonal variation among Yankan, Shanjiang, and Zhuigaolai Xong is significantly smaller or larger than the degree of tonal variation among any other three varieties of Xong spoken within Fenghuang County (or at least among any other three varieties in similar geographic proximity to each other).

Unfortunately, since the author only had access to a single speaker for each of Shanjiang and Zhuigaolai Xong, the descriptions of these varieties' tone systems are necessarily less thorough than the description of Yankan Xong's. Furthermore, while the description of Yankan Xong's tone system in Section 3.5.2 is one of the most detailed published to date for any Xong variety, it is still far from being entirely comprehensive. To some degree, this is probably unavoidable. Suprasegmental phenomena like tone are notoriously difficult to study in the field due to their heavy context-dependence and high level of interspeaker variation (Himmelmann and Ladd 2008), and the degree of tonal variation found among the Xong varieties spoken within Fenghuang County is significant – for example, the author has often observed noticeable differences in tonal phonetics even among Xong varieties spoken in neighboring villages, varieties whose segmental phonological systems are completely identical. A comprehensive phonetic and phonological (to say nothing of sociolinguistic) account of tonal variation within Fenghuang Xong would likely end up constituting a full book-length study of its own. Still, it is hoped that the data and analyses provided in the following sections can at least serve as a foundation for a more thorough future study of the topic.

3.5.2 The tone system of Yankan Xong

The description in this section is based primarily on the speech of Mrs. Haili Shi (*Shí Hǎilì* 石海丽), a female primary school teacher from Yankan Village who had lived and worked for several years in La'ershan Town at the time of the author's fieldwork (see Section 2.6.2 for more background information on this consultant). Unlike the situation with the tone system descriptions of Shanjiang Xong and Zhuigaolai Xong in Section 3.5.3, though, the author had the opportunity to confirm the information in this section with several other speakers from Yankan Village, including both males and females. No significant interspeaker variation was found – or, at the very least, there was significantly less variation with respect to tonal phonetics and phonology between any two Yankan Xong speakers than there was between any Yankan Xong speaker and any speaker of another Xong variety (aside from the fact that male speakers had significantly lower and narrower pitch ranges than female speakers, of course).

3.5.2.1 Tones appearing on monosyllabic forms produced in isolation

With the exception of certain toneless particles and interjections (see Section 3.6), every syllable in Yankan Xong will bear one of eight lexically specified tones. Table 3.5 presents some impressionistic phonetic characteristics of each of these eight tones. The structure of Table 3.5 is explained immediately following the table itself, as are the terms used in it.

The initial TONE NUMBER column in Table 3.5 gives each tone a unique identifying number, which is used when marking that tone in any phonological transcription. The subsequent TONE LETTER column provides an additional "tone letter" for each tone, which is used both to mark tone in orthographic transcriptions (see Section 4.4) and to refer to specific tones in running text (e.g. "Tone *-b* is a falling tone, while tone *-x* ... "). Thus, for example, the Xong form meaning 'frost' would have its tone marked

Table 3.5: Phonetic characteristics of Yankan Xong tones.

TONE NUMBER	TONE LETTER	PITCH HEIGHT/CONTOUR (INFORMAL)	PITCH HEIGHT/CONTOUR (NUMERIC SCALE)	PHONATION TYPE
1	*-b*	*mid-high to low fall*	[41]	*modal*
2	*-x*	*mid-high to high to mid-high peak*	[454]	*modal*
3	*-d*	*mid-high to mid fall*	[43]	*modal*
4	*-l*	*mid-high to mid fall*	[43]	*breathy*
5	*-t*	*low to mid-high rise*	[14]	*modal*
6	*-s*	*mid-low level*	[22]	*breathy*
7	*-k*	*mid-low level*	[22]	*modal*
8	*-f*	*mid-low to low fall*	[21]	*breathy*

with <5> in a phonological transcription (i.e. /tɛɰ5/) and with <t> in an orthographic transcription (i.e. <dout>).

Similar to the five-level notation systems used in many descriptions of East and Southeast Asian tonal languages, the next two columns – PITCH HEIGHT/CONTOUR (INFORMAL) and PITCH/HEIGHT CONTOUR (NUMERIC SCALE) – are based on a scale which divides each speaker's pitch range into five levels of roughly equal height, each of which is then referred to with a number (note that this notation system was first proposed in Chao 1930). From highest to lowest, these levels are: [5], or "high", [4], or "mid-high", [3], or "mid", [2], or "mid-low", and [1], or "low". Thus a tone which involved a fall from the very top of a speaker's pitch range to the very bottom would be represented numerically as [51], one which involved a rise from a point near the bottom of a speaker's pitch range to a point near the top would be [24], and one which involved a level pitch at the midpoint of a speaker's pitch range would be [33]. It is important to understand that these numeric descriptions (e.g. [51], [24], etc.) refer only to the phonetic properties of Xong's tones, and also to understand that Xong's tones are atomic (i.e. not composed of any smaller phonological units). Thus, for instance, tone *-b* in Yankan Xong is phonetically [41] (a mid-high to low fall), but phonologically it is an indivisible unit; it cannot be phonologically analyzed as a mid-high tone followed by a low tone any more than the English affricate /tʃ/ can be phonologically analyzed as an alveolar stop followed by a postalveolar fricative. This is in contrast to the situation in (for example) many African tonal languages, where contour tones on monosyllabic forms often *can* be analyzed as sequences of multiple level tones compressed onto a single syllable.

Finally, the PHONATION TYPE column lists the phonation type associated with each tone. In the case of Yankan Xong, each tone is generally produced with either modal or breathy voicing, although some tones are produced with creaky voicing in other varieties of Fenghuang Xong (see Section 3.5.3.2).

Figure 3.1 below presents pitch plots for eight Yankan Xong syllables produced by Mrs. Haili Shi (see Section 2.6.2 for more information on this speaker). These eight syllables are /tɛɰ1/ <doub> 'to answer', /tɛɰ2/ <doux> 'to gamble', /tɛɰ3/ <doud> 'to skin', /tɛɰ4/ <doul> 'hand', /tɛɰ5/ <dout> 'frost', /tɛɰ6/ <dous> 'to stop emission of liquid from the body (e.g. blood, tears, urine, etc.)', /tɛɰ7/ <douk> 'to amuse, to play with', and /tɛɰ8/ <douf> 'poison'. All eight syllables are segmentally identical, but each carries a different tone. Since these eight syllables clearly differ in meaning, they thus constitute a "minimal octuplet" which demonstrates that all eight tones are contrastive on monosyllabic forms produced in isolation.

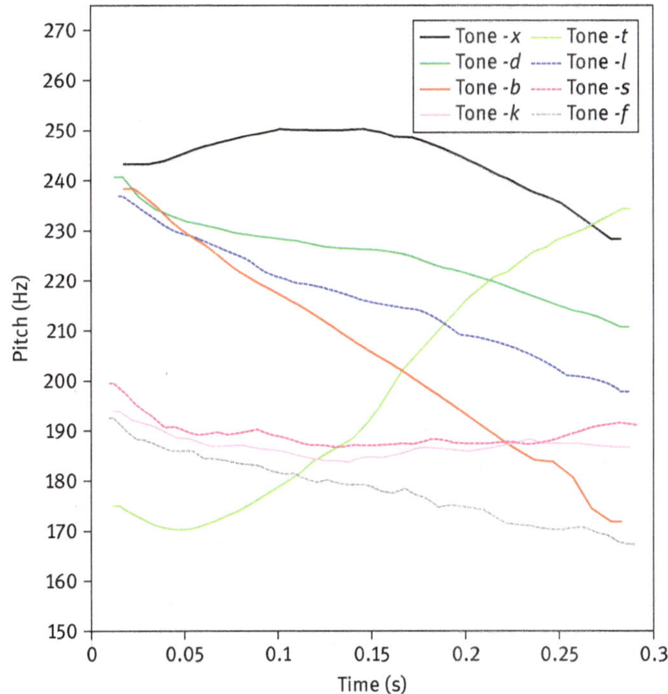

Figure 3.1: Pitch plots of Yankan Xong tones.

Note that the pitch plots of tones produced with modal voicing (i.e. tones *-b*, *-x*, *-d*, *-t*, and *-k*) have been represented with solid lines in Figure 3.1, while the pitch plots of tones produced with breathy voicing (i.e. tones *-l*, *-s*, and *-f*) have been represented with dashed lines.

It is important to understand that the pitch plots in Figure 3.1 are each based on a single token produced in a carrier sentence rather than an average of multiple tokens, and thus the reader should be careful not to overestimate their representativeness.[51] Even discounting the effects of tone sandhi (see Section 3.5.2.2), the exact suprasegmental characteristics of any given Xong syllable can vary widely depending on a number of factors. These include position within an utterance (for example, an *-s* or *-k* tone early in an utterance may be produced with a higher pitch than the same tone later in the utterance) and the tones on preceding and following syllables (for example, a *-t* tone immediately preceding a *-b*, *-x*, *-d*, or *-l* tone will generally end at a higher point than one preceding an *-s*, *-k*, or *-f* tone), not to mention the additional prosodic factors discussed in Section 3.6. Still, it is possible to give general phonetic descriptions of Yankan Xong's tones as they appear in relatively "neutral" phonetic environments.

Tone *-b* is a mid-high to low falling tone, starting from near the top of the speaker's pitch range and ending at the bottom of it. It is thus represented with [41] in Table 3.5. Tone *-b* is typically produced with modal voicing, although it is unique among the tones of Yankan Xong in that it is occasionally produced with light creaky voicing instead. Examples of syllables that carry tone *-b* when produced in isolation include /pi1/ <bib> 'hair', /pɛɰ1/ <boub> '1PL', /^{n}kɑ1/ <nggaob> 'medicine', /qwɤ1/ <gueub> 'white', /ɕõ1/ <Xonb> 'Miao', and /m̩1/ <mb> 'to hurt (intrans.), to be sick; illness'.

Tone *-x* is a mid-high to high to mid-high peaking tone, and it is thus represented with [454] in Table 3.5. This tone is always produced with modal voicing. Examples of syllables that carry tone *-x* when produced in isolation include /pɤ̃j2/ <beinx> 'flower', /tɕo2/ <jox> 'nine', /tɕi2/ <jix> 'NEG$_1$', /mɛ2/ <mex> 'to exist', /nja2/ <niax> 'meat', and /ljo2/ <liox> 'big'.

Tone *-d* is fairly similar to tone *-b* in terms of its pitch contour and phonation type. It differs primarily in that it does not fall to nearly as low a level as *-b* does, although it still begins at roughly the same level as *-b*. Tone *-d* is thus represented with [43] in Table 3.5. Examples of syllables that carry tone *-d* when produced in isolation include /pɑ̃3/ <baond> 'to shoot', /pjɛɰ3/ <bioud> 'home, family', /kɤ3/ <geud> 'to hold', /^{n}q^{h}ɛ3/ <nkhed> 'to look', /n^{ɦ}ɤ̃j3/ <hneind> 'to wear', and /ɕɑ̃3/ <xaond> 'not yet'.

Tone *-l* is in turn quite similar to tone *-d* in most respects. Both tones are nearly identical in terms of pitch height (though tone *-l* is sometimes very slightly lower than tone *-d*) and pitch contour; they differ primarily in that tone *-l* is produced with strong breathy voicing while tone *-d* is produced with modal voicing. The presence of breathy voicing on tones that descend from the historical tones 4 and 6 of Proto-Miao-Yao is common in many modern Miao-Yao languages (Niederer [1998: 65]; see also further below in this section). Yankan Xong's modern tone *-l* is the result of a merger between historical tones 4 and 8, and so its breathy voicing is unsurprising. Examples of syllables that carry tone *-l* when produced in isolation include /tju4/ <diul> 'to complete',

51 The specific carrier sentence used was _____ *aod-leb ndeud neind wel jix sheib puk* [_____ one-CLF word this 1SG NEG$_1$ able.to speak] 'I don't know how to say the word _____'.

/ʈʂɑ4/ <zhaol> 'non-Miao', /mɤ̃j4/ <meinl> 'CLF:person', /ŋɑ4/ <ngaol> 'narrow', /lo4/ <lol> 'to come', and /ʋɛ4/ <wel> '1SG'.

Tone *-t* is a sharply rising modal tone, beginning at the bottom of a speaker's pitch range and rising to near the top. It is thus represented with [14]. Examples of syllables that carry tone *-t* when produced in isolation include /tɑ5/ <daot> 'to kill', /^{n}tj^{h}o5/ <ntiot> 'smoky; smoke', /^{n}ts^{h}o5/ <ncot> 'to wash (clothing)', /qwɑ5/ <guaot> 'to pass', /m^{ɦ}ɑ̃5/ <hmaont> 'evening', and /ʐaw5/ <raut> 'good'.

Tone *-s* is a mid-low level tone, represented with [22] in Table 3.5. It is always accompanied by strong breathy voicing. Since the tone *-s* of modern Yankan Xong descends straightforwardly from the historical tone 6 of Proto-Miao-Yao, this breathy voicing is unsurprising (see also the discussion of tone *-l* above). Examples of syllables that carry tone *-s* when produced in isolation include /^{n}ts^{h}ɑ6/ <ncaos> 'to be done', /tɕõ6/ <jons> 'seven', /ʈʂɑ̃6/ <zhaons> 'fat', /qɑ̃6/ <ghans> 'to see', /nɛ6/ <nes> 'to ask', and /m̩6/ <ms> 'aunty'.

Tone *-k* is similar to tone *-s* in most respects: it too is a mid-low level tone, and it too is represented with [22] in Table 3.5. However, tone *-k* is produced with modal rather than breathy voicing. The difference between tones *-k* and *-s* thus parallels the difference between tones *-d* and *-l*. Examples of syllables that carry tone *-k* when produced in isolation include /p^{h}u7/ <puk> 'to speak', /^{n}p^{h}ɑ7/ <npaok> 'woman', /pjaw7/ <biauk> 'dark', /^{n}tju7/ <ndiuk> 'to peck', /q^{h}aw7/ <khauk> 'hole, cave', and /haw7/ <hauk> 'to drink'.

Finally, tone *-f* is a breathy, mid-low to low falling tone, represented with [21] in Table 3.5. Examples of syllables that carry tone *-f* when produced in isolation include /p^{h}ɛɰ8/ <pouf> 'paternal grandfather', /t^{h}i8/ <tif> 'stomach', /ts^{h}ɤ̃j8/ <ceinf> 'clear (e.g. water)', /mɑ̃8/ <maonf> 'thin', /n^{ɦ}ɛ8/ <hnef> 'day; CLF:day', and /hɛɰ8/ <houf> 'noisy'.[52]

52 An in-depth discussion of the historical development of Fenghuang Xong's tone systems (here including those of Yankan Xong, Shanjiang Xong, and Zhuigaolai Xong) lies outside the scope of this grammar. However, it is worth pointing out that most of Fenghuang Xong's eight modern tones seem to descend in relatively straightforward fashion from the eight tones that historically developed in most Miao-Yao languages after initial voiced and voiceless obstruents merged, thereby doubling the number of tones in these languages from four to eight (He 2009: 97; Niederer 1998: 249; Ratliff 2010: 184, 185). Similar processes of course took place in Vietnamese as well as in many Sinitic and Tai-Kadai languages. However, the reader should note that Fenghuang Xong's modern tone 8 (or *-f*) appears to have arisen due to a relatively recent split in historical tone 2, with the new tone 8 (or *-f*) subsequently drawing in several syllables that historically carried tone 1 (though it seems that in Zhuigaolai Xong rather fewer such syllables were drawn in than in Yankan or Shanjiang Xong; see Section 3.5.3.2 for details). The factors conditioning this recent split in historical tone 2 are currently unknown, but it appears that most of the historically tone 1 syllables that were subsequently drawn into the new tone 8 (or *-f*) begin with either aspirated or breathy consonants. Thus, unlike the situation in many other Miao-Yao languages, the tone 8 (or *-f*) of modern Fenghuang Xong does *not* represent a preservation of Miao-Yao's historical tone 8, which fully merged with historical tone 4 in all Fenghuang Xong varieties known to the author.

3.5.2.2 Tones and tone sandhi in polysyllabic sequences

There are several major tone-related phenomena in Yankan Xong that only become apparent in disyllabic and longer sequences. Many of Xong's tones participate in sandhi processes, in which a syllable that bears a particular tone in isolation is realized with a different tone when it occurs in certain phonologically defined environments. While most tones that participate in sandhi processes do so uniformly (in the sense that, e.g., all syllables that bear tone *-b* in isolation will behave identically in all sandhi contexts), those syllables that bear tone *-f* when produced in isolation can be divided into two groups based on their differing tonal behavior in certain polysyllabic sequences. The remainder of this section will be spent discussing and exemplifying all of these various phenomena. Note, though, that this section focuses only on tone sandhi processes in disyllabic sequences, as tone sandhi processes in trisyllabic and longer sequences will require further investigation before they can be described.

First, though, it must be made clear that in this grammar the term "tone sandhi" is used only to refer to major, phonologically triggered changes in the surface suprasegmental characteristics of syllables bearing a particular tone, changes which are not easily explained as simple cases of phonetic assimilation. All tones in Xong often undergo minor assimilatory processes in polysyllabic sequences, even in relatively slow and careful speech, but such processes are not considered tone sandhi here. For instance, tone *-d* is described as a mid-high to mid falling tone (i.e. [43]) in Table 3.5 above, and this is indeed its most common realization in monosyllabic utterances. However, when a syllable bearing tone *-d* immediately precedes a syllable bearing tone *-k* (which is a mid-low level tone, or [22]), the pitch on the syllable bearing tone *-d* often falls particularly low, all the way down to level [2]. This would not be considered an example of tone sandhi for two reasons: the change involved is phonetically a very minor one (specifically, it only involves a change from a [43] contour to a [42] one), and it can easily be explained as a case of anticipatory assimilation.

While some precise details of the system remain to be worked out, overall it appears that tone sandhi in Yankan Xong is not particularly complicated, especially in comparison to the extremely intricate sandhi systems found in Ḩmong, Ahmao, and other Chuanqiandian Miao languages (see Mortensen 2004). Four of Yankan Xong's eight tones – namely tones *-x*, *-t*, *-s*, and *-k* – are all "inert" with respect to tone sandhi, in the sense that a syllable which bears one of these four tones when produced in isolation will always be realized with that same tone in disyllabic and longer sequences. For example, a syllable which is pronounced with tone *-t* in isolation will always be pronounced with tone *-t* in longer sequences as well, regardless of the tones on the preceding and following syllables, the overall length of the sequence, and the grammatical structure of the sequence. It thus makes sense to speak of a particular syllable as having one of tone *-x*, tone *-t*, tone *-s*, or tone *-k* "underlyingly" and as also being realized with that same tone "on the surface".

In contrast, any syllable that is pronounced with tone *-b* (phonetically [41], with modal voicing), tone *-d* ([43], modal), or tone *-l* ([43], breathy) in isolation will always be realized with one of two surface tonal patterns in longer sequences: either with the same tone that it bears in isolation, or with tone *-k* ([22], modal). Specifically, syllables bearing any of tones *-b*, *-d*, or *-l* in isolation will be realized with tone *-k* when they occur in one of two environments: when immediately preceding a syllable that bears tone *-b* in isolation, or when immediately preceding certain syllables that bear tone *-f* in isolation (though not all *-f*-tone syllables, as will be discussed further below). These sandhi processes are thus all examples of regressive (or anticipatory) tone sandhi, in that the tone of the second (or following) syllable triggers a change in the tone of the first (or preceding) syllable rather than vice versa. For example, every syllable in examples (3.1–3.4) below bears tone *-b* when produced in isolation. However, when two such *-b*-tone syllables are produced in sequence, the tone of the first syllable changes to *-k*, while the tone of the second remains unchanged.[53]

(3.1)	/qɑ1-n̥aw1/	→	/qɑ7-n̥aw1/
	/qɑ^{41M}-n̥aw^{41M}/		/qɑ^{22M}-n̥aw^{41M}/
	<ghaob-nhaub>		<ghaok-nhaub>
	NOM-seed		NOM-seed
	'seed'		'seed'

(3.2)	/pu1-lɛ1/	→	/pu7-lɛ1/
	/pu^{41M}-lɛ^{41M}/		/pu^{22M}-lɛ^{41M}/
	<bub-leb>		<buk-leb>
	three-CLF		three-CLF
	'three (of something)'		'three (of something)'

(3.3)	/pɛɰ1	n̥o1/	→	/pɛɰ7	n̥o1/
	/pɛɰ^{41M}	n̥o^{41M}/		/pɛɰ^{22M}	n̥o^{41M}/
	<boub	nhob>		<bouk	nhob>
	1PL	walk		1PL	walk
	'We're walking.'			'We're walking.'	

53 These and all other examples in this section each consist of two sets of five horizontal lines, with the leftward set and the rightward set being separated by a rightward-pointing arrow. In both sets, the first line gives an IPA-like phonemic transcription in which each syllable's tone is indicated with a single, non-superscript tone number (see Table 3.5 above), the second line gives an IPA-like phonemic transcription in which each syllable's tone is represented with superscript numerals and a superscript letter <M> or <B> (the numerals indicate pitch height and contour, while the letter indicates modal vs. breathy voicing; again, see Table 3.5 above), the third line gives a transcription in the author's practical orthography (see Section 4.4), the fourth line gives a morpheme-by-morpheme gloss, and the fifth line gives a free English translation. The first three lines of each leftward set show the tones that each syllable would bear when produced in isolation, while the first three lines of each rightward set show the tones that each syllable would bear when occurring in the disyllabic sequence in question.

(3.4)	/kja1	^{n}kɤ1/	→	/kja7	^{n}kɤ1/
	/kja^{41M}	^{n}kɤ^{41M}/		/kja^{22M}	^{n}kɤ^{41M}/
	<giab	nggeub>		<giak	nggeub>
	stir.fry	mushroom		stir.fry	mushroom
	'to stir-fry mushrooms'			'to stir-fry mushrooms'	

In each of examples (3.5–3.8), the first syllable bears tone *-d* in isolation, while the second syllable bears tone *-b*. When produced in sequence, though, the tone of the first syllable changes to *-k*, while the tone of the second syllable remains unchanged.

(3.5)	/qwɛɰ3	qwɛ1/	→	/qwɛɰ7	qwɛ1/
	/qwɛɰ^{43M}	qwɛ^{41M}/		/qwɛɰ^{22M}	qwɛ^{41M}/
	<guoud	gueb>		<guouk	gueb>
	dog	black		dog	black
	'black dog'			'black dog'	

(3.6)	/qɑ3-qa1/	→	/qɑ7-qa1/
	/qɑ^{43M}-qa^{41M}/		/qɑ^{22M}-qa^{41M}/
	<ghaod-ghab>		<ghaok-ghab>
	feces-chicken		feces-chicken
	'chicken droppings'		'chicken droppings'

(3.7)	/ɑ3-lɛ1/	→	/ɑ7-lɛ1/
	/ɑ^{43M}-lɛ^{41M}/		/ɑ^{22M}-lɛ^{41M}/
	<aod-leb>		<aok-leb>
	one-CLF		one-CLF
	'one (of something)'		'one (of something)'

(3.8)	/^{n}q^{h}ɛ3	pɛɰ1/	→	/^{n}q^{h}ɛ7	pɛɰ1/
	/^{n}q^{h}ɛ^{43M}	pɛɰ^{41M}/		/^{n}q^{h}ɛ^{22M}	pɛɰ^{41M}/
	<nkhed	boub>		<nkhek	boub>
	look	1PL		look	1PL
	'Look at us.'			'Look at us.'	

Similarly, in each of examples (3.9–3.12), the first syllable bears tone *-l* in isolation, while the second syllable bears tone *-b*. When produced in sequence, the tone of the first syllable changes to *-k*, while the tone of the second syllable remains unchanged.

(3.9)	/mɛ4	qwɛ1/	→	/mɛ7	qwɛ1/
	/mɛ^{43B}	qwɛ^{41M}/		/mɛ^{22M}	qwɛ^{41M}/
	<mel	gueb>		<mek	gueb>
	horse	black		horse	black
	'black horse'			'black horse'	

(3.10)	/tɛɰ4	qwɛ1/	→	/tɛɰ7	qwɛ1/
	/tɛɰ^{43B}	qwɛ^{41M}/		/tɛɰ^{22M}	qwɛ^{41M}/
	<doul	gueb>		<douk	gueb>
	hand	black		hand	black
	'dirty hand'			'dirty hand'	

(3.11)	/mjɛɰ4	qwɤ1/	→	/mjɛɰ7	qwɤ1/
	/mjɛɰ^{43B}	qwɤ^{41M}/		/mjɛɰ^{22M}	qwɤ^{41M}/
	<mioul	gueub>		<miouk	gueub>
	fish	white		fish	white
	'white fish'			'white fish'	

(3.12)	/ku4-lɛ1/	→	/ku7-lɛ1/
	/ku^{43B}-lɛ^{41M}/		/ku^{22M}-lɛ^{41M}/
	<gul-leb>		<guk-leb>
	ten-CLF		ten-CLF
	'ten (of something)'		'ten (of something)'

One could thus say that in each of these disyllabic constructions (and others like them), the initial syllable has tone *-b*, tone *-d*, or tone *-l* underlyingly but is realized with tone *-k* on the surface. In contrast, the final syllable in each of these constructions has tone *-b* underlyingly and is also realized with tone *-b* on the surface.

Moving on, examples (3.13) and (3.14) show syllables that bear tone *-b* in isolation followed by syllables that bear tone *-f* in isolation, examples (3.15) and (3.16) show syllables that bear tone *-d* in isolation followed by syllables that bear tone *-f* in isolation, and examples (3.17) and (3.18) show syllables that bear tone *-l* in isolation followed by syllables that bear tone *-f* in isolation. In each example, the tone on the first syllable changes to *-k*, while the tone on the second syllable remains unchanged.

(3.13)	/pɛɰ1	p^{h}ɛɰ8/	→	/pɛɰ7	p^{h}ɛɰ8/
	/pɛɰ^{41M}	p^{h}ɛɰ^{21B}/		/pɛɰ^{22M}	p^{h}ɛɰ^{21B}/
	<boub	pouf>		<bouk	pouf>
	1PL	paternal.grandfather		1PL	paternal.grandfather
	'our paternal grandfather'			'our paternal grandfather'	

(3.14)	/qɑ1-t^{h}i8/	→	/qɑ7-t^{h}i8/
	/qɑ^{41M}-t^{h}i^{21B}/		/qɑ^{22M}-t^{h}i^{21B}/
	<ghaob-tif>		<ghaok-tif>
	NOM-stomach		NOM-stomach
	'stomach'		'stomach

			→		
(3.15)	/po3	p^{h}ɛɰ8/	→	/po7	p^{h}ɛɰ8/
	/po^{43M}	p^{h}ɛɰ^{21B}/		/po^{22M}	p^{h}ɛɰ^{21B}/
	<bod	pouf>		<bok	pouf>
	tell	paternal.grandfather		tell	paternal.grandfather
	'to tell (one's) paternal grandfather'			'to tell (one's) paternal grandfather'	

			→		
(3.16)	/tɕɑ3	t^{h}i8/	→	/tɕɑ7	t^{h}i8/
	/tɕɑ^{43M}	t^{h}i^{21B}/		/tɕɑ^{22M}	t^{h}i^{21B}/
	<jaod	tif>		<jaok	tif>
	bad	stomach		bad	stomach
	'to have an evil heart (lit. 'stomach')'			'to have an evil heart (lit. 'stomach')'	

			→		
(3.17)	/ʋɛ4	p^{h}ɛɰ8/	→	/ʋɛ7	p^{h}ɛɰ8/
	/ʋɛ^{43B}	p^{h}ɛɰ^{21B}/		/ʋɛ^{22M}	p^{h}ɛɰ^{21B}/
	<wel	pouf>		<wek	pouf>
	1SG	paternal.grandfather		1SG	paternal.grandfather
	'my paternal grandfather'			'my paternal grandfather'	

			→		
(3.18)	/ju4	n^{ɦ}ɛ8/	→	/ju7	n^{ɦ}ɛ8/
	/ju^{43B}	n^{ɦ}ɛ^{21B}/		/ju^{22M}	n^{ɦ}ɛ^{21B}/
	<yul	hnef>		<yuk	hnef>
	again	CLF:day		again	CLF:day
	'another day'			'another day'	

In examples (3.13–3.18), then, each initial syllable bears tone *-b*, tone *-d*, or tone *-l* underlyingly but is realized with tone *-k* on the surface. Each final syllable is realized with tone *-f* on the surface, though simply specifying the "underlying" tone of these final syllables as *-f* would be an oversimplification due to certain factors that are discussed further below.

However, in each of examples (3.19–3.22), despite the fact that the second syllable bears tone *-f* when produced in isolation, the first syllable – which bears either *-d* or *-l* in isolation – does not undergo tone sandhi; in other words, it does not change to tone *-k*, instead being realized with its underlying tone. Furthermore, note that the second syllable in each example changes from tone *-f* to tone *-x* when following a syllable that bears a *-d* or *-l* tone.

		→	
(3.19)	/qɑ3-jõ8/	→	/qɑ3-jõ2/
	/qɑ^{43M}-jõ^{21B}/		/qɑ^{43M}-jõ^{454M}/
	<ghaod-yonf>		<ghaod-yonx>
	feces-goat		feces-goat
	'goat droppings'		'goat droppings'

(3.20)	/tɕɑ3	njɛ8/	→	/tɕɑ3	njɛ2/
	/tɕɑ^{43M}	njɛ^{21B}/		/tɕɑ^{43M}	njɛ^{454M}/
	<jaod	nief>		<jaod	niex>
	bad	water.buffalo		bad	water.buffalo
	'to be a bad water buffalo'			'to be a bad water buffalo'	

(3.21)	/mĩ4-jõ8/	→	/mĩ4-jõ2/
	/mĩ^{43B}-jõ^{21B}/		/mĩ^{43B}-jõ^{454M}/
	<minl-yonf>		<minl-yonx>
	AUG-goat		AUG-goat
	'big goat'		'big goat'

(3.22)	/pɤ̃j4	jõ8/	→	/pɤ̃j4	jõ2/
	/pɤ̃j^{43B}	jõ^{21B}/		/pɤ̃j^{43B}	jõ^{454M}/
	<beinl	yonf>		<beinl	yonx>
	frighten	goat		frighten	goat
	'to frighten goats'			'to frighten goats'	

Next consider examples (3.23) and (3.24) below, which contain the same syllables that are produced with tone *-f* in isolation as examples (3.19–3.22) above (i.e. the terms for 'water buffalo' and 'goat'). In each of these two examples, the second syllable is realized with tone *-f* in isolation and when following an underlyingly *-b*-tone syllable. However, the initial *-b*-tone syllable in each of these examples does undergo tone sandhi and change to tone *-k* when followed by either of the *-f*-tone syllables in question, just as was the case in examples (3.13) and (3.14) above.

(3.23)	/tɑ1-njɛ8/	→	/tɑ7-njɛ8/
	/tɑ^{41M}-njɛ^{21B}/		/tɑ^{22M}-njɛ^{21B}/
	<daob-nief>		<daok-nief>
	AN-water.buffalo		AN-water.buffalo
	'water buffalo'		'water buffalo'

(3.24)	/tɑ1-jõ8/	→	/tɑ7-jõ8/
	/tɑ^{41M}-jõ^{21B}/		/tɑ^{22M}-jõ^{21B}/
	<daob-yonf>		<daok-yonf>
	AN-goat		AN-goat
	'goat'		'goat'

Comparing examples (3.13–3.18) with examples (3.19–3.24) shows that not all syllables that bear tone *-f* in isolation behave identically in disyllabic utterances. In fact, these examples suggest that the set of syllables that bear tone *-f* in isolation needs to be divided into two smaller sets. The members of the first set behave exactly like underlyingly *-b*-tone syllables in that they trigger tone sandhi on a preceding syllable that bears tone *-b*, *-d*, or *-l*, as is shown in examples (3.13–3.18). In contrast, the members of the second set trigger tone sandhi on a preceding syllable that bears tone *-b* (as is shown in examples (3.23) and (3.24)), but they do not trigger tone sandhi on a preceding syllable that bears tone *-d* or tone *-l* (as is shown in examples (3.19–3.22)). Furthermore, although the members of this second set are produced with tone *-f* in isolation, they are produced with tone *-x* in certain longer sequences (as, again, is shown in examples (3.19–3.22)).

For the remainder of this section, the first set of syllables will be referred to as *-f(b)*-tone syllables (since in disyllabic sequences they behave exactly like *-b*-tone syllables in terms of triggering tone sandhi), while the second set of syllables will be referred to as *-f(x)*-tone syllables (since they are realized with tone *-x* in certain environments).[54] In subsequent sections and chapters, though, the distinction between these two sets will be ignored, and both *-f(b)* and *-f(x)* syllables will simply be marked with the tone letter *-f* (as in, e.g., <tif> 'stomach', <yonf> 'goat', etc.). This is done both for convenience and for consistency, since in general tone sandhi is not marked in the Xong forms and example sentences included in this grammar.

There is a great deal of further evidence to support the author's proposed division between *-f(b)*-tone and *-f(x)*-tone syllables. Note that in each of examples (3.25) and (3.26) below, the initial syllable bears tone *-f* in isolation. However, when followed by a syllable that bears tone *-b* in isolation, the tone on the first syllable becomes tone *-k*, just as occurred with the initial underlyingly *-b*-tone syllables in examples (3.1–3.4) above. The form /pʰɛɰ8/ <pouf> 'paternal grandfather' in the examples below thus clearly belongs to the set of *-f(b)*-tone syllables, as do other forms that behave similarly like /tʰi8/ <tif> 'stomach' and /nʱɛ8/ <hnef> 'day; CLF:day'.

(3.25)	/pʰɛɰ8	qwɤ1/	→	/pʰɛɰ7	qwɤ1/
	/pʰɛɰ^{21B}	qwɤ^{41M}/		/pʰɛɰ^{22M}	qwɤ^{41M}/
	<pouf	gueub>		<pouk	gueub>
	paternal.grandfather	white		paternal.grandfather	white
	'braggart'			'braggart'	

(3.26)	/pʰɛɰ8	n̥o1/	→	/pʰɛɰ7	n̥o1/
	/pʰɛɰ^{21B}	n̥o^{41M}/		/pʰɛɰ^{22M}	n̥o^{41M}/
	<pouf	nhob>		<pouk	nhob>
	paternal.grandfather	walk		paternal.grandfather	walk
	'(My) paternal grandfather is walking.'			'(My) paternal grandfather is walking.'	

54 For some discussion of the historical origins of *-f(b)* and *-f(x)* syllables, see the final footnote in Section 3.5.2.1 above.

However, this process does not affect *-f(x)*-tone syllables when they precede a *-b*-tone syllable, as examples (3.27) and (3.28) below show. In these examples, the initial *-f(x)*-tone syllable is realized with tone *-x* when preceding a *-b*-tone syllable, rather than being realized with tone *-k*.

(3.27)	/jõ8	qwɛ1/	→	/jõ2	qwɛ1/
	/jõ^{21B}	qwɛ^{41M}/		/jõ^{454M}	qwɛ^{41M}/
	<yonf	gueb>		<yonx	gueb>
	goat	black		goat	black
	‘black goat’			‘black goat’	

(3.28)	/ʐ̩õ8	qwɤ1/	→	/ʐ̩õ2	qwɤ1/
	/ʐ̩õ^{21B}	qwɤ^{41M}/		/ʐ̩õ^{454M}	qwɤ^{41M}/
	<ronf	gueub>		<ronx	gueub>
	dragon	white		dragon	white
	‘white dragon’			‘white dragon’	

Still more evidence for the division between *-f(b)*-tone and *-f(x)*-tone syllables is given in examples (3.29–3.32). In examples (3.29) and (3.30), every syllable bears tone *-f* in isolation. However, when produced in sequence, the tone on the first syllable in each example changes to *-k*, while the tone on the second syllable remains unchanged. The behavior of both initial and final syllables in (3.29) and (3.30) is thus similar to the behavior of the initial and final *-b*-tone syllables in examples (3.1–3.4): in each of the six examples under discussion, the initial syllable is realized with tone *-k*, while the final syllable is realized with the same tone that it bears when produced in isolation. Each syllable in examples (3.29) and (3.30) thus belongs to set *-f(b)*.

(3.29)	/n^{ɦ}ɛ8-n^{ɦ}ɛ8/	→	/n^{ɦ}ɛ7-n^{ɦ}ɛ8/
	/n^{ɦ}ɛ^{21B}-n^{ɦ}ɛ^{21B}/		/n^{ɦ}ɛ^{22M}-n^{ɦ}ɛ^{21B}/
	<hnef-hnef>		<hnek-hnef>
	CLF:day-CLF:day		CLF:day-CLF:day
	‘every day’		‘every day’

(3.30)	/ts^{h}ɛɰ8	lj^{ɦ}o8/	→	/ts^{h}ɛɰ7	lj^{ɦ}o8/
	/ts^{h}ɛɰ^{21B}	lj^{ɦ}o^{21B}/		/ts^{h}ɛɰ^{22M}	lj^{ɦ}o^{21B}/
	<couf	hliof>		<couk	hliof>
	vinegar	many		vinegar	many
	‘a lot of vinegar’			‘a lot of vinegar’	

In examples (3.31) and (3.32), every syllable, both initial and final, again bears tone *-f* when produced in isolation. However, when produced as part of the disyllabic sequences shown in these examples, each initial syllable is realized with tone *-x* (rather than with tone *-k*, as happened in examples (3.29) and (3.30)), and each final syllable can optionally be realized with either tone *-x* or tone *-f* (rather than obligatorily being realized with tone *-f*, as again was the case in examples (3.29) and (3.30)). Each syllable in examples (3.31) and (3.32) thus belongs to the set of *-f(x)*-tone syllables.

(3.31) /ẓõ8-jõ8/ → /ẓõ2-jõ2/
/ẓõ^{21B}-jõ^{21B}/ /ẓõ^{454M}-jõ^{454M}/
<ronf-yonf> <ronx-yonx>
dragon-goat dragon-goat
'goat-like dragon' 'goat-like dragon'

or
/ẓõ2-jõ8/
/ẓõ^{454M}-jõ^{21B}/
<ronx-yonf>
dragon-goat
'goat-like dragon'

(3.32) /ẓõ8-njɛ8/ → /ẓõ2-njɛ2/
/ẓõ^{21B}-njɛ^{21B}/ /ẓõ^{454M}-njɛ^{454M}/
<ronf-nief> <ronx-niex>
dragon-water.buffalo dragon-water.buffalo
'water-buffalo–like dragon' 'water-buffalo–like dragon'

or
/ẓõ2-njɛ8/
/ẓõ^{454M}-njɛ^{21B}/
<ronx-nief>
dragon-water.buffalo
'water-buffalo–like dragon'

The tonal behavior of *-f(b)*-tone syllables has already been described fairly comprehensively, at least with respect to disyllabic sequences. However, there are still some remaining descriptive issues regarding the tonal behavior of *-f(x)*-tone syllables. First, it was shown in examples (3.19–3.22) above that syllables belonging to set *-f(x)* are produced with tone *-x* when they follow a syllable bearing tone *-d* or tone *-l*. As examples (3.33–3.36) below show, *-f(x)*-tone syllables are also produced with tone *-x* when they precede a syllable that bears tone *-d* or tone *-l*, or when they precede or follow a syllable that bears tone *-t*.

(3.33)	/ẓõ8-qwɛɰ3/	→	/ẓõ2-qwɛɰ3/
	/ẓõ^{21B}-qwɛɰ^{43M}/		/ẓõ^{454M}-qwɛɰ^{43M}/
	<ronf-guoud>		<ronx-guoud>
	dragon-dog		dragon-dog
	'dog-like dragon'		'dog-like dragon'

(3.34)	/jõ8-ṭṣɑ4/	→	/jõ2-ṭṣɑ4/
	/jõ^{21B}-ṭṣɑ^{43B}/		/jõ^{454M}-ṭṣɑ^{43B}/
	<yonf-zhaol>		<yonx-zhaol>
	goat-non.Miao		goat-non.Miao
	'sheep'		'sheep'

(3.35)	/ẓõ8	^{n}tɕ^{h}ĩ5/	→	/ẓõ2	^{n}tɕ^{h}ĩ5/
	/ẓõ^{21B}	^{n}tɕ^{h}ĩ^{14M}/		/ẓõ^{454M}	^{n}tɕ^{h}ĩ^{14M}/
	<ronf	nqint >		<ronx	nqint>
	dragon	red		dragon	red
	'red dragon'			'red dragon'	

(3.36)	/tɑ5	ẓõ8/	→	/tɑ5	ẓõ2/
	/tɑ^{14M}	ẓõ^{21B}/		/tɑ^{14M}	ẓõ^{454M}/
	<daot	ronf>		<daot	ronx>
	kill	dragon		kill	dragon
	'to kill a dragon'			'to kill a dragon'	

In fact, *-f(x)*-tone syllables will be produced with tone *-x* in all environments except for the following ones: (i) in isolation, (ii) when immediately following a syllable that bears tone *-b* in isolation, (iii) when immediately preceding or following a syllable that bears tone *-x* in isolation, and (iv) optionally when immediately following another syllable that also belongs to set *-f(x)*. In these four environments alone, syllables belonging to set *-f(x)* will be produced with tone *-f* (though only optionally so in the fourth environment). Examples (3.37) and (3.38) below demonstrate that syllables belonging to set *-f(x)* are produced with tone *-f* when following a syllable that bears tone *-x* in isolation, while examples (3.39) and (3.40) (repeated from examples (3.23) and (3.24) above) demonstrate that syllables belonging to set *-f(x)* are produced with tone *-f* when following a syllable that bears tone *-b* in isolation. Note also that the *-b* tone on each initial syllable in examples (3.39) and (3.40) changes to a *-k* tone due to the presence of the *-f* tone on the following syllable.

(3.37)	/nja2-ẓõ8/	→	/nja2-ẓõ8/
	/nja^{454M}-ẓõ^{21B}/		/nja^{454M}-ẓõ^{21B}/
	<niax-ronf>		<niax-ronf>
	meat-dragon		meat-dragon
	'dragon meat'		'dragon meat'

(3.38)	/nja2-jõ8/	→	/nja2-jõ8/
	/nja^{454M}-jõ^{21B}/		/nja^{454M}-jõ^{21B}/
	<niax-yonf>		<niax-yonf>
	meat-goat		meat-goat
	'mutton'		'mutton'

(3.39)	/tɑ1-njɛ8/	→	/tɑ7-njɛ8/
	/tɑ^{41M}-njɛ^{21B}/		/tɑ^{22M}-njɛ^{21B}/
	<daob-nief>		<daok-nief>
	AN-water.buffalo		AN-water.buffalo
	'water buffalo'		'water buffalo'

(3.40)	/tɑ1-jõ8/	→	/tɑ7-jõ8/
	/tɑ^{41M}-jõ^{21B}/		/tɑ^{22M}-jõ^{21B}/
	<daob-yonf>		<daok-yonf>
	AN-goat		AN-goat
	'goat'		'goat'

Examples (3.41) and (3.42) demonstrate that *-f(x)*-tone syllables are also produced with tone *-f* when they precede a syllable that bears tone *-x* in isolation.

(3.41)	/jõ8	qwɣ̃j2/	→	/jõ8	qwɣ̃j2/
	/jõ^{21B}	qwɣ̃j^{454M}/		/jõ^{21B}	qwɣ̃j^{454M}/
	<yonf	gueinx>		<yonf	gueinx>
	goat	yellow		goat	yellow
	'yellow goat'			'yellow goat'	

(3.42)	/ẓõ8	ljo2/	→	/ẓõ8	ljo2/
	/ẓõ^{21B}	ljo^{454M}/		/ẓõ^{21B}	ljo^{454M}/
	<ronf	liox>		<ronf	liox>
	dragon	big		dragon	big
	'big dragon'			'big dragon'	

For evidence that *-f(x)*-tone syllables can be produced either with tone *-f* or with tone *-x* when immediately following another syllable that belongs to set *-f(x)*, see examples (3.31) and (3.32) earlier in this section.

Taking all of the above into account, the tone sandhi system of Yankan Xong can so far be summarized as follows:

(i) **Inert tones:** Tones *-x*, *-t*, *-s*, and *-k* are "inert" in terms of tone sandhi, in the sense that a syllable which bears one of these tones when produced in isolation will always bear that same tone in disyllabic and longer sequences.

(ii) **Subsets of *-f*-tone syllables:** Syllables that bear tone *-f* in isolation can be divided into two sets: the *-f(b)* set, whose members behave like *-b*-tone syllables in terms of tone sandhi, and the *-f(x)* set, whose members are realized with tone *-x* in certain environments.

(iii) **Tones *-b*, *-d*, *-l*, and *-f(b)* followed by tone *-b*:** When a syllable that bears tone *-b*, tone *-d*, or tone *-l* in isolation precedes a syllable that bears tone *-b* in isolation, the tone on the first syllable changes to *-k*, while the tone on the second syllable remains *-b*. The same process occurs when a syllable that belongs to set *-f(b)* precedes a syllable that bears tone *-b* in isolation: the tone on the initial *-f(b)* syllable changes to *-k*, while the tone on the final *-b* syllable remains *-b*.

(iv) **Tones *-b*, *-d*, *-l*, and *-f(b)* followed by tone *-f(b)*:** When a syllable that bears tone *-b*, tone *-d*, or tone *-l* in isolation precedes a syllable that belongs to set *-f(b)*, the tone on the first syllable changes to *-k*, while the second syllable is realized with tone *-f*. When two syllables belonging to set *-f(b)* occur in sequence, the first syllable is realized with tone *-k*, while the second is realized with tone *-f*.

(v) **Tones *-b*, *-d*, and *-l* followed by tone *-f(x)*:** When a syllable that bears tone *-b* in isolation precedes a syllable that belongs to set *-f(x)*, that initial syllable will be realized with tone *-k*. However, when a syllable that bears tone *-d* or tone *-l* in isolation precedes a syllable that belongs to set *-f(x)*, that initial syllable will be realized with its underlying *-d* or *-l* tone, not with tone *-k*. See point (vi) immediately below for information on the realization of the final *-f(x)* syllable in such sequences.

(vi) **Surface realization of *-f(x)*-tone syllables:** When a syllable that belongs to set *-f(x)* is produced (a) in isolation, (b) immediately following a syllable that bears tone *-b* in isolation, or (c) immediately preceding or following a syllable that bears tone *-x* in isolation, it will be realized with tone *-f*. When a syllable that belongs to set *-f(x)* is produced immediately following another syllable that belongs to set *-f(x)*, that second *-f(x)*-tone syllable can be realized with either tone *-x* or tone *-f* in apparently free variation. In all other environments (including immediately preceding another syllable that belongs to set *-f(x)*), syllables belonging to set *-f(x)* are realized with tone *-x*.

(vii) **Remaining issues:** The surface tonal patterns of disyllabic *-f(b)* + *-f(x)* sequences and *-f(x)* + *-f(b)* sequences remain unknown, as the author has not yet been able to elicit any reliable data involving such sequences.

(viii) **Other cases:** In all disyllabic sequences not covered by (i–vii) above, each syllable will be realized with the same tone that it bears when produced in isolation.

Finally, note that all sandhi processes described in this section seem to be triggered purely phonologically, with no regard for the grammatical relationships between the forms involved.

3.5.3 Tone systems of other Fenghuang Xong varieties

3.5.3.1 The tone system of Shanjiang Xong

Like La'ershan, Shanjiang is a major Xong-speaking town in Fenghuang County, and the two towns are located less than an hour's drive away from each other. The description of Shanjiang Xong in this section is based on the speech of Mrs. Chenghua Long (*Lóng Chénghuā* 龙成花), a female primary school teacher from Shanjiang Town who had lived and worked for several years in La'ershan at the time of the author's fieldwork. See Section 2.6.2 for more background information on this consultant.

Shanjiang Xong's tone system is quite similar to Yankan Xong's. Just as in Yankan Xong, any given monosyllabic form produced in isolation in Shanjiang Xong will be accompanied by one of eight lexically specified tones. There is a high degree of lexical correspondence among tones in Yankan and Shanjiang Xong (so that, for example, any monosyllabic lexical item that bears tone *-b* in Yankan Xong will almost always bear tone *-b* in Shanjiang Xong as well), and also a high degree of phonetic similarity between most corresponding tones in the two varieties.

Table 3.6 gives some impressionistic phonetic characteristics for each of Shanjiang Xong's eight tones. See the commments regarding Table 3.5 in Section 3.5.2.1 above for information on this table's organization and the terms used within it.

Table 3.6: Phonetic characteristics of Shanjiang Xong tones.

TONE NUMBER	TONE LETTER	PITCH HEIGHT/CONTOUR (INFORMAL)	PITCH HEIGHT/CONTOUR (NUMERIC SCALE)	PHONATION TYPE
1	*-b*	*mid-high to low fall*	[41]	*modal*
2	*-x*	*mid-high to high to mid-high peak*	[454]	*modal*
3	*-d*	*mid-high to mid fall*	[43]	*modal*
4	*-l*	*mid-high to mid fall*	[43]	*breathy*
5	*-t*	*low to mid-high rise*	[14]	*modal*
6	*-s*	*mid-low to mid rise*	[23]	*breathy*
7	*-k*	*mid-low to mid rise*	[23]	*modal*
8	*-f*	*mid-low to low fall*	[21]	*breathy*

As a comparison between Tables 3.5 and 3.6 will show, the phonetic realizations of most tones are nearly identical in Yankan Xong and Shanjiang Xong. In fact, the only noteworthy difference is that tones *-s* and *-k* are mid-low to mid rising tones (phonetically [23]) in Shanjiang Xong, while they are mid-low level tones (phonetically [22]) in Yankan Xong. In each variety, though, tone *-s* and tone *-k* are virtually identical to each other in terms of their pitch height and pitch contour, with the primary difference between them being that tone *-s* is produced with breathy voicing while tone *-k* is produced with modal voicing.

While the behavior of Shanjiang Xong's tones in polysyllabic sequences has not been investigated as thoroughly as the behavior of Yankan Xong's (see Section 3.5.2.2 above), on the whole the relevant phenomena seem to be quite similar in both varieties. Most polysyllabic sequences that display tone sandhi in Yankan Xong also display tone sandhi in Shanjiang Xong, and generally in the same way. Furthermore, syllables that bear tone *-f* when produced in isolation in Shanjiang Xong can be divided into *-f(b)* and *-f(x)* classes based on their tonal behavior in polysyllabic sequences, just as in Yankan Xong.

However, there is one significant difference between tone sandhi processes in the two varieties. In Yankan Xong, there are a number of circumstances in which a syllable that does not bear tone *-k* when produced in isolation will nevertheless be realized with tone *-k* when it precedes certain other syllables. Specifically, this occurs when a syllable that either bears any of tones *-b*, *-d*, or *-l* in isolation or belongs to set *-f(b)* precedes a syllable that either bears tone *-b* in isolation or belongs to set *-f(b)*, or when a syllable that bears tone *-b* in isolation precedes a syllable belonging to set *-f(x)*.

In Shanjiang Xong, these same disyllabic sequences also trigger tone sandhi on their initial syllable, just as in Yankan Xong. However, instead of the affected syllable acquiring tone *-k*, it acquires a unique sandhi tone *-c*. In phonetic terms, this sandhi tone is modally voiced and bears a high level pitch, meaning that its pitch height and contour can be represented with [55]. While this tone *-c* is phonetically quite distinct from each of the eight tones described in Table 3.6 above, it is not listed in the table because it never occurs on monosyllabic forms produced in isolation. Instead, it occurs only in two types of obligatorily polysyllabic environments. The first of these are the sandhi environments described in the preceding paragraph. The second are a handful of recent disyllabic borrowings from Sinitic varieties, including *sic.jic* 'driver' (cf. Standard Mandarin *sījī* 司机), *kaoc.feic* 'coffee' (cf. Standard Mandarin *kāfēi* 咖啡), *xaonc.joc* 'banana' (cf. Standard Mandarin *xiāngjiāo* 香蕉), *Shanc.xic* 'Shanxi (Province)' (cf. Standard Mandarin *Shānxī* 山西), *weif.**douc*** 'flavor' (cf. Standard Mandarin *wèidao* 味道), and *Bol.**toc*** 'Bo To (personal name)' (cf. Standard Mandarin *Bó Tāo* 薄涛). Note that most (though not all) of these disyllabic Xong forms bear tone *-c* on each syllable, while most (though, again, not all) of the equivalent Standard Mandarin forms bear a first tone on each syllable.[55] Note also that the Standard Mandarin first tone is a high level tone produced with modal voicing, just like the tone *-c* of Shanjiang Xong.

55 Most of these forms are not listed in He's 2009 description of Fenghuang Chinese (see Section 2.5.3.1), and so their tonal characteristics in that variety are unknown.

3.5.3.2 The tone system of Zhuigaolai Xong

Zhuigaolai is a Xong-speaking village located about half an hour's walk from La'ershan Town. The description of Zhuigaolai Xong in this section is based on the speech of Mrs. Shixiang Wu (*Wú Shìxiāng* 吴世香), a female primary school teacher from Zhuigaolai who had lived and worked for several years in La'ershan at the time of the author's fieldwork. See Section 2.6.2 for more background information on this consultant.

The tone system of Zhuigaolai Xong is much more different from those of Yankan and Shanjiang Xong than either of those systems is from the other. While it is true of all three systems that any given monosyllabic form produced in isolation will be accompanied by one of eight lexically specified tones, tone *-f* is strikingly rarer in Zhuigaolai Xong than it is in Yankan or Shanjiang Xong. Most (though not all) monosyllabic forms which bear tone *-f* when produced in isolation in Yankan and Shanjiang Xong instead bear some other tone when produced in Zhuigaolai Xong.[56] This is particularly common for the set of *-f(b)*-tone syllables described in Section 3.5.2.2 above, almost all of which simply bear tone *-b* in Zhuigaolai Xong. It is somewhat less common for the set of *-f(x)*-tone syllables (again, see Section 3.5.2.2), some of which simply bear tone *-x* in Zhuigaolai Xong, some of which bear tone *-l*, and some of which still bear tone *-f(x)*. Aside from these points, though, there is still a fairly high degree of lexical correspondence between Zhuigaolai Xong's tones on the one hand and Yankan and Shanjiang Xong's tones on the other (in the sense that if a particular monosyllabic lexical item has, e.g., tone *-d* in Yankan and Shanjiang Xong, it will usually have tone *-d* in Zhuigaolai Xong as well), though not quite as high a degree as exists between Yankan and Shanjiang Xong.

However, many of Zhuigaolai Xong's tones are phonetically quite distinct from the corresponding tones in Yankan and Shanjiang Xong. Table 3.7 gives some impressionistic phonetic characteristics for each of the variety's eight tones. See the commments regarding Table 3.5 in Section 3.5.2.1 above for information on this table's organization and the terms used within it.

Table 3.7: Phonetic characteristics of Zhuigaolai Xong tones.

TONE NUMBER	TONE LETTER	PITCH HEIGHT/CONTOUR (INFORMAL)	PITCH HEIGHT/CONTOUR (NUMERIC SCALE)	PHONATION TYPE
1	*-b*	*mid-low to low to mid-low dip*	[212]	*creaky*
2	*-x*	*mid-high to high to mid-high peak*	[454]	*modal*

56 Because of this, the tonal minimal octuplet given in Section 3.5.2.1 is not actually a minimal octuplet in Zhuigaolai Xong, since the form meaning 'poison' bears tone *-l* rather than tone *-f* in this variety. However, a minimal octuplet can still be produced for Zhuigaolai Xong by replacing 'poison' with 'to hammer', which is /tɛɰ8/ <douf> in Zhuigaolai Xong (although it is /tɛɰ2/ <doux> in Yankan and Shanjiang Xong).

Table 3.7 (continuted)

TONE NUMBER	TONE LETTER	PITCH HEIGHT/CONTOUR (INFORMAL)	PITCH HEIGHT/CONTOUR (NUMERIC SCALE)	PHONATION TYPE
3	*-d*	*mid to mid-low fall*	[32]	*modal*
4	*-l*	*mid to mid-low fall*	[32]	*breathy*
5	*-t*	*low to mid-high rise*	[14]	*modal*
6	*-s*	*mid-high level*	[44]	*breathy*
7	*-k*	*mid-high level*	[44]	*modal*
8	*-f*	*mid-low to low to mid-low dip*	[212]	*breathy*

As Table 3.7 shows, the phonetic characteristics of tones *-b* and *-f* in Zhuigaolai Xong are quite different from those of the corresponding tones in Yankan and Shanjiang Xong. These two tones have identical pitch heights and pitch contours in Zhuigaolai Xong, differing solely in that tone *-b* is produced with creaky voicing while tone *-f* is produced with breathy voicing. Zhuigaolai Xong's tone *-b* is thus the only tone regularly produced with creaky voicing in any of the Xong tone systems surveyed in this chapter. Furthermore, while tones *-b* and *-f* are falling in both Yankan Xong and Shanjiang Xong, they are dipping (i.e. involving both an initial fall and a final rise) in Zhuigaolai Xong.

Tones *-x* and *-t* in Zhuigaolai Xong are similar to their equivalents in Yankan and Shanjiang Xong. Tones *-d* and *-l* are also fairly similar across these three varieties, though they are typically produced slightly lower in Zhuigaolai Xong (where they are phonetically [32]) than in Yankan or Shanjiang Xong (where they are phonetically [43]). Tones *-s* and *-k* are mid-high level tones (phonetically [44]) in Zhuigaolai Xong, while they are mid-low level tones (phonetically [22]) in Yankan Xong and mid-low to mid rising tones (phonetically [23]) in Shanjiang Xong. Just as in Yankan and Shanjiang Xong, though, in Zhuigaolai Xong tones *-d* and *-l* and tones *-s* and *-k* appear to be distinguished primarily by their phonation type: the tones *-d* and *-k* are modal, while the tones *-l* and *-s* are breathy. However, as was mentioned above, Zhuigaolai Xong differs from those other two varieties in that it also has a third pair of tones distinguished primarily by phonation type: its tone *-b* and tone *-f* are virtually identical in terms of pitch height and pitch contour, with the only significant difference between them being that tone *-b* is produced with creaky voicing and tone *-f* with breathy voicing.

Regrettably, the author has not yet had the opportunity to investigate tonal behavior in Zhuigaolai Xong's polysyllabic sequences in any real depth. However, it is at least clear that Zhuigaolai Xong, like Shanjiang Xong, has a unique sandhi tone *-c* which is phonetically distinct from the eight tones described in Table 3.7 and which only appears in polysyllabic sequences, never on monosyllabic forms produced in isolation. In phonetic terms, this tone is modally voiced and bears a high level pitch (phonetically [55]), just as is the case in Shanjiang Xong. Also like in Shanjiang Xong, in Zhuigaolai Xong this sandhi tone *-c* generally appears in the same phonological environments in which the sandhi-triggered *-k*-tone appears in Yankan Xong; see Section 3.5.3.1 for details. Significantly, though, Zhuigaolai Xong differs from Shanjiang Xong in that its sandhi tone *-c* never occurs in lexically specified fashion in recent borrowings from Sinitic varieties; instead, it only occurs in sandhi environments. Nevertheless, the existence of such a sandhi tone in both Zhuigaolai and Shanjiang Xong but not in Yankan Xong is somewhat remarkable given that, in general, the tone systems of Shanjiang and Yankan Xong resemble each other much more than either one resembles the tone system of Zhuigaolai Xong.

3.6 A note on non-tonal suprasegmental phenomena

Like many (perhaps even all) tone languages, Fenghuang Xong appears to feature an additional intonational system that is both distinct from and superimposed upon its tone system (see Section 3.5). This intonational system appears to make use of (at least) distinctive pitch heights, distinctive pitch contours, and distinctive durations, and it appears to operate at the level of the polysyllabic phonological phrase rather than at the level of the individual syllable. Unfortunately, the author did not have sufficient time while in the field to investigate Xong's intonational system to any real degree, and thus it cannot yet be described in any detail. This section instead merely lays out four pieces of preliminary evidence for the existence of such a system in the language. Comprehensively describing Xong's intonational system and its interactions with the language's tone system remains an important task for future scholars.

First, Xong features several particles and interjections (see Sections 9.2.1 and 11.3, respectively) that do not bear any lexically specified tone. Instead, the surface suprasegmental realization of any such particle or interjection will vary widely from utterance to utterance in terms of (at least) pitch height, pitch contour, and duration. The different suprasegmental realizations of these toneless syllables do not seem to correlate with the tone of the preceding syllable or any other obvious phonological factors, but in many cases they do appear to correlate with certain distinctions in sentence modality and speaker attitude. Second, a noticeable fall in pitch occurs at the end of many pragmatically neutral declarative utterances, regardless of the tones that the final few syllables in the utterance bear. This fall is most obvious when eliciting lexical items in isolation, but it regularly occurs in naturalistic speech as well. Third, there appears to be some way of signaling emphasis or focus through suprasegmental means in Xong, in particular by "exaggerating" the tones on the syllables in question (e.g. producing level tones with a particularly long duration, producing falling tones with a particularly sharp fall, etc.). Fourth and finally, there are a number of utterances in the author's corpus which consultants unanimously agree are intended to have interrogative force, despite the fact that this force is not overtly signaled through the presence of any segmental interrogative markers, unusual tonal behavior, or distinctive interrogative syntax. The author suspects that intonation plays at least some role in signaling that these utterances are interrogative, although admittedly it is also possible that speakers identify them as interrogative simply by relying on context and pragmatic knowledge instead.

3.7 Alternate syllable structure analyses

The syllable structure assumed so far in this chapter is (C)V^{T}, with each syllable consisting of an optional initial consonant, an obligatory vowel, and an obligatory tone. The only syllable types which violate this phonotactic template are those which consist of a syllabic nasal and an accompanying tone (see Section 3.3.4) and those which do not bear any lexically specified tone (Section 3.6).

Still, this (C)V^{T} template is not the only logically possible one. For instance, up until now it has simply been assumed that phonetically complex onsets like [^{n}ts^{h}], [^{ŋ}kj^{h}], [ŋw], and [m^{ɦ}] are unitary phonemes rather than sequences or clusters of phonemes. In theory, though, a putative phoneme like /^{n}ts^{h}/ could alternately be analyzed as a polyphonemic sequence of /n/ followed by /ts^{h}/, or as /^{n}ts/ followed by /h/, or as any one of a number of other possibilities. However, after careful consideration of all the available data, the author has still not arrived at any conclusion regarding which of these possibilities is the most likely. There does not appear to be any conclusive evidence one way or the other regarding whether Xong's phonetically complex syllable onsets should be analyzed as unitary, monophonemic consonants or as polyphonemic consonant clusters (or, for that matter, whether some complex onsets should be analyzed as unitary consonants and others as polyphonemic clusters).[57]

The author suggests that this lack of evidence should not be regarded as a failure of description or analysis, since the issue does not appear to have any great consequences for Xong phonology as a whole. While Xong's phonetically complex onsets are considered to be unitary phonemes throughout the majority of this chapter for the sake of convenience, few if any aspects of the author's description of Xong phonology would need to undergo any changes if they were instead analyzed as polyphonemic

57 The author would argue, however, that Xong's four diphthongal vowels /ɛɰ, aw, ɤj, ɤ̃j/ (see Section 3.3.3) should indeed be analyzed as unitary phonemes rather than as polyphonemic sequences. This is because (i) the offglide [ɰ] in the vowel /ɛɰ/ does not occur independently as either a glide */ɰ/ or a vowel */ɯ/, (ii) both the nucleus and offglide portions of the vowel /ɤ̃j/ are nasalized, but no nasal versions of either /ɤ/ or /j/ occur independently in the language (though a nasal vowel /ĩ/ does admittedly occur), and (iii) although Xong features seven monophthongal oral vowels and four monophthongal nasal vowels, it features only four diphthongal vowels, which is rather fewer than might be expected if those diphthongal vowels were underlyingly sequences of two vowels or of a vowel and a following glide.

consonant clusters. The most accurate analysis might actually be one in which Xong's syllables are simply divided into "initials" (i.e. onsets) and "finals" (i.e. rhymes), with the analyst remaining agnostic as to whether any given initial or final is monophonemic or polyphonemic. This approach is in fact the one typically taken in analyses performed within the framework of traditional Chinese linguistic theory (see Section 1.2.1 for further discussion of this issue, and see also Section 2.5.1 for more on traditional Chinese linguistic theory in general).

In any case, the remainder of this Section 3.7 discusses five particular types of evidence that may have some bearing on the issue, though, again, the majority of this evidence is rather inconclusive.

3.7.1 Restrictions on possible combinations

If Xong's complex onsets were analyzed as polyphonemic consonant clusters, then only a small number of the many logically possible clusters would be allowed. For instance, prenasalization could be analyzed as underlyingly being an independent nasal phoneme (or phonemes), but it would be one that can only co-occur with plosives within a single cluster (as in, e.g., /^{n}p/ or /^{n}ts/), not with fricatives or approximants or laterals. Affricates could similarly be analyzed as underlyingly being stop–fricative clusters, but only three of the many logically possible stop–fricative combinations actually occur (namely /t/ plus /s/, /t/ plus /ɕ/, and /t/ plus /ʂ/). Labialization could be analyzed as being underlyingly caused by the presence of /ʋ/ in a cluster, but such labialization can only occur with uvular plosives, the velar nasal /ŋ/, and the glottal "fricative" /h/. However, palatalization (which could be analyzed as being underlyingly caused by the presence of /j/ in a cluster) is admittedly something of an exception, since it can occur with a wide variety of syllable onsets (including bilabial, alveolar, and velar stops, the nasals /m, n/, and the laterals /l, l^{ɦ}/).[58]

While not definitive, the fact that only a few of the many logically possible complex syllable onsets actually occur is perhaps more consistent with an analysis of those onsets as unitary phonemes than as clusters. Of course, it is also possible that some of those complex onsets are unitary phonemes while others are clusters, and in that case the evidence presented in this section suggests that palatalized

58 Furthermore, Xong's alveolo-palatal consonants /tɕ, tɕ^{h}, ^{n}tɕ, ^{n}tɕ^{h}, ɕ/ could in theory be analyzed as clusters of alveolar sibilant consonants followed by the glide /j/, so that /tɕ/ would be underlyingly /tsj/, /ɕ/ would be underlyingly /sj/, and so on. While this analysis is phonetically plausible, there does not appear to be any independent evidence for it. In particular, note that the vowel /i/ never co-occurs with /j/ or with a palatalized consonant within the same syllable, but it readily co-occurs with alveolo-palatal consonants, as in /tɕi2/ <jix> 'NEG$_{1}$' or /ɕi1/ <xib> 'hungry'.

complex onsets are perhaps the most likely candidates for underlyingly being clusters.

3.7.2 Impossibility of epenthetic vowel insertion

No two adjacent phonetic constituents in any of Xong's complex syllable onsets can ever be separated by epenthetic vowels, even in extremely slow, emphatic speech. Such vowels can thus never be inserted between the nasal portion of a prenasalized plosive and the following stop or affricate portion, between a stop and a following labial or palatal glide, and so on. This is unlike the situation in, for example, English, where just such a test can be used to distinguish between initial consonant clusters and initial affricates. In response to the question *Did you just say "keen"?*, one can say, *No, I said "clean, [kə.lin] clean"*, with an epenthetic vowel inserted between /k/ and /l/ in the onset of the word *clean*. However, in response to the question *Did you just say "sheer"?*, one cannot say, **No, I said "cheer, [tə.ʃiɻ] cheer"*, with an epenthetic vowel inserted between [t] and [ʃ] in the onset of the word *cheer*. In this respect, all Xong syllables with complex onsets universally behave like English *cheer* rather than English *clean*. While hardly conclusive on its own, this is nevertheless the sort of behavior more typically associated with unitary phonemes than with consonant clusters.

3.7.3 Independent occurrence of putative cluster constituents

Nearly all phonetic constituents of Xong's complex syllable onsets can also occur as independent phonemes in syllable-initial position. For instance, the stop and fricative portions of each putative affricate can each occur as independent phonemes, the language features two voiced approximant phonemes (/ʋ/ and /j/) that are phonetically similar to labialization and palatalization, and a variety of nasal consonant phonemes (phonetically similar to prenasalization) occur independently as well. While aspiration could hardly be said to occur as an independent phoneme in Xong, note that two independent phonemes /h/ and /hw/ do occur in the language, and these are typically realized as nothing more than a period of initial voicelessness on the following vowel (with accompanying lip rounding for /hw/ as well; see Section 3.2.4 for details). The only phonetic constituent to which this does not apply is breathy voicing (occurring with the consonants /m^{ɦ}, n^{ɦ}, l^{ɦ}, lj^{ɦ}/), as there is no evidence whatsoever for the existence of an independent phoneme */ɦ/ in Xong.[59]

59 However, since there is never any contrast between phonetically aspirated consonants and phonetically breathy consonants in Xong, breathy voicing on a consonant could in theory be analyzed as an allophone of /h/, one that only occurs with nasals and laterals and not with plosives.

However, the fact that most of these phonetic constituents can also occur as independent phonemes is equally consistent with an analysis in which Xong complex onsets are considered unitary phonemes and with one in which they are considered consonant clusters. If none (or even just a very few) of these constituents could occur as independent phonemes, then that would indeed be an argument in favor of analyzing these complex onsets as unitary phonemes. The reverse, though, is not true, and so the evidence presented in this section is inconclusive as well.

3.7.4 Ordering restrictions

If Xong's complex syllable onsets are in fact analyzable as consonant clusters, then they are clusters which obey very strict ordering rules. If prenasalization (i.e. /n/ or some other nasal phoneme) is present, it will always occur first. If a stop is present, it will always occur after prenasalization but before any other constituents. If a fricative is present, it will always occur after a stop but before any glides. If a glide is present, it will always occur after a stop or fricative but before aspiration (i.e. /h/). Finally, if aspiration is present, it will always occur last.

Just as with the evidence presented in Section 3.7.3 above, though, these ordering restrictions are consistent with either analysis. If the ordering possibilities of the internal phonetic constituents of Xong's complex syllable onsets were relatively free, then that could be considered positive evidence that those onsets are indeed polyphonemic clusters. However, a lack of such freedom does not necessarily suggest that Xong's complex onsets are monophonemic, and so this evidence too is inconclusive.

3.7.5 Morphophonological evidence

Simply put, the author is not aware of any morphophonological evidence that has any bearing one way or the other on whether Xong's phonetically complex syllable onsets should be analyzed as consonant clusters or as unitary phonemes. Xong does not have a particularly rich morphological system to begin with, and its few arguably morphophonological processes (e.g. the [*did-lib-did*-VERB] construction described in Section 10.5.2, or certain ideophone templates described in Section 11.1) are equally consistent with either analysis.

3.8 Some final notes on interspeaker and intervarietal variation

As previous sections of this chapter showed, there is a significant amount of low-level phonetic variation among Xong speakers from different parts of Fenghuang County. In some cases the author has observed minor differences even between speakers born and raised in the same village. These differences are most pronounced in the tone systems of Fenghuang Xong speakers (see Section 3.5); vowels and especially consonants show much less variation. Phonologically, though, Fenghuang Xong is if anything surprisingly uniform given the variety's large speaker population and geographic extent. Furthermore, while the author's consultants were quite conscious that speakers from different areas spoke differently, they were unanimous in claiming that this variation never affected intelligibility within the bounds of Fenghuang County (or, in other words, that all Xong speakers from within the county could understand the speech of all other Xong speakers from within the county). In contrast, these consultants generally reported that Xong speakers from outside Fenghuang County were much less intelligible to them, with the reported level of intelligibility unsurprisingly tending to decrease as distance from Fenghuang County increased (see Section 2.2.2 for details). While some individual Xong speakers naturally have opinions about which Xong variety they think "sounds the best", there does not appear to be any variety of Xong which is widely recognized in Fenghuang County as being the most prestigious, or the most standard, or anything of the sort. This includes the governmentally recognized "standard" variety of Xong spoken in Jiwei Township in Huayuan County, as was discussed in Section 2.4.

There is also a significant amount of lexical variation among the author's consultants, although a full survey of the topic lies outside the scope of this study.[60] Most of what was said about phonetic and phonological variation above also applies to lexical variation: speakers are quite aware of it, but they claim it never affects mutual intelligibility among Xong speakers within Fenghuang County. The author has also observed a small amount of grammatical variation among the idiolects of his primary consultants, although it is not yet clear to what extent this reflects true "dialectal" variation as opposed to merely idiolectal differences. In general, the author's consultants seemed to be much less conscious of grammatical variation than they were of phonological and lexical variation, and they were also much less accepting of it. Rather than simply allowing that a certain grammatical construction or phrasing might be used in certain villages or towns but not in others (as generally happened when instances of phonological or lexical variation were encountered), the author's consultants would often argue over the "correct" way to phrase a particular utterance. A comprehensive survey of grammatical variation among different varieties of Fenghuang Xong has yet to be completed, but those points of variation which the author has so far observed will be noted wherever relevant in subsequent chapters.

It is worth mentioning here that the author's consultants always explained the intervarietal phonological and lexical differences they were aware of in terms of geography. For example, the author would often be told that certain lexical items were

60 Because of this variation, in this grammar the same lexical item will sometimes be transcribed differently in examples from different speakers, or even in different examples from the same speaker.

only used in certain villages, or that his attempted pronunciation of a certain tone resembled the way the tone was produced in a certain town. His consultants never explained these intervarietal differences in terms of non-geographic factors like gender, age, or differing clan or lineage group membership. The author himself is not aware of any specific effects that such non-geographic factors have had on variation within Fenghuang Xong, although he cannot unequivocally rule out their existence.

Previously published accounts of Xong rarely if ever mention any of this variation. Most of these accounts restrict their description to the speech of a single town or village. For instance, Xiang (1999) focuses solely on the variety of Xong spoken in Jiwei Township in Huayuan County, Chen (2009) solely on the Xong spoken in Daxing Town in Songtao County, and Yu (2011) solely on the Xong spoken in Aizhai Town (administratively part of Jishou City). Even Yang (2004), which contains what is by far the most thorough study of variation within Xong published to date, only provides information on three "representative" Xong varieties (see Section 2.5.2.3 for details). However, at least in Fenghuang County, even speakers from neighboring villages – or in some cases, even different parts of the same village – can have noticeable differences in their speech. It is unclear whether the degree of interspeaker and intervarietal variation found in Fenghuang County is unusually high compared to other areas in which Xong is spoken or whether previous scholars have simply not reported the variation that they encountered, although the author rather suspects the latter. In any case, dialectal and idiolectal variation within Fenghuang County and within the greater Xong-speaking region as a whole appears likely to be a promising topic for future research.

4 Orthographies

4.1 Introduction

The devotion of an entire chapter of a descriptive grammar to orthographic issues may seem unusual, but it is justified in Xong's case by the close connection between the existence of a practical orthography and linguistic legitimacy in mainland China; see, for instance, Zhou (2000), Bulag (2003), and Groves (2008: 14, 15, 23, 24, 26, 27). The author's own experiences in China provide further, if only anecdotal, evidence for the existence of such a connection. While performing research on Xong in China, he was informed by several Chinese laypeople on several separate occasions that Xong is not a "real" language (or rather, a real *yuyan* – see Section 2.4) because (they believed) it lacks an orthography.

It is also justified in this case by the unusually diverse set of writing systems that have been used to transcribe Xong (and perhaps other Xiangxi Miao languages) over the past several centuries. These include several distinct orthographies developed by native Xong speakers, all of which are ultimately derived from Chinese characters and are primarily logographic, as well as a more recently developed standard orthography and its regional variants, all of which are ultimately derived from the Latin alphabet by way of the Standard Mandarin *pinyin* orthography.[61,62]

Nevertheless, despite their diversity and historical significance, the author does not wish to exaggerate the importance of these orthographies in the daily lives of his Xong-speaking consultants and other members of their communities. At least within Fenghuang County (see Section 2.7), Xong is essentially an unwritten language. In the author's experience, relatively few people in Fenghuang County are aware of the existence of any of the orthographies discussed in this chapter, with the only notable exceptions being schoolteachers (who, while often aware of the standard orthography's existence, do not generally use it in the classroom) and some government

61 Another Xong writing system was developed in the 1950s by the Miao ethnologist Qigui Shi, the author of *Xiangxi Miaozu Shidi Diaocha Baogao* [*Report on a Field Survey of the Miao People of Xiangxi*] (see the introduction to Section 2.5). Unlike all the other writing systems described in this chapter, Shi's orthography was purely syllabic, with each character representing a single Xong syllable rather than a single morpheme or phoneme. The origins of the characters in Shi's orthography are unclear, as they do not appear to be either Sinitic- or Latin-derived.

Since Shi's orthography was only ever used by Shi himself, never by any other members of the larger Xong-speaking community, it is not discussed in detail in this chapter. However, the interested reader is encouraged to consult Yang (2004: 19, 20) and Yang and Luo (2008) for further information.

62 The Xong term for "Xong orthography" or "Xong script" is <ndeud-Xonb> (phonologically /ntɤ3-ɕõ1/). Depending on context, the morpheme <ndeud> could be translated as 'script, orthography', as 'writing (in general)', as 'grapheme', or as 'paper', while the morpheme <Xonb> simply means 'Miao' (see also Section 2.2.3).

officials. For the great majority of Xong speakers in Fenghuang County, the only written language used in any social setting is written Chinese.

The remainder of this chapter is divided into three sections. Section 4.2 gives an overview of the various logographic Xong orthographies that have been developed by Xong speakers themselves, all of which (as mentioned above) are ultimately derived from Chinese characters. Section 4.3 then discusses the standard Latinate Xong orthography developed by Chinese linguists in the 1950s, which was primarily intended to transcribe the Xong variety spoken in Jiwei Township. Section 4.4 details the modified version of the standard orthography which the author of this grammar uses to transcribe Xong varieties spoken within Fenghuang County. Additionally, Sections 4.3 and 4.4 both present some information on phonological differences between Jiwei and Fenghuang Xong.

4.2 Sinitic-derived orthographies

Contrary to popular belief – and even contrary to the published opinions of some Xong specialists, like Xiang (1992: 165) or Xiang (1999: 123) – native speakers of Xong had already invented several writing systems to represent their own language well before the creation of the standard Jiwei-based orthography. All such orthographies were clearly derived from the logographic Chinese writing system, and they largely follow the same general compositional principles as that system. Each Xong character generally represents a single monosyllabic morpheme (Xong's rare disyllabic morphemes are sometimes represented with single characters and sometimes with sequences of two characters), and each is composed of the same smaller orthographic "radicals" that are used in Chinese characters. These Xong orthographies are thus in many respects structurally similar to the Japanese *kanji*, Korean *hanja*, Vietnamese *chữ nôm*, and Zhuang *sawndip* orthographies, as well as to several other Sinitic-derived orthographies used to represent other languages of the Sinosphere that are less well known in the West (see, e.g., Zhou [1998: 214–264]).

The use of these orthographies seems to have never spread beyond a fairly narrow segment of the Xong-speaking population, and most sources report that they were (and, in some cases, still are) used primarily for transcribing Xong songs. None of the author's own consultants or other Xong-speaking contacts in Fenghuang County have been aware of the existence of any of these Sinitic-derived writing systems.

Each of the four sections below (4.2.1 to 4.2.4) is devoted to one of the four Sinitic-derived Xong orthographies that have been described in the literature.

4.2.1 The Sinographic orthography

The Sinographic orthography differs from the other Sinitic-derived orthographies discussed in subsequent sections in that it uses only existing Chinese characters to transcribe Xong, rather than featuring any newly created characters not used in Chinese. It may be helpful to think of this orthography less as a single, unitary writing system and more as a set of such systems, encompassing all "idio-orthographies" in which Xong speakers used only previously existing Chinese characters (though sometimes modified by diacritics, as discussed below) to transcribe their language. However, despite the very large amount of inter-user variation found in this set of writing systems (Yang and Luo 2008: 131, 134), these systems' many commonalities justify discussing them as a group here, and for convenience the author will continue to use the term "Sinographic orthography" to refer to them collectively.[63]

Historically, the use of borrowed Chinese characters to represent non-Sinitic languages was widespread throughout the Sinosphere, and unsurprisingly the identity of the first Xong speaker to use such characters to transcribe their language is unknown (Yang and Luo 2008: 130). In theory, the first use of this Sinographic orthography may well have occurred centuries or even millennia ago, and the orthography may have been independently "invented" several times. This orthography not only served as the basis for the Sinitic-derived Bantang, Laozhai, and Guzhang orthographies discussed in Sections 4.2.2 to 4.2.4 below, it is in fact still used today in certain Xong-speaking areas to transcribe Xong songs (Yang 2004: 14; Yang and Luo 2008: 131).

While the particular Sinographic characters used can vary enormously from writer to writer and from text to text, most of these characters can be divided into three classes based on the relationship between their meaning and pronunciation in Xong and their meaning and pronunciation in the local Sinitic variety. The first of these classes contains the "direct reading" (*zhídú* 直读) characters (Yang 2004: 12). These are Chinese characters whose pronunciation in the local Sinitic variety was felt by the writer to be very similar to that of particular Xong syllables, and thus they are used simply for their pronunciation. An example would be the use of the Chinese character 猛, pronounced *měng* in Standard Mandarin and meaning 'fierce' or 'violent', to represent the Xong form /moŋ^{33}/, meaning 'to go', solely because of the phonetic similarity between the Sinitic and Xong forms in question (Yang 2004: 14).[64]

The second class of characters in the Sinographic orthography contains the "side reading" (*pángdú* 旁读) characters (Yang 2004: 12, 13). These characters are also used solely for their pronunciation, not their meaning, but each one is accompanied by a diacritic to signal that its pronunciation in the local Sinitic variety only roughly

63 The term "Sinographic" is derived from the term *Hanzi Miaowen* (*Hànzì Miáowén* 汉字苗文), which literally means "Sinographic Miao script" and which is used in Yang (2004) and Yang and Luo (2008) to refer to the script (or set of scripts) in question.

64 Note that the readings of all Chinese characters in this section are given only in Standard Mandarin, since their readings in the local Sinitic variety (and even the identity of the local Sinitic variety) are generally unknown. The phonological representations of all Xong forms in this section are taken directly from Yang (2004), although Yang does not make clear which particular Xong variety is their source.

approximates that of the Xong form it is intended to represent. These diacritics could be of any shape, although small circles, triangles, and dots were especially common (Yang and Luo 2008: 131). An example would be the use of the Chinese character 告, pronounced *gào* in Standard Mandarin and meaning 'to tell', with an accompanying diacritic (e.g. 告°) to represent the Xong nominal prefix /qo^{31}/ 'NOM' (Yang 2004: 14). Since the Xong form in question begins with a uvular consonant and since such consonants are not found in any local Sinitic varieties, the writer in this case added a diacritic to signal that the Sinitic and Xong readings of the character were only roughly similar.

The third and final class of characters contains the "semantic reading" (*yìdú* 义读) characters (Yang 2004: 13). These characters bear the same diacritics as the *pangdu* characters just discussed, but here the diacritics signal that the characters are used solely for their meaning rather than their pronunciation. An example would be the use of the Chinese character 拉, pronounced *lā* in Standard Mandarin and meaning 'to pull', with an accompanying diacritic (e.g. 拉°) to represent the Xong form /ɕɯ^{44}/ 'to pull' (Yang 2004: 14). In this case the Sinitic pronunciation of the character in question is irrelevant, and the character is used only because its meaning is similar to that of the corresponding Xong form.

Obviously, from the point of view of a non-native speaker, the Sinographic orthography has several major shortcomings. Distinguishing between *pangdu* and *yidu* characters would be difficult for any reader not fluent in Xong, and the *pangdu* and even *zhidu* characters can only very roughly approximate the pronunciations of the Xong forms they represent. However, neither of these "flaws" would be a significant hindrance to the experienced Xong singers and songwriters who were (and are) the orthography's primary users (Yang 2004: 13).

Examples (4.1–4.5) below show the first five lines of a Xong wedding song transcribed using the Sinographic orthography. The full text of the song can be found in Yang (2004: 14–16). The Sinographic characters in the first lines and the phonological transcriptions in the second lines are copied directly from Yang (2004), but the glosses and free translations in the third and fourth lines have in some cases been modified for consistency and clarity.

(4.1)	贾	春	几	五°	猛	打°	鸟°
	ca^{44}	ʈhoŋ^{35}	tɕi^{44}	wu^{44}	moŋ^{33}	pɤ^{31}	nu^{11}
	PN	PN	DID	wander	go	hit	bird

'Gia Chong went everywhere hunting birds,' (Yang 2004: 14)

(4.2)	上°	单	告°	棒	太	花	山
	dʑhɯ^{35}	tɛ^{44}	qo^{31}	paŋ^{35}	thɛ^{35}	xwa^{53}	sɛ^{44}
	ascend	arrive	NOM	mountain.slope	PN	PN	mountain

'(He) climbed the slope of Taihua Mountain,' (Yang 2004: 14)

(4.3)

猛	碰°	阿	九	为°	麻	汝
moŋ^{33}	tsɯ^{31}	a^{44}	tɕɯ^{44}	ŋwei^{31}	ma^{31}	ʐu^{35}
go	meet	one	CLF	unmarried.woman	REL	good

'(He) met a beautiful girl,' (Yang 2004: 14)

(4.4)

弓	箭	拉°	成°	`几	干	甩°
koŋ^{44}	tɕɛ^{35}	ɕɯ^{44}	tɕe^{31}	tɕi^{44}	cɛ^{44}	ɛ^{44}
bow	arrow	pull	finish	NEG$_1$	dare	release

'(He) drew (his) bow but (he) couldn't release the arrow,' (Yang 2004: 14)

(4.5)

阿	个°	为°	忘°
a^{44}	le^{53}	ŋwei^{31}	noŋ^{44}
one	CLF	unmarried.woman	this

'(Ah,) this girl!' (Yang 2004: 15)

4.2.2 The Bantang orthography

This orthography was developed by the Xong singer and songwriter Bantang Shi (*Shí Băntáng* 石板塘; 1863–1928), who hailed from a village (also named Bantang) near what is now Longtan Town (*Lóngtán Zhèn* 龙潭镇) in Xiangxi Prefecture's Huayuan County (*Huāyuán Xiàn* 花垣县). Shi developed his orthography in order to transcribe Xong songs, including many that he wrote himself, and this orthography is in fact still used today by some Xong singers and songwriters in Longtan Town and the surrounding areas (Zhao and Liu 1990: 44; Yang 2004: 16).

The Bantang orthography originally contained over 1,000 unique logographic characters created by Shi (Zhao and Liu 1990: 44; Yang 2004: 16). Nearly all of these characters consisted of combinations of existing Chinese radicals, and nearly all fell into one of two of the six traditional structural classes (*liùshū* 六书) of Chinese characters. Most of the characters were "phonetic-semantic compounds" (*xíngshēngzì* 形声字), meaning they were composed of one radical used for its pronunciation and another radical used for its meaning. However, approximately one-tenth were "associative compounds" (*huìyìzì* 会意字), meaning they were composed of two (or sometimes more) radicals used solely for their meanings (Zhao and Liu 1990: 45, 46). In addition to these new characters created by Shi himself, documents written in the Bantang orthography made heavy use of the *pangdu* and *yidu* characters described in Section 4.2.1 above, and they also featured many unmodified (i.e. non–diacritic-bearing) Chinese characters which were used either for their pronunciation, their meaning, or both (Zhou 1998: 227; Yang 2004: 16).

Shi compiled all the characters used in his orthography into a dictionary, the *Miaowenzi Zhengpu* [*Authoritative Guide to the Miao Script*]. Two handwritten copies of this dictionary were produced, but neither one survives today. Zhao and Liu (1990: 44) report that one copy was borrowed by a company commander of the People's Liberation Army and then lost when that commander was later killed in battle. The other was destroyed in the Cultural Revolution. Sadly, this means that the Bantang characters still known today represent less than half of the thousand-plus characters created by Shi.

A large collection of Bantang Shi's Xong songs has been published (Zhao and Liu 1992), with each song accompanied by interlinear glosses and a free translation in Chinese. Unfortunately, the songs in the collection are transcribed using only the standard Latinate Xong orthography (see Section 4.3), and not Shi's own logographic orthography. Aside from this and the other sources cited in this section, further information on Shi's life and works can also be found in Liu (1982).

Some Xong verses transcribed in the Bantang orthography can be found in Zhao and Liu (1990: 48, 49); here, only a few example characters from the orthography will be given. Table 4.1 below presents five examples of the orthography's phonetic-semantic compounds, and Table 4.2 presents five examples of its associative compounds.[65] Note that the PRONUNCIATION column in each of the two tables gives the pronunciation of each character in the standard Jiwei Xong orthography (see Section 4.3). The MEANING/PRON. OF RADICALS column in Table 4.1 gives the meaning of each character's leftward (or upper, or outer) radical and the pronunciation of each character's rightward (or lower, or inner) radical in Standard Mandarin. Finally, the MEANING OF RADICALS column in Table 4.2 gives the meanings of each character's leftward and rightward (or upper and lower, or outer and inner) radicals.

Table 4.1: Phonetic-semantic compounds in the Bantang orthography.

CHARACTER	PRONUNCIATION	MEANING	COMPONENT RADICALS	MEANING/PRON. OF RADICALS	SOURCE
[illegible]	*nbeat*	'pig'	犭 + 罢	'dog' + *bà*	Zhao and Liu (1990: 45)
[illegible]	*ub*	'water'	氵 + 务	'water' + *wù*	Zhao and Liu (1990: 49)
[illegible]	*end*	'to look'	目 + 因	'eye' + *yīn*	Zhao and Liu (1990: 49)
[illegible]	*nongs*	'rain'	雨 + 奴	'rain' + *nú*	Zhao and Liu (1990: 45)
[illegible]	*sead*	'Xong song'	口 + 杀	'mouth' + *shā*	Zhao and Liu (1990: 49)

65 The author here wishes to thank his wife, Mrs. Xueqing Zhao, for (among so many other things) writing out the Xong characters in Tables 4.1 through 4.5 by hand.

Table 4.2: Associative compounds in the Bantang orthography.

CHARACTER	PRONUNCIATION	MEANING	COMPONENT RADICALS	MEANING OF RADICALS	SOURCE
⿰色白	*ghueub*	'white'	色 + 白	'color' + 'white'	Yang (2004: 17)
⿵门出	*blongl*	'to exit'	门 + 出	'door' + 'to exit'	Yang (2004: 17)
⿱合⿰目目	*ndeut ngheub* (disyllabic)	'to nap'	合 + 目 + 目	'to close' + 'eye' + 'eye'	Yang (2004: 17)
⿱流下	*neul*	'to flow'	流 + 下	'to flow' + 'to descend'	Yang (2004: 17)
⿱知面	*njot*	'to recognize'	知 + 面	'to know' + 'face'	Zhao and Liu (1990: 45)

4.2.3 The Laozhai orthography

The Laozhai orthography was created in the early 1950s, just a few years before the development of the standard Latinate Xong orthography (see Section 4.3). The creator, Chengjian Shi (*Shí Chéngjiàn* 石成鉴), was a native of Laozhai Village (*Lǎozhài Cūn* 老寨村), a subsidiary village of Malichang Town (*Málìchǎng Zhèn* 麻栗场镇) in Xiangxi Prefecture's Huayuan County. He was also the founder of a popular Xong musical troupe, and he originally developed his orthography to transcribe Xong songs (Zhao and Liu 1990: 44). The Laozhai orthography is reportedly still being used today for that very purpose by the current members of the troupe that Shi originally founded (Yang and Luo 2008: 131).

The general structural principles of the Laozhai orthography are quite similar to those of the Bantang orthography described in Section 4.2.2 above, although there is little or no overlap between the Xong-specific characters (as opposed to unmodified Chinese characters) used in each orthography. Only about 100 unique Laozhai characters have been attested, most of which are either phonetic-semantic compounds (composed of one radical signaling pronunciation and another signaling meaning) or associative compounds (composed of two or sometimes more radicals that signal only meaning). However, the ratio of phonetic-semantic compounds to associative compounds is somewhat lower in the Laozhai orthography than in the Bantang orthography, with only about three-fourths of the Laozhai characters being phonetic-semantic compounds (Zhao and Liu 1990: 44–46). Just as with the Bantang orthography (as well as with the Guzhang orthography discussed in Section 4.2.4 below),

Xong texts containing Laozhai characters also feature large numbers of unmodified Chinese characters, although it is unclear whether they also feature any examples of the diacritic-bearing *pangdu* or *yidu* characters described in Section 4.2.1 (Zhao and Liu 1990: 47; Yang and Luo 2008: 134).

The author does not have access to any complete texts (or even fragments of texts) written in the Laozhai orthography, but some of the orthography's phonetic-semantic and associative compounds are presented in Tables 4.3 and 4.4 below. The structure of these tables follows the same general pattern as that of Tables 4.1 and 4.2 in Section 4.2.2 above. Note, though, that the author was only able to find two clear examples of Laozhai phonetic-semantic compounds in the sources available to him.

Table 4.3: Phonetic-semantic compounds in the Laozhai orthography.

CHARACTER	PRONUNCIATION	MEANING	COMPONENT RADICALS	MEANING/PRON. OF RADICALS	SOURCE
	nbeat	'pig'	犭 + 八	'dog' + *bā*	Zhao and Liu (1990: 45)
	hliet	'cooked rice'	列 + 米	*liè* + 'rice'	Zhao and Liu (1990: 45)

Table 4.4: Associative compounds in the Laozhai orthography.

CHARACTER	PRONUNCIATION	MEANING	COMPONENT RADICALS	MEANING OF RADICALS	SOURCE
	nenl	'mouse, rat'	尖 + 口	'pointed' + 'mouth'	Zhao and Liu (1990: 46)
	hnangd	'to hear'	耳 + 口	'ear' + 'mouth'	Yang and Luo (2008: 132, 134)
	ad	'one'	扌 + 一	'hand' + 'one'	Yang (2004: 18)
	oub	'two'	扌 + 二	'hand' + 'two'	Yang (2004: 18)
	bub	'three'	扌 + 三	'hand' + 'three'	Yang (2004: 18)

4.2.4 The Guzhang orthography

Rather less is known about this orthography than about those discussed in the previous two sections. The only extant source in which examples of this orthography have been found is the *Guzhangping Ting Zhi* [*Gazetteer of Guzhangping Sub-Prefecture*], a late Qing era (1644–1912 C.E.) overview of what is now Guzhang County (*Gǔzhàng Xiàn* 古丈县) in Xiangxi Prefecture. This volume was compiled by Hongqin Dong (*Dǒng Hóngqín* 董鸿勤) in 1907, although Dong seems to have copied the Xong characters contained within it from some other, unknown source (Zhao and Liu 1990: 45; Yang 2004: 18; Yang and Luo 2008: 130). Unlike all the other Sinitic-derived Xong orthographies discussed in this chapter, the Guzhang orthography is no longer in use today. However, Zhao and Liu (1990: 44) reported that some elderly Xong speakers in Guzhang County had memories of a Sinitic-derived Xong orthography once being used in the area, so the orthography may still have been in use well into the first half of the twentieth century.

The structural principles of the Guzhang orthography are very similar to those of the Bantang and Laozhai orthographies described in Sections 4.2.2 and 4.2.3 above, although again there is little or no overlap among the Xong-specific characters used in the three orthographies. Approximately 100 unique Guzhang characters are found in the *Guzhangping Ting Zhi* (Zhao and Liu 1990: 44). Unlike those of the Bantang and Laozhai orthographies, nearly all of these Guzhang characters appear to be phonetic-semantic compounds rather than associative compounds. Yang and Luo (2008: 134) report that unmodified Chinese characters were used in Xong documents written in the Guzhang orthography just as heavily as they were in documents written in the Bantang and Laozhai orthographies, although it is not clear whether these documents also contained any *pangdu* or *yidu* characters (see Section 4.2.1).

Examples of some of the Guzhang orthography's phonetic-semantic compounds are given in Table 4.5 below. The structure of this table follows the same general pattern as that of Table 4.1 in Section 4.2.2. The reader should note, however, that the Guzhang Xong forms listed in the PRONUNCIATION column of Table 4.5 (all of which are taken from Yang and Luo [2008: 131]) are given in a modified version of IPA rather than in the standard Jiwei-based Xong orthography.

Table 4.5: Phonetic-semantic compounds in the Guzhang orthography.

CHARACTER	PRONUNCIATION	MEANING	COMPONENT RADICALS	MEANING/PRON. OF RADICALS	SOURCE
豝	/ba^{35}/	'pig'	豕 + 巴	'pig' + *bā*	Zhao and Liu (1990: 45)
氵五	/u^{54}/	'water'	氵 + 五	'water' + *wǔ*	Yang and Luo (2008: 131, 134)
雨送	/soŋ^{54}/	'thunder'	雨 + 送	'rain' + *sòng*	Yang (2004: 19)

Table 4.5 (continued)

CHARACTER	PRONUNCIATION	MEANING	COMPONENT RADICALS	MEANING/PRON. OF RADICALS	SOURCE
⿱雨戎	/ʑoŋ^{21}/	'dragon'	雨 + 戎	'rain' + *róng*	Yang and Luo (2008: 131, 134)
⿰足床	/ɖaŋ^{44}/	'to return'	足 + 床	'foot' + *chuáng*	Yang and Luo (2008: 131, 134)

4.3 The standard Jiwei-based Xong orthography

4.3.1 Historical background and current use

In 1956, a committee of Chinese linguists met in the city of Guiyang in Guizhou Province to develop practical orthographies for the four major Miao *fangyan* recognized at the time, one of which was Xiangxi Miao (Xiang 1992: 165; see also Section 2.4 of this grammar). Each of these four Miao orthographies was designed to represent a single "standard" variety of the *fangyan* in question. For Xiangxi Miao, the Xong variety spoken in Jiwei Township (*Jíwèi Xiāng* 吉卫乡) in Xiangxi Prefecture's Huayuan County (*Huāyuán Xiàn* 花垣县) was chosen as the standard, and thus the phonological distinctions represented in the orthography reflect those of Jiwei Xong. Like most new orthographies developed in China after the founding of the PRC in 1949 (including all Miao orthographies), this new Xong orthography was an alphabetic, Latinate writing system based primarily on Standard Mandarin *pinyin*.

From 1957 to 1959, the prefectural government of Xiangxi promoted the new orthography via a large-scale Xong literacy program. This program was directed mainly at illiterate adult speakers of Xong rather than school-age children. Official government figures claim that during this period over 120,000 speakers of Xong attended literacy classes, though they do not state what percentage of these were actually successful in achieving literacy. In addition, over a thousand teachers from Xiangxi Prefecture were taught the orthography themselves and received training in how to teach it to others. A "Miao Orthographic Oversight Committee" that reported to the prefectural government was set up in 1958, and it was ordered to begin work on translation and printing of Xong language materials (Yang 2004: 26, 27).

Unfortunately, the central government sharply reversed its position on minority language education in 1958, and in 1959 there was a complete cessation of all officially supported Xong literacy programs in Xiangxi (Zhou 2000: 132; Yang 2004: 27). The Cultural Revolution made educational programs of any sort very difficult for much of the 1960s and 1970s. A new Xong literacy program was initiated in 1983, although the focus of this program was still on adult monolingual literacy in Xong rather than on bilingual education for children. This program was on a much smaller scale than the one conducted in the 1950s. Yang (2004: 27, 28) reports that slightly over 4,000 speakers of Xong attended these literacy classes, 62% of whom received a passing grade.

The year 1985 finally saw the beginning of official efforts to promote bilingual Xong–Chinese education for Xong-speaking children attending primary school in Xiangxi Prefecture. In that year, 24 primary schools in Xiangxi's Huayuan and Fenghuang Counties began either Xong literacy classes or combined Xong–Chinese literacy classes (Yang 2004: 28). These programs differed from those of the 1950s in that they never had literacy in the standard Xong orthography as their ultimate goal. Instead, they were intended to use the Xong orthography as a stepping-stone to eventual literacy in Chinese. The standard Xong orthography continued to be taught in scattered primary schools throughout Xiangxi Prefecture in the 1990s and 2000s, though in recent years it has only very rarely been taught in any of the primary schools in Fenghuang County.

Overall, the standard Xong orthography does not appear to be nearly as widely used as certain other practical orthographies developed for other Miao-Yao languages, including Hmong's Romanized Popular Alphabet or the standard Qiandong Miao orthography used in Guizhou. Publications on Xong by Chinese linguists almost always use modified versions of IPA to transcribe Xong material. This is true even of those publications that describe the Jiwei Xong variety upon which the standard orthography is based. There have, however, been a number of Xong text collections produced using the standard orthography, or at least using minor variants thereof. Those that the author has been able to find include a large (nearly 400 pages in length) compendium of Xong songs and folktales (published anonymously in 1985), a collection of wedding songs (Zhang and Peng 1987), a collection of myths (Long and Long 1990), and a two-volume collection of courting songs (Long 2006a and 2006b). Yang (2004: 29) also reports that several technical and agricultural guides were published in the Xong orthography during the 1980s, as were a five-volume series of bilingual Xong–Chinese textbooks and several dozen issues of a local newspaper, although the author has not been able to find copies of these publications himself.

Finally, while it is not clear how popular the orthography currently is among Xong speakers in Jiwei Township itself and the surrounding regions, it appears to be largely unknown in Fenghuang County, and furthermore it is not especially popular among the few in Fenghuang who are aware of it (see also Section 2.7.2). Although there are a number of phonological distinctions in Fenghuang Xong which cannot be represented in the standard orthography (see Section 4.4.2), for the most part it does not appear that the orthography's unpopularity in Fenghuang County is due to any mismatch with Fenghuang Xong phonology. Rather, it appears to be primarily due to the fact that Xong literacy in any form is seen by many Xong speakers as essentially useless.

4.3.2 The orthography and its design principles

The standard Xong orthography uses the same basic organizing principles as most of the other standard (i.e. government-backed) orthographies developed for Miao languages in China since the founding of the PRC. Only letters from the English alphabet are used. In the case of the Xong orthography in particular, all such letters but <v> are used. Each orthographic syllable is composed of an optional initial consonant portion, an obligatory vowel portion (which may itself include an optional nasalization portion <n> or <ng>), and an obligatory final tone letter. Examples include <gangs> 'to give' (phonologically /kɑ̃6/), <npleut> 'to shout' (/^{n}pɹɤ5/), and <ngongx> 'silver' (/ŋõ2/) (Xiang 1999: 130).[66] As is shown in Tables 4.6 through 4.8 further below, digraphs, trigraphs, and even some tetragraphs are necessary to represent the many consonant and vowel phonemes of Jiwei Xong without using more than twenty-five letters.

In most texts written in the standard orthography, each syllable is separated from the preceding and following syllables by spaces, even in the case of relatively intimate grammatical constituents like nominal prefixes and their following noun roots (see Section 5.4) or the component syllables of ideophones (Section 11.1). Punctuation is used much the same as in English; at the very least, the author has not encountered any punctuation-related differences worth commenting on.

Tables 4.6 to 4.9 below present all orthographic units used in the Jiwei Xong orthography as well as their corresponding phonemic representation in a modified version of IPA.[67] Just as in Tables 3.1 to 3.4 in the previous chapter, the phonemic representation of each sound is given on the left and the corresponding orthographic representation is given in italics on the right. In Tables 4.6 and 4.7, manners of articulation are listed across the top of each table and places of articulation (including secondary articulations like labialization and palatalization) are given along the left side. Solely for convenience, prenasalization and aspiration are represented with superscript symbols in the phonemic transcription of each sound, while labialization, palatalization, rhotacization, and the fricative portions of affricate consonants are represented with ordinary (i.e. non-superscript) symbols.

---

66 In this chapter, just as in Chapter 3, transcriptions of Xong material given in a practical orthography (either the standard Xong orthography or the author's own) will be enclosed within angle brackets < >, while transcriptions given in more phonetic transcription systems (e.g. IPA) will be enclosed within slashes / /. In subsequent chapters, transcriptions of any Xong material given in a practical orthography will simply be italicized.

67 Phonological descriptions of Jiwei Xong often vary slightly from author to author; compare, for instance, the one in Wang (1985: 7–12), the one in Xiang (1999: 7–15), the one in Yang (2004: 80, 81), and the one inside the back cover of Shi (1997). The phonological system implied in this section represents an "average" of these four sources rather than a strict copy of any particular one of them.

Comments following each table will discuss some of the basic design principles of the orthography, especially those that may not be immediately intuitive to readers unfamiliar with Standard Mandarin *pinyin*.

Table 4.6: Plosive consonants in the standard Xong orthography.

	UNASPIRATED, NON-PRENASALIZED		ASPIRATED, NON-PRENASALIZED		UNASPIRATED, PRENASALIZED		ASPIRATED, PRENASALIZED	
PLAIN BILABIAL	p	*b*	p^{h}	*p*	^{n}p	*nb*	^{n}p^{h}	*np*
PALATALIZED BILABIAL	pj	*bi*	pj^{h}	*pi*	^{n}pj	*nbi*		
RHOTACIZED BILABIAL	pɹ	*bl*	pɹ^{h}	*pl*	^{n}pɹ	*nbl*	^{n}pɹ^{h}	*npl*
PLAIN ALVEOLAR	t	*d*	t^{h}	*t*	^{n}t	*nd*	^{n}t^{h}	*nt*
ALVEOLAR AFFRICATE	ts	*z*	ts^{h}	*c*	^{n}ts	*nz*	^{n}ts^{h}	*nc*
ALVEOLO-PALATAL	tɕ	*j*	tɕ^{h}	*q*	^{n}tɕ	*nj*	^{n}tɕ^{h}	*nq*
RETROFLEX	ʈ	*zh*	ʈ^{h}	*ch*	^{n}ʈ	*nzh*	^{n}ʈ^{h}	*nch*
PALATAL	c	*gi*	c^{h}	*ki*	^{n}c	*ngi*	^{n}c^{h}	*nki*
PLAIN VELAR	k	*g*	k^{h}	*k*	^{n}k	*ngg*	^{n}k^{h}	*nk*
LABIALIZED VELAR	kw	*gu*	kw^{h}	*ku*	^{n}kw	*nggu*	^{n}kw^{h}	*nku*
PLAIN UVULAR	q	*gh*	q^{h}	*kh*	^{n}q	*ngh*	^{n}q^{h}	*nkh*
LABIALIZED UVULAR	qw	*ghu*	qw^{h}	*khu*	^{n}qw	*nghu*	^{n}qw^{h}	*nkhu*

Most of the orthographic design choices evident in Table 4.6 above are straightforward, but there are a few that merit some comment. As the table shows, the standard Xong orthography uses initial <n> to represent prenasalization at all places of articulation, and it uses medial <u> and <i> to represent labialization and palatalization (rather than, e.g., <w> and <j>).[68] The symbols <u> and <i> are also used to represent the vowels /u/ and /i/, but this never results in confusion since labialized and

68 Every publication on Xong phonology with which the author is familiar includes a series of palatal stops /c, c^{h}, ^{n}c, ^{n}c^{h}/. These stops are analyzed as palatalized velar ones in this grammar (see Section 3.2.1.10).

non-labialized consonants are not contrastive before /u/, and palatalized and non-palatalized consonants are not contrastive before /i/.

The phonemes /^{n}k/ and /^{n}kw/ are represented by <ngg> and <nggu> rather than (as one might expect) <ng> and <ngu>, since the latter two orthographic representations are used for the nasals /ŋ/ and /ŋw/ instead (see Table 4.7 below). Uvular consonants are represented by adding a following <h> to the orthographic representation of the corresponding velar consonant.

Perhaps the least intuitive aspects of Table 4.6 for most readers are the use of <z>, <c>, <nz>, and <nc> to represent the alveolar affricates, the use of <j>, <q>, <nj>, and <nq> to represent the alveolo-palatal affricates, and the use of <zh>, <ch>, <nzh>, and <nch> to represent the retroflex plosives (these last correspond to the apical–post-alveolar affricates of Fenghuang Xong; see Section 3.2.1.8). However, all of these are derived quite straightforwardly from the *pinyin* system used for Standard Mandarin, in which <z> and <c> represent alveolar affricates, <j> and <q> represent alveolo-palatal affricates, and <zh> and <ch> represent apical–post-alveolar affricates.

Table 4.7: Non-plosive consonants in the standard Xong orthography.

	UNASPIRATED NASAL		ASPIRATED NASAL		UNASPIRATED LATERAL		ASPIRATED LATERAL		VOICELESS FRICATIVE		OTHER VOICED	
PLAIN BILABIAL	m	*m*	m^h	*hm*							β	*w*
PALATALIZED BILABIAL	mj	*mi*										
RHOTACIZED BILABIAL	mɹ	*ml*										
LABIODENTAL									f	*f*		
PLAIN ALVEOLAR	n	*n*	n^h	*hn*	l	*l*	l^h	*hl*				
PALATALIZED ALVEOLAR					lj	*li*	lj^h	*hli*				
ALVEOLAR SIBILANT									s	*s*		
ALVEOLO-PALATAL	ȵ	*ni*							ɕ	*x*	ʑ	*y*
RETROFLEX	ɳ	*nh*							ʂ	*sh*	ʐ	*r*
PLAIN VELAR	ŋ	*ng*										

Table 4.7 (continued)

	UNASPIRATED NASAL	ASPIRATED NASAL	UNASPIRATED LATERAL	ASPIRATED LATERAL	VOICELESS FRICATIVE	OTHER VOICED
LABIALIZED VELAR	ŋw *ngu*					
GLOTTAL					h *h*	
LABIALIZED GLOTTAL					hw *hu*	

As Table 4.7 shows, "aspirated" nasals and laterals (see Sections 3.2.2.2 and 3.2.3 for discussion of the actual phonetic realization of these consonants) are represented with an initial <h> preceding the orthographic representation of the corresponding unaspirated consonant: /m^{h}/ <hm>, /l^{h}/ <hl>, etc. The reasoning behind the orthographic representations of the alveolo-palatal and retroflex consonants in Table 4.7 may not be immediately obvious, but in most cases they are straightforwardly derived from Standard Mandarin *pinyin*.

Table 4.8 gives the oral monophthongal vowels of Jiwei Xong along with their orthographic representations in the standard orthography. Note that the mid-low front vowel /ɛ/ is represented with <an> despite the fact that it is non-nasalized in the Jiwei variety of Xong. As Xiang (1999: 127) explains, the corresponding vowel in most varieties of Xong *is* nasalized, and so <an> was chosen to represent the vowel in question.

Table 4.8: Oral monophthongs in the standard Xong orthography.

	FRONT (UNROUNDED)		CENTRAL (UNROUNDED)		BACK UNROUNDED		BACK ROUNDED	
HIGH	i	*i*			ɯ	*ou*	u	*u*
MID	e	*e*			ɤ	*eu*	o	*o*
MID-LOW	ɛ	*an*					ɔ	*ao*
LOW			a	*ea*	ɑ	*a*		

In addition to the oral monophthongs presented in Table 4.8, Jiwei Xong also has four nasal monophthongs /ĩ/ <in>, /ẽ/ <en>, /ɑ̃/ <ang>, and /õ/ <ong>, as well as a single (oral) diphthong /ei/ <ei>. The standard Xong orthography thus represents nasal front vowels by appending <n> to the orthographic representation of the corresponding oral vowel (/i/ <i>, /e/ <e> vs. /ĩ/ <in>, /ẽ/ <en>), but it represents nasal back vowels by appending <ng> instead (/ɑ/ <a>, /o/ <o> vs. /ɑ̃/ <ang>, /õ/ <ong>).

Table 4.9 presents the six tones of Jiwei Xong and the tone letters used to represent them in the standard orthography.[69] Each orthographic Xong syllable has one of these six tone letters appended to it. The numbers in the HISTORICAL TONE CATEGORY column show which of the eight historical Miao-Yao tones each modern Jiwei Xong tone corresponds to; see Section 3.5.2.1 for more information. The PHONETIC VALUE column gives the typical pitch contour of each tone, with the numerals <5> and <1> representing pitches near the high and low ends (respectively) of a speaker's pitch range. These values often vary slightly from author to author; the ones given in Table 4.9 are taken from Xiang (1999), as are all example syllables in the table.

Table 4.9: Tones in the standard Xong orthography.

HISTORICAL TONE CATEGORY	TONE LETTER	PHONETIC VALUE	EXAMPLE SYLLABLE (ORTHOGRAPHY)	EXAMPLE SYLLABLE (MODIFIED IPA)	EXAMPLE SYLLABLE (GLOSS)
1	<b>	[35]	*bib*	/pi1/	'hair'
2	<x>	[31]	*bix*	/pi2/	'to repay'
3/7 (merged)	<d>	[44]	*bid*	/pi3/	'fruit'
4/8 (merged)	<l>	[33]	*bil*	/pi4/	'pen, pencil'
5	<t>	[53]	*bit*	/pi5/	'to compare'
6	<s>	[42]	*bis*	/pi6/	'to shave one's head'

Some tone sandhi does occur in Jiwei Xong (Xiang 1999: 14, 15), but this sandhi is never represented in the standard orthography. In other words, the tone letter of each orthographic Xong syllable always represents the syllable's underlying tone, never its surface sandhi tone. No toneless syllables (see Sections 3.6 and 4.4.2 of this grammar) have been reported in Jiwei Xong, and thus there are no provisions for representing such syllables in the standard orthography.

69 These same tone letters are used in several different alphabetic, Latinate practical orthographies developed for Miao languages in China after the founding of the PRC (see also Section 4.4.2 below). In all of these orthographies, tone letter <b> is regularly used for a reflex of historical tone 1, <x> for historical tone 2, <d> for historical tone 3, <l> for historical tone 4, <t> for historical tone 5, <s> for historical tone 6, <k> for historical tone 7, and <f> for historical tone 8. However, even after discussing the issue with several Miao-Yao specialists, the author has still not been able to determine why these particular, apparently random letters were originally chosen to represent modern reflexes of the eight historical tones of Miao-Yao.

4.3.3 A sample text in the orthography

A short text transcribed in the Jiwei Xong orthography is provided below.[70] The text is taken from Xiang (1992: 167), and the free English translation given below the text is based on the free Chinese translation found in that source. Since Xiang (1992) does not provide interlinear glosses, none are given here. The text describes an episode in the life of Feng Lei (*Léi Fēng* 雷锋; 1940–1962), a young soldier in the People's Liberation Army who was held up by Chairman Mao as an example of a model citizen, soldier, and Chinese Communist Party member.

Guat Gioux
Leil Fongd xub deb ghob ngangx, hneb hneb mongl ngoub ndeud, deit lies nhaob guat ad doul gioux. Mex ad hneb dax zheax nongs, Leil Fongd nhangs dab leb bit wul ghad xub nangd tongl xol mongl ngoub ndeud. Jid mix nhaob dand deut gioux, zead ub jid piaob guat gioux jul. Leil Fongd pud: "Lol! Wel bul manx guat gioux." Leil Fongd geud jid mix ad leb ad leb nangd bul guat gioux mongl. Fangb xol nzhangd lol, Leil Fongd yeab geud jid mix ad leb ad leb nangd bul guat gioux lol.

Crossing the Bridge
When Feng Lei was a child, every day he had to cross a bridge to get to school. One day it was raining very heavily, and Feng Lei was on his way to school with several of his younger classmates. They got to the bridge and saw that the river waters had risen to cover it. Feng Lei said: "Come on! I'll carry you across." He carried them across the bridge one by one. After school, on their way home, Feng Lei again carried them across the bridge one by one.

4.4 An orthography for Fenghuang Xong

4.4.1 Overview

The orthography used in this grammar is largely based on the standard *pinyin*-derived Xong orthography that was developed to represent Jiwei Xong (see Section 4.3 above). Each orthographic syllable in the author's orthography is composed of an optional initial consonant portion, an obligatory vowel (or, occasionally, syllabic nasal) portion, and an obligatory final tone letter.[71] Just as in the standard orthography, the vowel portion of a syllable in the author's orthography may itself include an optional nasalization portion. Examples of syllables in the author's orthography

70 Because examples of the author's practical orthography for Fenghuang Xong can be found throughout this grammar (see in particular Texts 1 and 2), no equivalent sample text for that orthography is given in Section 4.4.
71 Note that Xong forms and utterances transcribed in this grammar generally do not indicate tone sandhi, although exceptions to this do occur in the description of tone sandhi itself in Section 3.5.2.2.

include <bioud> ‘home, family’ (phonologically /pjɛɰ3/), <ndanb> ‘to jump’ (/^{n}tã1/), and <eint> ‘to fly’ (/ɤ̃j5/).

The orthographic units used to transcribe segmental phonemes in the author’s practical orthography are presented in Tables 3.1 to 3.4 and the accompanying comments in Section 3.1. While these tables specifically focus on Yankan Xong, the high degree of phonological similarity across most of the Xong varieties spoken in Fenghuang County means that the orthographic units in Tables 3.1 to 3.4 can in fact be used to represent all phonemic segmental distinctions in all varieties of Fenghuang Xong known to the author. The orthographic units used to transcribe tones in the author’s orthography are presented in Table 3.5 in Section 3.5.2.1 (for Yankan Xong), Table 3.6 in Section 3.5.3.1 (for Shanjiang Xong), and Table 3.7 in Section 3.5.3.2 (for Zhuigaolai Xong), along with the accompanying comments in each of these sections. While the phonetic details provided in these latter three tables often vary depending on the variety in question, the orthographic units presented in them are identical.

However, the significant phonological differences between Fenghuang Xong and Jiwei Xong mean that there are necessarily some major differences between the standard Xong orthography and the one used in this grammar. Among the most obvious phonological differences are an additional two tones in Fenghuang Xong, the presence of certain consonants in Fenghuang Xong that are not found in Jiwei Xong (e.g. palatalized alveolar stops) and vice versa (e.g. rhotacized bilabial consonants), and fairly divergent vowel systems. There are also certain aspects of the standard orthography which seem difficult to justify on purely linguistic grounds, and these too have been changed. The most notable of these is the use of <n> to mark nasalization on some vowels and <ng> to mark nasalization on others, which is avoided in the orthography used here. These and many other differences between the two orthographies are discussed in detail in Section 4.4.2 below.

Still, the reader may question the author’s choice to use a practical orthography at all, rather than simply using IPA. There were two primary motivations behind the decision. The first of these is simple convenience. Although it successfully represents all phonemic distinctions made in Fenghuang Xong, the practical orthography used in this grammar makes use of only 25 letters of the English alphabet (no <v>) and no diacritics or superscript symbols. In the author’s experience, this makes it much faster to type and much less susceptible to transcription errors than IPA. The second reason for choosing to use a practical orthography is that in mainland China there is a close association between linguistic legitimacy and the existence of such an orthography, as was discussed in Section 4.1 above.

Furthermore, there is some precedent for using variants of the standard Jiwei-based orthography to transcribe other varieties of Xong. For instance, Luo (2005: 4–7) presents a variant of the standard orthography for use in transcribing Songtao Xong, and Yang et al. (2004: 8, 9) discuss some of the issues involved in adapting the standard orthography to represent the Xong variety spoken in Xiaomaopoying Village (*Xiǎomáopōyíng Cūn* 小茅坡营村), located in Hubei Province.[72]

The orthography used in this grammar was developed primarily for use in academic contexts such as field transcriptions and linguistic publications, although in theory its lack of unusual symbols and its many similarities to Standard Mandarin *pinyin* should make it well suited for use as a "real" practical orthography by Xong speakers themselves (this is true of the standard Xong orthography as well, for that matter). However, most of the author's consultants and other Xong-speaking contacts in Fenghuang County have shown little interest when presented with documents printed in the standard Xong orthography or with notes taken in the author's own orthography. The author has no reason to expect that his own or any other practical orthography will be widely adopted by Fenghuang Xong speakers at any point in the near future.

4.4.2 Differences between the Jiwei and Fenghuang Xong orthographies

Each difference between the standard Xong orthography and the practical orthography used in this grammar is listed below, along with the author's justification for the change in question.

1. Jiwei Xong has a series of rhotacized bilabial consonants /pɹ, pɹ^h, ^{n}pɹ, ^{n}pɹ^h, mɹ/, which are represented in the standard orthography with <bl, pl, nbl, npl, ml>. In all varieties of Fenghuang Xong known to the author, the rhotacized and palatalized bilabial consonants have merged into a single palatalized series (see Sections 3.2.1.3 and 3.2.2.1), and so <bl, pl, nbl, npl, ml> are not used in the author's orthography.

2. All varieties of Fenghuang Xong known to the author have a series of palatalized alveolar stops /tj, tj^h, ^{n}tj, ^{n}tj^h/ that are not found in Jiwei Xong (the cognates of syllables that begin with palatalized alveolar stops in Fenghuang Xong generally begin with alveolo-palatal affricates in Jiwei Xong). The author uses <di, ti, ndi, nti> to represent these stops via analogy with the orthographic units used to represent the palatalized bilabial and palatalized velar stops.

72 More precisely, Xiaomaopoying Village is located in Gaoluo Township (*Gāoluó Xiāng* 高罗乡), Xuan'en County (*Xuān'ēn Xiàn* 宣恩县), in the Enshi Tujia and Miao Autonomous Prefecture (*Ēnshī Tǔjiāzú Miáozú Zìzhìzhōu* 恩施土家族苗族自治州) in southwestern Hubei Province. Xiaomaopoying Xong had slightly over 300 speakers as of 2004 (Yang et al. 2004: 5), and it is notable for being the only known Xong variety spoken in Hubei Province, and thus the northernmost Xong variety spoken in China. However, it is not necessarily a last northerly holdout from an era in which Xong had a wider geographic distribution, since residents of Xiaomaopoying report that their ancestors fled northward to Hubei from Xiangxi's Huayuan County (in western Hunan Province) in the mid eighteenth century after one of the period's major Miao rebellions there ended in defeat (Yang et al. 2004: 5). For further information on Xiaomaopoying Xong, see also Zhao (2005).

3. Jiwei Xong makes a distinction between the labialized velar stops /kw, kw^h, ^{n}kw, ^{n}kw^h/ (represented with <gu, ku, nggu, nku> in the standard orthography) and the labialized uvular stops /qw, qw^h, ^{n}qw, ^{n}qw^h/ (represented with <ghu, khu, nghu, nkhu>). Since these two series have merged into a single series of labialized uvular stops in all varieties of Fenghuang Xong with which the author is familiar (see Section 3.2.1.12), only a single orthographic series is necessary to represent them. While in articulatory terms the stops in question are indeed more uvular than velar, the orthographic units <gu, ku, nggu, nku> (used for the labialized velar stops in the standard orthography) are used in this grammar for simplicity's sake.

4. Jiwei Xong distinguishes the vowels /e/ (represented with <e> in the standard orthography) and /ɛ/ (represented with <an> in the standard orthography, despite the fact that the vowel in question is not nasalized; see Section 4.3.2), while Fenghuang Xong has only a single mid front vowel /ɛ/. That vowel /ɛ/ is thus simply represented with <e> in the author's orthography.

5. Jiwei Xong distinguishes the vowels /a/, /ɑ/, and /ɔ/, represented in the standard orthography with <ea>, <a>, and <ao>. Fenghuang Xong lacks /ɔ/, instead distinguishing only /a/ and /ɑ/. In the author's orthography, the symbol <a> was chosen to represent /a/, since using the symbol <a> to represent the phoneme /a/ should be relatively intuitive for those readers who are already familiar with IPA. The digraph <ao> is then used to represent /ɑ/, while <ea> is not used at all.

6. The vowel /ɯ/ in Jiwei Xong corresponds to the vowel /ɛɰ/ in Fenghuang Xong. The author thus uses the digraph <ou> to represent /ɛɰ/ in his orthography, as the same digraph is used to represent /ɯ/ in the standard orthography.

7. Jiwei Xong features the vowels /ei/ and /ẽ/, represented with <ei> and <en> in the standard orthography. Fenghuang Xong lacks both of these vowels, but it does feature four additional vowels not found in Jiwei Xong: /ã/, /ɤj/, /ɤ̃j/, and /aw/. These four have been represented with <an>, <ei>, <ein>, and <au> in the author's practical orthography.[73] Note that <au> is distinct from <ao>, with the latter digraph being used to represent /ɑ/ in the author's orthography.

8. In the standard orthography, certain nasal vowels are represented by appending <n> to the orthographic representation of the corresponding oral vowel (e.g. <in> for /ĩ/), while other nasal vowels are represented by appending <ng> (e.g. <ong> for /õ/). For consistency's sake, in the author's orthography all nasal vowels are represented by appending <n> to the orthographic representation of the corresponding oral vowel.

---

73 The vowels /ɤj/ and /ɤ̃j/ were represented orthographically with <ai> and <ain> in Sposato (2012), but they are represented with <ei> and <ein> in this grammar to better reflect the phonetic height of the sounds in question.

9. In the author's orthography, orthographic syllables of the form <mX> are used to represent syllables featuring a syllabic bilabial nasal (see Section 3.3.4), with <X> being any tone letter. Examples include <mb> 'to hurt (intrans.), to be sick; illness' (phonologically /m̩1/) and <ms> 'kiwifruit' (phonologically /m̩6/). This convention is not used in the standard orthography, as no syllabic nasals are reported to occur in Jiwei Xong. (Note that orthographic <nh> is also used in the author's orthography to represent a Xong interjection glossed as 'uh-huh'. See Section 11.3.1 for details on the phonetic realization of this form.)

10. Since most varieties of Fenghuang Xong have eight contrastive syllable-level tones while Jiwei Xong has only six, two additional syllable-final tone letters <k> and <f> are used to represent tones 7 and 8 in the author's orthography.[74] These particular letters were chosen via analogy with the practical orthographies developed for other Miao languages in China with eight or more tones, in which syllable-final <k> and <f> are typically used to represent the modern reflexes of historical tones 7 and 8 (respectively). For example, this is the case in the practical orthographies developed for Hmu, Hmong, and Ahmao (Wang 1985: 157), as well as in the one developed for Mashan Miao (Wu and Yang 2010: 62).

It is important to note, though, that the eighth tone of modern Fenghuang Xong – i.e. the one represented with <f> in the author's practical orthography – does *not* represent a reflex of Miao-Yao's historical tone 8, which fully merged with historical tone 4 in all Fenghuang Xong varieties known to the author. Instead, this modern tone 8 appears to be the result of a relatively recent split in tone 2, with the new tone 8 subsequently drawing in several syllables that historically carried tone 1. See Section 3.5.2.1 for more details.

11. Toneless syllables in Fenghuang Xong (see Section 3.6) are indicated with syllable-final <h> in the author's orthography (e.g. <ih> 'EMPH', <lah> 'PRF'). No such syllables are reported in Jiwei Xong, and so there is no provision for representing them in the standard orthography.

74 A ninth tone (phonetically high, level, and modal, and represented with a tone letter <c> in this grammar) is found in the speech of two of the author's primary consultants, Mrs. Chenghua Long of Shanjiang Town and Mrs. Shixiang Wu of Zhuigaolai Village. This tone is somewhat marginal in that it generally only occurs as a non-underlying, sandhi-triggered surface tone in certain phonological environments, though for Mrs. Long alone it also occurs as an underlying, lexically specified tone in a small number of recent disyllabic borrowings from Sinitic (e.g. *xaonc.joc* 'banana', from Standard Mandarin *xiāngjiāo* [香蕉] or a cognate form in another Sinitic variety). See Section 3.5.3 for discussion.

4.4.3 Miscellaneous orthographic issues

In the Xong utterances and texts transcribed in this grammar, punctuation symbols (commas, periods, question marks, etc.) are generally used as in English. The initial letter of each personal and place name is capitalized, as is the initial letter of the term <Xonb> 'Miao'. Personal names are given in the translation of each Xong example as in the Xong transcription itself, except that periods between syllables are replaced with spaces, the first letter of each syllable is capitalized, and all tone letters are deleted. This can be seen in example (4.6) below.

(4.6) *Shif.jek gaons banb nggaob.*
PN give CLF:some medicine
'It was medicine from Shi Je.' (Haili Shi, in *Tooth Conversation*)

When a polymorphemic place name includes the locative prefix <dib-> 'LOC' (see Section 5.4.2.9) as its initial morpheme, the initial letters of both that locative prefix and the following syllable are capitalized. For example, the term for the county seat of Fenghuang County is transcribed as <Dib-Zhes> in this grammar, with the first letters of both <dib-> ('LOC') and <Zhes> ('Fenghuang') capitalized.

As in many of the isolating languages of mainland Southeast Asia, the issue of wordhood in Xong is a problematic one. Nevertheless, hyphens are used to connect the component morphemes of certain grammatical constituents, including (among others) noun compounds (see Section 5.3), numeral-classifier phrases (Section 6.1.2), polymorphemic pronominal forms (Sections 7.1.2 and 7.1.3), and morphologically complex constructions derived from verbal roots (Section 10.5). Periods are used to connect the component syllables of polysyllabic Xong morphemes and ideophones (see Section 11.1 for information on the latter) as well as the component syllables of certain recent borrowings from Sinitic varieties (see Section 5.3.4). Finally, spaces are used to separate any adjacent syllables not connected by hyphens or periods.

5 Nouns

5.1 Introduction

Nouns are a major open lexical category in Fenghuang Xong. In the most general terms, Xong nouns are roughly equivalent in function to nouns in major world languages like English or Standard Mandarin. A Xong noun will generally serve as either a component of a larger noun phrase or as a noun phrase in its own right, with a Xong noun phrase in turn being able to serve a variety of grammatical and discourse functions, including serving as an argument of a verb, as a possessor or possessum, and so on. Xong nouns also cover much of the same semantic territory as nouns in English, Mandarin, and other well known languages do, as they include terms referring to inanimate objects and substances (*ghaob-chek* [NOM-vehicle] 'vehicle', *aub* 'water', *hlit* 'cooked rice'), living organisms (*ghaob-ndaut* [NOM-tree] 'tree', *daob-mioul* [AN-fish] 'fish', *deb-deb* [child-RED] 'child'), and abstract concepts (*ghaob-ped* [NOM-matter] 'matter, affair', *ghaob-raos* [NOM-clever] 'cleverness, intelligence').

In phonological and morphological terms, though, Xong nouns (or rather, noun roots) are much more similar to their counterparts in Mandarin than in English, since they are generally monosyllabic and the only significant morphological processes they undergo are compounding (see Section 5.3) and some amount of affixation (Section 5.4). Xong nouns do not regularly participate in any number, case, or gender/noun class systems. While certain pronouns (which are arguably a subset of nouns) can take a plural suffix (see Sections 7.1.2.1 and 7.1.4), no non-pronominal nouns ever do. And while nominal prefixes (see Section 5.4) show certain superficial similarities with gender or noun class systems in other languages, they are unlike canonical examples of these systems in that they never trigger any sort of agreement and in that some nouns can simultaneously bear multiple such prefixes, while many nouns take no prefixes at all. Finally, no Xong nouns of any sort ever bear any overt case markers.

To avoid confusion in subsequent sections of this chapter, a few terminological issues must be clarified here. The term *noun root* is used to refer to a single (usually monosyllabic) nominal morpheme. This term is generally used in the context of discussing morphological processes that such roots undergo, such as prefixation or compounding. The term *noun compound* is used to refer to compounds composed of multiple noun roots either with or without a preceding nominal prefix. The broader term *noun* encompasses any form that displays the characteristic properties of nouns discussed in Section 5.2.1 below. It thus includes monomorphemic noun roots that occur in isolation as well as polymorphemic constructions like noun roots modified by a preceding prefix and noun compounds. Finally, the term *noun phrase* is used to refer to any syntactic phrase which follows the noun phrase structure rules laid out in Chapters 5 through 8 of this grammar. The term is generally used in the context of discussing syntactic constructions in which such phrases participate, and in such cases it can be used to refer to a phrase consisting of a noun root in isolation, to a more complex phrase consisting of a noun plus other noun-phrase–internal constituents (e.g. numeral-classifier phrases, demonstratives, relative clauses, etc.), or even to a phrase that contains no noun at all (e.g. a noun phrase consisting solely of a numeral-classifier phrase and a demonstrative, or one consisting solely of a relative clause).

The remainder of this chapter is structured as follows. Section 5.2 below outlines the basic grammatical and referential properties that characterize Xong nouns as a lexical category. Section 5.3 then covers noun compounds and subclasses thereof, while Section 5.4 examines Xong's system of nominal prefixes. Finally, Sections 5.5 and 5.6 discuss locative nouns and reduplicated nouns, respectively.

5.2 Properties of nouns

5.2.1 Grammatical properties of nouns

In addition to the rather vague semantic and functional properties described in Section 5.1, canonical Xong nouns also share two objective, testable, language-specific properties that define them as a lexical category: they can co-occur with a preceding numeral-classifier phrase (see Section 6.1.2), and they can be modified by a *manx* relative clause (Section 8.1.4). Each of these properties is discussed at length further below in this section. However, it should be understood that neither of these properties is diagnostic in isolation, as each of them also applies to at least some non-nominal forms in at least some constructions. Canonical Xong nouns are identified as such by the combination of both these properties rather than by any particular one of them.[75]

As in many languages of East and Southeast Asia, one of the most obvious characteristics of nouns in Xong is their ability to co-occur with a preceding numeral-classifier phrase. In fact, canonical Xong nouns cannot occur with a preceding bare numeral; instead, a classifier must intervene between the two. Examples (5.1–5.3) below show the nouns *deb-npaok* [DIM-woman] 'young woman', *deb-guk* [DIM-frog] 'frog', and *nzot* 'uncooked rice' each preceded by a numeral-classifier phrase. Note that none of these three examples would be grammatical if the post-numeral, pre-nominal classifiers were removed.

75 Xong also features at least three sets of "defective" or non-canonical nouns, which are forms that show significant functional, distributional, and/or referential overlap with canonical nouns but which do not strictly satisfy the two diagnostic criteria used to define nouns here. The first of these sets (locative nouns) is discussed in Section 5.5, while the second (pronouns) is discussed in Section 7.1. However, the third set (proper nouns) is not discussed at length anywhere in this grammar. Proper nouns in Xong do resemble other non-canonical nouns in that they can neither readily co-occur with a preceding numeral-classifier phrase nor be readily modified by a *manx* relative clause. Aside from this, though, there appears to be relatively little to say about them.

(5.1) *Mex* ***aod-meinl*** ***deb-npaok,*** *raut* *deb-npaok* *guaot.*
exist **one-CLF:person** **DIM-woman** good DIM-woman pass
'There was a young woman, a very beautiful young woman.' (Xingyu Shi, in *Deb Guk Ronf*)

(5.2) ***Aod-ngonl*** ***deb-guk*** *doub* *zhaos* *deb-pinf* *ndanb* *bionl* *lol.*
one-CLF:animate **DIM-frog** then$_1$ from DIM-bottle jump exit come
'Then the frog jumped out of the bottle.' (Chenghua Long, in *Frog, Where Are You?*)

(5.3) *Gaons* ***oub-xinb*** ***nzot*** ***bub-xinb*** ***nzot.***
give **two-CLF:sheng** **uncooked.rice** **three-CLF:sheng** **uncooked.rice**
'(Workers) would be given two or three *sheng* (unit of volume) of uncooked rice (per day).' (Qiusheng Long, in *Ngel.kanx*)

Examples (5.4–5.6) demonstrate that it is not possible for classifiers, ideophones, or most verbs to similarly co-occur with a preceding numeral-classifier phrase.[76]

(5.4) **aod-leb* *leb/* **aod-leb* *ngonl/* **aod-leb* *meinl*
one-CLF CLF/ one-CLF CLF:animate/ one-CLF CLF:person
(intended: 'one thing/animal/person')

(5.5) **aod-leb* *jel.jel/* **aod-leb* *biaol.biaol*
one-CLF IDEO:A:shiningly/ one-CLF IDEO:A:sour
(intended: 'one instance of shininess/sourness, one shiny/sour thing')

(5.6) **aod-leb* *nonx/* **aod-leb* *jont/* **aod-leb* *nqint*
one-CLF eat/ one-CLF sit/ one-CLF red
(intended: 'one instance of eating/sitting/being red, one edible thing/place to sit/red thing')

However, this property is not strictly diagnostic in isolation because certain property-denoting verbs can be preceded by a numeral-classifier phrase when that phrase

76 The sequences *aod-leb nonx*, *aod-leb jont*, and *aod-leb nqint* in example (5.6) are still interpretable utterances, though they sound somewhat unnatural to the author's consultants when produced in isolation. However, these consultants were quite clear that these sequences can only be interpreted as clauses, with each such clause consisting of a verb (*nonx* 'to eat', *jont* 'to sit', or *nqint* 'red') and its sole argument (*aod-leb* 'one [of something]'). The sequences in question cannot be interpreted as noun phrases referring to a single entity or event. Thus, for example, *aod-leb nonx* can only mean 'one is eating', not 'one who eats' or 'one act of eating' or 'one edible thing'. In contrast, the various sequences in examples (5.4) and (5.5) are simply uninterpretable.

serves to measure the property in question (and note that the mensural classifiers in such phrases can be distinguished from other classifiers only on semantic grounds, not grammatical ones; see Sections 6.1.2.2 and 6.1.4.8). Example (5.7) shows one instance of this, with the numeral-classifier phrase *oub-mix* [two-CLF:meter] 'two meters' preceding the verb *shanb* 'tall'.

(5.7) *Beul mex* ***oub-mix shanb.***
3 exist **two-CLF:meter tall**
'He's two meters tall.' (Haili Shi, fieldnotes)

Furthermore, it is not uncommon for demonstratives and relative clauses to co-occur with a preceding numeral-classifier phrase without any intervening noun, nor is it uncommon for numeral-classifier phrases to occur as noun phrases in their own right. Example (5.8) below shows a numeral-classifier phrase preceding a demonstrative, example (5.9) shows a numeral-classifier phrase preceding a *manx-naond* relative clause (the latter constituent has been enclosed within brackets), and example (5.10) shows a numeral-classifier phrase serving as an independent noun phrase (one which in this case functions as an argument of the verb *gaons* 'to give').

(5.8) *Gaons monx* ***aod-bub neind*** *leh.*
give 2SG **one-CLF:inanimate.group this** LEH
'(The Communist Party) would give you (all sorts of) these things.' (Qiusheng Long, in *Ngel.kanx*)

(5.9) *Wel lis* ***aod-leb [manx liox naond].***
1SG want **one-CLF [REL big ASSOC]**
'I want a big one.' (Chenghua Long, fieldnotes)

(5.10) *Gaons beul* ***oub-shauk.***
give 3 **two-CLF:yuan**
'Give him two *yuan* (unit of currency).' (Yan Long, fieldnotes)

The second major diagnostic property of Xong nouns is their ability to be modified by a *manx* relative clause. Examples (5.11–5.13) show the nouns *eud* 'clothing', *daob-jod* [AN-tiger] 'tiger', and *ob-def* [NOM-place] 'place' as they are modified by various types of *manx* relative clauses (see Section 8.1.4 for further discussion of these types). Note that the relative clauses in each of these examples have been enclosed within brackets.

(5.11) *aod-hnanf* ***eud [manx lis hneind]***
one-CLF:clothing **clothing [REL want wear]**
'an article of clothing that is to be worn (as opposed to sold)' (Haili Shi, fieldnotes)

(5.12) *Aod-roul* *Dol.xid* *jix* *doul* ***[manx nonx miex***
one-CLF:time$_1$ La'ershan NEG$_1$ remain **[REL eat person**
naond] daob-jod.
ASSOC] AN-tiger
'Nowadays there aren't any man-eating tigers around La'ershan.' (Haili Shi, fieldnotes)

(5.13) *Boub naond Ngel.kanx ob-def neind nins leb*
1PL ASSOC Yankan NOM-place this COP CLF
[manx jaod] ob-def.
[REL bad] NOM-place
'(When I was a boy,) this Yankan (Village) of ours was a bad place.'
(Qiusheng Long, in *Ngel.kanx*)

In contrast, examples (5.14–5.16) show that *manx* relative clauses cannot modify classifiers, verbs, or ideophones.

(5.14) **leb/*ngonl/*meinl [manx liox]*
CLF/CLF:animate/CLF:person [REL big]
(intended: 'a big object/animal/person')

(5.15) **nonx/*jont/*nqint [manx hliof]*
eat/sit/red [REL many]
(intended: 'to eat/sit a lot, to be very red; many instances of eating/sitting, many red things')

(5.16) **jel.jel/*biaol.biaol [manx hliof]*
IDEO:A:shiningly/IDEO:A:sour [REL many]
(intended: 'many instances of shininess/sourness, many shiny/sour things')

Still, it should be kept in mind that while *manx* relative clauses are often used to modify nouns, this is not their sole function. They can also co-occur with a preceding numeral-classifier phrase with no intervening noun, as in example (5.9) above, and they can occur as independent noun phrases in their own right, as in example (5.17) below.

(5.17) *Jix mex* ***[manx nonx]*** *jix mex* ***[manx hneind].***
NEG$_1$ exist **[REL eat]** NEG$_1$ exist **[REL wear]**
'(We) had nothing to eat and nothing to wear.' (Shixiang Wu, fieldnotes)

In addition to the two diagnostics just discussed (i.e. the ability to co-occur with a preceding numeral-classifier phrase and the ability to undergo modification by a *manx* relative clause), there are a number of other logically possible tests for nounhood in Xong. These include (i) the ability to serve as a possessor and/or possessum, (ii) the ability to be modified by a *naond* relative clause, (iii) the ability to co-occur with a following demonstrative, (iv) the ability to undergo certain morphological processes like compounding and prefixation, and (v) the ability to serve as an argument of a verb or other predicate. However, upon closer examination each of these tests turns out to be unsatisfactory as a diagnostic for nounhood, or at least much less satisfactory than the two tests discussed above.

First, the ability to serve as a possessor and/or possessum is really a property of noun phrases rather than of nouns. For instance, it is true that the nouns *daod* 'older brother' and *sond-guaod* [bone-back] 'back' each serve as a possessum in examples (5.18) and (5.19), and that the noun *daob-nbat* [AN-pig] 'pig' serves as a possessor in example (5.19) as well. Note that in these and similar examples below, each possessor phrase and possessum phrase has been enclosed within brackets, while each larger noun phrase composed of a possessor phrase and a possessum phrase together has been bolded.

(5.18) *Aod-leb* *nieus* *zhut* **[*boub* *naond*]** **[*daod*]**.
one-CLF buy reach **[1PL ASSOC]** **[older.brother]**
'One (of those people) bought my older brother.' (Qiusheng Long, in *Ngel. kanx*)[77]

(5.19) *nzaont* **[*daob-nbat* *naond*]** **[*sond-guaod*]**
ride **[AN-pig ASSOC]** **[bone-back]**
'to ride on a pig's back' (Haili Shi, fieldnotes)

However, more complex noun phrases can also serve as possessor and possessum just as easily. In example (5.20), a complex noun phrase consisting of an initial numeral-classifier phrase, a noun, and a final demonstrative (together meaning 'this fish') serves as the possessum of *wel* '1SG', and in example (5.21) the same complex noun phrase serves as the possessor of *ghaob-nheis* [NOM-scale] 'scales'.

(5.20) **[*Wel* *naond*]** **[*aod-ngonl* *mioul* *neind*]** *liox* *guaot!*
[1SG ASSOC] **[one-CLF:animate fish this]** big pass
'This fish of mine is really big!' (Shixiang Wu, fieldnotes)

77 The translation of *boub* '1PL' as 'my' rather than 'our' is correct here; see Section 8.2.1 for details.

(5.21) *Mx* *geud* ***[aod-ngonl*** ***mioul*** ***neind*** ***naond]***
2SG hold **[one-CLF:animate fish this ASSOC]**
[ghaob-nheis] *guaox* *sheub.*
[NOM-scale] scrape leave
'Scrape the scales off this fish.' (Shixiang Wu, fieldnotes)

Second, the ability to be modified by a *naond* relative clause (see Section 8.1.2) should in theory serve as just as satisfactory a diagnostic for Xong nouns as the ability to be modified by a *manx* relative clause. The primary function of both types of relative clause is, after all, to modify (i.e. restrict the reference of) nouns. In practice, though, the wide range of functions that the form *naond* 'ASSOC' serves – including marking relative clauses, marking possessive phrases, and serving as a clause-final marker (see Section 9.2.3.2) – means that constructions headed by *naond* can modify many different types of constituents, not just nouns. In contrast, the form *manx* 'REL' serves only to mark relative clauses. The identification of *manx* relative clauses is thus often easier than the identification of *naond* relative clauses, in the sense that a construction containing *manx* generally allows for fewer possible analyses than one containing *naond*. Using *manx* relative clauses to test for nounhood therefore provides all the advantages of using *naond* relative clauses for the same purpose, and with fewer complications. Still, as far as the author has been able to determine, all nouns which pass the *manx* relative clause test for nounhood would also pass the *naond* relative clause test, and vice versa.

Third, while Xong nouns often co-occur with a following demonstrative within a single noun phrase, there is evidence to suggest that such attributive demonstratives in Xong actually serve to modify a preceding classifier rather than the preceding noun. In other words, it appears that a noun itself cannot serve as the head of a noun-phrase–internal attributive demonstrative (see Section 7.2 for further discussion). This, coupled with the pragmatic oddness of certain noun–demonstrative combinations (especially when dealing with nouns referring to abstract concepts), makes the ability to co-occur with (much less be modified by) a demonstrative less than ideal as a test for nounhood in Xong.

Fourth, although Xong nouns display relatively little morphology compared to nouns in many of the world's other languages, there are two specific morphological processes which do operate on many of Xong's noun roots: compounding (see Section 5.3) and prefixation (Section 5.4). It thus seems natural to consider the ability to undergo these processes as a potential criterion for nounhood. However, while compounding may be a very productive morphological process for Xong nouns, it is not restricted to them, as Xong classifiers, numerals, and even verbs can all undergo processes that are at least superficially similar to compounding. And while many noun roots can take a preceding nominal prefix (as in, e.g., *daob-maonb* [AN-cat] 'cat', *ghaob-tif* [NOM-stomach] 'stomach', or *minl-aub* [AUG-water] 'river'), many other clearly nominal roots cannot (e.g. *feinx* 'rice noodles', *niax* 'meat', or *daut* 'speech').

Furthermore, certain nominal prefixes can modify classifiers, numerals, and/or verbs as well as nouns; see Section 5.4 for details and examples.

Fifth, using the ability to serve as an argument of a verb or other predicate as a criterion for nounhood in Xong is problematic for at least two reasons. First, these functions are not served by nouns per se, but rather by noun phrases. Second, these functions can also be served by other types of constituents (such as clauses) as well. See Section 9.1.1 for further discussion.

5.2.2 Referential properties of nouns

As was briefly mentioned in Section 5.1, Xong nouns serve to express many of the same concepts that nouns express in major world languages like English or Standard Mandarin. These include terms referring to entities in the natural world, including natural phenomena and substances (e.g. *nbet* 'snow', *git* 'wind', *bid-gheul* [FRT-mountain] 'mountain'), plants and animals (e.g. *bid-lid* [FRT-plum] 'plum', *daob-guoud* [AN-dog] 'dog', *daob-neinb* [AN-snake] 'snake'), and human beings (e.g. *miex/mianx* 'person', *ghaob-Xonb* [NOM-Miao] 'Miao [person, ethnicity]', *deb-ghot* [DIM-old] 'old person'), terms referring to inanimate objects, including foodstuffs (e.g. *hlit* 'cooked rice', *feinx* 'rice noodles', *niax* 'meat'), tools (e.g. *ghaob-wanl* [NOM-pot] 'pot', *bid-kied* [FRT-bullet] 'bullet', *beub* 'quilt'), and manmade structures (e.g. *bioud* 'home, house', *xox.ndaonf* 'school', *gieux* 'bridge'), and terms referring to abstract concepts (e.g. *ghaob-ped* [NOM-matter] 'matter, affair', *ghaob-raos* [NOM-clever] 'cleverness, intelligence', *faonk.faof* 'method').

Of course, providing any sort of comprehensive survey of the semantic or referential territory covered by Xong's nouns would take up a great deal of space while being of only questionable value, and so only a few representative examples have been given above. Still, there are some general referential properties of Xong nouns which are strikingly different from those of nouns in English or other European languages, although these same properties are not especially unusual for an isolating language of East or Southeast Asia.[78]

Among the most striking of these unusual (at least from a European perspective) properties is the fact that Xong nouns very often occur without any overt marking of

78 Perhaps unsurprisingly, these properties have received little to no discussion in most Chinese-language descriptions of Xong. This oversight is arguably another example of the Sinocentric bias found in many descriptive studies written within the framework of traditional Chinese linguistic theory, which is discussed in more detail in Section 2.5.1 of this grammar. Still, "arguably" is the operative word here, since – to be fair – it is easy to imagine a scholar working within the framework of traditional Chinese linguistic theory in turn arguing that this author's attention to these properties is in fact an example of his own Anglocentric (or at least Eurocentric) bias.

number or definiteness whatsoever.[79] Only context, the structure of the current discourse, and real-world knowledge allow listeners to determine whether a particular "bare" noun of this sort refers to a single entity or to multiple entities, or to determine whether the noun's referent is a specific, identifiable one or not. For instance, example (5.22) is felicitous regardless of the actual number of cows involved, and regardless of whether or not the speaker is discussing specific cows that are known to the addressee.

(5.22) *Monx lieus dut* ***daob-yul?***
2SG guard obtain **AN-cow**
'You'd be able to take care of the cow/the cows/a cow/some cows/cows?'
(Xingyu Shi, in *Deb Guk Ronf*)

Similarly, example (5.23) can be used regardless of whether it was one bowl or multiple bowls that fell, and regardless of whether or not the bowls in question were specific ones known to the addressee.

(5.23) ***Aob-zhet*** *zhaok lah.*
NOM-bowl fall PRF
'The bowl/the bowls/a bowl/some bowls/bowls fell.' (Chenghua Long, fieldnotes)

Example (5.24) provides one final instance of this with the noun *jeud* 'alcohol'. Note in particular that this noun demonstrates the same referential properties as *daob-yul* [AN-cow] 'cow' and *aob-zhet* [NOM-bowl] 'bowl' in examples (5.22) and (5.23) above. This is true even though cows and bowls are intuitively more like count nouns (in the sense that the component members of a set of cows or bowls are obviously discrete and easily distinguished), while alcohol is intuitively more like a mass noun (in the sense that a mass of alcohol cannot be easily divided into discrete component members).

---

79 Of course, Xong nouns are also unmarked for case and for gender or noun class. However, these topics are not discussed in this section for two reasons. First, neither case nor gender/noun class is as obviously a referential property (as opposed to, say, a grammatical property) as number, definiteness, or specificity. Second, it appears to be much more common for languages to lack case systems and gender/noun class systems than it is for them to lack number systems, making Xong's lack of case and gender/noun classes somewhat less remarkable than its lack of number. For instance, 100 of the 261 languages (≈ 38%) examined in Iggesen (2013) lack any sort of case marking, and 145 of the 257 languages (≈ 56%) examined in Corbett (2013) lack any sort of gender or noun class system. However, only 98 of the 1,066 languages (≈ 9%) examined in Dryer (2013a) lack plural marking, and can thus in most cases be assumed to lack any sort of nominal number system.

(5.24) *Monx lis jix lis hauk* ***jeud?***
2SG want NEG_1 want drink **alcohol**
'Do you want to drink the alcohol/some alcohol/alcohol?' (unknown Xong consultant, fieldnotes)

In fact, there is little evidence that Xong nouns can be meaningfully subdivided into classes like "mass nouns" or "count nouns". With respect to quantification, nouns like *aub* 'water' and *ngonx* 'silver' behave very similarly to nouns like *ghaob-doul* [NOM-hand] 'hand' or *daob-maonb* [AN-cat] 'cat', with the only apparent differences between them being easily explainable on semantic and pragmatic grounds.

The author does not wish to give the impression that the "bare" Xong nouns under discussion are necessarily *ambiguous* with respect to number and definiteness, but rather that they are simply *vague* with respect to them. As mentioned above, the number and definiteness of a particular bare noun will often be obvious from context, discourse structure, and/or real-world knowledge, and in many other cases it may simply be irrelevant. Furthermore, a number of optional methods of quantification are available when the quantity of a particular noun is important and not obvious from context (see Chapter 6). For instance, a numeral-classifier phrase can be added before the noun within the noun phrase (as in examples (5.25) and (5.26)), or a quantifier like *yaod(.yaod)* 'all' (see Section 9.2.3.1) can be added outside the noun phrase (as in example (5.27)). In these examples, note that the relevant quantifiers have been bolded, while the noun phrases whose referents those quantifiers serve to quantify have been enclosed within brackets.

(5.25) [***Aod-ngonl*** *guoud dox*] *ghab ninx.*
[**one-CLF:animate** dog that] bite NEX
'That dog bites people.' (Yan Long, fieldnotes)

(5.26) *Doul* [***oub-bub-bioud*** *miex*] *leh.*
remain [**two-three-CLF:home** person] LEH
'(After the bandits started raiding our village,) there were only two or three families (still living here).' (Qiusheng Long, in *Ngel.kanx*)

(5.27) *Hnant* [*aod-gheul miex naond deb-ngueif,*
call [one-CLF:village person ASSOC DIM-unmarried.woman
deb-npaok] ***yaod.yaod*** *hnant lol reinb nqad*
DIM-woman] **all** call come determine CLF:half.of.pair
xut.npeif nins leb naond xut.npeif.
shoe COP who ASSOC shoe
'Call (for me) all the unmarried women, all the young women in the village. Call them to come and determine who this shoe belongs to.' (Xingyu Shi, in *Oub Meinl Yaos Geud*)

Similarly, there are also ways to clearly express (in)definiteness in Fenghuang Xong without the use of articles or other such dedicated forms. For instance, despite the lack of any sort of indefinite article, the noun phrase *ngonl deb-ghot* [CLF:animate DIM-old] 'an old person' in example (5.28) below clearly has indefinite reference, since it occurs in the *mex* presentational construction that is often used to introduce new participants into a discourse (see Section 9.1.3.2).

(5.28) *Manx.eib.manx.ab* *mex* ***ngonl*** ***deb-ghot*** *jix* *mex*
a.long.time.ago exist **CLF:animate** **DIM-old** NEG_1 exist
deb *mex* *giad.*
child exist grandchild
'A long time ago, there was an old person who had no children or grandchildren.' (Xingyu Shi, in *Deb Guk Ronf*)

The presence of the bare classifier *ngonl* 'CLF:animate' before the noun *deb-ghot* in example (5.28) also makes it clear that the referent in this case is a single individual rather than multiple such individuals (see Section 6.1.3.1).

In contrast, the noun phrase *aod-ghoub sheinf.jind dox* [one-CLF:flexible.length nerve that] 'the nerve' in example (5.29) below clearly has definite reference due to the presence of the noun-phrase–final demonstrative *dox* 'that'.

(5.29) *Aod* *ghab* *beul* *doub* *naonb.nex* *zhut*
as.soon.as bite 3 $then_1$ seem reach
aod-ghoub ***sheinf.jind*** ***dox*** *lah.*
one-CLF:flexible.length **nerve** **that** PRF
'As soon as (I) bit down it was like I'd hit the nerve (in my tooth).' (Haili Shi, in *Tooth Conversation*)

5.3 Noun compounds

Noun compounding – that is, the simple concatenation of multiple nouns into a single larger noun (using the definition of "noun" provided in Section 5.1) – is an extremely common and highly productive morphological process in Xong.[80] The language's noun compounds can be divided into at least three well defined subtypes on the basis of their syntactic, morphological, and semantic properties. These subtypes are referred to here as the *attributive*, *reciprocal*, and *generic* subtypes, each of which

80 The author argues that constructions in which a property-denoting verb like *liox* 'big' or *gueinx* 'yellow' serves to attributively modify a noun within a noun phrase actually involve unflagged relative clauses rather than any sort of compounding. Constructions like *bioud liox* [home big] 'big home' and *guoud gueinx* [dog yellow] 'yellow dog' are thus discussed in Section 8.1.5 rather than here.

is discussed in more detail in one of Sections 5.3.1 to 5.3.3 below.[81] Section 5.3.4 then discusses noun compounds involving forms that have been recently borrowed into Xong from Sinitic languages, many of which violate the compound formation rules discussed in Sections 5.3.1 to 5.3.3.

Note that this section deals only with compounds that involve two or more non-prefixal, non-locative noun roots, although these compounds can also involve nominal prefixes and locative nouns as well.[82] Although some of the morphological processes in which nominal prefixes and locative nouns participate share certain similarities with the more canonical noun compounding processes discussed in this section, the additional unique properties that these prefixal and locative forms display mean that they are more appropriately discussed in later sections of their own (specifically, see Section 5.4 for nominal prefixes and Section 5.5 for locative nouns).

5.3.1 Attributive compounds

Attributive compounds are by far the most common subtype of noun compound (in the sense that the vast majority of distinct noun compounds which the author has encountered are attributive), and they appear to be the subtype with the fewest structural restrictions. In an attributive compound, one constituent noun (or noun root) clearly serves as the semantic head of the compound while the other serves as a modifier of that head. In other words, in attributive compounds the referent of the head noun (or noun root) is modified (i.e. restricted) by the referent of the attributive, or modifier, noun (or noun root). For instance, in example (5.30) below the head noun root *bioud* 'home' is modified (i.e. has its reference restricted) by the attributive noun root *ndaut* 'tree, wood', and in example (5.31) the head noun root *neus* 'egg' is modified by the attributive noun root *naus* 'duck'.[83]

---

81 Although many of the details differ, a number of the ideas presented in this section – especially those related to subtypes of noun compounds – were first inspired by Mortensen's 2003 study of coordinate compounds in Hmong.

82 Thus, for example, the form *ghaob-nheis-mioul* [NOM-scale-fish] 'fish scale' is still discussed in Section 5.3.1, because even though it involves the nominal prefix *ghaob-* 'NOM', it also involves two noun roots. Similarly, *daob-ghab-daob-naus* [AN-chicken-AN-duck] 'poultry' is still discussed in Section 5.3.3, since it still involves two noun roots (even though these roots are not immediate constituents of the compound as a whole) in addition to two instances of the nominal prefix *daob-* 'AN'. However, forms like *ghaob-doul* [NOM-hand] 'hand' and *leut-aub* [top-water] 'on the water' are not discussed in any part of Section 5.3, since each one involves only a single non-prefixal, non-locative noun root.

83 The Xong noun root *naus* refers to both 'ducks' in particular and 'birds' in general. Thus, depending on the context, a phrase like *aod-ngonl daob-naus* (with *aod-ngonl* [one-CLF:animate] and *daob-* 'AN') can mean either 'one duck' or 'one bird (regardless of kind)'. The root *naus* is variably glossed as either 'duck' or 'bird' in this grammar according to its intended meaning in each instance.

(5.30) *bioud-ndaut*
home-wood
'wooden home' (Haili Shi, fieldnotes)

(5.31) *neus-naus*
egg-duck
'duck egg' (Haili Shi, fieldnotes)

Similar semantic relationships between the head nouns (or noun roots) and attributive nouns (or noun roots) of noun compounds can be seen in examples (5.32–5.38) below.

(5.32) *khauk-bioud*
hole-home
'window' (Chenghua Long, in *Frog, Where Are You?*)

(5.33) *aub-gheb*
water-eye
'tears' (Xingyu Shi, in *Oub Meinl Yaos Geud*)

(5.34) *maonl-ded*
small.flying.insect-honey
'honeybee' (Chenghua Long, in *Frog, Where Are You?*)

(5.35) *niax-nbat/yul/guoud*
meat-pig/cow/dog
'pork/beef/dog meat' (Haili Shi, fieldnotes)

(5.36) *zhonx-hlod*
length-bamboo
'length of bamboo' (Xingyu Shi, in *Oub Meinl Yaos Geud*)

(5.37) *eud-beinx*
clothing-flower
'patterned clothing' (unknown Xong consultant, fieldnotes)

(5.38) *npaok-Xonb*
woman-Miao
'Miao woman' (Chenghua Long, fieldnotes)

Aside from this, though, attributive compounds display the same general referential properties as Xong nouns in general, as such compounds are unspecified for number and definiteness when they appear "bare" in Xong clauses (see Section 5.2.2)

In terms of their grammatical properties, Xong's attributive compounds also generally behave like the other canonical nouns described in Section 5.2.1 above. They can easily be quantified by a preceding numeral-classifier phrase, as in example (5.39), and they can also easily be modified by a *manx* relative clause, as in example (5.40).

(5.39)	***bub-leb***	*ghaob-zeint-bias*
	three-CLF	NOM-ceramic.jar-pickled.cabbage

'three jars for storing pickled cabbage' (Shixiang Wu, fieldnotes)

(5.40)	*Wel*	*nieus*	*aod-njaod*	***manx***	***raut***	*deud-yul.*
	1SG	buy	one-CLF:piece	**REL**	**good**	skin-cow

'I bought a nice cowhide.' (Haili Shi, fieldnotes)

Thus, attributive compounds are distinguished from noun roots more in terms of their internal structure than in terms of their grammatical or referential properties. However, the grammatical and referential properties of attributive compounds are still useful for distinguishing them from other subtypes of noun compounds, like the reciprocal and generic compounds discussed in Sections 5.3.2 and 5.3.3 below.

In general, attributive compounds have recursive, binary, hierarchical constituent structures. They are recursive in the sense that an attributive compound can itself serve as a constituent of a larger attributive compound, binary in the sense that every such compound can be subdivided into exactly two immediate constituents, each of which can be further subdivided into exactly two more immediate constituents, and so on until individual morphemes are reached, and hierarchical in the sense that each immediate constituent of an attributive compound either modifies or is modified by the other immediate constituent, rather than simply being coordinate with it.

As the examples in this section have demonstrated, the ordering of head noun (or noun root) and modifier noun (or noun root) in Xong's attributive compounds is generally Head–Modifier (also represented as NMod). New compounds created on the fly by the author's consultants consistently have NMod order, and the only non-sporadic exceptions to this NMod order are seen in recent borrowings from Sinitic languages (see Sections 2.7.2 and 5.3.4), as these languages have predominantly ModN order in their own noun compounds. It should be noted, though, that in many cases it is unclear whether a polysyllabic borrowed form with apparent ModN order should be analyzed as a compound or simply as an atomic borrowing with no internal structure. See Section 5.3.4 for further discussion of this issue.

Finally, while most attributive compounds involve only two noun roots, a few instances of such compounds involving three or even more noun roots have been attested. Some representative examples are given in (5.41–5.44) below, with the internal modification structure of each example being given in its first line.

(5.41) [[X-X]-X]
neus-ghab-naus
egg-chicken-duck
'duck egg' (Haili Shi, fieldnotes) (cf. *neus-ghab* 'chicken egg', **ghab-naus*)

(5.42) [X-[X-X]]
ghaob-deud-guk-ronf
NOM-skin-frog-dragon
'the skin of a dragon-frog' (Xingyu Shi, fieldnotes) (cf. *ghaob-deud* 'skin')

(5.43) [[X-X]-[X-X]]
neus-ghab-naus-ngonx
egg-chicken-bird-goose
'goose egg' (Haili Shi, fieldnotes) (cf. *neus-ghab* 'chicken egg', *naus-ngonx* 'goose')

(5.44) [[X-X]-[X-X]]
zhonx-hlod-aub-gheb
length-bamboo-water-eye
'a length of bamboo filled with tears' (Xingyu Shi, in *Oub Meinl Yaos Geud*)

Although no specific instances have been encountered, the author has no reason to suspect that even longer attributive compounds are impossible, or that they would behave differently in any way from the shorter examples discussed above. In any given case, each constituent of an attributive compound (whether that constituent is a noun root, a noun root with a preceding nominal prefix, or a noun compound itself) will usually only ever be modified by a following constituent, not by a preceding one.

From here on, the internal modification structure of each attributive noun compound will not be indicated in this grammar. Thus, for instance, it will not be indicated whether a given three-root compound has the structure [[X-X]-X] or [X-[X-X]]. There do not appear to be any grammatical differences associated with attributive compounds that have different internal modification structures, and in most cases the modification structure of a given compound will be obvious to the reader. However, the existence of these alternate internal modification structures should still be kept in mind whenever an example of an attributive compound is encountered in a subsequent section.

5.3.2 Reciprocal compounds

Xong's reciprocal compounds show very different structural, grammatical, and referential properties compared to the attributive compounds just discussed. Every reciprocal compound consists of exactly two noun roots, never three or more, and no reciprocal compound will ever feature a nominal prefix (see Section 5.4). Furthermore, while in attributive compounds more rightward roots serve to modify (i.e. restrict the reference of) more leftward roots, this is not the case with reciprocal compounds. Instead, each reciprocal compound refers to a particular kinship relation (e.g. siblings, mother and child, or husband and wife), with the first root referring to one necessary member of the relation (e.g. an older sibling, a mother, or a husband) and the second referring to the other necessary member of the relation (e.g. a younger sibling, a child, or a wife). These unusual referential properties result in reciprocal compounds behaving differently from attributive compounds with respect to quantification, as is discussed in more detail below. Finally, reciprocal compounds differ from all other types of compound in that they refer only to kinship-based concepts (although some attributive and generic compounds also refer to kinship-based concepts as well), and in that they appear to constitute a closed class.

So far the author has only been able to find nine clear examples of reciprocal compounds that are readily accepted by all of his consultants. These nine are presented in (5.45–5.53) below. Note that examples (5.45) through (5.49) involve cosanguineal kinship relations, while examples (5.50) through (5.53) involve affinal ones.

(5.45) *naob-geud*
older.brother-younger.sibling
'older brother(s) and younger sibling(s)' (Haili Shi, fieldnotes)[84]

(5.46) *yaos-geud*
older.sister-younger.sibling
'older sister(s) and younger sibling(s)' (Xingyu Shi, in *Oub Meinl Yaos Geud*)

(5.47) *maot-deb*
father-child
'father(s) and child(ren)' (Haili Shi, fieldnotes)

(5.48) *nek-deb*
mother-child
'mother(s) and child(ren)' (Haili Shi, fieldnotes)

84 There is some disagreement among the author's consultants about the applicability of *naob-geud* (in example (5.45)) and *yaos-geud* (in example (5.46)) to groups of siblings of mixed gender. Most of the author's consultants say that these compounds can be applied to any group of siblings as long as the oldest member of the group is of the appropriate gender, so that *naob-geud* can be applied to any group of siblings as long as the oldest one is male and *yaos-geud* can be applied to any group of siblings as long as the oldest one is female. However, a minority of the author's consultants say that they would only use *naob-geud* to refer to a group of siblings of which all members are male, and they would only use *yaos-geud* to refer to a group of siblings of which all members are female. It is not yet clear whether this reflects a dialectal difference or merely an idiolectal one.

(5.49) *poub-giad*
paternal.grandfather-grandchild
'paternal grandfather(s) and grandchild(ren)' (Shixiang Wu, fieldnotes)

(5.50) *baox-minl*
father-mother
'parents, father(s) and mother(s)' (Shixiang Wu, fieldnotes)

(5.51) *nek-maot*
mother-father
'parents, mother(s) and father(s)' (Shixiang Wu, fieldnotes)[85]

(5.52) *pouf-niaox*
paternal.grandfather-paternal.grandmother
'paternal grandparents' (Haili Shi, fieldnotes)[86]

(5.53) *bod-oud*
husband-wife
'spouses, married couple(s)' (Haili Shi, fieldnotes)

Note that in each of the nine examples above, the two roots together define a kinship relation, with each root of the compound referring to one necessary member of the relation in question. Thus, in example (5.45), the reciprocal compound *naob-geud* refers to the kinship relation between older brothers and their younger siblings, with the first root *naob* meaning 'older brother' and the second root *geud* meaning 'younger sibling'. One's status as an older brother entails that one has at least one younger sibling, and one's status as a younger sibling entails that one has at least one older sibling (though not necessarily an older brother in particular, of course). In other words, one's status as an older brother is defined by one's having a younger sibling, and vice versa. Similarly, in example (5.47), the reciprocal compound *maot-deb* refers to the kinship relation between fathers and their children, with the first root *maot* meaning 'father' and the second root *deb* meaning 'child'. Again, in this

85 There is no clear semantic difference between the roots *baox* and *maot*, both of which mean 'father', although the former root is used independently (i.e. not as part of a compound) to mean 'father' much more frequently than the latter one. The same is true of *minl* and *nek*, both of which mean 'mother', with *minl* being used independently much more frequently than *nek*. While the forms *baox* and *maot* seem to only function as nouns meaning 'father', note that the form *nek* also functions as a female nominal prefix (see Section 5.4.2.8) and the form *minl* also functions as an augmentative nominal prefix (Section 5.4.2.4). Reciprocal compounds "mixing" these sets of terms – e.g. **baox-nek* or **maot-minl* – are not accepted by the author's consultants.

86 The transcription of 'paternal grandfather' as *poub* in example (5.49) and as *pouf* in example (5.52) reflects dialectal variation.

case one's status as a father entails that one has at least one child, and one's status as a child entails that one has a father. Both of these examples are very different from attributive compounds like *eud-beinx* [clothing-flower] 'patterned clothing', in which the existence of clothing does not entail the existence of flowers (nor vice versa), and in which the second root serves solely to restrict the reference of the first root.

In addition to the nine clear examples of reciprocal compounds given above, two slightly more questionable examples are given in (5.54) and (5.55) below. The author's consultants report that neither compound is one that they would normally use, but that both were perfectly intelligible and sounded like something one might hear a native Xong speaker produce.

(5.54) ??*niaox-giad*
paternal.grandmother-grandchild
(intended: 'paternal grandmother[s] and grandchild[ren]')

(5.55) ??*daob-daok*
maternal.grandfather-maternal.grandmother
(intended: 'maternal grandparents')

Interestingly, while the reciprocal compound involving paternal grandfathers and grandchildren (*poub-giad*, in example (5.49) above) is perfectly acceptable and the one involving paternal grandmothers and grandchildren (*niaox-giad*, in example (5.54) above) is marginally acceptable, the corresponding reciprocal compounds involving maternal grandparents and grandchildren are completely unacceptable. This is shown in examples (5.56) and (5.57) below.

(5.56) **daob-giad*
maternal.grandfather-grandchild
(intended: 'maternal grandfather[s] and grandchild[ren]')

(5.57) **daok-giad*
maternal.grandmother-grandchild
(intended: 'maternal grandmother[s] and grandchild[ren]')

The formation of reciprocal compounds does not appear to be productive for modern Xong speakers. A number of additional constructed reciprocal compounds were presented to the author's consultants, including compounds involving teachers and students, boys and girls, boyfriends and girlfriends, and various combinations of aunts, uncles, nieces, and nephews, but all of these were rejected. Nevertheless, at this point it would be premature to unequivocally rule out the existence of at least a few further reciprocal compounds.

Reciprocal compounds behave somewhat differently with respect to quantification than do attributive compounds. While both types of compound can be readily quantified, reciprocal compounds are more restricted in the types of quantifying expressions they can take than are attributive compounds. In particular, reciprocal compounds can only be quantified by an expression that refers to more than one entity, such as a verb like *hliof/hliob* 'many' or a numeral-classifier phrase involving a numeral greater than *aod* 'one' and/or involving an inherently plural classifier like *deib* 'CLF:pair$_2$'. For instance, examples (5.58) and (5.59) below show that the reciprocal compound *naob-geud* 'older brother(s) and younger sibling(s)' can be readily quantified by the numeral-classifier phrase *oub-leb* [two-CLF] 'two (of something)', but not by *aod-leb* [one-CLF] 'one (of something)'.

(5.58) *Beul baox beul minl yab jix doul, doul*
3 father 3 mother also NEG$_1$ remain remain
mianx ***oub-leb naob-geud***
person **two-CLF older.brother-younger.sibling**
'Their father and mother had passed away, leaving only the two brothers.'
(Chunman Tang, in *Oub Leb Naob Geud*)

(5.59) **aod-leb naob-geud*
one-CLF older.brother-younger.sibling
(intended: 'one brother')

The next three examples demonstrate that the reciprocal compound *yaos-geud* 'older sister(s) and younger sibling(s)' can be quantified by an inherently plural classifier like *deib* 'CLF:pair$_2$' or by a numeral-classifier phrase containing the ignorative numeral *mins* 'how many, a few' (see Section 7.3.2.3), but not by the numeral-classifier phrase *aod-leb* [one-CLF] 'one (of something)'.

(5.60) *Manx.eib.manx.ab, mex* ***deib yaos-geud.***
a.long.time.ago exist **CLF:pair$_2$ older.sister-younger.sibling**
'A long time ago, there were two sisters.' (Xingyu Shi, in *Oub Meinl Yaos Geud*)

(5.61) *Mex* ***mins-leb yaos-geud?***
exist **how.many-CLF older.sister-younger.sibling**
'How many sisters do (you) have?' (Haili Shi, fieldnotes)

(5.62) **aod-leb yaos-geud*
one-CLF older.sister-younger.sibling
(intended: 'one sister')

Examples (5.63) and (5.64) provide similar evidence for the reciprocal compound *bod-oud* 'spouses, married couple(s)'.

(5.63) *aod-deib* *bod-oud*
one-CLF:pair$_2$ husband-wife
'a husband and wife, a married couple' (Haili Shi, fieldnotes)

(5.64) **aod-leb* *bod-oud*
one-CLF husband-wife
(intended: 'one spouse, one husband or wife' *or* 'one married couple')

If a speaker did need to refer to, e.g., 'one younger sibling' or 'one wife', they would simply use a different (though often obviously related) lexical item rather than a reciprocal compound, as in examples (5.65) and (5.66) below.

(5.65) *aod-leb* *deb-geud*
one-CLF DIM-younger.sibling
'one younger sibling' (Haili Shi, fieldnotes)

(5.66) *aod-leb* *npaok*
one-CLF woman
'one wife' (Haili Shi, fieldnotes)

Reciprocal compounds also differ from attributive compounds in that they can only be used to refer to heterogeneous sets of entities that include at least one individual instance of the referent of each of the compound's constituent roots. Thus, for instance, *naob-geud* [older.brother-younger.sibling] 'older brother(s) and younger sibling(s)' cannot be used to refer to two older brothers from two different families, or three younger siblings from three different families. It can only be used to refer to a set of necessarily heterogeneous individuals, some of whom are older brothers and the rest of whom are younger siblings.[87] This same restriction also applies to all other reciprocal compounds discussed in this section.

87 Although it is difficult to get clear judgments on the issue from some consultants, it appears that the use of a reciprocal compound strongly implies, but does not actually entail, that the referents of the reciprocal compound in question have the appropriate kinship relation with each other, and not just with some other entity not currently being referred to. Thus, in practice, one would almost always use *naob-geud* [older.brother-younger.sibling] 'older brother(s) and younger sibling(s)' to refer to siblings who share the same parents, but it would not be incorrect to use it to refer to a group consisting of the oldest brother from one family and the youngest sibling from another family (although in most circumstances it would certainly be pragmatically odd to do so).

This is in clear contrast to attributive compounds, which are used to refer to individuals or to homogeneous sets of individuals. For example, the attributive compound *neus-naus* [egg-duck] 'duck egg' can be used to refer either to a single duck egg or to a homogeneous set of duck eggs (homogeneous in the sense that all members of the set are duck eggs, not in the sense that all members are identical in every respect), but it would not be used to refer to a heterogeneous set containing both ducks and eggs.

Reciprocal compounds also possess two other properties that are worth mentioning here, although these properties are not diagnostic since they are also shared by the attributive compounds discussed in Section 5.3.1 above (though not by the generic compounds discussed in Section 5.3.3 below). First, the constituent roots of a reciprocal compound cannot be linked by the form *ox/ux* 'and' (see Section 8.3). Attempting to do so always results in an ungrammatical (though generally still interpretable) utterance, as examples (5.67–5.70) demonstrate.

(5.67) **bub-meinl* *naob* ***ox*** *geud*
three-CLF:person older.brother **and** younger.sibling
(intended: 'three brothers')

(5.68) *bub-meinl* *naob-geud*
three-CLF:person older.brother-younger.sibling
'three brothers' (Haili Shi, fieldnotes)

(5.69) **manx* *oub-leb* *bod* ***ox*** *oud*
2PL two-CLF husband **and** wife
(intended: 'you two, husband and wife' [addressing a married couple])

(5.70) *manx* *oub-leb* *bod-oud*
2PL two-CLF husband-wife
'you two, husband and wife' (addressing a married couple) (Haili Shi, fieldnotes)

Second, constituent ordering within reciprocal compounds is fixed. Reversing the order of any of the reciprocal compounds given in this section will result in an ungrammatical utterance, although sometimes one that is still interpretable. Thus, while *poub-giad* 'paternal grandfather(s) and grandchild(ren)' and *bod-oud* 'spouses, married couple(s)' are perfectly acceptable, the reversed versions in (5.71) and (5.72) below are not.

(5.71) **giad-poub*
grandchild-paternal.grandfather
(intended: 'paternal grandfather[s] and grandchild[ren]')

(5.72) **oud-bod*
wife-husband
(intended: 'spouses, married couple[s]')

However, there is one way in which reciprocal compounds differ from attributive compounds in terms of ordering constraints. As the examples in Section 5.3.1 showed, in attributive compounds the general ordering principle is that rightward roots modify leftward roots or, conversely, that leftward roots serve as semantic heads for rightward roots. However, in reciprocal compounds neither root modifies the other; rather, both roots serve to define a reciprocal kinship relation. In these compounds, ordering appears to be determined largely on a semantic basis: roots referring to older referents (e.g. older siblings, parents, grandparents) precede those referring to younger referents (e.g. younger siblings, children, grandchildren), and roots referring to male referents (e.g. husbands, fathers) precede those referring to female referents (e.g. wives, mothers). The sole exception to this generalization is the compound *nek-maot* [mother-father] 'parents, mother(s) and father(s)', in which a root with a female referent precedes a root with a male referent. The source of this atypical order is unclear, but note that there exists an alternate compound *baox-minl* [father-mother], which involves different roots and displays the opposite order (i.e. male before female) but which has the same meaning.

5.3.3 Generic compounds

5.3.3.1 Overview

Generic compounds are superficially similar to reciprocal compounds in some respects, but they still possess a number of unique structural, grammatical, and referential properties that serve to distinguish them as a class from all other types of noun compound. Most obviously, generic compounds always consist of exactly four syllables with an [[X-X][X-X]] internal structure – in other words, the first two syllables form a constituent, as do the last two syllables, and those two disyllabic constituents then combine to form the generic compound as a whole. These generic compounds also display very distinct referential properties. The two immediate constituents of a generic compound (i.e. the two disyllabic halves of such a compound) each refer to a representative member of some larger, heterogeneous set of entities. For example, the first immediate constituent of the generic compound in (5.73) below is *ghaob-nbed* 'rice cake' and the second is *ghaob-nzaut* 'uncooked rice', each of which is a representative member of the larger set of foods in general (and that set is, of course, a heterogeneous one).

(5.73) *ghaob-nbed-ghaob-nzaut*
NOM-rice.cake-NOM-uncooked.rice
'food, foodstuffs, provisions' (Xiaohui Wu, fieldnotes)

A generic compound can be used to refer to any group of entities that is contained within the larger, heterogeneous set of entities of which the compound's immediate constituents are representative members, even if that group does not actually contain an instance of every type of entity found in the larger heterogeneous set. Such a compound can also be used to refer to the larger, heterogeneous set of entities itself. Thus, for instance, the generic compound *ghaob-nbed-ghaob-nzaut* given above can be used to refer to any particular group of foods, such as all the food in one's home or all the food laid out on a table, even if that group of foods does not actually contain any rice cakes (*ghaob-nbed*) or uncooked rice (*ghaob-nzaut*). It can also be used to refer to food in general (i.e. non-referentially), as in the following example.

(5.74) *Boub bioud jix doul* ***ghaob-nbed-ghaob-nzaut.***
1PL home NEG_1 remain **NOM-rice.cake-NOM-uncooked.rice**
'We don't have anything to eat at home.' (Xiaohui Wu, fieldnotes)

While the referential differences between generic compounds and attributive compounds (see Section 5.3.1) are obvious, the referential differences between generic compounds and reciprocal compounds (Section 5.3.2) are more subtle, although they still exist. A reciprocal compound can only be applied to groups of entities that contain at least one instance of the referent of each of the compound's constituent roots. For example, *maot-deb* [father-child] 'father(s) and child(ren)' can only be applied to groups that contain at least one father and at least one child. In contrast, a generic compound can be applied to groups of entities that only contain an instance of the referent of one of the compound's two immediate constituents, or even to groups of entities that contain no instances of the referents of either immediate constituent. The generic compound *ghaob-nbed-ghaob-nzaut*, for instance, can be applied to groups of entities that contain rice cakes but not uncooked rice, to groups of entities that contain uncooked rice but not rice cakes, and even to groups of entities that contain neither rice cakes nor uncooked rice (as long as such groups still consist of various foodstuffs, of course).

Before moving on to a more detailed examination of the properties that distinguish generic compounds from Xong's other noun compounds, it is worth mentioning that similar constructions are also found in many other isolating languages of East and Southeast Asia. Some examples include the Tibeto-Burman language Lahu (Matisoff 1973: 81–86), the Tai-Kadai language Lao (Enfield 2007: 304–306), the Austroasiatic language Vietnamese (Thompson 1965: 128, 129), and the Miao-Yao language Hmong (Mortensen 2003), among many others. Furthermore, Xong's own generic compounds have already attracted a great deal of attention from other scholars; see, for instance, Yang (2004: 136–138), Luo (2005: 133–147), and Yu (2004; 2006; 2011: 325–338). However, it is important to note that these scholars of Xong only discuss generic compounds as a subset of a larger set of "fixed tetrasyllabic expressions" (*sìyīn gécí* 四音格词), many of which contain both noun roots and other, non-nominal roots, and many others of which contain no noun roots at all. While there is some phonological evidence for treating all these "fixed tetrasyllabic expressions" as a single cohesive class in other varieties of Xong, there does not appear to be any such evidence in Fenghuang Xong itself (for details, see Section 5.3.3.2 below). In the absence of such phonological evidence, the many structural, grammatical, and referential differences between generic noun compounds and other fixed tetrasyllabic expressions make it difficult to justify describing all fixed tetrasyllabic expressions together in a single section of this grammar.[88] Thus, other, non-nominal types of these expressions are not discussed here, but rather in various places throughout subsequent chapters. See in particular Sections 6.1.3.3, 10.5.2, 10.5.3, and 12.2.2.

Naturally, unless otherwise specified, the claims made in this and the following sections only apply to generic compounds (as defined by this author) in Fenghuang Xong.

5.3.3.2 Structural and referential properties

Generic compounds in Fenghuang Xong display a fairly rigid internal structure, if not quite as rigid a one as is found in reciprocal compounds (see Section 5.3.2). As was mentioned in Section 5.3.3.1, they are always composed of exactly four monosyllabic morphemes with an [[X-X][X-X]] internal structure, so that the first and second syllables form one disyllabic constituent, the third and fourth syllables form another, and the resulting two disyllabic constituents then combine to form the generic compound as a whole. Each disyllabic constituent in a generic compound almost always consists of a nominal prefix (see Section 5.4) and a following noun root, with both disyllabic constituents having the same prefix but different roots. This usually results in an *ABAC* structure, where *A* is a nominal prefix and *B* and *C* are noun roots. This is shown in (5.75) and (5.76) below, in which the nominal prefixes have been bolded.

(5.75) ***daob***-*ronf*-***daob***-*gueinb*
AN-dragon-**AN**-ghost
'supernatural beings' (Shixiang Wu, fieldnotes)

(5.76) ***ghaob***-*beub*-***ghaob***-*loud*
NOM-quilt-**NOM**-bamboo.sleeping.mat
'bedding' (Shixiang Wu, fieldnotes)

88 Similarly, one would not typically devote a section of a descriptive grammar specifically to fixed disyllabic constructions, since the relatively superficial feature that all such constructions have in common (namely, consisting of two syllables) will generally be outweighed by the significant structural, grammatical, and referential differences among (e.g.) a disyllabic subject–predicate sequence, a disyllabic noun–modifier sequence, a disyllabic multiverbal construction, and other types of disyllabic constructions.

However, there are a handful of generic compounds that violate these general rules. In examples (5.77) and (5.78), for instance, all four syllables are noun roots, with the first two syllables combining to form an attributive compound, the last two syllables combining to form another, and the two resulting disyllabic attributive compounds then combining into a single tetrasyllabic generic compound.

(5.77) *aub-gheb-aub-mes*
water-eye-water-face
'a face covered with tears, a weeping countenance' (Haili Shi, fieldnotes)[89]

(5.78) *aub-gheb-ghaod-mieus*
water-eye-feces-nose
'tears and mucus' (Chenghua Long, fieldnotes)

Example (5.79) is similar to most other generic compounds in that its first and third syllables are both nominal prefixes, but it is unusual in that here two different nominal prefixes are involved.

(5.79) *bid-gheul-ghaob-chaut*
FRT-mountain-NOM-wilderness
'wilderness, untamed land' (Xingyu Shi, in *Oub Meinl Yaos Geud*)

Finally, in example (5.80), the first two syllables constitute a disyllabic but apparently (at least in synchronic terms) monomorphemic noun (*laod.gheb* 'eye'), while the last two syllables constitute a typical attributive compound (*khauk-mes* [hole-face] 'face'). Aside from this unusual structural feature, though, the generic compound in this example displays all the same grammatical and referential properties as Xong's other generic compounds.

(5.80) *laod.gheb-khauk-mes*
eye-hole-face
'face, countenance' (Xiaohui Wu, fieldnotes)

The author has not yet encountered any attributive or reciprocal compounds whose constituent morphemes can be rearranged without affecting grammaticality or meaning, but roughly half of all attested generic compounds allow their two immediate constituent nouns to freely occur in either order. Thus, for instance, the attributive

89 The meaning of this compound – 'a face covered in tears, a weeping countenance' – is seemingly less "generic" than those of the other compounds presented so far in this section and may involve some degree of metaphoric extension. As examples (5.117) and (5.118) further below show, this seems to be common with generic compounds whose immediate constituents refer to body parts (or, in this case, excretions from the body).

compound *eud-beinx* [clothing-flower] 'patterned clothing' cannot be changed to **beinx-eud*, and the reciprocal compound *naob-geud* [older.brother-younger.sibling] 'older brother(s) and younger sibling(s)' cannot be changed to **geud-naob*. However, the generic compound meaning 'winter precipitation' can be produced as either *ghaob-giand-ghaob-nbet* (as in (5.81) below) or *ghaob-nbet-ghaob-giand* (as in (5.82)) with no change in meaning or grammaticality.

(5.81) *ghaob-giand-ghaob-nbet*
NOM-ice-NOM-snow
'winter precipitation (ice, snow, sleet, hail, etc.)' (Shixiang Wu, fieldnotes)

(5.82) *ghaob-nbet-ghaob-giand*
NOM-snow-NOM-ice
'winter precipitation (ice, snow, sleet, hail, etc.)' (Shixiang Wu, fieldnotes) (same as (5.81) above)

Similarly, the generic compound meaning 'dining utensils' can be produced as either *ghaob-dal-ghaob-zhet* (as in (5.83) below) or *ghaob-zhet-ghaob-dal* (as in (5.84)).

(5.83) *ghaob-dal-ghaob-zhet*
NOM-child's.bowl-NOM-bowl
'dining utensils' (Chenghua Long, fieldnotes)

(5.84) *ghaob-zhet-ghaob-dal*
NOM-bowl-NOM-child's.bowl
'dining utensils' (Chenghua Long, fieldnotes) (same as (5.83) above)

However, this is not true of all generic compounds. There are a handful of such compounds for which both orders are possible, but one is strongly preferred. This is the case with the generic compound meaning 'food, foodstuffs, provisions', as shown in (5.85) and (5.86) below.

(5.85) *ghaob-nbed-ghaob-nzaut*
NOM-rice.cake-NOM-uncooked.rice
'food, foodstuffs, provisions' (Xiaohui Wu, fieldnotes)

(5.86) ??*ghaob-nzaut-ghaob-nbed*
NOM-uncooked.rice-NOM-rice.cake
(intended: 'food, foodstuffs, provisions')

Furthermore, approximately half of all generic compounds only allow one order, with the alternate order being quite ungrammatical (though often still interpretable). This can be seen with the generic compound meaning 'melons (in general)' in examples (5.87) and (5.88) below.

(5.87) *ghaob-dob-ghaob-guaob*
NOM-melon-NOM-cucumber
'melons (in general)' (Xiaohui Wu, fieldnotes)

(5.88) **ghaob-guaob-ghaob-dob*
NOM-cucumber-NOM-melon
(intended: 'melons [in general]')

There does not appear to be any way of predicting whether a particular generic compound will freely allow either order, will allow either order but strongly prefer one, or will only allow one order. The author has not yet had the opportunity to test the "reversability" of every generic compound with multiple consultants, and so it is possible that some degree of idiolectal variation is involved. However, the many generic compounds that freely allow either order clearly demonstrate that the tonal ordering restrictions which Yu (2011: 327–329) observed for tetrasyllabic noun compounds in Aizhai Xong do not apply to any of the varieties of Fenghuang Xong spoken by the author's primary consultants.[90] The factors determining the relative ordering of constituents within Fenghuang Xong's generic compounds currently remain unclear.

Regardless of their internal structure and ordering possibilities, most generic compounds can (as was noted above) be used to refer to any subset of some larger, heterogeneous set of entities of which the referents of the compound's two immediate constituents are representative members. (A few generic compounds seem to have undergone some degree of metaphorical extension or lexicalization since they were first coined, meaning this claim is not strictly true for every generic compound, only for most of them.) Thus, a generic compound like *daob-jod-daob-xint* [AN-tiger-AN-leopard] 'large, dangerous carnivores' can be used to refer to a set that contains both tigers and leopards, to one that contains leopards but not tigers (or vice versa), or

90 Specifically, Yu argues that the tone on the second syllable of such a compound must either "precede" or be identical to the tone on the fourth syllable in terms of the eight historical tones of Miao-Yao (see Section 3.5.2.1). For example, if the tone on the second syllable of such a compound is a reflex of historical tone 1, then the tone on the fourth syllable is unrestricted. If the tone on the second syllable is a reflex of historical tone 2, then the tone on the fourth syllable can be any but a reflex of historical tone 1. If the tone on the second syllable is a reflex of historical tone 3, then the tone on the fourth syllable can be any but a reflex of historical tone 1 or historical tone 2. This continues on up to instances where the tone on the second syllable is a reflex of historical tone 8, in which case the tone on the fourth syllable must also be a reflex of historical tone 8. See Sections 6.2.2 and 11.1.3 of this grammar for discussion of similar restrictions in Fenghuang Xong's numeral phrases and ideophones (respectively), and see also Mortensen (2006: 174–270) for more information on tonal ordering restrictions in the languages of greater mainland Southeast Asia in general.

even to one that contains neither tigers nor leopards (e.g. one that contains only bears and lions). This is in sharp contrast to reciprocal compounds (see Section 5.3.2), which can only be used to refer to sets that include one or more representatives of the referent of each of the compound's immediate constituents. Thus, for example, the reciprocal compound *naob-geud* [older.brother-younger.sibling] 'older brother(s) and younger sibling(s)' can only be used to refer to a group of entities containing at least one older brother and at least one younger sibling.

This observation about referentiality is made particularly clear when one attempts to link the immediate constituents of a generic compound with the form *ox/ux* 'and' (see Section 8.3). This generally results in an utterance which is still grammatical, but which has a very different meaning from the equivalent utterance without *ox/ux*. This can be seen in examples (5.89) and (5.90) below, either of which could be used as an excuse to take one's leave when visiting someone else's home but which still clearly differ in meaning. Example (5.89), which contains the generic compound *daob-guoud-daob-nbat* 'domestic animals, especially mammals', can be used if one has both dogs and pigs at home, if one has either dogs or pigs at home (but not both), or even if one has neither dogs nor pigs at home, but only other animals (e.g. cows or horses).

(5.89) *Wel naond bioud heit doul* ***daob-guoud-daob-nbat.***
1SG ASSOC home still remain **AN-dog-AN-pig**
'I've still got animals at home (to go take care of).' (Shixiang Wu, fieldnotes)

In contrast, example (5.90), which contains the nouns *daob-guoud* [AN-dog] 'dog' and *daob-nbat* [AN-pig] 'pig' now linked by *ox/ux* 'and', could only be used if one specifically had at least one dog and at least one pig at home.

(5.90) *Wel naond bioud heit doul* ***daob-guoud ox daob-nbat.***
1SG ASSOC home still remain **AN-dog and AN-pig**
'I've still got dogs and pigs at home (to go take care of).' (Shixiang Wu, fieldnotes)

5.3.3.3 Generic compounds and quantification

Unlike the other types of noun compound discussed earlier in this chapter, the behavior of generic compounds with respect to quantifying expressions is somewhat irregular. While attributive compounds can be quantified by any semantically appropriate quantifying expression (see Section 5.3.1) and reciprocal compounds can be quantified by any such expression that refers to more than one entity (Section 5.3.2), generic compounds can only be readily quantified by expressions referring to relatively large and/or non-specific amounts. For instance, the generic compounds in examples (5.91) and (5.92) below are easily quantified by a verb like *hliof/hliob* 'many' or a numeral-classifier phrase like *aod-bat-ngonl* [one-hundred-CLF:animate] 'one hundred (animate entities)'.

(5.91) *Aod-del* *ndaut* *dox* *mex* ***hliob*** ***daob-ginb-daob-npad***
one-CLF:rigid.length tree that exist **many** **AN-bug-AN-ant**
guaot!
pass
'There are a ton of bugs on that tree!' (Xiaohui Wu, fieldnotes)

(5.92) *Boub* *bioud* *mex* ***aod-bat-ngonl*** ***daob-ghab-daob-naus.***
1PL home exist **one-hundred-CLF:animate** **AN-chicken-AN-duck**
'Our family has a hundred head of poultry.' (Xiaohui Wu, fieldnotes)

In contrast, it is impossible to quantify a generic compound using a quantifying expression that refers to only one entity, just as was the case with reciprocal compounds.

(5.93) **aod-leb* *ghaob-dob-ghaob-guaob*
one-CLF NOM-melon-NOM-cucumber
(intended: 'one melon')

(5.94) **aod-ngonl* *daob-yul-daob-nief*
one-CLF:animate AN-cow-AN-water.buffalo
(intended: 'one cow', 'one water buffalo', *or* 'one bovine')

Attempting to quantify generic compounds using quantifying expressions that refer to small, specific amounts greater than one (e.g. expressions meaning 'three', 'eight', 'fifteen', etc.) yields conflicting results. For instance, one consultant accepted an utterance meaning 'ten melons' (see example (5.95)) but rejected one intended to mean 'ten bugs' (example (5.96)), even though both involved perfectly parallel generic compounds, identical syntactic structures, and even similar semantic structures.

(5.95) *gul-leb* *ghaob-dob-ghaob-guaob*
ten-CLF NOM-melon-NOM-cucumber
'ten melons' (Xiaohui Wu, fieldnotes)

(5.96) **gul-ngonl* *daob-ginb-daob-npad*
ten-CLF:animate AN-bug-AN-ant
(intended: 'ten bugs')

Similarly, two consultants firmly rejected the utterance intended to mean 'three brothers' in example (5.97), but they reluctantly accepted the equivalent utterance intended to mean 'four maternal grandparents' in example (5.98). The consultants in question said that example (5.98) was not actually wrong, but that it would sound better if the generic compound *ghaob-daob-ghaob-daok* [NOM-maternal.grandfather-NOM-maternal.grandmother] were replaced with the reciprocal compound *daob-daok* [maternal.grandfather-maternal.grandmother].

(5.97)	**bub-meinl*	*ghaob-naob-ghaob-geud*
	three-CLF:person	NOM-older.brother-NOM-younger.sibling
	(intended: 'three brothers')	

(5.98)	??*bieib-meinl*	*ghaob-daob-ghaob-daok*
	four-CLF:person	NOM-maternal.grandfather-NOM-maternal.grandmother
	(intended: 'four maternal grandparents')	

The three examples below provide further conflicting evidence, as most of the author's consultants readily accepted examples (5.99) and (5.100) but firmly rejected example (5.101).

(5.99)	*il-ngonl*	*daob-nief-daob-yul*
	eight-CLF:animate	AN-water.buffalo-AN-cow
	'eight bovines, eight water buffalo and/or cows' (Shixiang Wu, fieldnotes)	

(5.100)	*bub-bok*	*ghaob-ngonx-ghaob-ngieb*
	three-CLF:bag	NOM-silver-NOM-gold
	'three bags of treasure' (Xiaohui Wu, fieldnotes)	

(5.101)	**Boub*	*mex*	*bub-moux*	*dib-laut-dib-laos.*
	1PL	exist	three-CLF:mu	LOC-land-LOC-field
	(intended: 'We have three *mu* [unit of area] of land.')			

The restriction against generic compounds co-occurring with quantifying expressions that refer to just one entity is easy enough to explain on semantic grounds, since generic compounds are only used to refer to sets of entities, not to individual ones (this is true of reciprocal compounds as well). The other quantifier-related restrictions shown above are more difficult to explain, especially since generic compounds are almost never quantified when they appear in the naturalistic Xong texts collected by the author. Additional fieldwork may reveal some singular semantic or grammatical principle underlying these restrictions, but it is also possible that they are caused instead by one or more factors that are not, strictly speaking, either semantic or grammatical in nature.

Specifically, it seems to the author that there may be something of a stylistic clash between the specific quantification of some small amount and the poetic, somewhat exaggerated or dramatic register with which generic compounds are normally associated (see Section 5.3.3.4 below). There may also be some pragmatic clash between the specific quantification of some small amount and the degree of internal variety, or heterogeneity, that is strongly implied by the use of a generic compound. Although (as was explained above) a generic compound can be used to refer to a set of entities that contains instances of the referents of both, either, or even neither of its immediate constituents, in many cases there is a very strong implicature (if not actually an entailment) that the set of entities to which a particular generic compound refers actually does contain at least one representative of each of the compound's constituents.

Consider examples (5.91) and (5.92) above. Both contain quantified generic compounds that are readily accepted by consultants, with the one in (5.91) meaning 'a ton of bugs' and the one in (5.92) meaning 'a hundred head of poultry'. The fact that these utterances are readily accepted is unsurprising, since such large, imprecise amounts accord well with the internal variety that the use of a generic compound implies: it is very possible that a set of entities made up of 'a ton of bugs' contains more than one type of bug, and that a set made up of 'a hundred head of poultry' contains multiple types of poultry (rather than, e.g., all chickens).[91] In addition, the use of these large, imprecise amounts (as opposed to a smaller one like 'ten or so' or a more specific one like 'ninety-seven') also fits – or at least does not clash with – the dramatic or exaggerated register with which generic compounds are associated.

However, using a generic compound when referring to smaller, more specific amounts like 'ten melons' (see example (5.95) above) or 'eight bovines' (example (5.99)) is somewhat odd, since sets with such small, specific numbers of members may very well not involve any internal variety. For instance, the melons involved may well be all watermelons, and the bovines involved may well be all water buffalo. And even if these sets did contain different types of entities, the numbers in question are small enough that one could just specify the members involved by saying, for example, 'five watermelons and five cucumbers' rather than just 'ten melons' (the author's consultants made this particular point to him several times while working with him on these compounds).

The issue of poetic or dramatic register may be relevant here as well. Consider examples (5.100) and (5.101) above, in which 'three bags of treasure' is accepted but

91 While 'a hundred' is obviously not imprecise in the same way that 'a ton' is, the author's consultants report that the 'hundred head of poultry' in example (5.92) could easily be referring to a group of poultry that actually numbers slightly more or less than one hundred. This is in contrast to quantifying expressions with more specific meanings like 'ninety-eight head of poultry' or 'one hundred and three head of poultry', which consultants report would only be used when referring to the exact amount in question (for obvious pragmatic reasons).

'three *mu* of land' is not, despite the very similar grammatical and semantic structures of the two utterances. This may be because 'three bags of treasure' implies more internal variety than 'three *mu* of land' (consultants report that the bags in question presumably contain various precious gems and metals rather than just gold or just silver, while the three *mu* of land may well be relatively homogeneous farmland), and also because 'three bags of treasure' seems more likely to be used in a poetic or dramatic context than 'three *mu* of land'. There are a number of relatively banal situations in which one might wish to refer to 'three *mu* of land', but it is difficult to imagine a likely situation in which one would need to refer to 'three bags of treasure' other than when reciting a folktale or something from a similarly dramatic genre.

Furthermore, in some cases this stylistic and/or pragmatic clash may be exacerbated by lexical blocking (see, e.g., Poser 1992). This may explain why example (5.97) above was rejected by the author's consultants, and why example (5.98) was accepted only reluctantly. In each case, the existence of a readily quantifiable reciprocal compound with a roughly similar meaning (*naob-geud* instead of *ghaob-naob-ghaob-geud* for 'brothers', and *daob-daok* instead of *ghaob-daob-ghaob-daok* for 'maternal grandparents') may explain consultants' reluctance to use a less readily quantifiable generic compound.

5.3.3.4 Pragmatic properties and semantic scope

All of the author's consultants have been very conscious of generic compounds in a metalinguistic sense. However, the author has not been able to elicit a Xong term that refers to these compounds, and his consultants simply refer to them with the Standard Mandarin term *chengyu* (*chéngyǔ* 成语, a term typically used to refer to certain tetrasyllabic idioms in Sinitic languages). The general consensus among the author's consultants is that the use of generic compounds is particularly associated with poetic or dramatic registers and is a mark of skilled (rather than merely competent or fluent) Xong speech. For instance, the author collected several texts from Mr. Qiusheng Long, an elderly Xong speaker from Yankan Village whose oratorical skills made him in great demand at weddings, funerals, and other important social events. Generic compounds were much more common in Mr. Long's texts than in texts collected from other speakers. Two examples can be seen in (5.102) below, and note also the parallelism of the two clauses involved.

(5.102) *Boub bex.seint jeub jud giet jont ninb*
1PL common.folk then$_3$ NEG$_2$ dare live at
dib-bioud-dib-deul, *jont ninb* ***khauk-raud-khauk-biat.***
LOC-home-LOC-firewood live at **hole-forest-hole-cliff**
'(Back when there were bandits everywhere,) we common folk didn't dare stay in our homes, (we had to) live out in the wilderness.' (Qiusheng Long, in *Ngel.kanx*)

It is unclear how productive generic compounds are, and whether they constitute a closed or an open class. Consultants have rejected some proposed generic compounds that seemed phonologically and semantically well formed to the author, but these same consultants have also said that other proposed generic compounds sound perfectly acceptable to them, even if they would not normally produce them themselves. If generic compounds are a closed class, though, they are certainly a very large one, with at least many dozens and perhaps even hundreds of members.[92]

Naturally, then, it would be impossible to exhaustively list all generic compounds here. However, examples (5.103–5.126) below do provide a representative sample of attested generic compounds to give the reader some idea of the sorts of meanings these compounds typically express (see also the many generic compounds given in earlier examples in Sections 5.3.3.1 through 5.3.3.3). First, examples (5.103–5.107) list several generic compounds referring to kin members (cf. the reciprocal compounds in Section 5.3.2 above).

(5.103) *ghaob-naob-ghaob-geud*
NOM-older.brother-NOM-younger.sibling
'brothers (in general)' (Haili Shi, fieldnotes)

(5.104) *ghaob-yaos-ghaob-geud*
NOM-older.sister-NOM-younger.sibling
'sisters (in general)' (Haili Shi, fieldnotes)

(5.105) *ghaob-deb-ghaob-nek*
NOM-child-NOM-mother
'mothers and children, mothers with (usually small) children' (Shixiang Wu, fieldnotes)

(5.106) *ghaob-deb-ghaob-giad*
NOM-child-NOM-grandchild
'children and grandchildren, descendants' (Shixiang Wu, fieldnotes)

(5.107) *ghaob-daob-ghaob-daok*
NOM-maternal.grandfather-NOM-maternal.grandmother
'maternal grandparents (in general)' (Haili Shi, fieldnotes)

92 Yu (2011: 425–455) lists several hundred fixed tetrasyllabic expressions in an appendix to her Aizhai Xong grammar, many of which are generic compounds. However, Yu's appendix also includes many tetrasyllabic expressions that would not be considered generic compounds according to the criteria used in this grammar, since they involve verbal, classifier, or other non-nominal roots.

There are a number of generic compounds referring to animals and plants as well. Examples (5.108–5.116) present some of the ones attested so far.

(5.108) *daob-jod-daob-xint*
AN-tiger-AN-leopard
'large, dangerous carnivores' (Chenghua Long, fieldnotes)

(5.109) *daob-yul-daob-nief*
AN-cow-AN-water.buffalo
'bovines' (Haili Shi, fieldnotes)

(5.110) *daob-guoud/yul-daob-nbat*
AN-dog/cow-AN-pig
'domestic animals, especially mammals' (Xiaohui Wu, fieldnotes)

(5.111) *daob-maonb-daob-guoud*
AN-cat-AN-dog
'domestic animals, especially mammals' (Xiaohui Wu, fieldnotes)

(5.112) *daob-ghab-daob-naus*
AN-chicken-AN-duck
'poultry' (Xiaohui Wu, fieldnotes)

(5.113) *daob-ginb-daob-npad*
AN-bug-AN-ant
'bugs, insects, small terrestrial invertebrates' (Shixiang Wu, fieldnotes)

(5.114) *ghaob-ndaut-ghaob-hlod*
NOM-tree-NOM-bamboo
'trees, bamboo, large plants in general' (Chenghua Long, fieldnotes)

(5.115) *ghaob-reib-ghaob-ncoud*
NOM-greens-NOM-grass
'grasses, vegetables, small plants in general' (Shixiang Wu, fieldnotes)

(5.116) *ghaob-janb-ghaob-nzaut*
NOM-???-NOM-uncooked.rice
'crops, domestic plants' (Shixiang Wu, fieldnotes)

As examples (5.117) and (5.118) below show, generic compounds whose immediate constituents refer to body parts often seem to involve some degree of metaphoric extension. This was also seen in example (5.77) above.

(5.117) *ghaob-tib-ghaob-xed*
NOM-stomach-NOM-intestine
'internal organs; personal character, moral fiber' (Shixiang Wu, fieldnotes)

(5.118) *ghaob-deut-ghaob-doul*
NOM-foot-NOM-hand
'quickness, alacrity, speed of action' (Shixiang Wu, fieldnotes)

Finally, examples (5.119–5.126) present a variety of generic compounds referring to other, more miscellaneous concepts.

(5.119) *ghaob/dib-laut-ghaob/dib-laos*
NOM/LOC-land-NOM/LOC-field
'land, croplands' (Shixiang Wu and Chenghua Long, fieldnotes)

(5.120) *ghaob-bioud-ghaob-deul*
NOM-home-NOM-firewood
'possessions, property, dwellings' (Xiaohui Wu, fieldnotes; cf. example (5.102) above)

(5.121) *ghaob-ngonx-ghaob-ngieb*
NOM-silver-NOM-gold
'wealth, treasure' (Shixiang Wu, fieldnotes)

(5.122) *ghaob/deb-janb-ghaob/deb-nghaot*
NOM/DIM-wealth-NOM/DIM-price
'wealth, money' (Xiaohui Wu, fieldnotes)

(5.123) *ghaob/baod-jaok-ghaob/baod-qanl*
NOM/BUG-prick-NOM/BUG-spike
'sharp things, pointy things' (Shixiang Wu, fieldnotes)

(5.124) *ghaob-neis-ghaob-mok*
NOM-machete-NOM-sickle
'bladed implements (in general)' (Chenghua Long, fieldnotes)

(5.125) *ghaob-wanl-ghaob-jut*
NOM-pot-NOM-kettle
'metal cookware (pots, pans, kettles, ladles, etc.)' (Chenghua Long, fieldnotes)

(5.126) *dib-gheul-dib-ronl*
LOC-village-LOC-???
'villages and towns, settlements' (Shixiang Wu, fieldnotes)

5.3.4 Compounds involving recent Sinitic borrowings

Many noun compounds in modern Xong involve forms recently borrowed from Sinitic, especially from the Standard Mandarin and Fenghuang Chinese varieties (see Section 2.7.2). Xong speakers are highly sensitive to this, and they are usually quite aware of which forms in their speech are recent Sinitic borrowings and which are "native" Xong forms.[93] Compounds that consist either partly or entirely of recent Sinitic borrowings are extremely common in Xong narratives and discourse, even among professedly monolingual Xong speakers, and furthermore such compounds often violate the various compound formation rules discussed in Sections 5.3.1 to 5.3.3 above. Thus, while the author's description of Xong phonology (see Chapter 3) largely ignores recent Sinitic borrowings, a comprehensive account of Xong's synchronic grammar requires that noun compounds featuring such borrowings be given some discussion here.

The simplest and most common compounds involving recent Sinitic borrowings are those which are clearly attributive in nature, but which consist entirely of Sinitic roots and display ModN order rather than NMod order (cf. Section 5.3.1).[94] The unusual ordering of these compounds is unsurprising, given that both Standard Mandarin and Fenghuang Chinese generally have ModN order in their own noun compounds. Examples of such compounds are given in (5.127–5.131) below, and many other similar examples (which are generally not marked as such) can be found in the Xong sentences and texts included in this grammar. In each example below, the Chinese characters, *pinyin* spelling, interlinear gloss, and meaning of the Standard Mandarin source form are given on the left, while the resulting Xong form, its meaning, and its source (in terms of the consultant who produced it) are given on the right.[95]

93 While the author's consultants are very conscious of recent borrowings from Sinitic in their own Xong speech, they do not readily distinguish between Xong's truly native forms and its many older borrowings from Sinitic. This is unsurprising given that many of these older borrowings were borrowed into Xong centuries or even millennia ago (see Section 3.1 of this grammar), and also given that many of them have undergone dramatic phonological changes since they were first borrowed. For instance, the author's consultants could hardly be blamed for failing to identify *raud* 'forest' as a very old Sinitic borrowing when its cognate form in Standard Mandarin is now *lín* (林), nor for failing to identify *niax* 'meat' as a borrowing when its Standard Mandarin cognate is now *ròu* (肉) (Yang 2004: 145, 147).

94 No clear examples of reciprocal compounds (see Section 5.3.2) or generic compounds (Section 5.3.3) involving obvious recent borrowings from Sinitic have yet been encountered.

95 While it is likely that some or even all of these forms were in fact borrowed from Fenghuang Chinese rather than from Standard Mandarin, only the (potential) Standard Mandarin source forms are

(5.127) 机枪
jī-qiāng → *jik-qaonk*
machine-gun
'machine gun' 'machine gun' (Qiusheng Long, in *Ngel.kanx*)

(5.128) 手机
shǒu-jī → *shoux-jik*
hand-machine
'cell phone' 'cell phone' (Haili Shi, in *Tooth Conversation*)

(5.129) 绿豆面
lǜdòu-miàn → *loux.doub-mianb*
mung.bean-noodles
'mung-bean noodles' 'mung-bean noodles' (Chenghua Long, fieldnotes)

(5.130) 英语老师
Yīngyǔ-lǎoshī → *Ink.ix-lox.sid*
English-teacher
'English teacher' 'English teacher' (Haili Shi, fieldnotes)

(5.131) 国王
guó-wáng → *guef-waonl*
country-king
'king' 'king' (Haili Shi, in *Guef Waonl Hauk Nggaob*)

In each of the compounds above, the semantic head of the compound appears last just as it does in the Standard Mandarin (or Fenghuang Chinese) source material, yielding ModN order rather than the more typically Xong NMod order. Of course, given their unusual constituent order and their obviously Sinitic sources, one could certainly argue that these particular compounds have not been productively formed by Xong speakers, but rather have simply been borrowed into Xong as atomic forms with no internal structure. In fact, the author rather suspects that this is the case, at least for most such compounds. However, in some cases Xong speakers will use either or both of the immediate constituents of these compounds independently, suggesting that at least some such compounds do have some degree of internal structure for at

presented here. Additionally, some constituents in these Standard Mandarin source forms which are themselves polymorphemic compounds – e.g. *lǜ-dòu* [green-bean] 'mung bean' in example (5.129) or *Yīng-yǔ* [English-language] 'English' in example (5.130) – are for simplicity's sake treated as atomic forms in these examples.

least some Xong speakers. For instance, while Xong's *Ink.ix-lox.sid* [English-teacher] 'English teacher' appears at first glance to be a straightforward borrowing of Standard Mandarin's *Yīngyǔ-lǎoshī* (or of the equivalent form in Fenghuang Chinese), note that both the first and second halves of the Xong form in question can also be used independently.

(5.132) *Puk* ***Ink.ix!***
speak **English**
'Speak English!' (Haili Shi, fieldnotes)

(5.133) *Beul* *nins* ***lox.sid.***
3 COP **teacher**
'He's a teacher.' (Haili Shi, fieldnotes)

Similarly, consultants regularly produce 'noodles' as just *mianb* (cf. *loux.doub-mianb* [mung.bean-noodles] 'mung-bean noodles' in example (5.129) above). Consultants are also quite aware that *guef* 'country' appears as the first syllable of a form meaning 'king' (see example (5.131) above) and also as the last syllable of several forms referring to particular countries (see example (5.138) below). All of this suggests that compounds like *Ink.ix-lox.sid* 'English teacher', *loux.doub-mianb* 'mung-bean noodles', and *guef-waonl* 'king' are in fact still analyzable (or morphologically transparent) to some degree even after they have been borrowed into Xong.[96]

Attributive compounds that feature both Xong roots and Sinitic roots are significantly rarer in the author's collected texts, although some examples do still occur. These compounds display Xong's "native" NMod order more often than the Sinitic-like

96 This raises some difficult questions about glossing such compounds. Due to the very large number of Sinitic borrowings in Xong, the high level of Standard Mandarin and/or Fenghuang Chinese proficiency found among many Xong speakers (including many of the author's consultants), and the high degree of typological similarity between Xong and the Sinitic languages, many Xong speakers must be aware of the original internal structures of many complex forms borrowed from Sinitic. However, it also stands to reason that many Xong speakers are likely unaware of the original internal structures of certain other such forms, especially for speakers less proficient in Sinitic varieties and for older borrowings that are less obviously similar to their modern Sinitic cognates. Thus, it is not always obvious whether such compounds should be glossed morpheme by morpheme or whether they should be given a single unitary gloss. For example, is 'cell phone' (see example (5.128)) better transcribed as *shoux-jik* or as *shoux.jik*, and is it better glossed as 'hand-machine' or simply as 'cell. phone'?

In this grammar the latter options are generally used (aside from in this Section 5.3.4 itself, that is), so that the form 'cell phone' is transcribed as *shoux.jik* rather than *shoux-jik* and is glossed as 'cell. phone' rather than 'hand-machine'. However, it should be noted that this is largely an arbitrary decision, and it should not be interpreted to mean that all such forms are morphologically atomic in Fenghuang Xong.

ModN order, and it seems even more likely that these compounds are still analyzable to modern Xong speakers. Five examples of such compounds are given in (5.134–5.138) below. In each case, the Sinitic source form is given in Chinese characters and *pinyin*, while any Xong forms are given in the author's practical orthography.

(5.134)			白菜		
	reib	+	*báicài*	→	*reib-bex.cef*
	vegetable		cabbage		vegetable-cabbage
	'vegetable'		'cabbage'		'cabbage' (Haili Shi, fieldnotes)

(5.135)			车		
	nek-geud	+	*chē*	→	*nek-geud-chek*
	AUG-road		vehicle		AUG-road-vehicle
	'road'		'vehicle'		'paved road' (Xiaohui Wu, in *Conversation in La'ershan*)

(5.136)	萝卜				
	luóbo	+	*doub*	→	*hlat.bous-doub*
	radish		earth		radish-earth
	'radish'		'earth'		'jícama, yam bean' (Chenghua Long, fieldnotes)

(5.137)	碟子				
	diézi	+	*sad*	→	*deb.zib-sad*
	disc		Xong.song		disc-Xong.song
	'DVD, CD'		'Xong song'		'DVD featuring traditional Xong songs' (Qiumei Wu, in *Conversation in Yankan*)

(5.138)	美国				
	Měiguó	+	*miex*	→	*Meix.guef-miex*
	U.S.		person		U.S.-person
	'the U.S.'		'person'		'American (person)' (Haili Shi, fieldnotes)

Note that the first four examples above all involve NMod order, while the fifth – *Meix.guef-miex* 'American (person)' – involves ModN order. Note also that in examples (5.134), (5.135), and (5.138) the head of each compound is a "native" Xong form while the modifier is a recent Sinitic borrowing, but in examples (5.136) and (5.137) the opposite is the case.

5.4 Nominal prefixes

5.4.1 Introduction

Like all varieties of Xong so far described in the literature, Fenghuang Xong features a set of bound monosyllabic morphemes which most often occur immediately preceding noun roots and which in most cases seem to have grammaticalized from noun roots themselves. These morphemes are referred to as *nominal prefixes* in this grammar. In addition to the fact that they are bound forms, these prefixes also differ from canonical noun roots in several other ways: their semantics are often relatively vague, many of them are optional in certain grammatical positions, some of them are interchangeable when they occur preceding certain noun roots, and overall they are much more productive (i.e. can combine with many more unique morphemes) than most other nominal forms. Some of these prefixes serve functions somewhat similar to those of derivational morphemes in other languages (e.g. changing lexical category or marking semantic sex – though *not* grammatical gender), others behave somewhat similarly to inflectional morphemes (e.g. in that they are obligatory in certain grammatical environments but do not have any clear lexical meaning), and many fall somewhere in between. Although it could be argued that their often optional nature and the fact that they do not trigger any sort of agreement mean that Xong's nominal prefixes do not bear a particularly heavy functional load in the language (certainly less so than, say, noun class prefixes in Bantu languages or gender marking in many European languages), their high frequency and relatively idiosyncratic grammatical behavior mean that these forms still merit thorough discussion here.

Xong's nominal prefixes have already attracted much attention from other scholars of the language. Previous studies specifically focusing on nominal prefixes in Xong include Luo (1980) and Guan (2006), and most longer descriptions of Xong grammar have also included a section devoted to these forms; see, for instance, Luo (1990: 85–106), Xiang (1999: 21–23), Yang (2004: 133–136, 161, 162, 166), Luo (2005: 115–132), Chen (2009: 37–52), and Yu (2011: 29–37). There have also been a number of studies that discuss nominal prefixes in the Miao-Yao family in general, including Chen (1993), Li (2002, 2003, 2006, 2007), and (in English) Ratliff (2006) and (2010: 200–206).

However, there appear to be significant differences between the behavior of nominal prefixes in the speech of the author's own consultants from Fenghuang County and the behavior of nominal prefixes in other Xong varieties as reported in previous studies, although it is unclear whether this is due to actual linguistic differences or merely to differences of analysis (or perhaps to a combination of both). In particular, Fenghuang Xong's system of nominal prefixes is much "messier" than the nominal prefix systems described in earlier publications by other scholars. Most such publications imply that Xong's nominal prefixes constitute a neatly paradigmatic system, with little interspeaker (much less intraspeaker) variation and with fairly regular grammatical behavior.

In Fenghuang Xong, though, nothing could be further from the truth. Nominal prefixes display more interspeaker variation than perhaps any other similarly sized set of morphemes in Fenghuang Xong, and in many cases this variation appears to be due to purely idiolectal preferences. Furthermore, individual speakers often give conflicting grammaticality judgments on specific examples. For instance, they might report that a certain nominal prefix is obligatory in a certain grammatical position during one elicitation session, and then report that it is completely optional in that same position during a subsequent session. Unfortunately, in many cases this means that it is impossible to give rigorous formulations of the rules governing the grammatical behavior of Fenghuang Xong's nominal prefixes, and in the sections that follow the author is often forced to resort to vague statements about how certain prefixes "usually" or "typically" behave. Because of this, the author suspects that examining the *frequency* with which Xong's nominal prefixes display certain optional behaviors in different grammatical environments would be a very fruitful method of investigation, although this would have to wait until much larger, much more diverse Xong corpora are collected.

Due to the significant functional and grammatical differences found among Fenghuang Xong's nominal prefixes, Section 5.4.2 has been divided into ten subsections, each of which discusses a particular prefix individually (the sole exception is Section 5.4.2.10, which discusses two distinct "quasi-prefixes"). As the descriptions in Section 5.4.2 make clear, the large amount of grammatical and semantic variation among Xong's nominal prefixes makes it impossible to give a strict list of criteria that would clearly delimit the set of nominal prefixes from the language's other, more canonical nominal morphemes. There is instead a continuum from the most "prefix-like" prefixes (e.g. *ghaob-* 'NOM' and *daob-* 'AN'), which are very frequently dropped and which rarely contribute any lexical meaning to the nouns in which they occur, to the least "prefix-like" prefixes (e.g. *baod-* 'BUG' and *bid-* 'FRT'), which could arguably be analyzed as canonical noun roots with unusually broad semantic ranges.

5.4.2 Individual nominal prefixes

5.4.2.1 The prefix *ghaob-/ob-/aob-* 'NOM'

The nominal prefix *ghaob-* 'NOM' is by far the most frequent one in Fenghuang Xong. The etymology of this prefix is unknown, but it currently exists in several phonological variants, with *ob-* used in Yankan Village, *aob-* used in Shanjiang Town (or at least by the author's consultant from Shanjiang), and *ghaob-* used in La'ershan Town and its surrounding villages (with the exception of Yankan). Many consultants also freely switch back and forth between two or even all three of these variants. For convenience's sake, though, these variants are generally ignored in running text within this grammar, so that the prefix in question is simply referred to as *ghaob-* (overall the most common variant) rather than as *ghaob-/ob-/aob-*.

The form *ghaob-* 'NOM' has two major functions: it occurs in lexically specified fashion on a wide variety of noun roots, and it serves as a nominalizer of certain non-nominal roots (including verbs, classifiers, numerals, and demonstratives). When serving in the former capacity, *ghaob-* 'NOM' usually does not make any contribution to the semantics of the noun as a whole, and it can often be dropped without affecting meaning or grammaticality. Since *ghaob-* has no clear lexical meaning of its own and often serves a nominalizing function, it is glossed as 'NOM', from 'nominal'.

Most of the noun roots that obligatorily occur with a preceding *ghaob-* 'NOM' (at least when produced in isolation) can be grouped into five broad semantic categories, although many of these categories have little if anything in common with any of the others. Furthermore, there are many other noun roots which seem as though they fall into one of these five semantic categories and yet never occur with *ghaob-* 'NOM', meaning that the occurrence of *ghaob-* on any given noun root is not predictable. In many cases there is also a significant degree of interspeaker variation in terms of whether a given noun root will occur with *ghaob-* 'NOM', with some other nominal prefix, or with no prefix at all. Similarly, whether or not any particular non-nominal root can undergo nominalization through the use of *ghaob-* is not entirely predictable, especially in the case of verbs.

The first of the five broad semantic categories into which *ghaob*-bearing noun roots can be grouped contains those that have human referents. Examples of noun roots referring to humans that obligatorily (at least for most consultants) occur with a preceding *ghaob-* 'NOM' when produced in isolation are given in (5.139–5.142). However, many other noun roots with human referents occur with *deb-* 'DIM' instead (see Section 5.4.2.3) or with no prefix at all.

(5.139) *ghaob-Xonb*
NOM-Miao
'Miao person, (the) Miao people' (Haili Shi, fieldnotes)[97]

(5.140) *ghaob-zhaol*
NOM-non.Miao
'non-Miao person, (the) non-Miao peoples' (Haili Shi, fieldnotes)

(5.141) *ghaob-npaok*
NOM-woman
'woman' (Shixiang Wu, fieldnotes)

97 See Section 2.2.3 for more information on the meaning of this term and on the meaning of the term *ghaob-zhaol* [NOM-non.Miao] in example (5.140).

(5.142) *ghaob-nint*
NOM-man
'man' (Shixiang Wu, fieldnotes)

The second category contains noun roots referring to body parts (both human and animal), although certain other such roots instead occur with *bid-* 'FRT' (see Section 5.4.2.5), with *baod-* 'BUG' (Section 5.4.2.6), or with no prefix whatsoever.

(5.143) *ghaob-doul*
NOM-hand
'hand' (Haili Shi, fieldnotes)

(5.144) *ghaob-deud*
NOM-skin
'skin' (Haili Shi, fieldnotes) (cf. *bid-deud* [FRT-skin] 'tail')

(5.145) *ghaob-sond*
NOM-bone
'bone' (Haili Shi, fieldnotes)

(5.146) *ghaob-deik*
NOM-wing
'wing' (Haili Shi, fieldnotes)

The third category contains roots referring to plants or parts of plants, although certain other such roots bear *bid-* 'FRT' (see Section 5.4.2.5) or *baod-* 'BUG' (Section 5.4.2.6) instead.

(5.147) *ghaob-ndaut*
NOM-tree
'tree' (Haili Shi, fieldnotes)

(5.148) *ghaob-hlod*
NOM-bamboo
'bamboo' (Shixiang Wu, fieldnotes)

(5.149) *ghaob-ncoud*
NOM-grass
'grass' (Haili Shi, fieldnotes)

(5.150) *ghaob-nhaub*
NOM-seed
'seed' (Haili Shi, fieldnotes)

The fourth category contains most noun roots referring to handheld tools and many noun roots referring to other kinds of inanimate objects. Still, certain other roots with similar semantics occur with a different prefix instead (often *baod-* 'BUG') or with no prefix at all.

(5.151) *ghaob-dab*
NOM-box
'box' (Haili Shi, fieldnotes)

(5.152) *ghaob-njib*
NOM-scissors
'scissors' (Shixiang Wu, fieldnotes)

(5.153) *ghaob-hlat*
NOM-rope
'rope' (Haili Shi, fieldnotes)

(5.154) *ghaob-roub*
NOM-stone
'stone, rock' (Haili Shi, fieldnotes)

The fifth and final category contains noun roots with relatively abstract or intangible referents, although many other such roots (especially those that have been recently borrowed from a Sinitic language) occur with no prefix at all.

(5.155) *ghaob-shob*
NOM-sound
'sound, voice' (Shixiang Wu, fieldnotes)

(5.156) *ghaob-lis*
NOM-gift
'gift' (Shixiang Wu, fieldnotes)

(5.157) *ghaob-ped*
NOM-matter
'matter, affair' (Shixiang Wu, fieldnotes)

(5.158) *aob-ngaonf*
NOM-time
'time' (Chenghua Long, in *Frog, Where Are You?*)

Along with *daob-* 'AN' (see Section 5.4.2.2), *ghaob-* 'NOM' is one of the most readily "droppable" prefixes. For a majority of consultants, the nouns in examples (5.139–5.158) above will always occur with an initial *ghaob-* 'NOM' when produced in isolation. However, in many situations the nouns in these examples can optionally occur without an initial *ghaob-*, and in such cases this dropping of *ghaob-* has no effect on either meaning or grammaticality. Whether or not *ghaob-* 'NOM' can be dropped from a particular noun depends on at least three factors: (i) the particular noun in which the prefix is occurring, (ii) the idiolectal preferences of the speaker, and (iii) the grammatical environment in which the noun is occurring. No obvious patterns have been found with regard to the first two of these factors. It appears that some nouns which bear *ghaob-* in isolation are simply more likely to drop it in running speech than other nouns, and that some speakers are simply more likely to drop *ghaob-* (at least from certain nouns in certain grammatical environments) than other speakers. The grammatical environments which permit or even require the dropping of *ghaob-* are not yet fully understood either, but it is at least possible to point out some general tendencies.

If a given noun bears *ghaob-* 'NOM' when produced in isolation, it will also bear *ghaob-* when it (i) occurs in clause-initial position, (ii) occurs in fronted preverbal position (see Section 9.1.3.1), (iii) serves as a possessor or possessum in the *naond* possessive construction (see Section 8.2.1), or (iv) occurs immediately following the copular verb *nins* 'COP'. For instance, most consultants report that *ghaob-* 'NOM' is obligatory in examples (5.159–5.162) below.

(5.159) ***Aob-roub*** *id-lons* *leut-gheul,* *geud* *roub* *zox.*
NOM-stone DID-gather top-place$_2$ hold stone smash
'(The villagers) gathered stones at the top (of the cliff, then they) attacked (the bandits) with them.' (Qiusheng Long, in *Ngel.kanx*)

(5.160) *Beul* ***ghaob-nhaub,*** ***ghaob-hlat,*** ***ghaob-mok*** *at* *mex.*
3 **NOM-seed** **NOM-rope** **NOM-sickle** SAT exist
'(They've got everything at that store,) they've got seeds, rope, and sickles.' (Xingyu Shi, fieldnotes)

(5.161) *Beul* *naond* ***ob-doul*** *gueub* *npeif.npeif!*
3 ASSOC **NOM-hand** white IDEO:A:white
'His hands are so white!' (Haili Shi, fieldnotes)

(5.162) *Beul* *jix* *nins* ***ghaob-Xonb.***
3 NEG$_1$ COP **NOM-Miao**
'He's not Miao.' (Shixiang Wu, fieldnotes)

Conversely, if a given noun bears *ghaob-* 'NOM' when produced in isolation, that *ghaob-* will generally be optional when the noun (i) is immediately preceded by a classifier, (ii) occurs as the initial constituent of an attributive compound, or (iii) immediately follows a verb other than *nins* 'COP'. This can be seen in examples (5.163–5.166) below, in which most consultants report that *ghaob-* 'NOM' is completely optional.

(5.163) *oub-leb* ***(ghaob-)dab***
two-CLF **(NOM-)box**
'two boxes' (Haili Shi, fieldnotes)

(5.164) *(ghaob-)deud-guoud*
(NOM-)skin-dog
'dog skin' (Shixiang Wu, fieldnotes)

(5.165) *Beul baox noul keuf zhut* ***(ob-)raonf.***
3 father catch shut reach **(NOM-)cage**
'His father caught (the bird) and shut (it) in a cage.' (Xingyu Shi, in *Oub Meinl Yaos Geud*)

(5.166) *Wel lis nieus* ***(ghaob-)njib.***
1SG want buy **(NOM-)scissors**
'I want to buy some scissors.' (Shixiang Wu, fieldnotes)

Finally, a noun that bears *ghaob-* 'NOM' when produced in isolation generally cannot bear *ghaob-* when occurring as a non-initial constituent of an attributive compound (see Section 5.3.1). For instance, both *ghaob-sond* 'bone' and *ghaob-doul* 'hand' bear *ghaob-* 'NOM' when produced in isolation. However, while 'hand bones, the bones of one's hand' can be produced as either *ghaob-sond-doul* [NOM-bone-hand] or *sond-doul* [bone-hand], it is never **ghaob-sond-ghaob-doul* [NOM-bone-NOM-hand] or **sond-ghaob-doul* [bone-NOM-hand].

It is important to note that *ghaob-* 'NOM' does not appear to mark any sort of discourse-related notion like definiteness, specificity, or topicality – or, at the very least, it appears that marking any of these notions cannot be its primary function. For instance, the noun *ob-deud-guk* [NOM-skin-frog] 'frog skin' clearly has a definite, specific referent in example (5.167) below, but its initial prefix *ob-* 'NOM' is completely optional.

(5.167) *Beul naond npaok ghans beul chaot dut*
3 ASSOC woman see 3 look.for obtain
beul naond aod-xeub ***(ob-)deud-guk*** *leh.*
3 ASSOC one-CLF:body **(NOM-)skin-frog** LEH
'His wife saw that he had found his frog skin.' (Xingyu Shi, in *Deb Guk Ronf*)

Conversely, the noun *ghaob-zhous* [NOM-chopstick] 'chopsticks' clearly has an indefinite, non-specific referent in example (5.168) (the speaker in this case was asking for any pair of chopsticks, not for some particular pair), but here too *ghaob-* 'NOM' is entirely optional.

(5.168) *Gaons wel aod-ngonl* ***(ghaob-)zhous.***
give 1SG one-CLF:pair$_1$ **(NOM-)chopstick**
'Give me a pair of chopsticks.' (Shixiang Wu, fieldnotes)

While nouns that occur with *ghaob-* 'NOM' when produced in isolation will also tend to occur with it in clause-initial position, these same nouns will occur with *ghaob-* in many other syntactic environments as well. Furthermore, nouns that do not occur with *ghaob-* when produced in isolation will not occur with it in clause-initial position either.

As was mentioned earlier in this section, *ghaob-* 'NOM' is also used to nominalize certain non-nominal roots. These include a small, non-predictable subset of Xong's verbs, some of which are shown in examples (5.169–5.172) below.

(5.169) *ghaob-raos*
NOM-clever
'cleverness, intelligence' (Shixiang Wu, fieldnotes)

(5.170) *ghaob-jaok*
NOM-prick
'thorn' (Haili Shi, fieldnotes) (cf. example (5.237) below)

(5.171) *ghaob-zhat*
NOM-step.on
'foot (of animal or inanimate object)' (Chenghua Long, fieldnotes)

(5.172) *aob-bix*
NOM-compare
'object of comparison, standard' (Chenghua Long, fieldnotes)

The prefix *ghaob-* 'NOM' can also occur on a variety of other non-nominal roots with varying grammatical, semantic, and pragmatic effects. These include classifiers (see Section 6.1.3.3), numerals (Section 6.2.2), demonstratives (Section 7.2), and ignoratives (Section 7.3). 7.7

Finally, note that *ghaob-* 'NOM' appears in a number of locative nouns, including *ghaob-bol* 'underside', *ghaob-zheud* 'edge, rim', and *ghaob-nhaons* 'inside'. See Sections 5.5.2.4 through 5.5.2.7 for further information.

5.4.2.2 The prefix *daob-* 'AN'

The semantics of this prefix are relatively clear, as it occurs almost exclusively on roots which refer to non-human animate entities. In practice, this means it mostly occurs on roots referring to animals (never on roots referring to humans, plants, or fungi), although it also occurs on several roots referring to mythological or supernatural beings, e.g. *daob-ronf* 'dragon' or *daob-gueinb* 'ghost'. The prefix in question is thus glossed as 'AN', for 'animal'. No phonological variants of this prefix have yet been attested.

While most terms referring to animals will occur with *daob-* 'AN', there are several exceptions. These include (i) some animal terms that occur with the prefix *baod-* 'BUG' instead (e.g. *baod-jant* 'weasel' or *baod-ghaut.biaok* 'cricket'; see Section 5.4.2.6), (ii) some animal terms recently borrowed from Sinitic that occur with no nominal prefix at all (e.g. *sib.zib* 'lion' or *hex.teinl* 'dolphin', from Standard Mandarin *shīzi* [狮子] and *hǎitún* [海豚] or cognate forms in another Sinitic variety), and (iii) a handful of apparently native animal terms that also occur with no prefix at all (e.g. *jis.jis* 'hedgehog' or *bot.geub* 'spider').

All of the author's consultants report that *daob-* 'AN' has no meaning of its own, although all of them are quite conscious of the fact that for the most part it occurs only in terms referring to animals, and that it occurs in almost all such terms. Based on apparently cognate forms in several other Miao languages, Gerner and Bisang (2010: 598) argue that *daob-* has grammaticalized from what was originally a classifier for animate entities, a hypothesis which appears plausible to this author.

A representative sample of nouns featuring *daob-* 'AN' is given below. Note that the forms in examples (5.173–5.182) refer to animals, while those in examples (5.183–5.185) refer to mythological or supernatural beings.

(5.173) *daob-maonb*
AN-cat
'cat' (Haili Shi, fieldnotes)

(5.174) *daob-ginb*
AN-bug
'bug, insect, small terrestrial invertebrate' (Chenghua Long, fieldnotes)

(5.175) *daob-mel*
AN-horse
'horse' (Chenghua Long, fieldnotes)

(5.176) *daob-naus*
AN-duck/bird
'duck; bird' (Shixiang Wu, fieldnotes)

(5.177) *daob-job*
AN-monkey
'monkey' (Chenghua Long, fieldnotes)

(5.178) *daob-neinb*
AN-snake
'snake' (Haili Shi, fieldnotes)

(5.179) *daob-ghab*
AN-chicken
'chicken' (Haili Shi, fieldnotes)

(5.180) *daob-shauk*
AN-centipede
'centipede' (Shixiang Wu, fieldnotes)

(5.181) *daob-guk*
AN-frog
'frog' (Chenghua Long, fieldnotes)

(5.182) *daob-mioul*
AN-fish
'fish' (Haili Shi, fieldnotes)

(5.183) *daob-ronf*
AN-dragon
'dragon' (Haili Shi, fieldnotes)

(5.184) *daob-gueinb*
AN-ghost
'ghost' (Shixiang Wu, fieldnotes)

(5.185) *daob-sob*
AN-thunder
'thunder, lightning, the Thunder God' (Haili Shi, fieldnotes)

Unlike *ghaob-* 'NOM', the prefix *daob-* 'AN' never serves as a nominalizer of originally non-nominal forms (e.g. classifiers or verbs). Aside from this, though, the grammatical properties of *ghaob-* 'NOM' (at least when it occurs on underlyingly nominal roots) and *daob-* 'AN' are nearly identical for most consultants, especially with respect to the particular environments in which these forms can be dropped without affecting meaning.

5.4.2.3 The prefix *deb-* 'DIM'

The high-frequency nominal prefix *deb-* 'DIM' (from 'diminutive') has grammaticalized from *deb* 'child', which is still a commonly used noun in Fenghuang Xong. In most instances the prefix *deb-* occurs in a lexically specified, non-productive fashion on nouns referring to small and/or young entities. The nouns in examples (5.186–5.192) below occur with such an initial *deb-* in the speech of all the author's primary consultants, although there are many other nouns that occur with *deb-* in the speech of some consultants but not in that of others.

(5.186) *deb-ngaok*
DIM-baby
'baby, infant' (Shixiang Wu, fieldnotes)

(5.187) *deb-bab*
DIM-leg
'calf (of leg)' (Shixiang Wu, fieldnotes) (cf. *minl-bab* [AUG-leg] 'thigh')

(5.188) *deb-npaok/nint*
DIM-woman/man
'girl/boy' (Haili Shi, fieldnotes)

(5.189) *deb-ngueif*
DIM-unmarried.woman
'unmarried woman' (Haili Shi, fieldnotes)

(5.190) *deb-nceik*
DIM-young.man
'young man' (Haili Shi, fieldnotes)

(5.191) *deb-geud*
DIM-younger.sibling
'younger sibling' (Haili Shi, fieldnotes)

(5.192) *deb-miaos*
DIM-orphan
'orphan' (Shixiang Wu, fieldnotes)

The prefix *deb-* 'DIM' also functions as a non-productive nominalizer of certain property-denoting verbs, with the resulting noun referring to a person possessing the property in question.

(5.193) *deb-liot/kod*
DIM-wealthy/poor
'wealthy/poor person' (Qiusheng Long, in *Ngel.kanx*)

(5.194) *deb-ghot*
DIM-old
'old person' (Shixiang Wu, fieldnotes) (though note that *ghot* can itself function as a noun meaning 'old person')

The prefix *deb-* 'DIM' generally does not contrast with *minl-* 'AUG' (see Section 5.4.2.4 below) in examples (5.186–5.194), in the sense that replacing *deb-* 'DIM' with *minl-* 'AUG' in any of these examples will usually result in an uninterpretable utterance. The sole exception is *deb-bab* [DIM-leg] 'calf (of leg)' in (5.187), which contrasts with *minl-bab* [AUG-leg] 'thigh'.

It is difficult to make any grammatical generalizations about *deb-* 'DIM' when it occurs in lexically specified fashion, as in examples (5.186–5.194) above. In some cases, consultants report that *deb-* 'DIM' can be dropped from nouns in which it is lexically specified to occur with no change in meaning or grammaticality, at least in certain grammatical positions (e.g. immediately after a classifier). This is the case with *deb-ghot* [DIM-old] 'old person' in example (5.194). In other cases, *deb-* 'DIM' can still be dropped, but this results in a slight change of meaning. For instance, dropping *deb-* from *deb-npaok* [DIM-woman] 'girl' (see example (5.188)) or replacing it with *ghaob-* 'NOM' results in an expression that means 'woman' rather than 'girl'. In still other cases, *deb-* cannot be dropped without resulting in a complete change of meaning, which may well yield a nonsensical utterance. This is the case with *deb-miaos* [DIM-orphan] 'orphan' in example (5.192), as *miaos* can only mean 'bamboo shoot' when produced without a preceding prefix. Furthermore, judgments about the acceptability of forms with or without an initial *deb-* 'DIM' often vary significantly among the author's consultants.

It is important to note, though, that in most cases the prefix *deb-* 'DIM' cannot productively attach to noun roots to yield expressions meaning 'a small NOUN' or 'a young NOUN'. To refer to young animals or plants, a particular type of attributive compound (see Section 5.3.1) is used instead. The immediate constituents of such a compound are (i) *deb-ngaok* 'baby, infant', which itself consists of *deb-* 'DIM' and the bound noun root *-ngaok* 'baby, infant', and (ii) a noun root referring to the type of animal or plant in question. For example, 'kitten' is *deb-ngaok-maonb* [DIM-baby-cat] rather than ??*deb-maonb*, and 'sapling' is *deb-ngaok-ndaut* [DIM-baby-tree] rather than ??*deb-ndaut*. To refer to young humans, speakers will generally use a noun containing a lexically specified instance of *deb-*, like *deb-ngaok* [DIM-baby] 'baby, infant' or *deb-npaok* [DIM-woman] 'girl'. To refer to small (rather than young) referents, a periphrastic construction involving a relative clause (see Section 8.1) will typically be used.

However, contrastive contexts constitute an important exception, as in such contexts *deb-* 'DIM' can in fact productively attach to noun roots. Such a contrastive context can either be implicit or explicit, and in the latter case it will involve two occurrences of the same noun root, one preceded by *deb-* 'DIM' and one preceded by *minl-* 'AUG' (see Section 5.4.2.4 below). Thus, while ??*deb-wanl* [DIM-pot] 'small pot' and ??*minl-wanl* [AUG-pot] 'big pot' are generally rejected by consultants when produced in isolation or in non-contrastive contexts, they are readily accepted in an utterance like the one in example (5.195).

(5.195) *Mx* *geud* ***minl-wanl*** *dieud* *hlit,* *geud* ***deb-wanl***
2SG hold **AUG-pot** boil.rice cooked.rice hold **DIM-pot**
giab *reib-yeus.*
stir.fry vegetable-cooked.meat
'Use the big pot to boil rice and the small pot to cook the main course.'
(Shixiang Wu, fieldnotes)

In addition to serving as a noun meaning 'child' and as a nominal prefix, the form *deb* can also serve as a classifier suffix (see Section 6.1.3.4) and as a quantifier (Section 9.2.3.3).

5.4.2.4 The prefix *minl-* 'AUG'

The prefix *minl-* 'AUG' (from 'augmentative') clearly derives from *minl* 'mother', a noun which is still very commonly used in Fenghuang Xong. No phonological variants of *minl-* 'AUG' have yet been attested, although consultants occasionally use *nek-* as an augmentative prefix in addition to *minl-*, at least in some forms (see Section 5.4.2.8 below for details). As a nominal prefix, *minl-* 'AUG' exists in semantic opposition to *deb-* 'DIM' (see Section 5.4.2.3 above), and much of what was said about the functions and productivity of *deb-* applies to *minl-* as well. Where *deb-* 'DIM' often occurs in a lexically specified, non-productive fashion on nouns referring to small and/or young entities, *minl-* 'AUG' often occurs in a similar fashion on nouns referring to large and/or old entities.

(5.196) *minl-mianx*
AUG-person
'adult' (Shixiang Wu, fieldnotes)

(5.197) *minl-aub*
AUG-water
'river, lake, large body of water' (Haili Shi, fieldnotes)

(5.198) *minl-bab*
AUG-leg
'thigh' (Shixiang Wu, fieldnotes) (cf. *deb-bab* [DIM-leg] 'calf [of leg]')

(5.199) *minl-naob/yaos*
AUG-older.brother/older.sister
'the oldest of several brothers/sisters' (Shixiang Wu, fieldnotes)

In this role, *minl-* 'AUG' is very similar to *deb-* 'DIM' both in terms of its grammatical behavior (especially its ability – or lack thereof – to be dropped without affecting meaning or grammaticality) and in terms of its high degree of interspeaker variation. Note, though, that *minl-* 'AUG' generally does not contrast with *deb-* 'DIM' in examples (5.196–5.199), with the exception of *minl-bab* [AUG-leg] 'thigh' vs. *deb-bab* [DIM-leg] 'calf (of leg)'. Some nouns are simply lexically specified as occurring with *minl-* 'AUG' (never *deb-* 'DIM'), while others are lexically specified as occurring with *deb-* 'DIM' (never *minl-* 'AUG'). Furthermore, just as with *deb-* 'DIM', *minl-* 'AUG' cannot be productively used to modify noun roots, except in contrastive contexts (see example (5.195) above). In non-contrastive contexts, consultants will typically use a periphrastic construction (often one involving a relative clause) to express that a particular referent is unusually large or old.

In addition to serving as a nominal prefix, *minl-* 'AUG' also occurs as a classifier prefix in a particular type of tetrasyllabic construction. See Section 6.1.3.3 for discussion.

5.4.2.5 The prefix *bid-* 'FRT'

The prefix *bid-* 'FRT' has clearly grammaticalized from the noun root *bid* 'fruit', although that latter form generally bears a preceding *ghaob-* 'NOM' (see Section 5.4.2.1) when produced in isolation. Unlike certain other nominal prefixes discussed in this chapter, *bid-* 'FRT' does not show any noteworthy phonological or grammatical variation among the author's consultants.

As a nominal prefix, *bid-* 'FRT' occurs primarily on noun roots referring to sweet, edible parts of plants. These include most plant parts that would be classified as fruits in an English folk taxonomy, as well as some that would be classified as vegetables and some that would be classified as nuts. A representative set of examples is given in (5.200–5.205) below.

(5.200) *bid-neb*
FRT-date
'date (fruit)' (Shixiang Wu, fieldnotes)

(5.201) *bid-guax*
FRT-peach
'peach' (Shixiang Wu, fieldnotes)

(5.202) *bid-lid*
FRT-plum
'plum' (Shixiang Wu, fieldnotes)

(5.203) *bid-ghand*
FRT-grape
'grape' (Shixiang Wu, fieldnotes)

(5.204) *bid-yaonx.ib*
FRT-potato
'potato' (Shixiang Wu, fieldnotes)

(5.205) *bid-ros*
FRT-chestnut
'chestnut' (Haili Shi, fieldnotes)

However, some recent borrowings from Sinitic never occur with this prefix even though they refer to sweet, edible parts of plants. Two examples are *xik.guaok* 'watermelon' and *xaonk.jok* 'banana', from Standard Mandarin *xīguā* (西瓜) and *xiāngjiāo* (香蕉) or from cognate forms in another Sinitic variety.

When occurring before a noun root that refers to a sweet, edible plant part, the prefix *bid-* 'FRT' displays a number of semantic and grammatical similarities with canonical noun roots, especially with those roots that serve as the initial constituents of attributive compounds (see Section 5.3.1). In such cases *bid-* appears to function as the semantic head of the noun in which it occurs, and if removed it yields an ungrammatical (and often uninterpretable) utterance. For instance, the forms meaning 'pork', 'beef', and 'mutton' in examples (5.206) and (5.207) and the forms meaning 'apricot', 'pear', and 'tangerine' in examples (5.208) and (5.209) display very similar semantic structures and grammatical properties.

(5.206) *Wel yeb nonx* ***niax-nbat/yul/yonf.***
1SG like eat **meat-pig/cow/goat**
'I like pork/beef/mutton.' (Haili Shi, fieldnotes)

(5.207) **Wel yeb nonx* ***nbat/yul/yonf.***
1SG like eat **pig/cow/goat**
(intended: 'I like pork/beef/mutton.')

(5.208) *Wel yeb nonx* ***bid-bonb/raox/lieus.***
1SG like eat **FRT-apricot/pear/tangerine**
'I like apricots/pears/tangerines.' (Haili Shi, fieldnotes)

(5.209) **Wel yeb nonx* ***bonb/raox/lieus.***
1SG like eat **apricot/pear/tangerine**
(intended: 'I like apricots/pears/tangerines.')

In cases such as these, it seems to the author that *bid-* could easily be analyzed as a noun root meaning 'fruit' instead of as a nominal prefix 'FRT'. Indeed, if *bid-* only co-occurred with noun roots referring to sweet, edible parts of plants, there would be little motivation for analyzing it as a nominal prefix at all. However, *bid-* also occurs preceding a number of noun roots whose referents are not plant parts, as is shown in examples (5.210–5.216) below. Most of these other noun roots still have some semantic features in common with those that refer to fruits and other sweet, edible plant parts, as they generally have referents that are both round (in either a spherical or cylindrical sense) and relatively small.

(5.210) *bid-ndaod*
FRT-finger
'finger' (Haili Shi, fieldnotes)

(5.211) *bid-deut*
FRT-foot
'toe' (Haili Shi, fieldnotes) (cf. the locative noun *deut* 'foot' in Section 5.5.2.4 below)

(5.212) *bid-dius*
FRT-knee
'knee' (Shixiang Wu, fieldnotes)

(5.213) *bid-deud*
FRT-skin
'tail' (Haili Shi, fieldnotes) (cf. *ghaob-deud* [NOM-skin] 'skin')

(5.214) *bid-ghob*
FRT-blister
'blister, boil' (Shixiang Wu, fieldnotes)

(5.215) *bid-zheux*
FRT-miliaria
'miliaria (i.e. sweat rash)' (Haili Shi, fieldnotes)

(5.216) *bid-zhonx*
FRT-length
'length, segment' (Xingyu Shi, in *Oub Meinl Yaos Geud*)

In all cases given so far, removing *bid-* will at the very least result in a change of meaning, and in many cases it will result in an utterance that is ungrammatical or even uninterpretable.[98]

However, there are two high-frequency noun roots which usually occur with a preceding *bid-* 'FRT' but which differ from the other noun roots discussed so far in this section in that (i) their meanings do not seem to obviously involve the notions of either "smallness" or "roundness" and (ii) they sometimes occur without a preceding *bid-* 'FRT' with no change in meaning, especially when immediately following a verb or classifier.

The first of these unusual roots is *deul* 'fire' (homophonous with *deul* 'firewood'), which is generally produced as *bid-deul* [FRT-fire] but which sometimes occurs as just *deul* in certain grammatical environments. This is shown in (5.217) and (5.218) below, in both of which *bid-* 'FRT' is in fact disallowed.

(5.217) *Beul ndout* ***(*bid-)deul.***
3 warm.oneself **(FRT-)fire**
'He's warming himself by the fire.' (Chenghua Long, fieldnotes)

(5.218) *Beul monl ghat khauk* ***(*bid-)deul*** *did-fand*
3 go go.to CLF:place$_2$ **(FRT-)fire** DID-turn.over
did-fand.
DID-turn.over
'He went to the fire-pit and poked through it.' (Xingyu Shi, in *Oub Meinl Yaos Geud*)

The second such noun root is *gheul* 'mountain' (homophonous with *gheul* 'village' and *gheul* 'place'; see Section 5.5.2.3). For all consultants, 'mountain' is usually expressed as *bid-gheul* [FRT-mountain], at least in isolation. However, in certain grammatical environments (especially when immediately preceded by a classifier or verb), the prefix *bid-* can be dropped with no change in meaning, so that 'mountain' is expressed as only *gheul*. This can be seen in examples (5.219) and (5.220), in both of which *bid-* 'FRT' is optional.

98 There is one general exception to this, though. A noun root which typically occurs with a preceding *bid-* 'FRT' when produced in isolation can often occur without *bid-* when serving as a non-initial constituent of an attributive compound (see Section 5.3.1). For example, 'apricot' can only be expressed as *bid-bonb* [FRT-apricot], not **bonb*, but 'apricot tree' can be expressed as either *ndaut-bid-bonb* [tree-FRT-apricot] or *ndaut-bonb* [tree-apricot].

(5.219) *aod-leb* ***(bid-)gheul***
one-CLF **(FRT-)mountain**
'one mountain' (Shixiang Wu, fieldnotes)

(5.220) *Tat-hnef* *monx* *lis* *jix* *lis* *ndieut* ***(bid-)gheul?***
this-CLF:day 2SG want NEG_1 want ascend **(FRT-)mountain**
'Will you go mountain-climbing today?' (unknown Xong consultant, fieldnotes)

Finally, the author has encountered two forms in which *bid-* 'FRT' appears to serve a nominalizing function. This first of these is shown in example (5.221), where *bid-* is used to derive a noun meaning 'heel' from the verb *zhox* 'to kick'. The second is shown in example (5.222), where *bid-* is used to derive a noun meaning 'hook, button' from the verb *gheud* 'to get stuck'. Note that this noun meaning 'hook, button' can alternately be realized with *baod-* 'BUG' in place of *bid-* 'FRT' (cf. example (5.238) below).

(5.221) *bid-zhox*
FRT-kick
'heel' (Shixiang Wu, fieldnotes)

(5.222) *bid-gheud*
FRT-get.stuck
'hook (e.g. fishing hook), button (e.g. of a shirt)' (Shixiang Wu, fieldnotes)

In summary, *bid-* 'FRT' is admittedly more similar to a canonical noun root than most of Xong's other nominal prefixes, as it often has fairly compositional semantics and usually cannot be dropped without affecting meaning or grammaticality. However, *bid-* is still classified as a nominal prefix here because (i) it occurs unexpectedly in forms meaning 'fire' and 'mountain', (ii) there are still some instances in which it can be dropped without affecting meaning or grammaticality, and (iii) it appears to serve as a nominalizer in the forms *bid-zhox* [FRT-kick] 'heel' and *bid-gheud* [FRT-get.stuck] 'hook, button'.

5.4.2.6 The prefix *baod-* 'BUG'

The prefix *baod-* 'BUG' derives its gloss from 'bug', since this form appears in a number of nouns whose referents are small, often unpleasant or undesirable animals. These include several types of insects as well as a few vertebrates like tadpoles, crows, and weasels (see examples (5.223–5.229) below). The etymology of *baod-* 'BUG' is unclear; although it is homophonous with *baod-* 'ML' (see Section 5.4.2.7), the two forms are not obviously related. No phonological variants of *baod-* 'BUG' have yet been attested.

(5.223) *baod-zhal*
BUG-dragonfly
'dragonfly' (Haili Shi, fieldnotes)

(5.224) *baod-bous*
BUG-butterfly
'butterfly, moth' (Haili Shi, fieldnotes)

(5.225) *baod-ghaut.biaok*
BUG-cricket
'cricket' (Shixiang Wu, fieldnotes)

(5.226) *baod-mx-deul*
BUG-???-fire
'firefly' (Haili Shi, fieldnotes) (note that **baod-mx* and **mx-deul* are meaningless)

(5.227) *baod-mx-guk*
BUG-???-frog
'tadpole' (Haili Shi, fieldnotes) (note that **baod-mx* and **mx-guk* are meaningless)

(5.228) *baod-aut*
BUG-crow
'crow' (Shixiang Wu, fieldnotes)

(5.229) *baod-jant*
BUG-weasel
'weasel' (Chenghua Long, fieldnotes)

It is important to note that the occurrence of *baod-* 'BUG' on noun roots referring to small, unpleasant or undesirable animals is lexically specified, as not all semantically appropriate noun roots allow a preceding *baod-*. For instance, 'spider' is *bot.geub*, never **baod-bot.geub* or **baod-geub*, and 'ant' is *daob-npand* [AN-ant], never **baod-npand*.

In addition to occurring in certain animal terms, *baod-* 'BUG' also occurs in a number of terms referring to parts of living things. These include some human body parts, some animal body parts, and even some parts of plants, as can be seen from examples (5.230–5.237) below.

(5.230) *baod-nins*
BUG-beard
'beard, mustache' (Shixiang Wu, fieldnotes)

(5.231) *baod-mieus*
BUG-nose
'nose' (Chenghua Long, in *Conversation in La'ershan*)

(5.232) *baod-niub*
BUG-lip
'lip' (Shixiang Wu, fieldnotes)

(5.233) *baod-gieb*
BUG-horn
'horn (e.g. of cow)' (Shixiang Wu, fieldnotes)

(5.234) *baod-ndiuk*
BUG-peck
'beak (of bird); tip (of blade)' (Haili Shi, fieldnotes)

(5.235) *baod-giat*
BUG-claw
'claw' (Haili Shi, fieldnotes)

(5.236) *baod-jonx*
BUG-root
'root (of plant or of tooth)' (Haili Shi, fieldnotes)

(5.237) *baod-jaok*
BUG-prick
'thorn' (Haili Shi, fieldnotes) (cf. example (5.170) above)

A few of the examples just given merit some additional comment. First, in examples (5.234) and (5.237), the prefix *baod-* 'BUG' appears to be serving as a nominalizer, yielding *baod-ndiuk* 'beak (of bird); tip (of blade)' and *baod-jaok* 'thorn' from the verbs *ndiuk* 'to peck' and *jaok* 'to prick'. Second, regarding example (5.237) in particular, note that 'thorn' can also be expressed as *ghaob-jaok* [NOM-prick].

The prefix *baod-* 'BUG' has also been attested in a handful of other nouns that appear to share few if any semantic features with the nouns given earlier in this section. These are shown in (5.238–5.240) below. Note that the first of these, *baod-gheud* 'hook, button', appears to be derived from the verb *gheud* 'to get stuck', and that this same noun can alternately be realized with *bid-* 'FRT' in place of *baod-* 'BUG' (cf. example (5.222) above).

(5.238) *baod-gheud*
BUG-get.stuck
'hook (e.g. fishing hook), button (e.g. of a shirt)' (Shixiang Wu, fieldnotes)

(5.239) *baod-biaok*
BUG-thief
'thief, pickpocket' (Shixiang Wu, fieldnotes)

(5.240) *baod-giet*
BUG-scorched.rice.cake
'scorched-rice cake' (Haili Shi, fieldnotes)

In addition to the idiosyncratic cases shown in (5.234), (5.237), and (5.238) above, the prefix *baod-* can also serve as a nominalizer of certain other verbs, although there are significant restrictions on which verbs can be nominalized in this way and on the meanings of the resulting nouns. Specifically, only verbs referring to what are seen by Xong speakers as negative or undesirable properties, states, or habitual activities can be nominalized by *baod-* 'BUG', and the resulting nouns can only be used to refer to human referents. For instance, the verbs in examples (5.241–5.247) below all refer to what are seen by Xong speakers as negative, undesirable qualities (e.g. fatness, blindness, stupidity, a propensity for crying, etc.), and the referents of the nouns in these examples can only be humans (rather than, e.g., animals).

(5.241) *baod-zhaons*
BUG-fat
'fat person' (Haili Shi, fieldnotes)

(5.242) *baod-nzeit*
BUG-skinny
'scrawny person' (Haili Shi, fieldnotes)

(5.243) *baod-ngaod*
BUG-short
'short person' (Haili Shi, fieldnotes)

(5.244) *baod-giaol*
BUG-stupid
'stupid person, idiot' (Shixiang Wu, fieldnotes)

(5.245) *baod-giul*
BUG-blind
'blind person' (Shixiang Wu, fieldnotes)

(5.246) *baod-daub*
BUG-deaf
'deaf person' (Haili Shi, fieldnotes)

(5.247) *baod-nied-giaol*
BUG-cry-???
'person who's always crying, crybaby' (Haili Shi, fieldnotes)[99]

This nominalizing use of *baod-* 'BUG' appears to have some lexical restrictions as well as semantic ones, since some semantically well formed constructions (or at least some constructions which appear semantically well formed to the author) are rejected by consultants.

(5.248) **baod-ngox*
BUG-fierce
(intended: 'mean person, shrewish person')

(5.249) **baod-laox*
BUG-slow
(intended: 'slow person, slowpoke')

Finally, *baod-* 'BUG' also serves as the initial morpheme in a handful of locative nouns (specifically, those referring to 'left' and 'right') and in certain reflexive pronouns. See Section 5.5.2.9 below for details on the former expressions and Section 7.1.3 for details on the latter.

The prefix *baod-* 'BUG' displays a relatively large amount of lexical variation across the author's primary consultants, in the sense that many nouns that bear *baod-* in the speech of one consultant will bear another prefix (or sometimes no prefix at all) in the speech of another. However, the form displays very little grammatical variation: for all of the author's consultants and in all grammatical environments, *baod-* can never be dropped from a noun (or verb) root on which it occurs. Attempting to do so will result in an utterance that is at the very least ungrammatical, and often even uninterpretable.[100]

---

99 Consultants report that *nied-giaol* is simply a disyllabic version of the verb *nied* 'to cry'. The meaning of the second syllable *-giaol* is unclear, although it is homophonous with *giaol* 'stupid'.

100 There is one minor exception to this claim: noun roots which ordinarily follow *baod-* 'BUG' when produced in isolation will generally occur without a preceding *baod-* when serving as a non-initial constituent of an attributive compound (see Section 5.3.1). For instance, 'nose' can only be expressed as *baod-mieus* [BUG-nose], not **mieus*, but 'nosebleed' can only be expressed as *nqind-mieus* [blood-nose], not **nqind-baod-mieus* [blood-BUG-nose].

Overall, *baod*- 'BUG' appears to function as a sort of less productive, less frequent version of *ghaob*- 'NOM' (see Section 5.4.2.1). Like *ghaob*- 'NOM', it occurs in a wide variety of nouns, most of which can be grouped into a few fairly distinct semantic categories (e.g. small unpleasant animals, body parts, etc.). Also like *ghaob*-, it occasionally serves to nominalize certain non-nominal roots. However, *baod*- 'BUG' is very much unlike *ghaob*- 'NOM' in that it can never be dropped without affecting meaning or grammaticality.

5.4.2.7 The prefix *baod*- 'ML'

Although homophonous with *baod*- 'BUG' (see Section 5.4.2.6 above), the prefix *baod*- 'ML' (from 'male') has a clearly distinct meaning, and so it is analyzed here as a different morpheme. This prefix occurs preceding noun roots that refer to non-human animates or, in a few rare cases, plants, and it serves to indicate that the referent of the noun in question is semantically male (though not grammatically masculine). It is not readily applied to nouns referring to smaller animals like snakes, frogs, or insects, as consultants report that it is difficult to imagine a situation in which it would be necessary to specify the sex of such an animal.

Examples (5.250–5.255) below show several roots that can co-occur with a preceding *baod*- 'ML', including some that refer to animals, some that refer to supernatural entities, and some that refer to plants.

(5.250) *baod-job*
ML-monkey
'male monkey' (Haili Shi, fieldnotes) (cf. *daob-job* [AN-monkey] 'monkey')

(5.251) *baod-guoud*
ML-dog
'male dog' (Haili Shi, fieldnotes) (cf. *daob-guoud* [AN-dog] 'dog')

(5.252) *baod-gueinb*
ML-ghost
'male ghost' (Haili Shi, fieldnotes) (cf. *daob-gueinb* [AN-ghost] 'ghost')

(5.253) *baod-ronf*
ML-dragon
'male dragon' (Haili Shi, fieldnotes) (cf. *daob-ronf* [AN-dragon] 'dragon')

(5.254) *baod-ndaut*
ML-tree
'male tree' (Hemin Long, fieldnotes) (cf. *ghaob-ndaut* [NOM-tree] 'tree')

(5.255) *baod-beinx*
ML-flower
'male flower' (Hemin Long, fieldnotes) (cf. *beinx* 'flower')

As these examples suggest, *baod-* 'ML' replaces *daob-* 'AN' (or, in the case of example (5.254), *ghaob-* 'NOM') rather than preceding or following it. As far as the author has been able to determine, *baod-* 'ML' cannot occur on roots referring to animals that do not bear *daob-* 'AN' when produced in isolation, including those discussed in Section 5.4.2.2 that take no prefix and those discussed in Section 5.4.2.6 that take *baod-* 'BUG' instead. However, since such roots generally refer to the sorts of animals for which consultants are reluctant to specify sex anyway (e.g. *jis.jis* 'hedgehog', *bot.geub* 'spider', *baod-aut* [BUG-crow] 'crow', etc.), it is unclear whether this should be interpreted as a real grammatical restriction or simply as a sign of the pragmatic oddness of the resulting constructions.

The form *baod-* 'ML' resembles canonical noun roots in that it can never be dropped without affecting meaning, but it is still classified as a prefix here because (i) it replaces the nominal prefixes *daob-* 'AN' and *ghaob-* 'NOM' rather than co-occurring with them (see examples (5.250–5.254) above) and (ii) it occurs preceding the semantic head of a polymorphemic noun rather than following it. For instance, in the attributive noun compound in example (5.256), what consultants identify as the semantic head occurs initially, but in the prefix-bearing noun in example (5.257), what consultants identify as the semantic head occurs finally.[101]

(5.256) ***ndaut**-guax*
tree-peach
'peach tree' (Shixiang Wu, fieldnotes)

(5.257) *baod-**ndaut***
ML-**tree**
'male tree' (Hemin Long, fieldnotes) (repeated from (5.254) above)

No phonological variants of *baod-* 'ML' have yet been encountered, and the author has not noticed any significant grammatical differences among his primary consultants with respect to this prefix. The etymology of *baod-* 'ML' is unclear; while it is segmentally homophonous with *baox* 'father', the two forms bear different tones.

101 Consultants identify the noun root *ndaut* 'tree' as the semantic head of example (5.256) in the sense that they consider *ndaut-guax* [tree-peach] 'peach tree' to be a type of tree rather than a type of peach. Similarly, they identify that same root *ndaut* 'tree' as the semantic head of example (5.257) in the sense that they consider *baod-ndaut* [ML-tree] 'male tree' to be a type of tree rather than a type of male.

5.4.2.8 The prefix *nek-* 'FM'

This prefix is simply the female counterpart of *baod-* 'ML', and so nearly everything that was said about the semantics, productivity, and grammatical properties of *baod-* in Section 5.4.2.7 above also applies here. Just as with *baod-* 'ML', *nek-* 'FM' (from 'female') occurs preceding noun roots that refer to non-human animates or plants to indicate that the referent of the noun in question is semantically female. All of the examples in Section 5.4.2.7 that can occur with *baod-* 'ML' can also occur with *nek-* 'FM' instead, with the expected change in semantics. Consultants are just as reluctant to apply *nek-* to roots referring to smaller animals like snakes, frogs, or insects as they are to apply *baod-* to such roots. The prefix *nek-* 'FM' replaces *daob-* 'AN' just as *baod-* 'ML' does, and like *baod-* it cannot be dropped without affecting meaning. Also like *baod-*, no phonological variants of *nek-* have yet been attested. However, the etymology of the prefix *nek-* 'FM' is clearer than that of *baod-* 'ML', as it has almost certainly grammaticalized from the noun *nek* 'mother'.

Interestingly, there are two particular forms in which *nek-* appears to function as an augmentative prefix (cf. *minl-* 'AUG' in Section 5.4.2.4 above) rather than as a female prefix (and as the examples below show, in such cases *nek-* is glossed as 'AUG' rather than as 'FM'). First, most of the author's consultants allow the notion 'big needle' to be expressed as either ***minl**-jub* [**AUG**-needle] or ***nek**-jub* [**AUG**-needle]. A few consultants allow only the former variant, but there does not appear to be any way to generalize about these consultants in terms of gender, age, hometown, or other obvious factors. In any case, an instance of the latter variant can be seen in example (5.258).

(5.258) *Gaons monx* ***nek-jub****.*
give 2SG **AUG-needle**
'Here, take this big (*female) needle.' (Qiumei Wu, in *Conversation in Yankan*)

Second, for all of the author's consultants, the notion 'road' is ordinarily expressed as ***nek**-geud* [**AUG**-road], at least in isolation. Consultants also allow ***minl**-geud* [**AUG**-road] in certain contexts (see Section 5.4.2.4), but only with the meaning 'big road', not just 'road'. The initial syllable of *nek-geud* 'road' is analyzed as 'AUG' rather than as 'FM' here due to the semantics of the entire disyllabic form (in particular, many roads are large, but none are female) and due to the precedent set by the existence of the form *nek-jub* [AUG-needle] 'big needle', in which *nek-* is clearly functioning as 'AUG' rather than as 'FM'.

(5.259) *Dob bob guaot, jix dut* ***nek-geud*** *nzhaod.*
deep forest pass NEG_1 obtain **AUG-road** return
'The forest was so deep, (she) couldn't find the way (*the big way/*the big road) back.' (Xingyu Shi, in *Oub Meinl Yaos Geud*)

This variation between *nek-* and *minl-* is not particularly surprising, since these two prefixes appear to have grammaticalized from distinct but synonymous nouns (see Section 5.3.2). However, it is important to note that this variation has significant restrictions. Not only is it apparently limited to the two forms discussed above (and for the first of those two forms, it is further limited to only certain consultants), but it is also unidirectional: while all consultants occasionally use *nek-* to mean 'AUG', no consultant ever uses *minl-* to mean 'FM'.

5.4.2.9 The prefix *dib-/ib-/jeub-/jil-* 'LOC'

This prefix is most commonly realized as *dib-*, and it is glossed as 'LOC' (from 'locative') since it only occurs in nouns referring to locations. The exact semantic contribution of *dib-* 'LOC' to a noun in which it occurs is often unclear, nor is it clear what factors determine whether or not *dib-* can occur on a semantically appropriate noun root. In many cases, *dib-* appears to be completely optional, so that its presence or absence does not have any clear effect on the meaning or pragmatics of the utterance in which it appears. For instance, consultants report that *dib-* is entirely optional in examples (5.260–5.262) below.

(5.260) *Beul zhaok* ***(dib-)aub.***
3 fall **(LOC-)water**
'He fell into the water.' (Haili Shi, fieldnotes)

(5.261) *Wel ninb* ***(dib-)bioud.***
1SG at **(LOC-)home**
'I'm at home.' (Shixiang Wu, fieldnotes)

(5.262) *Aod-jel* ***(dib-)laos*** *neind nins boub naond.*
one-CLF:agricultural.field **(LOC-)field** this COP 1PL ASSOC
'This field is ours.' (Haili Shi, fieldnotes)

In examples (5.263–5.265), however, the author's consultants report that *dib-* 'LOC' is obligatory. Note that in example (5.265) the nouns bearing *dib-* 'LOC' refer to temporal rather than spatial location.

(5.263) *Wel aod-roul ninb* ***dib-laos.***
1SG one-CLF:time$_1$ at **LOC-field**
'I'm in the fields right now.' (Shixiang Wu, fieldnotes)

(5.264) *Beul* *doub* *bianb* *chauk* *aod-ngonl* *naus* *eint*
3 then$_1$ change.into do one-CLF:animate bird fly
***dib-doub*.**
LOC-earth
'Then he changed into a bird and flew all around the world.' (Chunman Tang, in *Oub Leb Naob Geud*)

(5.265) *Wel* ***dib-hnef*** *chauk* *geud.donb,* ***dib-hmaont*** *beut* *nggueb.*
1SG **LOC-day** do work **LOC-evening** lie.down sleep
'I work during the day and sleep at night.' (Haili Shi, fieldnotes)

Although the etymology of *dib-* 'LOC' is currently unknown, it occurs as the initial element of several place names in Xiangxi Prefecture (see Section 2.2.1). For some of these place names, *dib-* 'LOC' is obligatory when the name is pronounced in isolation, but it can be dropped in certain grammatical environments, especially in immediate postverbal position (this is somewhat similar to the behavior of *ghaob-* 'NOM' and *daob-* 'AN', as discussed in Sections 5.4.2.1 and 5.4.2.2 above). This is the case with the place name *Dib-Zhes* [LOC-Fenghuang], which refers to the county seat of Fenghuang County (see Section 2.7). For other place names, though, *dib-* appears to be obligatory in all grammatical environments. This is the case with, for instance, *Dib-Weis* [LOC-Jiwei] 'Jiwei Township' (*Jíwèi Xiāng* 吉卫乡).

This prefix has perhaps more phonological variants than any other. Although it is most commonly realized as *dib-*, it has also been attested as *ib-*, *jeub-*, and *jil-*, and in many cases a single consultant will use several of these variants in apparently free variation. While the author has not encountered any noteworthy interspeaker variation in terms of the grammatical behavior of *dib-* 'LOC', this prefix is one of the less frequently occurring ones in the author's corpus, and so any such variation would likely be difficult to detect even if it did exist.

5.4.2.10 The "quasi-prefixes" *aod-* 'KIN' and *leud-/lod-* 'FAM'

Fenghuang Xong also features two "quasi-prefixes", which are idiosyncratic forms that display certain similarities with the nominal prefixes discussed in Sections 5.4.2.1 through 5.4.2.9 above but that differ from them in that they never occur on canonical noun roots.

The first such quasi-prefix is *aod-* 'KIN' (from 'kin'), which occurs in only a single form in Fenghuang Xong. That form is the interjection *aod-minl(-nek)* [KIN-mother (-mother)], which serves to express shock or dismay (somewhat like English *Oh, man!* or *Jesus!*, as is described in Section 11.3.5). While naturally a morpheme that occurs in only a single lexical item is very far indeed from being a canonical nominal prefix (which are, overall, much more productive than most noun roots), the form *aod-* is still discussed here because it appears to be cognate with a much more productive nominal prefix that occurs in other Xong varieties spoken outside Fenghuang County. That prefix is usually phonologically *aod-* or *ad-* (i.e. /ɑ3/ or /a3/), depending on the specific variety of Xong in question, and it is typically reported to occur only on noun roots referring to kin members older than the speaker; see, for example, Xiang (1999: 21), Luo (2005: 37), or Yu (2011: 31). In Fenghuang Xong, though, consultants reject the addition of this prefix to semantically appropriate noun roots in all grammatical environments.

The second quasi-prefix in Fenghuang Xong is *leud-/lod-* 'FAM' (from 'familiar'), which signals familiarity or intimacy and which only ever occurs on personal names. Examples of this can be seen in (5.266) and (5.267) below.

(5.266) *Nins* *yaox,* ***leud-Huaok?***
COP right? **FAM-PN**
'Isn't that so, Huao?' (Shixiang Wu, fieldnotes)

(5.267) *Dand* *def* *nghauk* *aub* *leh,* *beul* *dand* *def* *nghauk*
arrive place bathe water LEH 3 arrive place bathe
aub *shib* *beul* *hnant* ***leud-Nhaonl*** *nghauk* *aub.*
water it's 3 call **FAM-PN** bathe water
'(They) arrived at the bathing spot, they arrived there and she told (her younger sister) Nhaon to go bathe.' (Xingyu Shi, in *Oub Meinl Yaos Geud*)

Consultants report that *leud-/lod-* 'FAM' can occur prefixed to the name of anyone that the speaker knows reasonably well; it is not, for instance, restricted just to kin members or just to very close friends. Furthermore, it can occur on any syllable of a personal name. Surnames of Xong speakers in Fenghuang County are always monosyllabic, and given names are either monosyllabic or disyllabic. Accordingly, *leud-/lod-* 'FAM' can occur prefixed to a surname, prefixed to a monosyllabic given name, or prefixed to either syllable of a disyllabic given name. Thus, for instance, Mrs. Haili Shi, whose Xong surname is *Shif* and whose Xong given name is *Hex Lib*, could be addressed as *leud-Shif*, *leud-Hex*, or *leud-Lib* (or as *lod-Shif*, *lod-Hex*, or *lod-Lib*). Finally, note that *leud-/lod-* can be used for both address and reference, as can be seen by comparing example (5.266) (in which it is used to address someone directly) with example (5.267) (in which it is used to refer to someone indirectly).

The form 'FAM' has two phonological variants, *leud-* and *lod-*. It is unclear what factors determine which variant is used in any particular utterance, though overall *leud-* is significantly more common in the author's corpus than *lod-*. Both variants may well be borrowings of Standard Mandarin *lǎo* (老), with which they display significant phonetic, grammatical, and semantic similarities, or of a cognate form from another Sinitic variety.

5.5 Locative nouns

5.5.1 Properties and functions of locative nouns

Fenghuang Xong has a closed set of about twenty locative nouns (the exact count varies from consultant to consultant) that serve to express various spatial concepts like 'top', 'inside', 'front', and 'left (side)'. These forms display many structural and grammatical similarities with the more canonical nouns discussed in earlier sections of this chapter, but they also display certain unique properties that justify treating them as a distinct, non-canonical subclass of noun.

Like other non-canonical nouns (e.g. pronouns and proper nouns; see Section 5.2.1), locative nouns do serve many of the same functions as more canonical nouns. These primarily include functioning as noun phrases in their own right and functioning as components of larger noun phrases, with those noun phrases in turn being able to serve a wide variety of grammatical and discourse roles. For instance, in example (5.268), the locative noun *geud-neul* 'front' constitutes a noun phrase that serves as an argument of the verb *ninb* 'at'.

(5.268) *Monx jont ninb* ***geud-neul.***
2SG sit at **place$_1$-front**
'You go sit up front.' (Haili Shi, fieldnotes)

In example (5.269), the locative noun *geud-zheit* 'outside' constitutes a noun phrase that serves as an argument of the verb *ghat* 'to go to'.

(5.269) *Wel lis bionl monl aod-tit-deb ghat*
1SG want exit go one-CLF:time$_3$-DIM go.to
geud-zheit.
place$_1$-outside
'I need to leave home for a little while.' (Xingyu Shi, in *Oub Meinl Yaos Geud*)

In example (5.270), the locative noun *baod-zhax* 'right' constitutes a noun phrase that serves as the possessor (in a grammatical sense) of the noun phrase *aod-leb bioud dox* [one-CLF home that] 'that house'.

(5.270) ***Baod-zhax*** *naond aod-leb bioud dox nins ceink.zhaont*
BUG-right ASSOC one-CLF home that COP village.head
naond.
ASSOC
'That house on the right (lit. 'that house of the right's') belongs to the village head.' (Shixiang Wu, fieldnotes)

In example (5.271), the locative noun *geud-neul* 'front' constitutes a noun phrase that serves as the possessum of the noun phrase *wel* '1SG'.

(5.271)	*Mx*	*ghaod.maons*	*xeud*	*ninb*	*wel*	*naond*	***geud-neul.***
	2SG	NEG.IMP	stand	at	1SG	ASSOC	**place$_1$-front**

'Don't stand in front of me (lit. 'at my front').' (Shixiang Wu, fieldnotes)

Finally, in example (5.272) the locative noun *laot-gheul* 'top' constitutes a noun phrase that serves as the possessum of the preceding noun phrase *bid-gheul* 'mountain', and in (5.273) the locative noun *geud-zheit* 'back' constitutes a noun phrase that serves as the possessor of the following noun phrase *aod-taont faonx dox* [one-CLF:dwelling room that] 'that room'.

(5.272)	*Bid-gheul*	***laot-gheul***	*mex*	*aod-ngonl*	*daob-mel.*
	FRT-mountain	**top-place$_2$**	exist	one-CLF:animate	AN-horse

'There's a horse on the mountain (lit. 'on the mountain's top').' (Shixiang Wu, fieldnotes)

(5.273)	***Geud-zheit***	*naond*	*aod-taont*	*faonx*	*dox*	*nins*
	place$_1$-back	ASSOC	one-CLF:dwelling	room	that	COP

	boub	*baox*	*beut*	*naond.*
	1PL	father	lie.down	ASSOC

'That room in the back (lit. 'that room of the back's') is where my father sleeps.' (Shixiang Wu, fieldnotes)

When a noun phrase consisting of an independent locative noun serves as the possessor or possessum of another noun phrase, the intervening associative marker *naond* 'ASSOC' is generally optional (see Sections 8.2.1 and 8.2.2), although the author has encountered a handful of such instances where consultants report that the presence of *naond* is (for unclear reasons) either obligatory or disallowed.

In addition to occurring as noun phrases in their own right, locative nouns also very often occur as the first elements of *locative compound nouns*, which consist of an initial locative noun *X* and a following non-locative noun *Y* (this non-locative noun can consist of a single noun root, a nominal prefix plus one or more following noun roots, or a noun compound) and which mean roughly 'the *X* of *Y*' or 'at the *X* of *Y*'.[102]

102 As far as the author has been able to determine, any given locative noun can refer either to a particular side or face of an entity or to the space extending outward or inward from that side or face. Thus, for instance, *chek naond geud-neul* [vehicle ASSOC place$_1$-front] can be used to refer to the front side of a car (in the sense of *There's a scratch **on the front of** your car*), to refer to the space in front of a car (in the sense of *Don't start driving yet, there's a dog standing **in front of** the car*), or even to refer to the front half of a car's interior (in the sense of *Go sit **in the front of** the car, next to the driver*).

Structurally, these are very similar to the attributive compounds discussed in Section 5.3.1, since in both cases there is clearly a hierarchical semantic relationship between the compounds' immediate constituents, with the more head-like element preceding the more modifier-like element. This can be seen in the locative compound nouns given in examples (5.274) and (5.275) below. In (5.274) two instances of the locative noun *ob-zheud* 'edge' are modified by the noun roots *aub* 'water' and *jet* 'pool' in turn, and in (5.275) the locative noun *leut* 'top' is modified by the attributive noun compound *zeint-bias* 'pickled-cabbage jar'.

(5.274) *Dand* ***ob-zheud****-aub,* *dand* ***ob-zheud****-jet.*
arrive **NOM-edge**-water arrive **NOM-edge**-pool
'(She) went to the edge of the water, to the edge of the pool.' (Xingyu Shi, in *Oub Meinl Yaos Geud*)

(5.275) *Aod-ngonl* *deb-guk* *jont* *leb*
one-CLF:animate DIM-frog sit CLF
leut*-zeint-bias*
top-ceramic.jar-pickled.cabbage
'The frog was sitting on a pickled-cabbage jar.' (Xingyu Shi, in *Deb Guk Ronf*)

However, despite being able to serve as independent noun phrases and as heads of compound nouns, locative nouns differ from canonical nouns in that they do not strictly satisfy the two diagnostic criteria for Xong nounhood given in Section 5.2.1. First, the author has not encountered any instances of a locative noun (or a locative compound noun) being modified by a *manx* relative clause in any of his collected Xong texts, nor has he been able to elicit any from his consultants. Second, while locative nouns (or locative compound nouns) can occur with a preceding numeral-classifier phrase, they do so only very rarely, and consultants generally reject constructed examples in which a numeral-classifier phrase precedes such a noun.

Finally, all disyllabic locative nouns can undergo partial reduplication to indicate 'the very *X*, the *X*most'. (Certain other, non-locative nouns can also undergo reduplication, but without the same semantic effect; see Section 5.6 below for details.) In such partial reduplication, the second syllable of a locative noun is repeated, yielding a trisyllabic form [A-B-B] from the original disyllabic form [A-B]. Thus, for instance, *laot-gheul* [top-place$_2$] 'top' can be partially reduplicated to yield *laot-gheul-gheul* [top-place$_2$-RED] 'the very top, the topmost', and *geud-neul* [place$_1$-front] 'front' can be partially reduplicated to yield *geud-neul-neul* [place$_1$-front-RED] 'the very front, the frontmost'. This appears to be true regardless of whether the semantic head of the original disyllabic form was the initial syllable or the final syllable, as can be seen by comparing the reduplicated versions of *laot-gheul* [top-place$_2$] 'top' (whose semantic head is its first syllable) and *geud-neul* [place$_1$-front] 'front' (whose semantic head is its second syllable) just given. In terms of their grammatical behavior, these reduplicated locative nouns do not appear to differ from their non-reduplicated counterparts in any way.

An example of a reduplicated locative noun can be seen in (5.276) below, where the reduplicated form of *manx-nzhonb* [AT-middle] 'middle, center' is used to refer to 'the very center (of the city)'.

(5.276) *Boub jed jont ninb* ***manx-nzhonb-nzhonb***.
1PL older.sister live at **AT-middle-RED**
'My older sister lives in the very center (of the city).' (Haili Shi, fieldnotes)

Although locative nouns do share enough morphological and syntactic similarities to meaningfully discuss them as a group, they can be somewhat "messy" forms in practice. Different locative nouns often display slightly different grammatical properties, and many locative nouns have several variant forms. Furthermore, many of the constituent morphemes of locative nouns are semi-fossilized and have relatively opaque meanings. For all these reasons, it is necessary to briefly discuss each locative noun and its constituent morphemes individually, which is done in Section 5.5.2 below. First, though, some of the more basic properties of Fenghuang Xong's locative nouns are summarized in Table 5.1.

Table 5.1: Summary of Xong locative nouns.

LOCATIVE NOUN	GLOSS	TRANSLATION	MONOSYLLABIC VARIANT	SECTION DISCUSSED IN	OTHER NOTES
geud-neul	place_1-front	'front'	None	5.5.2.1	Can be used in temporal sense
geud-zheit	place_1-back/outside	'back, behind; outside'	*zheit-*	5.5.2.2	Can be used in temporal sense
zheit-gheul	back/outside-place_2	'back, behind; outside'	*zheit-*	5.5.2.2	Can be used in temporal sense
laot-/leut-/leux-gheul	top-place_2	'top, above'	*laot-/leut-/leux-*	5.5.2.3	None
daod-haond	place_3-bottom	'bottom'	*haond*	5.5.2.4	*Haond* can serve as NP
gix.bob/gix.bof	underneath	'underneath'	None	5.5.2.4	None
ghaob-bol	NOM-underside	'underside'	*bol-*	5.5.2.4	None
ghaob-deut	NOM-foot	'(at the) foot (of)'	*deut-*	5.5.2.4	None

Table 5.1 (continued)

LOCATIVE NOUN	GLOSS	TRANSLATION	MONOSYLLABIC VARIANT	SECTION DISCUSSED IN	OTHER NOTES
geud-deut	place$_1$-foot	'(at the) foot (of)'	*deut-*	5.5.2.4	None
ghaob-giaok	NOM-side	'side'	*giaok-*	5.5.2.5	None
ghaob-biank	NOM-side	'side'	None	5.5.2.5	*Biank* can serve as classifier
ghaob-zheud	NOM-edge	'edge, rim'	None	5.5.2.6	None
ghaob-sheint	NOM-edge	'edge, rim'	None	5.5.2.6	None
ghaob-deind	NOM-edge	'edge, rim'	None	5.5.2.6	None
ghaob-nhaons	NOM-inside	'inside'	*nhaons*	5.5.2.7	*Nhaons* can serve as NP
nhaons-naub/ -ndaub	inside-place$_4$	'inside'	*nhaons*	5.5.2.7	*Nhaons* can serve as NP
daod-nzhonb	place$_3$-middle	'middle, center'	None	5.5.2.8	None
manx-nzhonb	AT-middle	'middle, center'	None	5.5.2.8	None
baod-liak	BUG-left	'left'	None	5.5.2.9	None
baod-nins	BUG-left	'left'	None	5.5.2.9	None
baod-zhax	BUG-right	'right'	None	5.5.2.9	None

5.5.2 Inventory of locative nouns

All attested locative nouns are described and exemplified in Sections 5.5.2.1 to 5.5.2.9 below. These sections have been organized in terms of rough semantic categories, but this has been done solely for the reader's convenience and should not be taken as implying any sort of grammatical classification.

5.5.2.1 Forms meaning 'front'

The form *geud-neul* 'front' is one of Xong's more straightforward locative nouns. The first morpheme of this form, *geud-*, is glossed as 'place$_1$' when it appears in examples, since this same morpheme appears as a component in a number of other expressions referring to spatial concepts, like *geud-zheit* [place$_1$-back/outside] 'back, behind;

outside' and *geud-deut* [place$_1$-foot] '(at the) foot (of)'.[103] The second morpheme, -*neul*, is simply glossed as 'front' when it appears in examples, although consultants report that this syllable does not mean anything when produced in isolation.

The disyllabic noun *geud-neul* 'front' has no monosyllabic variant, not even when it functions as the head of a locative compound noun (as in example (5.277) below). No other forms meaning 'front' have yet been attested.

(5.277) *Beul* ***geud-neul**-bioud* *mex* *hot* *hliob* *ghaob-ndaut.*
3 **place$_1$-front**-home exist how.much many NOM-tree
'There are a lot of trees in front of his home.' (Shixiang Wu, fieldnotes)

(5.278) *Ninb* ***geud-neul*** *aod-doul* *chek* *dox* *nins* *wel*
at **place$_1$-front** one-CLF:hand vehicle that COP 1SG
naond.
ASSOC
'The car in front is mine.' (Shixiang Wu, fieldnotes)

The form *geud-neul* can also be used in a temporal sense to mean 'earlier, before', as in example (5.279) below.

(5.279) *Mx* *beut* *nggueb* *naond* ***geud-neul*** *lis* *xank*
2SG lie.down sleep ASSOC **place$_1$-front** want first
geud *zol.niel* *chauk* *diul.*
hold homework do complete
'You need to finish your homework before you go to sleep.' (Shixiang Wu, fieldnotes)

5.5.2.2 Forms meaning 'back, behind' or 'outside'

The forms *geud-zheit* and *zheit-gheul* can both be used to mean either 'back, behind' or 'outside'. While these two forms appear to be completely interchangeable for all consultants, it is unclear whether their meanings should be interpreted as a case of monosemy, polysemy, or ambiguity (see Gil 2004), and the root *zheit* is glossed as either 'back' or 'outside' when it appears in examples depending on the most appropriate English translation in each instance.

The first morpheme in *geud-zheit* 'back, behind; outside' is the same as the first morpheme in *geud-neul* 'front', and so it is similarly glossed as 'place$_1$'. However, unlike the root -*neul* 'front', which always occurs preceded by *geud-* (see Section 5.5.2.1 above), the root *zheit* often appears without a preceding *geud-* when it serves

103 Xiang (1999: 23) very plausibly argues that this bound form *geud-* 'place$_1$' has grammaticalized from the homophonous free noun root *geud* 'road'.

as the head of a locative compound noun. An example of this can be seen in (5.282) below, where *zheit-zhauf* [back-door] 'behind the door' is used rather than the equally acceptable *geud-zheit-zhauf* [place$_1$-back-door].

The second morpheme in *zheit-gheul* is homophonous with *gheul* 'village' and *gheul* 'mountain' (although 'mountain' is generally expressed as *bid-gheul*, with an initial prefix *bid-* 'FRT'), and all three of these morphemes may well be etymologically related. However, the author's consultants interpret the second morpheme of *zheit-gheul* 'back, behind; outside' as being only accidentally homophonous with *gheul* 'village' and *gheul* 'mountain'. Since this same *-gheul* morpheme also occurs in a locative noun meaning 'top, above' (see Section 5.5.2.3 below), it is simply glossed as 'place$_2$' when it appears in examples.

Finally, note that neither **geud-* nor **-gheul* can occur on its own to mean either 'back, behind' or 'outside'.

(5.280) *Shaont gid, mx naond* ***geud-zheit*** *mex ngonl*
fast run 2SG ASSOC **place$_1$-back** exist CLF:animate
guoud miauk!
dog crazy
'Run, there's a mad dog behind you!' (Shixiang Wu, fieldnotes)

(5.281) *Mx geud ghaob-nbed.sed biat zhaut* ***zheit-gheul.***
2SG hold NOM-garbage pour reach **outside-place$_2$**
'Take the garbage out.' (Shixiang Wu, fieldnotes)

(5.282) *Wel ninb* ***zheit****-zhauf guax fub huaob.*
1SG at **back**-door hang CLF:painting painting
'I hung a painting on the back of the door.' (Haili Shi, fieldnotes)

Both *geud-zheit* [place$_1$-back] and *zheit-gheul* [back-place$_2$] can also be used in a temporal sense to mean 'later on, afterward' (cf. *geud-neul* 'front' in Section 5.5.2.1 above). Instances of the former form being used in such a sense can be seen in example (5.283) below.

(5.283) ***Geud-zheit*** *doul Niaox.nhaonl ox beul naond bod,*
place$_1$-back remain PN and 3 ASSOC husband
geud-zheit *doub doul manx raut lex lah.*
place$_1$-back then$_1$ remain REL good only PRF
'From then on it was just Niao Nhaon and her husband, from then on there were only good things (for them).' (Xingyu Shi, in *Oub Meinl Yaos Geud*)

5.5.2.3 Forms meaning 'top, above'

The form meaning 'top, above' is *laot-gheul* for most consultants, although the variants *leut-gheul* and *leux-gheul* have also been attested. The first morpheme of this form, *laot-/leut-/leux-*, is glossed as 'top' when it appears in examples. Like *zheit* 'back, behind; outside' (see Section 5.5.2.2 above), the morpheme *laot-/leut-/leux-* 'top' often occurs alone (i.e. without a following *-gheul*) as the head of a locative compound noun. An example of this can be seen in (5.284) below, where *leut-zeint-bias* [top-ceramic.jar-pickled.cabbage] 'on a pickled-cabbage jar' is used rather than the equally acceptable *leut-gheul-zeint-bias* [top-place$_2$-ceramic.jar-pickled.cabbage].

The second morpheme of *laot-gheul* 'top, above' is the same as the second morpheme of *zheit-gheul* 'back, behind; outside' (again, see Section 5.5.2.2), and so it too is glossed as 'place$_2$' when it occurs in examples. While this morpheme is homophonous with *gheul* 'village' and *gheul* 'mountain', all three appear to be distinct morphemes in modern Xong. Example (5.285) below makes this particularly clear for the two forms *-gheul* 'place$_2$' and *gheul* 'mountain', which occur together within a single noun phrase to express 'the top of the mountain'.

(5.284) *Aod-ngonl* *deb-guk* *jont* *leb*
one-CLF:animate DIM-frog sit CLF
***leut**-zeint-bias.*
top-ceramic.jar-pickled.cabbage
'The frog was sitting on a pickled-cabbage jar.' (Xingyu Shi, in *Deb Guk Ronf*) (repeated from (5.275) above)

(5.285) *Boub* *gheul* *ninb* *bid-gheul* ***laot-gheul.***
1PL village at FRT-mountain **top-place$_2$**
'My village is at the top of the mountain.' (Haili Shi, fieldnotes)

5.5.2.4 Forms meaning 'bottom' or 'underneath'

Four distinct locative nouns are grouped together here since they all involve the notion of one entity being below or lower than another, but the semantic differences among all four forms are still fairly clear. The semantically broadest of these four forms is *daod-haond*, which could be translated as 'bottom', 'below', 'under(neath)', or 'lower than' depending on the context. The first morpheme of *daod-haond* can also serve as a non-locative (i.e. canonical) noun meaning 'place', and so it is glossed as 'place$_3$' when it occurs in examples. The second morpheme, *haond*, is simply glossed as 'bottom'. The form *daod-haond* is a somewhat atypical locative noun in that while it does have a monosyllabic variant (namely *haond*), this monosyllabic variant can never occur as the head of a locative compound noun, but instead only as an independent noun phrase (as in example (5.287) below). This is the precise opposite of nearly all other locative nouns with monosyllabic variants, since those variants can typically occur as the heads of locative compound nouns but not as independent noun phrases (the only other exception besides *haond* 'bottom' is *nhaons* 'inside', which is discussed in Section 5.5.2.7 below).

(5.286) *Beul ninb ghaob-ndaut* ***daod-haond.***
3 at NOM-tree **place$_3$-bottom**
'He's (sitting) under the tree.' (Shixiang Wu, fieldnotes)

(5.287) *Yab jix dut lot* ***haond*** *monl nieus nggaob.*
also NEG$_1$ obtain descend **bottom** go buy medicine
'(I) didn't have the chance to go down (to the main street in town) to buy medicine.' (Haili Shi, in *Tooth Conversation*)

The locative noun *gix.bob* (or *gix.bof*, for consultants from Yankan Village) is glossed as 'underneath' when it occurs in examples, although its precise meaning is a bit narrower than that of English *underneath*. It seems to specifically mean something like 'directly underneath some structure which extends past the referent in all horizontal directions'. It could thus be used for some small entity (e.g. insects, as in example (5.288) below) located underneath a table or a bed, but not for someone standing at the foot of a mountain or directly underneath a ceiling fan. Note that the form *gix.bob* does not have any monosyllabic variant, and this form is unique among all the locative nouns discussed in this chapter in that both of its syllables have completely opaque meanings (and so they are not given individual glosses).

(5.288) ***Gix.bob****-zonf mex hot hliob daob-ginb!*
underneath-bed exist how.much many AN-bug
'There are bugs all under the bed!' (Shixiang Wu, fieldnotes)

The locative noun *ghaob-bol* [NOM-underside] 'underside' can be used to refer to three types of referents: (i) the bottom surface of a solid three-dimensional object (e.g. the underside of a laptop computer), (ii) either face of the bottom surface of a hollow three-dimensional object (e.g. the upward face or downward face of the bottom surface of a bucket), and (iii) the lowest object in a vertical stack of objects (e.g. the lowest book in a stack of books, as in example (5.289) below). Like most other locative noun roots, the root *bol* 'underside' can also occur independently as the head of a locative compound noun.

(5.289) *Nins* ***ghaob-bol-bol*** *aod-beint dox.*
COP **NOM-underside-RED** one-CLF:book that
'(The book you're looking for) is the very bottom one (in that pile of books).' (Chenghua Long, fieldnotes)

The final locative noun to be discussed in this section means roughly 'foot' or 'base', as in 'at the foot (or base) of a mountain' or 'at the foot (or base) of a large tree'. More precisely, it seems to refer to the lower portion of an entity that is above and in contact with a horizontal two-dimensional plane, as well as to the portion of that plane immediately surrounding the entity in question. This locative noun has two variants, *ghaob-deut* [NOM-foot] and *geud-deut* [place$_1$-foot] (for information on the meaning of *geud-* 'place$_1$', see Section 5.5.2.1 above). Most of the author's consultants report that both variants are freely interchangeable for them. Like *bol* 'underside' and most other locative noun roots, the root *deut* 'foot' often occurs alone (i.e. without a preceding *ghaob-* or *geud-*) as the head of a locative compound noun. This can be seen in example (5.291) below.

(5.290) *Boub gheul ninb* ***ghaob-deut****-gheul.*
1PL village at **NOM-foot**-mountain
'My village is at the foot of the mountain.' (Shixiang Wu, fieldnotes)

(5.291) *Aod-gud nzhaond dand* ***deut****-ndaut.*
one-CLF:human.group return arrive **foot**-tree
'Everyone returned to the foot of the tree.' (Chenghua Long, in *Conversation in La'ershan*)

5.5.2.5 Forms meaning 'side'

The forms *ghaob-giaok* and *ghaob-biank* are both used to mean 'side' in Xong. Both forms consist of the nominal prefix *ghaob-* 'NOM' followed by a root that itself means 'side', either *giaok* or *biank*. The author has not yet been able to determine whether there is any semantic or pragmatic difference between the roots *giaok* and *biank*, and in many cases the two are interchangeable. However, they do differ in at least three ways.

First, the root *giaok* 'side' can optionally appear on its own without a preceding *ghaob-* 'NOM' when serving as the head of a locative compound noun, as is exemplified in (5.292).

(5.292) *Boub* ***giaok****-bioud mex aod-bons nbed.sed.*
1PL **side**-home exist one-CLF:pile garbage
'There's a trashpile next to our house.' (unknown Xong consultant, fieldnotes)

This is not true for *biank* 'side', which is always preceded by *ghaob-* 'NOM' even when serving as the head of a locative compound noun. For instance, the locative compound noun *ghaob-biank-laut* [NOM-side-land] 'along the sides of the garden' in example (5.293) cannot be replaced with **biank-laut* [side-land].

(5.293)

***Ghaob-biank**-laut*	*nins*	*reib-xeb,*	*manx-nzhonb-laut*	*nins*
NOM-side-land	COP	vegetable-oil	AT-middle-land	COP
bex.cef				
cabbage				

'(The plants) along the sides of the garden are rapeseed, (and the plants) in the middle are cabbage.' (Haili Shi, fieldnotes)

The second major difference between the two roots is that *biank* 'side' can also be used as a classifier meaning 'CLF:side', as in example (5.294) below (see also Section 6.1.4.5). In contrast, the root *giaok* 'side' can only be used as a locative noun, not as a classifier. This may be due to the third major difference between the two forms, namely that *biank* is an obvious recent borrowing of a Sinitic form (and is readily identified as such by consultants) that can similarly serve as either a classifier or a locative noun in the source language (the Sinitic form in question is either Standard Mandarin *biān* [边] 'side' or a cognate form from another Sinitic variety). This is not true of *giaok* 'side'. While the etymology of *giaok* is unclear at present, it is at least not an obvious borrowing from Sinitic, nor is it identified as such by consultants.

(5.294)

Aod-ngonl	*daob-jod*	*doub*	*nkhed*	*maox.loub*	***oub-biank***
one-CLF:animate	AN-wolf	then$_1$	look	road	**two-CLF:side**

zhaonl	*bed*	*manx*	*seik.xed*	*naond*	*beinx.*
grow	full	REL	fresh	ASSOC	flower

'The wolf saw fresh flowers growing on both sides of the road.' (Haili Shi, in *Xaub Honl Mob*)[104]

5.5.2.6 Forms meaning 'edge' or 'rim'

There are three forms meaning 'edge' or 'rim' in Xong: *ghaob-zheud*, *ghaob-sheint*, and *ghaob-deind*. Most of the author's consultants use all three of these forms, and there do appear to be some slight semantic differences among them. Unfortunately, different consultants describe these semantic differences in different ways, and the author is not yet able to precisely characterize them. All three forms are thus simply glossed as 'edge' whenever they appear in examples.

The forms *ghaob-zheud*, *ghaob-sheint*, and *ghaob-deind* all have the nominal prefix *ghaob-* 'NOM' as their first morpheme. This prefix appears to be obligatory when appearing in any of these locative nouns, even when the locative noun is modified by a following noun root. For instance, in example (5.295), *ghaob-zheud-lieux* [NOM-edge-well] 'the edge of the well' cannot be replaced with **zheud-lieux* [edge-well].

104 The form *jod* (often preceded by *daob-* 'AN') can be used to refer to both wolves and tigers in Fenghuang Xong; compare, for instance, this example (5.294) with examples (5.12) and (5.108) above.

(5.295) ***Ghaob-zheud**-lieux ngeul hint.*
NOM-edge-well slippery very
'The edge of the well is really slippery.' (Haili Shi, fieldnotes)

(5.296) *Minl-aub naond **ghaob-sheint** mex hliof ghaob-ndaut.*
AUG-water ASSOC **NOM-edge** exist many NOM-tree
'There are trees all along the river.' (Haili Shi, fieldnotes)

(5.297) *Jaont dand leb **ob-deind**-aub manh, aod-tit*
herd arrive CLF **NOM-edge**-water PART one-CLF:time$_3$
*beul minl zhaok aub leb **ob-deind**-aub dox.*
3 mother fall water CLF **NOM-edge**-water that
'(The boy) would herd (his cows) to the water's edge, to the water's edge where his mother had fallen in.' (Xingyu Shi, in *Oub Meinl Yaos Geud*)

5.5.2.7 Forms meaning 'inside'

Most of the author's consultants use two different forms that both mean 'inside'. The first of these is *ghaob-nhaons* for all consultants, with an initial nominal prefix *ghaob-* 'NOM' followed by the root *nhaons* 'inside'. Like certain other locative noun roots, *nhaons* often occurs alone (i.e. without a preceding *ghaob-* 'NOM') when serving as the head of a locative compound noun. For example, the locative compound noun *ghaob-nhaons-tief.tonx* [NOM-inside-bucket] 'inside the bucket' in example (5.298) could be expressed equally well as just *nhaons-tief.tonx* [inside-bucket].

(5.298) *Monx geud aub biat zhut **ghaob-nhaons**-tief.tonx.*
2SG hold water pour reach **NOM-inside**-bucket
'Pour the water into the bucket.' (Haili Shi, fieldnotes)

The root *nhaons* 'inside' is like *haond* 'bottom' (see Section 5.5.2.4) but unlike all other locative noun roots in that it can also occur as an independent, monosyllabic noun phrase in its own right. An example of this is given in (5.299) below.

(5.299) *Keuf oub-meinl doub ndax beul, wanx lot,*
shut two-CLF:person then$_1$ lift.up 3 throw descend
*wanx lot **nhaons**, wanx lot aub oh.*
throw descend **inside** throw descend water PART
'(Once the lid of the cage was) shut, the two of them lifted it up and then threw it down, they threw it down into the water.' (Xingyu Shi, in *Oub Meinl Yaos Geud*)

The second form that means 'inside' is *nhaons-naub* for some consultants and *nhaons-ndaub* for others. As mentioned above, the root *nhaons* 'inside' can occur alone as the head of a locative compound noun or as an independent noun phrase. The morpheme *-naub/-ndaub* never occurs independently, but it does occur as the second morpheme of the expressions *neind-naub* (or *neind-ndaub*) 'here' and *dox-naub* (or *dox-ndaub*) 'there', whose first morphemes are the demonstratives *neind* 'this' and *dox* 'that' (see Section 7.2). Thus, while the meaning of the form *-naub/-ndaub* itself is somewhat opaque, it only occurs in expressions that refer to location in some way, and so it is glossed as 'place$_4$' wherever it appears (as in (5.300) below).

(5.300) *Xik.guaok naond* ***nhaons-ndaub*** *nins manx nqint naond.*
watermelon ASSOC **inside-place$_4$** COP REL red ASSOC
'The inside of a watermelon is red.' (Shixiang Wu, fieldnotes)

5.5.2.8 Forms meaning 'middle' or 'center'

There are two forms used to express 'middle' or 'center' in Xong: *daod-nzhonb* and *manx-nzhonb*. The first of these is composed of *daod* 'place$_3$' (see Section 5.5.2.4 above) followed by *nzhonb* 'middle, center', and the second is composed of *manx* followed by *nzhonb*. Although homophonous with *manx* '2PL' and *manx* 'REL', the meaning of *manx* in the expression *manx-nzhonb* 'middle, center' is completely opaque to the author's consultants. In this it is similar to the syllable *manx* that appears in the fixed expressions *manx-eib* and *manx.eib.manx.ab*, both meaning roughly 'long ago, a long time ago' (see Section 7.2). Since it only appears in a few fixed expressions, all of which relate to spatial or temporal location, the form *manx* is given the intentionally vague gloss 'AT', from 'at' (note that the lowercase gloss 'at' is not used in this case since it is already used for the high-frequency verbs *ninb* 'at' and *deib* 'at').

Both *daod-nzhonb* and *manx-nzhonb* only ever appear as full disyllabic expressions (or as trisyllabic ones, if reduplicated), never as shortened monosyllabic ones. In other words, 'middle, center' is always expressed as *daod-nzhonb* or *manx-nzhonb*, never as just **nzhonb*, even when appearing as part of a larger locative compound noun.

(5.301) *Oub-zhaus ndaut* ***daod-nzhonb*** *mex aod-diaond*
two-CLF:vertical.plant tree **place$_3$-middle** exist one-CLF:lump
ghaob-roub.
NOM-stone
'Between the two trees there was a large rock.' (Shixiang Wu, fieldnotes)

(5.302) ***Manx-nzhonb*** *nins boub lox.sid.*
AT-middle COP 1PL teacher
'(The one in) the middle is my teacher.' (Haili Shi, fieldnotes)

5.5.2.9 Forms meaning 'right' or 'left'

The final locative nouns to be discussed in this chapter are *baod-liak* 'left', *baod-nins* 'left', and *baod-zhax* 'right'. The two forms meaning 'left' appear to be completely interchangeable, and most of the author's consultants readily use both forms. None of these three forms appear to significantly differ from Xong's other locative nouns in terms of their grammatical behavior, but note that they do differ from all other locative nouns in that their initial morpheme is the nominal prefix *baod-* 'BUG' (see Section 5.4.2.6). The forms *baod-liak* 'left', *baod-nins* 'left', and *baod-zhax* 'right' are also alike in that they never appear in a reduced monosyllabic form like **liak*, **nins*, or **zhax*, even when serving as the head of a locative compound noun (as in example (5.303) below).

(5.303) ***Baod-liak***-*nek-geud* *mex* *leb* *xox.ndaonf,* ***baod-zhax***-*nek-geud*
BUG-left-AUG-road exist CLF school **BUG-right**-AUG-road
mex *aod-leb* *fanb.dieb.*
exist one-CLF restaurant
'There's a school on the left side of the road and a restaurant on the right side of the road.' (Haili Shi, fieldnotes)

(5.304) ***Baod-liak*** *mex* *minl-aub,* ***baod-zhax*** *mex* *leb* *bioud.*
BUG-left exist AUG-water **BUG-right** exist CLF home
'There's a lake on the left and a house on the right.' (Haili Shi, fieldnotes)

5.6 Nominal reduplication

A handful of canonical Xong nouns can undergo reduplication, although this does not appear to have any noticeable semantic or pragmatic effect (cf. the discussion of reduplicated locative nouns in Section 5.5.1 above). Only four nouns capable of undergoing such reduplication have been attested so far, each of which is exemplified below.

(5.305) *Monx* *leb* *dauk,* *monx* *dionb* *ix* *dut* ***deb-deb.***
2SG CLF REFL 2SG lead NEG$_1$ obtain **child-RED**
'You can't care for the child on your own.' (Xingyu Shi, in *Oub Meinl Yaos Geud*)

(5.306) *Fanx.zheinb* *aod-leb* ***khauk-khauk*** *dox* *loux* *hint.*
anyway one-CLF **hole-RED** that long.time very
'Anyway that hole's been there (in my tooth) for a long time.' (Haili Shi, in *Tooth Conversation*)

(5.307) *Wel* *aod-khauk* *dox* *wel* *baol,* *doul* *leb*
1SG one-CLF:place$_2$ that 1SG break.down remain CLF
baod-jonx-jonx
BUG-root-RED
'That (tooth) of mine is broken, there's only a little bit of the root left.' (Haili Shi, in *Tooth Conversation*)

(5.308) *Aod-leb* ***deb-nceik-nceik*** *dox* *xonx* *hint* *aoh!*
one-CLF **DIM-young.man-RED** that attractive very PART
'That young man is really handsome!' (unknown Xong consultant, fieldnotes)

In each of examples (5.305–5.308), consultants report that the reduplicated noun could be replaced with its non-reduplicated version with no change in meaning or pragmatics.

Consultants have not produced any additional reduplicated canonical nouns aside from the four shown in (5.305–5.308), and they have uniformly rejected all other constructed examples of reduplicated canonical nouns that the author has suggested. Of course, there may well be additional reduplicable nouns in Xong that have simply escaped notice so far, but in any case it is clear that reduplication of canonical nouns does not play a particularly prominent role in Xong grammar. However, note that certain other types of Xong forms undergo reduplication much more readily than canonical nouns do, and with much clearer semantic and/or pragmatic effects. See, for instance, Section 5.5.1 on reduplicated locative nouns, Section 6.1.3.2 on reduplicated classifiers, and Section 10.5.4 on reduplicated verbs.

6 Classifiers and numerals

As in many languages of East and Southeast Asia (including all extant Miao-Yao languages reported in the literature), numerals in Xong generally cannot be used to quantify nouns directly. Instead, a Xong numeral must first combine with a following classifier to form a numeral-classifier phrase, which can only then be used to quantify a following noun. For instance, the noun *miex/mianx* 'person' cannot be directly quantified by a numeral like *aod* 'one', but only by a numeral-classifier phrase such as *aod-meinl* [one-CLF:person]. Similarly, the noun *yaok.saob* 'toothbrush' cannot be directly quantified by a numeral like *bub* 'three', but only by a numeral-classifier phrase like *bub-del* [three-CLF:rigid.length].

Fenghuang Xong features a robust, well developed set of at least several dozen dedicated classifiers (i.e. forms which only ever function as classifiers) whose individual meanings range from the very general (e.g. *ngonl* 'CLF:animate', which can be used with any noun that has an animate referent) to the very specific (e.g. *baonx* 'CLF:honeybee.hive', which – as its gloss suggests – can only be used with honeybee hives). Besides these dedicated classifiers, many nominal and verbal forms can serve as classifiers without any overt derivational marking. In addition to quantifying referents, Xong's classifiers and numeral-classifier phrases also serve a variety of other minor grammatical functions in the language (including marking duration, quantifying events or occurrences, and expressing the quantity, degree, or extent of certain property-denoting verbs), and numeral-classifier phrases in particular very often occur as noun phrases in their own right, with no noun occurring within the same noun phrase at all.[105] While Xong's numerals, classifiers, and numeral-classifier phrases are broadly similar to those of Standard Mandarin in terms of their syntactic, semantic, functional, and discourse-pragmatic properties, a comparison of this chapter with the relevant Standard Mandarin data will show that they (unsurprisingly) differ in many particulars.[106]

105 It is perhaps also worth mentioning here certain functions that classifiers and numeral-classifier phrases are not used for in Xong, especially when those functions are commonly performed by classifiers and numeral-classifier phrases in other languages of greater mainland Southeast Asia (see Bisang 1999). Most significantly, it appears that classifiers and numeral-classifier phrases are not used to signal (in)definiteness or (non)specificity in Xong, or at least not in any clear way. While it is conceivable that a large-scale corpus study might reveal some correlation between the tendency to use a classifier or numeral-classifier phrase in a noun phrase and the definiteness or specificity of the noun phrase's referent, no such correlation is obvious in the author's own corpus. In addition, the author also argues that Xong classifiers are not used to mark relativization or possession; see Sections 8.1.3 and 8.2.2 (respectively) for details.

106 This comparison to Standard Mandarin is made solely for the sake of convenience, since it is likely that many users of this grammar are already somewhat familiar with Standard Mandarin's numerals, classifiers, and numeral-classifier phrases. Comparisons to many other isolating languages of East and Southeast Asia (especially Sinitic and Miao-Yao ones) would be equally appropriate, but perhaps not as useful.

The remainder of this chapter is structured as follows. Section 6.1 discusses Xong classifiers, with Section 6.1.1 covering some terminological and other preliminary issues, Section 6.1.2 covering numeral-classifier phrases, Section 6.1.3 covering various other constructions that feature classifiers, and Section 6.1.4 covering classifier semantics. Section 6.2 then examines Xong numerals along with a variety of related topics, including numeral phrases, expressions of approximate quantity, and fractions and multiples.

Finally, while classifiers and numerals certainly carry a heavy functional load when it comes to nominal quantification in Xong, the language does feature several other methods of nominal quantification that do not rely solely on these forms. These include forms and constructions with meanings roughly equivalent to *some X*, *no X*, and the like in English and other European languages. However, these forms and constructions do not in any way constitute a natural grammatical class in Xong as they do in English (in which *some*, *no*, and similar quantifying forms all clearly belong to the class of determiners), and so they are discussed in various places throughout this grammar rather than together in this chapter. In particular, see Sections 9.1.3.1, 9.2.3.1, and 9.2.3.3.

6.1 Classifiers

6.1.1 Terminological and other preliminary issues

Before moving on to detailed discussions of the grammatical constructions in which Xong classifiers occur (see Sections 6.1.2 and 6.1.3) and the semantic characteristics of those classifiers (Section 6.1.4), there are several terminological and other issues which must be dealt with first. The term *classifier* is used in a technical sense in this grammar to refer to any Xong form which satisfies two definitional criteria: (i) it can co-occur with a preceding numeral, and (ii) it can occur reduplicated to convey the meaning 'every, each'.[107, 108] Example (6.1) below demonstrates that classifiers can readily co-occur with a preceding numeral, while examples (6.2–6.4) demonstrate that (some) nouns, (some) verbs, and ideophones cannot. Note that certain other nouns and verbs in Xong do indeed satisfy these definitional criteria, as is discussed

107 Since they combine with a preceding numeral (rather than, for instance, with a possessive marker or demonstrative), in crosslinguistic terms Xong's classifiers could be more precisely characterized as "numeral classifiers" (see Gil 2013). However, the term "numeral classifier" is not used in this grammar for two reasons. First, no other type of grammatical constituent is referred to as a "classifier" in this grammar, and so there is no need to disambiguate the classifiers discussed in this Section 6.1 from any other type of classifier. Second, avoiding the term "numeral classifier" ensures that there will be no confusion with the term "numeral-classifier phrase", which *is* frequently used in this grammar.

108 Note, though, that Xong features a handful of "defective" or non-canonical classifiers, which are forms that do not strictly satisfy these two definitional criteria but still generally pattern with Xong's canonical classifiers in grammatical and functional terms. See Sections 6.1.4.1 and 6.1.4.5 for details.

further below in this section. This does not appear to be the case with ideophones, though, which show no grammatical overlap with classifiers at all.

(6.1) *aod-meinl/aod-ngonl/aod-zheinb*
one-CLF:person/one-CLF:animate/one-CLF:tool
'one (person/animate entity/tool)' (Haili Shi, fieldnotes)

(6.2) **aod-guoud/*aod-miex/*aod-hlit*
one-dog/one-person/one-cooked.rice
(intended: 'one dog/person/grain of cooked rice')

(6.3) **aod-nonx/*aod-jont/*aod-nqint*
one-eat/one-sit/one-red
(intended: 'one instance of eating/drinking/being red, one edible thing/place to sit/red thing')

(6.4) **aod-jel.jel/*aod-biaol.biaol*
one-IDEO:A:shiningly/one-IDEO:A:sour
(intended: 'one instance of shininess/sourness, one shiny/sour thing')

Grammatical constituents composed of a numeral or numeral phrase (see Section 6.2.1) and a following classifier (as in example (6.1) above) are referred to as *numeral-classifier phrases* in this grammar; see Section 6.1.2 below for more information on these. A classifier that occurs in non-reduplicated form without a preceding numeral is referred to as a *bare classifier*, examples of which are given in (6.5) and (6.6) below. Note that this term does not refer to a type of classifier, but rather to a syntactic position in which a classifier can occur. Any classifier, whether dedicated or derived (see below in this section), can occur as either a bare classifier or as the second constituent of a numeral-classifier phrase.

(6.5) *Aod-ngonl* *deb-guk* *jont* ***leb***
one-CLF:animate DIM-frog sit **CLF**
leut-zeint-bias.
top-ceramic.jar-pickled.cabbage
'The frog was sitting on a pickled-cabbage jar.' (Xingyu Shi, in *Deb Guk Ronf*)

(6.6) *Aod-dieud* *dox* *Sank.ux.baob* *naond* *qik.zib* *mex*
one-CLF:time$_2$ that PN ASSOC wife exist
ngonl *deb-deb.*
CLF:animate child-RED
'At that time San U Bao's wife had a child.' (Qiusheng Long, in *Ngel.kanx*)

Examples (6.7–6.10) below demonstrate that classifiers can occur reduplicated to mean 'every, each', and that (some) nouns, (some) verbs, and ideophones cannot do so. See Section 6.1.3.2 below for more on such reduplicated classifiers.

(6.7) *Meinl-meinl/ngonl-ngonl/zheinb-zheinb* *at*
CLF:person-CLF:person/CLF:animate-CLF:animate/CLF:tool-CLF:tool SAT
raut.
good
'Every/each one (person/animate entity/tool) was good.' (Haili Shi, fieldnotes)

(6.8) **Guoud-guoud*/**miex-miex*/**hlit-hlit* *at* *raut.*
dog-dog/person-person/cooked.rice-cooked.rice SAT good
(intended: 'Every/each dog/person/grain of cooked rice was good.')

(6.9) **Nonx-nonx*/**jont-jont*/**nqint-nqint* *at* *raut.*
eat-eat/sit-sit/red-red SAT good
(intended: 'Every/each instance of eating/drinking/being red was good, every/each edible thing/place to sit/red thing was good.')

(6.10) **Jel.jel-jel.jel*/**biaol.biaol-biaol.biaol* *at*
IDEO:A:shiningly-IDEO:A:shiningly/IDEO:A:sour-IDEO:A:sour SAT
raut.
good
(intended: 'Every instance of shininess/sourness was good, every/each shiny/sour thing was good.')

The term *classifier role* is used to refer to any (or all) of the grammatical functions that classifiers characteristically serve. The most common of these are (i) serving as the second constituent of a numeral-classifier phrase (see example (6.1) above) and (ii) occurring in reduplicated form to mean 'every, each' (see example (6.7) above). See Sections 6.1.2 and 6.1.3 below for discussion of these and other, less frequent classifier roles that classifiers can serve.

Forms that serve classifier roles can be divided into two groups. Certain forms only serve classifier roles and never function as nouns or verbs. Examples of such forms include *zheinb* 'CLF:tool', *ngonl* 'CLF:animate', and *shauk* 'CLF:yuan'. These are referred to as *dedicated classifiers* in this grammar. Other forms can freely serve classifier roles, but they can also function as nouns or verbs. Examples of these forms include *zhet* 'CLF:bowl', which can also function as a noun meaning 'bowl', *ndeind* 'CLF:knife', which can also function as a noun meaning 'knife', and *giud* 'CLF:pinch' (as in *aod-**giud** njeud* [one-**CLF:pinch** salt] 'a pinch of salt'), which can also function as a verb meaning 'to pinch'. These forms are referred to as *derived classifiers* (at least when they are serving a classifier role, rather than functioning as nouns or verbs).[109] Only a small subset of nouns and an even smaller subset of verbs have been attested as derived classifiers in the author's corpus, and there are many nouns and verbs which consultants do not allow to serve any classifier roles (e.g. *aub* 'water', *ghab* 'chicken', *nqint* 'red', *daos* 'to die'). However, it is unclear whether this reflects a grammatical restriction, which would mean that some nouns and verbs can occur as derived classifiers while others simply cannot, or merely a semantic-pragmatic one, which would mean that any noun or verb could in theory occur as a derived classifier given an appropriate enough context (though for some nouns and verbs, like *aub* 'water' or *nqint* 'red', it is difficult to imagine what an appropriate enough context could possibly be).

There are two final preliminary issues that the reader may wish to keep in mind while continuing through the following subsections of this Section 6.1. First, Xong classifiers arguably do not serve to classify nouns themselves, since many (perhaps most) nouns can occur with multiple distinct classifiers (see Section 6.1.4). Instead, it might be more accurate to say that a classifier serves to indicate the unit (e.g. bowls, animate entities, herds, units of time/length/volume, etc.) that is being used in a particular instance to quantify a particular referent. Second, there is some evidence to suggest that the syntactic head of a Xong noun phrase containing a classifier is in fact the classifier itself, rather than the noun or any other noun-phrase–internal constituent. See Section 7.2 for further discussion of this latter issue.

6.1.2 Numeral-classifier phrases

6.1.2.1 Numeral-classifier phrases as constituents of larger noun phrases

Xong's numeral-classifier phrases most often occur as constituents of larger noun phrases. A numeral-classifier phrase serving as such a constituent will occur after the noun phrase's possessor (see Section 8.2), if there is one, and before the noun phrase's noun (see Chapter 5), if there is one. This is demonstrated in examples (6.11–6.13) below. In each of these three examples, each numeral-classifier phrase has been bolded, and each possessor phrase, numeral-classifier phrase, and noun has been enclosed within

---

109 The term "derived classifier" is perhaps less than ideal, since it is not entirely clear to the author that any sort of meaningful derivation is occurring when these forms serve classifier roles rather than serving as nouns or verbs (there is certainly no morphological marking of any derivational processes, at least). It might, for instance, be more accurate to say that certain Xong forms can only serve as classifiers, others can only serve as nouns, others can only serve as verbs, and still others can serve more than one of these functions (e.g. classifier and noun, classifier and verb, etc.). However, in some situations it is still desirable to distinguish between forms that only ever serve classifier roles and forms that can both serve classifier roles and serve as nouns and/or verbs, and the author has been unable to come up with a better term than "derived classifier" for the latter.

brackets. Note that this bracketing has been done solely for convenience, and it does not necessarily reflect the actual constituent structure of the noun phrases in question.

(6.11) [*Wel naond*] [***aod-ngonl***] [*mioul*] *neind liox guaot!*
[1SG ASSOC] [**one-CLF:animate**] [fish] this big pass
'This fish of mine is really big!' (Shixiang Wu, fieldnotes)

(6.12) [*Boub naond*] [***aod-ndaut***] [*aub*] *neind ik.zhil*
[1PL ASSOC] [**one-CLF:river**] [water] this all.the.way
tonk dand Laok.doux.yaonb.
pass.through arrive Liangtouyang
'This river of ours flows all the way to Liangtouyang (Village).' (Qiusheng Long, in *Ngel.kanx*)

(6.13) [*Mx naond*] [***aod-ngonl***] [*nbat*] *dox mex*
[2SG ASSOC] [**one-CLF:animate**] [pig] that exist
hot heind?
how.much heavy
'How heavy is that pig of yours?' (Shixiang Wu, fieldnotes)

However, the relative ordering possibilities for numeral-classifier phrases and prenominal relative clauses within the same noun phrase are flexible: both of these constituent types must occur after the possessor phrase (if present) and before the noun (if present), but they can occur in either order relative to each other. See Sections 8.1.2 (particularly examples (8.24–8.29)) and 8.1.4 for further information.

Aside from the ordering restrictions just discussed, there appear to be very few restrictions on the structure of a noun phrase that contains a numeral-classifier phrase. Additional material within such a noun phrase can consist of any one or any combination of the following: a noun (see Chapter 5), a demonstrative (Section 7.2), a relative clause (Section 8.1), or a possessor phrase (Section 8.2).[110] For instance, examples (6.14–6.16) below each feature a noun phrase containing a numeral-classifier phrase and a demonstrative, but no other material. In these examples, the noun phrases in question have been enclosed within brackets, and their numeral-classifier phrases have been bolded.

110 Of course, a Xong noun phrase can also consist of any one or any combination of these constituents without a numeral-classifier phrase, but noun phrases with no numeral-classifier phrase naturally lie outside the scope of this section.

(6.14) [***Aod-bix*** *neind*] *hnant dib?*
[**one-CLF:place$_1$** this] call which
'What's the name of this place?' (Haili Shi, fieldnotes)

(6.15) *Geud-zheit naond daut leh, guaot diul*
place$_1$-back ASSOC speech LEH pass complete
[***aod-dieud*** *dox*]...
[**one-CLF:time$_2$** that]
'Afterward, after that time had passed...' (Qiusheng Long, in *Ngel.kanx*)

(6.16) [***Aod-meinl*** *dib*] *ghaod raut deb,* [***aod-meinl***
[**one-CLF:person** which] more good child [**one-CLF:person**
dib] *ghaod kint nied, ghaod mex hliof aub-gheb...*
which] more often cry more exist many water-eye
'Whichever (of you two girls) is the better child, whichever of you weeps more, (she'll) have more tears...' (Xingyu Shi, in *Oub Meinl Yaos Geud*)

Examples (6.17–6.20) below each show one or more noun phrases that consist of a numeral-classifier phrase and a following noun, but no other material. Here, too, the noun phrases in question have been enclosed within brackets and their numeral-classifier phrases have been bolded.

(6.17) *Mex* [***aod-meinl*** *deb-npaok*] *leh...*
exist [**one-CLF:person** DIM-woman] LEH
'There (once) was a girl...' (Haili Shi, in *Xaub Honl Mob*)

(6.18) [***Aod-ngonl*** *guk*] *deit ndanb.*
[**one-CLF:animate** frog] still jump
'The frog kept jumping (into the old woman's bucket).' (Xingyu Shi, in *Deb Guk Ronf*)

(6.19) *Wel lis* [***oub-gul-leb*** *neus-ghab*].
1SG want [**two-ten-CLF** egg-chicken]
'I want twenty chicken eggs.' (unknown Xong consultant, fieldnotes)

(6.20) [***Aod-ngonl*** *guoud*] *leh, ghans mex*
[**one-CLF:animate** dog] LEH see exist
[***aod-baonx*** *maonl-ded*].
[**one-CLF:honeybee.hive** small.flying.insect-honey]
'The dog saw there was a beehive (there).' (Chenghua Long, in *Frog, Where Are You?*)

Example (6.21) shows two noun phrases that each contain a numeral-classifier phrase and a relative clause, but no other material.

(6.21) *Beul heit reinb.weif nins* [***aod-ngonl*** *manx rel.xins*
3 still believe COP [**one-CLF:animate** REL kind
naond], [***aod-ngonl*** *manx raons deul*].
ASSOC] [**one-CLF:animate** REL cut.firewood firewood]
'She still thought (he) was a kind (person), a woodcutter.' (Haili Shi, in *Xaub Honl Mob*)

Finally, examples (6.22–6.24) below show a variety of more complex noun phrases that each consist of a numeral-classifier phrase and multiple other noun-phrase–internal constituents, including possessors, nouns, demonstratives, and relative clauses. For instance, example (6.22) features a noun phrase consisting of an initial numeral-classifier phrase (*aod-meinl* [one-CLF:person] 'one [person]'), with that numeral-classifier phrase first being followed by a noun (*deb-ghot* [DIM-old] 'old person'), then a relative clause (*manx fuk jeud* [REL drink alcohol] ' ... who's drinking alcohol'), and then finally a demonstrative (*dox* 'that').

(6.22) [***Aod-meinl*** *deb-ghot manx fuk jeud dox*]
[**one-CLF:person** DIM-old REL drink alcohol that]
nins boub ceit.
COP 1PL paternal.uncle
'That old man drinking alcohol (over there) is my uncle.' (Shixiang Wu, fieldnotes)[111]

Example (6.23) shows a noun phrase whose first constituent is a single lengthy relative clause (*nieux-hnef nhaons wel chauk.geud lot Zhes naond* [yester-CLF:day with 1SG together descend Fenghuang ASSOC] ' ... who went to Fenghuang with me yesterday'), with that initial relative clause being followed by a numeral-classifier phrase (*oub-ngonl* [two-CLF:animate] 'two [animate entities]') and then a noun (*zhaol* 'non-Miao').

(6.23) [*Nieux-hnef nhaons wel chauk.geud lot Zhes*
[yester-CLF:day with 1SG together descend Fenghuang
naond ***oub-ngonl*** *zhaol*] *liot guaot.*
ASSOC **two-CLF:animate** non.Miao] wealthy pass
'Those two (non-Miao) people who went to Fenghuang with me yesterday are very wealthy.' (Haili Shi, fieldnotes)

111 The translation of *boub* '1PL' as 'my' rather than 'our' is correct here; see Section 8.2.1 for details.

Example (6.24) in turn shows a noun phrase consisting of five noun-phrase–internal constituents that occur in the following order: (i) a possessor phrase (*beul naond* [3 ASSOC] 'her, of hers'), (ii) a relative clause (*hauk aub naond* [drink water ASSOC] '... that are drinking water'), (iii) a numeral-classifier phrase (*oub-meinl* [two-CLF:person] 'two [people]'), (iv) a noun (*deb-deb* [child-RED] 'child'), and (v) a demonstrative (*dox* 'that').

(6.24) [*beul naond hauk aub naond* ***oub-meinl***
[3 ASSOC drink water ASSOC **two-CLF:person**
deb-deb dox]
child-RED that]
'those two children of hers that are drinking water' (Chenghua Long, fieldnotes)

6.1.2.2 Numeral-classifier phrases that do not serve as constituents of larger noun phrases

In addition to occurring as constituents of larger noun phrases, it is also quite common for a numeral-classifier phrase to occur as a noun phrase in its own right, with no other material occurring within that same noun phrase. This can be seen in examples (6.25–6.27) below, where each such numeral-classifier phrase functions as an argument of a verb. Note that the relevant numeral-classifier phrases in these examples have been bolded, and the coterminous noun phrases that they constitute have been enclosed within brackets.

(6.25) *Bioud.nhol* [***aod-bioud***] *jix doul, Ndaut.guax*
village.name [**one-CLF:home**] NEG_1 remain village.name
[***aod-bioud***] *jix doul, Bul.ncout* [***aod-bioud***]
[**one-CLF:home**] NEG_1 remain village.name [**one-CLF:home**]
at jix doul.
SAT NEG_1 remain
'There wasn't a single family left in (the village of) Biou Nho, there wasn't a single family left in (the village of) Ndau Gua, and there wasn't a single family left in (the village of) Bu Ncou.' (Qiusheng Long, in *Ngel.kanx*)

(6.26) *Oub-meinl at zeink.jaok ganx.qinf,* [***aod-meinl***]
two-CLF:person SAT increase emotion [**one-CLF:person**]
yeb [***aod-meinl***].
like [**one-CLF:person**]
'The two grew closer, (they grew to) love one another.' (Xingyu Shi, in *Deb Guk Ronf*)

(6.27) *Gaons* *wel* [***bub-leb***].
give 1SG [**three-CLF**]
'Give me three (pieces of candy).' (Haili Shi, fieldnotes)

In addition to serving as arguments of verbs, numeral-classifier phrases that occur as noun phrases in their own right can also serve in more adjunct-like roles. For instance, the numeral-classifier phrase in example (6.28) below serves to indicate the time at which the utterance in question holds, while the numeral-classifier phrases in examples (6.29–6.32) serve to indicate the number of times that an event or action occurs.

(6.28) [***Aod-roul***] *Dol.xid* *jix* *doul* *manx* *nonx* *miex*
[**one-CLF:time$_1$**] La'ershan NEG$_1$ remain REL eat person
naond *daob-jod.*
ASSOC AN-tiger
'Nowadays there aren't any man-eating tigers around La'ershan.' (Haili Shi, fieldnotes)

(6.29) *Wel* *puk* [***bub-dob***] *leh.*
1SG say [**three-CLF:occurrence**] LEH
'I've (already) said (it) three times.' (Xingyu Shi, fieldnotes)

(6.30) *Beul* *monl* [***oub-taonb***] *leh.*
3 go [**two-CLF:trip**] LEH
'They've been (there) twice.' (Haili Shi, fieldnotes)

(6.31) *Mx* *lis* *tiut* [***oub-tiut***].
2SG want press.down [**two-CLF:press.down**]
'You need to press (it) twice.' (Shixiang Wu, fieldnotes)

(6.32) *Beul* *ceut* *beul* [***bub-ndeind***].
3 chop 3 [**three-CLF:knife**]
'He slashed him three times (with a knife).' (Haili Shi, fieldnotes)

There are also at least two constructions in which a numeral-classifier phrase might appear, at first glance, to form a constituent with an adjacent noun in the same way as is described in Section 6.1.2.1 above, though more subtle grammatical evidence shows that this is not in fact the case. The first of these constructions involves dedicated verbal classifiers like *dob* 'CLF:occurrence', *cif* 'CLF:occurrence', and *taonb* 'CLF:trip' (see examples (6.29) and (6.30) above, as well as Section 6.1.4.9 below). These are classifiers which simultaneously belong to the set of dedicated classifiers (see Section 6.1.1) and to the set of verbal classifiers (Section 6.1.4.9), and which also display unique ordering properties with respect to adjacent nouns. Although a numeral-classifier phrase featuring one of these dedicated verbal classifiers will often occur without any adjacent noun whatsoever, it will occasionally occur with a following one, as in examples (6.33) and (6.34) below.

(6.33) *Tat-jut* *wel* *dand* ***oub-dob*** ***Dib-Zhes.***
this-CLF:year 1SG arrive **two-CLF:occurrence** **LOC-Fenghuang**
'I've been to Fenghuang twice this year.' (Xingyu Shi, fieldnotes)

(6.34) *Boub* *lol* ***aod-cif*** ***neind-naub*** *leh.*
1PL come **one-CLF:occurrence** **this-place$_4$** LEH
'We came here once.' (Qiusheng Long, in *Ngel.kanx*)

On the surface, it appears that one could argue that the numeral-classifier phrases in examples like (6.33) and (6.34) above combine with the following nouns to form larger noun phrases, ones that then serve as arguments of the preceding verbs. In other words, one might be tempted to argue that the utterances in (6.35) and (6.36) below have very similar semantic and grammatical structures, with the numeral-classifier phrase and its following noun forming a larger noun phrase in both cases.

(6.35) *Tat-hnef* *wel* *nonx* ***oub-zhet*** ***hlit.***
this-CLF:day 1SG eat **two-CLF:bowl** **uncooked.rice**
'I ate two bowls of rice today.' (Haili Shi, fieldnotes)

(6.36) *Tat-hnef* *wel* *guaot* ***oub-taonb*** ***aub.***
this-CLF:day 1SG pass **two-CLF:trip** **water**
'I crossed the river twice today.' (Haili Shi, fieldnotes)

However, it turns out that when a verb is followed by both (i) a numeral-classifier phrase containing a dedicated verbal classifier (e.g. *oub-taonb* [two-CLF:trip]) and (ii) a noun (e.g. *aub* 'water'), the ordering of these two postverbal constituents is in fact flexible. Thus, while examples (6.33), (6.34), and (6.36) above each feature a numeral-classifier phrase followed by a noun, they can also be rephrased (with no discernible change in meaning or pragmatics) so that the noun precedes the numeral-classifier phrase. This is shown in (6.37–6.39) below.

(6.37) *Tat-jut* *wel* *dand* ***Dib-Zhes*** ***oub-dob.***
this-CLF:year 1SG arrive **LOC-Fenghuang** **two-CLF:occurrence**
'I've been to Fenghuang twice this year.' (Xingyu Shi, fieldnotes) (cf. example (6.33) above)

(6.38) *Boub lol* ***neind-naub aod-cif*** *leh.*
1PL come **this-place$_4$ one-CLF:occurrence** LEH
'We came here once.' (Qiusheng Long, in *Ngel.kanx*) (cf. example (6.34) above)

(6.39) *Tat-hnef wel guaot* ***aub oub-taonb.***
this-CLF:day 1SG pass **water two-CLF:trip**
'I crossed the river twice today.' (Haili Shi, fieldnotes) (cf. example (6.36) above)

This is not true of numeral-classifier phrases containing more canonical, non-verbal classifiers, as examples (6.40) and (6.41) show. Neither is it true of numeral-classifier phrases containing derived (as opposed to dedicated) verbal classifiers (see Section 6.1.4.9), as can be seen from example (6.42).

(6.40) **Tat-hnef wel nonx* ***hlit oub-zhet.***
this-CLF:day 1SG eat **cooked.rice two-CLF:bowl**
(intended: 'I ate two bowls of rice today.') (cf. example (6.35) above)

(6.41) **Wel lis* ***neus-ghab oub-gul-leb.***
1SG want **egg-chicken two-ten-CLF**
(intended: 'I want twenty chicken eggs.') (cf. example (6.19) above)

(6.42) **Beul ceut* ***bub-ndeind beul.***
3 chop **three-CLF:knife 3**
(intended: 'He slashed him three times [with a knife].') (cf. example (6.32) above)

This suggests that when a numeral-classifier phrase containing a dedicated verbal classifier is followed by a noun, the two do not form a constituent. Instead, the numeral-classifier phrase constitutes one noun phrase, and the following noun another. Thus, it appears that the constituent structure shown in example (6.43) below is inaccurate, and it should instead be the one shown in (6.44).[112] The same applies to other, similar examples.

(6.43) **Tat-hnef wel guaot* [***oub-taonb aub***].
this-CLF:day 1SG pass [**two-CLF:trip water**]
'I crossed the river twice today.' (Haili Shi, fieldnotes)

112 The asterisk preceding (6.43) merely indicates that the constituent structure analysis shown in the example is inaccurate. The utterance transcribed in the example is perfectly grammatical, as a comparison with examples (6.36) and (6.44) will readily demonstrate.

(6.44) *Tat-hnef* *wel* *guaot* [***oub-taonb***] [***aub***].
this-CLF:day 1SG pass [**two-CLF:trip**] [**water**]
'I crossed the river twice today.' (Haili Shi, fieldnotes)

The second construction in which a numeral-classifier phrase appears to (but, this author would argue, does not actually) form a constituent with an adjacent noun in the way described in Section 6.1.2.1 involves a particular non-canonical subset of nouns, namely pronouns (see Section 7.1). Pronouns differ from more canonical nouns in that they are never preceded by a numeral-classifier phrase, but are instead often followed by one, as in (6.45) and (6.46) below.

(6.45) ***Manx*** ***oub-leb*** *fanb* *guaot.*
2PL **two-CLF** annoying pass
'You two are really annoying.' (Yan Long, fieldnotes)

(6.46) ***Beul*** ***bub-meinl*** *puk* *raut* *guaot.*
3 **three-CLF:person** say good pass
'Those three speak (Standard Mandarin) very well.' (Yan Long, fieldnotes)

Despite the fact that the numeral-classifier phrases in these examples follow the adjacent pronouns rather than precede them, they seem to serve essentially the same quantifying function that numeral-classifier phrases do when they precede a canonical (i.e. non-pronominal) noun. Thus, one could in theory argue that it is simply an idiosyncrasy of Xong grammar that numeral-classifier phrases precede canonical nouns within the same noun phrase but follow pronouns within the same noun phrase.

It appears, though, that a post-pronominal numeral-classifier phrase like the ones in examples (6.45) and (6.46) above does not form a noun phrase with its preceding pronoun, or at least not in the same way that a numeral-classifier phrase forms a noun phrase with a following (non-pronominal) noun. The most obvious evidence for this is the fact that a semantically appropriate canonical noun can be added after the numeral-classifier phrases in examples (6.45) and (6.46) with no discernible change in meaning (although consultants report that doing so is somewhat redundant), so that each numeral-classifier phrase is preceded by a pronoun and followed by a canonical noun. This is shown in examples (6.47) and (6.48) below.

(6.47) ***Manx*** ***oub-leb*** ***miex*** *fanb* *guaot.*
2PL **two-CLF** **person** annoying pass
'You two are really annoying.' (Yan Long, fieldnotes) (cf. example (6.45) above)

(6.48) ***Beul*** ***bub-meinl*** ***miex*** *puk raut guaot.*
3 **three-CLF:person** **person** say good pass
'Those three speak (Standard Mandarin) very well.' (Yan Long, fieldnotes) (cf. example (6.46) above)

The most parsimonious explanation for this would be that in examples (6.47) and (6.48) (and others like them), each numeral-classifier phrase combines first with the following noun to form a larger noun phrase, which then in turn combines appositively with the preceding pronoun to form an even larger noun phrase. This is shown in examples (6.49) and (6.50) below.

(6.49) [[***Manx***] [***oub-leb*** ***miex***]] *fanb guaot.*
[[**2PL**] [**two-CLF** **person**]] annoying pass
'You two are really annoying.' (Yan Long, fieldnotes)

(6.50) [[***Beul***] [***bub-meinl*** ***miex***]] *puk raut guaot.*
[[**3**] [**three-CLF:person** **person**]] say good pass
'Those three speak (Standard Mandarin) very well.' (Yan Long, fieldnotes)

This suggests that the grammatical structure of examples (6.45) and (6.46) above is *not* the one shown in (6.51) and (6.52) below, in which each pronoun simply combines with the following numeral-classifier phrase to form a larger noun phrase just as a canonical noun would combine with a preceding numeral-classifier phrase to form a larger noun phrase.[113]

(6.51) *[***Manx*** ***oub-leb***] *fanb guaot.*
[**2PL** **two-CLF**] annoying pass
'You two are really annoying.' (Yan Long, fieldnotes)

(6.52) *[***Beul*** ***bub-meinl***] *puk raut guaot.*
[**3** **three-CLF:person**] say good pass
'Those three speak (Standard Mandarin) very well.' (Yan Long, fieldnotes)

Rather, it is the one shown in (6.53) and (6.54) below, in which each initial pronoun constitutes one noun phrase and each following numeral-classifier phrase constitutes another, with the two then combining appositively to form a larger noun phrase. This differs from the way in which a canonical noun forms a more

113 Just as was the case with example (6.43) above, the asterisks in examples (6.51) and (6.52) each indicate an inaccurate constituent structure analysis rather than an ungrammatical utterance.

immediate constituent with a preceding numeral-classifier phrase, with no "intermediate" steps of analysis needed.[114]

(6.53) [[***Manx***] [***oub-leb***]] *fanb* *guaot.*
[[**2PL**] [**two-CLF**]] annoying pass
'You two are really annoying.' (Yan Long, fieldnotes) (cf. example (6.51) above)

(6.54) [[***Beul***] [***bub-meinl***]] *puk* *raut* *guaot.*
[[**3**] [**three-CLF:person**]] say good pass
'Those three speak (Standard Mandarin) very well.' (Yan Long, fieldnotes) (cf. example (6.52) above)

Finally, there is at least one (fairly low-frequency) construction in Xong in which a numeral-classifier phrase appears to form a constituent with a following verb.[115] In this construction, a numeral-classifier phrase immediately precedes a property-denoting verb (e.g. *shanb* 'tall', *liox* 'big', *heind* 'heavy'), with the numeral-classifier phrase serving to express the quantity, degree, or extent of the property referred to by the subsequent verb. Examples of this construction are given bolded and within brackets in (6.55–6.58) below.

(6.55) *Beul* *mex* [***oub-mix*** ***shanb***].
3 exist [**two-CLF:meter** **tall**]
'He's two meters tall.' (Haili Shi, fieldnotes)

(6.56) *Aod-meinl* *neind* *mex* [***bub-xeub*** ***shanb***].
one-CLF:person this exist [**three-CLF:body** **tall**]
'The (giant) was as tall as three men.' (Haili Shi, fieldnotes)

(6.57) *Mex* [***bub-ceinf*** ***doud***].
exist [**three-CLF:cun** **long**]
'(The stick) was three *cun* long.' (Chenghua Long, fieldnotes)

---

114 Note, though, that while a canonical noun does indeed form a "more immediate" constituent with a preceding numeral-classifier phrase than a pronoun does with a following numeral-classifier phrase (in the sense that it appears that a numeral-classifier phrase serves as the head of a following noun, while it is in apposition to a preceding pronoun), the resulting [NUMERAL-CLASSIFIER NOUN] construction is still rather "loose" in grammatical terms, since other constituents (like relative clauses) can occur between the numeral-classifier phrase and the following noun. See Section 6.1.2.1 for details.

115 The existence of this construction, in which a numeral-classifier phrase forms a constituent with a following verb rather than (as is typical) with a following noun, again raises some interesting questions about the nature of lexical categories in Xong. See Section 1.2.2 for discussion.

(6.58) *Wel lis aod-njaod manx* [***oub-gaonb heind***] *naond.*
1SG want one-CLF:piece REL [**two-CLF:catty heavy**] ASSOC
'I want a piece (of meat) that weighs two catties.' (Shixiang Wu, fieldnotes)

It appears that any semantically appropriate classifier can occur in this construction, although the fact that the final verb in the construction must be a property-denoting one means that classifiers with mensural semantics (see Section 6.1.4.8) tend to do so much more frequently than other classifiers.

6.1.3 Other constructions involving classifiers

In addition to the numeral-classifier phrases discussed in Section 6.1.2 above, Xong classifiers also participate in a variety of other, less frequent constructions as well. Each of the five subsections below is devoted to one such construction.

6.1.3.1 Bare classifiers

When a numeral-classifier phrase consists of the numeral *aod* 'one' and a following classifier, the initial numeral can be dropped so that the classifier occurs "bare". However, the reverse is not true: no numeral, including *aod* 'one', can occur without a following classifier (this applies also to numeral phrases; see Section 6.2.1). This is demonstrated by examples (6.59–6.64) below. These two triplets of examples show that a noun phrase consisting of a numeral-classifier phrase and some additional material is acceptable (see examples (6.59) and (6.62)), as is a noun phrase consisting of a bare classifier (i.e. one without a preceding numeral) and some additional material (see examples (6.60) and (6.63)). However, a noun phrase containing a numeral without a following classifier will be uniformly rejected by consultants (see examples (6.61) and (6.64)). Note that the relevant noun phrases in each of these examples have been enclosed within brackets.

(6.59) [*Aod-leb/ngonl/hnanf/zhet/donb neind*] *nins*
[one-CLF/CLF:animate/CLF:clothing/CLF:bowl/CLF:building this] COP
naonb?
what
'What is this (thing/animal/article of clothing/bowl/building)?' (Haili Shi, fieldnotes)

(6.60) [*Leb/ngonl/hnanf/zhet/donb neind*] *nins naonb?*
[CLF/CLF:animate/CLF:clothing/CLF:bowl/CLF:building this] COP what
'What is this (thing/animal/article of clothing/bowl/building)?' (Haili Shi, fieldnotes)

(6.61) *[*Aod neind*] *nins naonb?*
[one this] COP what
(intended: 'What is this?')

(6.62) *Wel jix ndiot* [*aod-leb/meinl/ngonl mianx dox*].
1SG NEG_1 recognize [one-CLF/CLF:person/CLF:animate person that]
'I don't know that person.' (Shixiang Wu, fieldnotes)

(6.63) *Wel jix ndiot* [*leb/meinl/ngonl mianx dox*].
1SG NEG_1 recognize [CLF/CLF:person/CLF:animate person that]
'I don't know that person.' (Shixiang Wu, fieldnotes)

(6.64) **Wel jix ndiot* [*aod mianx dox*].
1SG NEG_1 recognize [one person that]
(intended: 'I don't know that person.')

The fact that classifiers regularly occur as components of larger noun phrases without a preceding numeral, while numerals never occur as components of larger noun phrases without a following classifier, strongly suggests that the syntactic head of a numeral-classifier phrase is best analyzed as being the classifier, rather than the numeral.[116]

Unlike full numeral-classifier phrases, bare classifiers do not occur as independent noun phrases, though noun phrases containing bare classifiers (like those seen in examples (6.60) and (6.63) above) can still have any degree of structural complexity and occur in any syntactic position. However, bare classifiers are particularly common in two syntactic environments: (i) as the first element of a noun phrase that occurs in immediate postverbal position (see examples (6.65) and (6.66) below), and (ii) in noun-phrase–internal position between a preceding possessor phrase or relative clause and a following noun (see examples (6.67) and (6.68) below, as well as Sections 8.1.3 and 8.2.2). Note that in the examples below each bare classifier has been bolded and each noun phrase containing a bare classifier has been enclosed within brackets.

(6.65) *Manx.eib.manx.ab mex* [***ngonl*** *deb-ghot*] *jix mex*
a.long.time.ago exist [**CLF:animate** DIM-old] NEG_1 exist
deb mex giad.
child exist grandchild
'A long time ago, there was an old person who had no children or grandchildren.' (Xingyu Shi, in *Deb Guk Ronf*)

116 As was mentioned earlier in Section 6.1.1, there is also some evidence that the head of a larger noun phrase that contains both a classifier (either bare or within a numeral-classifier phrase) and some additional material (e.g. a noun, a relative clause, a demonstrative, etc.) is best analyzed as being the classifier rather than any of the noun phrase's other constituents. See Section 7.2 for details.

(6.66) *Beul bod deb-ghot, beul niab: "Minl aoh, heut*
3 tell DIM-old 3 say mother PART help
wel nes [***leb*** *npaok*]."
1SG find.a.wife [**CLF** woman]
'He told the old woman, he said: "Mother, help me find a wife."' (Xingyu Shi, in *Deb Guk Ronf*)

(6.67) *Naont beul jeub chaot dut* [*beul* ***ngonl*** *daob-guk*].
thus 3 then$_3$ look.for obtain [3 **CLF:animate** AN-frog]
'Then he found his frog.' (Chenghua Long, in *Frog, Where Are You?*)

(6.68) [*Zhanx* ***hant*** *ghaob-hlat neind*] *jaod nkhed daos.*
[tie **CLF:PL** NOM-rope this] bad look die
'These ropes that (you've) tied are really ugly.' (Haili Shi, fieldnotes)

In all relevant cases attested so far, consultants report that there is no semantic difference between a noun phrase containing a bare classifier and one containing a numeral-classifier phrase in which the numeral is *aod* 'one'. In other words, whenever a bare classifier has been encountered, consultants report that *aod* 'one' can be inserted before that classifier with no change in meaning, although they often say that doing so would be redundant or unnecessarily long-winded. The specific factors determining when a Xong speaker uses a numeral-classifier phrase in which the numeral is *aod* 'one' and when he or she uses a bare classifier instead have yet to be identified.

6.1.3.2 Reduplicated classifiers

Every canonical Xong classifier, regardless of its semantics and regardless of its status as dedicated or derived (see Section 6.1.1 above), can occur reduplicated to mean 'every, each'. This is true definitionally, since one of the defining characteristics of the set of classifiers in Xong is the ability to occur in this reduplicated construction. Some examples of this construction are given in (6.69–6.72) below. Note that reduplicated classifiers are often, though not obligatorily, followed by *(s)at* 'SAT' (see Section 9.2.3.1), but they are never preceded by any numeral or numeral phrase.

(6.69) *Aod-gheul dox* ***bioud-bioud*** *at liot.*
one-CLF:village that **CLF:home-CLF:home** SAT wealthy
'In that village, every family is wealthy.' (Haili Shi, fieldnotes)

(6.70) *Beul* ***roul-roul*** *at xib hlit.*
3 **CLF:time$_1$-CLF:time$_1$** SAT hungry cooked.rice
'He's always hungry.' (Shixiang Wu, fieldnotes)

(6.71) ***Leb-leb*** *at* *nes,* ***leb-leb*** *at* *niab* *jix* *ghans.*
CLF-CLF SAT ask **CLF-CLF** SAT say NEG_1 see
'(She) asked everyone (if they'd seen her shoe), but everyone said they hadn't seen (it).' (Xingyu Shi, in *Oub Meinl Yaos Geud*)

(6.72) *Aod-ngonl* *deb-guk* ***hnef-hnef*** *deit* *cot,*
one-CLF:animate DIM-frog **CLF:day-CLF:day** still argue
hnef-hnef *deit* *hnant.*
CLF:day-CLF:day still call
'Every day the frog continued to argue (with the old woman), every day (he) continued to ask (her to find him a wife).' (Xingyu Shi, in *Deb Guk Ronf*)

There appears to be a very strong preference for a reduplicated classifier phrase to occur independently rather than as a component of a larger noun phrase. The author's primary consultants only grudgingly accept constructions like the ones in examples (6.73) and (6.74) below, in which reduplicated classifier phrases appear in prenominal position within a noun phrase (i.e. where a noun-phrase–internal numeral-classifier phrase would typically occur), and they never produce such constructions themselves.

(6.73) ??[***Meinl-meinl*** *miex* *neind*] *at* *shanb.*
[**CLF:person-CLF:person** person this] SAT tall.
(intended: 'Every one of these people is tall.')

(6.74) ??[*Wel* *naond* ***ngonl-ngonl*** *daob-yul*] *at* *zhaons.*
[1SG ASSOC **CLF:animate-CLF:animate** AN-cow] SAT fat
(intended: 'All of my cows are fat.')

Instead, the noun phrase referring to the set of entities that the reduplicated classifier construction quantifies typically either occurs in clause-initial position (see examples (6.75) and (6.76) below, as well as example (6.69) above) or does not occur overtly at all (see example (6.77) below, as well as example (6.71) above). The reduplicated classifier construction itself then occurs in a more immediately preverbal position, though, as mentioned above, often with *(s)at* 'SAT' intervening between it and the following verb.

(6.75) *Aod-ncaod* *miex* *neind,* ***meinl-meinl***
one-CLF:animate.group person this **CLF:person-CLF:person**
at *shanb.*
SAT tall
'Every one of these people is tall.' (Haili Shi, fieldnotes) (cf. example (6.73) above)

(6.76) *Wel naond daob-yul* ***ngonl-ngonl*** *at zhaons.*
1SG ASSOC AN-cow **CLF:animate-CLF:animate** SAT fat
'All of my cows are fat.' (unknown Xong consultant, fieldnotes) (cf. example (6.74) above)

(6.77) *Aod-roul* ***leb-leb*** *at nins naond.*
one-CLF:time$_1$ **CLF-CLF** SAT COP ASSOC
'Nowadays all (the young people) are like that (i.e. they tend to dress foolishly).' (unknown Xong consultant, in *Conversation in Yankan*)

6.1.3.3 Classifiers preceded by *ghaob-/ob-/aob-* 'NOM' and *minl-* 'AUG'

The nominal prefix *ghaob-* 'NOM' (see Section 5.4.2.1) can occur preceding certain classifiers, primarily those that refer in some way to physical size or shape or to groups of referents. An example of this is given in (6.78) below.

(6.78) *Monx geud aod-zhaonk ndeud xit chauk*
2SG hold one-CLF:sheet paper tear do
ghaob-nhaux.
NOM-CLF:broad.length
'Tear that sheet of paper into strips.' (Haili Shi, fieldnotes)

A disyllabic [NOM-CLF:X] constituent (like *ghaob-nhaux* [NOM-CLF:broad.length] in example (6.78) above) may optionally occur reduplicated. Such reduplication generally has no clear semantic or pragmatic effect on the utterance as a whole (though see further below in this section for one possible exception), as can be seen by comparing example (6.78) above with example (6.79) below.

(6.79) *Monx geud aod-zhaonk ndeud xit chauk*
2SG hold one-CLF:sheet paper tear do
ghaob-nhaux ghaob-nhaux.
NOM-CLF:broad.length NOM-CLF:broad.length
'Tear that sheet of paper into strips.' (Haili Shi, fieldnotes) (same as (6.78) above)

A [NOM-CLF:X (NOM-CLF:X)] constituent like the ones in examples (6.78) and (6.79) will typically be preceded by the verb *chauk* 'to do, to make', and that verb *chauk* will itself typically be preceded by another verb. The entire [VERB do NOM-CLF:X (NOM-CLF:X)] construction – that is, the whole sequence from the verb preceding *chauk* 'to do, to make' up to the final (optionally reduplicated) [NOM-CLF:X] constituent – then means 'to make *X* into *Y* by means of *Z*', where *X* is some referent (either understood from context or overtly expressed via a noun phrase), *Y* is the shape (or dimensions, or type of group, etc.) referred to by the classifier in question, and *Z* is the action indicated by the verb preceding *chauk* 'to do, to make'. For instance, in examples (6.78) and (6.79) above, the construction as a whole could be literally translated as 'make that sheet of paper into broad lengths by means of tearing', or, more colloquially, as 'tear that sheet of paper into strips'.

Examples (6.80–6.82) below each show a further instance of this construction. In each example, the entire [VERB do NOM-CLF:X (NOM-CLF:X)] construction has been bolded.

(6.80) *Wel* ***hlaok chauk ghaob-ghoub***
1SG **cut do NOM-CLF:flexible.length**
(ghaob-ghoub).
(NOM-CLF:flexible.length)
'I cut (the potato) into strips.' (Haili Shi, fieldnotes)

(6.81) *Mx lis nieus hant manx* ***hlaok chauk***
2SG want buy CLF:PL REL **cut do**
ghaob-njaod (ghaob-njaod) *naond niax.*
NOM-CLF:piece (NOM-CLF:piece) ASSOC meat
'Buy meat that's been cut into pieces.' (Shixiang Wu, fieldnotes)

(6.82) *Aod-leb deb-npaok dox geud beinx* ***zhanx chauk***
one-CLF DIM-woman that hold flower **tie do**
ghaob-doul (ghaob-doul).
NOM-CLF:hand (NOM-CLF:hand)
'The girl tied the flowers into bunches.' (Chenghua Long, fieldnotes)

There are still two aspects of this construction that remain somewhat unclear. First, consultants usually report that reduplicating a disyllabic [NOM-CLF:X] constituent has no effect on the meaning or pragmatic import of the utterance in which it occurs. However, a single pair of examples (given in (6.83) and (6.84) below) has been found in which the reduplication vs. non-reduplication of the constituent in question does in fact appear to have some semantic effect. Note that these two examples also show rare instances of the verb *chauk* 'to do, to make' occurring in this construction without another preceding verb.

(6.83) *Boub chauk* ***aob-ncaod*** *lot giak yaox?*
1PL do **NOM-CLF:animate.group** descend avenue right?
'Let's go for a walk as a (single) group, okay?' (Chenghua Long, fieldnotes)

(6.84) *Boub* *chauk* ***aob-ncaod*** ***aob-ncaod***
1PL do **NOM-CLF:animate.group** **NOM-CLF:animate.group**
lot *giak* *yaox?*
descend avenue right?
'Let's go for a walk in (multiple) groups, okay?' (Chenghua Long, fieldnotes)

This pair of examples seems to suggest that when a classifier referring to a type of group (see Section 6.1.4.4) occurs in this construction, the reduplication of the [NOM-CLF:X] constituent implies (or perhaps even entails) the existence of multiple such groups, rather than just a single one. However, the reader should keep in mind that at this point this is merely a tentative hypothesis based on a very small amount of data.

Second, in some cases even the prefix *ghaob-* 'NOM' appears to be optional in this construction. Compare examples (6.85) and (6.86) below, which the speaker insisted were completely synonymous.

(6.85) *Dions* *ndaut* *lis* *dions* *chauk* ***nbax.***
plant tree want plant do **CLF:row**
'When (you) plant the trees, plant them in rows.' (Chenghua Long, fieldnotes)

(6.86) *Dions* *ndaut* *lis* *dions* *chauk* ***ghaob-nbax.***
plant tree want plant do **NOM-CLF:row**
'When (you) plant the trees, plant them in rows.' (Chenghua Long, fieldnotes) (same as (6.85) above)

The same speaker also reported that the constituent *ghaob-nbax* [NOM-CLF:row] in this example could be reduplicated without any change in meaning.

(6.87) *Dions* *ndaut* *lis* *dions* *chauk* ***ghaob-nbax*** ***ghaob-nbax.***
plant tree want plant do **NOM-CLF:row** **NOM-CLF:row**
'When (you) plant the trees, plant them in rows.' (Chenghua Long, fieldnotes) (same as (6.85) and (6.86) above)

Further research is needed to determine whether the presence of the prefix *ghaob-* 'NOM' and the reduplication of the [NOM-CLF:X] constituent in such examples are truly optional, or whether they have some subtle semantic or pragmatic effects that have simply escaped notice so far.

Many classifiers that refer to physical size or shape or to groups of entities can also occur in a particular tetrasyllabic construction involving the prefix *minl-* 'AUG' (see Section 5.4.2.4). In this construction, the second and fourth syllables are each the classifier itself, while the first and third syllables are each *minl-* 'AUG'. This construction typically serves a predicative function (rather than, e.g., a referential or adverbial one), and it typically takes a noun phrase as its sole argument. More specifically, the construction serves to indicate that the referent of the noun phrase in question exists in the form of 'many large *X*' or 'all large *X*', where *X* is the size, shape, and/or type of group referred to by the classifier appearing in the construction. For instance, *minl-zhaus-minl-zhaus* [AUG-CLF:vertical.plant-AUG-CLF:vertical.plant] means 'taking the form of many tall plants, all existing in the form of tall plants', as in example (6.88).

(6.88) *Miant bioud naond hant ghaob-ndaut*
3PL home ASSOC CLF:PL NOM-tree
minl-zhaus-minl-zhaus.
AUG-CLF:vertical.plant-AUG-CLF:vertical.plant
'Their family's trees are all really big.' (Shixiang Wu, fieldnotes)

Further examples are given in (6.89–6.92). Note that example (6.89) begins with an unflagged prenominal relative clause (see Section 8.1.3) *aod-zhaus ndaut dianx* [one-CLF:vertical.plant tree finish], meaning ' ... that are growing on the tree'. This relative clause combines with the following classifiers and noun *hant leb bid-guax* [CLF:PL CLF FRT-peach], meaning 'the peaches', to form a larger noun phrase that then means 'the peaches growing on the tree'. Finally, that larger noun phrase serves as the sole argument of *minl-leb-minl-leb* [AUG-CLF-AUG-CLF].

(6.89) *Aod-zhaus ndaut dianx hant leb bid-guax*
one-CLF:vertical.plant tree finish CLF:PL CLF FRT-peach
minl-leb-minl-leb.
AUG-CLF-AUG-CLF
'The peaches growing on the tree are all huge.' (Shixiang Wu, fieldnotes)

(6.90) *Aod-bons hlat neind*
one-CLF:pile rope this
minl-nhaux-minl-nhaux.
AUG-CLF:broad.length-AUG-CLF:broad.length
'The ropes in this pile are all very thick.' (Chenghua Long, fieldnotes)

(6.91) *Chauk hant ob-heik* ***minl-zheinb-minl-zheinb,*** *jont*
do CLF:PL NOM-chair **AUG-CLF:tool-AUG-CLF:tool** sit
sat jix raut jont.
SAT NEG_1 good sit
'The chairs (in this mahjong parlor) are all so huge, they're not even comfortable to sit on.' (Haili Shi, fieldnotes)

In example (6.92), the tetrasyllabic construction in question occurs noun-phrase–internally within a *naond* relative clause (see Section 8.1.2).

(6.92) *Aod-hant* ***minl-bons-minl-bons*** *naond leb.beul*
one-CLF:PL **AUG-CLF:pile-AUG-CLF:pile** ASSOC unshelled.rice
bat ninb boub bioud naond.
put at 1PL home ASSOC
'There are great big piles of rice (drying) at our home.' (Haili Shi, fieldnotes)

This construction is obligatorily tetrasyllabic; disyllabic versions like **minl-bons* [AUG-CLF:pile] or **minl-nhaux* [AUG-CLF:broad.length] are uniformly rejected by consultants. Because of this, and because this construction always has the same [AUG-CLF:X-AUG-CLF:X] structure without the possibility of any intervening linguistic material, the four syllables of the construction are connected with hyphens in this grammar.

6.1.3.4 Classifiers followed by *-deb* 'DIM'

Any classifier can be followed by a diminutive suffix *-deb* 'DIM'. This is true of both dedicated classifiers (see examples (6.93) and (6.94) below) and derived classifiers (examples (6.95) and (6.96)), and it is true of bare classifiers as well as classifiers that occur as part of a numeral-classifier phrase (compare example (6.94) with others in this section). The semantics of *-deb* 'DIM' are essentially what one would expect from its gloss, as the form serves primarily to highlight the unusually small size or paucity of the referent of the noun phrase in which it occurs.

(6.93) *Mx ml xot aod-roul-**deb**.*
2SG go rest one-CLF:time$_{1}$-**DIM**
'Go rest for a little bit.' (Lijun Wu, fieldnotes)

(6.94) *Leb-**deb** neind nins naonb?*
CLF-**DIM** this COP what
'What is this (small object)?' (Haili Shi, fieldnotes)

(6.95) *Wel nonx oub-zhet-**deb** hlit.*
1SG eat two-CLF:bowl-**DIM** cooked.rice
'I (only) had two small bowls of rice.' (Lijun Wu, fieldnotes)

(6.96) *Wel nanx ceut oub-ndeind-**deb**.*
1SG only chop two-CLF:knife-**DIM**
'I only gave it two little chops.' (Shixiang Wu, fieldnotes)

This suffix has not yet been observed signaling intimacy or endearment, as diminutives in many other languages do, but it does sometimes convey a slightly pejorative meaning (so that sometimes a [CLF:X-DIM] construction is better translated as 'a measly *X*' than as 'a small *X*'). This can be seen by examining the context in which examples (6.97) and (6.98) below were uttered.

(6.97) *Beul-god chad jef.feink aod-jut-***deb***!*
3-PL not.until marry one-CLF:year-**DIM**
'They've only been married for one measly year, (and the husband's already having an affair!)' (unknown Xong consultant, fieldnotes)

(6.98) *Wel lis nieus aod-gaonb-***deb** *nzaut!*
1SG want buy one-CLF:catty-**DIM** uncooked.rice
'I just want to buy one measly little catty (unit of mass) of rice, (and you won't even sell that to me?)' (Lijun Wu, fieldnotes)

The diminutive suffix *-deb* 'DIM' never attaches to nouns, although Fenghuang Xong does feature a homophonous (and probably etymologically related) diminutive nominal prefix that shows some degree of functional overlap with the suffix under discussion here; see Section 5.4.2.3 for details.

6.1.3.5 Classifiers serving as arguments of property-denoting verbs

Certain classifiers can occur independently (i.e. not as a component of a larger numeral-classifier phrase or noun phrase) as an argument of a preceding property-denoting verb that refers to a physical property or dimension, such as *liox* 'big', *xub* 'small', *ndoud* 'long', or *xonx* 'attractive'. Two initial examples of this construction are given in (6.99) and (6.100) below. In these and all similar examples in this section, the relevant property-denoting verbs and their following classifiers have been enclosed within brackets, while the classifiers in question have also been bolded.

(6.99) *Aod-ngonl daob-neinb neind [ndoud/led* ***ngonl***] *guaot.*
one-CLF:animate AN-snake this [long/short **CLF:animate**] pass
'This snake is really long/short.' (Shixiang Wu, fieldnotes)

(6.100) *Aod-zhons ndaut neind [shanb/ngaod/liox/xub*
one-CLF:vertical.plant tree this [tall/short/big/small
zhons] *guaot.*
CLF:vertical.plant] pass
'This tree is really tall/short/big/small.' (Haili Shi, fieldnotes)

The data available to the author is still fairly scant, but it so far appears that classifiers referring to some sort of physical shape (or to a group or part thereof) participate in this construction most readily, with such classifiers including the most semantically general classifier *leb* 'CLF' (see Section 6.1.4.1) as well as most of the classifiers listed in Sections 6.1.4.2 through 6.1.4.5. In contrast, classifiers with relatively abstract meanings cannot (or at the very least tend not to) participate at all. Such abstract classifiers include at least the forms *hant* 'CLF:PL', *gians* 'CLF:kind$_1$', *yaonk* 'CLF:kind$_2$', and *zhonx* 'CLF:kind$_3$' (see Section 6.1.4.1), mensural classifiers in general (Section 6.1.4.8), and verbal classifiers in general (Section 6.1.4.9). However, the author has not had the opportunity to explicitly test every attested classifier to see whether it can occur in this construction or not, and furthermore his consultants' judgments about which classifiers can occur in this construction occasionally differ across consultants and across elicitation sessions.

The precise meaning of this construction is difficult to pin down. In most cases, removing the classifier from the construction does not result in any obvious semantic or pragmatic changes. For instance, example (6.101) shows an utterance containing one instance of this construction (with the classifier *leb* 'CLF' preceded by the property-denoting verb *xub* 'small'), while example (6.102) shows the same utterance with the classifier *leb* 'CLF' removed. Consultants report that the members of this pair of examples (and of other similar pairs) are synonymous.

(6.101) *Aod-hant ghaob-roub dox yaod.yaod* [*xub* ***leb***] *guaot.*
one-CLF:PL NOM-stone that all [small **CLF**] pass
'Those stones are all really small.' (Chenghua Long, fieldnotes)

(6.102) *Aod-hant ghaob-roub dox yaod.yaod xub guaot.*
one-CLF:PL NOM-stone that all small pass
'Those stones are all really small.' (Chenghua Long, fieldnotes) (same as (6.101) above)

However, it appears to the author that the addition of a classifier after a property-denoting verb (as in examples (6.99–6.101) above) may place a slight emphasis on the particular physical shape (or group or part thereof) referred to by the classifier. Some possible evidence for this is provided by examples (6.103) and (6.104) below, but more data will be needed before this hypothesis can be confirmed.

(6.103) *Aod-hant beinx dox* [*liox* ***zhoud***] *guaot.*
one-CLF:PL flower that [big **CLF:bloom**] pass
'Those flowers (i.e. the blooms themselves) are really big.' (Chenghua Long, fieldnotes)

(6.104) *Aod-hant beinx dox* [*liox* ***zhaus***] *guaot.*
one-CLF:PL flower that [big **CLF:vertical.plant**] pass
'Those flowers (i.e. the entire plants, from the roots to the blooms) are really big.' (Chenghua Long, fieldnotes)

6.1.4 Classifier semantics

It is difficult to provide any sort of concise, useful summary of the semantic characteristics of Xong classifiers. To give just a few examples, some classifiers refer primarily to the physical shape of the referent of the noun phrase in which they appear (e.g. *nzhoud/zhoud* 'CLF:bloom' or *zhaonk* 'CLF:sheet'; see Section 6.1.4.2 below), others refer to temporal or locative concepts (e.g. *jut* 'CLF:year' or *bix* 'CLF:place$_{1'}$'; see Sections 6.1.4.6 and 6.1.4.7), and still others refer to groups of multiple referents (e.g. *ncaod* 'CLF:animate.group' or *bub* 'CLF:inanimate.group'; see Section 6.1.4.4) or to portions of some larger referent (e.g. *njaod* 'CLF:piece' or *gut* 'CLF:portion'; see Section 6.1.4.5). A variety of other semantic categories of classifiers are laid out in Sections 6.1.4.1 through 6.1.4.9 below, but a survey of these sections will show that some classifiers do not easily fit into any category, while it could be argued that many others fit into two or more categories equally well.

The selectional restrictions of classifiers (that is, the semantic restrictions on which classifiers can co-occur with which nouns within a single noun phrase) are similarly varied. Some classifiers, like *hant* 'CLF:PL' or *yaonk* 'CLF:kind$_{2'}$', can co-occur with almost any noun, while others, like *dib* 'CLF:fire' or *baonx* 'CLF:honeybee.hive', only co-occur with a handful of nouns that satisfy very particular semantic requirements. Some classifiers, especially verbal classifiers (see Section 6.1.4.9) and classifiers referring to temporal concepts (Section 6.1.4.6), rarely if ever co-occur with any noun within a single noun phrase.[117] There is also a fair amount of intervarietal and even interspeaker variation regarding which classifiers can co-occur with which nouns, though impressionistically this variation is still rather less than what is found with Xong's nominal prefixes (cf. Section 5.4.1).

The fact that classifiers encompass such a broad and varied semantic territory is not surprising, since these forms constitute an open lexical category in Xong just as nouns and verbs do. Several dozen dedicated classifiers have so far been attested, and the author strongly suspects that additional work on Xong would eventually reveal many more. Furthermore, the existence of derived classifiers (see Section 6.1.1), or forms that can function as both a classifier and a noun or as both a classifier and a verb, means that it is impossible to provide an exhaustive list of Xong classifiers. In

---

117 Conversely, some nouns tend to only co-occur with one particular classifier within a single noun phrase, while others can co-occur with any one of several classifiers, each of which highlights a different aspect of the noun's referent. Nouns with human referents, for example, can co-occur with *ngonl* 'CLF:animate', *leb* 'CLF', or *meinl* 'CLF:person', in ascending order of formality, or they can co-occur with a classifier that refers to a group (e.g. *deib* 'CLF:pair$_{2}$') if more than one referent is involved. Similarly, nouns with flower referents can co-occur with the classifier *nzhoud/zhoud* 'CLF:bloom', which highlights the flower itself (i.e. the reproductive organs) of the plant in question, with *zhons/zhaus* 'CLF:vertical.plant', which highlights the plant as a whole, or with *god* 'CLF:bunched.plant', which would indicate a small cluster of flowers growing closely together.

fact, some forms (like *bioud* 'home; CLF:home', *gheul* 'village; CLF:village', or *biank* 'side; CLF:side') occur both very frequently as nouns and very frequently as classifiers, to the point that it is unclear whether they should be considered nouns that can also function as classifiers or classifiers that can also function as nouns.[118]

In any case, Sections 6.1.4.1 through 6.1.4.9 below each discuss and (non-exhaustively) exemplify one rough semantic category of classifiers (e.g. "classifiers referring to physical shape", "classifiers referring to groups", etc.). At the beginning of each section, the classifiers discussed in the section are listed; classifiers discussed in multiple sections appear in multiple lists. The author here wishes to stress that the semantic categories on which these sections are based have been delineated solely for ease of discussion, and it would be difficult, if not impossible, to justify many of them on language-internal grounds. Furthermore, as mentioned above, the borders between these categories overlap significantly, and many classifiers arguably belong to several categories at the same time. Of course, any attempt to divide the members of another open lexical category (like nouns or verbs) into rough semantic categories would face similar difficulties. (It is perhaps worth mentioning here that no attempt is made to categorize Xong nouns or verbs on a semantic basis in this grammar simply because those two lexical categories are much more common crosslinguistically, and so most readers will already have some reasonable intuitions about the sorts of meanings that Xong nouns and verbs possess. The same is not necessarily true of classifiers.)

6.1.4.1 Classifiers with very few selectional restrictions

leb 'CLF'
hant 'CLF:PL'
gians 'CLF:kind$_1$'
yaonk 'CLF:kind$_2$'
zhonx 'CLF:kind$_3$'

There are five classifiers in Fenghuang Xong that can each be used to refer to a very wide variety of referents and can thus co-occur with a similarly wide variety of nouns. The first of these is *leb*, which is simply glossed as 'CLF'. This is the most semantically general classifier in Xong, and it is roughly equivalent in terms of function and meaning to (e.g.) *gè* (个), the most semantically general classifier in Standard Mandarin. The classifier *leb* 'CLF' is homophonous with (and probably etymologically related to) the dual pronominal suffix *-leb* 'DU' (see Section 7.1.2.1), the ignorative pronoun *leb* 'who, someone' (Section 7.3.2.1), and certain syllables occurring within reflexive pronouns (Section 7.1.3).

118 In reality, the author suspects that this may not even be a meaningful question to ask. See Section 1.2.2 for discussion of some of the issues involved.

This classifier can co-occur with (i) nouns with human referents, like *miex/mianx* 'person' and *lox.sid* 'teacher' (but see also Section 6.1.4.3 below), (ii) nouns with small and/or round referents, including rice grains and corn kernels (e.g. *aod-**leb** bob. mins* [one-**CLF** corn] 'one corn kernel'), pills and tablets (e.g. *aod-**leb** nggaob* [one-**CLF** medicine] 'one pill, one tablet'), drops of liquid (e.g. *aod-**leb** aub* [one-**CLF** water] 'one drop of water'), and fruits and vegetables like *bid-guax* [FRT-peach] 'peach' and *hlat.jub* 'spicy pepper' (note, though, that different classifiers are used to refer to the plants on which such fruits or vegetables are growing; see Section 6.1.4.3 for details), (iii) nouns referring to certain body parts like *ghoud.mx* 'heart' and *baod-mieus* [BUG-nose] 'nose' (though many other body parts take different classifiers; see Section 6.1.4.5), (iv) nouns referring to certain buildings, tools, and other man-made artifacts, including *bioud* 'home, house', *jet* 'traditional rice cooker', and *mok.kud* 'hat', (v) nouns with abstract referents, like *xos.qif* 'semester', *xox.shif/xox.shib* 'hour', and *faonk.faof* 'method', and (vi) various other nouns that do not take any more semantically specific classifier.

Examples of nouns from various semantic categories co-occurring with *leb* 'CLF' are given in (6.105–6.108) below.

(6.105) *Aod-**leb** pinf.gox neind gint-lib-gint-daod, deit nonx*
one-**CLF** apple this rot-LIB-rot-DAOD still eat
ix dut.
NEG_1 obtain
'This apple is (only) a little bit rotten, (but you) still shouldn't eat it.' (Chenghua Long, fieldnotes)

(6.106) *Wel doub nins aod-hnef dox, wel nonx **leb***
1SG $then_1$ COP one-CLF:day that 1SG eat **CLF**
jik.zaox.zaod.
chicken.claw
'That day I just ate a chicken's foot.' (Haili Shi, in *Tooth Conversation*)

(6.107) *Naonb.naont boub-leb nbanx **leb** banb.faox geud beul*
thus 1PL-DU think **CLF** solution hold 3
daot id-daos diex.
kill DID-die finish
'Then let's the two of us think of a way to kill her instead.' (Xingyu Shi, in *Oub Meinl Yaos Geud*)

(6.108) *Aod-**leb** bioud dox raut bioud guaot.*
one-**CLF** home that good home pass
'That house is a good one.' (Shixiang Wu, fieldnotes)

The classifier *hant* 'CLF:PL' can co-occur with virtually any noun. The 'PL' in this form's gloss is derived from 'plural', though (as is further discussed below in this section) this should not be taken to mean that *hant* simply marks plurality. In any case, examples of *hant* 'CLF:PL' functioning as a fairly canonical classifier are given in (6.109) and (6.110).

(6.109) *Naont* ***hant*** *daob-ginb doub zhaok bionl yaox?*
thus **CLF:PL** AN-bug then$_1$ fall exit right?
'So then the bugs just fall out (of your mouth), right?' (Shixiang Wu, in *Tooth Conversation*)

(6.110) *Wel naond eud lous aod-**hant** ghaod.laox neind.*
1SG ASSOC clothing dirty one-**CLF:PL** mud this
'My clothes have gotten dirty from this mud.' (Chenghua Long, fieldnotes)

While this form often serves more or less the same functions that canonical classifiers do, it displays several idiosyncratic grammatical properties. First, *hant* 'CLF:PL' is arguably a "defective" (or at least non-canonical) classifier in that it always occurs either bare or preceded by the numeral *aod* 'one', with its most reasonable English translation in either case being 'some' or 'a few' (or 'these' or 'those' when it also co-occurs with a demonstrative like *neind* 'this' or *dox* 'that'). It never occurs reduplicated, and it never occurs with a preceding numeral or numeral phrase other than *aod* 'one'. Second, it occasionally occurs preceding another bare classifier or numeral-classifier phrase within a single noun phrase, with the presence of *hant* in such cases having no obvious semantic or pragmatic effect. This latter property can be seen in examples (6.111) and (6.112) below, in which both *hant* 'CLF:PL' and the following bare classifier or numeral-classifier phrase have been bolded.

(6.111) *Aod-zhaus ndaut dianx* ***hant leb*** *bid-guax*
one-CLF:vertical.plant tree finish **CLF:PL CLF** FRT-peach
minl-leb-minl-leb.
AUG-CLF-AUG-CLF
'The peaches growing on the tree are all huge.' (Shixiang Wu, fieldnotes) (repeated from (6.89) above)

(6.112) *Aod-zhonx beinx neind naond* ***hant aod-kaok***
one-CLF:kind$_3$ flower this ASSOC **CLF:PL one-CLF:scent**
jeut.mos guaot.
fragrant pass
'The scent from this kind of flower is very nice.' (Haili Shi, fieldnotes)

While the semantics, high frequency, and idiosyncratic grammatical behavior of *hant* 'CLF:PL' might suggest that it is in the process of grammaticalizing as something like a plural marker, it is important to note that the great majority of noun phrases with semantically plural referents do not contain *hant*. Furthermore, consultants usually report that removing *hant* from a noun phrase in which it occurs has little or no effect on the overall meaning of the noun phrase (remember that Xong nouns themselves are unspecified with respect to number; see Section 5.2.2 for discussion). For the time being, it seems more prudent to regard *hant* 'CLF:PL' simply as a rather idiosyncratic member of the classifier class than as an incipient plural marker.

Xong also features three classifiers that refer to "kinds" or "types": *gians* 'CLF:kind$_1$', *yaonk* 'CLF:kind$_2$', and *zhonx* 'CLF:kind$_3$'. The form *gians* 'CLF:kind$_1$' can co-occur with any noun that has an inanimate referent, while *yaonk* 'CLF:kind$_2$' and *zhonx* 'CLF:kind$_3$' can co-occur with any noun regardless of whether the noun's referent is animate, inanimate, or even abstract. Aside from this one restriction on the use of *gians* 'CLF:kind$_1$', all three of these forms appear to be largely interchangeable. The forms *gians* 'CLF:kind$_1$' and *yaonk* 'CLF:kind$_2$' are exemplified in (6.113) and (6.114) below; for an instance of *zhonx* 'CLF:kind$_3$' in use, see example (6.112) above.

(6.113) *Boub* *mex* *bub-***gians** *nzaut.*
1PL exist three-**CLF:kind$_1$** uncooked.rice
'We have three kinds of rice (here in this store).' (unknown Xong consultant, fieldnotes)

(6.114) *Monx* *lis* *aod-***yaonk** *gil* *dib?*
2SG want one-**CLF:kind$_2$** tea which
'Which kind of tea do you want?' (Yan Long, fieldnotes)

6.1.4.2 Classifiers referring to physical shape

ghoub	'CLF:flexible.length'
del	'CLF:rigid.length'
nhaux	'CLF:broad.length'
ndaut	'CLF:river/needle/sentence'
zhaonk	'CLF:sheet'
gaol	'CLF:thick.sheet'
paond	'CLF:flat.tool'
diaond	'CLF:lump'
bud	'CLF:clump'
donx	'CLF:cylinder'
bons	'CLF:pile'

nzhoud/zhoud	'CLF:bloom'
xeub	'CLF:body'
miaux	'CLF:leaf'

A number of classifiers in Fenghuang Xong refer to physical shape, though some of these also refer to secondary characteristics like flexibility, texture, or function. For instance, there are at least four dedicated classifiers that each refer to a particular type of "length" (i.e. an entity that is saliently one-dimensional). The classifier *ghoub* 'CLF:flexible.length' is used with nouns like *(ghaob-)hlat* [(NOM-)rope] 'rope', *(ghaob-)zeif* [(NOM-)thread] 'thread', *(ghaob-)ncoud* [(NOM-)grass] 'grass', *bib* 'hair', and *tanf.huaond* '(coiled metal) spring'. The classifier *del* 'CLF:rigid.length' is used with nouns like *(ghaob-)ndaut* [(NOM-)tree] 'tree', *(ghaob-)xed/xand* [(NOM-)tooth] 'tooth', *bid-ndaod* [FRT-finger] 'finger', *yaok.saob* 'toothbrush', and *bix* 'writing utensil'. With lengths of relatively broad or thick referents, such as those referred to by *(ghaob-)hlat* [(NOM-)rope] 'rope' (at least when the ropes in question are rather thick ones), *nek-geud* [AUG-road] 'road', or *giak* 'avenue', the classifier *nhaux* 'CLF:broad.length' is used.

Compared to the three just discussed, the classifier *ndaut* 'CLF:river/needle/sentence' (homophonous with *ndaut* 'tree') has some rather unusual selectional restrictions: it only co-occurs with nouns referring to three specific types of "lengths", namely rivers, needles, and sentences. Thus 'a river' is expressed as *aod-**ndaut** aub* [one-**CLF:river** water], 'a needle' as *aod-**ndaut** jub* [one-**CLF:needle** needle], and 'a sentence' as *aod-**ndaut** daut* [one-**CLF:sentence** speech] (note that the gloss of *ndaut* varies in this grammar depending on the specific referent in question). It is possible that there is some semantic feature common to rivers, needles, and sentences that motivates the use of *ndaut* with these three types of referents and no others, but so far neither the author nor his consultants have been able to determine what that semantic feature might be.

Some examples of classifiers referring to "lengths" are given in (6.115–6.117) below.

(6.115) *Aod* *ghab* *beul* *doub* *naonb.nex* *zhut*
as.soon.as bite 3 then$_1$ seem reach
*aod-**ghoub*** *sheinf.jind* *dox* *lah.*
one-**CLF:flexible.length** nerve that PRF
'As soon as (I) bit down it was like I'd hit the nerve (in my tooth).' (Haili Shi, in *Tooth Conversation*)

(6.116) *Aod-**del*** *hlod* *liox* *hint* *leh.*
one-**CLF:rigid.length** bamboo big very LEH
'It was quite a large bamboo plant.' (Xingyu Shi, in *Oub Meinl Yaos Geud*)

(6.117) *Jud* *niel* *nhob* ***nhaux*** *dof* *raut,* *jont* *nied.*
NEG$_2$ know walk **CLF:broad.length** which good sit cry
'(She) didn't know which path she should take, (and so she) sat and wept.'
(Xingyu Shi, in *Oub Meinl Yaos Geud*)

Other classifiers refer to objects that are saliently two-dimensional. For example, the classifier *zhaonk* 'CLF:sheet' is used to refer to relatively thin sheets of material. It thus co-occurs with nouns like *ndeud* 'paper' or *jok* 'plastic', as in *aod-**zhaonk** ndeud* [one-**CLF:sheet** paper] 'a sheet of paper' or *bub-**zhaonk** jok* [three-**CLF:sheet** plastic] 'three (thin) sheets of plastic'. As its gloss suggests, the classifier *gaol* 'CLF:thick.sheet' is used to refer to thicker sheets of material. It thus co-occurs with nouns like *niax* 'meat', *cif.zhank* 'ceramic tile', *bok.lid* 'glass', and *hef.banx* 'blackboard', as in *aod-**gaol** hef.banx* [one-**CLF:thick.sheet** blackboard] 'a blackboard' or *oub-**gaol** niax* [two-**CLF:thick.sheet** meat] 'two (thick) sheets of meat, two steaks'. The classifier *paond* 'CLF:flat.tool' (see also Section 6.1.4.3 below) refers to both shape and function, as it co-occurs with nouns referring to tools (or sometimes articles of clothing) that are saliently two-dimensional.

Xong also features several classifiers that refer to saliently three-dimensional objects. The classifier *diaond* 'CLF:lump' is used for uneven, saliently three-dimensional masses of material, including *daob.hot* 'tofu', *nbet* 'snow', *niax* 'meat', and *(ghaob-)roub* [(NOM-)stone] 'stone'. The classifier *bud* 'CLF:clump' is also used for uneven, saliently three-dimensional masses of material, but it tends to be used with referents that have less structural integrity or are made up of relatively distinct component parts, like *doub* 'earth, soil' or *bid-ghand* [FRT-grape] 'grape' (as in *aod-**bud** bid-ghand* [one-**CLF:clump** FRT-grape] 'a bunch of grapes'). Some nouns can co-occur with either of these two classifiers with a corresponding difference in meaning: compare *aod-diaond nbet* [one-CLF:lump snow] 'a firmer, more compact ball of snow' with *aod-bud nbet* [one-CLF:clump snow] 'a larger, looser ball of snow'. Beyond these two, the classifier *donx* 'CLF:cylinder' is used with roughly cylindrical referents, and so it can co-occur with nouns like *bink.baonb* 'popsicle', *gied/giand* 'ice' (in the sense of 'icicle'), *jok* 'plastic' (in the sense of 'plastic cylinder'), or *ndeud* 'paper' (in the sense of 'roll of paper'). Finally, *bons* 'CLF:pile' is used to refer to loose piles of material, including *nbed.sed* 'garbage', *nbet* 'snow', *deul* 'firewood', and *leb.beul* 'unshelled rice'.

There are also at least two classifiers that refer to rather more specific shapes. The first of these is *nzhoud/zhoud* 'CLF:bloom', which is used to refer to "bloom-shaped" objects (i.e. objects that have a saliently one-dimensional "stalk" and a saliently two- or three-dimensional "head" connected to one end of that stalk). It can thus be used with *beinx* 'flower', *nggeub* 'mushroom', *bid-ghand* [FRT-grape] 'grape' (at least when referring to a bunch of grapes connected to a single stalk), *mieut* 'lung', and *shanb* 'liver'. The pronunciation *nzhoud* is used in Yankan Village and the pronunciation *zhoud* in Shanjiang Town, but it is unclear what pronunciation is used by speakers from La'ershan Town and its surrounding villages (other than Yankan, of course).

The second classifier that refers to a relatively specific shape is *xeub* 'CLF:body' (cf. the noun *(ghaob-)dieud* [(NOM-)body] 'body'). This classifier is occasionally used to refer to or quantify actual human bodies or entities that are body-like in shape or dimension, as in examples (6.118) and (6.119) below.

(6.118) *Aod-meinl* *neind* *mex* *bub-**xeub*** *shanb.*
one-CLF:person this exist three-**CLF:body** tall
'The (giant) was as tall as three men.' (Haili Shi, fieldnotes) (repeated from (6.56) above)

(6.119) *Tat-hnef* *monx* ***xeub*** *eud* *neind* *raut* *nkhed* *guaot.*
this-CLF:day 2SG **CLF:body** clothing this good look pass
'Your outfit looks great today.' (unknown Xong consultant, fieldnotes)

More commonly, though, *xeub* 'CLF:body' will occur in the numeral-classifier phrase *aod-xeub* [one-CLF:body], which will then either (i) co-occur with a following noun to mean 'a body completely covered with NOUN' or (ii) co-occur with a following property-denoting verb to mean (sometimes in a rather idiomatic sense) 'a body that's completely VERB' (for more on the latter construction, see also Section 6.1.2.2). An instance of *xeub* 'CLF:body' co-occurring with a following noun can be seen in example (6.120), and an instance of it co-occurring with a following property-denoting verb can be seen in (6.121).

(6.120) *Nkhed* *monx* ***aod-xeub*** ***qub*** *lah!*
look 2SG **one-CLF:body** **water** PRF
'Look at you, your whole body is soaking wet!' (Haili Shi, fieldnotes)

(6.121) *Chauk* *hant* *neind* *aob-naonb* *ix* *dut,* *nanx* *dut*
do CLF:PL this NOM-what NEG_1 obtain only obtain
aod-xeub ***mos.***
one-CLF:body **tired**
'(I) got nothing out of doing all this, all I got was tired.' (Chenghua Long, fieldnotes)

Example (6.122) shows the numeral-classifier phrase *aod-xeub* [one-CLF:body] followed by the form *mb*, which can function as either a verb meaning 'to be sick' or a noun meaning 'illness'. It is unclear (and probably indeterminate – see Section 1.2.2) whether *mb* in this example is functioning as a noun or a verb, and the form in question has been arbitrarily glossed as 'illness' rather than 'sick'.

(6.122) *Beul at raont zad.zat, doub dut*
3 SAT young IDEO:A:young then$_1$ obtain
aod-xeub mb.
one-CLF:body illness
'He's so young, and still (he) got so sick.' (Haili Shi, fieldnotes)

So far the only attested example of a derived classifier that refers primarily to physical shape is *miaux* 'CLF:leaf' (from the noun *miaux* 'leaf'). This classifier can be used to refer either to sheets of paper (so that *aod-**miaux** ndeud* [one-**CLF:leaf** paper] and *aod-zhaonk ndeud* [one-CLF:sheet paper] are synonymous) or to actual plant leaves (as in *aod-**miaux** miaux-ndaut* [one-**CLF:leaf** leaf-tree] 'a tree leaf').

6.1.4.3 Classifiers referring to taxonomic essence

meinl	'CLF:person'
ngonl	'CLF:animate'
leb	'CLF'
zheinb	'CLF:tool'
doul	'CLF:hand'
paond	'CLF:flat.tool'
hnanf	'CLF:clothing'
beint	'CLF:book'
bioud	'CLF:home'
donb	'CLF:building'
gheul	'CLF:village'
zhons/zhaus	'CLF:vertical.plant'
god	'CLF:bunched.plant'
dib	'CLF:fire'
pax	'CLF:text'

Many classifiers in Xong make reference to "taxonomic essence", by which is meant the (language-specific) general semantic category that a referent falls into.[119] Among the most frequent of these are *meinl* 'CLF:person' and *ngonl* 'CLF:animate'. The classifier *meinl* 'CLF:person' solely refers to individual humans. It thus only co-occurs with nouns that have human referents, including *miex/mianx* 'person' as well as more specific nouns like *deb-npaok* [DIM-woman] 'girl', *ghaob-Xonb* [NOM-Miao] 'Miao (person)', or *lox.sid* 'teacher'.

119 The term "taxonomic essence" is borrowed from Enfield (2007:147).

(6.123) *Mex aod-**meinl** deb-deb, sat mex oub-jut.*
exist one-**CLF:person** child-RED SAT exist two-CLF:year
'(They) had a child, (who was) already two years old.' (Xingyu Shi, in *Oub Meinl Yaos Geud*)

In contrast, the classifier *ngonl* 'CLF:animate' can be used with any animate entity, from insects to humans. Note that this form is homophonous with *ngonl* 'CLF:pair$_1$' (see Section 6.1.4.4), although there is no obvious etymological link between the two. Examples (6.124) and (6.125) show *ngonl* 'CLF:animate' being used to refer to a human referent and an animal referent, respectively.

(6.124) *Aod-**ngonl** dox nzeit guaot, piaf aod-kaok*
one-**CLF:animate** that skinny pass blow one-CLF:weather
git leh, beul at lis ghok lol.
wind LEH 3 SAT want fall.over come
'That (person's) so skinny a gust of wind could knock him over.' (Haili Shi, fieldnotes)

(6.125) *Naont beul ah, aod-**ngonl** naus zos ninb*
thus 3 PART one-**CLF:animate** bird land at
*sond-guaod-yul beul jix beinl **ngonl** deb-naus,*
bone-back-cow 3 NEG$_1$ frighten **CLF:animate** DIM-bird
jix eint sheub.
NEG$_1$ fly leave
'And so, when the bird landed on the back of a cow, (the child) didn't frighten it, and (it) didn't fly away.' (Xingyu Shi, in *Oub Meinl Yaos Geud*)

The only other classifier that is regularly used with individual human referents is *leb* 'CLF' (see Section 6.1.4.1).[120] This yields a three-way formality contrast among classifiers used with such referents, with *meinl* 'CLF:person' being the most formal, *ngonl* 'CLF:animate' the least formal, and *leb* 'CLF' somewhere between the other two. Consultants generally reject the use of *ngonl* 'CLF:animate' as impolite when applied to human referents in the author's own constructed sentences, but it is applied to such referents very frequently in these consultants' own naturalistic speech, especially – but not solely – when referring to children. In such cases, consultants insist that no impoliteness or disrespect to the referent is intended; they say that they are merely speaking "casually" or "informally". The difference in formality between *leb* 'CLF' (when used with human referents) and *meinl* 'CLF:person' is less sharp, and in most cases either classifier can be used equally well to refer to any human referent.

120 There are also several classifiers that can be used to refer to groups of humans; see Section 6.1.4.4.

Consultants unanimously agree, though, that with such referents the use of *meinl* 'CLF:person' is a bit more "formal" or "proper" (but certainly no more common) than the use of *leb* 'CLF'.

Xong also features at least five classifiers referring to human artifacts: *zheinb* 'CLF:tool', *doul* 'CLF:hand', *paond* 'CLF:flat.tool', *hnanf* 'CLF:clothing', and *beint* 'CLF:book'. All of these are dedicated classifiers except for *doul* 'CLF:hand' (cf. the noun *(ghaob-)doul* [(NOM-)hand] 'hand').[121] The classifiers *zheinb* 'CLF:tool', *doul* 'CLF:hand', and *paond* 'CLF:flat.tool' all co-occur with nouns referring to human tools (or sometimes items of furniture or articles of clothing), though there is little overlap among the particular nouns that can co-occur with each form. (Some consultants do occasionally report that a particular noun can co-occur with more than one of these three classifiers, but such reports are rarely consistent across consultants.) The classifier *zheinb* 'CLF:tool' can co-occur with nouns like *(ghaob-)mok* [(NOM-)sickle] 'sickle', *(ghaob-)daut* [(NOM-)axe] 'axe', *(ghaob-)heik* [(NOM-)chair] 'chair', and *beub* 'quilt', while *doul* 'CLF:hand' co-occurs with nouns like *(ghaob-)doux* [(NOM-)hammer] 'hammer', *(ghaob-)zhob* [(NOM-)broom] 'broom', *put* 'gun', and *zonf* 'bed'. The classifier *paond* 'CLF:flat.tool' (see also Section 6.1.4.2 above) co-occurs with nouns that refer to saliently two-dimensional tools (or sometimes articles of clothing), like *(ghaob-)sek* [(NOM-)umbrella] 'umbrella', *(ghaob-)miaok* [(NOM-)fan] '(folding) fan', *xaont* 'towel', *guk* 'conical bamboo hat', and *xut.mes* 'turban' (which is saliently two-dimensional when unwrapped). This means that *paond* 'CLF:flat.tool' refers to shape as well as taxonomic essence.

The classifier *hnanf* 'CLF:clothing' could perhaps be more precisely glossed as 'CLF:article.of.clothing', though for the sake of brevity it will continue to be glossed as just 'CLF:clothing' in this grammar. It co-occurs with nouns like *eud* 'clothing', *cheinf.shank* 'shirt', *jeub.nkheud* 'pants', and *qinf* 'dress, skirt', as in *aod-**hnanf** eud* [one-**CLF:clothing** clothing] 'an article of clothing' or *oub-**hnanf** jeub.nkheud* [two-**CLF:clothing** pants] 'two pairs of pants'. Finally, the classifier *beint* 'CLF:book' co-occurs with nouns referring to types of books, like *beinx.ndeud* 'book', *bif.jib.beinx* 'notebook', or *xox.sheb* 'novel'.[122]

There are at least three classifiers that refer to human dwellings or to collections thereof (classifiers referring to animal dwellings are discussed in Section 6.1.4.4). These are *bioud* 'CLF:home', *donb* 'CLF:building', and *gheul* 'CLF:village'. The form *donb* 'CLF:building' is a dedicated classifier, while *bioud* 'CLF:home' and *gheul* 'CLF:village' are arguably derived, as *bioud* often occurs as a noun meaning 'home,

121 The form *doul* 'CLF:hand' can also function as a verbal classifier; see Section 6.1.4.9.

122 For the sake of convenience, the forms *beinx.ndeud* 'book' and *bif.jib.beinx* 'notebook' are here glossed as though they were monomorphemic, but it is clearly no accident that the first syllable of ***beinx**.ndeud* 'book' and the last syllable of *bif.jib.**beinx*** 'notebook' are segmentally homophonous with *beint* 'CLF:book'. Both *beint* and *beinx* are likely borrowings of Standard Mandarin *běn* (本), meaning 'CLF:book', or of a cognate form from another Sinitic variety.

house, family' and *gheul* often occurs as a noun meaning 'village'. The classifier *bioud* 'CLF:home' can co-occur with nouns that have human referents to refer to 'a family, a household' of the referent in question, as in *aod-**bioud** miex* [one-**CLF:home** person] 'a family/household', *oub-**bioud** ghaob-Xonb* [two-**CLF:home** NOM-Miao] 'two Miao families/households', etc. It can also co-occur with nouns referring to inanimate objects or materials to indicate 'a houseful of' (or 'a house full of') the referent of the noun in question, as in example (6.126) below.

(6.126) *Boub at mex aod-**bioud** deul.*
1PL SAT exist one-**CLF:home** firewood
'We have a whole house full of firewood.' (Chenghua Long, fieldnotes)

The classifier *bioud* 'CLF:home' can also be used to refer to or quantify relatively low (i.e. single- or two-story) buildings or homes, in which case it typically occurs without a following noun.

The fairly low-frequency classifier *donb* 'CLF:building' is used to refer to or quantify taller buildings, generally ones at least three stories in height. In such cases it usually only co-occurs with the noun *bioud* 'home, house', so that (for instance) *aod-**donb** bioud* [one-**CLF:building** home] means 'a (tall) building'. The classifier *gheul* 'CLF:village' is used to refer to or quantify villages or their inhabitants, and so it generally co-occurs with nouns that have human referents. Thus, *aod-**gheul** miex* [one-**CLF:village** person] means 'one village (of people)' or 'the people of one village', *oub-**gheul** ghaob-zhaol* [two-**CLF:village** NOM-non.Miao] means 'two non-Miao villages' or 'the non-Miao people of two villages', and *bub-**gheul** deb-ghot* [three-**CLF:village** DIM-old] means 'three villages of elderly people' or 'the elderly people of three villages'.

(6.127) *Beul nins aod-**gheul** dib naond?*
3 COP one-**CLF:village** which ASSOC
'Which village is he from?' (Shixiang Wu, fieldnotes)

Xong also has two classifiers that refer specifically to individual plants, although these both make reference to shape as well as to taxonomic essence (see also Sections 6.1.4.2 and 6.1.4.4 for other classifiers that can be used to refer to plants or to parts or groups thereof). The classifier *zhons/zhaus* 'CLF:vertical.plant' (the former pronunciation is used in Yankan Village, while the latter is used in other parts of Fenghuang County) co-occurs with nouns referring to plants that are saliently vertical, like *(ghaob-) ndaut* [(NOM-)tree] 'tree', *(ghaob-)hlod* [(NOM-)bamboo] 'bamboo', *bob.mins* 'corn', and *yed/yand* 'tobacco'. In constrast, the classifier *god* 'CLF:bunched.plant' is used to refer to less saliently vertical plants, including *reib-beinx* [vegetable-flower] 'cauliflower', *hlat.bous* 'radish', *dob* 'melon', and *yaonb* 'young rice plant'. Note that these two classifiers are generally used only to refer to entire plants, and not to individual fruits, flowers, branches, or other plant parts. Some nouns referring to plants can co-occur with both classifiers, though there is sometimes a change of meaning or emphasis involved. For instance, compare *aod-**zhaus** ncoud* [one-**CLF:vertical.plant** grass] 'a blade of grass' with *aod-**god** ncoud* [one-**CLF:bunched.plant** grass] 'a clump of grass'.

Finally, there are two taxonomic essence classifiers that do not easily fit into any of the categories already discussed in this section. First, the classifier *dib* 'CLF:fire' is used to refer to fires, candles, and oil-lamps. This means that this classifier only co-occurs with two nouns, *deul* 'fire' (also 'firewood') and *xeb/xanb* 'candle, oil-lamp' (also 'oil'). Note that *dib* 'CLF:fire' can co-occur with *xeb/xanb* 'candle, oil-lamp' even when the candle or oil-lamp in question is not lit, as in example (6.129) below.

(6.128)

Lol	*mianx-khat*	*lah,*	*jeud-shaont*	*deid*	*aod-**dib***
come	person-guest	PRF	DID-fast	burn	one-**CLF:fire**

deul	*jeud-raut.*
fire	DID-good

'The guests have arrived, hurry up and start a nice fire (for them).'
(Chenghua Long, fieldnotes)

(6.129)

*Aod-**dib***	*xeb*	*dox*	*jix*	*raut,*	*ntiot*	*hint.*
one-**CLF:fire**	oil.lamp	that	NEG_1	good	smoky	very

'That (currently unlit) oil-lamp is no good, it produces too much smoke.'
(unknown Xong consultant, fieldnotes)

Second, the classifier *pax* 'CLF:text' is used with nouns like *sad* '(traditional) Xong song', *ndeud* 'writing' (also 'paper'), and *daut* 'speech' to refer to individual songs, texts, or lengths of speech. For example, *aod-**pax** sad* [one-**CLF:text** Xong.song] means 'a (traditional) Xong song', *aod-**pax** ndeud* [one-**CLF:text** writing] means 'a (written) text', and *aod-**pax** daut* [one-**CLF:text** speech] means 'a speech, a length of speech'.

6.1.4.4 Classifiers referring to groups

god/gud	'CLF:human.group'
ncaod	'CLF:animate.group'
bub	'CLF:inanimate.group'
ngonl	'CLF:$pair_1$'
deib	'CLF:$pair_2$'
roul	'CLF:nest/brood'
baonx	'CLF:honeybee.hive'
yonx	'CLF:column'
pax/nbax	'CLF:row'

bob	'CLF:forest'
raud	'CLF:forest'
jel	'CLF:agricultural.field'

Xong has a variety of classifiers that refer to groups of entities, among the most common of which are *god/gud* 'CLF:human.group', *ncaod* 'CLF:animate.group', and *bub* 'CLF:inanimate.group'. Each of these forms can be used with a group of entities of any size, ranging from a group with just two members to one with several hundred members. Just as their glosses suggest, *god/gud* 'CLF:human.group' can be used with any group composed solely of humans, *ncaod* 'CLF:animate.group' can be used with any group composed of humans and/or animals, and *bub* 'CLF:inanimate.group' can be used with any group composed solely of inanimate entities. Regarding the form meaning 'CLF:human.group' in particular, note that the pronunciation *gud* is used by speakers from Shanjiang Town while *god* is used by speakers from La'ershan Town and its surrounding villages. Note also that there exists a homophonous (and likely etymologically related) plural suffix *-god/-gud* 'PL' (see Section 7.1.2.1).

Examples of each of these three classifiers are given in (6.130–6.132) below.

(6.130) *Doul* ***god*** *manx shaod xut.npeif naond*
remain **CLF:human.group** REL try shoe ASSOC
yaod.yaod jix nins, yaod.yaod nzhaod diul khad.
all NEG_1 COP all return complete dry
'All of the others who'd tried on the shoe and had it not fit, they all went back too.' (Xingyu Shi, in *Oub Meinl Yaos Geud*)

(6.131) *Aod-**ncaod** daob-guoud dox aod-ngonl ghab*
one-**CLF:animate.group** AN-dog that one-CLF:animate bite
aod-ngonl.
one-CLF:animate
'Those dogs are all biting each other.' (Shixiang Wu, fieldnotes)

(6.132) *Aod-**bub** eud neind lis ncot*
one-**CLF:inanimate.group** clothing this want wash.clothing
yaox?
right?
'These clothes need to be washed, right?' (unknown Xong consultant, fieldnotes)

While the three classifiers discussed above do not entail any notion of permanence or organization in the group in question, Xong also features several other group classifiers that do. Examples of such classifiers include *ngonl* 'CLF:pair$_1$' (homophonous with *ngonl* 'CLF:animate'; see Section 6.1.4.3 above), *deib* 'CLF:pair$_2$', *roul* 'CLF:nest/

brood', *baonx* 'CLF:honeybee.hive', *yonx* 'CLF:column', and *pax/nbax* 'CLF:row'. The meanings of each of these forms are discussed in the following paragraphs.

The classifiers *ngonl* 'CLF:pair$_1$' and *deib* 'CLF:pair$_2$' are each used with a relatively small set of nouns, although there appears to be no overlap between nouns which occur with the former classifier and nouns which occur with the latter. Nouns that can occur with *ngonl* 'CLF:pair$_1$' include *waox.zid* 'sock', *shoux.tof* 'glove', *xut.npeif* 'shoe', and *(ghaob-)zhous* [(NOM-)chopstick] 'chopstick'. An example of this classifier in use is given in (6.133) below.

(6.133) *Oub-nqad* *did-buk* *ghad* *nins* *aod-**ngonl**.*
two-CLF:half.of.pair DID-combine then$_2$ COP one-**CLF:pair$_1$**
'When put together, the two (shoes) were clearly a pair.' (Xingyu Shi, in *Oub Meinl Yaos Geud*)

Nouns that can occur with the classifier *deib* 'CLF:pair$_2$' include *laod.gheb* 'eye', *zhoux.miouf* 'ear', *miex/mianx* 'person', and reciprocal noun compounds (see Section 5.3.2) like *bod-oud* [husband-wife] 'spouses, married couple(s)' and *yaos-geud* [older.sister-younger.sibling] 'older sister(s) and younger sibling(s)'. This classifier appears to be a borrowing of Standard Mandarin *duì* (对) 'CLF:pair' or of a cognate form from another Sinitic variety.

(6.134) *Manx.eib.manx.ab,* *mex* ***deib*** *yaos-geud.*
a.long.time.ago exist **CLF:pair$_2$** older.sister-younger.sibling
'A long time ago, there were two sisters.' (Xingyu Shi, in *Oub Meinl Yaos Geud*)

Neither *ngonl* 'CLF:pair$_1$' nor *deib* 'CLF:pair$_2$' is ever used with the nouns *(ghaob-)doul* [(NOM-)hand] 'hand' or *(ghaob-)bab* [(NOM-)leg] 'leg'. To refer to a pair of hands or legs, speakers simply use the numeral-classifier phrase *oub-nqad* [two-CLF:half.of.pair] instead. See Section 6.1.4.5 below for more on the form *nqad* 'CLF:half.of.pair'.

The classifiers *baonx* 'CLF:honeybee.hive' and *roul* 'CLF:nest/brood' are used to refer to groups of animals and/or to animal dwellings. Unsurprisingly, *baonx* 'CLF:honeybee.hive' can only be used to refer to hives of honeybees (not to hives of ants, termites, wasps, or even other kinds of bees), either in the sense of the physical hive structure itself or in the sense of the sum total of all the individual honeybees living in such a structure. Consultants report that this classifier can only combine with a single noun, namely *maonl-ded* [small.flying.insect-honey] 'honeybee', as in *oub-**baonx** maonl-ded* [two-**CLF:honeybee.hive** small.flying.insect-honey] 'two honeybee hives, two hives of honeybees'.[123]

123 The existence of this classifier *baonx* 'CLF:honeybee.hive' is somewhat surprising given how uncommon and economically insignificant beekeeping and honey-collecting are in modern La'ershan

The classifier *roul* 'CLF:nest/brood' (homophonous with *roul* 'CLF:time$_1$'; see Section 6.1.4.6 below) can co-occur with almost any noun that refers to a (non-human) terrestrial animal, from insects all the way up to large terrestrial vertebrates like horses and bears. It can have either of two meanings. First, it can refer to the natural (not man-made) dwelling place of an animal or group of animals, and second, it can refer to a brood or litter of animals (i.e. to all the animals born to a particular mother at a particular time). This form is glossed as 'CLF:nest' when the former meaning is intended and as 'CLF:brood' when the latter is intended, as can be seen in example (6.135) below.

(6.135) *Aod-**roul*** *neind* *mex* *bieib-leb* *neus-naus.*
one-**CLF:nest** this exist four-CLF egg-bird
'There were four bird eggs in the nest.' (Haili Shi, fieldnotes)

Note that *roul* can also function as a noun meaning 'nest', in which case it is often preceded by the nominal prefix *ghaob-* 'NOM' (see Section 5.4.2.1).

The classifiers *yonx* 'CLF:column' and *pax/nbax* 'CLF:row' (the latter pronunciation is used by speakers from Shanjiang Town, while the former is used by speakers from La'ershan Town and its surrounding villages) can refer to any group of entities whose constituent members are arranged into lines, including everything from people to plants to pencils. The classifier *yonx* 'CLF:column' is used to refer to entities arranged in lines parallel to the speaker's line of sight (i.e. extending from front to back), while *pax/nbax* 'CLF:row' is used to refer to entities arranged in lines perpendicular to the speaker's line of sight (i.e. extending from left to right). An example of each form is given in (6.136) and (6.137) below.

(6.136) *Aod-**yonx*** *deb-deb* *neind* *jix* *gaons* *ml.*
one-**CLF:column** child-RED this NEG$_1$ give go
'This group of children (lined up one behind another) can't go (outside to play).' (Shixiang Wu, fieldnotes)

(6.137) *Dions* *ndaut* *lis* *dions* *chauk* ***nbax.***
plant tree want plant do **CLF:row**
'When (you) plant the trees, plant them in rows.' (Chenghua Long, fieldnotes) (repeated from (6.85) above)

There are also at least three classifiers that are used to refer to large groups of plants or to the locations (see also Section 6.1.4.7 below) in which such plants are growing

---

and nearby areas, but it might perhaps suggest that these activities were more widespread and more economically significant at some point in the past.

(this is similar to the way that *baonx* 'CLF:honeybee.hive' can be used to refer to all the honeybees living in a hive or to the actual hive itself). Two of these, *bob* 'CLF:forest' and *raud* 'CLF:forest', are derived classifiers, while one, *jel* 'CLF:agricultural.field', appears to be a dedicated classifier. The semantic differences between *bob* 'CLF:forest' and *raud* 'CLF:forest' are unclear: some consultants claim that *bob* is typically used to refer to larger groups of plants than *raud* is, while other consultants claim the opposite. Regardless, consultants agree that these two forms can only co-occur with the nouns *(ghaob-)ndaut* [(NOM-)tree] 'tree' and *(ghaob-)hlod* [(NOM-)bamboo] 'bamboo' as well as with nouns referring to specific types of trees or bamboo. In contrast, the classifier *jel* 'CLF:agricultural.field' is used to refer to any bounded area of land on which plants are cultivated or to the sum total of cultivated plants growing in such an area. It can thus co-occur with any noun referring to a type of cultivated plant, including *hlat.bous* 'radish', *dob* 'melon', *yaonb* 'young rice plant', *mioux* 'mature rice plant', and so on. It can also co-occur with the nouns *laos* 'field' and *laut* 'land' when the area of land in question is fallow or when no particular type of cultivated plant need be specified.

6.1.4.5 Classifiers referring to parts or portions

banb	'CLF:half/some'
nqaos	'CLF:half.of.animate'
nqad	'CLF:half.of.pair'
biank	'CLF:side'
njaod	'CLF:piece'
gut	'CLF:portion'
kheut	'CLF:rigid.segment'
geul	'CLF:body.part'

Some classifiers specifically refer to parts or portions of larger entities or masses. For instance, Xong features three classifiers that refer to halves: *banb* 'CLF:half/some', *nqaos* 'CLF:half.of.animate', and *nqad* 'CLF:half.of.pair'. The first of these, *banb* 'CLF:half/some', occurs either bare or with a preceding numeral *aod* 'one' to mean 'half of *X*, half an *X*', with the referent of *X* either indicated by a following noun or simply understood from context. An example of this is given in (6.138) below.

(6.138) *Wel gaons monx aod-**banb**.*
1SG give 2SG one-**CLF:half**
'I'll give you half (of the money).' (Chenghua Long, fieldnotes)

More often, though, *banb* simply means 'some' rather than specifically 'half', as in example (6.139).

(6.139) *Ranf.houb* *nieux-hnef* *nex* *heut* *wel* *nieus* ***banb***
afterward yester-CLF:day NEX help 1SG buy **CLF:some**
nggaob.
medicine
'And then, yesterday (my husband) bought some medicine for me.' (Haili Shi, in *Tooth Conversation*)

As examples (6.138) and (6.139) above show, *banb* is glossed as either 'CLF:half' or 'CLF:some' depending on which meaning is intended in any particular case. It is unclear at present whether *banb* can occur reduplicated or whether it can co-occur with any numerals or numeral phrases other than *aod* 'one'; if it cannot, then that would mean that *banb* 'CLF:half/some' is a "defective" or non-canonical classifier just as *hant* 'CLF:PL' is (see Section 6.1.4.1). However, it appears that *banb* can at least co-occur with any noun whose referent is amenable to division, either into halves or into less precisely defined portions.

The classifier *nqaos* 'CLF:half.of.animate' only co-occurs with the noun *miex/mianx* 'person' and with nouns referring to types of animals. When co-occurring with the noun *miex/mianx* 'person', *nqaos* means 'half of a married couple', as in *aod-**nqaos** miex* [one-**CLF:half.of.animate** person] 'a spouse'. Note that *nqaos* cannot co-occur with any other nouns referring to people, not even *bod* 'husband' or *oud* 'wife'. In contrast, when this classifier co-occurs with a noun referring to a type of animal, it means 'half of a slaughtered (animal)'. Thus, for instance, *aod-**nqaos** nbat* [one-**CLF:half.of.animate** pig] means 'half of a pig', as one might find for sale in a butcher's shop.

The classifier *nqad* 'CLF:half.of.pair' co-occurs with nouns whose referents characteristically come in pairs, and in such cases it naturally refers to one half of such a pair. It can thus co-occur with (i) nouns referring to certain paired body parts, like *(ghaob-)doul* [(NOM-)hand] 'hand', *(ghaob-)bab* [(NOM-)leg] 'leg', *zhoux.miouf* 'ear', and *laod.gheb* 'eye', (ii) nouns referring to certain paired articles of clothing or other wearable items, like *xut.npeif* 'shoe', *shoux.tof* 'glove', *hod.lob* 'earring', and *donl-eud* [sleeve-clothing] 'sleeve', and (iii) the noun *(ghaob-)zhous* [(NOM-)chopstick] 'chopstick'. For example, *aod-**nqad** laod.gheb* [one-**CLF:half.of.pair** eye] means 'an eye', while *oub-**nqad** shoux.tof* [two-**CLF:half.of.pair** glove] means 'a pair of gloves'.

The classifier *biank* 'CLF:side' is arguably derived (rather than dedicated), since there exists a locative noun *ghaob-biank* [NOM-side] 'side' as well (see Section 5.5.2.5). Both classifier and noun are used to refer to one or more sides of an entity or location, or to the space extending inward or outward from such a side or sides. For instance, in example (6.140), *biank* 'CLF:side' is used to refer to the side of a car (i.e. to part of the actual physical structure of the car itself, rather than to the space extending outward or inward from that part).

(6.140) *Deit doul aod-**biank** chek jix nzad diul.*
still remain one-**CLF:side** vehicle NEG_1 wash complete
'There's still one side of the car that hasn't been washed yet.' (Haili Shi, fieldnotes)

In contrast, in example (6.141), *biank* 'CLF:side' is used to refer to the space extending inward from one particular side of a store.

(6.141) *Louf.caof ninb aod-**biank** dox.*
green.tea at one-**CLF:side** that
'The green tea is over on that side (of the store).' (Haili Shi, fieldnotes)

Classifiers with slightly less specific semantics include *njaod* 'CLF:piece' and *gut* 'CLF:portion'. The former classifier is used to refer to a piece of some material (e.g. *niax* 'meat', *bok.lid* 'glass', *jok* 'plastic') regardless of the size or shape of the piece in question, while the latter is used to refer to any portion or subset of some mass or group. Note that the form *gut* 'CLF:portion' is also used to express fractions and multiples in Xong, as is discussed in more detail in Section 6.2.3. Both classifiers are exemplified in (6.142) and (6.143) below.

(6.142) *Aod-**njaod** ndeinb neind nak nqint nqint.*
one-**CLF:piece** cloth this extremely red red
'This piece of cloth is such a bright red.' (Haili Shi, fieldnotes)

(6.143) *Nieux.ghoub wel nieus dut hliof bid-hex.qif, beb monx*
just.now 1SG buy obtain many FRT-tomato share 2SG
*aod-**gut**, Xaont.*
one-**CLF:portion** PN
'I just bought a ton of tomatoes, so I'll give you some, Xaon.' (Chenghua Long, fieldnotes)

Finally, there are two types of parts or portions that take more specific classifiers. First, rigid segments of some longer length generally take the classifier *kheut* 'CLF:rigid.segment'. Thus, for instance, *aod-**kheut** ndaut* [one-**CLF:rigid.segment** tree] means 'a segment/length of wood', and *aod-**kheut** nek-geud* [one-**CLF:rigid.segment** AUG-road] means 'a segment/length of road'. Second, all the paired body parts that can take the classifier *nqad* 'CLF:half.of.pair' can also take the classifier *geul* 'CLF:body.part' instead, with no change in meaning. Thus *aod-**geul** doul* [one-**CLF:body.part** hand] means 'a hand', *aod-**geul** laod.gheb* [one-**CLF:body.part** eye] means 'an eye', and so on. However, unlike *nqad* 'CLF:half.of.pair', the classifier *geul* 'CLF:body.part' only co-occurs with nouns referring to body parts, never with nouns referring to wearable items or other objects.[124]

With the possible exception of *biank* 'CLF:side', all classifiers discussed in this section appear to be dedicated rather than derived.

6.1.4.6 Temporal classifiers

hnef/hneb	'CLF:day'
hlaot	'CLF:month'
jut	'CLF:year'
dat	'CLF:morning'
hmaont	'CLF:evening'
is	'CLF:night'
feink.zhonk	'CLF:minute'
roul	'CLF:time$_1$'
dieud	'CLF:time$_2$'
tit	'CLF:time$_3$'
died.zhonk/ diand.zhonk	'CLF:o'clock'

There are roughly a dozen dedicated classifiers that are regularly used in Xong to refer to periods of time or to points in time. Classifiers used to refer to (relatively) clearly bounded periods of time include *hnef/hneb* 'CLF:day' (with the former pronunciation being used in Yankan Village and Shanjiang Town and the latter being used in La'ershan Town and its surrounding villages, aside from Yankan), *hlaot* 'CLF:month', *jut* 'CLF:year', *dat* 'CLF:morning', *hmaont* 'CLF:evening', *is* 'CLF:night', and *feink.zhonk* 'CLF:minute' (with that last form appearing to be a relatively recent borrowing of Standard Mandarin *fēnzhōng* [分钟] or of a cognate form from another Sinitic variety). These forms combine with a preceding numeral or numeral phrase to yield a numeral-classifier phrase that indicates a quantity of the periods of time in question, e.g. *bub-hnef* [three-CLF:day] 'three days', *biaob-dat* [five-CLF:morning] 'five mornings', or *jox-is* [nine-CLF:night] 'nine nights'. Just as with Xong's other classifiers, these forms can occur reduplicated to mean 'every, each', as in *hlaot-hlaot* [CLF:month-CLF:month] 'every/each month' or *jut-jut* [CLF:year-CLF:year] 'every/each

124 Any body part term that does not co-occur with *nqad* 'CLF:half.of.pair' or *geul* 'CLF:body.part' will instead co-occur with one of a variety of other classifiers depending on the salient semantic features of the body part term in question. For example, the nouns *(ghaob-)xed/xand* [(NOM-)tooth] 'tooth' and *bid-ndaod* [FRT-finger] 'finger' both co-occur with *del* 'CLF:rigid.length' (see Section 6.1.4.2), the nouns *(ghaob-)tif* [(NOM-)stomach] 'stomach' and *baod-mieus* [BUG-nose] 'nose' both co-occur with *leb* 'CLF' (Section 6.1.4.1), and the noun *sheinf.jind* 'nerve' co-occurs with *ghoub* 'CLF:flexible.length' (Section 6.1.4.2).

year'. Examples of classifiers referring to (relatively) clearly bounded periods of time can be seen in (6.144) and (6.145) below.

(6.144) ***Hnef-hnef*** *choud nex naond deb monl jaont*
CLF:day-CLF:day send NEX ASSOC child go herd
*yul, **hnef-hnef** monl chaut chauk geud.donb.*
cow **CLF:day-CLF:day** go wilderness do work
'Every day (the evil stepmother) sent (her husband's) child out to herd the cows, every day (she sent him) out into the wilderness to work.' (Xingyu Shi, in *Oub Meinl Yaos Geud*)

(6.145) *Oub-bub-**jut*** *ix.houf mex leb deb-deb.*
two-three-**CLF:year** later exist CLF child-RED
'Two or three years later (they) had a child.' (Xingyu Shi, in *Oub Meinl Yaos Geud*)

The notions 'hour' and 'week' are expressed with nouns in Xong rather than with classifiers, just as is the case in Standard Mandarin. The noun meaning 'hour' in Xong is either *xox.shif* or *xox.shib* (with the former pronunciation being used by speakers from Yankan Village and the latter by speakers from other parts of Fenghuang County), and the noun meaning 'week' is either *xink.qif* or *xink.kif* (with both pronunciations appearing to be in free variation for most consultants). These nouns only ever co-occur with the classifier *leb* 'CLF' (see Section 6.1.4.1) within a single noun phrase. Unsurprisingly, the Xong forms *xox.shif/xox.shib* 'hour' and *xink.qif/xink.kif* 'week' appear to be recent borrowings of either the equivalent forms in Standard Mandarin (in which 'hour' is *xiǎoshí* [小时] and 'week' is *xīngqī* [星期]) or cognate forms in another Sinitic variety.

The three classifiers *roul* 'CLF:time$_1$', *dieud* 'CLF:time$_2$', and *tit* 'CLF:time$_3$' are used to refer to less clearly bounded periods of time. All three of these forms are fairly high-frequency ones, and all three appear to be more or less interchangeable. These forms can each be used to refer to a period of time as short as a few minutes or as long as several years. Each of them can also co-occur with the noun *(ghaob-)ngaonf* [(NOM-)time] 'time' within a single noun phrase, with the presence or absence of *(ghaob-)ngaonf* 'time' having no obvious semantic or pragmatic effect on the noun phrase as a whole. An instance of each of these three forms can be seen in examples (6.146–6.148) below.

(6.146) *Aod-**roul*** *ngaonf dox wel zhaons guaot.*
one-**CLF:time$_1$** time that 1SG fat pass
'I was very fat back then.' (unknown Xong consultant, fieldnotes)

(6.147) *Gank.ceib geud shoux.jik deib Bes.doub caof* ***dieud.***
simply hold cell.phone at Baidu search **CLF:time$_2$**
'(I) just used my cell phone to search on (the popular Chinese search engine) Baidu for a while.' (Haili Shi, in *Tooth Conversation*)

(6.148) *Monx nzhaod monl nghauk manx deb-ghot aod-**tit**.*
2SG return go visit 2PL DIM-old one-**CLF:time$_3$**
'You should go back to visit your (father) for a while.' (Xingyu Shi, in *Oub Meinl Yaos Geud*)

The numeral-classifier phrases *aod-roul* [one-CLF:time$_1$] and *aod-tit* [one-CLF:time$_3$] can also be used in isolation (i.e. not as part of a larger noun phrase) to mean 'now' and 'then (in the past)', respectively.

(6.149) ***Aod-roul*** *nex-god yaod.yaod ndiot beul.*
one-CLF:time$_1$ NEX-PL all recognize 3
'Now everyone knows him.' (Haili Shi, fieldnotes)

(6.150) *Jaont dand leb ob-deind-aub manh,* ***aod-tit***
herd arrive CLF NOM-edge-water PART **one-CLF:time$_3$**
beul minl zhaok aub leb ob-deind-aub dox.
3 mother fall water CLF NOM-edge-water that
'(The boy) would herd (his cows) to the water's edge, to the water's edge where his mother had fallen in.' (Xingyu Shi, in *Oub Meinl Yaos Geud*)

To refer to a specific clock time (e.g. 'one o'clock', 'seven o'clock', etc.), the classifier *died.zhonk/diand.zhonk* 'CLF:o'clock' is used (with the former pronunciation being used by speakers from Yankan Village and the latter by speakers from other parts of Fenghuang County). This form is another recent borrowing from Standard Mandarin or another Sinitic variety, with the equivalent form in Standard Mandarin being *diǎnzhōng* (点钟). Example (6.151) below demonstrates how *died.zhonk/diand.zhonk* 'CLF:o'clock' is used to refer to a specific time.

(6.151) *Wel bieib-**died.zhonk** ghat manx bioud.*
1SG four-**CLF:o'clock** go.to 2PL home
'I'll come to your house at four o'clock.' (Haili Shi, fieldnotes)

The classifiers discussed in this section occasionally co-occur with a preceding verb (and sometimes with a following noun as well) to indicate the length of time that an activity or event lasts. Examples of this are given in (6.152) and (6.153) below, where the relevant classifiers have been bolded.

(6.152) *Wel ninb beul bioud beux oub-**hmaont** maos.jaonb.*
1SG at 3 home hit two-**CLF:evening** mahjong
'I spent two evenings playing mahjong at her house.' (Chenghua Long, fieldnotes)

(6.153) *Monx heut wel teuf aod-**tit** aub gaons wel hauk.*
2SG help 1SG scoop one-**CLF:time$_3$** water give 1SG drink
'Go get some water (lit. 'scoop water for some time') for me to drink.' (Xingyu Shi, fieldnotes)

No clear examples of derived temporal classifiers have yet been attested.

6.1.4.7 Locative classifiers

bix 'CLF:place$_1$'
khauk 'CLF:place$_2$'
bioud 'CLF:home'
gheul 'CLF:village'
bob 'CLF:forest'
raud 'CLF:forest'
biank 'CLF:side'
baont 'CLF:slope'
bas 'CLF:expanse'

Fenghuang Xong features two dedicated classifiers that are used solely to refer to locations. The first of these is *bix* 'CLF:place$_1$', which has significant selectional restrictions. It only ever co-occurs with the numeral *aod* 'one' within a numeral-classifier phrase, never with any other numerals or numeral phrases, and it only ever co-occurs with the noun *(ghaob-)def* [(NOM-)place] 'place', never with any other nouns. Of course, like all other classifiers, *bix* 'CLF:place$_1$' often occurs bare (i.e. without a preceding numeral), and it often occurs without any following noun at all. In most cases, a noun phrase in which the classifier is *bix* will also contain a demonstrative such as *neind* 'this' or *dox* 'that', with the noun phrase as a whole then meaning 'here, this place' or 'there, that place'. This can be seen in example (6.154) below.

(6.154) *Aod-**bix** neind raut jeus bioud guaot.*
one-**CLF:place$_1$** this good build home pass
'This place would be really good for building homes.' (Shixiang Wu, fieldnotes)

The second Xong classifier that is used solely to refer to locations is *khauk* 'CLF:place$_2$'. This classifier has fewer selectional restrictions than *bix* 'CLF:place$_1$'. It can co-occur with any preceding numeral or numeral phrase, with the resulting numeral-classifier phrase then meaning 'two (places)', 'three (places)', and so on depending on the numeral or numeral phrase in question. And while *khauk* 'CLF:place$_2$' can co-occur with the noun *(ghaob-)def* [(NOM-)place] 'place' just as *bix* 'CLF:place$_1$' can, it can also co-occur with a variety of other nouns referring to types of plants or types of terrain, as in example (6.155) below.

(6.155)	*Aod-**khauk***	*hlat.bous*	*neind*	*nins*	*boub*	*naond.*
	one-**CLF:place$_2$**	radish	this	COP	1PL	ASSOC

'This plot of radishes belongs to us.' (unknown Xong consultant, fieldnotes)

The etymology of *bix* 'CLF:place$_1$' is unclear, but it seems likely that *khauk* 'CLF:place$_2$' is related to the noun *khauk* 'hole, cave'. Note, though, that the noun *khauk* 'hole, cave' never co-occurs with the classifier *khauk* 'CLF:place$_2$' within a single noun phrase; instead, *khauk* 'hole, cave' will typically co-occur with *leb* 'CLF' (see Section 6.1.4.1).

Derived classifiers (or at least arguably derived classifiers) that can be used to refer to locations include *bioud* 'CLF:home' and *gheul* 'CLF:village' (see Section 6.1.4.3), *bob* 'CLF:forest' and *raud* 'CLF:forest' (Section 6.1.4.4), *biank* 'CLF:side' (Section 6.1.4.5), *baont* 'CLF:slope', *bas* 'CLF:expanse', and classifiers derived from various other nouns with locative semantics.

6.1.4.8 Mensural classifiers

ceinf/ceinb	'CLF:cun (unit of length equivalent to ~3.33 centimeters)'
chix/qiaok	'CLF:chi (unit of length equivalent to 10 *cun*, or ~33.33 centimeters)'
zhaonb	'CLF:zhang (unit of length equivalent to 10 *chi*, or ~3.33 meters)'
mix	'CLF:meter (standard international unit of length)'
hnant	'CLF:li (unit of length equivalent to 500 meters)'
feinb	'CLF:area.fen' (unit of area equivalent to ~66.66 square meters)'
moux	'CLF:mu (unit of area equivalent to 10 *fen*, or ~666.66 square meters)'
xinb	'CLF:sheng (unit of volume equivalent to ~1 liter)'
doud	'CLF:dou (unit of volume equivalent to 10 *sheng*, or ~10 liters)'
danb	'CLF:dan (unit of volume equivalent to 10 *dou*, or ~100 liters)'
gheb	'CLF:mace (unit of mass equivalent to 5 grams)'
jix	'CLF:tael (unit of mass equivalent to 10 mace, or 50 grams)'
gaonb	'CLF:catty (unit of mass equivalent to 10 taels, or 500 grams)'

feink	'CLF:currency.fen (unit of currency equal to 0.01 *yuan*)'
giux	'CLF:jiao (unit of currency equal to 0.1 *yuan*)'
shauk/kuex	'CLF:yuan (unit of currency equal to 10 *jiao* or 100 *fen*)'

Xong has a variety of mensural classifiers, which are classifiers that refer to strictly defined units of some physical property (length, area, volume, or mass) or of currency.[125] Despite their relatively distinct semantics, in terms of their grammatical behavior Xong's mensural classifiers appear to be fully canonical members of the classifier class (see, for instance, examples (6.156–6.164) in this section). Etymologically, though, these forms are unusual in that most of them are recent borrowings of Sinitic mensural classifiers, which makes it difficult to provide glosses for them that are both succinct and accurate. For instance, *ceinf/ceinb* 'CLF:cun' could be glossed as 'CLF:3.33.cm', sacrificing elegance for accuracy, or it could be glossed as 'CLF:inch', sacrificing accuracy (since an international inch is 2.54 centimeters, not 3.33 centimeters) for elegance. The solution adopted in this grammar is to gloss each Sinitic-derived mensural classifier with the *pinyin* spelling of the equivalent Standard Mandarin form, even when the classifier in question may have been borrowed from a Sinitic variety other than Standard Mandarin (note, though, that some minor exceptions to this rule are discussed in the following paragraphs). Thus, in this grammar *ceinf/ceinb* is simply glossed as 'CLF:cun', since the *pinyin* spelling of the equivalent form in Standard Mandarin is *cùn*.

First, there are five commonly used mensural classifiers that refer to length, all of which are dedicated rather than derived. Three of these – *ceinf/ceinb* 'CLF:cun', *chix/qiaok* 'CLF:chi', and *zhaonb* 'CLF:zhang' – are clear borrowings of Sinitic measurement terms. The form *ceinf/ceinb* 'CLF:cun' (from Standard Mandarin *cùn* [寸]) refers to a unit of length that is equivalent to approximately 3.33 centimeters, with the pronunciation *ceinf* being used in Yankan Village and Shanjiang Town and *ceinb* being used in La'ershan Town and nearby villages (aside from Yankan). Ten *ceinf/ceinb* then yield a *chix/qiaok*, which is thus roughly equivalent to 33.33 centimeters. This latter form, glossed as 'CLF:chi' (from Standard Mandarin *chǐ* [尺]), is pronounced as *chix* in Yankan Village and as *qiaok* in other areas of Fenghuang County. A *zhaonb* 'CLF:zhang' (from Standard Mandarin *zhàng* [丈]) is then equal to ten *chix/qiaok*, or approximately 3.33 meters.

125 The fact that this Section 6.1.4.8 discusses classifiers referring to physical properties and currency but not classifiers referring to time (see Section 6.1.4.6) may strike the reader as somewhat arbitrary, since certain temporal classifiers (like *feink.zhonk* 'CLF:minute' or *jut* 'CLF:year') refer to units that are just as strictly defined as those referred to by any length, volume, or mass classifiers. Still, the author felt that discussing temporal classifiers and (non-temporal) mensural classifiers separately might make things clearer to the reader, and in any case the boundaries of most of the categories discussed in these Sections 6.1.4.1 through 6.1.4.9 are arbitrary to at least some degree.

In addition to these three, Fenghuang Xong speakers also regularly use *mix* 'CLF:meter', borrowed either from Standard Mandarin *mǐ* (米) or from a cognate form in another Sinitic variety. A Xong *mix*, just like a Standard Mandarin *mǐ*, is identical in length to a standard international meter. Finally, the author's consultants all report that a *hnant* 'CLF:li' is identical to a *lǐ* (里), a modern Chinese unit of length equivalent to 500 meters, and so the form in question is glossed as 'CLF:li' in this grammar. However, the Xong classifier *hnant* is clearly not a borrowing of Standard Mandarin *lǐ* or any cognate forms in other Sinitic varieties, though it is homophonous with (and perhaps etymologically related to) the Xong verb *hnant* 'to shout'.

Examples of mensural classifiers referring to length are given in (6.156) and (6.157) below.

(6.156) *Aod-hnanf* *eud* *lis* *mins-**qiaok*** *ndeib?*
one-CLF:clothing clothing want how.many-**CLF:chi** cloth
'How many *chi* of cloth will it take to make one article of clothing?'
(Chenghua Long, fieldnotes)

(6.157) *Zhaos* *Dol.xid* *ghat* *Biax.guk* *mex* *oub-gul-**hnant*** *geud.*
from La'ershan go.to Shanjiang exist two-ten-**CLF:li** road
'It's twenty *li* from (the town of) La'ershan to (the town of) Shanjiang.'
(Chenghua Long, fieldnotes)

Only two classifiers that refer to units of area have been attested, both of which are dedicated rather than derived. The classifier *feinb* 'CLF:area.fen' (from Standard Mandarin *fēn* [分]) refers to a unit of area roughly equivalent to 66.66 square meters. Note that this form is glossed as 'CLF:area.fen' rather than just 'CLF:fen' in order to distinguish it from *feink* 'CLF:currency.fen' (see below in this section). The classifier *moux* 'CLF:mu' (from Standard Mandarin *mǔ* [亩]) refers to an area of ten *feinb*, or roughly 666.66 square meters. Both *moux* 'CLF:mu' and *feinb* 'CLF:area.fen' occur in example (6.158) below.

(6.158) *Boub* *manx* *nieus* *jel* *laos* *dox* *mex*
1PL 2PL buy CLF: agricultural.field field that exist
*aod-**moux*** *yab* *il-**feinb**.*
one-**CLF:mu** also eight-**CLF:area.fen**
'That field that we and you (pl.) bought together is one *mu* and eight *fen* in area.' (Chenghua Long, fieldnotes)

The three classifiers most commonly used to refer to standardized units of volume are *xinb* 'CLF:sheng' (from Standard Mandarin *shēng* [升]), *doud* 'CLF:dou' (from Standard Mandarin *dǒu* [斗]), and *danb* 'CLF:dan' (from Standard Mandarin *dàn* [石]). A *xinb* is roughly equivalent to a liter, a *doud* to ten liters, and a *danb* to one hundred liters. While there are few (if any) derived classifiers in Xong that refer to length, area, mass, or currency, there are a great many derived classifiers that refer to volume. Virtually any noun that refers to some sort of three-dimensional container can also function as a derived classifier referring to volume, including *zhet* 'bowl; CLF:bowl', *tont* 'bucket; CLF:bucket', *beix* 'cup; CLF:cup', *pinf* 'bottle; CLF:bottle', *dab* 'box; CLF:box', and *did* 'cylindrical basket worn on one's back; CLF:cylindrical.basket.worn.on.back'. Of course, derived volume classifiers like these typically refer to units of volume that are much less standardized than those referred to by dedicated volume classifiers like *xinb* 'CLF:sheng', *doud* 'CLF:dou', or *danb* 'CLF:dan'.

Examples of classifiers referring to volume are given in (6.159) and (6.160) below. Example (6.159) features a derived classifier, while example (6.160) features a dedicated one.

(6.159) *Gul-**pinf** beul hauk ix dut.*
ten-**CLF:bottle** 3 drink NEG_1 obtain
'He won't be able to drink ten bottles (of beer).' (unknown Xong consultant, fieldnotes)

(6.160) *Zeix aod-taonb mianx-khat neind lis dieud*
invite one-CLF:trip person-guest this want boil.rice
*aod-**danb** nzaut.*
one-**CLF:dan** uncooked.rice
'For these guests that have been invited (lit. 'for inviting this trip of guests'), (we'll) need to boil one *dan* of rice.' (Shixiang Wu, fieldnotes)

Xong also features three dedicated classifiers that refer to units of mass: *gheb* 'CLF:mace', *jix* 'CLF:tael', and *gaonb* 'CLF:catty'. A *gheb* is equivalent to 5 grams, a *jix* is equivalent to 50 grams (or ten *gheb*), and a *gaonb* is equivalent to 500 grams (or ten *jix*). The meanings of these three forms are identical to the meanings of three Chinese units of mass, which in Standard Mandarin are referred to as the *qián* ([钱], equivalent to a Xong *gheb*), the *liǎng* ([两], equivalent to a Xong *jix*), and the *jīn* ([斤], equivalent to a Xong *gaonb*). However, since the Xong classifiers in question bear little or no phonetic resemblance to the equivalent Standard Mandarin terms, the author glosses them with the standard English translations of those Mandarin terms rather than with their *pinyin* spelling. Thus *gheb* is glossed as 'CLF:mace' (rather than 'CLF:qian'), *jix* is glossed as 'CLF:tael' (rather than 'CLF:liang'), and *gaonb* is glossed as 'CLF:catty' (rather than 'CLF:jin'). Note that no examples of derived classifiers referring to units of mass have been attested.

Examples (6.161) and (6.162) show classifiers referring to units of mass in use.

(6.161) *Nieux-hnef* *wel* *nieus* *niax,* *nex* *lox.banx* *yut*
yester-CLF:day 1SG buy meat NEX boss few
wel *aod-**jix**.*
1SG one-**CLF:tael**
'Yesterday I bought some meat, and the seller shorted me one tael.' (Haili Shi, fieldnotes)

(6.162) *Nieus* *naont* *hliob,* *yut* *aod-**gheb**-deb* *jix* *hnaond.*
buy thus many few one-**CLF:mace**-DIM NEG$_1$ sense
'(When you) buy this much (tea), (if you were) shorted one measly mace (you) wouldn't even notice.' (Shixiang Wu, fieldnotes)

Finally, there are four classifiers used to refer to units of currency. The classifiers *shauk* and *kuex* are completely synonymous, and both are glossed as 'CLF:yuan' in this grammar. These two forms both refer to the *yuán* (元), the standard unit of currency in the People's Republic of China. The origin of the form *shauk* is unknown, but the form *kuex* appears to be a borrowing of Standard Mandarin *kuài* ([块], a colloquial term for the Chinese *yuán*) or of a cognate form in another Sinitic variety. One-tenth of a *shauk* (or *kuex*) is then referred to with *giux* 'CLF:jiao' (from Standard Mandarin *jiǎo* [角]), and one-tenth of a *giux* is referred to with *feink* 'CLF:currency.fen' (from Standard Mandarin *fēn* [分]). Note that *feink* is glossed as 'CLF:currency.fen' rather than just 'CLF:fen' in order to distinguish it from *feinb* 'CLF:area.fen' (see above in this section). No examples of derived classifiers referring to units of currency have been attested.

Instances of classifiers referring to units of currency can be seen in examples (6.163) and (6.164) below. Both of these examples show speakers bemoaning the rapidly rising cost of living in China, which has made currency denominations smaller than one *yuán* virtually worthless.

(6.163) *Aod-gud* *deb-deb* *aod-roul* *ngaonf* *beb*
one-CLF:human.group child-RED one-CLF:time$_1$ time share
*aod-**giux*** *daont* *at* *ix* *lis.*
one-**CLF:jiao** money SAT NEG$_1$ want
'These children nowadays, (if you only) give (them) one *jiao*, (they) won't even take it.' (Chenghua Long, fieldnotes)

(6.164) *Aod-roul* *neind* *ghat* *dib* *at* *jix* *ghans* *mex*
one-CLF:time$_1$ this go.to which SAT NEG$_1$ see exist
leb *yonb* *aod-**feink*** *daont.*
who use one-**CLF:currency.fen** money
'These days, no matter where (you) go, (you) won't see anybody using *fen*.' (Haili Shi, fieldnotes)

6.1.4.9 Verbal classifiers

dob	'CLF:occurrence'
cif	'CLF:occurrence'
taonb	'CLF:trip'
miaok	'CLF:fan'
jub	'CLF:needle'
ndeind	'CLF:knife'
daut	'CLF:axe'
put	'CLF:gun'
doul	'CLF:hand'
deik	'CLF:wing'
gheb	'CLF:eye'
mes	'CLF:face'
ghaok	'CLF:hug'
giud	'CLF:pinch'
zhox	'CLF:kick'
zaonb	'CLF:crash.into'
qonf	'CLF:shove'
tiut	'CLF:press.down'

Xong's verbal classifiers are distinct from other classifiers in that they serve to quantify events or occurrences rather than more time-stable referents (e.g. animate beings, inanimate entities, or abstract concepts). Most of these verbal classifiers are essentially adverbial in function, in the sense that their primary purpose is to modify verbs (hence the term *verbal classifier*). Some of them also display unique ordering properties or unique selectional restrictions. However, it should be noted that none of these properties apply exceptionlessly to every verbal classifier in the language. This means that these forms only constitute a general semantic category of classifiers, and not a grammatically defined subclass of them.

Verbal classifiers can be divided into three groups: dedicated verbal classifiers, verbal classifiers derived from nouns, and verbal classifiers derived from verbs. Xong's dedicated verbal classifiers include *dob* 'CLF:occurrence', *cif* 'CLF:occurrence', and *taonb* 'CLF:trip'. While there appear to be only three dedicated verbal classifiers in the language, all three are relatively high-frequency forms, at least compared to the other verbal classifiers discussed in this section. Note that the meanings of *dob* 'CLF:occurrence' and *cif* 'CLF:occurrence' appear to be identical, with consultants reporting that the sole difference between them is that *dob* is a more "native" Xong form while *cif* is a recent borrowing from Sinitic (either of Standard Mandarin *cì* [次] or of a cognate form from another Sinitic variety). The forms *dob* 'CLF:occurrence' and *cif* 'CLF:occurrence' can be used to quantify essentially any event or occurrence, while *taonb* 'CLF:trip' is used to quantify events or occurrences that involve an entity (or entities) moving from one location to another.

Each of these three dedicated verbal classifiers can be seen exemplified in (6.165–6.167) below. In these and all other examples in this section, each instance of a verbal classifier has been bolded.

(6.165) *Aod-**dob*** *neind* *nex* *ghaod.gueb* *lol*
one-**CLF:occurrence** this NEX government.official come
jex.ncaof *job.ngab,* *wel* *at* *gueil* *lah.*
inspect teaching.plan 1SG SAT dodge PRF
'This time when the government official came to inspect our teaching plans, he didn't inspect mine (lit. 'I dodged him').' (unknown Xong consultant, fieldnotes)

(6.166) *Hmaont-dius* *wel* *at* *gox* *oub-**cif*** *deit*
evening-??? 1SG SAT do two-**CLF:occurrence** still
jix *raut.*
NEG_1 good
'That evening I used (the medicine) twice but it still wasn't working.' (Haili Shi, in *Tooth Conversation*)

(6.167) *Tat-hnef* *wel* *guaot* *oub-**taonb*** *aub.*
this-CLF:day 1SG pass two-**CLF:trip** water
'I crossed the river twice today.' (Haili Shi, fieldnotes) (repeated from (6.36) above)

Although Xong's dedicated verbal classifiers do occasionally co-occur with a following noun (as in example (6.167) above), it appears that the classifier and noun in such cases do not actually form a constituent together. The primary evidence for this lies in the fact that the relative ordering of classifier and noun in such cases is flexible: the classifier (either bare or within a numeral-classifier phrase) can occur first, with the noun following, or the noun can occur first, with the classifier following. In this respect dedicated verbal classifiers differ from both non-verbal classifiers (see Sections 6.1.4.1 through 6.1.4.8) and derived verbal classifiers (see further below in this section), neither of which display any flexible ordering properties with respect to adjacent nouns. See Section 6.1.2.2 above for further discussion and examples.

In addition to dedicated verbal classifiers, Xong also features a group of verbal classifiers that are derived from nouns. Around a dozen such classifiers have so far been attested (though the author has no reason to suspect that more such forms will not be encountered in the future), all of which are derived from nouns that refer to either types of tools or body parts. These include *miaok* 'CLF:fan', *jub* 'CLF:needle', *ndeind* 'CLF:knife', *daut* 'CLF:axe', *put* 'CLF:gun', *doul* 'CLF:hand' (note that this form in particular can also function as a taxonomic essence classifier; see Section 6.1.4.3), *deik* 'CLF:wing', *gheb* 'CLF:eye', and *mes* 'CLF:face'.

The choice of which noun-derived verbal classifier to use in any particular situation will naturally vary depending on the tool or body part used to carry out the event or activity in question. This can be seen in examples (6.168–6.170) below.

(6.168)

Beul	*baond*	*aod-ngonl*	*nbat-doub*	*dox*	*bub-**put**,*
3	shoot	one-CLF:animate	pig-earth	that	three-**CLF:gun**

beul	*deit*	*jix*	*daos.*
3	still	NEG$_1$	die

'He shot the wild pig three times (with a gun), but it still didn't die.' (Shixiang Wu, fieldnotes)

(6.169)

Daob-naus	*eint*	*aod-**deik***	*zos*	*aod-**deik**,*	*eint*
AN-bird	fly	one-**CLF:wing**	land	one-**CLF:wing**	fly

jix	*dut*	*hot*	*ghoub*	*yab*	*zos*	*aod-dieud*	*daonl.*
NEG$_1$	obtain	how.much	far	also	land	one-CLF:time$_2$	wait

'The bird would fly for a bit and then land for a bit. Before it flew too far, it would stop and wait for a while.' (Xingyu Shi, in *Oub Meinl Yaos Geud*)

(6.170)

Wel	*nkhed*	*beul*	*aod-**gheb**.*
1SG	look	3	one-**CLF:eye**

'I glanced at him (once).' (Haili Shi, fieldnotes)

Numeral-classifier phrases containing a verbal classifier derived from a noun never co-occur with a following noun. They may, however, co-occur with a preceding noun phrase, as in examples (6.168) and (6.170) above. In such cases the numeral-classifier phrase and the preceding noun phrase do not appear to form a constituent, as evidenced by the fact that the noun phrase in question can itself contain a different numeral-classifier phrase (e.g. *aod-ngonl* [one-CLF:animate] in example (6.168)). Instead, the noun phrase serves as an argument of the preceding verb, while the numeral-classifier phrase serves a more adjunct-like role.

Xong's third and final group of verbal classifiers includes those that are derived from verbs, such as *ghaok* 'CLF:hug' (from the verb *ghaok* 'to hug'), *giud* 'CLF:pinch' (from *giud* 'to pinch'), *zhox* 'CLF:kick' (from *zhox* 'to kick'), *zaonb* 'CLF:crash.into' (from *zaonb* 'to crash into'), *qonf* 'CLF:shove' (from *qonf* 'to shove'), and *tiut* 'CLF:press.down' (from *tiut* 'to press down'). These forms generally serve to indicate the number of times that an event or activity occurs, just as other verbal classifiers do, but in some cases they instead function as something like mensural classifiers (see Section 6.1.4.8) in order to quantify some referent.

When serving to indicate the number of times that an event or activity occurs, verbal classifiers derived from verbs behave very similarly to the verbal classifiers derived from nouns discussed earlier in this section. A numeral-classifier phrase containing such a classifier will not co-occur with a following noun, but it may co-occur with a preceding noun phrase (e.g. *monx* '2SG' in example (6.171) below). That noun phrase and the following numeral-classifier phrase do not form a constituent; instead, the noun phrase serves as an argument of the preceding verb while the numeral-classifier phrase serves as something like an adjunct.

(6.171) *Wel zhox monx aod-**zhox**.*
1SG kick 2SG one-**CLF:kick**
'I'll give you a kick.' (Chenghua Long, fieldnotes)

In most instances of this construction, a single underlyingly verbal form will occur twice: first as a verb that expresses the main predication of the clause, and then again as a derived classifier that quantifies the event or activity referred to by that verb. This can be seen in example (6.171) above, where *zhox* occurs once as a verb meaning 'to kick' and once as a classifier meaning 'CLF:kick'. It can also be seen in example (6.172) below, where *tiut* occurs once as a verb meaning 'to press down' and once as a classifier meaning 'CLF:press.down'.

(6.172) *Mx lis tiut oub-**tiut**.*
2SG want press.down two-**CLF:press.down**
'You need to press (it) twice.' (Shixiang Wu, fieldnotes) (repeated from (6.31) above)

When serving to quantify a referent (rather than an event or activity), verbal classifiers derived from verbs function very similarly to the mensural classifiers described in Section 6.1.4.8 above. A numeral-classifier phrase containing such a classifier can function as a noun phrase in its own right, with the identity of the referent in question being understood from context (as in example (6.173)), or it can combine with a following noun (one that overtly expresses the identity of the referent) to form a larger noun phrase (as in example (6.174)).

(6.173) *Wel chaot bub-**ghaok**.*
1SG look.for three-**CLF:hug**
'I found three armfuls (of firewood).' (Haili Shi, fieldnotes)

(6.174) *Wel giud oub-**giud** nzot.*
1SG pinch two-**CLF:pinch** uncooked.rice
'I got two pinches of rice.' (Haili Shi, fieldnotes)

6.2 Numerals

6.2.1 Cardinal numerals and numeral phrases

It appears that all Fenghuang Xong speakers have two sets of numeral forms, both of which are decimal (i.e. base-10). One of these sets is composed of what are seen by Xong speakers as "native" Xong forms, while the other set consists of forms that these same speakers identify as having been borrowed relatively recently from a Sinitic variety.[126] These two distinct sets are present even in the idiolects of speakers who are for most practical purposes essentially monolingual in Xong. Both of these sets are presented in Table 6.1 below, but first some initial comments are in order.

The "native" numerals of Fenghuang Xong display much less cross-dialectal (or at least cross-idiolectal) variation, and so they have been arranged in a single column in Table 6.1. Only two of these "native" numerals display any phonological variation among the author's primary consultants. The form meaning 'six' is *zhut* for speakers from Yankan Village and Shanjiang Town, but *zhaut* for speakers from La'ershan Town and nearby villages (aside from Yankan Village). The form meaning 'hundred million' is *ik* for speakers from Shanjiang Town, but *ib* for all other speakers. (For more information on the author's primary consultants and their hometowns, see Sections 2.6.2 and 2.7.1.)

The "Sinitic" numerals display a much higher level of phonological (specifically, tonal) variation among the author's consultants, and so these have been divided into three columns in Table 6.1. The first of these columns shows the forms used in Yankan Village, the second shows the forms used in Shanjiang Town, and the third shows the forms used in La'ershan Town and nearby villages (again, not including Yankan). Most of these forms are relatively straightforward, but note that while the author's consultants report that the forms for 'hundred', 'ten thousand', and 'hundred million' are identical in both sets of numerals, they report that the "native" set of numerals simply lacks a form for 'zero'. Note also that the phonetic realization of the "Sinitic" numeral *erk/erb* 'two' is discussed in the introduction to Section 3.3.

In addition to the numerals presented in Table 6.1, Fenghuang Xong also features two non-integer numerals, *daob* 'a few' and *mins* 'how many'. These two forms differ from Xong's other, more canonical numerals in that they do not refer to integers ('one', 'two', 'ten', etc.), but they nevertheless pattern very similarly to Xong's

126 The origins of each set of numerals deserve a bit more comment here. First, it is unclear which particular Sinitic variety was the source of Fenghuang Xong's more "Sinitic-like" numerals, as the forms in question are roughly equally similar to the Fenghuang Chinese numerals listed in He (2011: 76, 77) and to the numerals of modern Standard Mandarin. Second, many of the supposedly "native" Xong forms that make up the other set of numerals may actually be very old borrowings from Sinitic or Tibeto-Burman. This may in fact be true of all the numerals in that other set aside from *oub* 'two' and *bub* 'three'; see Ratliff (2010: 214–218) for discussion.

Table 6.1: Numerals of Fenghuang Xong.

GLOSS	"NATIVE" XONG FORM	"SINITIC" FORM, YANKAN XONG	"SINITIC" FORM, SHANJIANG XONG	"SINITIC" FORM, LA'ERSHAN XONG
'zero'	n/a	*linf*	*linl*	*linl*
'one'	*aod*	*if*	*ib*	*il*
'two'	*oub*	*erk*	*erk*	*erb*
'three'	*bub*	*sank*	*sank*	*sank*
'four'	*bieib*	*sib*	*sib*	*sib*
'five'	*biaob*	*ux*	*ux*	*ux*
'six'	*zhut/zhaut*	*louf*	*louf*	*loul*
'seven'	*jons*	*qif*	*qif*	*qil*
'eight'	*il*	*baof*	*baof*	*baol*
'nine'	*jox*	*jeux*	*jeux*	*jeux*
'ten'	*gul*	*shif*	*shif*	*shil*
'hundred'	*bat*	*bat*	*bat*	*bat*
'thousand'	*canf*	*qed*	*qand*	*qand*
'ten thousand'	*wanb*	*wanb*	*wanb*	*wanb*
'hundred million'	*ib/ik*	*ib*	*ik*	*ib*

canonical numerals in terms of their syntactic properties. Both of these non-integer numerals are discussed in Section 6.2.2 below, and the form *mins* 'how many' is further discussed in Section 7.3.2.3 as well.

Although the basic structures of Xong's two sets of numerals are broadly similar (in the sense that both sets are base-10 systems populated solely by monosyllabic forms), in practice there is a fairly clear division of labor between them. The numerals that speakers view as "Sinitic" almost never co-occur with a following classifier to form a numeral-classifier phrase. Instead, these numerals are typically used only for a small, restricted set of functions, including the reading of telephone numbers, identification numbers (e.g. on one's national ID card), computer passwords, the names of years in the Gregorian calendar (e.g. 1949, 2015), and other similar tasks. In essence, then, these "Sinitic" numerals are not used to actually quantify referents; they are instead used whenever a string of digits is used as a unique identifier (like a telephone or ID number), with the actual digits involved having no real semantic content.[127]

127 One exception to this is the ordinal construction, which uses "Sinitic" numerals rather than "native" Xong ones. See Section 6.2.3 for details.

In contrast, the other, more "native" set of numerals is used for all other functions, primary among them being the quantification of referents via the use of a numeral-classifier phrase. This means that Xong's "native" numerals are rather more grammatically active and occur with a much higher frequency than its "Sinitic" numerals, and so the bulk of this section will be concerned only with those "native" numerals.

The numerals *aod* 'one' through *jox* 'nine' occur straightforwardly before a classifier to form a numeral-classifier phrase (see Section 6.1.2), as is shown in examples (6.175–6.183) below. In these examples, each numeral has been bolded.

(6.175) ***aod**-leb* *neind*
one-CLF this
'this (thing), this (one)' (Lijun Wu, fieldnotes)

(6.176) ***oub**-ngonl* *daob-yul*
two-CLF:animate AN-cow
'two cows' (Shixiang Wu, fieldnotes)

(6.177) ***bub**-meinl* *mianx*
three-CLF:person person
'three people' (Shixiang Wu, fieldnotes)

(6.178) ***bieib**-hnef*
four-CLF:day
'four days' (Haili Shi, fieldnotes)

(6.179) ***biaob**-shauk* *daont*
five-CLF:yuan money
'five *yuan* (unit of currency)' (Shixiang Wu, fieldnotes)

(6.180) ***zhut**-doul* *put*
six-CLF:hand gun
'six guns' (Haili Shi, fieldnotes)

(6.181) ***jons-**jut*
seven-CLF:year
'seven years' (Haili Shi, fieldnotes)

(6.182) *wel* *naond* ***il**-leb* *daonx* *neind*
1SG ASSOC **eight**-CLF candy this
'these eight pieces of candy of mine' (Long Chenghua, fieldnotes)

(6.183) ***jox**-gaonb* *niax-nbat*
nine-CLF:catty meat-pig
'nine catties (unit of mass) of pork' (Yan Long, fieldnotes)

For quantities from 'ten' to 'ninety-nine', a polymorphemic numeral phrase will be used rather than a single monomorphemic numeral (here the term *numeral phrase* simply refers to a polymorphemic grammatical unit composed solely of numerals). In such a numeral phrase, the first morpheme will be a numeral indicating the number of tens, the second will be the numeral *gul* 'ten' itself, and the third will be a numeral indicating the number of ones. Thus, for example, the quantity 'twenty-three' in Xong would be expressed as *oub-gul-bub* [two-ten-three], the quantity 'ninety-nine' would be expressed as *jox-gul-jox* [nine-ten-nine], and the quantity 'thirty' would be expressed as simply *bub-gul* [three-ten]. For quantities from 'ten' to 'nineteen' in particular, the initial *aod* 'one' is optional. This means that 'ten' can be expressed as either *gul* [ten] or *aod-gul* [one-ten], 'eleven' can be expressed as either *gul-aod* [ten-one] or *aod-gul-aod* [one-ten-one], and so on.

These more complex numeral phrases can combine with a following classifier to form a numeral-classifier phrase just as monomorphemic numerals can. Examples can be seen in (6.184–6.189) below, in which each numeral has been bolded.

(6.184) ***(aod-)gul**-meinl* *miex*
(one-)ten-CLF:person person
'ten people' (Haili Shi, fieldnotes)

(6.185) ***(aod-)gul-biaob**-shauk* *daont*
(one-)ten-five-CLF:yuan money
'fifteen *yuan* (unit of currency)' (Xingyu Shi, fieldnotes)

(6.186) ***oub-gul**-ngonl* *daob-ghab*
two-ten-CLF:animate AN-chicken
'twenty chickens' (Lijun Wu, fieldnotes)

(6.187) ***bub-gul-oub**-leb* *deb-deb*
three-ten-two-CLF child-RED
'thirty-two children' (Chenghua Long, fieldnotes)

(6.188) ***jons-gul-biaob**-jut*
seven-ten-five-CLF:year
'seventy-five years' (Haili Shi, fieldnotes)

(6.189) ***jox-gul-jox**-meinl* *zhaol-ginb*
nine-ten-nine-CLF:person non.Miao-soldier
'ninety-nine soldiers' (Chenghua Long, fieldnotes)

For quantities larger than 'ninety-nine', still more complex numeral phrases are used. These have the same general structure as the numeral phrases just discussed, with a numeral referring to the number of ones occurring last, preceded by the numeral *gul* 'ten', preceded by a numeral referring to the number of tens, preceded by the numeral *bat* 'hundred', preceded by a numeral referring to the number of hundreds, and so on. This means that the quantity '333' in Xong would be *bub-bat-bub-gul-bub* [three-hundred-three-ten-three] and '12,345' would be *aod-wanb-oub-canf-bub-bat-bieib-gul-biaob* [one-ten.thousand-two-thousand-three-hundred-four-ten-five], while the quantities '500', '5,000', and '50,000' would simply be *biaob-bat* [five-hundred], *biaob-canf* [five-thousand], and *biaob-wanb* [five-ten.thousand]. Examples of these more complex numeral phrases combining with a following classifier to form a numeral-classifier phrase are shown in (6.190–6.192) below. In these examples, each numeral has again been bolded.

(6.190) ***bub-bat-aod-gul-biaob**-leb* *neus-ghab*
three-hundred-one-ten-five-CLF egg-chicken
'315 chicken eggs' (Lijun Wu, fieldnotes)

(6.191) ***aod-canf-oub-bat**-meinl* *zos*
one-thousand-two-hundred-CLF:person people
'1,200 people' (Haili Shi, fieldnotes)

(6.192) ***jox-wanb-jox-canf-jox-bat-jox-gul-jox**-shauk*
nine-ten.thousand-nine-thousand-nine-hundred-nine-ten-nine-CLF:yuan
did.daont
money
'99,999 *yuan* (unit of currency)' (Shixiang Wu, fieldnotes)

To refer to large quantities in which the value of one or more non-initial, non-final decimal units is zero (e.g. '303', in which the tens unit is zero, or '1,005', in which both the tens and hundreds units are zero), a complex numeral phrase similar to the ones discussed above is used, with those decimal units whose values are zero simply being left out. Thus, for example, '303' would be expressed in Xong as *bub-bat-bub* [three-hundred-three] (cf. *bub-bat-bub-gul* [three-hundred-three-ten] '330'), while '1,005' would be expressed as *aod-canf-biaob* [one-thousand-five] (cf. *aod-canf-biaob-bat* [one-thousand-five-hundred] '1,500' and *aod-canf-biaob-gul* [one-thousand-five-ten] '1,050'). These numeral phrases combine with a following classifier to form a numeral-classifier phrase just as the numerals and numeral phrases in previous examples in this section do.

Finally, note that the "Sinitic" numeral *linf/linl* 'zero' cannot combine with a following classifier to form a numeral-classifier phrase, and Xong lacks a "native" form for 'zero'. To refer to the complete lack of a particular type of referent (or, in other words, to a group of referents whose quantity is zero), Xong speakers will typically use a periphrastic construction rather than a numeral. See Section 9.1.3.1 for further details.

6.2.2 Approximate quantification with numerals

There are three primary ways that numerals can be used to express approximate amounts (e.g. *about three*, *eight or nine*, *a few*) in Fenghuang Xong, all of which make use of Xong's "native" numerals rather than its "Sinitic" ones (see Section 6.2.1 above). The first of these involves the use of either of Xong's non-integer numerals, *daob* 'a few' or *mins* 'how many'.[128] In grammatical terms, these forms clearly belong to the class of numerals in Xong, since (i) they can co-occur with a following classifier to form a numeral-classifier phrase and (ii) they can co-occur with Xong's integer numerals to form larger numeral phrases. Both of these abilities are evident in examples (6.193–6.198) below.

(6.193) *Wel nanx mex* ***daob****-shauk daont.*
1SG only exist **a.few**-CLF:yuan money
'I only have a few *yuan* (unit of currency).' (Wu Lijun, fieldnotes)

(6.194) *Mex aod-gul-****daob****-leb.*
exist one-ten-**a.few**-CLF
'There are ten-plus (i.e. more than ten, less than twenty) (students outside).' (Haili Shi, fieldnotes)

(6.195) *Aod-leb dox raut guaot, lis* ***daob****-gul-shauk.*
one-CLF that good pass want **a.few**-ten-CLF:yuan
'That one's very nice, (it) costs a few dozen (lit. 'several tens of') *yuan*.' (unknown Xong consultant, fieldnotes)

(6.196) *Monx naond deb mex* ***mins****-jut?*
2SG ASSOC child exist **how.many**-CLF:year
'How old is your child?' (Haili Shi, fieldnotes)

128 Note, though, that the notion 'many' is typically expressed in Xong with the verb *hliof/hliob* 'many' rather than with a non-integer numeral.

(6.197) *Lis* ***mins****-bat-shauk* *daont?*
want **how.many**-hundred-CLF:yuan money
'(It) costs how many hundreds of *yuan*?' (Haili Shi, fieldnotes)

(6.198) *Beul mex oub-gul-****mins****-jut.*
3 exist two-ten-**how.many**-CLF:year
'She's in her twenties.' (Yan Long, fieldnotes)

The semantics of *daob* 'a few' are relatively straightforward. As the form's gloss suggests, it serves as an indefinite (never interrogative) numeral referring to an amount larger than one but smaller than ten or so. Thus, for example, *daob-meinl miex* [a.few-CLF:person person] 'a few people' could be used to refer to any group of people with at least two and no more than nine or so people, while *daob-gul-shauk daont* [a.few-ten-CLF:yuan money] 'a few tens of *yuan*' could be used to refer to any amount of money that is at least twenty and no more than ninety or so *yuan* in value.

The semantics of *mins* 'how many' are more complex, as this form belongs not only to the class of numerals but also to the class of ignoratives (see Section 7.3). This means it can essentially function as either an interrogative numeral ('how many?') or an indefinite one ('a few') depending on context, the structure of the current discourse, and the speaker's and listener's real-world knowledge. Some instances of this can be seen in examples (6.196) and (6.197) above, where *mins* occurs with interrogative force, and in the subsequent example (6.198), where it does not. Many more such instances can be found in Section 7.3.2.3, where *mins* is discussed in much more detail.

Another method of expressing approximate amounts in Xong is via the use of two (or, very rarely, three or more) consecutive numerals in sequence within a single numeral phrase, with that numeral phrase then being followed by the appropriate classifier. For instance, 'two or three' can be expressed in Xong as *oub-bub-leb* [two-three-CLF] and 'four or five' can be expressed as *bieib-biaob-leb* [four-five-CLF], as in the following examples.

(6.199) *Daod neind mex* ***oub-bub-leb*** *bid-lieus.*
place$_3$ this exist **two-three-CLF** FRT-tangerine
'There are two or three tangerines here (on the table).' (Shixiang Wu, fieldnotes)

(6.200) *Zheit-zhauf mex* ***bub-bieib-meinl*** *miex nghauk.zaol.*
outside-door exist **three-four-CLF:person** person play
'There are three or four people playing outside.' (Haili Shi, fieldnotes)

(6.201) *Nieux-hnef wel nieus eud, yonb diul*
yester-CLF:day 1SG buy clothing use complete
bieib-biaob-bat-shauk.
four-five-hundred-CLF:yuan
'Yesterday I bought some clothes, and (I) spent four or five hundred *yuan* (on them).' (Haili Shi, fieldnotes)

This same construction can also be used for approximate amounts greater than ten, with the consecutive numerals able to occur in any position (e.g. ones, tens, hundreds, etc.) within a numeral phrase. Thus, for instance, 'twenty-two or twenty-three' can be expressed as *oub-gul-oub-bub-leb* [two-ten-two-three-CLF] and 'twenty-four or twenty-five' can be expressed as *oub-gul-bieib-biaob-leb* [two-ten-four-five-CLF], with the consecutive numerals in these cases still occurring in the ones position. 'Twenty or thirty' can correspondingly be expressed as *oub-bub-gul-leb* [two-three-ten-CLF] and 'forty or fifty' as *bieib-biaob-gul-leb* [four-five-ten-CLF], with the consecutive numerals here occurring in the tens position. Approximate amounts greater than one hundred can be expressed similarly.

However, there are certain restrictions on which particular numerals can thus occur in sequence within a single numeral phrase. In particular, the combinations 'one or two' and 'eight or nine' are strongly dispreferred by all of the author's primary consultants, and the combination 'nine or ten' is simply not allowed. This is true regardless of the position occupied by these combinations within the numeral phrase (e.g. in the ones position, the tens position, the hundreds position, etc.). Examples (6.202–6.204) below demonstrate these restrictions.

(6.202) ??*Mex* ***aod-oub****-gul-ngonl deb-deb.*
exist **one-two**-ten-CLF:animate child-RED
(intended: 'There are ten or twenty children [in each class].')

(6.203) ??*Aod-gaonb lis* ***il-jox****-shauk.*
one-CLF:catty want **eight-nine**-CLF:yuan
(intended: '[It] costs eight or nine *yuan* [unit of currency] per catty [unit of mass].')

(6.204) **Beul lis* ***jox-gul****-leb.*
3 want **nine-ten**-CLF
(intended: 'He wants nine or ten.')

The motivations for these restrictions seem fairly clear, although they are not identical in all three cases. First, all of the author's consultants agree that *jox-gul-leb* [nine-ten-CLF] in example (6.204) above is in fact grammatical, but it can only be interpreted as 'ninety', not as 'nine or ten' (i.e. not as an approximate amount).

In contrast, the restrictions against the sequences meaning 'one or two' and 'eight or nine' appear to be phonologically motivated. In particular, it appears that when two consecutive numerals occur in sequence to indicate an approximate amount, the tone on the first numeral must either be identical to or "precede" the tone on the second numeral in terms of the eight historical tones of Miao-Yao (see also Sections 3.5.2.1, 5.3.3.2, and 11.1.3). The Xong numerals *oub* 'two', *bub* 'three', *bieib* 'four', and *biaob* 'five' all bear the same tone (a reflex of Miao-Yao's historical tone 1), and so the combinations 'two or three', 'three or four', and 'four or five' are acceptable. Since the tone on *zhut/zhaut* 'six' is a reflex of Miao-Yao's historical tone 5, the tone on *jons* 'seven' is a reflex of historical tone 6, and the tone on *il* 'eight' is a reflex of historical tone 8, the combinations 'five or six', 'six or seven', and 'seven or eight' do not present any problems either. However, the tone on *aod* 'one' is a reflex of historical tone 3, meaning that it cannot comfortably precede *oub* 'two', whose tone is a reflex of historical tone 1. Similarly, since the tone on *il* 'eight' is a reflex of historical tone 8, it cannot comfortably occur before *jox* 'nine', whose tone is a reflex of historical tone 2.[129]

A third and final way of expressing approximate amounts in Xong is through the use of a numeral preceded by the nominal prefix *ghaob-* 'NOM' (see Section 5.4.2.1 for more on this form) and followed by the appropriate classifier. The nominal prefix *ghaob-* can only precede certain numerals in Xong, namely the non-integer numeral *mins* 'how many' (but not the non-integer numeral *daob* 'a few') and those integer numerals which are multiples of ten (*gul* 'ten', *bat* 'hundred', *canf* 'thousand', etc.). It can also precede both *mins* 'how many' and a multiple-of-ten integer numeral within the same numeral phrase (see example (6.210) below), but it never combines with integer numerals smaller than ten (i.e. *aod* 'one' through *jox* 'nine').

When it does combine with a following numeral, the prefix *ghaob-* 'NOM' has one of two semantic effects depending on the numeral in question. If the numeral is a multiple of ten, the resulting construction means 'approximately *X*, about *X*', with *X* being the numeral following *ghaob-*. This can be seen in examples (6.205–6.207) below, where *ob-gul-shauk* [NOM-ten-CLF:yuan] means 'about ten *yuan*', *ghaob-bat-meinl* [NOM-hundred-CLF:person] means 'about a hundred (teachers)', and *ghaob-canf-shauk* [NOM-thousand-CLF:yuan] means 'about a thousand *yuan*'.

129 Full credit for this observation about tonal ordering restrictions goes to the scholar Jinzhi Yu; see, for instance, Yu (2011: 69, 70). Interestingly, Yu reports that the combination 'six or seven' is disallowed in the Aizhai variety of Xong that she describes, despite the fact that the tone on 'six' is a reflex of historical tone 5 and the tone on 'seven' is a reflex of historical tone 6. Yu has no explanation for this in her 2011 work, but note that the combination 'six or seven' is fully allowed in Fenghuang Xong. This means that there is actually more evidence for Yu's tonal ordering theory in Fenghuang Xong than there is in the Aizhai Xong that Yu herself describes. (For more information on tonal ordering restrictions in the languages of greater mainland Southeast Asia in general, see Mortensen [2006: 174–270].)

(6.205) *Aod-roul* *aod-gaonb* *bid-hex.ndof* *hat* *nins*
one-CLF:time$_1$ one-CLF:catty FRT-walnut still COP
ob-gul-shauk *daont* *leh.*
NOM-ten-CLF:yuan money LEH
'Now a catty (unit of mass) of walnuts still costs about ten *yuan* (unit of currency).' (Haili Shi, fieldnotes)

(6.206) *Boub* *xox.ndaonf* *mex* ***ghaob-bat-meinl*** *lox.sid.*
1PL school exist **NOM-hundred-CLF:person** teacher
'Our school has about a hundred teachers.' (Haili Shi, fieldnotes)

(6.207) *Boub* *mex* ***ghaob-canf-shauk.***
1PL exist **NOM-thousand-CLF:yuan**
'We have about a thousand *yuan* (unit of currency).' (unknown Xong consultant, fieldnotes)

However, when the non-integer numeral *mins* 'how many' follows *ghaob-* 'NOM', the resulting construction instead means 'many' (i.e. a large but indeterminate amount). Note that the presence of a preceding *ghaob-* forces a non-interrogative reading of the ignorative *mins* (cf. Section 7.3.2.3).

(6.208) *Wel* *mex* ***ghaob-mins-leb*** *geub.bul.*
1SG exist **NOM-how.many-CLF** friend
'I have many friends.' (Lijun Wu, fieldnotes)

(6.209) *Nzaut* *ghot,* *sat* *nins* *hant* *manx* *dianx*
uncooked.rice old SAT COP CLF:PL REL finish
aob-mins-jut *naond.*
NOM-how.many-CLF:year ASSOC
'(It was) old rice, (it) had already been stored for many years.' (Xiaohui Wu, in *Conversation in La'ershan*)

(6.210) *Beul* *mex* ***ghaob-mins-bat-ngonl*** *daob-ghab.*
3 exist **NOM-how.many-hundred-CLF:animate** AN-chicken
'They have many hundreds of chickens.' (Lijun Wu, fieldnotes)

6.2.3 Other numeral-related topics

Ordinality is most often expressed in Xong by means of a construction consisting of an initial ordinal prefix *dib-* 'ORD', one of the "Sinitic" numerals discussed in Section

6.2.1 above (or a numeral phrase composed of multiple such numerals, e.g. *erk-shif-if* [two-ten-one] 'twenty-one'), and a following classifier – and then, optionally, a following noun. Examples of this can be seen in (6.211–6.214) below. Note that the phonetic form, the grammatical environment in which it occurs, and the meaning of *dib-* 'ORD' all suggest that it is a borrowing of the Standard Mandarin ordinal marker *dì* (第) or of a cognate form from another Sinitic variety.

(6.211) *Wel lis* ***dib-if/erk/sank/sib/ux/louf/qif/baof/jeux/shif-leb.***
1SG want **ORD-one/two/three/four/five/six/seven/eight/nine/ten-CLF**
'I want the first/second/third/fourth/fifth/sixth/seventh/eighth/ninth/tenth one.' (Haili Shi, fieldnotes)

(6.212) *Wel nins boub xox.ndaonb* ***dib-erk-meinl*** *Tof.box*
1SG COP 1PL school **ORD-two-CLF:person** Taobao
naond mianx.
ASSOC person
'Out of all the people at our school, I use (the popular Chinese shopping website) Taobao the second most.' (Chenghua Long, fieldnotes)

(6.213) *Wel* ***dib-sib-cif*** *ghat Dol.xid.*
1SG **ORD-four-CLF:occurrence** go.to La'ershan
'(This is) my fourth time coming to La'ershan.' (unknown Xong consultant, fieldnotes)

(6.214) *Boub bioud nins* ***dib-sank-donb.***
1PL home COP **ORD-three-CLF:building**
'Our home is (in) the third building (on the left there).' (Shixiang Wu, fieldnotes)

While Xong lacks any "native" way of referring to most ordinal concepts, 'first' and 'last' can be expressed via the forms *ghaob-kit* [NOM-begin] and *ghaob-biaob* [NOM-last]. Note that the form *kit* itself is a verb meaning 'to begin', while *ghaob-biaob* (never just **biaob*) is an idiosyncratic form that is only ever used to mean 'last' (see Section 5.4.2.1 for information on the nominal prefix *ghaob-* 'NOM'). The forms *ghaob-kit* 'first' and *ghaob-biaob* 'last' are then followed by a noun phrase that expresses the referent in question, with this noun phrase obligatorily containing a classifier. In examples (6.215–6.218) below, both *ghaob-kit/ghaob-biaob* and their following noun phrases have been bolded.

(6.215) ***Ghaob-kit oub-hnef*** *nins manx raut zhel naond,*
NOM-begin two-CLF:day COP REL good sun ASSOC
geud-zheit oub-hnef dad.kit daox nons.
place$_I$-back two-CLF:day not.until precipitate rain
'The first two days were nice and sunny, it was only raining for the next two days.' (Haili Shi, fieldnotes)

(6.216) ***Ob-kit meinl*** *beux hlit dut hliof niax*
NOM-begin CLF:person hit cooked.rice obtain many meat
guaot, geud-zheit aod-god lol beux doub
pass place$_I$-back one-CLF:human.group come hit then$_1$
jix doul niax.
NEG$_1$ remain meat
'The first person who got food (from the school cafeteria) took a ton of meat, so there wasn't any left for the people after him.' (Haili Shi, fieldnotes)

(6.217) ***Ghaob-biaob aod-meinl miex*** *lis keuf baod-zhauf.*
NOM-last one-CLF:person person want shut BUG-door
'The last person (to leave) should shut the door.' (Haili Shi, fieldnotes)

(6.218) ***Ghaob-biaob bub-ndaut*** *nins wel puk naond.*
NOM-last three-CLF:sentence COP 1SG speak ASSOC
'The last three sentences were mine.' (Shixiang Wu, fieldnotes)

Fractions and multiples can be expressed in Xong via use of the classifier *gut* 'CLF:portion' (see also Section 6.1.4.5). Fractions are syntactically discontinuous in Xong, since the denominator is represented as a numeral-classifier phrase in fronted preverbal position (with the phrase's numeral being the denominator itself, and the classifier being *gut* 'CLF:portion') while the numerator is represented as another numeral-classifier phrase in postverbal position later within the same clause (with this phrase's numeral being the numerator itself, and the classifier here again being *gut* 'CLF:portion'). The denominator expression can optionally be followed by a canonical noun expressing the referent in question (as in example (6.221) below) or by a locative noun meaning 'inside' (i.e. *ghaob-nhaons*, *nhaons-naub*, or *nhaons-ndaub*; see Section 5.5.2.7, as well as example (6.222) below). Examples of fractions are given in (6.219–6.222), where all elements of each fractional expression have been bolded.

(6.219) ***Bub-gut*** *gaons monx* ***oub-gut.***
three-CLF:portion give 2SG **two-CLF:portion**
'(I'll) give you two-thirds (of the money).' (Xingyu Shi, fieldnotes)

(6.220) ***Biaob-gut*** *wel nonx diul* ***bieib-gut.***
five-CLF:portion 1SG eat complete **four-CLF:portion**
'I ate four-fifths (of the candy).' (Shixiang Wu, fieldnotes)

(6.221) ***Bieib-gut mianx*** *monl diul* ***bub-gut.***
four-CLF:portion person go complete **three-CLF:portion**
'Three-fourths of the people have left.' (Chenghua Long, fieldnotes)

(6.222) ***Bub-gut nhaons-naub*** *wel lis* ***aod-gut.***
three-CLF:portion inside-place$_4$ 1SG want **one-CLF:portion**
'I want one-third (of the cake).' (Haili Shi, fieldnotes)

Multiples are also expressed by means of a numeral-classifier phrase containing *gut* 'CLF:portion'. The numeral within that numeral-classifier phrase refers to the multiple in question, although the original amount (i.e. the divisor of the multiple) can be expressed in a variety of different ways or simply left to context. Examples of multiples can be seen in (6.223) and (6.224) below, in which the relevant numeral-classifier phrases have been bolded.

(6.223) *Wel lis yaonl beul naond* ***bub-gut.***
1SG want much 3 ASSOC **three-CLF:portion**
'I want three times as much as him.' (Haili Shi, fieldnotes)

(6.224) *Wel oub-gul-jut, beul liox wel* ***oub-gut.***
1SG two-ten-CLF:year 3 big 1SG **two-CLF:portion**
'I'm twenty years old, and he's twice as old as me.' (Chenghua Long, fieldnotes)

Multilingual Xong speakers will generally simply switch to a Sinitic variety when there is a need to express other mathematical concepts beyond the ones already discussed in this section, including simple arithmetic. Monolingual Xong speakers make use of a variety of periphrastic constructions (often displaying significant interspeaker variation) to express the same.

7 Deictic forms

This chapter covers three small and closed (but very high-frequency) sets of forms: pronouns such as *wel* '1SG' and *manx* '2PL', demonstratives such as *neind* 'this' and *dox* 'that', and ignoratives such as *naonb* 'what, something' and *mins* 'how many, a few' (these last are forms which can essentially function as either interrogative or indefinite pro-forms depending on the discourse context; see Wierzbicka 1980). As the remainder of this chapter makes clear, these are three very distinct sets of forms, each of which has unique grammatical, referential, and functional properties. However, they are grouped together in a single chapter here because they all involve some inherent degree of deixis and because they all occur most often as either noun phrases in their own right or as constituents of larger noun phrases.

7.1 Pronouns

7.1.1 Monomorphemic personal pronouns

As is typical for the Miao-Yao family, Fenghuang Xong has a fairly small inventory of monomorphemic personal pronouns. Every variety of Fenghuang Xong investigated by the author so far has only five or six such pronouns, with the exact number depending on the particular variety in question. These inventories are thus much more similar in size and complexity to those of the Sinitic languages than to those of widely spoken mainland Southeast Asian languages like Vietnamese (see Thompson 1965: 248–252) or Lao (Enfield 2007: 77–84).

The pronominal system characteristic of Xong speakers from Yankan Village and Shanjiang Town features the five monomorphemic forms presented in Table 7.1 below.

Table 7.1: Monomorphemic pronouns of Yankan and Shanjiang Xong.

	1ST PERSON	2ND PERSON	3RD PERSON
SINGULAR	*wel*	*monx*	*beul*
PLURAL	*boub*	*manx*	

In general, the semantics of Xong's first- and second-person pronouns are exactly what their glosses would lead one to expect.[130] The form *wel* '1SG' is used to refer

130 One minor exception is that the singular pronouns *wel* '1SG' and *monx* '2SG' are strongly dispreferred (though not, strictly speaking, ungrammatical) as possessors of certain nouns, including primarily kin terms (compare *boub baox* [1PL father] 'my/our father' and ??*wel baox* [1SG father] 'my father'). See Section 8.2.1 for further discussion.

to the speaker, *monx* '2SG' to refer to a singular addressee, *boub* '1PL' to refer to any group of referents that includes the speaker (which means this form is unspecified with respect to clusivity; cf. Section 7.1.2.2), and *manx* '2PL' to refer to multiple addressees or to a group of referents that includes the addressee(s). Each of these four monomorphemic pronouns is exemplified in clause-initial position in (7.1–7.4) below.

(7.1) ***Wel*** *ghans* *ngonl* *deb-npaok* *raut* *guaot,* ***wel*** *yeb* *guaot.*
1SG see CLF:animate DIM-woman good pass **1SG** like pass
'I saw a very pretty girl, (and) I really liked her.' (Xingyu Shi, in *Deb Guk Ronf*)

(7.2) ***Boub*** *ghad* *lis* *beul* *diex.*
1PL NEG.IMP want 3 finish
'Let's just get rid of her and be done with it.' (Xingyu Shi, in *Oub Meinl Yaos Geud*)

(7.3) *Aod-ngonl* *deb-npaok* *neind,* ***monx*** *lis* *ghat* *dib* *monl?*
one-CLF:animate DIM-woman this **2SG** want go.to which go
'Little girl, where are you going?' (Haili Shi, in *Xaub Honl Mob*)

(7.4) ***Manx*** *oub-leb* *liox* *miex* *lah...*
2PL two-CLF big person PRF
'You two are all grown up...' (Xingyu Shi, in *Oub Meinl Yaos Geud*)

The system laid out in Table 7.1 features only a single third-person pronoun *beul* '3' This pronoun is regularly used to refer to both singular referents (as in example (7.5) below) and plural referents (as in examples (7.6) and (7.7)), and so it is treated here as being unspecified for number.

(7.5) ***Beul*** *jeub* *xeud* *ninb* *khauk-bioud* *hnant* *daob-guk.*
3 $then_3$ stand at hole-home call AN-frog
'He (i.e. the boy) then stood by the window and shouted for the frog.' (Chenghua Long, in *Frog, Where Are You?*)

(7.6) *Gonb.canx.daonx* *aod-god* *dox,* ***beul*** *lis* *nonx*
Communist.Party one-CLF:human.group that **3** want eat
niax-miex.
meat-person
'(The landlords lied to us villagers, they said that) those Communists, they were all cannibals.' (Qiusheng Long, in *Ngel.kanx*)

(7.7) ***Beul*** *bub-meinl* *puk* *raut* *guaot.*
3 three-CLF:person speak good pass
'Those three speak (Standard Mandarin) very well.' (Yan Long, fieldnotes)

In example (7.8) below, *beul* '3' occurs three times. It has a singular referent (namely, the father of the two sisters in question) the first and second times it occurs, but a plural referent (namely, the two sisters themselves) the third time it occurs.

(7.8) ***Beul*** *puk* *diex* *naond,* *aod-meinl* *gaons* *aod-leb*
3 speak finish ASSOC one-CLF:person give one-CLF
bid-zhonx-hlod, ***beul*** *monl* *lah.* ***Beul*** *baox* *monl* *lah.*
FRT-length-bamboo **3** go PRF **3** father go PRF
'He (i.e. the two sisters' father) finished speaking, gave each (sister) a length of bamboo, and then he left. Their (i.e. the two sisters') father left.' (Xingyu Shi, in *Oub Meinl Yaos Geud*)

The pronoun *beul* '3' is most commonly used with human referents (see examples (7.5–7.8) above), but it has also been attested being used with other animate referents (see example (7.9) below) and with inanimate referents (see example (7.10)).

(7.9) ***Beul*** *doub,* *aod-houd* *doub* *geud* *Xaub.Honl.Mob*
3 then$_1$ one-CLF:mouthful then$_1$ hold Little.Red.Hat
naond *daok* *ngheut* *ghat* *ghaob-tif.*
ASSOC maternal.grandmother swallow go.to NOM-stomach
'He (i.e. the wolf) then swallowed up Little Red Hat's (maternal) grandmother in one bite.' (Haili Shi, in *Xaub Honl Mob*)

(7.10) *Naont* ***beul*** *mb* *guaot.*
thus **3** hurt pass
'So it (i.e. my tooth) really hurt.' (Haili Shi, in *Tooth Conversation*)

Unlike Xong speakers from Yankan Village and Shanjiang Town, speakers from La'ershan Town and many of its surrounding villages (aside from Yankan, that is) have a distinct third-person plural pronoun *miant* '3PL'. Even for these speakers, *beul* '3' can still be used for either singular or plural referents, but *miant* '3PL' can naturally only be used for plural referents. Examples of *miant* '3PL' can be seen in (7.11) and (7.12) below.

(7.11) ***Miant*** *sheib* *beux* *pax.*
3PL able.to hit playing.card
'They know how to play cards.' (Shixiang Wu, fieldnotes)

(7.12) ***Miant*** *aod-meinl* *chot* *daut* *aod-leb* *bid-raox.*
3PL one-CLF:person take obtain one-CLF FRT-pear
'Each of them took one pear.' (Lijun Wu, in *Pear Story*)

Note also that many of these speakers from La'ershan Town and its surrounding villages (aside from Yankan) regularly produce '2SG' as *mx* rather than *monx* (cf. the discussion of syllabic bilabial nasals in Yankan Xong in Section 3.3.4). The monomorphemic pronominal system of these speakers is represented in Table 7.2 below.

Table 7.2: Monomorphemic pronouns of La'ershan Xong.

	1ST PERSON	2ND PERSON	3RD PERSON
SINGULAR	*wel*	*mx*	*beul*
PLURAL	*boub*	*manx*	*miant*

As was briefly mentioned earlier in Section 5.2.1, Xong's personal pronouns can be considered "defective" or non-canonical nouns in that they show significant functional and distributional overlap with Xong's canonical nouns but do not strictly satisfy the two diagnostic criteria that are used in this grammar to define nounhood (namely, the ability to co-occur with a preceding numeral-classifier phrase and the ability to be modified by a *manx* relative clause). Functionally, Xong's pronouns strongly resemble canonical nouns in that they very often serve as noun phrases which in turn serve as arguments of verbs (see examples (7.13) and (7.14)) or as possessors of other noun phrases (examples (7.15) and (7.16)).

(7.13) ***Wel*** *at* *niab* *del* ***beul*** *gint* *diul* *khad.*
1SG SAT say let **3** rot complete dry
'I say just let it (i.e. my tooth) rot.' (Haili Shi, in *Tooth Conversation*)

(7.14) ***Beul*** *baond* *aod-hmaont* *jik.qaonk.*
3 shoot one-CLF:evening machine.gun
'He fired the machine gun all evening.' (Qiusheng Long, in *Ngel.kanx*)

(7.15) *Aod-ngonl* *guk* *ndanb* *ghat* ***wel*** ***ob-nqad,*** *minx.xaond*
one-CLF:animate frog jump go.to **1SG** **NOM-bucket** dirty
wel ***naond*** ***aub.***
1SG **ASSOC** **water**
'The frog jumped into my bucket, it got my water all dirty.' (Xingyu Shi, in *Deb Guk Ronf*)

(7.16) *Geud,* *geud,* ***boub*** ***baox*** *nzhaod.*
younger.sibling younger.sibling **1PL** **father** return
'Little sister, little sister, our father has returned.' (Xingyu Shi, in *Oub Meinl Yaos Geud*)

However, Xong's personal pronouns generally cannot be possessed by other noun phrases. Two minor exceptions to this are the fixed expressions given in (7.17) and (7.18) below, which are used as intimate terms of address between spouses.

(7.17) *wel* *naond* *mx*
1SG ASSOC 2SG
'you, my spouse (lit. 'my you')' (Xiaohui Wu, fieldnotes)

(7.18) *mx* *naond* *wel*
2SG ASSOC 1SG
'I, your spouse (lit. 'your me')' (Xiaohui Wu, fieldnotes)

Also like canonical nouns, pronouns often co-occur with a numeral-classifier phrase, typically one featuring one of the three classifiers *leb* 'CLF', *meinl* 'CLF:person', and *ngonl* 'CLF:animate'. However, while numeral-classifier phrases precede canonical (i.e. non-pronominal) nouns (see Section 6.1.2.1), they instead follow pronouns, as in examples (7.19–7.21) below. (Example (7.21) has been repeated from (7.7) above.) Furthermore, there is evidence that such post-pronominal numeral-classifier phrases do not form a constituent with their preceding pronouns, or at least not in the same way that prenominal numeral-classifier phrases form a constituent with their following nouns; see Section 6.1.2.2 for details.

(7.19) ***Boub*** ***bieib-meinl*** *at* *sheib* *puk.*
1PL **four-CLF:person** SAT able.to speak
'The four of us can all speak (Xong).' (Chenghua Long, fieldnotes)

(7.20) ***Manx*** ***oub-leb*** *jont* *bioud,* *ghad.maons* *id-beux* *id-ndaot.*
2PL **two-CLF** live home NEG.IMP DID-hit DID-curse
'You two stay here, not fighting and not arguing.' (Xingyu Shi, in *Oub Meinl Yaos Geud*)

(7.21) ***Beul*** ***bub-meinl*** *puk* *raut* *guaot.*
3 **three-CLF:person** speak good pass
'Those three speak (Standard Mandarin) very well.' (Yan Long, fieldnotes)

It is very difficult to get consultants to accept pronouns that co-occur with a preceding numeral-classifier phrase or with a *manx* relative clause, which again are the two diagnostic characteristics of Xong nouns laid out in Section 5.2.1.

(7.22) ??*bub-leb* ***boub***
three-CLF **1PL**
(intended: 'three of us, the three of us')

(7.23) ??*manx* *nonx* *hlit* *naond* ***manx***
REL eat cooked.rice ASSOC **2PL**
(intended: 'those of you who are eating, you who are eating')

Consultants will sometimes accept constructions like those in examples (7.22) and (7.23) when presented with a suitably bizarre scenario (e.g. one involving cloning, resulting in multiple "me's" or multiple "you's"), but they only do so grudgingly, and they never produce such constructions themselves. While this may be due more to the pragmatic oddness of the constructions in question than to their strict ungrammaticality, this restriction – whatever its cause – still means that Xong pronouns cannot be considered canonical examples of Xong nouns.

Finally, just as with canonical nouns, Xong's pronouns never vary for case or noun class/gender. However, these pronouns are much more active with respect to number than are canonical nouns. Aside from the distinct singular and plural monomorphemic pronouns already discussed in this section (e.g. *wel* '1SG' vs. *boub* '1PL'), Xong speakers also make use of several morphological strategies for marking pronominal number. These strategies are discussed in Section 7.1.2 below.

7.1.2 Polymorphemic personal pronouns

In addition to the monomorphemic personal pronouns discussed in Section 7.1.1 above, Fenghuang Xong speakers also regularly make use of a variety of morphologically complex pronouns. These are derived from monomorphemic pronouns via processes of suffixation, compounding, or both.

7.1.2.1 Pronouns with dual or plural suffixes

Any monomorphemic non-singular pronoun (i.e. *boub* '1PL', *manx* '2PL', *beul* '3', and *miant* '3PL') can take either the dual suffix *-leb* 'DU' or the plural suffix *-god/-gud* 'PL' (note that the form *-god* is characteristic of speakers from La'ershan Town and its surrounding villages, while speakers from Shanjiang Town have *-gud*). For all speakers, this includes the first-person and second-person plural pronouns *boub* '1PL' and *manx* '2PL', as shown in examples (7.24–7.27) below. Pronouns bearing the plural suffix *-god/-gud* 'PL' can be used to refer to groups of two referents or to groups of more than two referents, while those bearing the dual suffix *-leb* 'DU' can only be used to refer to groups of exactly two referents.

(7.24) ***Boub-leb*** *nieus* *reib-yeus.*
1PL-DU buy vegetable-cooked.meat
'Let's we two go buy groceries.' (Yan Long, fieldnotes)

(7.25) ***Manx-leb*** *ox beul monl ngheint aub.*
2PL-DU and 3 go carry.on.shoulder.pole water
'You two go with him to get water (using shoulder-poles).' (Haili Shi, fieldnotes)

(7.26) ***Boub-gud*** *ox monx monl puk, ix mex nqat naond.*
1PL-PL and 2SG go speak NEG_1 exist fear ASSOC
'We'll go with you to explain, there's nothing to be afraid of.' (Chenghua Long, fieldnotes)

(7.27) ***Manx-god*** *jont chauk-naonb?*
2PL-PL sit do-what
'What are you all doing sitting (there)?' (Shixiang Wu, fieldnotes)

For those consultants whose only monomorphemic third-person pronoun is *beul* '3' (see Section 7.1.1 above), the suffixes *-leb* 'DU' and *-god/-gud* 'PL' can attach to it as well. The resulting form *beul-leb* [3-DU] is used to refer to groups of exactly two referents, and the resulting form *beul-god* (or *beul-gud*) [3-PL] is used to refer to groups of two or more referents.

(7.28) ***Beul-leb*** *nins wel naond geub.bul.*
3-DU COP 1SG ASSOC friend
'Those two are my friends.' (Yan Long, fieldnotes)

(7.29) ***Beul-gud*** *niab, ix bud beul.*
3-PL say NEG_1 tell 3
'They (i.e. everyone) said not to tell him.' (Chenghua Long, in *Conversation in La'ershan*)

(7.30) ***Beul-god*** *nzhaod dand diex roul-deb, aod-ngonl*
3-PL return arrive finish CLF:$time_1$-DIM one-CLF:animate
deb-guk sat nzhaod dand.
DIM-frog SAT return arrive
'A little while after they (i.e. the woman and her mother-in-law) had returned, the frog returned as well.' (Xingyu Shi, in *Deb Guk Ronf*)

However, for those consultants who have a distinct monomorphemic third-person plural pronoun *miant* '3PL' (again, see Section 7.1.1), the suffixes *-leb* 'DU' and *-god/-gud* 'PL' will generally only be used with that third-person plural pronoun, not with *beul* '3'. These consultants do not outright reject the use of *beul-leb* and *beul-god*, but they report that they would almost always use *miant-leb* and *miant-god* instead.

(7.31) ***Miant-leb*** *deib* *dox* *nghauk.zaol.*
3PL-DU at that play
'Those two are playing over there.' (Lijun Wu, fieldnotes)

(7.32) ***Miant-god*** *yaod.yaod* *at* *monl.*
3PL-PL all SAT go
'They've all left.' (Shixiang Wu, fieldnotes)

The semantics of *-leb* 'DU' are fairly clear: the use of a monomorphemic pronoun bearing this suffix entails that the members of the referent group are exactly two in number. It is important to note here that the monomorphemic non-singular pronouns *boub* '1PL', *manx* '2PL', *beul* '3', and (for consultants who have it) *miant* '3PL' can also be used for referent groups whose members are two in number; the difference is that these monomorphemic pronouns can also be used for referent groups larger in number, while pronouns bearing *-leb* 'DU' cannot.[131]

Etymologically, the suffix *-leb* 'DU' itself seems likely to be the result of a shortening of *oub-leb* [two-CLF] 'two (people, things)' (for more information on *leb* 'CLF', see Section 6.1.4.1). In fact, monomorphemic non-singular pronouns followed by *oub-leb* [two-CLF] are also very often used to refer to groups of two referents.

(7.33) ***Boub*** ***oub-leb*** *nins* *manx* *raut* *geub.bul.*
1PL **two-CLF** COP REL good friend
'We two are good friends.' (Yan Long, fieldnotes)

(7.34) ***Beul*** ***oub-leb*** *deit* *npieut* *ah,* *deit* *npieut* *ah,* *ix* *hnaond*
3 **two-CLF** still shout PART still shout PART NEG_1 hear
daob-guk *doub.*
AN-frog answer
'They two (i.e. the boy and his dog) kept shouting and shouting, (but) they didn't hear the frog reply.' (Chenghua Long, in *Frog, Where Are You?*)

However, it seems clear that at this point *-leb* 'DU' is quite grammaticalized, and thus its gloss of 'DU' (rather than simply 'CLF') is justified. Other semantically similar classifiers like *meinl* 'CLF:person' and *ngonl* 'CLF:animate' can never be used as dual suffixes, and *-leb* 'DU' can only attach to (non-singular) pronouns, never to canonical nouns or other forms.

The exact semantic contribution of *-god/-gud* 'PL' to pronouns on which it appears is less clear. After fairly extensive investigation of the topic with several

131 This is similar to the way in which, for example, English *we* can be used for groups of two referents or more than two referents, but *we two* can only be used for groups of exactly two referents.

different consultants on several different occasions, it seems that in every situation in which a monomorphemic pronoun bearing the suffix *-god/gud* 'PL' can be used, that same monomorphemic pronoun could also be used without the plural suffix, with no change in meaning. Effectively, this means that *-god/ -gud* 'PL' is always optional, including in examples (7.35) and (7.36) below and in other examples throughout this section.

(7.35)	***Beul(-god)***	*nins*	*ghaob-zhaol.*
	3(-PL)	COP	NOM-non.Miao

'They're not Miao.' (Haili Shi, fieldnotes)

(7.36)	*Kiot,*	***beul(-gud)***	*deit*	*lis*	*ndanx*	*nzhaod.*
	strange	**3(-PL)**	still	want	lift.up	return

'(I thought it was) strange, they still wanted to carry (the old woman's body) back (to her village).' (Chenghua Long, in *Conversation in La'ershan*)

Both the author's own observations and his consultants' explicit comments suggest that the addition of *-god/-gud* 'PL' to a pronoun simply serves to emphasize the plurality of the pronoun's referents, rather than to explicitly signal it.

Etymologically, it seems likely that the suffix *-god/-gud* 'PL' is related to the homophonous classifier *god/gud* 'CLF:human.group' (see Section 6.1.4.4), instances of which can be seen in (7.37) and (7.38) below.

(7.37)	*Monx*	*ix*	*nianl,*	*aod-**gud***	*nzhaond*	*dand*	*deut-ndaut...*
	2SG	NEG_1	know	one-**CLF:human.group**	return	arrive	foot-tree

'Don't you know, (when) everyone had returned to the foot of the tree...' (Chenghua Long, in *Conversation in La'ershan*)

(7.38)	*Aod-**gud***	*deb-deb*	*xeud*	*chauk*	*nbax.*
	one-**CLF:human.group**	child-RED	stand	do	CLF:row

'The children are standing in a row.' (Chenghua Long, fieldnotes)

Just as with *-leb* 'DU', *-god/-gud* 'PL' can never occur as a plural suffix on canonical (i.e. non-pronominal) nouns, although unlike *-leb* it can attach to the "semi-pronominal" form *nex/ninx* 'NEX'; see Section 7.1.4 for discussion.

All attested combinations of monomorphemic pronouns, dual suffixes, and plural suffixes are represented in Tables 7.3 and 7.4 below. Table 7.3 represents the speech of Xong speakers from Yankan Village and Shanjiang Town, while Table 7.4 represents that of Xong speakers from La'ershan Town and its surrounding villages (aside from Yankan). For simplicity's sake, alternate pronunciations of particular morphemes (e.g. *-god/-gud* 'PL') are ignored within these two tables.

Table 7.3: Monomorphemic and suffix-bearing pronouns of Yankan and Shanjiang Xong.

<table>
<tr><th></th><th>1ST PERSON</th><th>2ND PERSON</th><th>3RD PERSON</th></tr>
<tr><td>MONOMORPHEMIC SINGULAR</td><td>wel</td><td>monx</td><td rowspan="2">beul</td></tr>
<tr><td>MONOMORPHEMIC PLURAL</td><td>boub</td><td>manx</td></tr>
<tr><td>SUFFIX-BEARING DUAL</td><td>boub-leb</td><td>manx-leb</td><td>beul-leb</td></tr>
<tr><td>SUFFIX-BEARING PLURAL</td><td>boub-god</td><td>manx-god</td><td>beul-god</td></tr>
</table>

Table 7.4: Monomorphemic and suffix-bearing pronouns of La'ershan Xong.

	1ST PERSON	2ND PERSON	3RD PERSON
MONOMORPHEMIC SINGULAR	*wel*	*mx*	*beul*
MONOMORPHEMIC PLURAL	*boub*	*manx*	*miant*
SUFFIX-BEARING DUAL	*boub-leb*	*manx-leb*	*miant-leb*
SUFFIX-BEARING PLURAL	*boub-god*	*manx-god*	*miant-god*

7.1.2.2 Clusive pronouns

Fenghuang Xong features two *clusive pronouns*, which are trimorphemic pronominal forms that differ from all pronouns discussed in earlier sections of this chapter in at least two respects: they are specified for clusivity (i.e. each is either obligatorily inclusive or exclusive), and they each contain two of the monomorphemic personal pronouns discussed in Section 7.1.1.

The first of these clusive pronouns is *boub-leb-monx* (or *boub-leb-mx* for some speakers) [1PL-DU-2SG] 'we two (inclusive)'. This form contains the monomorphemic pronouns *boub* '1PL' and *monx/mx* '2SG', which are joined together by an intervening *-leb* 'DU'. It is used only to refer to the (singular) speaker, the (singular) addressee, and no other referents, and it thus serves as an inclusive dual pronoun. Examples of its use can be seen in (7.39) and (7.40).

(7.39) ***Boub-leb-mx*** *kiad* *njaonx.*
1PL-DU-2SG attend weekly.market
'Let's you and I go to the weekly market.' (Shixiang Wu, fieldnotes)

(7.40) ***Boub-leb-monx*** *nins* *manx* *raut* *geub.bul.*
1PL-DU-2SG COP REL good friend
'You and I are good friends.' (Haili Shi, fieldnotes)

The second clusive pronoun is *boub-leb-beul* [1PL-DU-3] 'we two (exclusive)'. This contains the monomorphemic pronouns *boub* '1PL' and *beul* '3' joined by an intervening *-leb* 'DU'. It is used only to refer to the (singular) speaker and to some other (singular) referent who is *not* the addressee, and it thus serves as an exclusive dual pronoun. Examples of its use can be seen in (7.41) and (7.42).

(7.41) *Nins* ***boub-leb-beul*** *naond.*
COP **1PL-DU-3** ASSOC
'It belongs to me and him.' (Yan Long, fieldnotes)

(7.42) ***Boub-leb-beul*** *yanb did-ndaot yaonl.*
1PL-DU-3 like DID-curse much
'She and I really like arguing with each other.' (Shixiang Wu, fieldnotes)

While the structural and semantic differences between these two clusive pronouns and the other pronominal forms already discussed in Sections 7.1.1 and 7.1.2.1 are fairly clear, care must be taken to distinguish them from certain other, superficially similar pronominal constructions that have not yet been discussed. In particular, it is not uncommon for two pronouns to occur in juxtaposition to each other (i.e. in zero-marked conjunction; see Section 8.3), which sometimes results in constructions that greatly resemble (at least in terms of surface structure) the clusive pronouns just introduced. Examples of such juxtaposed pronominal constructions are given in (7.43–7.46) below.

(7.43) ***Manx-leb wel*** *jix nins geub.bul.*
2PL-DU 1SG NEG$_1$ COP friend
'You two and I (*you [sg.] and I) aren't friends.' (Yan Long, fieldnotes)

(7.44) ***Manx-leb beul*** *deib chauk naonb oh?*
2PL-DU 3 at do what PART
'What are you two and he/she/they (*you [sg.] and he/*you [sg.] and she/*you [sg.] and they) up to?' (Haili Shi, fieldnotes)

(7.45) ***Beul-leb wel*** *jix monl.*
3-DU 1SG NEG$_1$ go
'They two and I (*he and I/*she and I) aren't going.' (Yan Long, fieldnotes)

(7.46) ***Boub-god beul*** *yaod.yaod nins ghaob-Xonb.*
1PL-PL 3 all COP NOM-Miao
'We and she (i.e. we three teachers and this young girl) are all Miao.' (Shixiang Wu, fieldnotes)

On the surface, the juxtaposed pronominal constructions in examples (7.43–7.46) greatly resemble the clusive pronouns *boub-leb-monx* 'we two (incl.)' and *boub-leb-beul* 'we two (excl.)'. Like those clusive pronouns, each of these juxtaposed constructions involves an initial non-singular monomorphemic pronoun (*boub* '1PL', *manx* '2PL', or *beul* '3'), a following dual (or sometimes plural) suffix, and a final monomorphemic pronoun that can be used to refer to a singular referent (*wel* '1SG', *monx* '2SG', or *beul* '3.).

However, in terms of semantic structure there is a very clear difference between the clusive pronouns *boub-leb-monx* 'we two (incl.)' and *boub-leb-beul* 'we two (excl.)' on the one hand and the juxtaposed constructions in (7.43–7.46) on the other: namely, the semantics of the juxtaposed constructions are fully predictable from the semantics of their constituent pronouns, while this is not true for the clusive pronouns. This is clearly demonstrated by the ability of the juxtaposed pronominal constructions in examples (7.43–7.46) to have their constituents overtly joined by *ox/ux* 'and' (rather than merely juxtaposed) with no change in meaning (for more on the form *ox/ux*, see Section 8.3). This can be seen by comparing examples (7.47–7.50) below, which contain *ox/ux* 'and', with examples (7.43–7.46) above, which do not. The meanings of the two members of each of these four pairs of examples (i.e. examples (7.43) and (7.47), (7.44) and (7.48), (7.45) and (7.49), and (7.46) and (7.50)) are identical, regardless of the presence or absence of *ox/ux*.

(7.47) ***Manx-leb ox wel*** *jix nins geub.bul.*
2PL-DU and 1SG NEG_1 COP friend
'You two and I (*you [sg.] and I) aren't friends.' (Yan Long, fieldnotes)

(7.48) ***Manx-leb ox beul*** *deib chauk naonb oh?*
2PL-DU and 3 at do what PART
'What are you two and he/she/they (*you [sg.] and he/*you [sg.] and she/*you [sg.] and they) up to?' (Haili Shi, fieldnotes)

(7.49) ***Beul-leb ox wel*** *jix monl.*
3-DU and 1SG NEG_1 go
'They two and I (*he and I/*she and I) aren't going.' (Yan Long, fieldnotes)

(7.50) ***Boub-god ox beul*** *yaod.yaod nins ghaob-Xonb.*
1PL-PL and 3 all COP NOM-Miao
'We and she (i.e. we three teachers and this young girl) are all Miao.' (Shixiang Wu, fieldnotes)

Thus, for example, the meaning of the juxtaposed pronominal construction *manx-leb wel* [2PL-DU 1SG] 'you two and I' is identical to the combined meanings of *manx-leb* [2PL-DU] 'you two' and *wel* [1SG] 'I', and the meaning of *manx-leb beul* [2PL-DU 3] 'you two and he/she/they' is identical to the combined meanings of *manx-leb* [2PL-DU] 'you two' and *beul* [3] 'he/she/they'.

However, this is not true for the clusive pronouns *boub-leb-monx* 'we two (incl.)' and *boub-leb-beul* 'we two (excl.)'. The meaning of the pronoun *boub-leb-monx* [1PL-DU-2SG] 'we two (incl.)' is *not* identical to the combined meanings of *boub-leb* [1PL-DU] 'we two' and *monx* [2SG] 'you (sg.)', and the meaning of the pronoun *boub-leb-beul* [1PL-DU-3] 'we two (excl.)' is *not* identical to the combined meanings of *boub-leb* [1PL-DU] 'we two' and *beul* [3] 'he/she/they'. This can be seen most clearly by joining the constituents of these clusive pronouns with *ox/ux* 'and'. While this does not result in ungrammatical utterances, the resulting constructions necessarily refer to at least three referents, while the clusive pronouns *boub-leb-monx* and *boub-leb-beul* necessarily refer to exactly two referents. This is shown in examples (7.51) and (7.52) below.

(7.51) ***Boub-leb*** *ox* ***monx*** *chauk.geud monl chauk miex-khat.*
1PL-DU **and** **2SG** together go do person-guest
'We two and you (sg.) (*I and you [sg.]) are going to visit someone (lit. 'are going to be guests').' (Yan Long, fieldnotes) (cf. *boub-leb-monx* [1PL-DU-2SG] 'I and you [sg.]')

(7.52) ***Boub-leb*** *ox* ***beul*** *yaod.yaod nins Dol.xid naond.*
1PL-DU **and** **3** all COP La'ershan ASSOC
'We two and he/she/they (*I and he/she/they) are all from La'ershan.' (Haili Shi, fieldnotes) (cf. *boub-leb-beul* [1PL-DU-3] 'I and he/she/they')

7.1.3 Reflexive pronouns

Reflexive constructions (i.e. monoclausal constructions in which two or more noun phrases with distinct semantic roles are coreferential) in Fenghuang Xong obligatorily involve one of three morphologically complex reflexive pronouns: *daut-leb* [REFL-CLF] 'oneself', *baod-dauk* [BUG-REFL] 'oneself', or *baod-dauk-leb* [BUG-REFL-CLF] 'oneself'. These three forms are obviously related, with each of them involving the morpheme *daut/dauk* 'REFL' (the *-t* ~ *-k* tonal variation here is at present inexplicable), and furthermore the trimorphemic form *baod-dauk-leb* appears to simply be the result of a merger between the dimorphemic forms *baod-dauk* and *daut-leb* (or, conversely, the latter two forms may be the result of a split in the former form). All three forms seem to be completely interchangeable, with no discernible differences in meaning or pragmatic import among them, although individual consultants tend to favor the use of just one or two particular forms rather than freely switching among all three.

These reflexive forms can also be considered non-canonical (or "defective") examples of nouns. Like the personal pronouns discussed in Sections 7.1.1 and 7.1.2 above, they show a large degree of functional overlap with canonical nouns, as they very often function as noun phrases which in turn function as arguments of verbs or as possessors of other noun phrases (see examples (7.53–7.57) below). However, unlike canonical nouns, reflexive pronouns in Xong cannot be modified by *manx* relative clauses and generally cannot co-occur with a preceding numeral-classifier phrase (although one minor exception to the latter claim about numeral-classifier phrases is discussed at the end of this section).

Each of examples (7.53–7.58) below features a reflexive pronoun. In examples (7.53) and (7.54), each reflexive pronoun's antecedent noun phrase is *monx* '2SG', which occurs in initial position in example (7.53) and midway through example (7.54). Note that in addition to such antecedent noun phrases, all three of the reflexive forms under discussion here – *daut-leb*, *baod-dauk*, and *baod-dauk-leb* – also always have the option of being immediately preceded by a coreferential personal pronoun, with the presence or absence of this pronoun having no apparent effect on meaning or pragmatics.

(7.53) *Monx ghad.maons beux (monx)* ***daut-leb*** *lah!*
2SG NEG.IMP hit (2SG) **REFL-CLF** PRF
'Don't hit yourself!' (Haili Shi, fieldnotes)

(7.54) *Bionl dand geud-zheit monx lis tank raut (monx)*
exit arrive place$_1$-outside 2SG want take.care.of good (2SG)
baod-dauk-leb.
BUG-REFL-CLF
'You need to take care of yourself while you're away from home.' (Chenghua Long, fieldnotes)

In example (7.55), the reflexive pronoun's antecedent noun phrase is *wel* '1SG', and in examples (7.56) and (7.57), the reflexive pronoun's antecedent noun phrase is *beul* '3'. All of these antecedent noun phrases occur clause-initially, and, again, the reflexive pronouns in these examples also have the option of being immediately preceded by a coreferential personal pronoun.

(7.55) *Wel kif (wel)* ***daut-leb*** *naond guaot.*
1SG angry (1SG) **REFL-CLF** ASSOC pass
'I'm really angry at myself.' (Chenghua Long, fieldnotes)

(7.56) *Beul zhaos job.gind nhaons-daub ghans (beul)* ***daut-leb.***
3 from mirror inside-place$_4$ see (3) **REFL-CLF**
'She saw herself in the mirror.' (Shixiang Wu, fieldnotes)

(7.57) *Beul ghab (beul)* ***daut-leb.***
3 bite (3) **REFL-CLF**
'It (i.e. the dog) bit itself.' (Chenghua Long, fieldnotes)

In example (7.58), *daut-leb* [REFL-CLF] is coreferential with the clause-initial noun phrase *monx* '2SG', but it serves as the possessor of the noun phrase *deb-geud* 'little sister' rather than as an argument of any verb (the form *lieif* 'even' is non-verbal).

(7.58) *Monx lieif (monx)* ***daut-leb*** *naond deb-geud at*
2SG even (2SG) **REFL-CLF** ASSOC DIM-younger.sibling SAT
jix ndiot!
NEG_1 recognize
'You don't even recognize your own little sister!' (Haili Shi, fieldnotes)

Any of Xong's reflexive pronouns can be used in an emphatic function, similar to the emphatic use of English reflexive pronouns in expressions like *I'll do it (all by)* ***myself***.[132] In fact, this usage is if anything even more frequent than the usage of these pronouns in canonical reflexive constructions, at least in the author's own collected Xong texts. When serving this emphatic function, Xong's reflexive pronouns are usually preceded by a coreferential personal pronoun that makes clear the referent of the reflexive pronoun itself. This can be seen in examples (7.59–7.62) below.

(7.59) *Aod-dieud dox leh,* ***wel daut-leb*** *dieud hlit*
one-$CLF:time_2$ that LEH **1SG REFL-CLF** boil.rice cooked.rice
daut-leb *nonx.*
REFL-CLF eat
'Back then, I'd boil rice all by myself and eat (it) all by myself.' (Qiusheng Long, in *Qiusheng Long's Life History*)

(7.60) ***Mx baod-dauk-leb*** *monl chauk.*
2SG BUG-REFL-CLF go do
'Go do it yourself.' (Shixiang Wu, fieldnotes)

(7.61) ***Monx*** *at* ***daut-leb*** *zhut beul, lis nieus nggaob hauk-naonb?*
2SG SAT **REFL-CLF** cure 3 want buy medicine do-what
'You can just treat it (i.e. your tooth) yourself, so what do you need to buy medicine for?' (Chenghua Long, in *Tooth Conversation*)

(7.62) *Daos nhaons-aub, doul* ***beul daut-leb*** *dionb deb nzhaod.*
die inside-water remain **3 REFL-CLF** lead child return
'(Her sister) drowned in the water, leaving only her to bring the child back.' (Xingyu Shi, in *Oub Meinl Yaos Geud*)

132 And also, for that matter, similar to the emphatic use of the Standard Mandarin reflexive form *zìjǐ* (自己) in expressions like *Wǒ zìjǐ lái zuò* (我自己来做) [1SG REFL come do] 'I'll do it myself'.

However, this preceding personal pronoun can be left out when the referent of the reflexive pronoun is obvious from context, as in examples (7.63) and (7.64), or when the reflexive pronoun has no specific referent, as in example (7.65).

(7.63) ***Daut-leb*** *chauk.*
REFL-CLF do
'Do it (your)self.' (Haili Shi, fieldnotes)

(7.64) *Tief.xok.yok* *haf* *deit* *nins* ***baod-dauk-leb*** *naond*
high.quality.medicine still still COP **BUG-REFL-CLF** ASSOC
aod-banb *dox,* *ux* *Hex* *yaox?*
one-CLF:some that and PN right?
'The best medicine is still that stuff of your own, isn't that right, He?' (Chenghua Long, fieldnotes)

(7.65) ***Baod-dauk*** *naond* *sib* ***baod-dauk*** *guant.*
BUG-REFL ASSOC matter **BUG-REFL** care
'One should take care of one's own affairs.' (Shixiang Wu, fieldnotes)

Reflexive pronouns in Xong can also serve a logophoric function in subordinate clauses (see Section 12.4), in that they can be used to explicitly signal the coreferentiality of a noun phrase in the subordinate clause with a noun phrase in the matrix clause. This logophoric use of reflexive pronouns is much less common than the emphatic use just discussed, but the relevant data does seem robust. For instance, note that the second occurrence of *beul* '3'(within a subordinate clause) in each of examples (7.66) and (7.67) below may – but need not – be coreferential with the first occurrence of *beul* '3' (within a matrix clause) in the same example.

(7.66) ***Beul*** *niab* ***beul*** *monl* *lah.*
3 say **3** go PRF
'He$_i$ said he$_i$ left.' *or* 'He$_i$ said he$_j$ left.' (Shixiang Wu, fieldnotes)

(7.67) ***Beul*** *niel* ***beul*** *jix* *sheib* *yeb* *nonx.*
3 know **3** NEG$_1$ able.to like eat
'She$_i$ knew she$_i$ wouldn't like (the food).' *or* 'She$_i$ knew she$_j$ wouldn't like (the food).' (Haili Shi, fieldnotes)

Examples (7.68) and (7.69) below are identical to examples (7.66) and (7.67) above except for the fact that the second occurrence of *beul* '3' (within the subordinate clause) in each example has been replaced with a reflexive pronoun. This replacement now forces a reading of each example in which the clause-initial *beul* '3' (within the matrix clause) is coreferential with the reflexive pronoun (within the subordinate clause).

(7.68) ***Beul*** *niab* ***daut-leb*** *monl* *lah.*
3 say **REFL-CLF** go PRF
'He$_i$ said he$_i$ left.' (*'He$_i$ said he$_j$ left.') (Shixiang Wu, fieldnotes)

(7.69) ***Beul*** *niel* ***baod-dauk-leb*** *jix* *sheib* *yeb* *nonx.*
3 know **BUG-REFL-CLF** NEG$_1$ able.to like eat
'She$_i$ knew she$_i$ wouldn't like (the food).' (*'She$_i$ knew she$_j$ wouldn't like [the food].') (Haili Shi, fieldnotes)

In examples (7.70) and (7.71) below, each subordinate clause now contains both an initial pronoun *beul* '3' and a following reflexive pronoun. Although the relevant data available to the author is still fairly scant, these two examples appear to show an interesting interaction between the emphatic and logophoric functions of reflexive pronouns in Xong. In example (7.70), one possible reading involves the coreferentiality of *beul* '3' in the matrix clause with the noun phrase *beul daut-leb* [3 REFL-CLF] in the subordinate clause. Under this reading, the reflexive pronoun is essentially serving a logophoric function, as it serves to mark the noun phrase in which it occurs as coreferential with *beul* '3' in the matrix clause.

(7.70) ***Beul*** *niab* ***beul*** ***daut-leb*** *monl* *lah.*
3 say **3** **REFL-CLF** go PRF
'He$_i$ said he$_i$ left.' *or* 'He$_i$ said he$_j$ left by himself.' (Shixiang Wu, fieldnotes)

However, another possible reading involves the *non*-coreferentiality of *beul* '3' in the matrix clause with *beul daut-leb* [3 REFL-CLF] in the subordinate clause. Under this reading, the reflexive pronoun is interpreted as being coreferential with the immediately preceding *beul* '3' (within the subordinate clause) alone, and it is also interpreted as serving an emphatic function rather than a logophoric one. Thus, example (7.70) above can mean either 'He$_i$ said he$_i$ left' or 'He$_i$ said he$_j$ left by himself'. It appears that only context allows the hearer to determine which of these two possible readings was the intended one.

In contrast, only one reading is possible for example (7.71) below, despite the fact that the subordinate clause in this example – like the one in example (7.70) above – contains both an initial pronoun *beul* '3' and a following reflexive pronoun. Here, the only possible reading involves the coreferentiality of *beul* '3' in the matrix clause with the noun phrase *beul baod-dauk-leb* [3 BUG-REFL-CLF] in the subordinate clause, with the reflexive pronoun essentially serving a logophoric function. Although more investigation is still needed, the author suspects that the impossibility of an emphatic (rather than logophoric) reading here is primarily due to a semantic clash between the high degree of agentivity associated with the emphatic use of reflexive pronouns in Xong and the low degree of agentivity associated with the verb *yeb* 'to like'.

(7.71) ***Beul*** *niel* ***beul*** ***baod-dauk-leb*** *jix* *sheib* *yeb* *nonx.*
3 know **3** **BUG-REFL-CLF** NEG_1 able.to like eat
'She$_i$ knew she$_i$ wouldn't like (the food).' (Haili Shi, fieldnotes) (same as (7.69) above)

Finally, although *daut/dauk* 'REFL' most often occurs as a constituent morpheme of one of the polymorphemic reflexive pronouns discussed above (e.g. *baod-dauk*, *daut-leb*), it occasionally occurs independently. In such cases it is always immediately preceded by either (i) a numeral-classifier phrase consisting of a numeral followed by *leb* 'CLF' or *meinl* 'CLF:person' (e.g. *aod-leb* [one-CLF], *oub-meinl* [two-CLF:person]) or (ii) a bare classifier *leb* 'CLF' or *meinl* 'CLF:person' (for more on numeral-classifier phrases and bare classifiers, see Sections 6.1.2 and 6.1.3.1, respectively).[133] This numeral-classifier phrase or bare classifier itself is in turn always preceded by a personal pronoun such as *boub* '1PL' or *monx* '2SG'. (Still, the fact that the reflexive form in question can occur with a preceding numeral-classifier phrase at all seems to suggest that it may once have been a fairly canonical member of the noun class.) When occurring independently like this, 'REFL' is always realized as *dauk*, never as **daut*, and furthermore it can only be used in an emphatic function, never in a logophoric or canonical reflexive one. Examples of this usage can be seen in (7.72–7.75) below.

(7.72) *Wel* ***aod-leb*** ***dauk*** *geud.*
1SG **one-CLF** **REFL** sweep
'I'll sweep (the floor) myself.' (Haili Shi, fieldnotes)

(7.73) *Boub* ***oub-leb*** ***dauk*** *chauk.*
1PL **two-CLF** **REFL** do
'We two will do it ourselves.' (Shixiang Wu, fieldnotes)

(7.74) *Monx* ***aod-meinl*** ***dauk*** *chauk.*
2SG **one-CLF:person** **REFL** do
'Do it yourself.' (Haili Shi, fieldnotes)

(7.75) *Monx* ***leb*** ***dauk,*** *monx* *dionb* *ix* *dut* *deb-deb.*
2SG **CLF** **REFL** 2SG lead NEG_1 obtain child-RED
'You can't care for the child on your own.' (Xingyu Shi, in *Oub Meinl Yaos Geud*)

133 The author's consultants do not allow the use of *ngonl* 'CLF:animate' in this reflexive construction, even though it seems to the author that it would be semantically appropriate. However, these consultants often reject the application of *ngonl* to human referents in constructed sentences, even though they themselves readily apply it to such referents in natural, unprompted speech (see Section 6.1.4.3). It is thus unclear how strict this restriction against the use of *ngonl* 'CLF:animate' in this reflexive construction actually is, although it is true that such use is at least so far unattested.

7.1.4 The "semi-pronominal" form *nex/ninx* 'NEX'

The form *nex/ninx* 'NEX' is regularly realized as *nex* by all of the author's consultants, while the alternate pronunciation *ninx* is occasionally used by speakers from Yankan Village, with the two pronunciations apparently being in free variation for those latter speakers. This high-frequency form serves three major, partially overlapping functions in Fenghuang Xong: (i) it can serve as a canonical noun meaning 'person', (ii) it can serve as a pronominal-like form very similar to *beul* '3' in terms of semantics and distribution, and (iii) it can serve as an associative plural marker (see Daniel and Moravcsik 2013). The form also serves a number of minor functions as well, though it is sometimes unclear (and perhaps unimportant) which of these should be considered distinct functions in their own right and which should be considered mere "sub-functions" of the three major functions just listed. The overlap among all these various functions makes it difficult to say whether *nex/ninx* should be considered an example of monosemy, polysemy, or ambiguity (see Gil 2004), and the form is thus referred to as a "semi-pronominal" one here. While each of *nex/ninx*'s functions is discussed separately below, the reader should understand that this is done primarily for the sake of presentational convenience, and it may not be truly reflective of the status of *nex/ninx* in the minds of Xong speakers. To err on the side of caution, though, the author glosses all occurrences of *nex/ninx* as 'NEX' regardless of the particular function that the form appears to be serving in any particular case.

Examples (7.76–7.79) below show that when *nex/ninx* serves as a canonical noun meaning 'person', it is usually interchangeable with the fully canonical noun *miex/mianx* 'person' (*miex* is the form used by speakers from Yankan Village, while *mianx* is the form used by other speakers; see Section 3.3.2.2).[134] Note that in examples (7.77), (7.78), and (7.79), *nex/ninx* 'NEX' displays the two diagnostic properties of canonical nouns in Xong: namely, the ability to be modified by a *manx* relative clause and the ability to co-occur with a preceding numeral-classifier phrase (see Section 5.2.1).

(7.76)	*Aod-ngonl*	*guoud*	*dox*	*ghab*	***ninx/miex.***
	one-CLF:animate	dog	that	bite	**NEX/person**

'That dog bites people.' (Yan Long, fieldnotes)

134 There is also a canonical noun *zos* 'people' in Fenghuang Xong. This grammatically unusual form seems to mean more or less the same thing as *miex/mianx* 'person', but while *miex/mianx* is unspecified for number, *zos* is only used when (i) its referent is semantically plural (and the greater in number the referent is, the more likely *zos* is to be used rather than *miex/mianx*) and (ii) its referent is explicitly quantified, e.g. by a preceding numeral-classifier phrase or by the verb *hliof/hliob* 'many'.

(7.77) *Manx mex daont naond* ***nex/miex*** *ghat dib at jix*
REL exist money ASSOC **NEX/person** go.to which SAT NEG$_1$
nhob geud, geud jont chek.
walk road hold sit vehicle
'People who have money don't need to walk anywhere, (they) can just take a car.' (Haili Shi, fieldnotes)

(7.78) *Manx bioud mex mins-meinl* ***nex/miex****?*
2PL home exist how.many-CLF:person **NEX/person**
'How many people are there in your family?' (Haili Shi, fieldnotes)

(7.79) *Lis zoux.zhil aod-hot* ***nex/mianx****.*
want organize one-CLF:team **NEX/person**
'(The People's Liberation Army soldiers) wanted to organize the villagers (into a militia unit).' (Shixiang Wu, fieldnotes)

However, in some cases *nex/ninx* 'NEX' is better translated as specifically 'other people' rather than just 'people' (or 'person'), and in such cases consultants do not allow the form's replacement with *miex/mianx* 'person'. This can be seen in examples (7.80) and (7.81) below.[135]

(7.80) *Ghaob-xed naond hant naond yaof-zhif jix diaos*
NOM-tooth ASSOC CLF:PL ASSOC tooth-quality NEG$_1$ catch.up.to
nex/*miex *ghaod ngeinb.*
NEX/*person more hard
'(As for) the quality of (my) teeth, (they're) just not as sturdy as other people's.' (Haili Shi, in *Tooth Conversation*)

(7.81) *Nek-deb-nek-giad chauk naonb nanx ix diaos*
mother-child-mother-grandchild do what only NEG$_1$ catch.up.to
nex/*mianx *shaont.*
NEX/*person fast
'Mothers with (young) children can't do anything as fast as other people.' (Chenghua Long, fieldnotes)

135 For discussion of the unusual grammatical structures seen in example (7.80), including two instances of *naond* 'ASSOC' occurring within a single possessive construction, see Text 2 near the end of this grammar. However, these unusual structures do not appear to have any bearing on the use of *nex* 'NEX' in this example.

When *nex/ninx* 'NEX' serves as a pronoun, it is third-person and unspecified with respect to number.[136] In this function, *nex/ninx* unsurprisingly shows a very high degree of functional and distributional overlap with *beul* '3' (and to a lesser extent with *miant* '3PL' for those speakers who use that form; see Section 7.1.1), and in some cases these forms are interchangeable (though in these cases *nex/ninx* is not interchangeable with *miex/mianx* 'person'). This can be seen in examples (7.82–7.84) below.

(7.82) *Dib.daont* *nins* ***ninx/beul*** *naond.*
money COP **NEX/3** ASSOC
'That money belongs to him.' (Haili Shi, fieldnotes)

(7.83) *Gaons* ***nex/beul*** *biaob-gaonb* *hlat.jub.*
give **NEX/3** five-CLF:catty hot.pepper
'(The villagers had to) give them (i.e. the bandits) five catties (unit of mass) of hot peppers.' (Qiusheng Long, in *Ngel.kanx*)

(7.84) *Ranf.houb* *nieux-hnef* ***nex/beul*** *heut* *wel* *nieus* *banb*
afterward yester-CLF:day **NEX/3** help 1SG buy CLF:some
nggaob.
medicine
'And then, yesterday he (i.e. my husband) bought some medicine for me.' (Haili Shi, in *Tooth Conversation*)

However, there are some cases in which *nex/ninx* 'NEX' in its pronominal capacity and *beul* '3' (or *miant* '3PL') are not interchangeable, or at least not without some change in pragmatic import. For instance, the author's collected texts strongly suggest that *nex/ninx* can be used to convey more respect or politeness than *beul* '3' or *miant* '3PL' would. The speaker in example (7.85) thus uses *nex* to refer to the oldest of his brothers, a person deserving of respect due to his seniority within the speaker's family. (Note that *naob* and *daod* are interchangeable terms for 'older brother', at least in Yankan Xong.)

136 All of the author's elicition sessions were conducted in Standard Mandarin, and his consultants very often translated *nex/ninx* into Standard Mandarin as *rénjiā* (人家). The exact function of this Standard Mandarin form is too complex to discuss in detail here, though Liu (2001), for instance, describes it as a "sympathetic antilogophor". Translating *nex/ninx* as *rénjiā* is certainly understandable, since the two forms do show a great deal of functional and distributional overlap. However, the two forms are not identical in every aspect of their grammatical behavior or referential properties, as a comparison between this Section 7.1.4 and (e.g.) Liu (2001) will show.

(7.85) *Aod-dieud dox wel mex bub-meinl*
one-CLF:time$_2$ that 1SG exist three-CLF:person
naob-geud. Minl-daod leh, ***nex*** *doub chauk*
older.brother-younger.sibling AUG-older.brother LEH **NEX** then$_1$ do
nex *naond giaok.*
NEX ASSOC home
'Back then I had three brothers. My oldest brother, he left home to start his own family.' (Qiusheng Long, in *Qiusheng Long's Life History*)

In example (7.86), the speaker is a poor old woman who has adopted a talking frog as her son, and the referent of *nex* is a wealthy landlord with a beautiful daughter. The respect or politeness due here arises from a difference in wealth and social status rather than seniority within a kin group.

(7.86) *Wel deb jix mex, giad jix mex, monx aod-ngonl*
1SG child NEG$_1$ exist grandchild NEG$_1$ exist 2SG one-CLF:animate
deb-guk, wel monl haut ***nex*** *saot deb-npaok?* ***Nex*** *chauk-dib*
DIM-frog 1SG go to **NEX** beg DIM-woman **NEX** do-which
gaons wel raut lah?
give 1SG good PRF
'I have no children, no grandchildren, and you're nothing but a frog. (Now you want) me to go ask him (i.e. the landlord) to give you his daughter in marriage? How on earth could he (i.e. the landlord) agree?' (Xingyu Shi, in *Deb Guk Ronf*)

In example (7.87) below, the referent of *nex* is (from the speaker's point of view) deserving of respect for several reasons: she was a very elderly person, she was the mother of the local school's principal (and note that the speaker is herself a teacher at said school), and at the time of utterance she was very recently deceased.

(7.87) *Hnef-doul* ***nex*** *chad.kit nzhaod.*
day-??? **NEX** not.until return
'She (i.e. the principal's mother) only went back (to her village) the day before yesterday.' (Chenghua Long, in *Conversation in La'ershan*)

In example (7.88), the referent of *nex* was the author himself, and the speaker was an elderly Xong-speaking woman who had never met a foreigner before. The use of *nex* here is unsurprising, as foreigners (in particular Westerners) are uniformly seen as wealthy and highly educated in most rural Xong-speaking communities. The context in example (7.88) is that of a discussion between two elderly women, who were lamenting the fact that (as they saw it) they had no stories or narratives of significance for the author to record.

(7.88) ***Nex*** *jix chauk manx zheinb, hliof daut yaonl.*
NEX NEG$_1$ do REL real many speech much
'If he (i.e. the author) didn't want (us) to talk about matters of importance, (well then we'd) have lots to say.' (Qiumei Wu, in *Conversation in Yankan)*

Occasionally *nex/ninx* occurs immediately before a coreferential noun rather than occurring independently, but even in these cases the form still appears to be signaling something like respect or politeness.

(7.89) *Chauk nex naond npaok, chauk* ***nex yes.web*** *naond nheinx.*
do NEX ASSOC woman do **NEX landlord** ASSOC daughter.in.law
'(She) became his (i.e. the landlord's son's) wife, she became the landlord's daughter-in-law.' (Xingyu Shi, in *Oub Meinl Yaos Geud*)

(7.90) ***Nex yux.sid-Xonb,*** *nex mex aod-zhonx manx niab nggaob chauk naont...*
NEX traditional.doctor-Miao NEX exist one-CLF:kind$_3$ REL say medicine do thus
'The traditional doctors, they have a kind of medicine that works like this...' (Chenghua Long, fieldnotes)

In other cases, *nex/ninx* 'NEX' is used as a pronoun not out of respect for the referent, but because the identity of the referent is non-specific and not particularly important. In these cases, *nex/ninx* can usually be translated quite accurately as (generic) *they* in English, as in ***They*** *say that it's going to rain tomorrow.* This can be seen in examples (7.91–7.93) below.

(7.91) ***Nex*** *hnant sheit tont.zhik ninb dox.*
NEX call write notice at that
'They told (me) to post a notice there.' (Chenghua Long, in *Conversation in La'ershan*)

(7.92) ***Nex*** *niab geud nhex sheub yol dions del manx xanb nins aod.sheit raut.*
NEX say hold pull.out leave again plant CLF:rigid.length REL new COP the.same good
'They say you can have (your old tooth) pulled out and then put a new (tooth) in, and the new tooth will be just as good as your old one.' (Chenghua Long, in *Tooth Conversation*)

(7.93) *Yul* *hnef* *zheinx.bif* *niab* *lis* ***nex*** *sheub.*
again CLF:day prepare say want **NEX** leave
'One of these days (I'm) going to have them take (my broken tooth) out.' (Haili Shi, in *Tooth Conversation*)

The two major functions of *nex/ninx* so far described – i.e. serving as a canonical noun and serving as a pronoun – seem to overlap in certain cases. For instance, in example (7.94) below, the speaker is recounting preparations that villagers in Yankan would make when a bandit raid was imminent. In this case, it seems to the author that *nex* could be translated equally well as 'people' or as '(generic) they', and his consultants' explanations seem to suggest the same.

(7.94) *Daob-nief* *daob-yul* *qek.bub* *yaod.yaod* *keuf,* *jud* *giet*
AN-water.buffalo AN-cow all all shut NEG$_2$ dare
jaont *bionl,* *jaont* *bionl* ***nex*** *doub* *ghons* *dut.*
release exit release exit **NEX** then$_1$ herd obtain
'The water buffalo and cattle were all shut (in mountain caves), (the villagers) didn't dare let them out, if they got out then people (or generic 'they') would go get them back.' (Qiusheng Long, in *Ngel.kanx*)

In example (7.95), the speaker is explaining how it can be difficult to find help in burying one's kin members if one has been away from home for too long. In this case, too, it seems that *nex* could be translated equally well as 'people' or as '(generic) they'.

(7.95) *Ix* *jont* *dib-gheul,* *ix* *daox.doub* ***nex,*** *sat*
NEG$_1$ live LOC-village NEG$_1$ greet **NEX** SAT
niul *yaox?*
unfamiliar right?
'(If you) don't live at home, (if you) don't greet people (or generic 'them'), (then you'll) be like a stranger (to them), right?' (Chenghua Long, in *Conversation in La'ershan*)

In addition to serving the functions already discussed, *nex/ninx* 'NEX' is often used as a possessive marker when (i) the possessor is a third-person referent (rather than the speaker or addressee) and (ii) the possessum is a kin term or one of a handful of other inalienably possessed nouns (e.g. *bioud* 'home, family', *gheul* 'village'). While this usage is discussed more thoroughly in Section 8.2.3, example (7.96) below shows one representative instance of it.

(7.96) ***Lod-Hex nex gheul*** *ndieut hant bid-gheul*
FAM-PN NEX village ascend CLF:PL FRT-mountain
nhob ndieut nhob lot.
walk ascend walk descend
'He's village is up in the mountains, (you need to) walk up and down and up and down to get there.' (Xiaohui Wu, in *Conversation in La'ershan*)

Note that *beul* '3' can also serve as a possessive marker in the same construction and with the same restrictions (again, see Section 8.2.3). This makes it unclear whether serving as a possessive marker should be considered a distinct function of *nex/ninx* 'NEX' or simply a logical result of the fact that *nex/ninx* patterns very similarly to *beul* '3' in many cases.

The third major function of *nex/ninx* 'NEX' is to serve as an associative plural marker (see Daniel and Moravcsik 2013). When serving this function, *nex/ninx* occurs immediately after a kin term or personal name, and the resulting construction as a whole means something like '*X* and the people characteristically associated with *X*' (where *X* is the referent of the kin term or personal name in question).

(7.97) ***Boub daok nex*** *aod-reux dox*
1PL maternal.grandmother NEX one-CLF:generation that
hlit-gil-sed sat nonx ix ncheut.
cooked.rice-???-powder SAT eat NEG_1 full
'People of my (maternal) grandmother's generation couldn't even eat their fill of porridge.' (Chenghua Long, fieldnotes)

(7.98) ***Beul baox nex*** *ninb bioud,* ***beul baox nex*** *hnaond.*
3 father NEX at home **3 father NEX** hear
'Her father and sister were at home, her father and sister (must have) heard (her calling).' (Xingyu Shi, in *Oub Meinl Yaos Geud*)[137]

(7.99) *Geud-neul aod-hmaont manx* ***Meik.jinb nex*** *nonx niax-guoud*
$place_I$-front one-CLF:evening REL **PN NEX** eat meat-dog
wel ix lot haond monl giat nex nonx manx mieil.
1SG NEG_1 descend bottom go share NEX eat REL spicy
'The night before (my tooth started hurting), when Mei Jin's family was having dog meat, I didn't go down (from the school where I live) to her home to eat spicy food (as I knew the dog meat would be).' (Haili Shi, in *Tooth Conversation*)

137 In this example, the interpretation of *beul baox nex* [3 father NEX] as 'her father and sister' (rather than 'her father and mother' or any other logical possibility) is determined by narrative context: the referent of *beul* '3' in the example is a young woman whose only surviving family members are her father and her older sister.

The form *nex/ninx* 'NEX' also has one final, minor function. Examples (7.100) and (7.101) below show that *nex/ninx* can occur with the plural suffix *-god/-gud* 'PL', in which case consultants generally translate the resulting dimorphemic form as 'everyone, everybody'.[138] The only other forms in Xong which can take the plural suffix are non-singular personal pronouns like *boub* '1PL' and *manx* '2PL' (see Section 7.1.2.1 above), and this is thus one of the clearest ways in which *nex/ninx* 'NEX' resembles a pronoun rather than a canonical noun.

(7.100) *Sox.ix* ***nex-god*** *yaod.yaod* *hnant* *beul* *hnant* *chauk* *Xaub.Honl.Mob.*
so **NEX-PL** all call 3 call do Little.Red.Hat
'And so everyone called her Little Red Hat.' (Haili Shi, in *Xaub Honl Mob*)

(7.101) *Aod-roul* ***nex-god*** *yaod.yaod* *ndiot* *beul.*
one-CLF:time$_1$ **NEX-PL** all recognize 3
'Now everyone knows him.' (Haili Shi, fieldnotes)

7.2 Demonstratives

Compared to many other Miao languages, Fenghuang Xong has a fairly simple system of demonstratives.[139] For all of the author's consultants, there is a basic two-way contrast between the proximal demonstrative *neind* 'this' and the distal demonstrative *dox* 'that'.[140, 141] These two demonstratives also contrast paradigmatically with the ignorative

---

138 Other ways of expressing 'everyone, everybody' include (i) the use of the apparently monomorphemic forms *chaot.shib* (characteristic of speakers from La'ershan and nearby villages, including Yankan) or *tat.shib* (characteristic of speakers from Shanjiang), and (ii) the use of reduplicated classifiers with human referents, such as *leb-leb* [CLF-CLF] or *meinl-meinl* [CLF:person-CLF:person] (see Section 6.1.3.2).

139 See Gerner (2009) for a survey of demonstrative systems in several Miao languages, including among them a variety of Xong spoken in Huayuan County (see Figure 2.6 in Section 2.7.1 of this grammar). It is interesting to note that the Xong variety described by Gerner (see in particular page 79 of his article) appears to feature five distinct demonstratives (not including any ignorative demonstratives, which Gerner does not discuss). Two of these, transcribed as /nən^{44}/ and /ei^{35}/, appear to be cognate with the Fenghuang Xong demonstratives *neind* 'this' and (archaic) *eib* 'yon' (see footnote below in this section), but the other three are unknown in Fenghuang Xong.

140 Note that the demonstrative *neind* 'this' is distinct from *tat-* 'this', with the latter being a bound non-demonstrative form that only occurs in a few fixed temporal expressions (e.g. *tat-hneb/tat-hnef* [this-CLF:day] 'today', *tat-hmaont* [this-CLF:evening] 'this evening', *tat-jut* [this-CLF:year] 'this year', etc.).

141 It seems likely that Fenghuang Xong once featured a third (non-ignorative) demonstrative *eib* 'yon'. This form appears in a few fixed expressions that all mean 'long ago, a long time ago', including *(aod-)roul eib* [(one-)CLF:time$_1$ yon], *manx-eib* [AT-yon] (see Section 5.5.2.8 for more on the form *manx* 'AT'), and *manx.eib.manx.ab* (this latter expression is morphemically [AT-yon-AT-???], but for convenience's sake it is simply glossed as 'a.long.time.ago' in this grammar). However, *eib* is not used

demonstrative *dib/dof* 'which, some(thing/one)', although this latter form is discussed in Section 7.3 below (where ignoratives in general are discussed) rather than here.

When serving an attributive function (i.e. as a constituent of a larger noun phrase), demonstratives always occur in noun-phrase–final position. This can be seen in examples (7.102–7.109) below. The type of constituent immediately preceding each demonstrative varies from example to example: it is a noun in examples (7.102) and (7.103), a relative clause in (7.104) and (7.105), a numeral-classifier phrase in (7.106) and (7.107), and a bare classifier in (7.108) and (7.109). Nevertheless, in all eight examples the demonstrative is invariably the final element of the noun phrase to which it belongs.

(7.102) *Boub naond aod-ndaut aub* ***neind*** *ik.zhil tonk*
1PL ASSOC one-CLF:river water **this** all.the.way pass.through
dand Laok.doux.yaonb.
arrive Liangtouyang
'This river of ours flows all the way to Liangtouyang (Village).' (Qiusheng Long, in *Ngel.kanx*)

(7.103) *Beul nzhaod ghat aod-leb khauk-lieux* ***dox.***
3 return go.to one-CLF hole-well **that**
'He returned to that well (where the old woman had been getting water).' (Xingyu Shi, in *Deb Guk Ronf*)

(7.104) *Aod-ngonl manx chauk xut.npeif* ***neind*** *at neub.*
one-CLF:animate REL do shoe **this** SAT skilled
'This (person) who made the shoe must be very skilled.' (Xingyu Shi, in *Oub Meinl Yaos Geud*)

(7.105) *Xaub.Honl.Mob doub ndiaox aod-banb manx nonx* ***dox*** *bionl*
Little.Red.Hat then$_1$ carry one-CLF:some REL eat **that** exit
bioud.
home
'Little Red Hat then carried the food out of the house.' (Haili Shi, in *Xaub Honl Mob*)

productively as a demonstrative by any of the author's consultants, even very elderly ones. Still, many consultants – even relatively young ones, in their twenties – report that they have heard it used productively before, although they typically cannot recall specific instances. Given its low frequency and productivity, it is not surprising that the semantics of *eib* 'yon' are somewhat unclear: most consultants simply report that *eib* could "probably" be used to refer to referents that are even further away (either in space or time) than those that are referred to with *dox* 'that'.

(7.106) *Naont sox.ix aod-hmaont* ***dox*** *taf jix dut.*
thus so one-CLF:evening **that** endure NEG_1 obtain
'So, that evening (I) couldn't bear (the pain).' (Haili Shi, in *Tooth Conversation*)

(7.107) *Jud.leb deib dut aod-nqad* ***neind,*** *doul*
who match obtain one-CLF:half.of.pair **this** remain
nqad, jud.leb doub chauk beul naond nheinx.
CLF:half.of.pair who $then_1$ do 3 ASSOC daughter.in.law
'Whoever could match this shoe, whoever had the other half of the pair, she would become his (i.e. the landlord's) daughter-in-law.' (Xingyu Shi, in *Oub Meinl Yaos Geud*)

(7.108) *Jix nconl, jix diaos Laox.guel nex hant* ***dox.***
NEG_1 steep NEG_1 catch.up.to PN NEX CLF:PL **that**
'(The road to that village) isn't steep, not like that (road) to Lao Gue's (village).' (Xiaohui Wu, in *Conversation in La'ershan*)

(7.109) *Dand hnef* ***dox*** *leh, dand hnef* ***dox*** *shib yaod.yaod lol...*
arrive CLF:day **that** LEH arrive CLF:day **that** it's all come
'When the day arrived, when the day arrived everyone came (to try on the shoe).' (Xingyu Shi, in *Oub Meinl Yaos Geud*)

Demonstratives can readily occur in a noun phrase that contains a preceding classifier (either bare or within a numeral-classifier phrase), regardless of whether the noun phrase contains any other constituents (see examples (7.102–7.109) above). However, demonstratives generally cannot occur in a noun phrase that contains a noun but lacks a classifier. Such noun phrases – i.e. with a noun and a demonstrative, but no classifier – do occur in running speech (as in example (7.110) below), but they do so only very occasionally. Furthermore, consultants generally reject similar constructions when produced by the author, they never produce such constructions themselves when speaking carefully, and they usually report that such constructions sound "better" or "more complete" if a classifier is inserted before the noun.

(7.110) *Deb-guk* ***neind*** *haut wel saot hliof guaot hliof yaonl.*
DIM-frog **this** to 1SG beg many pass many much
'This frog has been begging me and begging me (to find a wife for him).' (Xingyu Shi, in *Deb Guk Ronf*)

The utterances shown in examples (7.111) and (7.112) below are much more typical. These examples demonstrate that the demonstratives *neind* 'this' and *dox* 'that' can readily occur in a noun phrase containing a numeral-classifier phrase (see Section 6.1.2), regardless of whether the noun phrase contains a noun as well. However, consultants do not accept example (7.113), which features a noun phrase containing a demonstrative and a noun but no classifier.

(7.111) *Wel lis aod-ngonl daob-yul* ***neind/dox.***
1SG want one-CLF:animate AN-cow **this/that**
‘I want this/that cow.’ (Haili Shi, fieldnotes)

(7.112) *Wel lis aod-ngonl* ***neind/dox.***
1SG want one-CLF:animate **this/that**
‘I want this/that one (animal).’ (Haili Shi, fieldnotes)

(7.113) **Wel lis daob-yul* ***neind/dox.***
1SG want AN-cow **this/that**
(intended: ‘I want this/that cow.’)

The same is true of examples (7.114–7.116), although here a bare classifier is involved rather than a full numeral-classifier phrase.

(7.114) *Beul lis hant eud* ***neind/dox.***
3 want CLF:PL clothing **this/that**
‘He wants these/those clothes.’ (Shixiang Wu, fieldnotes)

(7.115) *Beul lis hant* ***neind/dox.***
3 want CLF:PL **this/that**
‘He wants these/those (things).’ (Shixiang Wu, fieldnotes)

(7.116) **Beul lis eud* ***neind/dox.***
3 want clothing **this/that**
(intended: ‘He wants these/those clothes.’)

It appears that – at least in careful speech – the presence of a preceding classifier in a noun phrase is a necessary condition for the presence of a demonstrative within that same noun phrase, but the presence or absence of a preceding noun is irrelevant. This suggests that Xong demonstratives actually serve to modify classifiers (or the numeral-classifier phrases in which they occur) rather than to modify nouns themselves. This in turn suggests that the grammatical head of a Xong noun phrase that contains a noun and a classifier may in fact be the classifier rather than the noun (although the noun may arguably still serve as the *semantic* head of the noun phrase; cf. Enfield’s [2007: 120] discussion of similar issues in the Tai-Kadai language Lao).

There are, however, at least two lexically specified exceptions to this restriction against nouns and demonstratives co-occurring within the same noun phrase without an accompanying classifier. The nouns *daod* ‘place$_3$’ (see Section 5.5.2.4 for more information on this form and its gloss) and *(ghaob-)def* [(NOM-)place] 'place' regularly occur with a following demonstrative even when not preceded by a classifier, and they do so even in slow, careful speech. Note that both of these nouns are high-frequency forms with relatively abstract, locative meanings, and their ability to co-occur with a following demonstrative without a preceding classifier may simply be the result of some degree of grammaticalization.

(7.117) *Wel ninb* ***daod*** ***neind!***
1SG at **place**$_3$ **this**
'I'm (over) here!' (Shixiang Wu, fieldnotes)

(7.118) *Boub naond Ngel.kanx* ***ob-def*** ***neind*** *nins leb manx jaod ob-def.*
1PL ASSOC Yankan **NOM-place** **this** COP CLF REL bad NOM-place
'(When I was a boy,) this Yankan (Village) of ours was a bad place.' (Qiusheng Long, in *Ngel.kanx*)

The demonstratives *neind* 'this' and *dox* 'that' can also occur in isolation (i.e. as noun phrases in their own right, rather than as constituents of some larger noun phrase). When doing so, these demonstratives generally serve a deictic locative function, so that *neind* in isolation is usually better translated as 'here' and *dox* in isolation as 'there' (for consistency's sake, though, these forms are still glossed as 'this' and 'that' even when occurring in isolation). Examples of this can be seen in (7.119–7.121) below.

(7.119) *Wel ninb* ***neind,*** *monx ninb* ***dox.***
1SG at **this** 2SG at **that**
'I'm (over) here, and you're (over) there.' (Haili Shi, fieldnotes)

(7.120) *Monx dand* ***neind*** *hauk-naonb, Nhaonl?*
2SG arrive **this** do-what PN
'What did you come here for, Nhaon?' (Xingyu Shi, in *Oub Meinl Yaos Geud*)

(7.121) *Beul doub lias beul deb-geud naond teid bat* ***dox.***
3 then$_1$ switch 3 DIM-younger.sibling ASSOC put.back put **that**
'She switched (the drinking water) into her younger sister's (length of bamboo).' (Xingyu Shi, in *Oub Meinl Yaos Geud*)

Demonstratives that thus occur in isolation with a deictic locative function may be optionally preceded by the nominal prefix *ghaob-* 'NOM' (see Section 5.4.2.1 and example (7.122) below) or followed by the noun root *-naub/-ndaub* 'place$_4$' (see Section 5.5.2.7 and example (7.123) below) with no change in meaning. Note, though, that when these demonstratives serve an attributive function (i.e. as constituents of a larger noun phrase), they are never preceded by *ghaob-* 'NOM' or followed by *-naub/ -ndaub* 'place$_4$'.

(7.122) *Beul deib* ***ob-dox.***
3 at **NOM-that**
'He's (over) there.' (Haili Shi, fieldnotes)

(7.123) *Boub lol* ***aod-cib*** ***neind-naub*** *leh.*
1PL come **one-CLF:occurrence** **this-place$_4$** LEH
'We came here once.' (Qiusheng Long, in *Ngel.kanx*)

In addition to using just *neind* or *dox* (or either of these forms with an attached *ghaob-* 'NOM' or *-naub/-ndaub* 'place$_4$'), it is also common for Xong speakers to express deictic location (e.g. 'here', 'there') by means of a bare classifier or numeral-classifier phrase followed by a demonstrative (with the classifier involved typically meaning something like 'CLF:place'). Examples of this are given in (7.124) and (7.125) below.

(7.124) ***Aod-bix*** ***neind*** *hnant dib?*
one-CLF:place$_1$ **this** call which
'What's the name of this place?' (Haili Shi, fieldnotes)

(7.125) *Ghans* ***khauk*** ***dox*** *mex leb roub ghaod shanb.*
see **CLF:place$_2$** **that** exist CLF stone more tall
'(The boy) saw that there was a taller stone over there.' (Chenghua Long, in *Frog, Where Are You?*)

Finally, Xong demonstratives are not used in isolation to refer to (non-locative) entities, as in English *I want* ***that*** or *Here, take* ***this.***

(7.126) ****Neind/*dox*** *nins wel naond.*
this/that COP 1SG ASSOC
(intended: 'This/that [thing] is mine.')

Instead, Xong speakers use a numeral-classifier phrase or bare classifier (with the choice of classifier depending on the referent) followed by a demonstrative, as in examples (7.127–7.130).

(7.127) *Beul niel lah,* ***aod-leb neind*** *nins manx giaox naond, jix*
3 know PRF **one-CLF this** COP REL fake ASSOC NEG_1
nins aub-gheb.
COP water-eye
'Then he knew, this (length of bamboo) was fake, it didn't contain tears at all (but rather only ordinary water).' (Xingyu Shi, in *Oub Meinl Yaos Geud*)

(7.128) ***Aod-banb neind*** *yaod.yaod zhix tonb naond.*
one-CLF:some this all cure pain ASSOC
'All of these things can be used as painkillers.' (Haili Shi, in *Tooth Conversation*)

(7.129) ***Leb dox*** *nins naonb?*
CLF that COP what
'What is that thing?' (Lijun Wu, fieldnotes)

(7.130) *Chauk* ***hant neind*** *aob-naonb ix dut, nanx dut*
do **CLF:PL this** NOM-what NEG_1 obtain only obtain
aod-xeub mos.
one-CLF:body tired
'(I) got nothing out of doing all this, all I got was tired.' (Chenghua Long, fieldnotes)

7.3 Ignoratives

7.3.1 Properties of the ignorative class

Ignoratives (the term is borrowed from Wierzbicka 1980) constitute a small, closed set of forms. These forms cover much of the same functional territory as interrogative and indefinite pronouns in (for example) European languages. However, there are no distinct interrogative vs. non-interrogative (i.e. indefinite) ignorative forms in Xong; instead, the interpretation of a given ignorative as interrogative or non-interrogative depends on context, the structure of the current discourse, and real-world knowledge, in a clear case of macrofunctionality (see Gil 2004).

For instance, consider the ignorative noun *naonb* 'what, something' in examples (7.131–7.136) below.[142] The first two of these examples are segmentally and tonally

142 As these and other examples in Section 7.3 show, Xong's ignorative forms are uniformly given English interrogative glosses when they appear in examples and texts in this grammar. For instance, *naonb* is always glossed as 'what' rather than 'something', *(dib.)leb/(jud.)leb* is always glossed as 'who' rather than 'someone', and so on. This glossing convention is adopted primarily for the sake of brevity, and it should not be interpreted as implying that the interrogative functions of Xong's ignoratives are somehow more basic or more primary than their non-interrogative functions.

identical (although unfortunately the author is unable to confirm whether or not they are identical in terms of non-tonal intonational contours), but they serve very different discourse functions. As example (7.131) shows, it is possible to interpret the utterance in question as a statement meaning 'I'm going to do something today' or 'I've got something to do today'. This is the preferred interpretation when the utterance is addressed to someone other than the speaker, but it is still a possible reading even when the utterance is addressed to oneself.

(7.131)	*Tat-hneb*	*wel*	*lis*	*chauk*	***naonb*.**
	this-CLF:day	1SG	want	do	**what**

'I'm going to do something today, I've got something to do today.' (Shixiang Wu, fieldnotes)

However, it is also possible to interpret the exact same utterance as a question meaning 'What am I going to do today?'. This reading appears to be equally possible in a situation in which the utterance is addressed to oneself and in one in which it is addressed to someone else.

(7.132)	*Tat-hneb*	*wel*	*lis*	*chauk*	***naonb*?**
	this-CLF:day	1SG	want	do	**what**

'What am I going to do today?' (Shixiang Wu, fieldnotes)

The next two examples below are also segmentally and tonally identical (again, though, the author is unable to confirm whether or not they are identical in terms of non-tonal intonational contours). The presence of the negative marker *(j)ix* 'NEG$_1$' makes a non-interrogative reading of this utterance (i.e. 'I'm not doing anything today' or 'I've got nothing to do today') strongly preferred regardless of the identity of the addressee.

(7.133)	*Tat-hneb*	*wel*	*jix*	*chauk*	***naonb*.**
	this-CLF:day	1SG	NEG$_1$	do	**what**

'I'm not doing anything today, I've got nothing to do today.' (Shixiang Wu, fieldnotes)

However, given an appropriate enough context, an interrogative reading of the same utterance is still possible. For instance, when consultants were presented with a situation in which the imagined speaker of the utterance was in the process of trying to change several bad habits over the course of several days (e.g. deciding to stop smoking one day, then to stop beating his children the next day, then to stop drinking the third day, etc.), they allowed an interrogative reading with a meaning something like 'What (bad habit) am I not doing today?'.

(7.134) *Tat-hneb* *wel* *jix* *chauk* ***naonb?***
this-CLF:day 1SG NEG_1 do **what**
'What am I not doing today?' (Shixiang Wu, fieldnotes)

The same is true of the next pair of examples, which can mean either 'You're not doing anything today' or 'What are you not doing today?'.

(7.135) *Tat-hneb* *mx* *jix* *chauk* ***naonb.***
this-CLF:day 2SG NEG_1 do **what**
'You're not doing anything today, you've got nothing to do today.' (Shixiang Wu, fieldnotes)

(7.136) *Tat-hneb* *mx* *jix* *chauk* ***naonb?***
this-CLF:day 2SG NEG_1 do **what**
'What are you not doing today?' (Shixiang Wu, fieldnotes)

Section 7.3.2 below is devoted to individual members of the ignorative class. In particular, Section 7.3.2.1 discusses the ignorative nouns *naonb* 'what, something' and *(dib.) leb/(jud.)leb* 'who, someone', Section 7.3.2.2 discusses the ignorative demonstrative *dib/dof* 'which, some(thing/one)', and Section 7.3.2.3 discusses the ignorative quantifiers *mins* 'how many, a few' and *haut/hot* 'how much, so much'. It is important to note that different ignorative forms in Xong display grammatical and distributional properties associated with different lexical categories. For example, *mins* 'how many, a few' greatly resembles Xong's numerals in terms of its grammatical and distributional properties, while *dib/dof* 'which, some(thing/one)' greatly resembles Xong's demonstratives. This means that the class of ignoratives is not actually a lexical category in the sense that nouns or verbs or classifiers are, since it can only be defined in terms of its members' referential properties and not their grammatical or distributional ones.

7.3.2 Individual ignorative forms

7.3.2.1 The ignorative nouns *naonb* 'what, something' and *(dib.)leb/(jud.)leb* 'who, someone'

The ignorative forms *naonb* 'what, something' and *(dib.)leb/(jud.)leb* 'who, someone' show a high degree of functional and distributional overlap with canonical nouns (and in the case of *[dib.]leb/[jud.]leb*, with pronouns as well), and these forms can thus be thought of as ignorative pro-forms for the class of nouns in general. The ignorative *naonb* is glossed as 'what' whenever it occurs in examples, although in non-interrogative contexts it is generally better translated into English as 'something' (see Section 7.3.1 above). Similarly, *(dib.)leb/(jud.)leb* is glossed as 'who' in all examples, although it is often better translated as 'someone' when not serving an interrogative function. As these glosses suggest, *naonb* is generally used for non-human referents and *(dib.)leb/(jud.)leb* for human ones.

The form *naonb* 'what, something' can occur as a noun phrase in its own right or as a modifier within a larger noun phrase. In either case, the presence of a preceding nominal prefix *ghaob-* 'NOM' (see Section 5.4.2.1) is generally optional, with the presence or absence of the prefix not having any appreciable semantic or pragmatic effects. For instance, in examples (7.137) and (7.138) below, *naonb* occurs as an independent noun phrase in postverbal position, and in both cases its preceding *ob-* 'NOM' is completely optional. Note that in the first of these examples, context and pragmatics produce a very strong preference to interpret *(ob-)naonb* as interrogative, while in the second example they produce a similarly strong preference to interpret it as non-interrogative.

(7.137) *Monx npof nonx* ***(ob-)naonb****?*
2SG desire eat **(NOM-)what**
'What do you feel like eating?' (Haili Shi, fieldnotes)

(7.138) *Wel jix npof chauk* ***(ob-)naonb****.*
1SG NEG_1 desire do **(NOM-)what**
'I don't want to do anything.' (Haili Shi, fieldnotes)

The nominal prefix is similarly optional in example (7.139), in which *(ghaob-)naonb* serves as a modifier within a larger noun phrase and in which it has a preferred interrogative interpretation. A comparison with the subsequent example (7.140) also demonstrates that when *(ghaob-)naonb* serves as a modifier within a noun phrase, it always occurs preceding its head noun, never following it.[143]

(7.139) *Mx ninb nonx* ***(ghaob-)naonb reib****?*
2SG at eat **(NOM-)what vegetable**
'What (type of) food are you eating?' (Shixiang Wu, fieldnotes)

(7.140) **Mx ninb nonx* ***reib (ghaob-)naonb****?*
2SG at eat **vegetable (NOM-)what**
(intended: 'What [type of] food are you eating?')

143 The form *ghaob-naonb* [NOM-what] can also occur following another noun phrase to mean 'and stuff, and the like', as in *Dib.daont* ***ghaob-naonb*** *sat jix ghans lah* [money NOM-what SAT NEG_1 see PRF] 'The money and stuff's all gone'. Note, though, that this usage of *ghaob-naonb* should probably be considered a distinct syntactic construction, since it involves a clearly different meaning (compare *ghaob-naonb dib.daont* [NOM-what money] 'what money' with *dib.daont ghaob-naonb* [money NOM-what] 'money and stuff, money and the like') and since in such cases *ghaob-naonb* appears to be in apposition to the preceding noun phrase rather than a modifier within it.

Examples (7.141) and (7.142) below show that *ghaob-* 'NOM' is optional with *naonb* 'what, something' even after the copular verb *nins* 'COP'. This is unlike most canonical nouns that can bear the prefix *ghaob-*, since for those nouns the prefix in question is normally obligatory when following *nins* 'COP' (see Section 5.4.2.1).

(7.141) *Nins* ***(ghaob-)naonb*** *nggaob?*
COP **(NOM-)what** medicine
'What kind of medicine was it?' (Shixiang Wu, in *Tooth Conversation*)

(7.142) *Aod-banb neind nins* ***(ob-)naonb?***
one-CLF:some this COP **(NOM-)what**
'What is this stuff?' (Haili Shi, fieldnotes)

However, there is at least one environment in which the presence of a nominal prefix on *naonb* is not optional: when *naonb* occurs in fronted preverbal position (see Section 9.1.3.1), either independently or as part of a larger noun phrase occurring in that position, the presence of an initial *ghaob-* 'NOM' is obligatory (note, though, that this is also true of most *ghaob*-bearing canonical nouns when they occur in the same position; see again Section 5.4.2.1). This can be seen by comparing examples (7.143) and (7.144) and examples (7.145) and (7.146). Note that in example (7.143) a non-interrogative interpretation of *naonb* is very strongly preferred, and in example (7.145) such an interpretation is in fact obligatory due to the presence of a following *at* 'SAT' (see Section 9.2.3.1).

(7.143) *Tat-hneb wel* ***ghaob-naonb*** *jix chauk.*
this-CLF:day 1SG **NOM-what** NEG_1 do
'I'm not doing anything today.' (Shixiang Wu, fieldnotes)

(7.144) **Tat-hneb wel* ***naonb*** *jix chauk.*
this-CLF:day 1SG **what** NEG_1 do
(intended: 'I'm not doing anything today.')

(7.145) *Wel* ***ghaob-naonb niax*** *at jix lis.*
1SG **NOM-what meat** SAT NEG_1 want
'I don't want any (sort of) meat.' (Haili Shi, fieldnotes)

(7.146) **Wel* ***naonb niax*** *at jix lis.*
1SG **what meat** SAT NEG_1 want
(intended: 'I don't want any [sort of] meat.')

A comparison of example (7.145) above with (7.147) below provides further evidence that when *naonb* 'what, something' occurs within a larger noun phrase, it always precedes its head noun rather than following it.

(7.147) *Wel **niax** ***(ghaob-)naonb*** *at* *jix* *lis.*
1SG **meat** **(NOM-)what** SAT NEG_1 want
(intended: 'I don't want any [sort of] meat.')

Finally, *naonb* also serves as the second morpheme of the fixed expression *chauk-naonb* 'why' (lit. [do-what]). This expression is sometimes realized as *hauk-naonb* in fast or casual speech, as in examples (7.152–7.154) below (note that examples (7.152) and (7.153) are repeated from (7.120) and (7.61), respectively).

(7.148) ***Chauk-naonb*** *naus* *at* *sheib* *ngheub* *sad?*
do-what bird SAT able.to sing Xong.song
'How is the bird able to sing Xong songs?' (Xingyu Shi, in *Oub Meinl Yaos Geud*)

(7.149) ***Chauk-naonb*** *monx* *lis* *hneind* *aod-xeub* *ob-deud-guk?*
do-what 2SG want wear one-CLF:body NOM-skin-frog
'Why would you want to wear a frog skin?' (Xingyu Shi, in *Deb Guk Ronf*)

(7.150) *Mx* ***chauk-naonb*** *xaont* *xox* *puk* *Xonb?*
2SG **do-what** wish study speak Xong
'Why do you want to learn Xong?' (Shixiang Wu, fieldnotes)

(7.151) *Monx* *lot* *Zhes* ***chauk-naonb****?*
2SG descend Fenghuang **do-what**
'Why are you going to Fenghuang?' (Haili Shi, fieldnotes)

(7.152) *Monx* *dand* *neind* ***hauk-naonb****,* *Nhaonl?*
2SG arrive this **do-what** PN
'What did you come here for, Nhaon?' (Xingyu Shi, in *Oub Meinl Yaos Geud*) (repeated from (7.120) above)

(7.153) *Monx* *at* *daut-leb* *zhut* *beul,* *lis* *nieus* *nggaob* ***hauk-naonb****?*
2SG SAT REFL-CLF cure 3 want buy medicine **do-what**
'You can just treat it (i.e. your tooth) yourself, so what do you need to buy medicine for?' (Chenghua Long, in *Tooth Conversation*)

(7.154) *Nbet* ***hauk-naonb*** *nins* *manx* *gueub* *naond?*
snow **do-what** COP REL white ASSOC
'Why is snow white?' (Shixiang Wu, fieldnotes)

Much of what was said above about *naonb* 'what, something' also applies to *(dib.) leb/(jud.)leb* 'who, someone' (the former pronunciation is by far the most common one, with *[jud.]leb* only occasionally being used by speakers from Yankan Village).

Although *(dib.)leb/(jud.)leb* never occurs with a preceding nominal prefix, it can readily occur as an argument of a verb (as in example (7.155) below), as a possessor (as in example (7.156)), and even in some cases as a possessum (as in examples (7.157) and (7.158)). Furthermore, as the transcription of *(dib.)leb/(jud.)leb* in each of these examples suggests, 'who, something' can be alternately realized as just *leb* for all consultants in all grammatical environments.

(7.155) *Nins* ***(dib.)leb*** *chauk naond?*
COP **who** do ASSOC
'Who did this?' (Haili Shi, fieldnotes)

(7.156) *Hnant lol reinb nqad xut.npeif nins* ***(jud.)leb***
call come determine CLF:half.of.pair shoe COP **who**
naond xut.npeif.
ASSOC shoe
'Call (all the young, unmarried women of the village) to come and determine who this shoe belongs to.' (Xingyu Shi, in *Oub Meinl Yaos Geud*)

(7.157) *Mx nins wel naond* ***(dib.)leb****?*
2SG COP 1SG ASSOC **who**
'What is your relationship to me?' (lit. 'You're my who?') (Shixiang Wu, fieldnotes)

(7.158) *Wel jix nins mx naond* ***(dib.)leb****.*
1SG NEG_1 COP 2SG ASSOC **who**
'I don't have any relationship to you.' (lit. 'I'm not your anyone.') (Shixiang Wu, fieldnotes)

Examples (7.157) and (7.158) above show that *(dib.)leb/(jud.)leb* 'who, someone' can serve either an interrogative or a non-interrogative function depending on the context just as *naonb* 'what, something' can. This is further demonstrated by examples (7.159–7.162) below. In the first two of these examples there is a strong preference to interpret the form meaning 'who, someone' as interrogative. There is a similarly strong preference to interpret it as non-interrogative in example (7.161), and a non-interrogative interpretation is actually obligatory in example (7.162) due to the presence of a following *at* 'SAT' (see Section 9.3.3.1).

(7.159) *Monx aod-ngonl daob-guk, monx at lis nes*
2SG one-CLF:animate AN-frog 2SG SAT want find.a.wife
npaok, ***jud.leb*** *lol kint ninb monx raut leh?*
woman **who** come willing marry 2SG good LEH
'You're (just) a frog, and you want to find a wife, but who would be willing to marry you?' (Xingyu Shi, in *Deb Guk Ronf*)

(7.160)

Leb-leb	*at*	*lol,*	*leb-leb*	*at*	*shaod,*	*jix*	*nins,*	*nins*	***leb***
CLF-CLF	SAT	come	CLF-CLF	SAT	try	NEG_1	COP	COP	**who**

zhut	*hox?*
wear.shoes	fit

'Everyone came, and everyone tried (on the shoe, but it) didn't fit. Who would the shoe fit?' (Xingyu Shi, in *Oub Meinl Yaos Geud*)

(7.161)

Nex	***dib.leb***	*lol*	*heut*	*monx*	*leh,*	*deit*	*nins*	*tit*	*jix*
NEX	**who**	come	help	2SG	LEH	still	COP	replace	NEG_1

dut	*naond.*
obtain	ASSOC

'No matter who comes to help you, they can't replace (you doing it yourself).' (Haili Shi, in *Guef Waonl Hauk Nggaob*)

(7.162)

Jix	*dut*	*def*	*chaot,*	*nes*	*nex*	***jud.leb***	*at*	*jix*	*ghans.*
NEG_1	obtain	place	look.for	ask	NEX	**who**	SAT	NEG_1	see

'(She) couldn't find (the shoe) anywhere, and everyone (she) asked said they hadn't seen (it).' (Xingyu Shi, in *Oub Meinl Yaos Geud*)

The etymological source of *(dib.)leb/(jud.)leb* is unclear at present, although it may not be a coincidence that the form's obligatory second syllable is homophonous with *leb* 'CLF' (see Section 6.1.4.1). Furthermore, the optional first syllable *dib* is homophonous with *dib* 'which, some(thing/one)' (see Section 7.3.2.2 below), although obviously this is not true of the optional first syllable *jud* in the alternate pronunciation *(jud.)leb.*

7.3.2.2 The ignorative demonstrative *dib/dof* 'which, some(thing/one)'

The form *dib/dof* occurs in essentially the same grammatical environments as the demonstratives *neind* 'this' and *dox* 'that', and it is thus analyzed here as the ignorative pro-form corresponding to the class of demonstratives. The pronunciation *dib* is regularly used by all of the author's consultants, while the pronunciation *dof* is occasionally used by consultants from Yankan Village and Shanjiang Town (though those same consultants also use *dib* as well, in apparently free variation). Since *dib* and *dof* do not appear to differ in any appreciable grammatical, semantic, or pragmatic respects, both are glossed as 'which' whenever they occur in examples, although in non-interrogative contexts they are often better translated as 'some *X*' (where *X* is the semantic head of the noun phrase in which *dib/dof* occurs).

Like other demonstratives, *dib/dof* 'which, some(thing/one)' most often occurs as the final element of noun phrases which contain a classifier but which need not contain a noun (see Section 7.2). This can be seen by comparing examples (7.163) and (7.164) with example (7.165).

(7.163) *Monx lis aod-ngonl daob-yus* ***dib?***
2SG want one-CLF:animate AN-cow **which**
'Which cow do you want?' (Haili Shi, fieldnotes)

(7.164) *Monx lis aod-ngonl* ***dib?***
2SG want one-CLF:animate **which**
'Which (cow) do you want?' (Haili Shi, fieldnotes)

(7.165) **Monx lis daob-yus* ***dib?***
2SG want AN-cow **which**
(intended: 'Which cow do you want?')

Unsurprisingly, *dib/dof* very often serves an interrogative function when it occurs in such a noun-phrase–final position, as examples (7.163) and (7.164) above and (7.166–7.169) below show.

(7.166) *Nins aod-leb* ***dib*** *chauk naond?*
COP one-CLF **which** do ASSOC
'Which one (of you) did this?' (Haili Shi, fieldnotes)

(7.167) *Naont mx geud gians* ***dib*** *zhaut?*
thus 2SG hold CLF:kind$_1$ **which** cure
'So which (folk remedy) did you use to fix (your tooth)?' (Shixiang Wu, in *Tooth Conversation*)

(7.168) *Mx ninb khauk* ***dib?***
2SG at CLF:place$_2$ **which**
'Where are you?' (Shixiang Wu, fieldnotes)

(7.169) *Daob-mioul, aod-yaonk* ***dib*** *raut nonx aod-yaonk* ***dib***
AN-fish one-CLF:kind$_2$ **which** good eat one-CLF:kind$_2$ **which**
jaod nonx?
bad eat
'As for fish, which kind tastes good and which kind tastes bad?' (unknown Xong consultant, in *Conversation in Yankan*)

However, just as with Xong's other ignoratives, the form *dib/dof* 'which, some(thing/one)' can also serve a non-interrogative function in the same syntactic position given an appropriate context. This can be seen in examples (7.170–7.173) below, in which *dib/dof* still occurs noun-phrase–finally but does not have any interrogative force.

(7.170) *Mx aod-dieud* ***dib*** *monl wel jix guant.*
2SG one-CLF:time$_2$ **which** go 1SG NEG$_1$ care
'I don't care when you leave.' (Shixiang Wu, fieldnotes)

(7.171) *Tat-hnef monx aod-bix* ***dib*** *at jix lis monl.*
this-CLF:day 2SG one-CLF:place$_1$ **which** SAT NEG$_1$ want go
'Don't go anywhere today.' (Haili Shi, fieldnotes)

(7.172) *Jud niel nhob nhaux* ***dof*** *raut, jont nied.*
NEG$_2$ know walk CLF:broad.length **which** good sit cry
'(The girl) didn't know which path she should take, (and so she) sat and wept.' (Xingyu Shi, in *Oub Meinl Yaos Geud*)

(7.173) *Aod-meinl* ***dib*** *ghaod raut deb, aod-meinl* ***dib***
one-CLF:person **which** more good child one-CLF:person **which**
ghaod kint nied, ghaod mex hliof aub-gheb.
more often cry more exist many water-eye
'Whichever of you is the better child, whichever of you weeps more, (she'll) have more tears.' (Xingyu Shi, in *Oub Meinl Yaos Geud*)

Semantically, the difference between *dib/dof* 'which, some(thing/one)' and *naonb* 'what, something' (see Section 7.3.2.1) appears to be broadly similar to the difference between English *which* and *what*, with the former generally being used when choosing from among a relatively restricted set of possibilities (e.g. ***Which*** *of you three will go with me?*) and the latter being used when choosing from among a much larger set of possibilities (e.g. ***What*** *do you want to be when you grow up?*).

Just like Xong's other demonstratives (see Section 7.2), *dib/dof* 'which, some(thing/one)' can also follow the nouns *daod* 'place$_3$' and *(ghaob-)def* 'place' even when these nouns are not preceded by a classifier. Examples of the former can be seen in (7.174) and (7.175) below. Note that in the first of these examples *dib/dof* 'which, some(thing/one)' serves an interrogative function, while in the second it serves a non-interrogative function.

(7.174) *Shif.jib.shaonb* ***daod dib*** *yab mex daob-ginb?*
in.reality **place$_3$ which** also exist AN-bug
'Seriously, how (lit. 'where') could you possibly have bugs in your teeth?' (Haili Shi, in *Tooth Conversation*)

(7.175) *Dand hmaont-dius beul xeub xut.npeif, jix ghans xut.npeif.*
arrive evening-??? 3 retrieve shoe NEG_1 see shoe
*Doul nqad leh, **daod dib** eit id-ngual chaot.*
remain CLF:half.of.pair LEH **$place_3$ which** still DID-circle look.for
'That evening she went to retrieve the shoes, (but she) saw that one was missing. Only one was left, (and so she) went around everywhere looking.' (Xingyu Shi, in *Oub Meinl Yaos Geud*)

Dof alone also appears in the fixed expression *ib-dof* (never **ib-dib*), meaning 'where'. The identity of this expression's first syllable is unclear, and so the expression is glossed as [???-which] when it occurs in examples and texts in this grammar.[144] Unsurprisingly, the expression *ib-dof* is used only by speakers from Yankan Village and Shanjiang Town, as is the case with *dof* itself.

(7.176) *Beul baox jud niel ghat **ib-dof** leh.*
3 father NEG_2 know go.to **???-which** LEH
'(She) didn't know where her father had gone.' (Xingyu Shi, in *Oub Meinl Yaos Geud*)

Also like other demonstratives, *dib/dof* can occur independently (i.e. as a noun phrase in its own right, rather than as a constituent of some larger noun phrase). In such cases *dib/dof* generally serves a deictic locative function, so that it is better translated as 'where' (or 'somewhere' or 'anywhere', depending on the context), although even in these cases *dib/dof* is still uniformly glossed as 'which'. Note that when *dib/dof* thus occurs in isolation with a locative function, it may optionally be preceded by the nominal prefix *ghaob-* 'NOM' (see Section 5.4.2.1 and examples (7.177) and (7.178) below) with no change in meaning.

(7.177) *Mox.shib deib **ob-dib**?*
bathroom at **NOM-which**
'Where's the bathroom?' (Haili Shi, fieldnotes)

(7.178) *Monx nins **ob-dib** naond?*
2SG COP **NOM-which** ASSOC
'Where are you from?' (Haili Shi, fieldnotes)

144 The identity of the first syllable in *ib-dof* [???-which] 'where' may be unclear, but note that it is homophonous with one variant of the nominal prefix *dib-/ib-/jeub-/jil-* 'LOC' (see Section 5.4.2.9) and that it shares the same vowel and tone as both the first syllable of *(dib.)leb* 'who, someone' (see Section 7.3.2.1) and *dib* 'which'.

(7.179) *Wel eint ghat* ***dib*** *monx nhob ghat* ***dib.***
1SG fly go.to **which** 2SG walk go.to **which**
'Wherever I fly, you walk.' (Xingyu Shi, in *Oub Meinl Yaos Geud*)

(7.180) *Monx zhaos* ***dib*** *dut niax-naus?*
2SG from **which** obtain meat-bird
'Where did you get bird meat from?' (Xingyu Shi, in *Oub Meinl Yaos Geud*)

(7.181) *Ob-ras ninb* ***dof?*** *Monx tout wel naond bat* ***dof?***
NOM-comb at **which** 2SG pick.up 1SG ASSOC put **which**
'Where is the comb? Where did you put (that comb) of mine?' (Xingyu Shi, in *Oub Meinl Yaos Geud*)

(7.182) *Nkhed ngonl guoud ix zhus* ***dib*** *leh.*
see CLF:animate dog NEG_1 suffer **which** LEH
'(The boy) saw that the dog wasn't hurt anywhere (on its body).' (Chenghua Long, in *Frog, Where Are You?*)

However, note that *dib/dof* 'which, some(thing/one)' never occurs with a preceding *ghaob-* 'NOM' when it occurs as a constituent of a larger noun phrase. Furthemore, *dib/dof* is unlike *neind* 'this' and *dox* 'that' in that it is never followed by the noun root *-naub* '$place_4$' (or its phonological variant, *-ndaub*) even when it occurs independently (cf. Sections 5.5.2.7 and 7.2).

Finally, *dib* and *dof* also occur as the second morphemes of the fixed expressions *chauk-dib* and *chauk-dof* 'how' (lit. [do-which]), which are sometimes realized as *hauk-dib* and *hauk-dof* in fast or casual speech (see examples (7.187) and (7.188) below, as well as the discussion of *chauk-naonb* 'why' in Section 7.3.2.1 above).

(7.183) *Aod-leb reib-yeus neind* ***chauk-dib*** *giab?*
one-CLF vegetable-cooked.meat this **do-which** stir.fry
'How do you cook this dish?' (Shixiang Wu, fieldnotes)

(7.184) *Monx* ***chauk-dib*** *giab at jud guant.*
2SG **do-which** stir.fry SAT NEG_2 care
'It doesn't matter how you cook it.' (Haili Shi, fieldnotes)

(7.185) *Wel lis* ***chauk-dib*** *chauk?*
1SG want **do-which** do
'How should I do it?' (unknown Xong consultant, fieldnotes)

(7.186) ***Chauk-dib*** *hnant* *jix* *doub* *leh.*
do-which call NEG$_1$ answer LEH
'No matter how (the girl) called, there was no answer.' (Xingyu Shi, in *Oub Meinl Yaos Geud*)

(7.187) *Beul* *jix* *niel* ***hauk-dib*** *jix* *doul* *aub.*
3 NEG$_1$ know **do-which** NEG$_1$ remain water
'She didn't know how the water kept disappearing.' (Xingyu Shi, in *Oub Meinl Yaos Geud*)

(7.188) *Seink.cheinf* *beul* *deit* *nins* *zhus* *daob-ginb* *konk,* *ix* *konk*
naturally 3 still COP suffer AN-bug burrow NEG$_1$ burrow
beul ***hauk-dib*** *dut* *daont?*
3 **do-which** obtain pass.through
'Well, logically, it must be that there's a bug (in your tooth), otherwise how would there be a hole there?' (Chenghua Long, in *Tooth Conversation*)

7.3.2.3 The ignorative quantifiers *mins* 'how many, a few' and *haut/hot* 'how much, so much'

There are two ignorative forms that refer to quantity in Fenghuang Xong. The first of these is *mins* 'how many, a few', which patterns very closely with Xong's numerals (see Section 6.2) in terms of its distributional and grammatical properties (e.g. occurring in immediate pre-classifier position to form a numeral-classifier phrase). It is uniformly glossed as 'how many', which is also the appropriate English translation for the form in interrogative contexts, as in examples (7.189–7.192) below.

(7.189) *Aod-hnanf* *eud* *lis* ***mins**-qaok* *ndeib?*
one-CLF:clothing clothing want **how.many**-CLF:chi cloth
'How many *chi* (unit of length) of cloth will it take to make one article of clothing?' (Chenghua Long, fieldnotes)

(7.190) *Monx* *naond* *deb* *mex* ***mins**-jut?*
2SG ASSOC child exist **how.many**-CLF:year
'How old is your child?' (Haili Shi, fieldnotes)

(7.191) *Manx* *bioud* *mex* ***mins**-meinl* *mianx?*
2PL home exist **how.many**-CLF:person person
'How many people are there in your family?' (Shixiang Wu, fieldnotes)

(7.192) *Aod-hant* *niux* *neind* *lis* ***mins**-shauk* *daont*
one-CLF:PL meat this want **how.many**-CLF:yuan money
aod-gaonb?
one-CLF:catty
'How many *yuan* (unit of currency) is this meat per catty (unit of mass)?'
(Shixiang Wu, fieldnotes)

Just like other ignorative forms, *mins* can also serve a non-interrogative function given an appropriate context. In such cases *mins* is usually better translated as 'a few' (or, in negative contexts, 'not even a few' or 'not many'), although even then it is still uniformly glossed as 'how many'. Examples of *mins* serving such a non-interrogative function can be seen in (7.193–7.195) below.

(7.193) *Wel* *mex* ***mins**-shauk* *daont.*
1SG exist **how.many**-CLF:yuan money
'I have a few *yuan* (unit of currency).' (Haili Shi, fieldnotes)

(7.194) *Mx* *heut* *wel* *chaot* ***mins**-ngonl* *zhous.*
2SG help 1SG look.for **how.many**-CLF:pair$_1$ chopstick
'Go find a few pairs of chopsticks for me.' (Shixiang Wu, fieldnotes)

(7.195) *Monl* *ghat* *Tonx.reinl* *jix* *lis* ***mins**-leb* *xox.shif.*
go go.to Tongren NEG$_1$ want **how.many**-CLF hour
'It doesn't take many hours to get to Tongren (City).' (Haili Shi, fieldnotes)

In some cases consultants report that both interrogative and non-interrogative interpretations of an utterance containing *mins* are equally likely, with only context allowing one to determine which meaning was intended. This is the case in examples (7.196) and (7.197) below, which are segmentally and suprasegmentally homophonous (at least insofar as the author and his consultants are able to determine) but which clearly differ in terms of meaning and pragmatic import.

(7.196) *Beul* *bioud* *mex* ***mins**-ngonl* *ghab.*
3 home exist **how.many**-CLF:animate chicken
'His family has a few chickens.' (Shixiang Wu, fieldnotes)

(7.197) *Beul* *bioud* *mex* ***mins**-ngonl* *ghab?*
3 home exist **how.many**-CLF:animate chicken
'How many chickens does his family have?' (Shixiang Wu, fieldnotes)

The ability of *mins* to serve both interrogative and non-interrogative functions depending on the context is further illustrated by the question-and-answer pair shown in example (7.198). In the first utterance within the example, *mins-bioud manx liot* [how.many-CLF:home REL wealthy] means 'how many wealthy families?' (i.e. it serves an interrogative function), while in the second utterance the exact same sequence means '(not even) a few wealthy families' (i.e. it serves a non-interrogative function). In addition to any contextual clues, the presence of *(j)ix* 'NEG$_1$' in the second utterance strongly encourages a non-interrogative reading.

(7.198) *"Manx naond Ngel.kanx ah, mex haut-yut, mex*
2PL ASSOC Yankan PART exist how.much-few exist
***mins**-bioud manx liot ah?" Beul niab: "Jix*
how.many-CLF:home REL wealthy PART 3 say NEG$_1$
*mex **mins**-bioud manx liot."*
exist **how.many**-CLF:home REL wealthy
'(The People's Liberation Army soldiers asked the landlord:) "How many wealthy families are there in this Yankan Village of yours?" He replied: "Barely any."' (Qiusheng Long, in *Ngel.kanx*)

Note that *mins* 'how many, a few' is typically used only to refer to quantities smaller than ten. For larger indeterminate quantities, *haut/hot* 'how much, so much' is generally used instead; see discussion further below in this section. However, *mins* 'how many, a few' resembles Xong's other numerals in that it can also occur preceding or following a numeral that refers to a multiple of ten (e.g. *gul* 'ten', *bat* 'hundred', etc.) as part of a numeral phrase (see Section 6.2.1). This is shown in examples (7.199) and (7.200) below. In both of these examples, *mins* 'how many, a few' could have either an interrogative or a non-interrogative interpretation depending on the context, although at the time the speaker of the first example actually intended her utterance as a question and the speaker of the second intended hers as a statement.

(7.199) *Lis **mins**-bat-shauk daont?*
want **how.many**-hundred-CLF:yuan money
'(It) costs how many hundreds of *yuan* (unit of currency)?' (Haili Shi, fieldnotes)

(7.200) *Beul mex oub-gul-**mins**-jut.*
3 exist two-ten-**how.many**-CLF:year
'She's in her twenties.' (Yan Long, fieldnotes)

The form *mins* 'how many, a few' can also occur with a preceding nominal prefix *ghaob-* 'NOM' (see Section 5.4.2.1), and the presence of this prefix has two semantic effects on *mins*. First, it forces a non-interrogative interpretation of the ignorative, and second, it changes the ignorative's meaning from 'a few' (i.e. a small but indeterminate amount) to 'many' (i.e. a large but indeterminate amount). Examples of this can be seen in (7.201) and (7.202) below.

(7.201) *Beul bioud heit doul* ***ghaob-mins****-ngonl daob-ghab.*
3 home still remain **NOM-how.many**-CLF:animate AN-chicken
'His family still has many chickens.' (*'His family still has a few chickens', *'How many chickens does his family still have?') (Haili Shi, fieldnotes)

(7.202) *Nzaut ghot, sat nins hant manx dianx*
uncooked.rice old SAT COP CLF:PL REL finish
aob-mins*-jut naond.*
NOM-how.many-CLF:year ASSOC
'It was old rice, it had already been stored for many years.' (*'It had already been stored for a few years', *'How many years had it already been stored for?') (Xiaohui Wu, in *Conversation in La'ershan*)

The other ignorative quantifier in Fenghuang Xong is *haut/hot* 'how much, so much'. The two pronunciations of this form are in free variation for most consultants, although some consultants tend to use one more than the other. Although *haut/hot* 'how much, so much' does show some functional overlap with *mins* 'how many, a few', the two forms occur in different syntactic environments and have distinct meanings. Most obviously, while *haut/hot* does serve an essentially quantifying function, it is unlike *mins* in that it does not pattern with Xong's numerals at all. It does not occur in immediate pre-classifier position, and it cannot occur in numeral phrases like those seen in examples (7.199) and (7.200) above.

Instead, *haut/hot* 'how much, so much' typically occurs before a verb that refers to a property or state, including verbs like *shanb* 'tall', *heind* 'heavy', *hliof/hliob* 'many', *loux* '(to be/to last) a long time', *yeb/yanb* 'to like', *ghoub* 'far', and so on. Examples are given in (7.203–7.210) below. Note that in examples (7.203–7.206) *haut/hot* serves an interrogative function, while in examples (7.207–7.210) it serves a non-interrogative one.

(7.203) *Monx mex* ***hot*** *shanb?*
2SG exist **how.much** tall
'How tall are you?' (Haili Shi, fieldnotes)

(7.204) *Mx naond aod-ngonl nbat dox mex* ***hot*** *heind?*
2SG ASSOC one-CLF:animate pig that exist **how.much** heavy
'How heavy is that pig of yours?' (Shixiang Wu, fieldnotes)

(7.205) *Beul mex* ***hot*** *hliob daont?*
3 exist **how.much** many money
'How much money does he have?' (Shixiang Wu, fieldnotes)

(7.206)

Monx	*heut*	*beul*	*diex*	***hot***	*loux*	*ah?*
2SG	help	3	finish	**how.much**	long.time	PART

'How long were you working for him?' (Qiusheng Long, in *Ngel.kanx*)

(7.207)

Pus.reinl	*hauk*	*diul*	***haut***	*hliof*	***haut***	*hliof*
servant	drink	complete	**how.much**	many	**how.much**	many
naond	*nggaob.*					
ASSOC	medicine					

'The servant drank tons and tons of medicine.' (Haili Shi, in *Guef Waonl Hauk Nggaob*)

(7.208)

Xaub.Honl.Mob	***hot***	*yeb*	*aod-banb*	*manx*	*yab*	*xonx*
Little.Red.Hat	**how.much**	like	one-CLF:some	REL	also	attractive
yab	*jeut.mos*	*naond*	*beinx!*			
also	fragrant	ASSOC	flower			

'Little Red Hat loved those beautiful, fragrant flowers so much!' (Haili Shi, in *Xaub Honl Mob*)

(7.209)

Monx	*jix*	*mex*	***hot***	*heind.*
2SG	NEG_1	exist	**how.much**	heavy

'You barely weigh anything.' (Haili Shi, fieldnotes)

(7.210)

Daob-naus	*eint*	*aod-deik*	*zos*	*aod-deik,*	*eint*	*jix*	*dut*
AN-bird	fly	one-CLF:wing	land	one-CLF:wing	fly	NEG_1	obtain
hot	*ghoub*	*yab*	*zos*	*aod-dieud*	*daonl.*		
how.much	far	also	land	one-CLF:$time_2$	wait		

'The bird would fly for a bit and then land for a bit. Before it flew too far, it would stop and wait for a while.' (Xingyu Shi, in *Oub Meinl Yaos Geud*)

As examples (7.203–7.206) above show, in an interrogative context the meaning of *haut/hot* is essentially 'how much' or 'to what degree'. In an affirmative non-interrogative context, though, *haut/hot* generally means something closer to 'so much' or 'to such a great degree'. This can be seen in examples (7.207) and (7.208) above. This is in sharp contrast to *mins* 'how many, a few', which in an affirmative non-interrogative context means 'a few' (i.e. some, but not many). Note, however, that examples (7.209) and (7.210) above show that this is not true of *haut/hot* in a negative non-interrogative context, in which case it means 'not much' or 'not at all'.

Finally, in any context *haut/hot* can optionally be followed by the verb *yut* 'few'. This does not result in any discernible change in meaning, and for convenience the author connects *haut/hot* 'how much, so much' and *yut* 'few' with a hyphen when they occur together like this. As examples (7.211–7.213) below demonstrate, the dimorphemic form *haut-yut* (or *hot-yut*) is then followed by the property or state verb that it serves to modify, just as *haut/hot* would be if it occurred alone.

(7.211) *Manx bioud mex* ***hot-yut*** *hliob zos?*
2PL home exist **how.much-few** many people
'How many people are there in your family?' (Shixiang Wu, fieldnotes)

(7.212) *Daob-waonl, monx pinb.shif, monx deib boub-god* ***haut-yut***
great-king 2SG usually 2SG to 1PL-PL **how.much-few**
raut ***haut-yut*** *raut...*
good **how.much-few** good
'O great king, you have always – you have been so good to us...' (Haili Shi, in *Guef Waonl Hauk Nggaob*)

(7.213) *Wel jix mex* ***hot-yut*** *hliob daont.*
1SG NEG_1 exist **how.much-few** many money
'I don't have much money.' (unknown Xong consultant, fieldnotes)

8 Complex nominal constructions

Much like the preceding Chapter 7, this chapter deals with several distinct grammatical topics. However, where the previous chapter dealt with certain sets of forms, this chapter deals with certain sets of grammatical constructions. In particular, this chapter covers three such sets: relative clauses (which are defined in this grammar as subordinate, noun-phrase–internal clauses that serve to restrict the reference of their head noun), possessive constructions (defined as constructions in which a possessum noun phrase is modified – i.e. has its reference restricted – by a possessor noun phrase within a single larger noun phrase), and nominal conjunction (in which two or more noun phrases are combined into a single larger noun phrase, with the noun phrases so combined being of roughly equal syntactic rank). Just as with the topics discussed in the previous Chapter 7, there are very significant grammatical and functional differences among these three sets of constructions, with little to no overlap among them. Still, they are grouped together in this chapter because all of them involve noun phrases with relatively complex internal structures: either noun phrases that contain a clause (in the case of relative clauses), or noun phrases that are made up of multiple smaller noun phrases (in the case of possessive constructions and nominal conjunction).

8.1 Relative clauses

8.1.1 Introduction

This section discusses relative clauses in Fenghuang Xong, which are defined in this grammar as noun-phrase–internal subordinate clauses that serve to modify (i.e. restrict the reference of) their head noun. Before beginning this discussion, though, there are several terminological issues which must be addressed.

First, when the term "unflagged" is used with respect to relative clauses (and with respect to possessive constructions as well, for that matter; see Section 8.2.2), it simply means "bearing no overt segmental or tonal marker" (the alternate term "unmarked" is not used due to its potential ambiguity; see Haspelmath 2006). Thus an unflagged relative clause is a relative clause that does not bear any overt marker of its relative clause status (i.e. it does not bear either *naond* 'ASSOC' or *manx* 'REL').

Second, when the term "head noun" is used with respect to relative clauses, it refers to a relative-clause–external noun that co-occurs with a relative clause within the same noun phrase. The use of this term should not be taken to imply that in a noun phrase containing both a relative-clause–external noun and a relative clause, the noun serves as the head of the relative clause in a strict grammatical sense. While this particular term is perhaps less than ideal, it is useful when discussing ordering constraints in noun phrases containing relative clauses. In addition, similar terminology is widely used in studies of relative clauses in other languages produced by other scholars, and so its use here may help facilitate crosslinguistic comparison.

Third, a "headless" relative clause is one that occurs in a noun phrase that lacks any relative-clause–external noun. In other words, a headless relative clause is one that does not co-occur with any relative-clause–external noun within the same noun phrase, though it may still co-occur with other noun-phrase–internal, relative-clause–external constituents (such as numeral-classifier phrases or demonstratives). Just as with the term "head noun" discussed above, one could argue that this terminology is less than ideal, but it is widespread in the existing typological literature on relative clauses.

Moving on, all Xong relative clauses share a number of grammatical properties. Among these properties are the following: (i) Xong relative clauses are always externally rather than internally headed, (ii) they always occur embedded within their main clause rather than adjoined to it, (iii) there are no differences between Xong relative clauses and main clauses in terms of verb finiteness or constituent order, and verbs in relative clauses do not bear any nominalizing or relativizing morphology, and (iv) the role of the head noun within a Xong relative clause is not marked in any way.[145]

Xong displays an unusually complex system of relative clause constructions for an isolating language of greater mainland Southeast Asia, and two publications specifically devoted to relative clauses in Xong have already appeared. One of these, Sposato (2012), is a relatively simple descriptive study produced by the author of this grammar early on in the course of his fieldwork (see Section 2.5.4), and Section 8.1 of this grammar supersedes it. The other relevant study, Wu (2011), is a master's thesis focusing on relative clause constructions in Gouliang Xong, the Xong variety spoken in Gouliang Village near the town of Shanjiang in Fenghuang County (see Sections 2.5.3.1 and 2.5.3.3 of this grammar). Although the author of this grammar has not worked with any Xong speakers from Gouliang Village itself, all of his primary consultants report that they can easily understand the Xong spoken in all villages around Shanjiang Town, presumably including Gouliang.[146] In any case, Wu's thesis is one of the better examples of recent descriptive work on Xong grammar, and Wu demonstrates much more familiarity with modern typological literature and analytical techniques than many other contemporary scholars writing on Xong in Chinese. Because of this – and because Wu (2011) is itself written in Chinese, and thus presumably

145 While it is certainly true that neither relative nor resumptive pronouns are used to mark the role of the head noun within a Xong relative clause, one could conceivably argue that the role of the head noun is still marked by gapping (i.e. by the absence of any overt expression of the head noun within the relative clause). However, it is unclear how relevant this notion of "gapping" is to a language like Xong, in which virtually any argument in any clause can be elided (see Section 9.1.2).

146 Because of this presumable mutual intelligibility, this author did not think it inappropriate to re-elicit certain examples originally provided in Wu (2011) with his own consultants. Several such examples have been included in Sections 8.1.2 through 8.1.5 below, though these examples often had to undergo some degree of rephrasing before the author's own consultants would accept them.

inaccessible to many readers of this grammar – the remainder of this introductory section is devoted to a critical review of Wu's work.

Wu divides her thesis into five main chapters. The first of these (Wu 2011: 1–8) contains a literature review and a discussion of the author's data sources, which included thirty hours of recorded Xong speech plus several Xong text collections produced by other scholars. This first chapter also discusses Wu's theoretical framework, which is a blend of basic linguistic theory and traditional Chinese linguistic theory (see Sections 2.5.1 and 2.6.1 of this grammar for more information). The second chapter (2011: 9–21) lays out Wu's classification scheme for Gouliang Xong relative clauses. There are two potentially controversial arguments in this chapter. First, Wu considers the most basic distinction among Xong relative clauses to be the one between headed and headless relative clauses, and the most basic distinction among headed relative clauses to be the one between prenominal and postnominal (or pre- and post-head) relative clauses (2011: 21). Second, Wu considers unflagged postnominal relative clauses (see Section 8.1.5 below) to be postnominal *manx* relative clauses from which the marker *manx* 'REL' has been elided (2011: 10).

However, it seems to this author that neither of these arguments is entirely supported by the linguistic evidence. First, there are a number of readily observable grammatical differences between postnominal relative clauses marked with *manx* 'REL' (see Section 8.1.4 below) and unflagged postnominal relative clauses (Section 8.1.5), and so it is unclear why Wu considers the latter to simply be an elided version of the former rather than a distinct type of relative clause.[147] Second, ignoring headless relative clauses for the moment, all relevant Xong data with which the author is familiar suggests that relative clauses which bear *naond* 'ASSOC' as the sole marker of their relative clause status differ significantly in terms of their structural constraints from those which bear both *manx* 'REL' and *naond* 'ASSOC' and those which bear *manx* 'REL' alone, certainly much more so than the latter two types of relative clause differ from each other. In other words, on purely language-internal criteria the most appropriate first-order division among Xong relative clauses must be one in which relative clauses bearing *naond* 'ASSOC' alone are divided from relative clauses bearing *manx* 'REL', not one in which prenominal relative clauses are divided from postnominal ones (especially because certain types of Xong relative clauses can occur in either prenominal or postnominal position). Detailed justification for this alternate classification can be found in Sections 8.1.2 through 8.1.5 below, although the same information can be obtained more quickly by comparing the summaries of Xong's relative clause types in Section 8.1.6.

Moving on, Wu's third chapter (2011: 22–36) provides a more detailed look at the grammatical properties of headed relative clauses in Gouliang Xong (2011: 22–25)

147 This is in contrast to prenominal relative clauses marked with *naond* 'ASSOC' (see Section 8.1.2) and unflagged prenominal relative clauses (Section 8.1.3), whose only meaningful grammatical difference appears to be that the former bear a final *naond* while the latter do not.

and an overview of the relative clause markers *manx* 'REL' and *naond* 'ASSOC' (2011: 26–30), as well as a somewhat puzzling discussion of possible semantic, pragmatic, and cognitive differences between prenominal and postnominal relative clauses (2011: 33–36). The most relevant section of the chapter with regard to this grammar is probably Wu's description of prenominal relative clauses "flagged" with a following bare classifier or numeral-classifier phrase (2011: 30, 31). The author of this grammar disagrees with Wu's analysis of these constructions, and an alternate analysis is discussed in detail in Section 8.1.3 below.

The fourth chapter discusses two major grammatical topics. The first of these is the set of possible syntactic roles (e.g. subject, direct object, indirect object, etc.) which the head nouns of both prenominal and postnominal Xong relative clauses can have within those relative clauses (Wu 2011: 37–46). Wu reports few restrictions on prenominal relative clauses, but she argues that postnominal relative clauses can only be used to directly relativize on subjects and obliques. She says that in order to relativize on a direct object, indirect object, or possessor with a postnominal relative clause, that argument must first be "promoted to subject position" by converting the clause to a "passive" one (and it appears that objects of comparison cannot be relativized on by a postnominal relative clause at all). However, Wu neglects to define several important grammatical terms in this section (including "subject", "object", and "passive", among others), which may be partially responsible for some of the significant differences between her analysis and the one provided in this grammar. See Section 8.1.4 below for details.

The second major topic covered in Wu's Chapter 4 is the set of strategies used in Gouliang Xong to signal the role of a head noun within its relative clause, namely gapping (though see this author's comments on "gapping" in Xong relative clauses earlier in this section) and resumptive pronouns (Wu 2011: 46, 47). Interestingly, the author of this grammar has not encountered any instances of resumptive pronouns in his own fieldwork, not even when working with a Xong speaker from Shanjiang Town, which is very near Wu's own fieldsite of Gouliang Village.[148]

The fifth and final chapter presents arguments for some of Wu's major conclusions. The most significant of these is that postnominal relative clauses are the older, more "native" method of relativization in Xong, with prenominal relative clauses being a more recent innovation. Although this author does not necessarily agree with every detail of Wu's arguments here, he does agree with her general conclusion. Furthermore, Wu deserves significant credit for considering Xong-internal factors as well as influence from Sinitic languages when discussing the origins of Xong's prenominal relative clauses (Wu 2011: 56–58).

148 Resumptive pronouns do occur in certain Standard Mandarin relative clauses; see Section 8.1.2 for some discussion. It is unclear whether resumptive pronouns occur in relative clauses in Fenghuang Chinese, which is the other major Sinitic variety spoken in Fenghuang County (see Section 2.7.2).

On the whole, while this author may not agree with all of the analyses it presents, Wu (2011) remains one of the strongest works on Xong grammar published to date, one that is certainly worth consulting for readers literate in Chinese. The remainder of this Section 8.1 covers many of the same topics that are discussed in Wu's work, although the organizational scheme used here is quite different from the one used by Wu. First, Section 8.1.2 focuses on *naond* relative clauses, which are obligatorily prenominal relative clauses flagged with a final associative marker *naond* 'ASSOC'. Section 8.1.3 discusses certain other prenominal relative clauses that are not flagged with a final *naond*. Section 8.1.4 examines *manx* relative clauses, which are flagged with an initial relative clause marker *manx* 'REL' and which can be divided into a number of subtypes based on where they occur in relation to their head noun and what, if any, additional relative clause markers they bear. Section 8.1.5 covers postnominal unflagged relative clauses, which are obligatorily postnominal relative clauses that bear no overt marker of their relative clause status. Finally, Section 8.1.6 briefly summarizes the differences among Xong's various relative clause types, and it also considers whether Xong is best analyzed (in word order typological terms) as a language in which prenominal relative clauses predominate (i.e. RelN, to use the terminology of Dryer 2013c), as one in which postnominal relative clauses predominate (i.e. NRel), or as one in which neither type predominates (i.e. "mixed").

8.1.2 *Naond* relative clauses

Xong's *naond* relative clauses are structurally and functionally very similar to Standard Mandarin's relative clauses, and they have fewer restrictions on their internal grammatical structure than any other type of Xong relative clause.[149] Relative clauses of this sort always precede their head nouns, and they are always accompanied by an invariant final associative marker *naond* 'ASSOC' (see Section 9.2.3.2) that serves as the only overt marker of their relative clause status (cf. the final associative marker *de* [的] that accompanies Standard Mandarin relative clauses). Examples are given in (8.1) and (8.2) below. In these and subsequent examples, each *naond* relative clause has been enclosed within brackets, and each relative clause's head noun has been bolded.

149 The author was able to perform a brief elicitation session on relative clauses in Fenghuang Chinese (see Section 2.7.2) with a few of his primary Xong-speaking consultants, as the consultants in question all speak Fenghuang Chinese as their second language (with Standard Mandarin then as their third). During the session, the author simply asked his consultants to translate a few utterances containing relative clauses from Standard Mandarin into Fenghuang Chinese. The results of this elicitation session should perhaps not be taken too seriously, since this was the only session the author conducted on Fenghuang Chinese and since it is possible that his consultants were to some degree simply doing morpheme-by-morpheme translations. Still, it is worth pointing out that the resulting Fenghuang Chinese relative clauses were fairly similar to both Standard Mandarin relative clauses and Xong's *naond* relative clauses, as they were obligatorily prenominal relative clauses marked with a final associative particle (which was segmentally [ti], with an uncertain pitch).

(8.1) [[*wel* *nieus*] *naond*] ***bid-deid***
[[1SG buy] ASSOC] **FRT-bean**
'the beans that I bought' (Yan Long, fieldnotes)

(8.2) [[*hlaok* *reib*] *naond*] ***ghaob-ndeind***
[[cut vegetable] ASSOC] **NOM-knife**
'a knife for chopping vegetables' (Haili Shi, fieldnotes)

Xong's *naond* relative clauses are like all other relative clauses in the language in that the role of the relative clause's head noun within the relative clause itself is not overtly indicated in any way (though see the discussion of "gapping" in Xong relative clauses in Section 8.1.1 above). Nevertheless, there appear to be relatively few restrictions on the possible roles a head noun can have within a *naond* relative clause. For instance, the head noun of each *naond* relative clause in examples (8.3–8.5) below functions as an AGENT (i.e. as the more agent-like argument of a semantically transitive verb or the most agent-like argument of a semantically ditransitive verb) within its relative clause. (See Section 9.1.1 for more on AGENTS, SUBJECTS, PATIENTS, and other grammaticalized syntactic roles in Xong.)

(8.3) [[*Hnef-hnef* *ngheint* *aub*] *naond*] ***miex***
[[CLF:day-CLF:day carry.on.shoulder.pole water] ASSOC] **person**
at *kut* *guaot.*
SAT bitter pass
'People who have to haul water every day really have it rough.' (Haili Shi, fieldnotes)

(8.4) *Aod-god* *miex* *dox,* *sat* *nins* [[*mex* *cef* *mex*
one-CLF:human.group person that SAT COP [[exist wealth exist
njel *mex* *nghaot*] *naond*] *aod-god* ***miex*** *dox*
wealth exist price] ASSOC] one-CLF:human.group **person** that
leh, *cos.yol.*
LEH lie
'Those people, all those wealthy, powerful people, they lied.' (Qiusheng Long, in *Ngel.kanx*)

(8.5) [[*Heut* *monx* *nieus* *niax*] *naond*] ***deb-nint*** *dox* *nins* *bix*
[[help 2SG buy meat] ASSOC] **DIM-man** that COP CLF:place_1
dib *naond?*
which ASSOC
'Where's that boy who buys meat for you from?' (unknown Xong consultant, fieldnotes)

In examples (8.6–8.8), the head noun of each *naond* relative clause functions as a SUBJECT (i.e. as the sole argument of a semantically intransitive verb) within its relative clause.

(8.6) [[*liox*] *naond*] ***daob-guoud***
[[big] ASSOC] **AN-dog**
'a big dog' (Shixiang Wu, fieldnotes)

(8.7) *Nins* [[*zeib* *kut*] *naond*] ***rib.zib***.
COP [[most bitter] ASSOC] **day**
'(Those) were (our) most difficult days.' (Qiusheng Long, in *Ngel.kanx*)

(8.8) *Pus.reinl* *hauk* *diul* [[*haut* *hliof* *haut* *hliof*]
servant drink complete [[how.much many how.much many]
naond] ***nggaob***.
ASSOC] **medicine**
'The servant drank tons and tons of medicine.' (Haili Shi, in *Guef Waonl Hauk Nggaob*)

The head noun of each *naond* relative clause in examples (8.9–8.11) functions as a PATIENT (i.e. as the more patient-like argument of a semantically transitive verb) within its relative clause.

(8.9) *Aod-ngonl* [[*lis* *beux*] *naond*] ***daob-nbat*** *nzeit* *guaot*.
one-CLF:animate [[want hit] ASSOC] **AN-pig** skinny pass
'That pig that's to be killed is very skinny.' (Shixiang Wu, fieldnotes)

(8.10) [[*Monx* *nieus*] *naond*] ***niax*** *jix* *raut* *nonx*.
[[2SG buy] ASSOC] **meat** NEG_1 good eat
'The meat that you bought doesn't taste good.' (Yan Long, fieldnotes)

(8.11) *Monx* *zhank.meinf* *yonb* [[*manx-eib* *did-lons*] *naond*]
2SG always use [[AT-yon DID-gather] ASSOC]
aod-hant ***dib.daont***.
one-CLF:PL **money**
'You're always spending the money that we saved up before.' (Haili Shi, fieldnotes)

Only a few examples of *naond* relative clauses have been attested in which the head noun functions as a RECIPIENT (i.e. as the most recipient-like argument of a semantically ditransitive verb) within its relative clause (as in English *the man that I lent money to*). However, the few relevant examples that have been found (given in (8.12–8.14) below) do not differ from other *naond* relative clauses in any appreciable way. Note in particular that the role of each head noun within its respective relative clause is still not indicated in any way. This is one significant difference between Xong relative clauses marked with *naond* and Standard Mandarin relative clauses marked with *de* (的), since the latter construction will typically make use of a resumptive pronoun when dealing with recipients, obliques, and other types of arguments lower on the Accessibility Hierarchy (for more on the Accessibility Hierarchy in general, see Keenan and Comrie 1977). Consultants do allow the insertion of resumptive pronouns in relative clauses such as the ones shown in (8.12–8.14) below, but they report that doing so results in an utterance that sounds less "natural" than one without a resumptive pronoun.

(8.12) [[*Lox.sik* *nieux.ghoub* *gaons* *taonx*] *naond*] *aod-ngonl*
[[teacher just.now give candy] ASSOC] one-CLF:animate
deb-deb *dox* *nins* *wel* *naond* *deb.*
child-RED that COP 1SG ASSOC child
'That kid who the teacher just gave candy to is my kid.' (Shixiang Wu, fieldnotes)

(8.13) [[*Nieux.ghoub* *mx* *gaons* *did.daont*] *naond*] *meinl*
[[just.now 2SG give money] ASSOC] CLF:person
mianx *dox* *nins* *leb?*
person that COP who
'Who's that person you just gave money to?' (Shixiang Wu, fieldnotes)

(8.14) *Aod-leb* *neind* *nins* *jix* *nins* [[*monx* *shab* *Xonb*]
one-CLF this COP NEG$_1$ COP [[2SG teach Xong]
naond] ***lox.web****?*
ASSOC] **white.foreigner**
'Is this the (white) foreigner that you're teaching Xong to?' (unknown Xong consultant, fieldnotes)

The head noun of each *naond* relative clause in examples (8.15–8.19) below functions as a relatively oblique-like argument within its relative clause. More specifically, the head nouns of the relative clauses in examples (8.15) and (8.16) are serving in an instrumental role, the head noun of the relative clause in example (8.17) is serving in a locative role, and the head nouns of the relative clauses in examples (8.18) and (8.19) are serving in a temporal role. In these cases, too, the role of each head noun within its relative clause is not indicated in any way. With respect to examples (8.17–8.19) in particular, note that the use of relative clauses with head nouns like *ghaob-def* [NOM-place] 'place' or *ob-ngaonf* [NOM-time] 'time' is in fact the standard way of expressing "where" and "when" clauses in Xong, though such clauses can also be expressed using the other types of relative clause discussed in Sections 8.1.3 through 8.1.5.

(8.15) *Beul ninb bioud mex zheinb deb-mok, [[raons*
3 at home exist CLF:tool DIM-sickle [[cut.firewood
deul] naond] ***mok.***
firewood] ASSOC] **sickle**
'They had a sickle at home, a sickle for cutting firewood.' (Xingyu Shi, in *Deb Guk Ronf*)

(8.16) [[*Nzad mes*] *naond*] ***ghaob-beinx*** *zeib jaod.*
[[wash face] ASSOC] **NOM-basin** most bad
'The face-washing basin is the shoddiest (of all our basins).' (Shixiang Wu, fieldnotes)

(8.17) *Aod-bix neind nins [[boub giab reib-yeus]*
one-CLF:place$_1$ this COP [[1PL stir.fry vegetable-cooked.meat]
naond] ***ghaob-def.***
ASSOC] **NOM-place**
'This is where we cook.' (Haili Shi, fieldnotes)

(8.18) [[*Beul hneind eud*] *naond*] ***ngaonf*** *leh, daob-guoud*
[[3 wear clothing] ASSOC] **time** LEH AN-dog
jeud-nggut leb pinf manh...
DID-enter CLF bottle PART
'While he (i.e. the boy) was getting dressed, the dog crawled into the bottle...' (Chenghua Long, in *Frog, Where Are You?*)

(8.19) *Deib [[Xaub.Honl.Mob mob ghaob-dieud monl liuk*
at [[Little.Red.Hat squat NOM-body go pluck
beinx] naond] ***ob-ngaonf,*** *aod-ngonl daob-jod doub*
flower] ASSOC] **NOM-time** one-CLF:animate AN-wolf then$_1$
gies.gies naond nhob sheub lah.
quietly ASSOC walk leave PRF
'When Little Red Hat squatted down to pluck flowers, the wolf quietly snuck away.' (Haili Shi, in *Xaub Honl Mob*)

In the author's corpus, there is only a single clear example of a *naond* relative clause in which the head noun functions as a possessor within the relative clause. Further research is needed to determine whether the paucity of such examples represents a real grammatical dispreference for them or whether it is simply an artifact of the author's small corpus size.

(8.20) *Aod-ngonl* [[*aob-mes* *shaonb*] *naond*] ***daob-guoud***
one-CLF:animate [[NOM-face wound] ASSOC] **AN-dog**
dox *nins* *boub* *giaok-bioud* *naond.*
that COP 1PL side-home ASSOC
'That dog with the wound on its face is our neighbor's.' (Chenghua Long, fieldnotes)

No examples of *naond* relative clauses in which the head noun serves as an object of comparison within the relative clause (as in English *the boy that I am taller than*) have yet been attested in the author's collected Xong texts, and attempts to elicit such relative clauses have so far proven unsuccessful. Just as with *naond* relative clauses in which the head noun serves as a possessor, it remains unclear whether this reflects an actual grammatical restriction against such relative clauses in Fenghuang Xong or whether it is merely a sign of their pragmatic oddness.

Finally, in some cases the head noun of a *naond* relative clause appears to have no semantic or grammatical role within its relative clause whatsoever (see also Comrie 1998 and Matsumoto, Comrie, and Sells 2017). Examples of this can be seen in (8.21–8.23) below. As these examples show, the head nouns of relative clauses of this sort usually have rather abstract meanings, like *nzeinx* 'kindness' or *sib* 'matter, affair'. Still, it seems clear that these constructions should still be considered typical examples of *naond* relative clauses, since they are still subordinate clauses marked with a final *naond* 'ASSOC' that serve to restrict the reference of their head noun.

(8.21) [[*Monx* *gieub* *wel* *deb-npaok*] *naond*] ***nzeinx*** *naonb*
[[2SG save 1SG DIM-woman] ASSOC] **kindness** as
gheul *shanb,* *naonb* *aub* *dob.*
mountain tall as water deep
'Your kindess in saving my daughter was as tall as the mountains, as deep as the sea.' (Chenghua Long, adapted from Xiang [1999: 193])

(8.22) *Wel* *lis* *geud* [[*mx* *tat-hnef* *ndaot* *lox.sik*]
1SG want hold [[2SG this-CLF:day curse teacher]
naond] ***sib*** *bod* *boub* *baox!*
ASSOC] **matter** tell 1PL father
'I'm going to tell our father about how you swore at the teacher today!' (unknown Xong consultant, fieldnotes)

(8.23) [[*Yux.sid-Xonb* *zhut* *mb*] *naond*] ***faonk.faob*** *nanb*
[[traditional.doctor-Miao cure pain] ASSOC] **method** really
kiot *kiot.*
strange strange
'The way the traditional doctor cures pain is really strange.' (Chenghua Long, fieldnotes)

Xong's *naond* relative clauses are not the only noun-phrase–internal elements that occur before the noun itself within a noun phrase: possessive phrases (see Section 8.2) and numeral-classifier phrases (Section 6.1.2) typically do so as well. Examples (8.24–8.29) below show that possessive phrases obligatorily occur in noun-phrase–initial position, but they also show that the relative ordering of prenominal numeral-classifier phrases and *naond* relative clauses is flexible within noun phrases that contain both. In these six examples, each possessive phrase, numeral-classifier phrase, and *naond* relative clause has been enclosed within brackets, and each noun has been bolded.

(8.24) [*boub naond*] [*bub-ngonl*] [[*beut nggueb*] *naond*]
[1PL ASSOC] [three-CLF:animate] [[lie.down sleep] ASSOC]
daob-yul *dox*
AN-cow that
'those three sleeping cows of ours' (Haili Shi, fieldnotes)

(8.25) [*boub naond*] [[*beut nggueb*] *naond*]
[1PL ASSOC] [[lie.down sleep] ASSOC]
[*bub-ngonl*] ***daob-yul*** *dox*
[three-CLF:animate] **AN-cow** that
'those three sleeping cows of ours' (Haili Shi, fieldnotes)

(8.26) *[[*beut nggueb*] *naond*] [*boub naond*]
[[lie.down sleep] ASSOC] [1PL ASSOC]
[*bub-ngonl*] ***daob-yul*** *dox*
[three-CLF:animate] **AN-cow** that
(intended: 'those three sleeping cows of ours')

(8.27) *[[*beut nggueb*] *naond*] [*bub-ngonl*] [*boub naond*]
[[lie.down sleep] ASSOC] [three-CLF:animate] [1PL ASSOC]
daob-yul *dox*
AN-cow that
(intended: 'those three sleeping cows of ours')

(8.28) *[*bub-ngonl*] [[*beut nggueb*] *naond*] [*boub naond*]
[three-CLF:animate] [[lie.down sleep] ASSOC] [1PL ASSOC]
daob-yul *dox*
AN-cow that
(intended: 'those three sleeping cows of ours')

(8.29) *[*bub-ngonl*] [*boub naond*] [[*beut nggueb*] *naond*]
[three-CLF:animate] [1PL ASSOC] [[lie.down sleep] ASSOC]

daob-yul *dox*
AN-cow that
(intended: 'those three sleeping cows of ours')

The form *naond* 'ASSOC' can also be used to create certain headless constructions that do not feature any head noun. Although strictly speaking these constructions are not relative clauses according to the definition used in this grammar (see Section 8.1.1 above), they greatly resemble *naond* relative clauses in structural terms (as they too consist of a subordinate clause followed by the associative marker *naond* 'ASSOC'), and so they are still discussed here. However, these headless *naond* relative clauses are quite different from their headed counterparts in functional terms. Rather than serving to modify a head noun, most such headless constructions serve one of three major functions: (i) they serve as a noun phrase in their own right (as in examples (8.30) and (8.31) below), (ii) they serve as a constituent of a larger noun phrase in what is still an essentially modifying function (as in examples (8.32) and (8.33)), or (iii) they follow the copular verb *nins* 'COP' to express some property or attribute of that copular verb's preceding (or elided) argument (as in examples (8.34) and (8.35); in such cases it is not clear whether there is any difference between using *nins* 'COP' plus a following relative clause and simply using the relativized clause in question as a non-relativized predicate).

(8.30) *Boub-gud ox monx monl puk, ix mex [[nqat] naond].*
1PL-PL and 2SG go speak NEG$_1$ exist [[fear] ASSOC]
'We'll go with you to explain, there's nothing to be afraid of.' (Chenghua Long, fieldnotes)

(8.31) *[[Kiak chek] naond] ix raut nghauk.zaol, [[baond put]*
[[drive vehicle] ASSOC] NEG$_1$ good play [[shoot gun]
naond] ghaod mex weik.
ASSOC] more exist interest
'The racing (computer game) isn't all that fun, but the shooting (computer game) is more interesting.' (unknown Xong consultant, fieldnotes)

(8.32) *[[Lanb] naond] aod-jut dox...*
[[chaotic] ASSOC] one-CLF:year that
'Back in the year of troubles...' (Qiusheng Long, in *Ngel.kanx*)

(8.33) *[[Jont ninb ghaob-deut-ndaut] naond] aod-meinl dox*
[[sit at NOM-foot-tree] ASSOC] one-CLF:person that
doub nins xob.zhaonx.
then$_1$ COP principal
'That person sitting under the tree is (our school's) principal.' (Haili Shi, fieldnotes)

(8.34) *Aod-banb* *neind* *nins* [[*zeib* *jex.bieb,*
one-CLF:some this COP [[most simple.and.convenient
zeib *jex.jef*] *naond*] *yaox?*
most quick.and.easy] ASSOC] right?
'These (folk remedies) are the simplest, the easiest, right?' (Haili Shi, in *Tooth Conversation*)

(8.35) *At* *nins* [[*ghous*] *naond*].
SAT COP [[trick] ASSOC]
'It was all a trick.' (Xingyu Shi, in *Oub Meinl Yaos Geud*)

8.1.3 Unflagged prenominal relative clauses

One other type of prenominal relative clause has occasionally been encountered in the speech of the author's consultants. This type has two variants, neither of which is nearly as common as the *naond* relative clauses just discussed.

In the first variant of this other prenominal relative clause type, the relative clause precedes a bare classifier (see Section 6.1.3.1) or a numeral-classifier phrase (Section 6.1.2), which in turn precedes the head noun. Examples of this can be seen in (8.36–8.39) below. In these examples, each relative clause, each bare classifier or numeral-classifier phrase, and each head noun has been enclosed within brackets, although no further constituent structures among them have been indicated.

(8.36) [*Zhanx*] [*hant*] [*ghaob-hlat*] *neind* *jaod* *nkhed* *daos.*
[tie] [CLF:PL] [NOM-rope] this bad look die
'These ropes that (you've) tied are really ugly.' (Haili Shi, fieldnotes)

(8.37) [*beut* *nggueb*] [*leb*] [*ghaob-def*]
[lie.down sleep] [CLF] [NOM-place]
'a place for sleeping' (Haili Shi, fieldnotes)

(8.38) [*Shab* *ndeud*] [*aod-meinl*] [*mianx*] *dox* *nins* *boub* *baox.*
[teach writing] [one-CLF:person] [person] that COP 1PL father
'That teacher is my father.' (Chenghua Long, fieldnotes)[150]

150 The translation of *boub* '1PL' as 'my' rather than 'our' is correct here; see Section 8.2.1 for details.

(8.39) [*Chauk donb*] [*aod-ncaod*] [*miex*] *dox nins*
[do work] [one-CLF:animate.group] [person] that COP
wel naond geub.bul.
1SG ASSOC friend
'Those people working there are my friends.' (Haili Shi, fieldnotes)

In the second variant, the relative clause immediately precedes its head noun with no intervening material whatsoever. Examples of this can be seen in (8.40) and (8.41) below. Note that while examples such as these are not particularly rare in naturalistic Xong speech, they are generally judged to be only marginally grammatical when they are pointed out to consultants or when they are produced in elicitation contexts. See further below in this section for details.

(8.40) [*Monx beut nggueb*] [*ghaob-ngaonf*] *dianx nbeit puk daut.*
[2SG lie.down sleep] [NOM-time] finish dream speak speech
'You were talking in your sleep.' (unknown Xong consultant, fieldnotes)

(8.41) *Aod-hant dox nins* [*monx nieus*] [*niax*].
one-CLF:PL that COP [2SG buy] [meat]
'That was the meat that you bought.' (Yan Long, fieldnotes)

Note also that in none of these cases does the associative marker *naond* 'ASSOC' appear.

Wu (2011: 14, 15, 30, 31) analyzes the bare classifiers in examples like (8.36) and (8.37) and the numeral-classifier phrases in examples like (8.38) and (8.39) as relative clause markers. In other words, she argues that the bare classifiers and numeral-classifier phrases in cases such as these are not merely serving their typical noun-phrase–internal functions (see Sections 6.1.2.1 and 6.1.3.1), they are also serving the same function that *naond* 'ASSOC' does in those relative clauses in which it appears: to occur as the final element of a prenominal relative clause and thereby mark it as such. Interestingly, Wu explicitly says that examples like (8.40) and (8.41), in which a relative clause directly precedes its head noun with no intervening material whatsoever, do not occur in Gouliang Xong (2011: 14, 31).

It seems to this author, however, that there is a better way to account for the relevant data than the one provided in Wu (2011).[151] In particular, this author would

151 The arguments in this section are generally similar to arguments given in Section 8.2.2 about the inability of classifiers to serve as possessive markers in Xong. Note, though, that the relevant linguistic facts (and thus the author's arguments about those facts) in these two sections are not completely identical. For instance, the author's consultants readily accept possessive constructions composed solely of an initial, unflagged possessor noun phrase and a following bare possessum noun (as in *wel daont* [1SG money] 'my money'). However, they only very grudgingly accept equivalent constructions

argue that the bare classifiers in examples like (8.36) and (8.37) and the numeral-classifier phrases in examples like (8.38) and (8.39) do not serve as relative clause markers, and they do not form a grammatical constituent with the preceding relative clause. Instead, the prenominal relative clauses in examples like these simply bear no overt marker of their relative clause status. In other words, this author would argue that the actual constituent structure in these sorts of constructions is *not* the one implied in Wu (2011) (shown in the diagram immediately below), in which a prenominal relative clause forms an immediate constituent with the following bare classifier or numeral-classifier phrase, with the resulting constituent then combining with the following noun to constitute the noun phrase in its entirety.

*[[RELATIVE.CLAUSE (NUM-)CLF] NOUN]

Rather, it is the one given below, in which the prenominal relative clause does not form an immediate constituent with the following bare classifier or numeral-classifier phrase. Note that here the exact higher-level relations between the noun phrase's final noun and its initial relative clause, or between its final noun and the preceding bare classifier or numeral-classifier phrase, are irrelevant. The key point is that the initial relative clause and the following bare classifier or numeral-classifier phrase do not form a constituent.

[[RELATIVE.CLAUSE] [(NUM-)CLF] [NOUN]]

The author has three main pieces of evidence to support this alternate analysis. First, it is significant that consultants only produce prenominal relative clauses without *naond* 'ASSOC' in fast, casual speech. In slower or more careful speech, they generally insist that *naond* be inserted immediately after such a prenominal relative clause, before any following material. This is true of prenominal relative clauses followed by a bare classifier (as in examples (8.36) and (8.37) above), of those followed by a full numeral-classifier phrase (as in examples (8.38) and (8.39)), and of those followed immediately by a noun (as in examples (8.40) and (8.41)). Thus, for instance, consultants report that example (8.42) below, which contains *naond* 'ASSOC', is preferable to example (8.43), which lacks it. The same is true of examples (8.44) and (8.45) and of examples (8.46) and (8.47).

(8.42) [*Zhanx* ***naond***] [*hant*] [*ghaob-hlat*] *neind jaod nkhed daos.*
[tie **ASSOC**] [CLF:PL] [NOM-rope] this bad look die
'These ropes that (you've) tied are really ugly.' (Haili Shi, fieldnotes)

---

composed solely of an initial, unflagged relative clause and a following bare head noun (as in ??*monx nieus niax* [2SG buy meat] 'the meat that you bought', which is at best marginally grammatical in slow and/or careful speech).

(8.43) [*Zhanx*] [*hant*] [*ghaob-hlat*] *neind jaod nkhed daos.*
[tie] [CLF:PL] [NOM-rope] this bad look die
'These ropes that (you've) tied are really ugly.' (Haili Shi, fieldnotes) (repeated from (8.36) above)

(8.44) [*Shab ndeud* ***naond***] [*aod-meinl*] [*mianx*] *dox nins boub baox.*
[teach writing **ASSOC**] [one-CLF:person] [person] that COP 1PL father
'That teacher is my father.' (Chenghua Long, fieldnotes)

(8.45) [*Shab ndeud*] [*aod-meinl*] [*mianx*] *dox nins boub baox.*
[teach writing] [one-CLF:person] [person] that COP 1PL father
'That teacher is my father.' (Chenghua Long, fieldnotes) (repeated from (8.38) above)

(8.46) [*Monx beut nggueb* ***naond***] [*ghaob-ngaonf*] *dianx nbeit puk daut.*
[2SG lie.down sleep **ASSOC**] [NOM-time] finish dream speak speech
'You were talking in your sleep.' (unknown Xong consultant, fieldnotes)

(8.47) [*Monx beut nggueb*] [*ghaob-ngaonf*] *dianx nbeit puk daut.*
[2SG lie.down sleep] [NOM-time] finish dream speak speech
'You were talking in your sleep.' (unknown Xong consultant, fieldnotes) (repeated from (8.40) above)

However, there is something of a grammaticality continuum involved here. While all consultants prefer any prenominal relative clause that is marked with *naond* 'ASSOC' over any such relative clause without *naond*, the various possible dispreferred constructions are not all equally "bad". Consultants judge examples like (8.40) and (8.41), with no classifier at all, to be the worst, and they judge examples like (8.38) and (8.39), with full numeral-classifier phrases, to be the least bad. Examples like (8.36) and (8.37), with a bare classifier but no numeral, are judged to fall somewhere in the middle.[152] Nevertheless, in all cases consultants prefer a prenominal relative clause with a following *naond* over one without it. This suggests that the bare classi-

152 Although a detailed investigation of the topic lies well outside the scope of the current study, it is not difficult to think of potential functional explanations for this grammaticality continuum. For instance, it may simply be that the more segmental material there is between a preceding unflagged relative clause and a following head noun, the less possibility there is of the listener misinterpreting the grammatical relationship between the relative clause and the noun.

fiers and numeral-classifier phrases in examples like (8.36–8.39) do not really substitute for *naond* 'ASSOC' in marking their preceding relative clauses as such, but rather that they merely happen to occur in the immediate post–relative-clause slot within their noun phrase, with there being no special grammatical relationship whatsoever between the bare classifier or numeral-classifier phrase and the preceding relative clause.

Second, although headless versions of relative clauses marked with *naond* 'ASSOC' are common, it is impossible to form a headless relative clause marked with a final bare classifier in slow or careful speech (examples of such constructions do very occasionally occur in particularly fast or casual speech, but consultants universally reject these examples as ungrammatical when they are pointed out to them). This can be seen from examples (8.48) and (8.49) below. This fact suggests that, unlike *naond* 'ASSOC', the bare classifiers in examples like (8.36) and (8.37) above do not form a constituent with their preceding relative clauses.

(8.48) *Nins* [[*hlaok* *niax*] ***naond***].
COP [[cut meat] **ASSOC**]
'(This knife) is for cutting meat.' (Yan Long, fieldnotes)

(8.49) **Nins* [[*hlaok* *niax*] ***zheinb***].
COP [[cut meat] **CLF:tool**]
(intended: '[This knife] is for cutting meat.')

In contrast, it is possible (though rather uncommon) to have a noun phrase that consists solely of an unflagged relative clause and a following numeral-classifier phrase, as in example (8.50) below. However, this fact has no bearing on either this author's arguments or the arguments presented in Wu (2011), as the existence of this sort of construction is consistent with either analysis. This author would argue that the relationship between the unflagged relative clause and the following numeral-classifier phrase in such constructions is similar to the one between the *naond* relative clause and the following numeral-classifier phrase in examples like (8.51) below (in which no head noun occurs, so that the relative clause is arguably serving to restrict the reference of the numeral-classifier phrase instead of the reference of a noun), while Wu would presumably analyze such constructions as headless relative clauses marked with a final numeral-classifier phrase.

(8.50) *Wel* *puk* *naond* *nins* [*hnef-hnef* *nied-giaol*]
1SG speak ASSOC COP [CLF:day-CLF:day cry-???]
[*aod-ngonl*].
[one-CLF:animate]
'I'm talking about the one (child) who cries every day.' (Haili Shi, fieldnotes)

(8.51) [[*Lanb*] ***naond***] [*aod-jut*] *dox...*
[[chaotic] **ASSOC**] [one-CLF:year] that
'Back in the year of troubles...' (Qiusheng Long, in *Ngel.kanx*) (repeated from (8.32) above)

Third, this alternate analysis readily accounts for the existence of examples like (8.40) and (8.41), in which a prenominal relative clause is immediately followed by its head noun with no intervening material whatsoever. If there exists no special grammatical relationship between the prenominal relative clauses and the classifiers in examples like (8.36–8.39), then the absence of classifiers in examples (8.40) and (8.41) is not difficult to explain. In examples (8.36–8.39), each prenominal relative clause is unflagged (i.e. bears no overt marker of its relative clause status) and happens to occur in a noun phrase containing a bare classifier or numeral-classifier phrase, and so the relative clause immediately precedes that classifier or numeral-classifier phrase. In examples (8.40) and (8.41), each prenominal relative clause is also unflagged in the same way, but each one happens to occur in a noun phrase that does not contain any classifier (which is itself not an unusual occurrence in Xong discourse). Because of this, the relative clauses in these latter two examples directly precede their head nouns. No additional explanation is necessary in either case. However, if one assumes that the bare classifiers and numeral-classifier phrases in examples like (8.36–8.39) are actually serving to mark the preceding relative clauses as such, then the existence of examples like (8.40) and (8.41) requires a more complex explanation, one that must account for prenominal relative clauses marked with *naond* 'ASSOC', for those marked with a bare classifier or numeral-classifier phrase, and for those marked with nothing at all.

The reader may have noticed that no mention has been made of the possible roles that the head noun of an unflagged prenominal relative clause (i.e. of the sort discussed in this section) can have within its relative clause. This lack of discussion is not accidental. The number of attested prenominal relative clauses that do not bear a final *naond* 'ASSOC' is fairly small to begin with, and eliciting relative clauses whose head nouns have uncommon roles (e.g. possessor, object of comparison, etc.) within their relative clause can be quite difficult. Still, the examples given earlier in this section do at least show that the head noun of an unflagged prenominal relative clause can serve as an AGENT within its relative clause (see examples (8.38) and (8.39)), as a PATIENT (examples (8.36) and (8.41)), or as a relatively oblique-like argument (examples (8.37) and (8.40)). (See Section 9.1.1 for more on AGENTS, PATIENTS, and other grammaticalized syntactic roles in Xong.) Examples (8.40) and (8.41) further show that these relative clauses have no restriction against relative-clause–internal preverbal arguments of the sort found in *manx* relative clauses and unflagged postnominal relative clauses (see Sections 8.1.4 and 8.1.5, respectively), and examples (8.36) and (8.41) show that they need not refer to inherent properties or habitual/characteristic activities of their head nouns, as unflagged postnominal relative clauses must (again, see Section 8.1.5). All these facts together suggest that the unflagged prenominal relative clauses discussed in this section are perhaps best analyzed as *naond* relative clauses from which the final associative marker *naond* 'ASSOC' has been elided, rather than as a distinct relative clause construction in their own right.

8.1.4 *Manx* relative clauses

Xong's *manx* relative clauses are those that bear an initial relative clause marker *manx* 'REL'. Like *naond* 'ASSOC', the form *manx* 'REL' never varies for any grammatical properties of its head noun. Unlike *naond*, though, *manx* serves only as a relative clause marker in Fenghuang Xong, not as a more general associative marker. In addition, all *manx* relative clauses share a significant restriction on their internal structure, one which does not apply to any of the other relative clause types discussed so far: namely, *manx* relative clauses show a very strong dispreference for relative-clause–internal preverbal arguments.

Despite sharing these common properties, *manx* relative clauses can still be divided into three subtypes based on which (if any) additional relative clause markers occur within the relative clause and where the relative clause occurs in relation to its head noun. The first subtype of *manx* relative clause is the postnominal *manx* relative clause, which follows its head noun and occurs with an initial *manx* 'REL' as its only relative clause marker. An example of this sort of relative clause is given in (8.52) below. Note that in this and all subsequent examples in this section, each *manx* relative clause has been enclosed within brackets and each head noun has been bolded.

(8.52) *Aod-meinl* ***deb-ghot*** [*manx* [*fuk* *jeud*]] *dox* *nins*
one-CLF:person **DIM-old** [REL [drink alcohol]] that COP
boub *ceit.*
1PL paternal.uncle
'That old man drinking alcohol (over there) is my paternal uncle.' (Shixiang Wu, fieldnotes)

The second subtype is the prenominal *manx* relative clause, which precedes its head noun and occurs with an initial *manx* 'REL' as its only relative clause marker. An example of this type of construction can be seen in (8.53) below.

(8.53) *Ngeuk* *Xob* *jud* *nianl* *beul* *daut* [*manx* [*jaod*]] ***mb****?*
PN Principal NEG_2 know 3 obtain [REL [bad]] **illness**
'Principal Ngeu didn't know that she was seriously ill?' (Shixiang Wu, in *Conversation in La'ershan*)

The third and final subtype of *manx* relative clause is the *manx-naond* relative clause, which precedes its head noun and occurs with two relative clause markers, an initial *manx* 'REL' and a final *naond* 'ASSOC'. Despite bearing a final *naond* and occurring only in prenominal position, *manx-naond* relative clauses are much more similar to other *manx* relative clauses in terms of restrictions on their internal structure than they are to *naond* relative clauses (see Section 8.1.2). An example of a *manx-naond* relative clause is given in (8.54) below.

(8.54) *Aod-roul* *Dol.xid* *jix* *doul* [*manx* [*nonx* *miex*]
one-CLF:time$_1$ La'ershan NEG$_1$ remain [REL [eat person]
naond] ***daob-jod.***
ASSOC] **AN-tiger**
'Nowadays there aren't any man-eating tigers around La'ershan.' (Haili Shi, fieldnotes)

As the rest of this section will show, the degree to which postnominal *manx*, prenominal *manx*, and *manx-naond* relative clauses should be considered distinct constructions as opposed to subtypes of a single construction will largely depend on the analyst's personal preferences. Although there are identifiable differences among postnominal *manx*, prenominal *manx*, and *manx-naond* relative clauses, these differences appear to be less substantial than those between *naond* relative clauses (see Section 8.1.2) and *manx* relative clauses, or those between unflagged postnominal relative clauses (Section 8.1.5) and *manx* relative clauses.

Just as with Xong's other relative clause types, the function of the head noun of any type of *manx* relative clause within the relative clause itself is not indicated in any way. Although there are more grammatical restrictions operating on *manx* relative clauses than on *naond* relative clauses, it appears that (contra Wu 2011 and Sposato 2012) these restrictions cannot be formulated in terms of the possible syntactic or semantic functions of the head noun within its relative clause.[153] For instance, the head noun of a *manx* relative clause can readily serve as an AGENT (i.e. as the more

153 In particular, Wu (2011: 38–45) argues that postnominal relative clauses in Gouliang Xong (including postnominal *manx* relative clauses and unflagged postnominal relative clauses, which Wu discusses together) have a restriction against directly relativizing on direct objects, indirect objects, and possessors. Wu claims that in order to relativize on a noun which would have the role of direct object, indirect object, or possessor within its (postnominal) relative clause, that noun must first be made the "subject" of a "passive" clause. However, the data presented in Wu (2011) is still consistent with the alternate analysis provided by this author in this section, and this author suspects that many of the differences between Wu's analysis and his own arise from differences in theoretical orientation. For instance, Wu does not actually define most of the grammatical terms used in her study (including "subject", "direct object", "indirect object", and "passive"), instead seeming to rely solely on intuition to identify grammatical constituents and constructions. This is not unusual for a work produced within the framework of (or at least heavily influenced by) traditional Chinese linguistic theory (see Section 2.5.1), but it may be responsible for some of the most important differences between Wu's analysis and this author's.

agent-like argument of a semantically transitive verb or the most agent-like argument of a semantically ditransitive verb) within its relative clause, as is shown in (8.55–8.57) below. (See Section 9.1.1 for more on AGENTS, SUBJECTS, PATIENTS, and other grammaticalized syntactic roles in Xong.)

(8.55) *Aod-ngonl* ***deb-deb*** *[manx [nied]] dox liax raut*
one-CLF:animate **child-RED** [REL [cry]] that resemble good
nins rant geud.
COP lose road
'It seems like that crying child is lost.' (Haili Shi, fieldnotes)

(8.56) *Beul deit chaot donb, jix nins* ***ghaob-npaok*** *[manx*
3 still look.for work NEG_1 COP **NOM-woman** [REL
[hneb-hneb jont ninb bioud]].
[CLF:day-CLF:day sit at home]]
'She's still looking for work, she's not (the sort of) woman who (just) sits at home every day.' (Shixiang Wu, fieldnotes)

(8.57) *Aod-meinl [manx [ndieut laot-tef puk daut]*
one-CLF:person [REL [ascend top-platform speak speech]
naond] ***lox.sik*** *dox nins xob.zhaont.*
ASSOC] **teacher** that COP principal
'That teacher who's going up to speak at the podium is the principal.' (Shixiang Wu, fieldnotes)

In examples (8.58–8.61) below, the head noun of each *manx* relative clause serves as a SUBJECT (i.e. as the sole argument of a semantically intransitive verb) within its relative clause.

(8.58) *Xaub.Honl.Mob liuk dut hliof banb [manx [raut*
Little.Red.Hat pluck obtain many CLF:some [REL [good
nkhed] naond] ***beinx*** *guaot.*
look] ASSOC] **flower** pass
'Little Red Hat picked a great many beautiful flowers.' (Haili Shi, in *Xaub Honl Mob*)

(8.59) *Aod-ngonl daob-jod doub nkhed maox.loub oub-biank*
one-CLF:animate AN-wolf $then_1$ look road two-CLF:side
zhaonl bed [manx [seik.xed] naond] ***beinx.***
grow full [REL [fresh] ASSOC] **flower**
'The wolf saw fresh flowers growing on both sides of the road.' (Haili Shi, in *Xaub Honl Mob*)

(8.60) *Daob-guk nins aod-ngonl* ***deb-nceik*** *[manx [xonx*
AN-frog COP one-CLF:animate **DIM-young.man** [REL [attractive
xonx]] dox.
attractive]] that
'The frog was (actually) that handsome young man.' (Xingyu Shi, in *Deb Guk Ronf*)

(8.61) *Beul nins [manx [jaod]]* ***mianx.***
3 COP [REL [bad]] **person**
'He's a bad guy.' (Chenghua Long, fieldnotes)

In example (8.62), the head noun of the *manx* relative clause is serving as a PATIENT (i.e. as the more patient-like argument of a semantically transitive verb) within its relative clause, while in example (8.63), the head noun of the *manx* relative clause is serving as a THEME (i.e. as the most theme-like argument of a semantically ditransitive verb). Note that the use of *lis* 'to want' in each example here is not coincidental. Consultants report that while examples (8.62) and (8.63) would not be ungrammatical if *lis* 'to want' were absent, the examples in question sound more "natural" when it is included. The use of *lis* in *manx* relative clauses in which the head noun has the role of PATIENT or THEME may thus serve (at least in part) to make the head noun more amenable to relativization.

(8.62) *Aod-hnanf [manx [lis hneind] naond]* ***eud***
one-CLF:clothing [REL [want wear] ASSOC] **clothing**
bat ninb bix neind.
put at CLF:place$_1$ this
'The article of clothing that is to be worn (as opposed to sold) is over here.' (Haili Shi, fieldnotes)

(8.63) *Aod-hant neind nins* ***did.daont*** *[manx [lis bid beul]].*
one-CLF:PL this COP **money** [REL [want return 3]]
'This is the money that (you) want to return to him.' (Shixiang Wu, fieldnotes)

It has not yet proven possible to elicit a *manx* relative clause in which the head noun serves as a RECIPIENT (i.e. as the most recipient-like argument of a semantically ditransitive verb) within its relative clause, and no clear examples of such are attested in the author's Xong corpus. It is unclear whether this reflects an actual grammatical restriction against such relative clauses or whether it merely indicates that they require a rather unusual discourse context.

In examples (8.64–8.67), the head noun of each *manx* relative clause serves as an oblique-like argument within its relative clause. In particular, the head noun of the relative clause in example (8.64) is serving in an instrumental role, the head noun of the relative clause in example (8.65) is serving in a temporal role, and the head nouns of the relative clauses in examples (8.66) and (8.67) are serving in a locative role.

(8.64) *Wel xaont nieus aod-giaob* ***jit.zid*** *[manx [beux bob.mins]].*
1SG wish buy one-CLF:machine **machine** [REL [hit corn]]
'I want to buy a corn-grinding machine.' (Chenghua Long, fieldnotes)

(8.65) *[manx [chad kek xox] naond]* ***ghaob-ngaonf***
[REL [not.until open study] ASSOC] **NOM-time**
'the time when school just started' (Haili Shi, fieldnotes)

(8.66) *Ghat nex* ***ghaob-def*** *[manx [yanb xib]] ml louf.*
go.to NEX **NOM-place** [REL [act play]] go record
'(You should) go to where people are performing plays to record (some Xong texts).' (Shixiang Wu, fieldnotes)

(8.67) *Ghaob-neind nins aod-ndaut* ***minl-aub*** *[manx ncot eud]].*
NOM-this COP one-CLF:river **AUG-water** [REL [wash.clothing clothing]]
'This is the river (we) wash clothing in.' (Haili Shi, fieldnotes)

The head noun of each *manx* relative clause in examples (8.68–8.70) appears to be serving as a possessor within its relative clause. Note that examples (8.68) and (8.69) each involve a semantically inalienable possessum (these are, respectively, teeth and livers), while example (8.70) involves a semantically alienable possessum (namely, a car). Note also that alienability is not discussed for other relative clause types in this chapter due to a simple lack of data.

(8.68) *Aod-meinl* ***mianx*** *[manx [nkhoud diul ghaob-xand]] dox nins beul poub.*
one-CLF:person **person** [REL [fall.out complete NOM-tooth]] that COP 3 paternal.grandfather
'That person whose teeth have all fallen out is his paternal grandfather.' (Shixiang Wu, fieldnotes)

(8.69) *[manx [xub shanb] naond]* ***deb-deb***
[REL [small liver] ASSOC] **child-RED**
'cowardly children (lit. 'children whose livers are small')' (Haili Shi, fieldnotes)

(8.70) *Aod-meinl* **sic.jic** [*manx* [*geud-neul* *oub-hnef* *baol*
one-CLF:person **driver** [REL [place$_1$-front two-CLF:day break.down
chek]] *dox* *tat-hnef* *yab* *zhus* *nex* *qaonx.*
vehicle]] that this-CLF:day also suffer NEX steal
'That driver whose car broke down a few days ago was robbed this morning.' (Chenghua Long, fieldnotes)[154]

Just as with *naond* relative clauses, it has so far proven impossible to elicit any examples of *manx* relative clauses in which the head noun serves as an object of comparison within the relative clause (as in English *the boy that I am taller than*), and none have yet been encountered in the author's collected Xong texts. However, at this point it is still unclear whether there is a real grammatical restriction against such relative clauses in Xong or whether they are merely pragmatically unusual.

The head nouns of some *manx* relative clauses have no semantic or grammatical role within their relative clause at all. In such cases, the head nouns themselves typically have fairly abstract meanings, as in (8.71) and (8.72) below.

(8.71) *Aod-leb* **sib** [*manx* [*daos* *guoud*]] *dox* *beul* *nianl* *xaond?*
one-CLF **matter** [REL [die dog]] that 3 know not.yet
'Does he know about the dog dying yet?' (Chenghua Long, fieldnotes)

(8.72) *Wel* *yanb* [*manx* [*daox* *nons*] *naond*] ***aob-shob.***
1SG like [REL [precipitate rain] ASSOC] **NOM-sound**
'I like the sound of rain.' (Chenghua Long, fieldnotes)

The reader may have noticed that every *manx* relative clause in every example given so far in this section shares a common restriction: none of them ever features a preverbal argument. A *manx* relative clause always has the relative clause marker *manx* 'REL' as its first element, with the second element after that relative clause marker usually being a verb, although in some cases it is a temporal or frequency expression like *chad* 'not until' (see example (8.65)) or *hneb-hneb* [CLF:day-CLF:day] 'every day' (example (8.56)), which is then followed by a verb.[155] However, it is typically impossible for a *manx* relative clause to have an argument immediately following the relative clause's initial *manx* 'REL' (one could in theory argue that the initial *manx*

---

154 For information on Mrs. Chenghua Long's tone -c (which appears on each syllable of the form *sic.jic* 'driver' in example (8.70)), see Section 3.5.3.1.

155 The author suspects that *manx* relative clauses could also begin with a variety of grammatical operators, including negative markers, the forms *(s)at* 'SAT' and *yaod(.yaod)* 'all', and various forms with temporal meanings like 'then', 'still', or 'again' (see Section 9.1.1). However, it must be stated that no examples of such relative clauses are attested in the author's Xong corpus, and he did not have the opportunity to attempt to elicit any while in the field.

'REL' form is itself occupying a preverbal argument slot, but while this may be consistent with the available data, the author has no independent evidence that it is in fact the case).[156] This restriction is shown in examples (8.73–8.75) below. In these ungrammatical examples, the head noun and the relative-clause–internal preverbal argument of each *manx* relative clause have been bolded, while each *manx* relative clause itself has been enclosed within brackets.

(8.73) **Aod-ngonl* ***daob-naus*** [*manx* [***monx*** *lis* *beux*]] *ninb*
one-CLF:animate **AN-duck** [REL [**2SG** want hit]] at
geud-zheit.
place$_I$-outside
(intended: 'The duck that you wanted to kill is outside.')

(8.74) **Boub* *bioud* *mex* *leb* ***ghaob-beinf*** [*manx* [***nex*** *beux* *deuk*]].
1PL home exist CLF **NOM-basin** [REL [**NEX** hit break]]
(intended: 'There's a basin that somebody broke in our house.')

(8.75) **Aod-ngonl* [*manx* [***daob-guoud*** *ghab* *daos*] *naond*]
one-CLF:animate [REL [**AN-dog** bite die] ASSOC]
deb-ngaok-ghab *neind* *nins* *wel* *naond.*
DIM-baby-chicken this COP 1SG ASSOC
(intended: 'This chick that was killed [lit. 'bitten to death'] by the dog is mine.')

Grammatical variants of examples (8.73–8.75) are provided in (8.76–8.78) below. In each case, the example in question is now grammatical because its *manx* relative clause no longer features a preverbal argument. In example (8.76), the change was accomplished simply by eliding the preverbal argument (which also resulted in a slight change of meaning); in examples (8.77) and (8.78), it was done by converting the original relative clause into a complement of the verb *zhus/zhaus* 'to suffer' (see Section 9.3.4).[157]

156 A single example of a *manx* relative clause with a relative-clause–internal preverbal argument occurs in Text 2 of this grammar. This is *geud-neul aod-hmaont* [*manx* [***Meik.jinb nex*** *nonx niax-guoud*]] (here brackets mark the boundaries of the relative clause in question, while bolding marks the relative-clause–internal preverbal argument), which is glossed as [place$_I$-front one-CLF:evening REL PN NEX eat meat-dog] and translated as 'the night before (my tooth started hurting), when Mei Jin's family was having dog meat'. Consultants did accept this example when it was pointed out to them, but the existence of this single, currently inexplicable exception does not disprove the claim that there is a general restriction against preverbal arguments in *manx* relative clauses.

157 Given that examples like (8.74) and (8.75) can be made grammatical by converting the original *manx* relative clause into a complement of the verb *zhus/zhaus* 'to suffer', one might reasonably suspect that Xong is on the verge of developing a "true" or canonical passive construction (cf. Section 9.3.4). This hypothesis is consistent with the available data, but the author is unaware of any positive evidence that it is in fact the case. It is equally possible that the use of *zhus/zhaus* 'to suffer' to

(8.76) *Aod-ngonl* ***daob-naus*** [*manx* [*lis* *beux*]] *ninb* *geud-zheit.*
one-CLF:animate **AN-duck** [REL [want hit]] at place$_1$-outside
'The duck that's to be killed is outside.' (Haili Shi, fieldnotes)

(8.77) *Boub* *bioud* *mex* *leb* ***ghaob-beinf*** [*manx* [***zhus*** *nex* *beux* *deuk*]].
1PL home exist CLF **NOM-basin** [REL [**suffer** NEX hit break]]
'There's a basin that somebody broke in our house.' (Haili Shi, fieldnotes)

(8.78) *Aod-ngonl* [*manx* [***zhaus*** *daob-guoud* *ghab* *daos*] *naond*]
one-CLF:animate [REL [**suffer** AN-dog bite die] ASSOC]
deb-ngaok-ghab *neind* *nins* *wel* *naond.*
DIM-baby-chicken this COP 1SG ASSOC
'This chick that was killed (lit. 'bitten to death') by the dog is mine.' (Shixiang Wu, fieldnotes)

Although there do not appear to be any noteworthy differences in the restrictions operating on *manx-naond* and postnominal *manx* relative clauses (aside from the fact that the former are obligatorily prenominal and bear a final *naond* 'ASSOC', while the latter are obligatorily postnominal and do not), there are some significant differerences between these two relative clause types on the one hand and prenominal *manx* relative clauses on the other. In particular, the author's consultants display a very strong preference for prenominal *manx* relative clauses to consist solely of a single property-denoting verb (*nqint* 'red', *nzeit* 'skinny', *liot* 'wealthy', etc.), with no other material occurring in the relative clause whatsoever (this appears to be a more extreme version of a similar restriction operating on unflagged postnominal relative clauses, as is discussed in Section 8.1.5 below). No such restriction is relevant to *manx-naond* or postnominal *manx* relative clauses, which can be of any length and any degree of complexity. Thus, examples (8.79–8.81) below, each of which contains a prenominal *manx* relative clause consisting of more than just a single property-denoting verb, are at best marginally grammatical, and consultants suggest that relative clauses such as the ones in these examples would be better rephrased as *naond*, *manx-naond*, postnominal *manx*, or (in some cases) postnominal unflagged relative clauses.

(8.79) ??[*manx* [*yab* *ngaod* *yab* *zhaons*]] ***deb-nceik***
[REL [also short also fat]] **DIM-young.man**
(intended: 'a short, fat young man')

"de-front" a preverbal argument within a *manx* relative clause is a diachronically stable feature of Xong, one that is not indicative of any incipient passive construction.

(8.80) ??[*manx* [*jaod guaot*]] ***ob-def***
[REL [bad pass]] **NOM-place**
(intended: 'a very bad place')

(8.81) ??[*manx* [*shab ndeud*]] ***miex***
[REL [teach writing]] **person**
(intended: 'a teacher') (and note that the alternate version ??*manx shab miex* [REL teach person] is, if anything, even less acceptable)

In contrast, examples (8.82–8.84), in which each prenominal *manx* relative clause consists solely of a single property-denoting verb, are judged fully grammatical by all consultants. Still, the relative clauses shown in these examples could also be rephrased as *naond*, *manx-naond*, postnominal *manx*, or postnominal unflagged relative clauses with no change in meaning or grammaticality.

(8.82) [*manx* [*ngaod/zhaons*]] ***deb-nceik***
[REL [short/fat]] **DIM-young.man**
'a short/fat young man' (Chenghua Long, fieldnotes)

(8.83) [*manx* [*raut*]] ***miex***
[REL [good]] **person**
'a good person' (Haili Shi, fieldnotes)

(8.84) *Boub naond Ngel.kanx ob-def neind nins leb*
1PL ASSOC Yankan NOM-place this COP CLF
[*manx* [*jaod*]] ***ob-def.***
[REL [bad]] **NOM-place**
'(When I was a boy,) this Yankan (Village) of ours was a bad place.' (Qiusheng Long, in *Ngel.kanx*)

Relative clauses such as these, in which the relative clause occurs before its head noun and is marked only with an initial (rather than a final) relative clause marker, are exceedingly rare among the languages of the world, with the only other examples known to the author being found in certain Semitic languages of Ethiopia (Tosco 1998) and in Sare, a Sepik language of New Guinea (Sumbuk 2002). However, it must be pointed out that such relative clauses are hardly the only ones possible in Xong, as the language also features several other types of prenominal relative clause (including *naond* relative clauses, unflagged prenominal relative clauses, and *manx-naond* relative clauses) as well as several types of postnominal relative clause (including postnominal *manx* relative clauses and unflagged postnominal relative clauses). Furthermore, the semantic and grammatical restrictions operating on this type of relative clause are perhaps heavier than the restrictions on any other type of Xong relative clause.[158]

The ordering possibilities of *manx* relative clauses vis-à-vis other noun-phrase–internal constituents are fairly easy to describe (in the interest of space, no examples specifically demonstrating these ordering possibilities are provided here, but relevant examples can be found throughout this Section 8.1.4). Xong's *manx-naond* relative clauses exhibit the same ordering possibilities as *naond* relative clauses: they must occur after any possessor phrase and before any head noun, but they can occur either before or after a numeral-classifier phrase (see examples (8.24–8.29) in Section 8.1.2 above). Postnominal *manx* relative clauses occur immediately after their head noun, with no intervening material possible (consultants generally do not allow a postnominal *manx* relative clause and an unflagged postnominal relative clause to modify the same noun). Finally, prenominal *manx* relative clauses occur immediately before their head noun, again with no intervening material possible (if a numeral-classifier phrase is inserted between a prenominal *manx* relative clause and its following head noun, consultants will generally insist that a final *naond* 'ASSOC' be added to the relative clause).

Just as was the case with the associative marker *naond* 'ASSOC' (see Section 8.1.2), the relative clause marker *manx* 'REL' can also serve to mark certain headless constructions that do not feature any head noun. Such constructions can optionally occur with a final *naond* 'ASSOC' as well, meaning that there exist headless counterparts of relative clauses marked with *manx* alone and of relative clauses marked with both *manx* and *naond*. Like the equivalent headless constructions with *naond* 'ASSOC', headless constructions with *manx* 'REL' do not serve to modify a noun, but rather they serve one of three other functions: (i) they serve as a noun phrase in their own right (as in examples (8.85) and (8.86) below), (ii) they serve as a constituent of a larger noun phrase in what is still an essentially modifying function (as in examples (8.87–8.89)), or (iii) they follow the copular verb *nins* 'COP' to express some property or attribute of that copular verb's preceding (or elided) argument (as in examples (8.90) and (8.91); in such cases it is not clear whether there is any difference between using *nins* 'COP' plus a following relative clause and simply using the relativized clause in question as a non-relativized predicate).

(8.85) *Jix* *mex* [*manx* [*nonx*]] *jix* *mex* [*manx* [*hneind*]].
NEG$_1$ exist [REL [eat]] NEG$_1$ exist [REL [wear]]
'(We) had nothing to eat and nothing to wear.' (Shixiang Wu, fieldnotes)

158 The typological noteworthiness of these relative clauses also varies depending on whether prenominal and postnominal *manx* relative clauses are analyzed as two distinct constructions, each of which obligatorily occurs on only one side of its head noun, or as subtypes of a single construction that can occur in either prenominal or postnominal position. The latter analysis would mean Xong's prenominal *manx* relative clauses are even less typologically remarkable, but the choice between the two analyses seems to the author to be a fairly arbitrary one.

(8.86) [*Manx* [*nqint*] *naond*] *raut* *nkhed.*
[REL [red] ASSOC] good look
'The red ones look the best.' (Yan Long, fieldnotes)

(8.87) *Aod-ngonl* [*manx* [*lis* *beux*]] *nzeit* *guaot.*
one-CLF:animate [REL [want hit]] skinny pass
'The one (pig) that's to be killed is very skinny.' (Haili Shi, fieldnotes)

(8.88) *Nins* *god* [*manx* [*sanb.minb*] *naond*].
COP CLF:human.group [REL [tell.fortune] ASSOC]
'(They're) fortune-tellers.' (Shixiang Wu, fieldnotes)

(8.89) *Beul* *heit* *reinb.weif* *nins* *aod-ngonl* [*manx* [*rel.xins*]
3 still believe COP one-CLF:animate [REL [kind]
naond], *aod-ngonl* [*manx* [*raons* *deul*]].
ASSOC] one-CLF:animate [REL [cut.firewood firewood]]
'She still thought (he) was a kind (person), a woodcutter.' (Haili Shi, in *Xaub Honl Mob*)

(8.90) *Aod-leb* *neind* *nins* [*manx* [*giaox*] *naond*].
one-CLF this COP [REL [fake] ASSOC]
'This one was fake.' (Xingyu Shi, in *Oub Meinl Yaos Geud*)

(8.91) *Aub-gheb* *ghad* *nins* [*manx* [*diaonl*]].
water-eye $then_2$ COP [REL [sweet]]
'Tears are (a bit) sweet.' (Xingyu Shi, in *Oub Meinl Yaos Geud*)

8.1.5 Unflagged postnominal relative clauses

Unflagged postnominal relative clauses are those which immediately follow their head noun and bear no overt marker of their relative clause status (i.e. no *naond* 'ASSOC', *manx* 'REL', or other similar marker). There are significant semantic and grammatical restrictions on unflagged postnominal relative clauses, which incidentally justify analyzing these relative clauses as a distinct construction type in Xong (rather than, e.g., as postnominal *manx* relative clauses whose initial *manx* 'REL' has been elided). Semantically, unflagged postnominal relative clauses can typically only be used to refer to inherent properties, or to habitual or characteristic activities or uses, of their head nouns. Grammatically, there is a very strong preference for such relative clauses to consist of either a verb alone or a verb and a following noun phrase, with that noun phrase generally consisting of a single monosyllabic noun. In running speech consultants occasionally produce slightly more complex unflagged postnominal relative clauses (e.g. ones containing multiple verbs, or containing a verb and a degree marker or temporal expression) or unflagged postnominal relative clauses that do not refer to inherent, habitual, or characteristic features of their head nouns, but when such relative clauses are pointed out to them they generally insist that they be replaced with either a *naond* or *manx* relative clause (see Sections 8.1.2 and 8.1.4 above), and they do not accept such constructions when produced by the author in elicitation sessions. None of the author's consultants have ever allowed (or produced themselves) an unflagged postnominal relative clause containing a preverbal argument (i.e. an argument that immediately follows the relative clause's head noun).

Most attested unflagged postnominal relative clauses can be placed into one of several rough categories based on the semantic relationship between the relative clause and its head noun. A few examples from each of these categories are provided below to give the reader some idea of the functions that these relative clauses serve in Fenghuang Xong. The categories have been ordered from most to least common, with the single most common one containing those unflagged postnominal relative clauses that refer to inherent (though not necessarily permanent) properties of their head nouns. Such relative clauses typically consist of a single verb expressing the property in question, as in examples (8.92–8.96) (for arguments that these constructions are not simply noun–verb compounds, see further below in this section). In these and all other examples below, each unflagged postnominal relative clause has been enclosed within brackets and each head noun has been bolded.

(8.92) ***guoud*** [*gueinx*]
dog [yellow]
'yellow dog' (Haili Shi, fieldnotes)

(8.93) ***maonb*** [*nzeit*]
cat [skinny]
'skinny cat' (Haili Shi, fieldnotes)

(8.94) ***miex*** [*zhaons*]
person [fat]
'fat person' (Haili Shi, fieldnotes)

(8.95) ***ndeud*** [*gueub*]
paper [white]
'white paper' (Shixiang Wu, fieldnotes)

(8.96) *Beul hneind aod-xeub* ***eud*** [*xeb*].
3 wear one-CLF:body **clothing** [new]
'He put on a new set of clothes.' (Xingyu Shi, in *Deb Guk Ronf*)

Note that in example (8.97) below, a *manx-naond* relative clause (see Section 8.1.4) is used to refer to an action being performed by the noun phrase's referent at the time of utterance (i.e. eating grass), while an unflagged postnominal relative clause is used to refer to an inherent property of that same referent (i.e. the property of blackness).

(8.97) *Mx nkhed aod-ngonl manx deib nonx reib naond* ***yul***
2SG look one-CLF:animate REL at eat greens ASSOC **cow**
[gueb] dox.
[black] that
'Look at that black cow that's eating grass.' (Shixiang Wu, fieldnotes)

The unflagged postnominal relative clauses in examples (8.98) and (8.99) differ from most attested examples of such relative clauses in that each of them features a non-verbal, non-nominal morpheme: the comparative marker *ghaod* 'more' in (8.98), and the manner marker *naont* 'thus' in (8.99).

(8.98) *Ghans khauk dox mex leb* ***roub*** *[ghaod shanb].*
see CLF:place$_2$ that exist CLF **stone** [more tall]
'(The boy) saw that there was a taller stone over there.' (Chenghua Long, in *Frog, Where Are You?*)

(8.99) *Monx ah nins aod-ngonl* ***deb-nceik*** *[naont xonx]...*
2SG PART COP one-CLF:animate **DIM-young.man** [thus attractive]
'You're such an attractive young man...' (Xingyu Shi, in *Deb Guk Ronf*)

The second most common semantic category into which unflagged postnominal relative clauses can be divided contains those relative clauses that refer to a purpose or activity, with the head noun referring to a tool or substance that is typically used for that purpose or activity. These relative clauses generally consist of either a verb and a following noun, as in examples (8.100–8.102), or a verb alone, as in example (8.103).

(8.100) *Aod-zheinb neind nins* ***ghaob-ndeind*** *[hlaok niax/reib].*
one-CLF:tool this COP **NOM-knife** [cut meat/vegetable]
'This is a knife for cutting meat/vegetables.' (Haili Shi, fieldnotes)

(8.101) *Beul geud* ***put*** *[beux naus] beux daos aod-ngonl*
3 hold **gun** [hit bird] hit die one-CLF:animate
nbat-doub.
pig-earth
'He killed a wild pig with a bird gun (lit. 'bird-shooting gun').' (Shixiang Wu, fieldnotes)

(8.102) *Mx geud* ***beinx*** *[nzad mes] meb lol.*
2SG hold **basin** [wash face] take come
'Bring the face-washing basin over.' (Shixiang Wu, fieldnotes)

(8.103) ***cant*** *[peub]*
shovel [dig]
'digging shovel' (Shixiang Wu, fieldnotes)

The unflagged postnominal relative clause in example (8.104) below differs from most other attested examples of such relative clauses in that it features two verbs along with a following noun. Note that in this case, the verb *geud* would be more idiomatically translated as 'to use' rather than 'to hold'.

(8.104) *Aod-tont dox nins* ***aub*** *[geud ncot eud].*
one-CLF:bucket that COP **water** [hold wash.clothing clothing]
'That bucket (contains) water for washing clothes.' (Haili Shi, fieldnotes)

A third category into which unflagged postnominal relative clauses can be divided contains relative clauses referring to an activity that is typically carried out at a particular location or time, with the head noun then referring to that location or time.

(8.105) ***Ghaob-def*** *[shok eud] ninb dox.*
NOM-place [dry.in.sun clothing] at that
'The place for hanging clothes out to dry is (over) there.' (Haili Shi, fieldnotes)

(8.106) *Beul ghad jix ndiot* ***geud*** *[nzhaod].*
3 $then_2$ NEG_1 recognize **road** [return]
'Then she didn't know the way home.' (Xingyu Shi, in *Oub Meinl Yaos Geud*)

(8.107) ***ghaob-ngaonf*** *[nonx hlit]*
NOM-time [eat cooked.rice]
'meal time, time for eating' (Haili Shi, fieldnotes)

(8.108) *Nins hlaot-bieib,* ***ob-ngaonf*** *[diaons yaonb]...*
COP month-four **NOM-time** [plant young.rice.plant]
'It was the fourth lunar month, the time to plant rice...' (Qiusheng Long, in *Long Qiusheng's Life History*)

Finally, some unflagged postnominal relative clauses have head nouns with human referents, with the relative clause itself referring to a characteristic or habitual activity performed by the referent. Examples of this can be seen in (8.109–8.111) below. The first of these examples is noteworthy in that its noun phrase *miex chauk donb* [person do work] has become lexicalized: it can only mean 'farmer', not *'person who works' or *'person who's working'. To express those latter meanings, one would have to use a *naond* or *manx* relative clause instead (e.g. *chauk donb naond miex* [do work ASSOC person]). See also further below in this section for some additional discussion of this issue.

(8.109)	*Beul*	*nins*	***miex***	*[chauk*	*donb].*
	3	COP	**person**	[do	work]

'He's a farmer.' (Haili Shi, fieldnotes)

(8.110)	*Mx*	*nins*	*aod-meinl*	***mianx***	*[shab*	*ndeud].*
	2SG	COP	one-CLF:person	**person**	[teach	writing]

'You're a teacher.' (Shixiang Wu, fieldnotes)

Example (8.111) below is noteworthy in that it contains two relative clauses modifying the same head noun (cf. example (8.97) above). A habitual activity performed by the referent (i.e. singing Xong songs) is referred to with an unflagged postnominal relative clause, while a more temporary, incidental characteristic of the referent (i.e. the fact that he has just arrived in La'ershan) is referred to with a *manx-naond* relative clause.

(8.111)	*Wel*	*ndiot*	*aod-meinl*	*manx*	*chad.chad*	*lol*	*dand*
	1SG	recognize	one-CLF:person	REL	not.until	come	arrive

Dol.xid	*naond*	***miex***	*[ngheub*	*sad].*
La'ershan	ASSOC	**person**	[sing	Xong.song]

'I know that Xong singer who just arrived in La'ershan.' (Haili Shi, fieldnotes)

Many unflagged postnominal relative clauses have undergone some degree of lexicalization (see, e.g., example (8.109) above). This, coupled with the relatively simple grammatical structure of most of these relative clauses and their lack of overt marking, might lead one to argue that relative clauses of this type should in fact be analyzed as morphological constituents of noun compounds rather than as any sort of syntactic construction. In other words, one might argue that the sequence *guoud gueinx* [dog yellow] 'yellow dog' (see example (8.92) above) is better analyzed as a compound *guoud-gueinx* [dog-yellow] than as a head noun *guoud* 'dog' followed by an unflagged postnominal relative clause *gueinx* 'yellow', and that similar analyses should be applied to the other unflagged postnominal relative clauses given in this section.

However, while the author does not have any particularly strong evidence against this analysis, neither does he have very much evidence in support of it. Unflagged postnominal relative clauses in Xong do not feature any of the sorts of evidence that might be used in other languages to distinguish compounds from syntactically formed constructions, such as the presence of unique tone sandhi patterns that do not occur in other environments, atypical word order properties (as in, e.g., English *pasta-maker* vs. *to make pasta*), or sharp restrictions on grammatical structure. With reference to that last point, note in particular that several examples of unflagged postnominal relative clauses in this section contain non-verbal, non-nominal material like comparative markers or manner markers (see examples (8.98) and (8.99) above), which would not normally be expected in a noun compound. Thus, on the basis of the data currently available to the author, there does not appear to be any clear, non-arbitrary motivation for analyzing Xong's unflagged postnominal relative clauses as anything other than relative clauses.

Finally, note that no headless versions of unflagged postnominal relative clauses have been attested.

8.1.6 Summary of Xong relative clause constructions

Table 8.1 below summarizes the major differences among Xong's various relative clause types. For ease of comparison, the three subtypes of *manx* relative clause (namely postnominal *manx*, prenominal *manx*, and *manx-naond*) have been listed separately in the table.

Table 8.1: Comparison of relative clause constructions in Fenghuang Xong.

RELATIVE CLAUSE TYPE	RELATIVE CLAUSE MARKER(S)	POSITION WITHIN NP	RESTRICTIONS	HEADLESS VERSION POSSIBLE?
Naond relative clause	Final *naond* 'ASSOC'	Prenominal, before or after numeral-classifier phrase	None apparent	Yes
Unflagged prenominal relative clause	None	Prenominal (see Section 8.1.3 for details)	Only occurs in fast and/or casual speech	No
Postnominal *manx* relative clause	Initial *manx* 'REL'	Immediately postnominal	No preverbal arguments in relative clause	Yes
Prenominal *manx* relative clause	Initial *manx* 'REL'	Immediately prenominal	No preverbal arguments in relative clause; strong preference for relative clause to consist solely of a single property-denoting verb	Yes
Manx-naond relative clause	Initial *manx* 'REL' and final *naond* 'ASSOC'	Prenominal, before or after numeral-classifier phrase	No preverbal arguments in relative clause	Yes
Unflagged postnominal relative clause	None	Immediately postnominal	Significant semantic and structural restrictions (see Section 8.1.5 for details)	No

Regardless of the exact number of distinct relative clause types that one counts, the wide structural variety evident in Xong's relative clauses presents certain difficulties for typological classification of Xong word order, in particular with respect to whether relative clauses in Xong should be considered predominantly prenominal, predominantly postnominal, or "mixed" prenominal/postnominal (see Dryer 2013c). Table 8.1 shows that Xong features several types of obligatorily prenominal relative clauses, including *naond* relative clauses, unflagged prenominal relative clauses, and *manx-naond* relative clauses (although unflagged prenominal relative clauses could arguably be analyzed as *naond* relative clauses from which the final *naond* marker has been elided), and that it features one type of obligatorily postnominal relative clause (namely, unflagged postnominal relative clauses). The language also arguably features one type of relative clause that can occur in either position (these are relative clauses marked with *manx* 'REL' alone), although the fact that there are slightly different restrictions on the internal structures of prenominal and postnominal relative clauses marked with *manx* 'REL' alone (see Section 8.1.4 for discussion) means that they could perhaps be analyzed as two distinct relative clause constructions, one of which is obligatorily prenominal and one of which is obligatorily postnominal.

Still, overall it seems clear that Xong should be considered a language in which prenominal relative clauses predominate over postnominal relative clauses, or, in other words, that Xong is a RelN language rather than an NRel or "mixed" one (again, see Dryer 2013c). There are three pieces of evidence in favor of this analysis. First, the relative clause type with the fewest grammatical and semantic restrictions (*naond* relative clauses) is obligatorily prenominal, while the type with the most such restrictions (unflagged postnominal relative clauses) is obligatorily postnominal. Second, in the author's collected Xong texts it appears that prenominal relative clauses of any type are much more common (at a rate of at least 2:1) than postnominal relative clauses of any type. Third, there is significantly more structural variety among Xong's prenominal relative clauses (which can be marked with a final *naond*, an initial *manx*, both, or neither) than among its postnominal relative clauses (which can be marked with either an initial *manx* or with nothing at all).[159]

159 Now that all types of Xong relative clause have already been introduced, it must be mentioned that relative clauses in the Miao language Hmyo (also known as Luopohe or Luobohe [罗泊河] Miao; ISO 639-3 code *hml*) are strikingly similar to relative clauses in Xong in overall structural terms (Yoshihisa Taguchi p.c. 2015). Hmyo has (i) a prenominal relative clause construction with a final marker /mo^{42}/ (equivalent to Xong's *naond* relative clauses), (ii) a prenominal relative clause construction with no marker (equivalent to Xong's unflagged prenominal relative clauses), (iii) a prenominal relative clause construction with both an initial marker /ta^{42}/ and a final marker /mo^{42}/ (equivalent to Xong's *manx-naond* relative clauses), and (iv) a postnominal relative clause construction with an initial marker /ta^{42}/ (equivalent to Xong's postnominal *manx* relative clauses), though apparently it does not have any equivalents to Xong's prenominal *manx* relative clauses or unflagged postnominal relative clauses. These similarities are at present inexplicable, since Hmyo and Xong are not particularly close in either genealogical or geographic terms (Hmyo is a member of the Chuanqiandian sub-branch

8.2 Possessive constructions

Fenghuang Xong features three possessive constructions: the *naond* possessive construction (discussed in Section 8.2.1 below), the unflagged possessive construction (discussed in Section 8.2.2), and the pronominal possessive construction (discussed in Section 8.2.3).[160] In all three constructions, the possessor invariably precedes its possessum.

8.2.1 The *naond* possessive construction

The single most common way to express possession in Fenghuang Xong is through the use of the *naond* possessive construction. In this construction, the possessor noun phrase occurs initially, followed by the invariant associative marker *naond* 'ASSOC' (see Section 9.2.3.2 for more on this form), followed in turn by the possessum noun phrase. Thus, such a possessive construction will have the following structure:

[[NP$_{\text{POSSESSOR}}$ *naond*] NP$_{\text{POSSESSUM}}$]

As this diagram suggests, the possessor noun phrase and its following *naond* 'ASSOC' form a single grammatical constituent, which then combines with the possessum noun phrase to form the possessive construction as a whole. That the possessor noun phrase and its following *naond* form a grammatical constituent is clear from the fact that headless possessive constructions (which consist of a possessor noun phrase followed by *naond* 'ASSOC', with no possessum at all) are common, while the opposite construction (which would consist of an initial *naond* 'ASSOC' and a following possessum noun phrase, but with no possessor) is completely ungrammatical, and generally even uninterpretable. This can be seen by comparing examples (8.112) and (8.113) below, which each feature several grammatical examples of headless possessive constructions, with examples (8.114) and (8.115), which each feature an ungrammatical

of Miao [see Section 2.3.4] and is spoken in central Guizhou Province) and since Hmyo's relative clause markers do not appear to be cognate with Xong's relative clause markers. See also Section 10.5.1 for discussion of further similarities between Xong and Hmyo in the realm of verbal prefixes.

160 Similar to the situation with the author's discussion of relative clauses in Section 8.1, the three grammatical structures examined here in Section 8.2 are referred to as distinct "constructions" solely for convenience, and other scholars would not necessarily be unjustified in dividing Xong's possessive expressions into a larger or smaller number of them. For instance, since there do not appear to be any significant grammatical differences between the so-called "*naond* possessive construction" and the so-called "unflagged possessive construction" aside from the presence of *naond* 'ASSOC' in the former and its absence in the latter, one could just as easily refer to these as a single construction that occurs with an optional possessive marker. Going in the opposite direction, one could consider the headless and headed versions of the *naond* possessive construction (see Section 8.2.1) as two distinct constructions, yielding a total of four possessive constructions instead of only three.

(and uninterpretable) construction composed of an initial *naond* and a following possessum noun phrase.

(8.112) *Hant neind nins [baox/minl/yaos naond].*
CLF:PL this COP [father/mother/older.sister ASSOC]
'These belong to (our) father/mother/older sister.' (Yan Long, fieldnotes)

(8.113) *Aod-leb dox nins [wel/monx/beul naond].*
one-CLF that COP [1SG/2SG/3 ASSOC]
'That one is mine/yours/hers.' (Yan Long, fieldnotes)

(8.114) **naond bioud*
ASSOC home
(intended: 'someone's home' or 'some sort of home')

(8.115) **naond daob-guoud*
ASSOC AN-dog
(intended: 'someone's dog' or 'some sort of dog')

There do not appear to be any purely grammatical restrictions on the structure of either the possessor or possessum noun phrases in a *naond* possessive construction. Given an appropriate enough discourse context, any Xong noun phrase can serve as either the possessor or possessum in such a construction, although in naturalistic contexts certain combinations of possessor and possessum (e.g. a noun phrase consisting solely of a numeral-classifier phrase possessing another similar noun phrase, or a noun phrase consisting solely of a headless relative clause possessing another similar noun phrase) occur rarely or not at all. For instance, examples (8.116–8.121) below contain possessor and/or possessum noun phrases that consist solely of a personal or reflexive pronoun (see Section 7.1), solely of a locative noun (see Section 5.5), solely of a canonical noun (see Chapter 5 in general), or solely of a numeral-classifier phrase (see Section 6.1.2), as well as several instances of more complex possessor or possessum noun phrases (incidentally, those latter instances demonstrate that the constituents of this possessive construction – i.e. the possessor and the possessum – should indeed be analyzed as noun phrases rather than as mere nouns). Note that in these and all subsequent examples in this section, the constituent structure of each possessive construction has been indicated with brackets.

(8.116) *Wel lis shud [[wel naond] daob-guk].*
1SG want look.for [[1SG ASSOC] AN-frog]
'I'm looking for my frog.' (Chenghua Long, in *Frog, Where Are You?*)

(8.117) *Monx lieif [[daut-leb naond] deb-geud] at jix*
2SG even [[REFL-CLF ASSOC] DIM-younger.sibling] SAT NEG_1
ndiot!
recognize
'You don't even recognize your own little sister!' (Haili Shi, fieldnotes)

(8.118) *Mx ghaod.maons xeud ninb [[wel naond] geud-neul].*
2SG NEG.IMP stand at [[1SG ASSOC] $place_1$-front]
'Don't stand in front of me.' (Shixiang Wu, fieldnotes)

(8.119) [[*Baod-zhax naond*] *aod-leb bioud dox*] *nins ceink.zhaont naond*
[[BUG-right ASSOC] one-CLF home that] COP village.head ASSOC
'That house on the right belongs to the village head.' (Shixiang Wu, fieldnotes)

(8.120) [[*Aod-bix dib naond*] *Ink.ix*] *puk naond zeib raut?*
[[one-CLF:$place_1$ which ASSOC] English] speak ASSOC most good
'Where is the best English spoken?' (Haili Shi, fieldnotes)

(8.121) [[*gul-jons-il-jut naond*] *deb-ngueif*]
[[ten-seven-eight-CLF:year ASSOC] DIM-unmarried.woman]
'a young woman of seventeen or eighteen years' (Xingyu Shi, in *Deb Guk Ronf*)

It is important to note that the possessor in a *naond* possessive construction merely serves to restrict the reference of its possessum in some way.[161] The specific semantic relationship between the possessor and possessum in this construction can thus vary widely, and only a few representative types of these relationships will be discussed here. For instance, in some cases the referent of a possessor noun phrase in a *naond* possessive construction "owns" the referent of the possessum noun phrase, as in examples (8.122) and (8.123) below.

(8.122) [[*Niaox.meib naond*] *leb zhonx-hlod*]
[[PN ASSOC] CLF length-bamboo]
'Niao Mei's length of bamboo' (Xingyu Shi, in *Oub Meinl Yaos Geud*)

(8.123) [[*Boub naond*] *aod-ndaut aub neind*] *ik.zhil*
[[1PL ASSOC] one-CLF:river water this] all.the.way
tonk dand Laok.doux.yaonb.
pass.through arrive Liangtouyang
'This river of ours flows all the way to Liangtouyang (Village).' (Qiusheng Long, in *Ngel.kanx*)

161 This is quite similar to the function of relative clauses in Xong, as was discussed in Section 8.1 above.

This same construction can also be used to express part-whole relationships, with the whole taking the role of the possessor and the part taking the role of the possessum. In such cases the possessum phrase will typically involve a locative noun, like *ghaob-nhaons* [NOM-inside] 'inside' in example (8.124) or *laot-gheul* [top-place$_2$] 'top' in example (8.125). See Section 5.5 for more on locative nouns in general.

(8.124) *Monx geud aub biat zhut [[tief.tonx naond] ghaob-nhaons].*
2SG hold water pour reach [[bucket ASSOC] NOM-inside]
'Pour the water into the bucket.' (Haili Shi, fieldnotes)

(8.125) *[[Bid-gheul naond] laot-gheul] mex hot hliof*
[[FRT-mountain ASSOC] top-place$_2$] exist how.much many
hot hliof nggeub.
how.much many mushroom
'There are a ton of mushrooms on top of the mountain.' (Yan Long, fieldnotes)

The *naond* possessive construction can also be used to refer to body parts, with the entity to whom the body part in question belongs naturally taking the role of the possessor and the body part itself taking the role of the possessum (though note that body part terms can also occur without any overtly expressed possessor in Xong).

(8.126) *Tat-hneb [[wel naond] sond-ghond] mex houd-deb xob.*
this-CLF:day [[1SG ASSOC] bone-neck] exist CLF:mouthful-DIM sore
'My neck's a little bit sore today.' (Shixiang Wu, fieldnotes)

(8.127) *Mx zhat zhaus [[wel naond] ghaob-doul]!*
2SG step.on reach [[1SG ASSOC] NOM-hand]
'You stepped on my hand!' (unknown Xong consultant, fieldnotes)

The possessor in a *naond* possessive construction can also serve to express the temporal or spatial location or origin of the possessum, as in examples (8.128) and (8.129) below.[162]

162 Note the recursive possessive construction in example (8.128), in which two instances of *naond* 'ASSOC' occur: *Dol.xid naond Banx.doul.gueb naond Lonf.zeib.xink* [La'ershan ASSOC village.name ASSOC PN], meaning '(the person) Lon Zei Xin from (the village) Ban Dou Gue belonging to (the town) La'ershan'.

(8.128) *Daob-maonb nins Banx.doul.gueb naond,* [[*Dol.xid naond*]
AN-cat COP village.name ASSOC [[La'ershan ASSOC]
[[*Banx.doul.gueb naond*] *Lonf.zeib.xink*]].
[[village.name ASSOC] PN]]
'The Cat (i.e. a bandit with that nickname) was from the village of Ban Dou Gue, (he was a man named) Lon Zei Xin from the village of Ban Dou Gue belonging to the town of La'ershan.' (Qiusheng Long, in *Ngel.kanx*)

(8.129) [[*Manx.eib.manx.ab naond*] *sib*] *leh, jix liax*
[[a.long.time.ago ASSOC] matter] LEH NEG$_1$ resemble
dieud neind.
CLF:time$_2$ this
'The things (that happened) in the old days, they weren't like (the things that happen) now.' (Xingyu Shi, in *Deb Guk Ronf*)

Lastly, the *naond* possessive construction can also be used to express both cosanguineal and affinal kinship relations.

(8.130) *Beul caont* [[*beul naond*] *npaok*] *ox* [[*beul naond*] *minl*].
3 meet [[3 ASSOC] woman] and [[3 ASSOC] mother]
'He met his wife and his mother.' (Xingyu Shi, in *Deb Guk Ronf*)

(8.131) *Aod-dieud dox* [[*Sank.ux.baob naond*] *qik.zib*] *mex*
one-CLF:time$_2$ that [[PN ASSOC] wife] exist
ngonl deb-deb...
CLF:animate child-RED
'At that time San U Bao's wife had a child...' (Qiusheng Long, in *Ngel.kanx*)

While most of the various semantic relationships that can hold between the possessor and possessum noun phrases in a possessive construction do not require any further comment, it is worth pointing out that possessive constructions which express a kinship relation have an additional restriction that is not operative in other such constructions. Specifically, if the possessor noun phrase in a possessive construction is a pronoun and the possessum noun phrase in the same construction refers to a kin member, there is a very strong preference for the possessor pronoun to be a monomorphemic non-singular one (i.e. *boub* '1PL', *manx* '2PL', *beul* '3', *miant* '3PL', or *nex/ninx* 'NEX', but not *wel* '1SG' or *monx/mx* '2SG'; see Section 7.1). This is true even if the possessor is in fact semantically singular, and it applies to unflagged possessive constructions (discussed in Section 8.2.2 below) just as it does to *naond* possessive constructions (it does not apply to the pronominal possessive construction discussed in Section 8.2.3, though, since the possessor in such a construction is never a pronoun).

Examples (8.132–8.134) below show that when the possessor of the noun phrase *baox* 'father' is a first-person pronominal one, there is a strong preference for using the monomorphemic non-singular pronoun *boub* '1PL' rather than the monomorphemic singular one *wel* '1SG' or the polymorphemic plural one *boub-god* [1PL-PL]. All consultants agree that this is true even when the possessor is semantically singular (e.g. even when the speaker's only living family member is his or her father, with the speaker's mother, siblings, and other family members all having passed away). Note that the presence or absence of *naond* 'ASSOC' has no discernible semantic or pragmatic effect in these cases.

(8.132) [[*Boub* (*naond*)] *baox*] *jix* *ninb* *bioud.*
[[1PL (ASSOC)] father] NEG_1 at home
'My/our father's not at home.' (Haili Shi, fieldnotes)

(8.133) ??[[*Wel* (*naond*)] *baox*] *jix* *ninb* *bioud.*
[[1SG (ASSOC)] father] NEG_1 at home
(intended: 'My father's not at home.')

(8.134) ??[[*Boub-god* (*naond*)] *baox*] *jix* *ninb* *bioud.*
[[1PL-PL (ASSOC)] father] NEG_1 at home
(intended: 'Our father's not at home.')

The same can be seen in examples (8.135–8.137) below. These examples show that when the possessor of the noun *jed* 'older sister' is a pronominal one (in this case second-person), there is a strong preference for using the monomorphemic non-singular pronoun *manx* '2PL' rather than the monomorphemic singular one *monx/ mx* '2SG' or the polymorphemic plural one *manx-god* [2PL-PL].[163] Again, this is true even when the possessor is semantically singular, and it is true regardless of whether *naond* 'ASSOC' intervenes between the possessor and possessum or not.

(8.135) [[*Manx* (*naond*)] *jed*] *mx* *at* *jix* *ndiot!*
[[2PL (ASSOC)] older.sister] 2SG SAT NEG_1 recognize
'You don't even recognize your own older sister!' (Shixiang Wu, fieldnotes)

(8.136) ??[[*Mx* (*naond*)] *jed*] *mx* *at* *jix* *ndiot!*
[[2SG (ASSOC)] older.sister] 2SG SAT NEG_1 recognize
(intended: 'You don't even recognize your own older sister!')

163 The form *jed* 'older sister' is a recent borrowing of Standard Mandarin *jiě* (姐) or of a cognate form from another Sinitic variety. The more "native" Xong form for 'older sister' is *yaos*, although it is possible that *yaos* itself is simply an older, less transparent borrowing from Sinitic.

(8.137) ??[[*Manx-god* *(naond)*] *jed*] *mx* *at* *jix* *ndiot!*
[[2PL-PL (ASSOC)] older.sister] 2SG SAT NEG$_1$ recognize
(intended: 'You don't even recognize your own older sister!')

This same preference for monomorphemic non-singular pronominal possessors also applies to possessum noun phrases that refer to a handful of other inalienably possessed entities, most notably *bioud* 'home, family' and *gheul* 'village'. Somewhat unexpectedly, though, it does not apply to possessum noun phrases referring to children or grandchildren (e.g *deb* 'child', *deb-deb* [child-RED] 'child', or *giad* 'grandchild'), which readily take singular pronominal possessors.

Finally, as was mentioned earlier in this section, headless possessive constructions with *naond* 'ASSOC' are also possible in Xong. These consist solely of a possessor noun phrase and a following *naond* 'ASSOC', with no possessum at all. These headless possessive constructions naturally do not serve the same function as headed *naond* possessive constructions: the latter serve to restrict the reference of a possessum noun phrase through the addition of a possessor noun phrase, while the former function as noun phrases themselves or follow the copular verb *nins* 'COP' to express some property (often but not always ownership) of that copular verb's preceding (or elided) argument. However, the significant structural similarities that headless *naond* possessive constructions share with their headed equivalents (aside from the lack of a possessum, of course) still justify discussing them in this section. Note that the functional and structural differences between headed and headless possessive constructions are similar to those between headed and headless relative clauses; see Section 8.1 above for more information.

Examples (8.138–8.141) below show a representative sample of headless *naond* possessive constructions, each of which has been enclosed within brackets.

(8.138) [*Bix.ndaut.doux.yeuf* *naond*] *doub* *nins* *Sank.ux.baob.*
[village.name ASSOC] then$_1$ COP PN
'(The bandit) from Bi Ndau Dou Yeu (Village) was (named) San U Bao.' (Qiusheng Long, in *Ngel.kanx*)

(8.139) *Aod-hant* *neind* *jix* *nins* [*mx* *naond*].
one-CLF:PL this NEG$_1$ COP [2SG ASSOC]
'These (things) aren't yours.' (Shixiang Wu, fieldnotes)

(8.140) *Beul* *naond* *npaok* *tout* [*beul* *naond*] *diet* *ncaos.*
3 ASSOC woman pick.up [3 ASSOC] hide be.done
'His wife took his (frog skin) and hid it away.' (Xingyu Shi, in *Deb Guk Ronf*)

(8.141) *Nins* [*boub-leb-beul* *naond*].
COP [1PL-DU-3 ASSOC]
'It's mine and hers.' (Yan Long, fieldnotes)

8.2.2 The unflagged possessive construction

Most of what was said about the *naond* possessive construction in Section 8.2.1 above also applies to the unflagged possessive construction. In fact, there appear to be only two noteworthy differences between the two. First, in the unflagged possessive construction the possessor noun phrase immediately precedes the possessum noun phrase, with no intervening material whatsoever. This means that an unflagged possessive construction will have the following grammatical structure:

$$[[NP_{\text{POSSESSOR}}] \quad NP_{\text{POSSESSUM}}]$$

Second, unlike with the *naond* possessive construction, there does not exist any corresponding headless version of the unflagged possessive construction.

Several representative examples of the unflagged possessive construction are given in (8.142–8.149) below. Just as in Section 8.2.1, the constituent structure of each possessive construction has been marked with brackets.

(8.142) [[*Beul*] *baox*] *leh,* *soud* *beul* *aod-deib*
[[3] father] LEH raise 3 one-CLF:pair$_2$
yaos-geud *liox* *miex* *lah.*
older.sister-younger.sibling big person PRF
'Their father raised them, the two sisters, to adulthood.' (Xingyu Shi, in *Oub Meinl Yaos Geud*)

(8.143) *Anb* *liax* *liax* *raut* [[*manx*] *gheul*].
really resemble resemble good [[2PL] village]
'(Principal Ngeu's village) is just like your village.' (Chenghua Long, in *Conversation in La'ershan*)

(8.144) *Monx* *nzhaod* *monl* *nghauk* [[*manx*] *deb-ghot*] *aod-tit.*
2SG return go visit [[2PL] DIM-old] one-CLF:time$_3$
'You should go back to visit your (father) for a while.' (Xingyu Shi, in *Oub Meinl Yaos Geud*)

(8.145) *Lis* *meb* [[*beul*] *aod-xeub* *ob-deud-guk*].
want take [[3] one-CLF:body NOM-skin-frog]
'(The dragon-frog) wanted to get his frog skin.' (Xiao Shi, in *Deb Guk Ronf*)

(8.146) *Doub* *nghaok* [[*ngonl* *daob-jod*] *ghaob-tif*]...
then$_1$ cut.with.scissors [[CLF:animate AN-wolf] NOM-stomach]
'Then (the hunter) cut the wolf's stomach open with the scissors...' (Haili Shi, in *Xaub Honl Mob*)

(8.147) *Dieud dox leh, dut [[Us.zhux] aod-peik*
CLF:time$_2$ that LEH obtain [[Wuchaohe] one-CLF:group
miex] noul geud keuf.
person] catch hold shut
'At that time, (they) caught and locked up a group (of rebels) from Wuchaohe (Village).' (Qiusheng Long, in *Ngel.kanx*)

(8.148) *[[Bid-gheul] laot-gheul] mex aod-ngonl daob-mel.*
[[FRT-mountain] top-place$_2$] exist one-CLF:animate AN-horse
'There's a horse on the mountain.' (Shixiang Wu, fieldnotes)

(8.149) *[[Oub-zhaus ndaut] daod-nzhonb] mex aod-diaond*
[[two-CLF:vertical.plant tree] place$_3$-middle] exist one-CLF:lump
ghaob-roub.
NOM-stone
'Between the two trees there was a large rock.' (Shixiang Wu, fieldnotes)

There do not appear to be any strict grammatical rules governing when a *naond* possessive construction is used versus an unflagged possessive construction, although there does seem to be a general tendency to use *naond* 'ASSOC' when the possessum is alienably possessed and to use an unflagged possessive construction when it is inalienably possessed. There is also a tendency to use the *naond* possessive construction in slower, more careful speech and the unflagged possessive construction in faster, more casual speech. However, this latter tendency appears to be weaker than the former one, so that (for example) possessed noun phrases whose referents are kin members will generally appear in the unflagged possessive construction rather than the *naond* one even in slow, careful speech. Note also that the preference for pronominal possessors of kin terms to be monomorphemic non-singular ones (see Section 8.2.1) applies to the unflagged possessive construction just as it does to the *naond* possessive construction.

It has been reported that bare classifiers can serve to mark possession in a number of other Miao-Yao varieties, including the Miao language Hmong (Bisang 1999: 148) and the Yao language Biao Min (Mao 2004: 263, 264). However, this does not appear to be the case for Fenghuang Xong. It is true that instances of a possessor noun phrase followed by a bare classifier (see Section 6.1.3.1) followed in turn by a seemingly possessed noun do occasionally occur in naturalistic Xong speech, as in examples (8.150) and (8.151) below. In these two examples, the sequences under discussion have been enclosed within brackets, but the sequences' internal constituent structures have not been further indicated.

(8.150) *Nins [boub zheinb mok] neind.*
COP [1PL CLF:tool sickle] this
'It's our sickle.' (Xingyu Shi, in *Deb Guk Ronf*)

(8.151) *Naont beul jeub chaot dut* [*beul ngonl daob-guk*].
thus 3 then$_3$ look.for obtain [3 CLF:animate AN-frog]
'Then he found his frog.' (Chenghua Long, in *Frog, Where Are You?*)

However, there is reason to believe that the bare classifiers in these constructions are not actually serving as noun-phrase–external possessive markers, but rather that they are merely serving as the first element of the possessum noun phrase in typical classifier fashion.[164] Significantly, consultants only produce these sorts of possessive constructions in fast, casual speech. In slower, more careful speech, they generally insist that *naond* 'ASSOC', *aod* 'one', or both *naond* and *aod* be inserted between each initial possessor noun phrase and the following bare classifier, and they report that doing so has no effect on the meaning of the resulting construction. Thus, examples (8.152–8.154) below are all perfectly valid rephrasings of example (8.150) above, and in slow and/or careful speech these rephrasings are actually preferred over the original version in example (8.150).

(8.152) *Nins* [[*boub* ***naond***] *zheinb mok neind*].
COP [[1PL **ASSOC**] CLF:tool sickle this]
'It's our sickle.' (Xingyu Shi, fieldnotes)

(8.153) *Nins* [[*boub*] ***aod****-zheinb mok neind*].
COP [[1PL] **one**-CLF:tool sickle this]
'It's our sickle.' (Xingyu Shi, fieldnotes)

(8.154) *Nins* [[*boub* ***naond***] ***aod****-zheinb mok neind*].
COP [[1PL **ASSOC**] **one**-CLF:tool sickle this]
'It's our sickle.' (Xingyu Shi, fieldnotes)

The simplest way to account for the data in examples (8.150–8.154) above (and in other examples like them) is to assume that the bare classifiers in examples (8.150) and (8.151) are simply ordinary noun-phrase–initial classifiers within the possessum noun phrase, and that the possessor and possessum noun phrases are simply juxtaposed in a typical unflagged possessive construction. Otherwise, one would be forced to conclude that *zheinb* 'CLF:tool' is serving as a possessive marker in example (8.150) but not in example (8.152), even though it occurs in the same immediately prenominal position in both cases. Similarly, one would be forced to conclude that the full numeral-classifier phrase *aod-zheinb* [one-CLF:tool] is serving to mark possession in example (8.153) (which would be unusual in and of itself), while the exact same

164 Similar (though not identical) arguments apply to prenominal relative clauses that do not bear any overt marker of their relative clause status; see Section 8.1.3 above for details.

numeral-classifier phrase is not serving to mark possession in example (8.154), even though in both cases it occurs in the same immediately prenominal position.

Furthermore, while headless *naond* possessive constructions that consist solely of a possessor noun phrase and a following *naond* 'ASSOC' are quite possible (see Section 8.2.1 as well as examples (8.155) and (8.157) below), it is generally impossible to form a corresponding headless possessive construction with just a possessor noun phrase and a following classifier (see examples (8.156) and (8.158) below). Such headless possessive constructions with a final classifier do occasionally occur in casual, naturalistic Xong speech (as in example (8.159), where *boub bioud ngonl* [1PL home CLF:animate] means 'my husband'), but only very rarely, and consultants reject similar constructed examples when produced by the author. This suggests that, unlike *naond* 'ASSOC', the bare classifiers in examples (8.150) and (8.151) above do not form a constituent with their preceding possessor noun phrases.

(8.155) *Nins* [*boub* *naond*].
COP [1PL ASSOC]
'It's ours.' (Xingyu Shi, fieldnotes)

(8.156) **Nins* [*boub* *zheinb*].
COP [1PL CLF:tool]
(intended: 'It's our tool.')

(8.157) *Naont* *beul* *jeub* *chaot* *dut* [*beul* *naond*].
thus 3 then$_3$ look.for obtain [3 ASSOC]
'Then he found his (thing, object, possession).' (Chenghua Long, fieldnotes)

(8.158) **Naont* *beul* *jeub* *chaot* *dut* [*beul* *ngonl*].
thus 3 then$_3$ look.for obtain [3 CLF:animate]
(intended: 'Then he found his [animate entity].')

(8.159) *Tit-deb* *wel* *eit* *hnant* [*boub* *bioud* *ngonl*]
CLF:time$_3$-DIM 1SG still call [1PL home CLF:animate]
heut *wel* *guaox* *deb* *shand*.
help 1SG peel DIM ginger
'After a while I asked my (husband) to peel some ginger for me.' (Haili Shi, in *Tooth Conversation*)

Thus, it appears that the best-supported grammatical analysis for examples like (8.150) and (8.151) is *not* the following one, in which the possessor noun phrase and the following bare classifier (here ostensibly serving as a possessive marker) form a grammatical constituent distinct from the following possessum noun phrase:

*[[NP$_{POSSESSOR}$ CLF] NP$_{POSSESSUM}$]

Instead, the best-supported analysis appears to be the one below, in which the possessor noun phrase is simply followed by the possessum noun phrase, with that possessum noun phrase incidentally having a bare classifier as its first element:

[[NP$_{POSSESSOR}$] NP$_{POSSESSUM}$]

8.2.3 The pronominal possessive construction

In this third and final possessive construction, either the third-person pronoun *beul* '3' (see Section 7.1.1) or the "semi-pronominal" form *nex/ninx* 'NEX' (Section 7.1.4) is itself used as a possessive marker. Just as with the *naond* and unflagged possessive constructions described above, in this construction the possessor still occurs initially and the possessum still occurs finally, with *beul* '3' or *nex/ninx* 'NEX' occurring between them. Examples of this can be seen in (8.160–8.163) below. The internal constituent structure of each pronominal possessive construction has been indicated with brackets in these examples, although evidence for these structures is not given until the end of this section.

(8.160) *Beul niab jix did-lieul leh, nins [Ngeuk Xob*
3 say NEG$_1$ DID-wrong LEH COP [PN Principal
[nex minl]].
[NEX mother]]
'He said he wasn't mistaken, it was Principal Ngeu's mother.' (Xiaohui Wu, in *Conversation in La'ershan*)

(8.161) *Naont [Ngeuk Xob [nex deb-geud]] niel*
thus [PN Principal [NEX DIM-younger.sibling]] know
ix niel?
NEG$_1$ know
'Then does Principal Ngeu's younger brother know?' (Haili Shi, in *Conversation in La'ershan*)

(8.162) *[Lod-Hex [nex gheul]] ndieut hant bid-gheul*
[FAM-PN [NEX village]] ascend CLF:PL FRT-mountain
nhob ndieut nhob lot.
walk ascend walk descend
'He's village is up in the mountains, (you need to) walk up and down and up and down to get there.' (Xiaohui Wu, in *Conversation in La'ershan*)

(8.163) *Beul* *nins* *puk* [*Lonf.yeb* [*beul* *minl*]].
3 COP speak [PN [3 mother]]
'He's talking about Lon Ye's mother.' (Haili Shi, fieldnotes)

There are no discernible pragmatic or semantic differences between the forms *nex/ninx* 'NEX' and *beul* '3' when they occur in this construction (cf. Section 7.1.4), although in the author's collected texts the appearance of *nex/ninx* in this construction is several times more common than the appearance of *beul*.

The grammatical and semantic restrictions operating on the pronominal possessive construction are much stricter than those operating on either the *naond* or unflagged possessive constructions, and so the former construction naturally occurs much less frequently in Xong narratives and discourse than the latter two. In particular, the possessor in this construction must consist solely of a person's name (or a person's name plus a following title, like *Ngeuk Xob* 'Principal Ngeu'), and the possessum must consist solely of a noun that refers to either a kin member (though not including *deb* 'child', *deb-deb* [child-RED] 'child', or *giad* 'grandchild') or one of a handful of other inalienably possessed entities like *bioud* 'home, family' or *gheul* 'village'.[165]

Finally, it seems clear that the possessum and its preceding *nex/ninx* 'NEX' or *beul* '3' form an immediate constituent in the pronominal possessive construction, with the possessor then combining with that constituent to form the possessive construction as a whole. This means that the constituent structure of this construction is the following one:

[$\text{NP}_{\text{POSSESSOR}}$ [*nex/ninx/beul* $\text{NP}_{\text{POSSESSUM}}$]]

This is the opposite of the constituent structure of the *naond* possessive construction described in Section 8.2.1 above (in which the initial possessor noun phrase forms an immediate constituent with its following possessive marker *naond* 'ASSOC'), and the relevant evidence here is essentially the opposite of what was given for the *naond* possessive construction's constituent structure: namely, it is quite possible to form a constituent of the type [*nex/ninx* + $\text{NP}_{\text{POSSESSUM}}$] or [*beul* + $\text{NP}_{\text{POSSESSUM}}$] (these are equivalent to unflagged possessive constructions of the type described in Section 8.2.2 above), but it is impossible to form one of the type *[$\text{NP}_{\text{POSSESSOR}}$ + *nex/ninx*] or *[$\text{NP}_{\text{POSSESSOR}}$ + *beul*].

165 It is interesting to note that the set of nouns that can serve as the possessum in this pronominal possessive construction is essentially the same as the set of nouns that can only very reluctantly be possessed by polymorphemic or singular pronouns in the *naond* and unflagged possessive constructions (see discussion in Sections 8.2.1 and 8.2.2 above). This could be taken as suggesting some sort of alienability distinction among possessed nouns in Fenghuang Xong, with the set of inalienable nouns encompassing kin terms (except for terms like *deb* 'child', *deb-deb* [child-RED] 'child', and *giad* 'grandchild') and a few other terms like *bioud* 'home, family' and *gheul* 'village', and the set of alienable nouns encompassing all other nouns.

8.3 Nominal conjunction

In Fenghuang Xong, one of the most common ways through which multiple noun phrases can be combined into a single, larger noun phrase is juxtaposition, in which one noun-phrase conjunct is placed after another to form a larger noun phrase without any overt marker of conjunction whatsoever.[166] Instances of such noun-phrase juxtaposition can be seen in (8.164–8.166) below, where each conjunct noun phrase has been enclosed within brackets.

(8.164)

[Niaox.meib]	*[Niaox.nhaonl]*	*zhaos*	*xub*	*jix*	*doul*	*minl,*
[PN]	[PN]	from	small	NEG_1	remain	mother

nanx	*doul*	*baox.*
only	remain	father

'(The sisters) Niao Mei and Niao Nhaon had no mother growing up, (they) had only their father.' (Xingyu Shi, in *Oub Meinl Yaos Geud*)

(8.165)

Beul	*jeub*	*dionb*	*[deb-guoud]*	*[deb-guk]*	*nzhaond*	*monl*	*lah.*
3	$then_3$	lead	[DIM-dog]	[DIM-frog]	return	go	PRF

'He then led the dog and the frog back home.' (Chenghua Long, in *Frog, Where Are You?*)

(8.166)

Boub	*[niax-nbat]*	*[niax-ghab]*	*[niax-mioul]*	*at*	*yanb*	*nonx.*
1PL	[meat-pig]	[meat-chicken]	[meat-fish]	SAT	like	eat

'We like eating pork, chicken, and fish.' (unknown Xong consultant, fieldnotes)

While there is a strong preference for juxtaposed noun phrases in Xong to have parallel constituent structures (e.g. both consisting of a noun alone, or both consisting of a noun plus a preceding numeral-classifier phrase, etc.), there appear to be few if any restrictions on those constituent structures themselves. For instance, note that in example (8.167) below each noun-phrase conjunct consists of a numeral-classifier phrase and a following noun, rather than just a noun alone.

(8.167)

Beul	*bioud*	*mex*	*[bub-leb*	*deb-nint]*	*[bub-leb*	*deb-npaok].*
3	home	exist	[three-CLF	DIM-man]	[three-CLF	DIM-woman]

'Their family has three sons and three daughters.' (Haili Shi, fieldnotes)

In example (8.168), each conjunct consists of a headless relative clause, with no nouns involved at all.

166 For discussion of disjunction (including nominal disjunction) in Xong, see Section 12.6.4.

(8.168) *Aod-dieud* *dox* [*manx* *nonx*] [*manx* *hneind*] *at* *jix* *mex.*
one-CLF:time$_2$ that [REL eat] [REL wear] SAT NEG$_1$ exist
'Back then (we) didn't have anything to eat or to wear.' (unknown Xong consultant, fieldnotes)

In examples (8.169) and (8.170), each conjunct is a complex noun phrase that consists of an initial possessor noun phrase and a following possessum noun phrase. Note that in example (8.169) each conjunct features a *naond* possessive construction (see Section 8.2.1), while in example (8.170) each conjunct features an unflagged possessive construction (Section 8.2.2).

(8.169) *Naont* [*beul* *naond* *deb*] [*beul* *naond* *nheinx*]
thus [3 ASSOC child] [3 ASSOC daughter.in.law]
nzhaod *monl* *nkhed* *Niaox.nhaonl* *naond* *baox.*
return go look PN ASSOC father
'And so his (son) and his daughter-in-law went back to visit Niao Nhaon's father.' (Xingyu Shi, in *Oub Meinl Yaos Geud*)

(8.170) [*Boub* *ceit*] [*boub* *bex.maok*] *at*
[1PL father's.older.brother] [1PL father's.older.brother's.wife] SAT
jix *ninb* *bioud.*
NEG$_1$ at home
'My uncle and aunt aren't at home.' (Shixiang Wu, fieldnotes)

Finally, in example (8.171) each conjunct is a noun phrase consisting solely of a personal pronoun.

(8.171) [*Boub-god*] [*beul*] *yaod.yaod* *nins* *ghaob-Xonb.*
[1PL-PL] [3] all COP NOM-Miao
'We and she (i.e. we three teachers and this young girl) are all Miao.' (Shixiang Wu, fieldnotes)

Care must be taken to distinguish juxtaposed noun phrases of the sort seen in examples (8.164–8.171) above from apparently similar constructions that actually have very different grammatical structures. In particular, juxtaposed noun phrases consisting solely of noun roots or noun compounds can appear quite similar to reciprocal or generic compounds (discussed in Sections 5.3.2 and 5.3.3, respectively), and those consisting solely of pronouns can appear quite similar to clusive pronouns (discussed in Section 7.1.2.2). The reader is encouraged to consult the sections just cited for more detailed information on how to distinguish juxtaposed noun phrases from these other, superficially similar constructions.

In addition to simple juxtaposition, Fenghuang Xong also features two monosyllabic verbs that often appear between two noun phrases with an essentially conjunctive function: *nhaons* 'with' and *ox/ux* 'and'. Both of these forms are clearly canonical members of the verb class in Xong, but they have taken on several functions that are more typically characteristic of nominal conjunctions in other languages. The remainder of this section is devoted to a description of the grammatical and semantic properties of *nhaons* 'with' and *ox/ux* 'and', along with some brief discussion of the functional, distributional, and semantic overlap that they share with nominal conjunctions in other languages.

First of all, both *nhaons* 'with' and *ox/ux* 'and' (the latter form is realized as *ux* by speakers from Shanjiang Town and as *ox* by speakers from other parts of Fenghuang County) can be directly negated by *(j)ix* 'NEG$_1$' and can undergo relativization through the use of *manx* 'REL', which are the two criteria used to define the class of verbs in this grammar (see Section 10.2). This is shown in examples (8.172) and (8.173). Incidentally, these two examples also demonstrate that *nhaons* and *ox/ux* can each serve as the sole verb in a main or relative clause.

(8.172)	*Wel*	*ix*	***nhaons/ux***	*monx*	*lah.*
	1SG	NEG$_1$	**with/and**	2SG	PRF

'I'm not (participating in this joint business venture) with you anymore.' (Chenghua Long, fieldnotes)

(8.173)	*Aod-ngonl*	*deb-deb*	*manx*	***nhaons/ux***	*baox*	*dox...*
	one-CLF:animate	child-RED	REL	**with/and**	father	that

'That child who's living with his father...' (Chenghua Long, fieldnotes)

The verb *nhaons* is consistently glossed as 'with' in this grammar and the verb *ox/ux* is consistently glossed as 'and', but depending on context the most appropriate English translation for each form can range from 'with, to be with' to 'to accompany' to 'to be together, to stay together'. The author's consultants report that the only notable semantic difference between the two is that the use of *nhaons* 'with' to conjoin two noun phrases does not entail that the conjoined entities performed the action (or underwent the process, etc.) referred to by the clause's main predicate together, while the use of *ox/ux* 'and' does in fact carry such an entailment. Given this, one might argue that it would make more sense to gloss *nhaons* as 'and' and to gloss *ox/ux* as 'with'. However, in this grammar *nhaons* is still glossed as 'with' and *ox/ux* as 'and' because in the author's collected Xong corpus *nhaons* more often appears in contexts where it is more appropriately translated into English as 'with', while *ox/ux* more often appears in contexts where it is more appropriately translated as 'and'.

Examples of *nhaons* 'with' and *ox/ux* 'and' occurring between two noun phrases with a function and meaning very similar to those of canonical nominal conjunctions in other languages (such as, e.g., English *and*) are given in (8.174–8.179) below.[167]

(8.174) *Daob-jod aod nonx [beul naond daok]*
AN-wolf as.soon.as eat [3 ASSOC maternal.grandmother]
nhaons *[Xaub.Honl.Mob]...*
with [Little.Red.Hat]
'As soon as the wolf had eaten Little Red Hat and her grandmother...' (Haili Shi, in *Xaub Honl Mob*)

(8.175) *Doub nghaok ngonl daob-jod ghaob-tif,*
then$_1$ cut.with.scissors CLF:animate AN-wolf NOM-stomach
doub geud [Xaub.Honl.Mob] ***nhaons*** *[beul*
then$_1$ hold [Little.Red.Hat] **with** [3
daok] giub bionl.
maternal.grandmother] rescue exit
'Then (the hunter) cut the wolf's stomach open with the scissors, then (he) rescued Little Red Hat and her grandmother.' (Haili Shi, in *Xaub Honl Mob*)

(8.176) *[Niaox.nhaonl naond bod]* ***nhaons*** *[beul baox] ninb bioud.*
[PN ASSOC husband] **with** [3 father] at home
'Niao Nhaon's husband and father were at home.' (Xingyu Shi, in *Oub Meinl Yaos Geud*)

(8.177) *Beul geud [leb baod-ndiuk-mok dox]* ***ox*** *[beul*
3 hold [CLF BUG-peck-sickle that] **and** [3
zheinb mok dox] deib.
CLF:tool sickle that] compare
'He took the sickle-tip and his own sickle and compared them.' (Xingyu Shi, in *Deb Guk Ronf*)

(8.178) *Ranf.houb [beul naond npaok]* ***ox*** *[beul naond minl]*
afterward [3 ASSOC woman] **and** [3 ASSOC mother]
chauk naont daut-leb nzhaod ghat bioud monl ah.
do thus REFL-CLF return go.to home go PART
'Afterward his wife and his mother went home by themselves.' (Xingyu Shi, in *Deb Guk Ronf*)

167 In these and all subsequent examples in this section, the forms *nhaons* and *ox/ux* are bolded, while the constituents that they link (in a general semantic sense, if not necessarily in the sense of strict grammatical conjunction) are enclosed within brackets.

(8.179) *Boub bioud heit doul* [*daob-guoud*] **ox** [*daob-nbat*].
1PL home still remain [AN-dog] **and** [AN-pig]
'I've still got dogs and pigs at home (to go take care of).' (Shixiang Wu, fieldnotes)

While sequences composed of an initial *nhaons* 'with' or *ox/ux* 'and' and a following noun phrase in examples such as these might display some superficial similarities with unflagged postnominal relative clauses (see Section 8.1.5), note that (i) such sequences do not serve to modify (i.e. restrict the reference of) any noun, which is a definining characteristic of relative clauses in this grammar, (ii) such sequences are not subject to any of the semantic or grammatical restrictions which unflagged postnominal relative clauses must obey, and (iii) the forms *nhaons* and *ox/ux* can be used to link constituents other than noun phrases, as is discussed further below in this section.

Examples (8.180–8.184) below show that various forms, including grammatical operators like *ghad* 'then$_2$', *deit* 'still', and *(s)at* 'SAT' (see Section 9.1.1) as well as the particle *leh* 'LEH' (Section 9.2.1.1), can occur between *nhaons* 'with' and the conjunct preceding it or between *ox/ux* 'and' and the conjunct preceding it. This is an unusual property for nominal conjunctions (see Brown and Dryer 2008), but it is perhaps unsurprising given the verbal nature of *nhaons* and *ox/ux*, as most other verbs in Xong can also occur in the same environment.

(8.180) *Xib hlit* [*manx*] *ghad* **nhaons** [*boub*] *chauk toux.feid.*
hungry cooked.rice [2PL] then$_2$ **with** [1PL] do bandit
'If you guys are hungry, then come be bandits with us.' (Qiusheng Long, in *Ngel.kanx*)

(8.181) [*Aod-ngonl guoud*] *leh, sat* **nhaons** [*beul*] *xeud*
[one-CLF:animate dog] LEH SAT **with** [3] stand
ninb khauk-bioud dox hnant daob-guk.
at hole-home that call AN-frog
'The dog stood with him at the window and called for the frog, too.' (Chenghua Long, in *Frog, Where Are You?*)

(8.182) *Naont shib* [*beul naond npaok*] *leh* **ox** [*beul naond*
thus it's [3 ASSOC woman] LEH **and** [3 ASSOC
minl] *doub ghans beul dut aod-xeub deud-guk.*
mother] then$_1$ see 3 obtain one-CLF:body skin-frog
'And so it was that his wife and his mother saw that he had found his frog skin.' (Xingyu Shi, in *Deb Guk Ronf*)

(8.183) [*Aod-leb baod-ndiuk-mok neind*] *wel niab chauk-dib* ***ox***
[one-CLF BUG-peck-sickle this] 1SG say do-which **and**
[*boub bioud zheinb mok leb baod-ndiuk-mok*] *did-deib?*
[1PL home CLF:tool sickle CLF BUG-peck-sickle] DID-compare
'This sickle-tip – I say, how can it be that it matches up with the sickle-tip from our own sickle?' (Xingyu Shi, in *Deb Guk Ronf*)

(8.184) [*Beul*] *deit* ***nhaons*** [*aod-ngonl deb-guk*] *puk...*
[3] still **with** [one-CLF:animate DIM-frog] speak
'He still said to the frog...' (Xingyu Shi, in *Deb Guk Ronf*)

Examples (8.185–8.190) below show that *nhaons* 'with' and *ox/ux* 'and' can also be used to link constituents other than noun phrases. In particular, examples (8.185–8.187) show that these two forms can be used to link clauses, while examples (8.188–8.190) show that they can be used to link certain noun-phrase–internal constituents. Note, though, that in most cases simple juxtaposition could be used for these same functions as well.

(8.185) [*Chaonb gok*] ***nhaons/ox*** [*tiob ux*] *mx yanb gians dib?*
[sing song] **with/and** [jump dance] 2SG like CLF:kind$_1$ which
'Which do you like more, singing or dancing?' (Shixiang Wu, fieldnotes)

(8.186) [*Fuk yank*] ***nhaons/ox*** [*fuk jeud*] *sat deib*
[drink tobacco] **with/and** [drink alcohol] SAT to
ghaob-dieud jix raut.
NOM-body NEG$_1$ good
'Smoking and drinking are both bad for you.' (Shixiang Wu, fieldnotes)

(8.187) [*Nbaod beinx*] ***nhaons/ux*** [*raul eud*] *aod.sheit*
[embroider flower] **with/and** [sew clothing] the.same
lis aod-jub aod-jub naond lol.
want one-CLF:needle one-CLF:needle ASSOC come
'Whether (you're) embroidering or sewing, (you) need to take it one stitch at a time.' (Chenghua Long, fieldnotes)

(8.188) *Boub bioud* [*daob-yul*] ***nhaons/ux*** [*daob-nbat*] *yaod.yaod sat*
1PL home [AN-cow] **with/and** [AN-pig] all SAT
mes diul khad.
sell complete dry
'Our family's sold all our cows and pigs.' (Chenghua Long, fieldnotes)

(8.189) *biaob-zhaut-ngonl* [*daob-nief*] ***nhaons/ox*** [*daob-yul*]
five-six-CLF:animate [AN-water.buffalo] **with/and** [AN-cow]
'five or six water buffalo and cows (i.e. five or six animals, some of which are water buffalo and some of which are cows)' (Shixiang Wu, fieldnotes)

(8.190) *Nins* [*wel naond*] ***nhaons/ox*** [*beul naond*] *dib.daont.*
COP [1SG ASSOC] **with/and** [3 ASSOC] money
'It's my and her money.' (Yan Long, fieldnotes)

Finally, the forms *nhaons* and *ox/ux* can each occur multiple times in a single clause to link three or more constituents, as in example (8.191) below. In this example, consultants report that *nhaons* 'with' could be freely replaced with *ox/ux* 'and' with no discernible change in meaning or pragmatics.

(8.191) [*Daob-guk*] ***nhaons*** [*daob-guoud*] ***nhaons*** [*beul*] *dianx leh*
[AN-frog] **with** [AN-dog] **with** [3] finish LEH
manx raut geub.bul.
REL good friend
'The frog and the dog and he (i.e. the boy) were all good friends.'
(Chenghua Long, in *Frog, Where Are You?*)

9 Clauses

This chapter discusses the basic structure of the Xong clause. It thus includes discussion of the most important sorts of clausal constituents and the ways in which these are combined to form larger syntactic units, as well as discussion of certain non-canonical clause types like comparative and interrogative clauses.

It is important to note that although multiverbal constructions play a very important role in Xong clausal grammar, such constructions are discussed in Chapter 12 rather than here. This is done partly because this way both chapters can be kept to manageable lengths, and partly because multiverbal constructions are not necessarily clause-level phenomena. This chapter thus mainly discusses clauses and clausal phenomena which need not involve more than one verb, though some exceptions to this general rule have been made wherever the author found it convenient (see, for instance, Sections 9.3.3 and 9.3.4).

The specific topics covered in this chapter have been organized as follows. Section 9.1 discusses the major constituents and overall structure of Xong clauses, along with important related phenomena like argument ellipsis and cross-clausal coreference restrictions (Section 9.1.2) and information structure (Section 9.1.3). Section 9.2 discusses certain forms which play important roles in Xong clausal syntax and which do not easily fit into any of the other chapters of this grammar, including most prominently particles (Section 9.2.1). Finally, Section 9.3 discusses several non-canonical clause types that display noteworthy syntactic or semantic properties, including imperative clauses (Section 9.3.1), interrogative clauses (Section 9.3.2), comparative clauses (Section 9.3.3), and Xong's so-called "passive" clauses (Section 9.3.4).

9.1 Basic clausal structure

9.1.1 Constituent types and ordering

Any pragmatically neutral, univerbal Xong clause will contain from zero to three arguments.[168] An example of such a clause with zero arguments is given in (9.1) below.

---

168 Verbless clauses do occur in Xong, though little attention is devoted to them in this description due to their relative infrequency and apparent lack of interesting syntactic properties. Two examples, though, would be *Tat-hnef xink.qif-sib* [this-CLF:day week-four] 'Today is Thursday' and *Bub-shauk aod-gaonb* [three-CLF:yuan one-CLF:catty] '(These vegetables cost) three *yuan* (unit of currency) per catty (unit of mass)'. Such verbless clauses most commonly contain either an expression referring to time or one referring to money, as in the examples just provided.

(9.1) *Raut.*
good
'Okay.' (Haili Shi, fieldnotes)

An example of such a clause with one argument is given in (9.2). In this and similar following examples in this section, each argument has been enclosed within brackets and each verb has been bolded.

(9.2) [*Beul baox*] ***monl*** *lah.*
[3 father] **go** PRF
'Their father left.' (Xingyu Shi, in *Oub Meinl Yaos Geud*)

An example of such a clause with two arguments is given in (9.3).

(9.3) [*Wel*] ***liaos*** [*monx*].
[1SG] **miss** [2SG]
'I've missed you.' (Xingyu Shi, in *Oub Meinl Yaos Geud*)

Finally, an example of such a clause with three arguments is given in (9.4).

(9.4) [*Wel*] ***bod*** [*mx*] [*aod-gians sib*].
[1SG] **tell** [2SG] [one-CLF:kind$_1$ matter]
'I'm going to tell you about something.' (Shixiang Wu, fieldnotes)

Note that this section concerns itself solely with pragmatically neutral, univerbal clauses in which all arguments are overtly expressed, as in examples (9.1–9.4) above. For discussion of clauses in which one or more arguments are elided, see Section 9.1.2. See also Sections 9.1.3 and 9.3 for discussion of less pragmatically neutral clauses, and see Chapter 12 for discussion of clauses containing multiple verbs.

There is little to no evidence for grammaticalized syntactic roles like "subject" or "direct object" in Xong in the form of (i) relativization restrictions (see Section 8.1), (ii) argument ellipsis restrictions or cross-clausal coreference restrictions (Section 9.1.2), (iii) any sort of passive construction (Section 9.3.4), or (iv) overt marking of any kind (e.g. case marking on nouns, argument marking on verbs, etc.). However, constituent ordering restrictions do provide evidence for a variety of grammaticalized syntactic roles in Xong, and many of these show some degree of functional overlap with canonical examples of grammaticalized syntactic roles in other languages.[169]

169 By "grammaticalized syntactic role", the author means a language-specific grammaticalized neutralization of semantic roles that (i) is associated with a single syntactic position (or, in some cases, with the possibility of freely occurring in either of two syntactic positions) and (ii) primarily functions as an argument of predicates.

The first syntactic role to be discussed in this section is the SUBJECT, which is the syntactic role associated with the sole argument of a semantically intransitive verb.[170, 171] A SUBJECT can typically occur in either preverbal or postverbal position, at least in pragmatically neutral, univerbal clauses (which, again, are the only sort of clauses under consideration in this section). Examples of SUBJECTS occurring in preverbal position are given in (9.5–9.7), and examples of them occurring in postverbal position are given in (9.8–9.10). In addition to being bracketed, each SUBJECT in these examples has also been marked with a following subscript <$_S$>. The sole verb in each clause has been bolded.

(9.5) *Dib-hnef [beul] jix anb* ***mb.***
LOC-day [3]$_S$ NEG$_1$ really **hurt**
'During the day it (i.e. my tooth) doesn't hurt all that much.' (Haili Shi, in *Tooth Conversation*)

(9.6) *Fanx.zheinb [aod-leb khauk-khauk dox]* ***loux*** *hint.*
anyway [one-CLF hole-RED that]$_S$ **long.time** very
'Anyway that hole's been there (in my tooth) for a long time.' (Haili Shi, in *Tooth Conversation*)

(9.7) *[Niaox.meib] ghaod* ***raos.***
[PN]$_S$ more **clever**
'Niao Mei was cleverer (than her sister).' (Xingyu Shi, in *Oub Meinl Yaos Geud*)

---

170 By "semantically intransitive verb", the author means a verb whose referent property (or action, or activity, etc.) could be held (or undertaken, or undergone, etc.) even if there were only a single entity in existence, and this could be done without that single entity simultaneously possessing two distinct semantic roles. For instance, one could easily *daos* ('to die') even if one were the sole entity in existence. However, one could not *daot* ('to kill') if one were the sole entity in existence, or at least not without one's simultaneously serving as killer and killed (i.e. committing suicide, and thereby simultaneously possessing two distinct semantic roles). For the purposes of this grammar, *daos* 'to die' is thus a semantically intransitive verb, while *daot* 'to kill' is not. A "semantically transitive verb", in contrast, is a verb whose referent action (or activity, etc.) would require a minimum of two entities in existence in order to be carried out. An example of such a verb would be *daot* 'to kill'. Finally, a "semantically ditransitive verb" would be a verb like *gaons* 'to give', whose referent action would require a minimum of three entities in existence in order to be carried out.

171 The name of each particular grammaticalized syntactic role is always given in small caps (e.g. SUBJECT, AGENT, etc.) in this description. It is important to note that these terms are intended to refer only to Xong-specific syntactic roles (i.e. grammaticalized neutralizations of semantic roles that are associated with particular syntactic positions and that primarily function as arguments of predicates). They do *not* refer to semantic roles, which are instead always referred to using ordinary (i.e. non–small-caps) terms. Thus, for instance, the terms "AGENT" and "PATIENT" refer to two particular grammaticalized syntactic roles in Xong, while the terms "agent" and "patient" refer to two particular semantic roles.

(9.8) ***Xub*** *[aub]* *hint.*
small [water]$_S$ very
'The water pressure (in our home) is really low.' (unknown Xong consultant, fieldnotes)

(9.9) ***Daox*** *[nons]* *lah.*
precipitate [rain]$_S$ PRF
'It's raining.' (Yan Long, fieldnotes)

(9.10) ***Mex*** *[ngonl* *deb-naus]*.
exist [CLF:animate DIM-bird]$_S$
'A little bird appeared.' (Xingyu Shi, in *Oub Meinl Yaos Geud*)

While it is true that a SUBJECT can typically occur in either preverbal or postverbal position in a canonical Xong clause, it is worth mentioning that it will always occur in postverbal position when its referent is first introduced into an ongoing discourse (see Section 9.1.3.2). Of course, it is quite likely that there exist additional factors determining whether a SUBJECT precedes or follows its verb in any given case, but these have yet to be identified.

The next two syntactic roles to be discussed are the AGENT and the PATIENT. The former is the syntactic role associated with the more agent-like argument of a semantically transitive verb, which will occur in preverbal position; the latter is the syntactic role associated with the more patient-like argument of a semantically transitive verb, which will occur in postverbal position (again, attention is here restricted solely to pragmatically neutral, univerbal clauses in which all arguments are overtly expressed).[172] Examples of (preverbal) AGENTS and (postverbal) PATIENTS can be seen in each of (9.11–9.15) below. In addition to being bracketed, each AGENT in these examples has been marked with a following subscript <$_A$>, and each PATIENT has been marked with a following subscript <$_P$>. The sole verb in each clause has again been bolded.

(9.11) *[Wel]* ***nonx*** *[leb* *jik.zaox.zaod]*.
[1SG]$_A$ **eat** [CLF chicken.claw]$_P$
'I ate a chicken's foot.' (Haili Shi, in *Tooth Conversation*)

(9.12) *[Wel]* ***liaos*** *[monx]*.
[1SG]$_A$ **miss** [2SG]$_P$
'I've missed you.' (Xingyu Shi, in *Oub Meinl Yaos Geud*)
(repeated from (9.3) above)

172 For information on two-argument clauses involving semantically intransitive verbs, see Section 10.4.

(9.13) [*Beul*] *ghad* ***cod*** [*deb-xut.npeif*].
[3]$_A$ then$_2$ **sew** [DIM-shoe]$_P$
'She (started to) sew some shoes.' (Xingyu Shi, in *Oub Meinl Yaos Geud*)

(9.14) [*Beul baox*] ***dand*** [*zheit-cheid*].
[3 father]$_A$ **arrive** [outside-gate]$_P$
'Their father arrived at the gate.' (Xingyu Shi, in *Oub Meinl Yaos Geud*)

(9.15) [*Yaos*] ***nbut*** [*Niaox.meib*], [*deb-geud*] ***nbut***
[older.sister]$_A$ **name** [PN]$_P$ [DIM-younger.sibling]$_A$ **name**
[*Niaox.nhaonl*].
[PN]$_P$
'The older sister was named Niao Mei, and the younger Niao Nhaon.' (Xingyu Shi, in *Oub Meinl Yaos Geud*)

The author is not aware of any cases in which an AGENT will occur in postverbal position in a univerbal clause. While an AGENT will occur postverbally when first introduced into an ongoing discourse through the use of the *mex* presentational construction (see Section 9.1.3.2) or through the use of a clause featuring *zhus/zhaus* 'to suffer' (Section 9.3.4), in such cases another verb will obligatorily occur following the AGENT. However, there are a variety of non-canonical clause types in which a PATIENT will occur in preverbal position even in a univerbal clause; these are discussed in detail in Section 9.1.3.1 below.

The last two syntactic roles to be discussed here are the RECIPIENT and the THEME. The RECIPIENT is the syntactic role associated with the most recipient-like argument of a semantically ditransitive verb, which will occur in immediate postverbal position. The THEME is the syntactic role associated with the most theme-like argument of a semantically distransitive verb, which will occur following the most recipient-like argument (i.e. following the RECIPIENT). Note that in all cases the most agent-like argument of a semantically ditransitive verb will behave identically to the more agent-like argument of a semantically transitive verb, and there is thus no need to distinguish the two; the term "AGENT" is sufficient to refer to both.

Examples of three-argument clauses featuring an AGENT, a RECIPIENT, and a THEME are given in (9.16–9.19) below. In addition to being bracketed, each AGENT in these examples has been marked with a following subscript <$_A$>, each RECIPIENT has been marked with a following subscript <$_R$>, and each THEME has been marked with a following subscript <$_T$>. Just as in earlier examples in this section, the sole verb in each clause has been bolded.

(9.16) [*Wel*] *aod-hnef* ***beb*** [*deb*] [*aod-shauk* *daont*].
[1SG]$_{A}$ one-CLF:day **share** [child]$_{R}$ [one-CLF:yuan money]$_{T}$
'Every day I give my child one *yuan* (unit of currency).' (Chenghua Long, fieldnotes)

(9.17) [*Beul*] ***giok*** [*wel*] [*Ink.ix*].
[3]$_{A}$ **teach** [1SG]$_{R}$ [English]$_{T}$
'He's teaching me English.' (Chenghua Long, fieldnotes)

(9.18) [*Wel*] ***bod*** [*mx*] [*aod-gians* *sib*].
[1SG]$_{A}$ **tell** [2SG]$_{R}$ [one-CLF:kind$_{1}$ matter]$_{T}$
'I'm going to tell you about something.' (Shixiang Wu, fieldnotes) (repeated from (9.4) above)

(9.19) *Naonb.roul* [*wel*] ***gaons*** [*manx* *oub-leb*] [*aod-leb* *zhonx-hlod*].
now [1SG]$_{A}$ **give** [2PL two-CLF]$_{R}$ [one-CLF length-bamboo]$_{T}$
'Now I'm going to give each of you (two) a length of bamboo.' (Xingyu Shi, in *Oub Meinl Yaos Geud*)

In pragmatically neutral, univerbal clauses in which all arguments are overtly expressed, RECIPIENTS and THEMES will always occur in postverbal position, as in examples (9.16–9.19) above. However, in less canonical clauses, one of these constituent types (never both at the same time) may occur in preverbal position instead; see Section 9.1.3.1 for discussion.

This section has so far described five distinct grammaticalized syntactic roles: (i) the SUBJECT (representing the sole argument of a semantically intransitive verb), (ii) the AGENT (representing the more agent-like argument of a semantically transitive verb or the most agent-like argument of a semantically ditransitive verb), (iii) the PATIENT (representing the more patient-like argument of a semantically transitive verb), (iv) the RECIPIENT (representing the most recipient-like argument of a semantically ditransitive verb), and (v) the THEME (representing the most theme-like argument of a semantically ditransitive verb). A natural next step would be to investigate whether any two (or even more) of these constituent types could be "merged" into a single type, as was already done earlier in this section for the more agent-like argument of a semantically transitive verb and the most agent-like argument of a semantically ditransitive verb. However, no such further mergers appear to be possible.

The AGENT already represents a merger of two constituent types (i.e. the more agent-like argument of a semantically transitive verb and the most agent-like argument of a semantically ditransitive verb), but it does not appear possible to further merge the AGENT with any other syntactic roles. It is impossible to merge the AGENT with the PATIENT, the RECIPIENT, or the THEME, as the ordering possibilities of the AGENT clearly differ from the ordering properties of each of those other three syntactic roles. This is made most obvious by the fact that an AGENT can co-occur within a single univerbal clause with a PATIENT, with a RECIPIENT, with a THEME, or with both a RECIPIENT and a THEME. In all such cases, the AGENT and the other argument(s) will occur in different syntactic positions.

Neither is it possible to merge the AGENT with the SUBJECT, since the two again clearly have different ordering properties. In pragmatically neutral, univerbal clauses, an AGENT will always occur in preverbal position, while a SUBJECT can usually occur on either side of its verb.

For much the same reasons, the SUBJECT cannot be merged with the PATIENT, the RECIPIENT, or the THEME. While a SUBJECT can typically appear in either preverbal or postverbal position in a univerbal, pragmatically neutral clause, PATIENTS, RECIPIENTS, and THEMES will always appear in postverbal position in such clauses.

Finally, although it does not appear possible to fully merge any two (or all three) of the PATIENT, RECIPIENT, and THEME, these three constituent types do seem to display certain similarities not shared by the SUBJECT or AGENT. It is true that the RECIPIENT and THEME are clearly distinct syntactic roles in univerbal clauses that feature three overtly expressed arguments. This is made most obvious by the fact that both a RECIPIENT and a THEME can co-occur in a single such clause, and when they do they will occur in different syntactic positions. However, when a clause that features a semantically distransitive verb occurs with either the RECIPIENT or THEME argument elided, the remaining (i.e. non-elided) argument seems to behave identically (at least in terms of constituent ordering) to the PATIENT argument of a clause that features a semantically transitive verb. In other words, when the RECIPIENT of a three-argument univerbal clause is elided, the remaining THEME behaves identically to the PATIENT of a two-argument univerbal clause, and when the THEME of a three-argument univerbal clause is elided, the remaining RECIPIENT behaves identically to the PATIENT of a two-argument univerbal clause.

Taking all of the information presented so far in this section into account, the basic structure of a pragmatically neutral, univerbal Xong clause with all arguments overtly expressed can be represented by the three schemas given in (9.20), (9.23), and (9.25) below. In particular, (9.20) represents a clause with only one argument, (9.23) represents a clause with two arguments, and (9.25) represents a clause with three arguments. The Xong sentences in (9.21), (9.22), (9.24), and (9.26) then each provide a representative example of the preceding clause type, with examples (9.21) and (9.22) in particular showing two equally acceptable orders for a single clause.

(9.20) SUBJECT VERB / VERB SUBJECT (two possible orders)

(9.21) [*Miex-khat*] ***lol*** *lah.*
[person-guest]$_S$ **come** PRF
'The guests have arrived.' (Chenghua Long, fieldnotes)

(9.22) ***Lol*** *[miex-khat]* *lah.*
come [person-guest]$_S$ PRF
'The guests have arrived.' (Chenghua Long, fieldnotes) (same as (9.21) above)

(9.23) AGENT VERB PATIENT

(9.24) *[Aod-ngonl* *naus]* *at* ***bob*** *[wel].*
[one-CLF:animate bird]$_A$ SAT **talk.about** [1SG]$_P$
'This bird's talking about me.' (Xingyu Shi, in *Oub Meinl Yaos Geud*)

(9.25) AGENT VERB RECIPIENT THEME

(9.26) *Naonb.roul* *[wel]* ***gaons*** *[manx* *oub-leb]* *[aod-leb* *zhonx-hlod].*
now [1SG]$_A$ **give** [2PL two-CLF]$_R$ [one-CLF length-bamboo]$_T$
'Now I'm going to give each of you (two) a length of bamboo.' (Xingyu Shi, in *Oub Meinl Yaos Geud*) (repeated from (9.19) above)

However, the schemas in (9.20), (9.23), and (9.25) are not complete, as they only indicate the relative positioning of verbs and arguments. In addition to the verb slot and the various argument slots shown in these schemas, two other important syntactic slots are found in the Xong clause.[173] The first of these is the *grammatical operator* (or 'GO') slot, which occurs between a verb and its preceding argument. Grammatical operators in Xong include negative markers like *(j)ix* 'NEG$_1$' and *xaond* 'not yet' (see Section 9.2.2), quantifying forms like *(s)at* 'SAT' and *yaod(.yaod)* 'all' (see Section 9.2.3.1), and various forms with temporal meanings like 'then', 'still', 'not until, only then', 'also', or 'again' (see the introduction to Section 9.2). Multiple grammatical operators can and often do co-occur in a single univerbal Xong clause, and when they do there appear to be certain rules governing their relative ordering (e.g. forms meaning 'still' precede negative markers, etc.). However, for the most part the precise syntactic relationships between different grammatical operators and between each grammatical operator and other elements of the clause have yet to be investigated.

Examples (9.27) and (9.28) below each show a clause featuring one (bolded) grammatical operator, while example (9.29) shows a clause featuring two (bolded) grammatical operators.

(9.27) *Wel* ***doub*** *beut* *lah.*
1SG **then$_1$** lie.down PRF
'I (was able to) go to sleep.' (Haili Shi, in *Tooth Conversation*)

173 Note that the description in this section is restricted to major constituents of Xong clauses, and so it does not discuss certain minor clausal constituent types like temporal phrases or degree markers.

(9.28) *Niaox.meib* ***yab*** *chauk beul naond npaok.*
PN **also** do 3 ASSOC woman
'(Now) Niao Mei would be his wife.' (Xingyu Shi, in *Oub Meinl Yaos Geud*)

(9.29) *Wel* ***at*** ***jix*** *nins nieux-hmaont...*
1SG **SAT** **NEG$_1$** COP yester-CLF:evening
'It's not just last night (that my tooth was hurting)...' (Haili Shi, in *Tooth Conversation*)

The final syntactic slot to be discussed in this section is the *clause-final form* (or 'CFF') slot, which naturally occurs clause-finally. This slot can be occupied by a toneless particle (see Section 9.2.1) or by one of a handful of tone-bearing, non-particle clause-final forms (Section 9.3.2.3). Both particles and non-particle clause-final forms typically have semantic scope over the entire clause in which they appear, and they tend to express relatively abstract grammatical or discourse-pragmatic notions (e.g. marking a clause as interrogative, or as emphatic, or as background information with respect to another clause). Unlike the grammatical operators described earlier in this section, it appears that only a single clause-final form can occur in any given clause.

Examples (9.30–9.32) each show a clause featuring one (bolded) clause-final form. This clause-final form is a particle in examples (9.30) and (9.31), but it is a non-particle clause-final form in example (9.32).

(9.30) *Beul baox monl* ***lah.***
3 father go **PRF**
'Their father left.' (Xingyu Shi, in *Oub Meinl Yaos Geud*) (repeated from (9.2) above)

(9.31) *Nieux-hnef wel chad beb monx oub-shauk ih!*
yester-CLF:day 1SG not.until share 2SG two-CLF:yuan EMPH
'I just gave you two *yuan* (unit of currency) yesterday!' (Haili Shi, fieldnotes)

(9.32) *Aod-banb neind nins zeib jex.bieb, zeib*
one-CLF:some this COP most simple.and.convenient most
jex.jef naond ***yaox?***
quick.and.easy ASSOC **right?**
'These (folk remedies) are the simplest, the easiest, right?' (Haili Shi, in *Tooth Conversation*)

Taking grammatical operators and clause-final forms into account, the structure of a pragmatically neutral, univerbal Xong clause with all arguments overtly expressed can be represented with the three schemas given in (9.33), (9.36), and (9.38) below. Just as with the schemas given in (9.20), (9.23), and (9.25) earlier in this section, the schema in (9.33) represents a clause with a single argument, the one in (9.36) represents a clause with two arguments, and the one in (9.38) represents a clause with three arguments. The Xong sentences in (9.34), (9.35), (9.37), and (9.39) then each provide a representative example of the preceding clause type, with examples (9.34) and (9.35) in particular showing two equally acceptable orders for a single clause.[174] Note that in these examples each argument has been enclosed within brackets and marked with a following subscript letter indicating its syntactic role (<$_{S}$> for SUBJECT, <$_{A}$> for AGENT, etc.). Each grammatical operator and clause-final form has also been enclosed within brackets; in addition, each grammatical operator has been marked with a following subscript <$_{GO}$> and each clause-final form has been marked with a following subscript <$_{CFF}$>. Finally, each clause's verb has been bolded.

(9.33) SUBJECT GO VERB CFF /
GO VERB SUBJECT CFF (two possible orders)

(9.34) [*Aub*] ***xub*** [*lah*].
[water]$_{S}$ **small** [PRF]$_{CFF}$
'The water pressure's dropped.' (Qiumei Wu, fieldnotes)

(9.35) ***Xub*** [*aub*] [*lah*].
small [water]$_{S}$ [PRF]$_{CFF}$
'The water pressure's dropped.' (Qiumei Wu, fieldnotes) (same as (9.34) above)

(9.36) AGENT GO VERB PATIENT CFF

(9.37) [*Oub-meinl*] [*doub*] ***ndax*** [*beul*]...
[two-CLF:person]$_{A}$ [then$_{1}$]$_{GO}$ **lift.up** [3]$_{P}$
'The two of them lifted (the cage) up...' (Xingyu Shi, in *Oub Meinl Yaos Geud*)

(9.38) AGENT GO VERB RECIPIENT THEME CFF

---

174 The reader will note that examples (9.34), (9.35), and (9.37) each contain either a grammatical operator or a clause-final form, but not both. This is not due to any restriction on grammatical operators and clause-final forms co-occurring within a single clause, as many clauses in the author's naturalistic Xong corpus (including example (9.39) as well as many clauses in the two texts provided at the end of this grammar) feature both types of forms. However, most of these clauses involve multiple verbs, non-canonical constituent ordering, and/or one or more elided arguments, making them unsuitable for inclusion in this Section 9.1.1 (which, again, restricts its attention to pragmatically neutral, univerbal clauses in which all arguments are overtly expressed).

(9.39)

Nieux-hnef	*[wel]*	*[chad]*	***beb***	*[monx]*	*[oub-shauk]*	*[ih]!*
yester-CLF:day	[1SG]$_A$	[not.until]$_{GO}$	**share**	[2SG]$_R$	[two-CLF:yuan]$_T$	[EMPH]$_{CFF}$

'I just gave you two *yuan* (unit of currency) yesterday!' (Haili Shi, fieldnotes) (repeated from (9.31) above)

The reader may have noticed that this section has made no mention of verb phrases. This is because there does not appear to be any significant evidence in Xong for postulating the "verb phrase" as a level of syntactic analysis distinct from the clause, and so verb phrases simply play no part in this description.

As a final note, the author wishes to reiterate that this section has concerned itself solely with pragmatically neutral, univerbal Xong clauses in which all arguments are overtly expressed. This was done primarily for the sake of ease of analysis and clarity of presentation. However, an examination of the texts provided at the end of this grammar will quickly show that such clauses in fact constitute only a very small minority in naturalistic Xong speech due to the pervasiveness of multiverbal constructions, argument ellipsis, and constituent reordering motivated by information structure concerns.

9.1.2 Argument ellipsis and cross-clausal coreference

As in many of the other isolating languages of East and Southeast Asia, nearly any argument in Xong can be elided when its role within a clause and the identity of its referent are either obvious from context or are unimportant. For instance, the AGENTS in examples (9.40–9.43) have been elided, as have the PATIENTS in examples (9.44–9.47) (see Section 9.1.1 above for more information on grammaticalized syntactic roles like AGENT and PATIENT in Xong). Each elided argument in these and similar examples in this section has been represented with a null symbol <Ø>, and the syntactic role of each elided argument has been represented with a subscript letter following that null symbol (<Ø$_A$> for an elided AGENT, <Ø$_P$> for an elided PATIENT, etc.). Note that the null symbols in question are used merely for presentational convenience, and they are not intended to represent "null arguments" in any theoretically significant sense.

(9.40)

Ø$_A$	*hnef-hnef*	*at*	*npod*	*mel*	*ah,*
	CLF:day-CLF:day	SAT	toss	stone.toss.game	PART

Ø$_A$	*zhox*	*ghab*	*lah,*	Ø$_A$	*ndanb*	*sheinb.kiet*	*lah,*
	kick	shuttlecock	PRF		jump	hopscotch	PRF

Ø$_A$	*hnef-hnef*	*nghauk.zaol*	*leh.*
	CLF:day-CLF:day	play	LEH

'Every day (she) played the stone-tossing game, (she) played shuttlecock, (she) played hopscotch, every day (she) was out playing.' (Xingyu Shi, in *Oub Meinl Yaos Geud*)

(9.41) $Ø_A$ *nonx zhaus naonb?*
eat suffer what
'What did (you) eat?' (Shixiang Wu, in *Tooth Conversation*)

(9.42) $Ø_A$ *ngheub sad gaons beul dont.*
sing Xong.song give 3 listen
'(The bird) sang a Xong song for him.' (Xingyu Shi, in *Oub Meinl Yaos Geud*)

(9.43) $Ø_A$ *hauk jix hauk jeud?*
drink NEG_1 drink alcohol
'Will (you) drink alcohol (with us)?' (unknown Xong consultant, fieldnotes)

(9.44) *Wel ghad jix monl nbaod* $Ø_P$.
1SG $then_2$ NEG_1 go fill.in
'But I'm not going to get (my tooth) filled in.' (Haili Shi, in *Tooth Conversation*)

(9.45) *Wel ob* $Ø_P$ *manh.*
1SG burn PART
'I burned (your comb).' (Xingyu Shi, in *Oub Meinl Yaos Geud*)

(9.46) *Beul ndok* $Ø_P$.
3 weave
'She wove (the cloth).' (Xingyu Shi, in *Oub Meinl Yaos Geud*)

(9.47) *Wel jix sheib puk* $Ø_P$.
1SG NEG_1 able.to speak
'I can't speak (English).' (unknown Xong consultant, fieldnotes)

In each of examples (9.48–9.51), both the AGENT and the PATIENT have been elided, leaving no overtly expressed arguments at all.

(9.48) $Ø_A$ *mok mok mok mok* $Ø_P$.
touch touch touch touch
'(He) touched (the bamboo plant) over and over and over again.' (Xingyu Shi, in *Oub Meinl Yaos Geud*)

(9.49) *Nins hmaont dox* $Ø_A$ *giaot zhus* $Ø_P$.
COP CLF:evening that chew suffer
'(But my tooth never hurt before,) it was just that night that (I) bit into (a chicken foot).' (Haili Shi, in *Tooth Conversation*)

(9.50) $Ø_A$ *nieus* $Ø_P$ *lah.*
buy PRF
'(Yes, I) bought (the vegetables you wanted).' (Yan Long, fieldnotes)

(9.51) $Ø_A$ *jix* *nonx* $Ø_P$.
NEG_1 eat
'(Americans) don't eat (chicken feet).' (Shixiang Wu, fieldnotes)

The SUBJECTS have been elided from examples (9.52–9.55), which in each case again results in a clause with no overtly expressed arguments whatsoever.

(9.52) $Ø_S$ *zhaons.*
fat
'(That dog's) fat.' (Chenghua Long, fieldnotes)

(9.53) $Ø_S$ *jix* *nkied.*
NEG_1 happy
'(She's) not happy.' (Yan Long, fieldnotes)

(9.54) *Naont* $Ø_S$ *raut* *jix* *raut?*
thus good NEG_1 good
'So did (the ginger) work (to cure your toothache)?' (Shixiang Wu, in *Tooth Conversation*)

(9.55) $Ø_S$ *anb* *chanf* *chanf.*
really gross gross
'(The traditional method for curing a toothache) is super gross.' (Chenghua Long, in *Tooth Conversation*)

Examples (9.56–9.63) show eight equally grammatical versions of a three-argument clause involving an AGENT (*wel* '1SG'), a RECIPIENT (*beul* '3'), and a THEME (*aod-zheinb ndeind* [one-CLF:tool knife] 'a knife'). In example (9.56), all three arguments are overtly expressed. In each of examples (9.57–9.59), one argument has been elided, while in each of examples (9.60–9.62), two arguments have been elided. Finally, in example (9.63), all three arguments have been elided.

(9.56) *Wel* *gaons* *beul* *aod-zheinb* *ndeind.*
1SG give 3 one-CLF:tool knife
'I gave him a knife.' (Haili Shi, fieldnotes)

(9.57) Ø$_A$ *gaons beul aod-zheinb ndeind.*
give 3 one-CLF:tool knife
'(I) gave him a knife.' (Haili Shi, fieldnotes)

(9.58) *Wel gaons* Ø$_R$ *aod-zheinb ndeind.*
1SG give one-CLF:tool knife
'I gave (him) a knife.' (Haili Shi, fieldnotes)

(9.59) *Wel gaons beul* Ø$_T$.
1SG give 3
'I gave him (a knife).' (Haili Shi, fieldnotes)

(9.60) Ø$_A$ *gaons* Ø$_R$ *aod-zheinb ndeind.*
give one-CLF:tool knife
'(I) gave (him) a knife.' (Haili Shi, fieldnotes)

(9.61) Ø$_A$ *gaons beul* Ø$_T$.
give 3
'(I) gave him (a knife).' (Haili Shi, fieldnotes)

(9.62) *Wel gaons* Ø$_R$ Ø$_T$.
1SG give
'I gave (him a knife).' (Haili Shi, fieldnotes)

(9.63) Ø$_A$ *gaons* Ø$_R$ Ø$_T$.
give
'(I) gave (him a knife).' (Haili Shi, fieldnotes)

It is important to note that Xong clauses from which one or more arguments have been elided are extremely common in Xong speech regardless of genre, formality level, or individual speakers' demographic characteristics (age, gender, etc.). In fact, it appears that clauses from which one or more arguments have been elided are even more common in naturalistic speech than clauses in which every argument is overtly expressed; see, for instance, the two extended Xong texts included at the end of this grammar. Clauses such as these are perfectly ordinary expressions in Xong; they are not pragmatically "marked" or unusual in any way. Needless to say, the extremely high prevalence of elided arguments in Xong speech does not appear to present any particular difficulties of interpretation or parsing for Xong speakers and listeners. This is true despite the fact that Xong verbs lack any sort of agreement morphology, which might be used in other, more morphologically complex languages to help manage reference to elided arguments.

Just as there are no apparent restrictions on argument elision in Xong, neither do there appear to be any restrictions on cross-clausal coreference, or at least none that can be formulated in terms of grammaticalized syntactic roles like AGENT or SUBJECT (again, see Section 9.1.1 for more on such roles in Xong). This is in contrast to the situation in, for instance, English, where an argument that occurs in each of two conjoined clauses can be elided in the second of those clauses only if it is the subject of each clause. For instance, *The man went into the forest and Ø killed the bear* is acceptable, as the argument *the man* is the subject (whether overt or elided) of each clause. The sentence *The bear went into the forest and Ø was killed by the man* is also acceptable, since the argument *the bear* is now the subject of each clause (though here a passive construction is needed to allow the semantically patient-like argument *the bear* to serve as the subject of the second conjoined clause). However, **The bear went into the forest and the man killed Ø* is unacceptable, since here *the bear* is serving as the subject of the first conjoined clause but as the object of the second. Similar but opposite arguments would apply to syntactically ergative languages, as in the well known case of Dyirbal (see, e.g., Dixon 1972).

In Xong, though, the interpretation of elided arguments in such clauses does not depend on grammaticalized syntactic roles like in English or in Dyirbal, but rather on the discourse context and on speakers' and listeners' real-world knowledge. Consider first example (9.64). In this example, consultants report that only the AGENT of the first clause can be interpreted as the elided SUBJECT of the second clause. In other words, the sentence can only be interpreted as meaning 'The child dropped the bowl on the floor and cried', not as meaning *'The child dropped the bowl on the floor and it (i.e. the bowl) cried'. Note that in this and similar examples below in this section, each overt AGENT or PATIENT argument has been enclosed within brackets, and the syntactic role of each such argument has been indicated with a following subscript letter (<$_A$> for AGENT and <$_P$> for PATIENT).

(9.64) [*Aod-ngonl* *deb* *dox*] *geud* [*ghaob-zhet*] *zhaok*
[one-CLF:animate child that]$_A$ hold [NOM-bowl]$_P$ fall
lot *daod.doub,* *nied* *lah.*
descend earth cry PRF
'The child dropped the bowl on the floor and cried.' (Haili Shi, fieldnotes)

Example (9.65) is similar, in that consultants again report that only the AGENT of the first clause can be interpreted as the elided SUBJECT of the second clause. Thus this sentence can only be interpreted as meaning 'He found a snake in the road and shouted (in fright)', not as meaning *'He found a snake in the road and it (i.e. the snake) shouted (in fright)'.

(9.65) *[Beul] caont [aod-ngonl neinb] ninb nek-geud, doub*
[3]$_{A}$ meet [one-CLF:animate snake]$_{P}$ at AUG-road then$_{1}$
hnant lah.
call PRF
'He found a snake in the road and shouted (in fright).' (Chenghua Long, fieldnotes)

However, in example (9.66) the opposite occurs. Here consultants report that only the PATIENT of the first clause can be interpreted as the elided SUBJECT of the second clause. Thus here the sentence can only be interpreted as meaning 'The child dropped the bowl on the floor and it broke', not as meaning *'The child dropped the bowl on the floor and broke'.

(9.66) *[Aod-ngonl deb dox] geud [ghaob-zhet] zhaok*
[one-CLF:animate child that]$_{A}$ hold [NOM-bowl]$_{P}$ fall
lot daod.doub, deuk lah.
descend earth break PRF
'The child dropped the bowl on the floor and (it) broke.' (Haili Shi, fieldnotes)

The same thing happens in example (9.67), in which consultants again report that only the PATIENT of the first clause can be interpreted as the elided SUBJECT of the second clause. Thus this sentence can only be interpreted as meaning 'He didn't frighten the bird and it didn't fly away', not as meaning *'He didn't frighten the bird and didn't fly away'.

(9.67) *[Beul] jix beinl [ngonl deb-naus], jix eint sheub.*
[3]$_{A}$ NEG$_{1}$ frighten [CLF:animate DIM-bird]$_{P}$ NEG$_{1}$ fly leave
'He didn't frighten the bird, and (it) didn't fly away.' (Xingyu Shi, in *Oub Meinl Yaos Geud*)

Thus, the elided SUBJECTS in the second clauses of examples (9.64) and (9.65) are interpreted as being coreferential with the preverbal AGENTS in the preceding clauses, while the elided SUBJECTS in the second clauses of examples (9.66) and (9.67) are interpreted as being coreferential with the postverbal PATIENTS in the preceding clauses. There are no restrictions on cross-clausal coreference of the type found in English or of the type found in Dyirbal. Instead, the preferred interpretations of the elided arguments in the second clauses of these four examples arise from the semantics of the arguments and predicates involved, from the discourse context, and from speakers' and listeners' real-world knowledge. Children are much more likely to cry than bowls, and bowls are much more likely to break than children. People are much more likely to cry out in fright than snakes, and birds are much more likely to fly away than people.

Further evidence for the lack of cross-clausal coreference restrictions on conjoined clauses in Xong is provided by examples (9.68–9.70) below. For each of these examples, two interpretations are possible, at least when the example is produced in isolation. Either the AGENT of the first clause can be interpreted as the elided SUBJECT of the second clause, or the PATIENT of the first clause can be interpreted as the elided SUBJECT of the second clause.

(9.68) [*Wel*] *beux* [*aod-ngonl* *neinb* *dox*], *doub* *sheub* *lah*
[1SG]$_A$ hit [one-CLF:animate snake that]$_P$ then$_1$ leave PRF
'I hit the snake and then fled.' *or* 'I hit the snake and then it fled.' (Haili Shi, fieldnotes)

(9.69) [*Aod-ngonl* *ronf*] *ghans* [*aod-ngonl* *daob-jod*],
[one-CLF:animate dragon]$_A$ see [one-CLF:animate AN-tiger]$_P$
doub *npieut* *lah.*
then$_1$ shout PRF
'The dragon saw the tiger and then (the dragon) roared.' *or* 'The dragon saw the tiger and then (the tiger) roared.' (Chenghua Long, fieldnotes)

(9.70) [*Aod-ngonl* *baod-aut*] *hnaond* [*aod-ngonl*
[one-CLF:animate BUG-crow]$_A$ hear [one-CLF:animate
naus-zeib], *doub* *eint* *sheub.*
bird-sparrow]$_P$ then$_1$ fly leave
'The crow heard the sparrow and then (the crow) flew away.' *or* 'The crow heard the sparrow and then (the sparrow) flew away.' (Shixiang Wu, fieldnotes)

This is because the meaning of the predicate in each example's second clause is compatible with the meaning of either argument in that example's first clause, and, again, because no cross-clausal coreference restrictions based on syntactic roles exist in Xong to govern the interpretation of elided arguments in the second of two conjoined clauses.

9.1.3 Information structure

Departures from the usual ordering constraints described in Section 9.1.1 above are not uncommon in Xong.[175] Since neither case marking nor verbal agreement marking are found in the language, the positioning of an argument within a clause does pro-

175 Nevertheless, it is still fully possible to distinguish predominant constituent orders for many types of constructions in Xong, or at least many of the types of constructions that word order typologists are interested in. For instance, in word order typological terms Xong is clearly SVO in transitive clauses, XVO in transitive clauses involving obliques, and so on (see Dryer 2013d). Furthermore,

vide the most significant overt indication of that argument's role within the clause in question. However, this positioning is less important than one might expect, and in many cases it appears that context and real-world knowledge are equally if not more important when it comes to assigning syntactic roles to arguments in naturalistic Xong speech. In addition, Xong speakers have access to a wide variety of "non-canonical" constituent ordering possibilities that serve a similarly wide variety of information structure functions (e.g. introducing new referents, emphasizing or de-emphasizing referents which have already been introduced, etc.), and it is these alternate constituent ordering possibilities that form the subject of this section.

Still, a full description of the constituent ordering possibilities in Xong clauses lies outside the scope of this grammar, and this author would argue that such a description would more properly constitute part of a comprehensive study of Xong discourse and pragmatics. Sections 9.1.3.1 and 9.1.3.2 below thus simply discuss some of the more common sorts of departures from Xong's canonical ordering constraints. In particular, Section 9.1.3.1 discusses apparent clausal "topics" in Xong as well as argument fronting to preverbal position, while Section 9.1.3.2 discusses the *mex* presentational construction (featuring the verb *mex* 'to exist') and other methods of referent introduction. Many other sorts of non-canonical constituent ordering can be found throughout the example sentences and texts included in this grammar.

9.1.3.1 "Topicalization" and argument fronting

While there has been a great deal of discussion on "topics" and "topic-prominence" in East and Southeast Asian languages over the past several decades (see Li and Thompson 1976 and Shi 2000, among many others), these notions do not appear to be particularly relevant to Xong.[176] It is admittedly quite common for arguments which would appear postverbally in a pragmatically neutral clause to instead appear in preverbal position in a less pragmatically neutral clause. In some cases such a preverbal argument will optionally be followed by one of a handful of certain particles (e.g. *leh*

---

sub-clausal phenomena in the language (such as noun phrases and their internal constituents) often have fairly rigid ordering constraints.

176 It is important to distinguish here between the grammatical notion "topic" (referring to a particular grammaticalized syntactic position in which an argument can occur, with said argument serving to express what the following clause is "about") and the information structure notion "topical" (referring to older, more presupposed information that has already been introduced into a discourse). In this grammar, all references to "topics" or "topicalization" (as in this Section 9.1.3.1) are intended to refer to the former notion only. The term "topical" (in its information structure sense) is not used in this grammar at all in order to avoid confusion with the term "topic" (in its grammatical sense). Instead, where other authors might use "topical", this author uses more periphrastic expressions like "previously introduced into a discourse". In the interest of symmetry, the term "focal" (referring to newer, less presupposed information that has not been previously introduced into a discourse) is not used in this description either, with the author again using more periphrastic expressions like "newly introduced into a discourse" instead.

'LEH' or *meh* 'BCKG'; see Section 9.2.1), and the argument in question could arguably be said to express what the following clause is "about".[177] These preverbal arguments do display a fair number of formal and functional similarities with canonical topics in other languages. Examples of such "topic-like" preverbal arguments have been enclosed within brackets in (9.71–9.79) below. Note that the relevant arguments in examples (9.71–9.77) are noun phrases, while the ones in examples (9.78) and (9.79) are clauses.

(9.71) [*Daob-mioul*], *aod-yaonk* *dib* *raut* *nonx* *aod-yaonk*
[AN-fish] one-CLF:kind$_2$ which good eat one-CLF:kind$_2$
dib *jaod* *nonx?*
which bad eat
'As for fish, which kind tastes good and which kind tastes bad?' (unknown Xong consultant, in *Conversation in Yankan*)

(9.72) [*Aod-leb* *zhonx-hlod*] *leh,* *nkhed* *manx* *oub-meinl*
[one-CLF length-bamboo] LEH look 2PL two-CLF:person
dib *ghaod* *raut* *deb.*
which more good child
'These lengths of bamboo, they'll show which of you is the better child.' (Xingyu Shi, in *Oub Meinl Yaos Geud*)

(9.73) *Naont* [*beul*] *ah,* *aod-ngonl* *naus* *zos* *ninb*
thus [3] PART one-CLF:animate bird land at
sond-guaod-yul *beul* *jix* *beinl* *ngonl* *deb-naus,*
bone-back-cow 3 NEG$_1$ frighten CLF:animate DIM-bird
jix *eint* *sheub.*
NEG$_1$ fly leave
'And so, as for him (i.e. the child), when the bird landed on the back of a cow, he didn't frighten it, and it didn't fly away.' (Xingyu Shi, in *Oub Meinl Yaos Geud*)

(9.74) [*Beul* *deb-geud* *naond*], *beul* *meb* *dut* *sheub.*
[3 DIM-younger.sibling ASSOC] 3 take obtain leave
'She took her younger sister's (tears) with her.' (Xingyu Shi, in *Oub Meinl Yaos Geud*)

177 "Aboutness" strikes the author as a rather subjective property, but it is nevertheless a key component of many definitions of the notion "topic" that have been used by prominent linguists over the years. See Gerner (2003: 954) for a partial list.

(9.75) *Beul baox leh, Niaox.meib leh, [baod-zhauf] at*
3 father LEH PN LEH [BUG-door] SAT
keuf [baod-cheid] at keuf.
shut [BUG-gate] SAT shut
'Her father, and (her sister) Niao Mei, they'd shut the door, and shut the gate.' (Xingyu Shi, in *Oub Meinl Yaos Geud*)

(9.76) *Aub nins manx uk.seb uk.weib, [houd-deb*
water COP REL colorless flavorless [CLF:mouthful-DIM
weib.dob] jix mex.
flavor] NEG_1 exist
'Water is colorless and tasteless, it doesn't have any flavor at all.' (Xingyu Shi, in *Oub Meinl Yaos Geud*)

(9.77) *[Aod-ngonl] at jix beux.*
[one-CLF:animate] SAT NEG_1 hit
'(He) won't even kill a single (bug).'
(Chenghua Long, fieldnotes)

(9.78) *[Saut] nex niab bionl ginb dant yaox?*
[smoke] NEX say exit bug truly right?
'He said that you can really smoke the bugs out, huh?' (Shixiang Wu, in *Tooth Conversation*)

(9.79) *[Zox nbed] manx zox mins-doud?*
[smash rice.cake] 2PL smash how.many-CLF:dou
'(When the New Year comes,) how many *dou* (unit of volume) of rice cakes is your family planning on making?' (Chenghua Long, fieldnotes)

As these examples show, a wide variety of grammatical, semantic, and information-structural relationships can hold between such a fronted argument and the following clause. Taking this variety into account along with the difficulty involved in rigorously defining and applying a slippery notion like "aboutness" and the fact that any overt marking of fronted arguments (with, e.g., *leh* 'LEH' or *meh* 'BCKG') is optional, it is not clear what is gained in terms of descriptive accuracy or economy by referring to any fronted argument in Xong as a "topic". Instead, simply referring to the argument in question as a "fronted" one would seem to be sufficient.

The remainder of this section will therefore ignore the notions of "topic" and "topic position" and instead concentrate on some of the more common functions that argument fronting (i.e. the occurrence in preverbal position of an argument which would normally appear in postverbal position in a more pragmatically neutral clause) can serve in Xong. Note that many of these functions appear to display some degree of overlap, so that a particular instance of argument fronting might serve multiple functions at the same time. Note also that aside from a handful of cases involving apparent speech errors or hesitation on the part of the speaker, there are no clear examples of clauses involving three or more preverbal arguments, which suggests that there are only two preverbal slots in a Xong clause (though only one slot will be occupied in a pragmatically neutral clause, as was described in Section 9.1.1 above).

First, in clauses involving a semantically transitive or ditransitive verb, Xong speakers occasionally use argument fronting of a PATIENT, RECIPIENT, or THEME combined with elision of an AGENT to de-emphasize the role of that AGENT (see Section 9.1.1 for more on semantically transitive and ditransitive verbs and on grammaticalized syntactic roles like AGENT, PATIENT, RECIPIENT, and THEME). While the author would not argue that this is a "passive" construction in any canonical sense of the term (see Section 9.3.4), it does naturally show some degree of functional overlap with passive constructions in other languages. Examples of this sort of clause are given in (9.80–9.83) below, where each fronted argument has been enclosed within brackets.

(9.80) [*Oub-nqad*] *did-buk* *ghad* *nins* *aod-ngonl.*
[two-CLF:half.of.pair] DID-combine then$_2$ COP one-CLF:pair$_1$
'When put together, the two (shoes) were clearly a pair.' (Xingyu Shi, in *Oub Meinl Yaos Geud*)

(9.81) [*Reib-yeus*] *at* *gaons* *houd-deb*
[vegetable-cooked.meat] SAT give CLF:mouthful-DIM
yut *yut.*
few few
'(He) would only receive a tiny little bit of meat and vegetables.' *or* 'Only a tiny little bit of meat and vegetables would be given (to him).' (Xingyu Shi, in *Oub Meinl Yaos Geud*)

(9.82) [*Hant* *ob-zeif*] *yaod* *det* *cef* *det*
[CLF:PL NOM-thread] all break ??? break
diul.
complete
'The threads were all snapped and broken.' (Xingyu Shi, in *Oub Meinl Yaos Geud*)

(9.83) [*Shand*] *doub* *kox.ix* *geud* *ghaod.lot.*
[ginger] then$_1$ can hold mouth
'(You) can put the ginger in your mouth.' *or* 'The ginger can be put in (one's) mouth.' (Haili Shi, in *Tooth Conversation*)

Second, preverbal positioning is generally associated with arguments whose referents have already been introduced into the current discourse (as opposed to arguments whose referents are being introduced for the first time; cf. Section 9.1.3.2 below), and so argument fronting is very frequently used with PATIENTS, RECIPIENTS, and THEMES whose referents have already been so introduced. (No such argument fronting could meaningfully be said to occur with a preverbal AGENT or SUBJECT, though, since even in a more pragmatically neutral clause the former would obligatorily occur in preverbal position and the latter could optionally do so.) In such cases the fronted PATIENT, RECIPIENT, or THEME will generally occur in the first preverbal slot rather than the second, so that it will sometimes be followed by a non-fronted preverbal AGENT (see examples (9.84–9.86) below). Subordinate clauses referring to previously introduced notions can appear in fronted position as well (see example (9.86)).

Examples of fronted PATIENTS, RECIPIENTS, and THEMES which refer to previously introduced referents are given in (9.84–9.89) below. Each such argument has been enclosed within brackets.

(9.84) *Ranf.houb [bid-ghaond] wel ix dut shaod.*
afterward [FRT-garlic] 1SG NEG$_1$ obtain try
'Afterward I didn't try the garlic.' (Haili Shi, in *Tooth Conversation*)

(9.85) [*Niax-naus*] *wel biat box.nhol manh.*
[meat-bird] 1SG pour throw.away PART
'I threw the bird meat away.' (Xingyu Shi, in *Oub Meinl Yaos Geud*)

(9.86) [*Bux donb*] *wel niel.*
[fill.in hole] 1SG know
'I know that I could get the hole (in my tooth) filled in.' (Haili Shi, in *Tooth Conversation*)

(9.87) [*Aod-ngonl naus*] *beux daos geud giab nonx.*
[one-CLF:animate bird] hit die hold stir.fry eat
'(I) killed the bird and cooked it (to eat).' (Xingyu Shi, in *Oub Meinl Yaos Geud*)

(9.88) [*Beul baox*] *jud niel ghat ib-dof leh.*
[3 father] NEG$_2$ know go.to ???-which LEH
'(She) didn't know where her father had gone.' (Xingyu Shi, in *Oub Meinl Yaos Geud*)

(9.89) [*Oub-nqad*] *meb gaons yes.web nkhed.*
[two-CLF:half.of.pair] take give landlord look
'(She) took both (shoes) and showed them to the landlord.' (Xingyu Shi, in *Oub Meinl Yaos Geud*)

While it is true that fronted PATIENTS, RECIPIENTS, and THEMES generally occur in the first preverbal slot of a Xong clause, there is one particular construction in which they occur in the second preverbal slot instead. In this construction, a PATIENT, RECIPIENT, or THEME that contains (i) an ignorative (see Section 7.3), (ii) a numeral-classifier phrase in which the numeral is *aod* 'one', or (iii) a bare classifier (see Section 6.1.3.1) occurs in the second preverbal slot of a clause, where it is then immediately followed by *(s)at (j)ix* [SAT NEG$_1$] (in rare cases, like in example (9.94) below, *[s]at* 'SAT' may be omitted). An AGENT can optionally occur before the fronted PATIENT, RECIPIENT, or THEME just described. The construction as a whole then means 'not even a single *X*' or 'not even a little *X*', where *X* is the referent of the fronted non-AGENT argument. Examples of this construction can be seen in (9.90–9.94) below, in which each fronted PATIENT, RECIPIENT, or THEME has been enclosed within brackets and each relevant instance of *(s)at* 'SAT' and *(j)ix* 'NEG$_1$' has been bolded.

(9.90)

[Ob-naonb	*weib.dob]*	***at***	***jix***	*mex,*	*doub*	*nins*	*aub.*
[NOM-what	flavor]	**SAT**	**NEG$_1$**	exist	then$_1$	COP	water

'It didn't have any flavor at all, it was just water.' (Xingyu Shi, in *Oub Meinl Yaos Geud*)

(9.91)

Tat-hnef	*monx*	*[aod-bix*	*dib]*	***at***	***jix***	*lis*	*monl.*
this-CLF:day	2SG	[one-CLF:place$_1$	which]	**SAT**	**NEG$_1$**	want	go

'Don't go anywhere today.' (Haili Shi, fieldnotes)

(9.92)

Wel	*jix*	*nonx*	*niax,*	*[aod-houd]*	***at***	***jix***	*nonx.*
1SG	NEG$_1$	eat	meat	[one-CLF:mouthful]	**SAT**	**NEG$_1$**	eat

'I don't eat meat, not even a single bite.' (Haili Shi, fieldnotes)

(9.93)

Beul	*[aod-ngonl]*	***at***	***jix***	*beux.*
3	[one-CLF:animate]	**SAT**	**NEG$_1$**	hit

'He won't even kill a single (bug).' (Chenghua Long, fieldnotes)

(9.94)

Aub	*nins*	*manx*	*uk.seb*	*uk.weib,*	*[houd-deb*
water	COP	REL	colorless	flavorless	[CLF:mouthful-DIM

weib.dob]	***jix***	*mex.*
flavor]	**NEG$_1$**	exist

'Water is colorless and tasteless, it doesn't have any flavor at all.' (Xingyu Shi, in *Oub Meinl Yaos Geud*) (repeated from (9.76) above)

9.1.3.2 Introduction of new referents

The two most common methods of introducing a new referent into an ongoing Xong discourse are (i) placing the argument referring to the referent in question in postverbal position (either immediately postverbal or following another postverbal argument) and (ii) making use of the *mex* presentational construction. Examples of the former method can be seen in (9.95–9.101) below, where each argument referring to a newly introduced referent has been enclosed within brackets and each verb immediately preceding such an argument has been bolded. Note that example (9.95) features a newly introduced PATIENT, example (9.96) features a newly introduced RECIPIENT, and example (9.97) features a newly introduced THEME, each of which has been marked with a following subscript letter indicating its syntactic role (e.g. <P> for PATIENT, etc.). See Section 9.1.1 above for more on these and other grammaticalized syntactic roles in Xong.

(9.95) *Jont zhonx-nbat, jix mex naonb sib chauk, beul*
live pen-pig NEG_1 exist what matter do 3
ghad ***cod*** *[deb-xut.npeif].*
$then_2$ **sew** $[DIM\text{-}shoe]_P$
'In the pig-pen there was nothing to do, so she started to sew some shoes.'
(Xingyu Shi, in *Oub Meinl Yaos Geud*)

(9.96) *Wel lis geud mx tat-hnef ndaot lox.sik naond*
1SG want hold 2SG this-CLF:day curse teacher ASSOC
sib ***bod*** *[boub baox]!*
matter **tell** $[1PL\ father]_R$
'I'm going to tell our father about how you swore at the teacher today!'
(unknown Xong consultant, fieldnotes)

(9.97) *Naonb.roul wel* ***gaons*** *manx oub-leb [aod-leb*
now 1SG **give** 2PL two-CLF [one-CLF
zhonx hlod].
length $bamboo]_T$
'Now I'm going to give each of you (two) a length of bamboo.' (Xingyu Shi, in *Oub Meinl Yaos Geud*) (repeated from (9.19) above)

A PATIENT, RECIPIENT, or THEME will generally occur in postverbal position even in more pragmatically neutral clauses that do not serve to introduce a new referent into an ongoing discourse (again, see Section 9.1.1). However, the same is not true of SUBJECTS, which can typically occur in either preverbal or postverbal position in such pragmatically neutral clauses. When a SUBJECT is introduced into a discourse for the first time, though, it loses that positional flexibility and must obligatorily occur in postverbal position, as in examples (9.98) and (9.99).

(9.98) *Oh, zhaos leb ob-def manx diet leb*
INTJ from CLF NOM-place REL hide CLF
ob-xed-ras dox ***bionl*** *[ngonl deb-npaok].*
NOM-tooth-comb that **exit** [CLF:animate DIM-woman]$_S$
'From the place where (he'd) hidden the comb-tooth there appeared a young woman.' (Xingyu Shi, in *Oub Meinl Yaos Geud*)

(9.99) *Ghad* ***zhax*** *[git] guaot...*
then$_2$ **strong** [wind]$_S$ pass
'A great wind blew through...' (Xingyu Shi, in *Oub Meinl Yaos Geud*)

Finally, when it comes to AGENTS, one might expect something of a "clash" between opposed ordering tendencies: newly introduced arguments in general typically occur in postverbal position in Xong, but AGENTS typically occur in preverbal position, at least in pragmatically neutral clauses (see Section 9.1.1). This potential clash is neatly resolved by the obligatory use of a multiverbal construction (see Chapter 12) whenever an AGENT is first introduced into an ongoing discourse. This multiverbal construction will usually involve either *mex* 'to exist' (see example (9.100) as well as further below in this section) or *zhus/zhaus* 'to suffer' (see example (9.101) as well as Section 9.3.4). The newly introduced AGENT will occur after *mex* or *zhus/zhaus* but before the verb with respect to which it is actually serving as an AGENT. In examples (9.100) and (9.101) below, each instance of *mex* 'to exist' and *zhus/zhaus* 'to suffer' has been bolded, as has each verb following an AGENT.

(9.100) ***Mex*** *[ngonl deb-naus]* ***niab*** *deux: "Leud-Nhaonl,*
exist [CLF:animate DIM-bird]$_A$ **say** QUOT FAM-PN
leud-Nhaonl, leud-Nhaonl..."
FAM-PN FAM-PN
'A little bird appeared and said: "Nhaon, Nhaon, Nhaon..."' (Xingyu Shi, in *Oub Meinl Yaos Geud*)

(9.101) *Miant bioud* ***zhaus*** *[zheinb.fux]* ***faol.kuanx.***
3PL home **suffer** [government]$_A$ **be.fined**
'Their family was fined by the government (for having too many children).' (unknown Xong consultant, fieldnotes)

In summary, not every postverbal argument in a Xong discourse necessarily serves to introduce a new referent into the discourse, but it does appear to be true that every time a new referent is first introduced it will occur in postverbal position. Conversely, not every argument referring to a previously introduced referent will necessarily occur in preverbal position (especially if the referent is relatively patient-like and/or not particularly important to the ongoing discourse), but it does appear to be the case that every preverbal argument will refer to a previously introduced referent.

The other common method of introducing a new referent into a Xong discourse is through the use of the *mex* presentational construction, an example of which was already seen in (9.100) above. Although it is consistently glossed as 'exist' in this grammar, the verb *mex* serves a variety of functions, including functioning as a verb meaning 'to have' and as a verb meaning 'wealthy'. It also serves to introduce new referents into a discourse, in which case the argument referring to the newly introduced referent appears immediately after *mex*. This *mex* presentational construction is very similar in both structural and functional terms to presentational constructions in certain other languages of East and Southeast Asia, including the Lao presentational construction involving the verb *mii2* 'to exist, to have' (Enfield 2007: 157–161) and the Standard Mandarin presentational construction involving the verb *yǒu* (有) 'to exist, to have'. Like these other constructions, the Xong construction in question can usually be translated into English as 'There is/are/was/were [REFERENT]'.

In examples (9.102–9.105), each instance of presentational *mex* 'to exist' has been bolded, and each argument referring to a newly introduced referent has been enclosed within brackets.

(9.102) *Manx.eib.manx.ab,* ***mex*** *[deib* *yaos-geud].*
a.long.time.ago **exist** [CLF:pair$_2$ older.sister-younger.sibling]
Yaos *nbut* *Niaox.meib,* *deb-geud*
older.sister name PN DIM-younger.sibling
nbut *Niaox.nhaonl.*
name PN
'A long time ago, there were two sisters. The older sister was named Niao Mei, and the younger Niao Nhaon.' (Xingyu Shi, in *Oub Meinl Yaos Geud*)

(9.103) *Wel* *jaont* *yul* *ninb* *dox* ***mex*** *[ngonl* *naus]*
1SG herd cow at that **exist** [CLF:animate bird]
hnef-hnef *ngheub* *sad,* *hnef-hnef* *at*
CLF:day-CLF:day sing Xong.song CLF:day-CLF:day SAT
niab *wel* *naond* *nbut.*
say 1SG ASSOC name
'I was herding cows out there and there was a bird that sings Xong songs every day, that says my name every day.' (Xingyu Shi, in *Oub Meinl Yaos Geud*)

(9.104) ***Mex*** *[ngonl deb-naus] shib ... zos ninb beul*
exist [CLF:animate DIM-bird] it's land at 3
jaont daob-yul naond sond-guaod-yul laot-gheul.
herd AN-cow ASSOC bone-back-cow top-place$_2$
'There was a little bird that landed on the back of a cow he was herding.' (Xingyu Shi, in *Oub Meinl Yaos Geud*)

(9.105) ***Mex*** *[hnef] beul ghad shok, ghad zhax git*
exist [CLF:day] 3 then$_2$ dry.in.sun then$_2$ strong wind
guaot meh, piaf raol git meh, dut beul
pass BCKG blow CLF:weather wind BCKG obtain 3
naond xut.npeif sat piaf sheub monl. ***Mex***
ASSOC shoe SAT blow leave go **exist**
[nqad] piaf sheub, doul nqad.
[CLF:half.of.pair] blow leave remain CLF:half.of.pair
'Then one day, as (the shoes) were drying, a great wind blew through, a gust of wind blew through, and it blew a shoe away. It blew away one shoe, leaving the other.' (Xingyu Shi, in *Oub Meinl Yaos Geud*)

Note that the *mex* presentational construction is arguably a subtype of the postverbal method for introducing new referents that was discussed previously in this section, since the argument referring to the newly introduced referent in this construction will occur in immediate post-*mex* (i.e. postverbal) position.

9.2 Particles, negative markers, and other grammatical forms

This section discusses a number of grammatical (as opposed to lexical) forms which play significant roles in Xong syntax but which do not easily fit into any other sections of this grammar. In particular, Section 9.2.1 discusses particles (though certain interrogative particles are discussed in more detail in Section 9.3.2.3), Section 9.2.2 discusses negative markers, and Section 9.2.3 discusses a variety of more idiosyncratic forms.

Note that this section does not discuss every grammatically significant form in Xong. In particular, there are a number of high-frequency grammatical operators (see Section 9.1.1) with temporal meanings that still await description. These include several forms meaning roughly 'not until, only then' (*dad.kit*, *shaod.kit*, *chad.kit*, and *kit*, all glossed as 'not.until'), several forms meaning roughly 'then' (*doub* 'then$_1$', *ghad* 'then$_2$', and *jeub* 'then$_3$'), and several forms meaning roughly 'still' (*deit*, *heit*, *eit*, *hat*, *haf*, and *haok*, all glossed as 'still'), as well as the forms *yul/yol* 'again' and *(y)ab* 'also'. Any future account of these forms' meanings, functions, and interactional properties (both with each other and with Xong's particles and aspectual-modal–marking verbs) would be of great significance to the field of Xong studies.

9.2.1 Particles

The term *particle* is used in a technical sense in this grammar to refer to the members of an apparently closed set of monosyllabic forms that display similar phonological, grammatical, and semantic properties. With respect to phonology, the most salient property of particles is that they are uniformly toneless (for more on toneless syllables in general, see Section 3.6). This is a necessary but not sufficient criterion for particlehood in Xong, since certain interjections are toneless as well (see Section 11.3). Every attested Xong particle also shares two other phonological properties: it begins either with a sonorant (i.e. non-plosive, non-fricative) consonant or with no consonant at all, and it features a monophthongal vowel rather than a diphthongal vowel. However, these latter two properties may be merely coincidental, since they are hardly rare among Xong's other, non-particle forms and since only about a dozen particles have been attested so far.

With respect to grammar, particles are distinct from other Xong forms in that each of them most often occurs in clause-final position, although a few of them can also occur in certain phrase-final positions within a clause as well (see Sections 9.2.1.1 and 9.2.1.2 below). With respect to semantics, particles are characterized by their having fairly abstract grammatical and discourse-pragmatic meanings, as opposed to the more lexical meanings typical of forms belonging to Xong's major lexical categories (i.e. nouns, classifiers, verbs, and ideophones).

Sections 9.2.1.1 through 9.2.1.4 below describe four non-interrogative particles which have relatively clear meanings and functions (clear, at least, compared to those of other attested particles) and which show relatively little variation in meaning and function across the author's consultants. Other attested particles are not described in this section, generally for one of three reasons. First, the interrogative particle *yoh/yah* 'QP.NTRL' is discussed in Section 9.3.2.3 further below rather than in this Section 9.2.1. Second, it is not yet possible to meaningfully characterize the meanings or functions of certain apparent particles that appear only a handful of times (or in some cases only once) in the author's corpus. Third, three or four particles (namely *manh*, *oh*, *aoh*, and *ah*, with the last two possibly being phonological variants of a single form) appear frequently in the author's corpus, but despite a fair amount of investigative work devoted just to these particular forms, their meanings and functions still remain largely opaque. Particles belonging to the latter two categories (i.e. low-frequency particles and the particles *manh*, *oh*, *aoh*, and *ah*) are not explicitly discussed anywhere in this grammar, but they are uniformly glossed as 'PART' (from 'particle') wherever they occur. In contrast, the particle *yoh/yah* 'QP.NTRL' (again, see Section 9.3.2.3) and the four particles discussed in Sections 9.2.1.1 through 9.2.1.4 below are each given a more specific gloss.

9.2.1.1 The particle *leh* 'LEH'

The particle *leh* 'LEH' is a very high-frequency form in Fenghuang Xong, although it appears to be much more common in narratives than in conversations or isolated utterances. For instance, it appears 75 times in the narrative titled *Oub Meinl Yaos Geud*, but only four times in the conversation titled *Tooth Conversation* (accordingly, most of the examples in this section are taken from the former text). Nevertheless, this form is rather difficult to characterize in semantic and functional terms. It most commonly serves as a clause linker or as a marker of certain clause-internal syntactic constituents, but it appears to serve certain other minor functions as well, and in many cases it occurs with no clear function whatsoever. The remainder of this section will discuss those functions of *leh* which the author has so far been able to discern, as well as the insertion possibilities of *leh* within Xong clauses. Note that *leh* is conservatively glossed as 'LEH' in this grammar, since the author feels that the meaning(s) and function(s) of the form are not yet well understood enough to justify a more specific gloss.

The single most common function of *leh* 'LEH' is to serve as a clause-linking particle. In such cases *leh* appears at the end of the first linked clause, before the second linked clause. When serving as a clause linker, the semantics of *leh* appear to be fairly general, as the particle seems to merely indicate that there is some sort of logical relationship between the two linked clauses. In some cases this is a relationship of temporal sequencing (so that [CLAUSE_1 *leh*, CLAUSE_2] means something like 'CLAUSE_1, then CLAUSE_2'), in others it is a relationship of reason or cause (so that [CLAUSE_1 *leh*, CLAUSE_2] means 'CLAUSE_1, because CLAUSE_2'), in others it is a relationship of purpose (so that [CLAUSE_1 *leh*, CLAUSE_2] means 'CLAUSE_1, in order to CLAUSE_2'), and in yet others it is a relationship of explanation (so that [CLAUSE_1 *leh*, CLAUSE_2] means 'CLAUSE_1, that is to say CLAUSE_2'). Examples of each of these types of logical relationship can be seen in (9.106–9.113) below.[178]

(9.106)	*Naont*	*meib-Nhaonl*	*beul*	*shib*	*jix*	*nzhaod*	***leh,***
	thus	younger.sister-PN	3	it's	NEG_1	return	**LEH**

	chauk	*nex*	*naond*	*npaok,*	*chauk*	*nex*	*yes.web*
	do	NEX	ASSOC	woman	do	NEX	landlord

	naond	*nheinx.*
	ASSOC	daughter.in.law

'And so little sister Nhaon didn't go back. She became (the landlord's son's) wife, she became the landlord's daughter-in-law.' (Xingyu Shi, in *Oub Meinl Yaos Geud*)

178 In the two texts included at the end of this grammar, *leh* 'LEH' sometimes occurs at the end of an orthographic sentence despite having an apparently clause-linking function. This merely indicates that there was a significant pause between the first clause (i.e. the one bearing *leh*) and the following clause. It has no effect on the meaning or function of *leh* 'LEH' or on the relationship between the initial *leh*-bearing clause and the following clause.

(9.107) *Manx nins deb-ngueif nins deb-npaok* ***leh,***
REL COP DIM-unmarried.woman COP DIM-woman **LEH**
xaond tad bioud naond jeub chauk wel
not.yet establish home ASSOC $then_3$ do 1SG
naond nheinx.
ASSOC daughter.in.law
'(If the person this shoe belongs to) is an unmarried woman, a young woman, if she hasn't yet started a family, then she can be my daughter-in-law.' (Xingyu Shi, in *Oub Meinl Yaos Geud*)

(9.108) *Naont beul doub kaot* ***leh,*** *jix gaons sheub, jix*
thus 3 $then_1$ stop **LEH** NEG_1 give leave NEG_1
gaons nzhaod ghat leb khauk-roub dox.
give return go.to CLF hole-stone that
'And so he stopped her, he didn't let her leave. He didn't let her go back to the hole in the stone (wall, where she had been hiding after being magically transformed into the tooth of a comb).' (Xingyu Shi, in *Oub Meinl Yaos Geud*)

(9.109) *Liaos naont wel gaons manx oub-leb bid-zhonx-hlod*
miss thus 1SG give 2PL two-CLF FRT-length-bamboo
leh, *gaons manx geud zhut aub-gheb.*
LEH give 2PL hold store water-eye
'(If you) missed me, then give me your two lengths of bamboo, the ones I gave you to store your tears with.' (Xingyu Shi, in *Oub Meinl Yaos Geud*)

(9.110) *Beul teuf dut aub* ***leh,*** *beul chot, chot nhob*
3 scoop obtain water **LEH** 3 take take walk
nzhaod gaons beul baox hauk.
return give 3 father drink
'She scooped up some water, and she started taking it back to give to her father to drink.' (Xingyu Shi, in *Oub Meinl Yaos Geud*)

(9.111) *Jix niel nhob ib-dof raut* ***leh,***
NEG_1 know walk ???-which good **LEH**
bid-gheul-ghaob-chaut bob-raud-ndaut.
FRT-mountain-NOM-wilderness forest-forest-tree
'(She) didn't know where she should go, (everywhere around her was) wilderness, deep forest.' (Xingyu Shi, in *Oub Meinl Yaos Geud*)

(9.112) *Jix mex aod-ngonl manx hox* ***leh.*** *Leb-leb*
NEG$_1$ exist one-CLF:animate REL fit **LEH** CLF-CLF
zhut at jix peif
wear.shoes SAT NEG$_1$ match
'No one was the right size. No one who tried on the shoe fit.' (Xingyu Shi, in *Oub Meinl Yaos Geud*)

(9.113) *Deb-deb naond baox nzhaod lol* ***leh,*** *nonx*
child-RED ASSOC father return come **LEH** eat
hlit nzod, nonx niax-naus.
cooked.rice early eat meat-bird
'The child's father came home. He ate some of the bird meat for breakfast.' (Xingyu Shi, in *Oub Meinl Yaos Geud*)

In some cases *leh* 'LEH' serves to link two identical (or nearly identical) repeated clauses, as in examples (9.114–9.117) below.

(9.114) *Dand hnef dox* ***leh,*** *dand hnef dox*
arrive CLF:day that **LEH** arrive CLF:day that
shib yaod.yaod lol id-reinb nqad xut.npeif
it's all come DID-determine CLF:half.of.pair shoe
dox nins leb naond.
that COP who ASSOC
'When the day arrived, when the day arrived everyone came to determine who the shoe belonged to.' (Xingyu Shi, in *Oub Meinl Yaos Geud*)

(9.115) *Diex gid.daud loux beul baox nzhaod lol* ***leh.***
finish extremely long.time 3 father return come **LEH**
Beul baox nzhaod, beul baox dand zheit-cheid.
3 father return 3 father arrive outside-gate
'After a very long time, their father returned. Their father returned, he arrived at the gate.' (Xingyu Shi, in *Oub Meinl Yaos Geud*)

(9.116) *Dand def nghauk aub* ***leh,*** *beul dand def nghauk*
arrive place bathe water **LEH** 3 arrive place bathe
aub shib beul hnant leud-Nhaonl nghauk aub.
water it's 3 call FAM-PN bathe water
'(They) arrived at the bathing spot, they arrived there and she told (her younger sister) Nhaon to go bathe.' (Xingyu Shi, in *Oub Meinl Yaos Geud*)

(9.117) *Niaox.meib ghad shaod* ***leh.*** *Shaod leh, sat jaok*
PN then$_2$ try **LEH** try LEH SAT prick
beul ghaod.lot.
3 mouth
'And so Niao Mei tried (the bird meat). She tried it, and (the bird's bones) pricked her mouth.' (Xingyu Shi, in *Oub Meinl Yaos Geud*)

The particle *leh* 'LEH' is also frequently used to mark certain noun phrases and temporal expressions (e.g. *nieux.ghoub* 'just now', *tat-hnef* [this-CLF:day] 'today', etc.) within a clause. It most often marks such phrases and expressions when they occur in clause-initial position, though it can mark certain non–clause-initial phrases and expressions as well; see further below in this section for details. The exact function of *leh* when it occurs following a noun phrase or temporal expression is unclear. In some cases it appears to be serving as something like a topic marker (though the notion of "topic" seems to be largely irrelevant to Xong grammar as a whole, as is discussed in Section 9.1.3.1), in others it seems to simply mark a pause between the preceding phrase or expression and the subsequent remainder of the clause, and in still others it occurs with no obvious function whatsoever.

Examples of *leh* serving to mark noun phrases and temporal expressions are given in (9.118–9.121) below.

(9.118) *Niaox.meib Niaox.nhaonl zhaos xub jix doul minl,*
PN PN from small NEG$_1$ remain mother
nanx doul baox. Beul baox ***leh,*** *soud beul*
only remain father 3 father **LEH** raise 3
aod-deib yaos-geud liox miex lah.
one-CLF:pair$_2$ older.sister-younger.sibling big person PRF
'The mother of (the two sisters) Niao Mei and Niao Nhaon passed away when they were very young, leaving only their father. This father, he raised them to adulthood.' (Xingyu Shi, in *Oub Meinl Yaos Geud*)

(9.119) *Niaox.meib* ***leh,*** *jaod deb hint, jix liaos baox naond.*
PN **LEH** bad child very NEG$_1$ miss father ASSOC
'Niao Mei, as for her, she was a very bad child. She didn't miss her father.' (Xingyu Shi, in *Oub Meinl Yaos Geud*)

(9.120) *Aod-leb zhonx-hlod* ***leh,*** *nkhed manx*
one-CLF length-bamboo **LEH** look 2PL
oub-meinl dib ghaod raut deb.
two-CLF:person which more good child
'These lengths of bamboo, they'll show which of you is the better child.' (Xingyu Shi, in *Oub Meinl Yaos Geud*) (repeated from (9.72) above)

(9.121) *Beul baox* ***leh,*** *Niaox.meib* ***leh,*** *baod-zhauf at*
3 father **LEH** PN **LEH** BUG-door SAT
keuf baod-cheid at keuf.
shut BUG-gate SAT shut
'Her father, and (her sister) Niao Mei, they'd shut the door, and shut the gate.' (Xingyu Shi, in *Oub Meinl Yaos Geud*) (repeated from (9.75) above)

In some cases *leh* seems to function as a contrastive marker, roughly translatable as 'but' or 'but as for'. When functioning as such a marker, *leh* can occur in either clause-internal position (as in example (9.122) below) or clause-final position (as in example (9.123)).

(9.122) *Hnef-hnef choud nex naond deb monl*
CLF:day-CLF:day send NEX ASSOC child go
jaont yul, hnef-hnef monl chaut chauk
herd cow CLF:day-CLF:day go wilderness do
geud.donb. Beul ***leh,*** *hnef-hnef ninb bioud jont konf.*
work 3 **LEH** CLF:day-CLF:day at home sit free.time
'Every day (the wicked stepmother) sent (her husband's) child out to herd the cows, every day she sent him out into the wilderness to work. But she, every day she stayed at home and relaxed.' (Xingyu Shi, in *Oub Meinl Yaos Geud*)

(9.123) *Fanx.zheinb deit taf dut, yul aod-hmaont* ***leh,***
anyway still endure obtain again one-CLF:evening **LEH**
mb guaot.
hurt pass
'(That evening) at least (I) was able to bear (the pain in my tooth). But the evening after that, it really hurt.' (Haili Shi, in *Tooth Conversation*)

The author's primary consultants report that *leh* is sometimes used as a placeholder while a speaker is thinking of what to say next (rather like English *um* ...), although the author does not yet have any clear examples of *leh* serving this function. Besides the functions so far discussed, *leh* 'LEH' often occurs with no apparent function whatsoever, and regardless of the particular function it serves in any particular instance, consultants generally report that *leh* can be removed from an utterance in which it occurs without affecting meaning or grammaticality.

While in the author's corpus *leh* 'LEH' generally occurs in either clause-final position or immediately following a clause-initial noun phrase or temporal expression, the particle can in fact be inserted in a wide variety of positions within a clause (note, though, that *leh* cannot occur between any two constituents of a noun phrase; in other words, it cannot occur noun-phrase–internally). For instance, in the constructed sentence given in example (9.124) below, consultants report that *leh* can be inserted in four different positions: following the clause-initial temporal expression *nieux. ghoub* 'just now', following the preverbal argument *wel* '1SG', following the postverbal argument *beul* '3', and following the postverbal argument *aod-banb bid-ghand* [one-CLF:some FRT-grape] 'some grapes'. Consultants also report that more than one instance of *leh* could be inserted in a single clause, but that doing so would in most cases sound somewhat "unnatural".

(9.124) *Nieux.ghoub (leh) wel (leh) gaons beul (leh)*
just.now (LEH) 1SG (LEH) give 3 (LEH)
aod-banb bid-ghand (leh).
one-CLF:some FRT-grape (LEH)
'I gave him some grapes just now.' (Haili Shi, fieldnotes)

In the constructed sentence given in example (9.125), consultants report that *leh* can occur in only two positions: following the preverbal argument *beul* '3', and following the postverbal argument *daob-ginb* [AN-bug] 'bugs'.

(9.125) *Beul (leh) deit ix beux daob-ginb (leh).*
3 (LEH) still NEG_1 hit AN-bug (LEH)
'He still doesn't kill bugs.' (Chenghua Long, fieldnotes)

Note that the form *leh* cannot occur (i) between two preverbal grammatical operators (e.g. between *deit* 'still' and *ix* 'NEG_1' in example (9.125)), (ii) between a preverbal grammatical operator and a following verb (e.g. between *ix* 'NEG_1' and *beux* 'hit' in example (9.125)), or (iii) between a verb and an immediately following argument (e.g. between *gaons* 'give' and *beul* '3' in example (9.124), or between *beux* 'hit' and *daob-ginb* [AN-bug] 'bugs' in example (9.125)). See Section 9.1.1 for more on grammatical operators in general.

As the punctuation in the examples given so far suggests, *leh* 'LEH' appears to form a constituent with the clause or phrase preceding it rather than with the one following it. There are three primary pieces of evidence for this. First, consultants almost always pause (and often for a significant length of time) immediately after *leh*, while they never pause immediately before it. Second, *leh* always occurs as the last element of the preceding intonational phrase rather than occurring as the first element of the following one or occurring as an independent intonational phrase. Third, several of Xong's particles (e.g. *ih* 'EMPH', *lah* 'PRF', *yoh/yah* 'QP.NTRL') clearly only ever occur in clause-final position, while no particle clearly only ever occurs in clause-initial (or phrase-initial) position. This suggests that in somewhat less clear cases involving other particles (as with *leh* 'LEH'), the null hypothesis should be that the particle in question forms a constituent with the preceding linguistic material rather than with the following linguistic material.

9.2.1.2 The particle *meh* 'BCKG'

The particle *meh* is glossed 'BCKG', from 'background'. As this gloss suggests, the function of *meh* seems to be to signal that the clause in which it occurs serves as background, or as an explanation, or as a reason for the following clause. In other words, a [CLAUSE_1 *meh*, CLAUSE_2] construction means something along the lines of 'CLAUSE_1, so CLAUSE_2'. Unsurprisingly, the particle *meh* 'BCKG' cannot occur at the end of a clause that is produced in isolation (i.e. without a second, following clause).[179]

(9.126) *Aod-roul* *ngaonf* *ceind* *guaot* ***meh,*** *shaont* *deb*
one-CLF:time_1 time cool pass **BCKG** fast DIM
heut *deb* *reus* *eud.*
help child add clothing
'It's really cool now, hurry up and help the child put on some more clothes.' (Chenghua Long, fieldnotes)

(9.127) *Naont* *deb-geud* *daos* ***meh,*** *naont* *jix* *doul*
thus DIM-younger.sibling die **BCKG** thus NEG_1 remain
leb *heut* *monx* *khauf* *deb* ***meh,*** *naont* *wel*
who help 2SG take.care.of child **BCKG** thus 1SG
heut *monx* *khauf* *deb* *diex.*
help 2SG take.care.of child finish
'My younger sister (i.e. your wife) is dead, and so now there's no one left to help you care for your child. So I'll just help you care for the child, and that'll be that.' (Xingyu Shi, in *Oub Meinl Yaos Geud*)

(9.128) *Aod-ngonl* *dox* *giaol* *guaot* ***meh,*** *nex* *puk*
one-CLF:animate that stupid pass **BCKG** NEX speak
ob-naonb *beul* *deit* *seinb.*
NOM-what 3 still believe
'That guy's so stupid, he'll believe anything you tell him.' (Haili Shi, fieldnotes)

Occasionally, *meh* 'BCKG' occurs clause-internally after a clause-initial noun-phrase argument. In such cases *meh* seems to be serving as a contrastive marker, as in examples (9.129) and (9.130) below. Note that *meh* is still glossed as 'BCKG' even when it occurs in this clause-internal position.

179 The comments about *leh* 'LEH' appearing at the end of an orthographic sentence (see Section 9.2.1.1) also apply to *meh* 'BCKG' when it appears in such a position.

(9.129) *Wel* ***meh,*** *liaos monx naond guaot, daonl jix*
1SG **BCKG** miss 2SG ASSOC pass wait NEG_1
niaons monx nzhaod, hnef-hnef nied nied nied.
ABIL 2SG return CLF:day-CLF:day cry cry cry
'But (unlike my sister) I missed you greatly, I couldn't wait for you to come back. Every day I wept and wept and wept.' (Xingyu Shi, in *Oub Meinl Yaos Geud*)

(9.130) *Naont meib-Nhaonl beul shib jix nzhaod leh,*
thus younger.sister-PN 3 it's NEG_1 return LEH
chauk nex naond npaok, chauk nex yes.web
do NEX ASSOC woman do NEX landlord
naond nheinx. Niaox.meib ***meh,*** *nzhaod.*
ASSOC daughter.in.law PN **BCKG** return
'And so little sister Nhaon didn't go back. She became (the landlord's son's) wife, she became the landlord's daughter-in-law. But (her sister) Niao Mei, she went back.' (Xingyu Shi, in *Oub Meinl Yaos Geud*)

Finally, just as with *leh* 'LEH' (see Section 9.2.1.1 above), *meh* 'BCKG' appears to form a constituent with the clause or phrase preceding it rather than with the one following it, and for the same reasons.

9.2.1.3 The particle *ih* 'EMPH'

The form *ih* 'EMPH' (from 'emphatic') is one of Fenghuang Xong's more straightforward particles. It simply serves to add a note of emphasis to the clause in which it appears, or (perhaps more accurately) to a particular constituent within that clause. It is not yet clear, though, how Xong speakers signal which particular constituent within a clause *ih* 'EMPH' is intended to emphasize. The two most obvious possibilities would seem to be (i) that no overt signaling is done at all, so that the listener relies solely on context to determine which constituent the speaker intended to emphasize, or (ii) that the signaling is done through intonational means (see Section 3.6). More research is needed to determine which (if either) of these two possibilities is the correct one.

(9.131) *Wel nins naont chauk* ***ih!***
1SG COP thus do **EMPH**
'I *am* doing it that way!' (Shixiang Wu, fieldnotes)

(9.132) *Beul nins manx liox naond* ***ih.***
3 COP REL big ASSOC **EMPH**
'He's the *boss*.' (Chenghua Long, fieldnotes)

(9.133) *Aod-hnanf* *eud* *dox* *xonx* *guaot* ***ih.***
one-CLF:clothing clothing that attractive pass **EMPH**
'That (shirt) is *really* pretty.' (Haili Shi, fieldnotes)

9.2.1.4 The particle *lah* 'PRF'

The particle *lah* is glossed as 'PRF', from 'perfect'. Some of the more common functions of this form are (i) signaling that an event or action occurred (or at least started occurring) in the past and still has current relevance as of the time of speaking, and (ii) signaling the onset of a state or property that still has current relevance as of the time of speaking. Examples of the former can be seen in (9.134–9.136), and examples of the latter can be seen in (9.137–9.139).[180]

(9.134) *Beul* *baox* *monl* ***lah.***
3 father go **PRF**
'Their father left.' (Xingyu Shi, in *Oub Meinl Yaos Geud*) (repeated from (9.2) above)

(9.135) *Aod* *ghab* *beul* *doub* *naonb.nex* *zhut*
as.soon.as bite 3 then$_1$ seem reach
aod-ghoub *sheinf.jind* *dox* ***lah.***
one-CLF:flexible.length nerve that **PRF**
'As soon as (I) bit down it was like I'd hit the nerve (in my tooth).' (Haili Shi, in *Tooth Conversation*)

(9.136) *Beul* *doub* *geud* *gaons* *beul* *deb-geud* ***lah.***
3 then$_1$ hold give 3 DIM-younger.sibling **PRF**
'She gave (her own drinking water) to her younger sister.' (Xingyu Shi, in *Oub Meinl Yaos Geud*)

(9.137) *Wel* *sout-hnef* *wel* *jix* *mb* ***lah.***
1SG past.few-CLF:day 1SG NEG$_1$ hurt **PRF**
'The past few days (my tooth) hasn't hurt (unlike during the preceding few days).' (Haili Shi, in *Tooth Conversation*)

180 Given the description of *lah* 'PRF' just provided, it may strike the reader as unusual that several of the examples in this section have non–past-tense translations. This is to some extent an artifact of translation, as any particular instance of a Xong verb will often have multiple, equally valid English equivalents. See Section 10.2 for some discussion.

(9.138) *Beul baox niel* ***lah,*** *niel beul jix dut dand neind.*
3 father know **PRF** know 3 NEG$_1$ obtain arrive this
'Then her father knew, he knew that she had never been there before.'
(Xingyu Shi, in *Oub Meinl Yaos Geud*)

(9.139) *Beul baox niab deux: "Manx oub-leb liox miex* ***lah,*** *sat*
3 father say QUOT 2PL two-CLF big person **PRF** SAT
mex aod-gul-jons-il-jut ***lah,*** *sat kox.ix cheinf.jaok* ***lah."***
exist one-ten-seven-eight-CLF:year **PRF** SAT can get.married **PRF**
'Their father said: "You two are all grown up, you're now seventeen or eighteen years old. Now you can get married."' (Xingyu Shi, in *Oub Meinl Yaos Geud*)

It is important to note that while *lah* 'PRF' is often used to signal the onset of a state or property that still has current relevance as of the time of speaking, this use of *lah* does not necessarily entail that the state or property in question still holds as of the time of speaking. As is described in more detail in Section 10.3, *lah* 'PRF' does appear to have this entailment property with certain state- or property-denoting verbs, but not with others. This can be seen by comparing examples (9.140) and (9.141), in which consultants report that the use of *lah* with a state- or property-denoting verb does not entail that 'VERB is the case now', with examples (9.142) and (9.143), in which consultants report that the use of *lah* with such a verb does in fact entail that 'VERB is the case now'.

(9.140) *Miaux-ndaut nqint* ***lah.***
leaf-tree red **PRF**
'The leaves turned red (though they are not necessarily still red now).'
(Shixiang Wu, fieldnotes)

(9.141) *Aod-roul gueinx mioux* ***lah.***
one-CLF:time$_1$ yellow mature.rice.plant **PRF**
'The rice plants turned yellow (though they are not necessarily still yellow now).' (Chenghua Long, fieldnotes)

(9.142) *Wel ninb xol.taonx* ***lah.***
1SG at school **PRF**
'I live at the school now.' (Shixiang Wu, fieldnotes)

(9.143) *Ntiot* ***lah!***
smoky **PRF**
'(The room's) filled with smoke!' (Haili Shi, fieldnotes)

Two other, less frequent functions of *lah* 'PRF' are (i) serving to mark the members of a list (see example (9.144) below and example (9.139) above) and (ii) serving as an emphatic marker (see examples (9.145) and (9.146) below). When *lah* 'PRF' is serving either of these functions, it may simultaneously be serving as a more canonical perfect marker as well, as in examples (9.139) and (9.146).

(9.144) *Hnef-hnef* *at* *npod* *mel* *ah,* *zhox*
CLF:day-CLF:day SAT toss stone.toss.game PART kick
ghab ***lah,*** *ndanb* *sheinb.kiet* ***lah,*** *hnef-hnef*
shuttlecock **PRF** jump hopscotch **PRF** CLF:day-CLF:day
nghauk.zaol *leh.*
play LEH
'Every day (she) played the stone-tossing game, (she) played shuttlecock, (she) played hopscotch, every day (she) was out playing.' (Xingyu Shi, in *Oub Meinl Yaos Geud*) (repeated from (9.40) above)

(9.145) *Nins* *naont* *raut* *guaot* ***lah!***
COP thus good pass **PRF**
'In that case (i.e. in the case that this shoe really does belong to you), excellent!' (Xingyu Shi, in *Oub Meinl Yaos Geud*)

(9.146) *Aod-minl-nek,* *wel* *naond* *deb* *gheil* *ghaod* *zhut*
KIN-mother-mother 1SG ASSOC child excrete feces reach
manx *bioud* ***lah!***
2PL home **PRF**
'Oh no, my kid's pooped (on the floor) in your house!' (unknown Xong consultant, fieldnotes)

Since in Standard Mandarin the emphatic perfect marker *la* (啦) can also serve as both a listing marker and an emphatic marker, and since there is a very high degree of phonetic similarity between Standard Mandarin *la* and Xong *lah*, the use of the Xong perfect marker for these two functions may be due at least in part to influence from Standard Mandarin (or to influence from another Sinitic variety in which similar facts hold).

9.2.2 Negative markers

Fenghuang Xong features four negative markers: *(j)ix* 'NEG$_1$', *jud* 'NEG$_2$', *xaond* 'not yet', and *ghad(.maons)/ghaod(.maons)* 'NEG.IMP'. The first three of these forms are discussed immediately below in Sections 9.2.2.1 through 9.2.2.3, while the fourth is discussed further below in Section 9.3.1.

9.2.2.1 The negative marker *(j)ix* 'NEG$_1$'

The form *(j)ix* 'NEG$_1$' is by far the most common negative marker in Fenghuang Xong, and also the most versatile. By definition, this form can be used to negate any verb, since one of the defining characteristics of the class of verbs in Xong is the ability to undergo negation by *(j)ix* (see Section 10.2). The form *(j)ix* typically appears immediately preceding the verb that it negates (see examples (9.147) and (9.148) below), although the degree marker *(n)anb* 'really' can occur between *(j)ix* and a following verb (see example (9.149)). The form *(j)ix* can also occur within (rather than preceding) certain multiverbal constructions (see example (9.150)), as is discussed in more detail in Section 12.3.3. Finally, note that *(j)ix* 'NEG$_1$' plays an important role in forming interrogative clauses in Xong, specifically through the use of the [C NEG C] construction. See example (9.151) below for one instance of this construction, which is discussed much more thoroughly in Section 9.3.2.2.

(9.147) *Wel* ***jix*** *zheb. Wel sout-hnef wel* ***jix*** *mb lah.*
1SG **NEG$_1$** pull.out 1SG past.few-CLF:day 1SG **NEG$_1$** hurt PRF
'I'm not going to get (my tooth) pulled out. The past few days it hasn't hurt.' (Haili Shi, in *Tooth Conversation*)

(9.148) *Beul ghad* ***jix*** *ndiot geud nzhaod.*
3 then$_2$ **NEG$_1$** recognize road return
'Then she won't know the way back.' (Xingyu Shi, in *Oub Meinl Yaos Geud*)

(9.149) *Aod-meinl ghaod jaod deb,* ***jix*** *nanb nied,* ***jix***
one-CLF:person more bad child **NEG$_1$** really cry **NEG$_1$**
liaos baox naond, ***jix*** *nied* ***jix*** *mex aub-gheb.*
miss father ASSOC **NEG$_1$** cry **NEG$_1$** exist water-eye
'Whichever (of you) is the worse child, whichever (of you) doesn't weep, doesn't miss her father, (she) won't cry and (she) won't have any tears.' (Xingyu Shi, in *Oub Meinl Yaos Geud*)

(9.150) *Naont sox.ix aod-hmaont dox taf* ***jix*** *dut.*
thus so one-CLF:evening that endure **NEG$_1$** obtain
'So, that evening (I) couldn't bear (the pain).' (Haili Shi, in *Tooth Conversation*)

(9.151) *Nhaonl, monx dand neind* ***jix*** *dand, Nhaonl?*
PN 2SG arrive this **NEG$_1$** arrive PN
'Nhaon, have you been here before, Nhaon?' (Xingyu Shi, in *Oub Meinl Yaos Geud*)

The negative marker under discussion here is transcribed as *(j)ix* in running text, since for most consultants it is realized as *jix* in slower or more careful speech and as *ix* in faster or more casual speech.

9.2.2.2 The negative marker *jud* 'NEG$_2$'

The form *jud* 'NEG$_2$' so far appears to be identical to *(j)ix* 'NEG$_1$' in terms of its grammatical behavior, but it has some additional selectional restrictions which *(j)ix* 'NEG$_1$' lacks. In particular, *jud* 'NEG$_2$' can only be used to negate a small set of certain verbs, including *niel/nianl* 'to know', *dut/daut* 'to obtain', *lis* 'to want', *sheib* 'to be able to', *guant* 'to care', and *giet* 'to dare', all of which can also be negated by *(j)ix* 'NEG$_1$' as well. As their glosses suggest, it is difficult to characterize these verbs semantically, although note that all of them have relatively abstract meanings (in the sense that none of them refer to easily observable properties or physical actions or events). In terms of frequency, *jud* 'NEG$_2$' occurs with *niel/nianl* 'to know' significantly more often than it does with all other verbs combined, at least in the author's Xong corpus. No phonological variants of *jud* 'NEG$_2$' have yet been attested. There may well be other subtle semantic, grammatical, and/or pragmatic differences between *jud* 'NEG$_2$' and *(j)ix* 'NEG$_1$', but neither the author nor his consultants have yet been able to identify any.

Instances of *jud* 'NEG$_2$' in use can be seen in examples (9.152–9.154) below.

(9.152) *Aod-roul* *neind* *yab* ***jud*** *dut* *def* *puk.*
one-CLF:time$_1$ this also **NEG$_2$** obtain place speak
'(I) don't know what to talk about this time either.' (Haili Shi, in *Tooth Conversation*)

(9.153) *Nghauk* *aub* *ox.sheib* ***jud*** *guant* *monl.*
bathe water perhaps **NEG$_2$** care go
'Perhaps (her husband) wouldn't care if (she) went bathing.' (Xingyu Shi, in *Oub Meinl Yaos Geud*)

(9.154) *Beul* *baox* ***jud*** *niel* *ghat* *ib-dof* *leh.*
3 father **NEG$_2$** know go.to ???-which LEH
'(She) didn't know where her father had gone.' (Xingyu Shi, in *Oub Meinl Yaos Geud*) (repeated from (9.88) above)

9.2.2.3 The negative marker *xaond* 'not yet'

Like *(j)ix* 'NEG$_1$' and *jud* 'NEG$_2$', the form *xaond* 'not yet' occurs immediately before the verb that it negates. Also like *(j)ix* 'NEG$_1$' (but unlike *jud* 'NEG$_2$'), *xaond* 'not yet' has no selectional restrictions and can be used to negate any verb. However, there exist at least a handful of minor grammatical differences between *(j)ix* 'NEG$_1$' and *jud* 'NEG$_2$' on the one hand and *xaond* 'not yet' on the other. First, *xaond* 'not yet' occasionally functions as a clause-final interrogative marker rather than as a negative marker, as is shown in examples (9.155) and (9.156) below (see also Section 9.3.2.3). Second, *xaond* 'not yet' does not occur in the [C NEG C] interrogative construction (see Section 9.3.2.2), nor does it appear as a medial negator in any multiverbal constructions (see Chapter 12).

There is also a clear semantic difference between the form *xaond* 'not yet' and the forms *(j)ix* 'NEG_1' and *jud* 'NEG_2'. In particular, *xaond* is used to negate verbs referring to actions (or events, or states, or properties, etc.) that have not yet happened, but which the speaker has reason to believe either (i) will happen at some point in the future or (ii) should have (or are likely to have) already happened.[181] The use of either *(j)ix* 'NEG_1' or *jud* 'NEG_2' carries no such implication. Thus, for instance, *xaond* 'not yet' could be readily used in Xong utterances equivalent to *I haven't eaten* or *She hasn't woken up*, since eating and waking up are events that are highly likely to happen to every person every day. However, it could not be used in Xong utterances equivalent to *I haven't been to Beijing* or *His sister hasn't beaten him*, or at least not unless it was an unusual situation in which the relevant semantic preconditions were met (e.g. if the speaker in question had an upcoming trip to Beijing already planned, or if the sister in question had already announced plans to beat her brother).

Instances of *xaond* 'not yet' in use can be seen in examples (9.155–9.157) below. Note that the utterance shown in example (9.155) is a fixed expression that serves as the most common greeting among Xong speakers in Fenghuang County.

(9.155) *Nonx hlit* ***xaond?***
eat cooked.rice **not.yet**
'Have (you) eaten yet?' (Yan Long, fieldnotes)

(9.156) "*Monx tad bioud* ***xaond?***" "*Wel* ***xaond*** *tad.*"
2SG establish home **not.yet** 1SG **not.yet** establish
'(The landlord asked:) "Have you married yet?" (The girl answered:) "I haven't."' (Xingyu Shi, in *Oub Meinl Yaos Geud*)

(9.157) *Zhet niax-naus leh? Nieux.ghoub wel* ***xaond*** *nonx diul.*
CLF:bowl meat-bird LEH just.now 1SG **not.yet** eat complete
'Where did that bowl of bird meat go? I hadn't finished eating it before.' (Xingyu Shi, in *Oub Meinl Yaos Geud*)

181 The author's consultants consistently translate *xaond* as *méi* (没) 'have not' when speaking Standard Mandarin. This is certainly understandable, as the two forms do show a significant amount of grammatical and semantic overlap. However, the Xong and Standard Mandarin forms in question are not exactly equivalent, most obviously in that the use of Standard Mandarin *méi* does not imply that the speaker has any reason to believe that the action (or event, etc.) referred to by the negated verb will happen at some point in the future or should have already happened.

9.2.3 Other grammatical forms

9.2.3.1 The forms *(s)at* 'SAT' and *yaod(.yaod)* 'all'

The high-frequency form *(s)at* 'SAT' has two phonological variants, both of which are regularly used by all of the author's consultants. The variant *sat* is more common in slow or careful speech, and the shortened variant *at* is more common in fast or casual speech. Both of these variants can often be translated as 'all' in English, but the precise functions of *(s)at* differ from those of English *all* enough that the author uses the gloss 'SAT' in this description instead.

Examples of *(s)at* 'SAT' functioning as a quantifier meaning roughly 'all' or 'whole, entire' can be seen in (9.158–9.163) below. As these and subsequent examples further below show, when serving this or any other function *(s)at* occurs in preverbal position following the relevant noun phrase (if that noun phrase is overtly expressed, which it need not be; see example (9.162)). Such noun phrases often consist solely of a numeral-classifier phrase or a reduplicated classifier (as in examples (9.158–9.161)), but they can contain other noun-phrase–internal constituents as well (as in example (9.163)).

(9.158) *Aod-hmaont* **at** *jix* *mb.*
one-CLF:evening **SAT** NEG_1 hurt
'(My tooth) didn't hurt the whole evening.' (Haili Shi, in *Tooth Conversation*)

(9.159) *Oub-meinl* **at** *liaos.*
two-CLF:person **SAT** miss
'(We) both missed (you).' (Xingyu Shi, in *Oub Meinl Yaos Geud*)

(9.160) *Hnef-hnef* **at** *npod* *mel* *ah,* *zhox*
CLF:day-CLF:day **SAT** toss stone.toss.game PART kick
ghab *lah,* *ndanb* *sheinb.kiet* *lah,* *hnef-hnef*
shuttlecock PRF jump hopscotch PRF CLF:day-CLF:day
nghauk.zaol *leh.*
play LEH
'Every day (she) played the stone-tossing game, (she) played shuttlecock, (she) played hopscotch, every day (she) was out playing.' (Xingyu Shi, in *Oub Meinl Yaos Geud*) (repeated from (9.40) above)

(9.161) *Leb-leb* **at** *lol,* *leb-leb* **at** *shaod,* *jix* *nins.*
CLF-CLF **SAT** come CLF-CLF **SAT** try NEG_1 COP
'Everyone came, and everyone tried (on the shoe, but it) didn't fit.' (Xingyu Shi, in *Oub Meinl Yaos Geud*)

(9.162) ***At*** *nins ghous naond*
SAT COP trick ASSOC
'It was all a trick.' (Xingyu Shi, in *Oub Meinl Yaos Geud*)

(9.163) *Hant bob.mins* ***sat*** *ghaus cef ghaus diul!*
CLF:PL corn **SAT** fall.over ??? fall.over complete
'The corn's all fallen over!' (Chenghua Long, fieldnotes)

In other cases, *(s)at* 'SAT' appears to function as a general intensifier, signaling emphasis, certainty, or degree depending on the specific syntactic and discourse environment in which it occurs. When serving this function, a variety of English translations for *(s)at* are possible, and sometimes there is no readily available translation at all. This can be seen in examples (9.164–9.169) below.

(9.164) ***Sat*** *lous ghaod-nbat ndeb meh.*
SAT dirty feces-pig wet BCKG
'(The shoes) were filthy with pig droppings, and wet.' (Xingyu Shi, in *Oub Meinl Yaos Geud*)

(9.165) *Wel* ***at*** *jix nins nieux-hmaont,* ***at*** *loux*
1SG **SAT** NEG_1 COP yester-CLF:evening **SAT** long.time
ob-hmaont daos lah.
NOM-evening die PRF
'It's not just last night (that my tooth was hurting), it's been a whole bunch of nights now.' (Haili Shi, in *Tooth Conversation*)

(9.166) *Monx* ***at*** *konk ginb.*
2SG **SAT** burrow bug
'You've got bugs (in your teeth).' (Chenghua Long, in *Tooth Conversation*)

(9.167) *Yab nhob nhob nhob nhob nhob nhob.* ***At*** *nhob gid.daud ghoub.*
also walk walk walk walk walk walk **SAT** walk extremely far
'So again (they) walked, and walked, and walked, and walked. They walked very, very far.' (Xingyu Shi, in *Oub Meinl Yaos Geud*)

(9.168) *Meib-Nhaonl jaod deb hint meh, wel* ***at***
younger.sister-PN bad child very BCKG 1SG **SAT**
qiaos.kueis hint manh.
suffer very PART
'Little sister Nhaon is such a bad child, I'm suffering so much (with her here).' (Xingyu Shi, in *Oub Meinl Yaos Geud*)

(9.169) *Monl* *diex* *aod-tit* *gid.daud* *loux* *leh,* ***sat***
go finish one-CLF:time$_3$ extremely long.time LEH **SAT**
monl *loux* *hint.*
go long.time very
'(The girls' father) was gone for a very long time, a very long time indeed.' (Xingyu Shi, in *Oub Meinl Yaos Geud*)

When *(s)at* 'SAT' occurs within a negative clause following an ignorative like *naonb* 'what, something', *(dib.)leb/(jud.)leb* 'who, someone', or *dib/dof* 'which, some(thing/one)' (see Section 7.3), the combination of the two serves essentially the same function that negative pronouns do in other languages. Thus *naonb* 'what, something' together with *(s)at* in a negative clause means 'nothing', *(dib.)leb/(jud.) leb* 'who, someone' together with *(s)at* in a negative clause means 'nobody', and so on. Examples of *(s)at* co-occurring with ignoratives in negative clauses are shown in (9.170–9.172) below.

(9.170) *Hnant* *monx* *chauk* ***naonb*** *monx* ***at*** *ghad* *monl.*
call 2SG do **what** 2SG **SAT** NEG.IMP go
'Whatever (she) tells you to do, don't do it.' (Xingyu Shi, in *Oub Meinl Yaos Geud*)

(9.171) *Nes* *nex* ***jud.leb*** ***at*** *jix* *ghans.*
ask NEX **who** **SAT** NEG$_1$ see
'Everyone (she) asked said they hadn't seen (the missing shoe).' (Xingyu Shi, in *Oub Meinl Yaos Geud*)

(9.172) *Tat-hnef* *monx* *aod-bix* ***dib*** ***at*** *jix* *lis* *monl.*
this-CLF:day 2SG one-CLF:place$_1$ **which** **SAT** NEG$_1$ want go
'Don't go anywhere today.' (Haili Shi, fieldnotes) (repeated from (9.91) above)

The form *yaod(.yaod)* 'all' is rather simpler to describe. This form has two variants, *yaod.yaod* and *yaod.* There are no obvious grammatical, semantic, or pragmatic differences between the two, although the disyllabic variant is much more common in naturalistic Xong speech than the monosyllabic variant. Whether disyllabic or monosyllabic, this form will either appear immediately following a noun-phrase argument (in which case it means 'all NP') or appear as a noun-phrase argument itself (in which case it means 'all *X*', with the referent of *X* being retrievable from context). There do not appear to be any clear semantic or pragmatic differences between *yaod(.yaod)* 'all' and *(s)at* 'SAT', at least when the latter is serving as a quantifier meaning 'all'. Unlike *(s)at*, though, *yaod(.yaod)* cannot serve as a general intensifier.

(9.173) *Aod caof, ab kox.ix geud shand, ab kox.ix*
as.soon.as search also can hold ginger also can
geud bid-ghaond, ab kox.ix geud weib.jink, yaox?
hold FRT-garlic also can hold MSG right?
Aod-banb neind ***yaod.yaod*** *zhix tonb naond.*
one-CLF:some this **all** cure pain ASSOC
'As soon as I searched (on the internet for information on curing a toothache), I found out you could use ginger, you could use garlic, you could use MSG (i.e. monosodium glutamate), all of these things can be used as painkillers.' (Haili Shi, in *Tooth Conversation*)

(9.174) *Naonb.naont, gaons wel hnant, hnant aod-gheul*
thus give 1SG call call one-CLF:village
miex naond deb-ngueif, deb-npaok ***yaod.yaod***
person ASSOC DIM-unmarried.woman DIM-woman **all**
hnant lol reinb nqad xut.npeif nins leb
call come determine CLF:half.of.pair shoe COP who
naond xut.npeif.
ASSOC shoe
'So, call for me all the unmarried women, all the young women in the village. Call them to come and determine who this shoe belongs to.' (Xingyu Shi, in *Oub Meinl Yaos Geud*)

(9.175) ***Yaod.yaod*** *monl shaod, monl zhut, zhut jix*
all go try go wear.shoes wear.shoes NEG_1
yaonx, zhut jix hox.
fit.into wear.shoes NEG_1 fit
'Everyone went to try, to try on the shoe, but it didn't fit for any of them, none of them were the right size.' (Xingyu Shi, in *Oub Meinl Yaos Geud*)

(9.176) *Ndok dut ninx naond baol diul khad* ***yaod.yaod.***
weave obtain NEX ASSOC break.down complete dry **all**
'In trying to weave it, she managed to ruin all of (her sister's cloth).' (Xingyu Shi, in *Oub Meinl Yaos Geud*)

(9.177) *Hant ob-zeif* ***yaod*** *det cef det diul.*
CLF:PL NOM-thread **all** break ??? break complete
'The threads were all snapped and broken.' (Xingyu Shi, in *Oub Meinl Yaos Geud*) (repeated from (9.82) above)

9.2.3.2 The form *naond* 'ASSOC'

Two of the most common functions of the associative marker *naond* 'ASSOC' are marking certain relative clause constructions and marking certain possessive constructions. These two functions are discussed in detail in Sections 8.1.2 and 8.2.1 (respectively), but two examples of *naond* 'ASSOC' serving each function are given in (9.178–9.181) below. Examples (9.178) and (9.179) each feature a relative clause (enclosed within brackets) marked with a final *naond*, while examples (9.180) and (9.181) each feature a possessive phrase (similarly enclosed within brackets) marked with a final *naond*.

(9.178) *Hat doul leb [zeib raut* ***naond****] faonk.faob.*
still remain CLF [most good **ASSOC**] method
'There's still an even better way.' (Chenghua Long, in *Tooth Conversation*)

(9.179) *[Monx nieus* ***naond****] niax jix raut nonx.*
[2SG buy **ASSOC**] meat NEG$_1$ good eat
'The meat that you bought doesn't taste good.' (Yan Long, fieldnotes)

(9.180) *[Meib-Nhaonl* ***naond****] bod kif.*
[younger.sister-PN **ASSOC**] husband angry
'Little sister Nhaon's husband was angry.' (Xingyu Shi, in *Oub Meinl Yaos Geud*)

(9.181) *[Monx* ***naond****] aob-xand daont khauk nins*
[2SG **ASSOC**] NOM-tooth pass.through hole COP
zhus daob-ginb konk aoh?
suffer AN-bug burrow PART
'Maybe it was a bug that made that hole in your tooth?' (Chenghua Long, in *Tooth Conversation*)

The form *naond* 'ASSOC' also occasionally appears in clause-final position with no obvious function whatsoever, and in such cases consultants generally report that *naond* can be removed from the utterance in question without affecting meaning or grammaticality. The author suspects that this clause-final use of *naond* serves some sort of discourse-pragmatic or information-structural function, but unfortunately the precise nature of that function is quite opaque at present.

Examples of *naond* 'ASSOC' occurring in clause-final position with no obvious function are given in (9.182) and (9.183) below.

(9.182) *Baox, meib-Nhaonl jaod deb guaot. Monx monl*
father younger.sister-PN bad child pass 2SG go

naont loux lol, nkhed beul jix liaos monx ***naond.***
thus long.time come look 3 NEG_1 miss 2SG **ASSOC**
'Father, little sister Nhaon is a very bad child. You were gone for such a long time, but look how she didn't miss you.' (Xingyu Shi, in *Oub Meinl Yaos Geud*)

(9.183) *Beul puk diex* ***naond,*** *aod-meinl gaons aod-leb*
3 speak finish **ASSOC** one-CLF:person give one-CLF
bid-zhonx-hlod, beul monl lah.
FRT-length-bamboo 3 go PRF
'He finished speaking, gave each (sister) a length of bamboo, and then he left.' (Xingyu Shi, in *Oub Meinl Yaos Geud*)

As is the case with a number of other apparently multifunctional forms in Xong (e.g. the "semi-pronominal" form *nex/ninx* 'NEX', described in Section 7.1.4, or the verbal prefix *[d]id-* 'DID', described in Section 10.5.1), the author has no strong evidence at this time regarding whether the various functions of *naond* 'ASSOC' should be considered an example of monosemy, polysemy, or ambiguity (see Gil 2004).

9.2.3.3 The form *deb* 'DIM'

In addition to serving as a diminutive nominal prefix (see Section 5.4.2.3) and a diminutive classifier suffix (Section 6.1.3.4), the form *deb* 'DIM' can also occur in postverbal position as a quantifier meaning essentially 'a bit, a little'. In such cases *deb* 'DIM' can optionally be followed by a noun-phrase argument. A [VERB DIM] construction (i.e. one without a following noun-phrase argument) means 'to VERB a bit, to VERB a little' (see examples (9.185) and (9.186) below), while a [VERB DIM NP] construction (i.e. one with a following noun-phrase argument) means 'to VERB a little NP, to VERB a bit of NP' (see example (9.184)).

Note that when *deb* 'DIM' appears in postverbal position with a following noun-phrase argument, it appears to be quantifying that following argument rather than quantifying the preceding verb. For example, *giab* ***deb*** *niax* [stir.fry **DIM** meat] means 'to stir-fry a bit of meat' rather than **'to stir-fry meat for a bit'. This is in fact the reason that *deb* 'DIM' is not connected to either the preceding or following forms with hyphens when it occurs as a postverbal quantifier. Semantically, *deb* 'DIM' appears to be more closely associated with the following noun-phrase argument (at least when there is one) than with the preceding verb. Syntactically, though, *deb* 'DIM' appears to be more closely associated with the preceding verb, since that preceding verb is obligatory while the following noun-phrase argument is optional. Given this conflicting evidence, the most conservative course of action would seem to be to transcribe the postverbal quantifier *deb* as an independent orthographic word, not connected to either the preceding verb or the following noun phrase.

Instances of *deb* 'DIM' serving as a postverbal quantifier can be seen in (9.184–9.186) below.

(9.184) *Nheis* **deb** *reib* *ah,* *nheis* *reib* *boub-leb*
gather **DIM** vegetable PART gather vegetable 1PL-DU
dieud *hlit* *gaons* *boub* *baox* *nonx.*
boil.rice cooked.rice give 1PL father eat
'Gather some vegetables, gather some vegetables and we'll cook some rice for our father.' (Xingyu Shi, in *Oub Meinl Yaos Geud*)

(9.185) *Naont* *beul* *mb* *guaot,* *naont* *doub* *aod-hmaont*
thus 3 hurt pass thus $then_1$ one-CLF:evening
dox *deit* *raut* ***deb.***
that still good **DIM**
'So it (i.e. my tooth) really hurt, but by the evening it was a little better.' (Haili Shi, in *Tooth Conversation*)

(9.186) *Wel* *aod* *giaot* *leux* ***deb.***
1SG as.soon.as chew shatter **DIM**
'As soon as I chewed (the ginger, my tooth) cracked a little bit.' (Haili Shi, in *Tooth Conversation*)

9.2.3.4 The form *shib* 'it's'

Despite the fact that this form occurs with very high frequency in naturalistic Xong texts (though it is virtually unattested in elicited utterances produced in isolation), the precise meaning and function of *shib* 'it's' are difficult to describe. The author strongly suspects that Xong *shib* is a borrowing of the Standard Mandarin copular verb *shì* (是) or of a cognate form from another Sinitic variety, as the Xong and Sinitic forms in question display high levels of phonetic similarity and distributional overlap. However, *shib* 'it's' is only very rarely used as a copula in Xong, for which purpose the verb *nins* 'COP' is generally used instead. Rather, *shib* appears to be an idiosyncratic form which can occur in a wide variety of positions within a clause and which (like Standard Mandarin *shì*) can in many cases be translated into English as 'it is the case that' or 'it's that' (though for the sake of convenience the form in question is simply glossed as 'it's' in this grammar). Xong's *shib* is unlike Standard Mandarin's *shì*, though, in that in many other cases it occurs without any discernible meaning or function whatsoever. Given the abstract meaning and (apparently) subtle grammatical and discourse-pragmatic functions of *shib*, it is not surprising that consultants have significant difficulty describing the purpose of the form in any particular instance, and they generally report that *shib* can be removed from an utterance in which it occurs without affecting the overall meaning or grammaticality of the utterance. A proper description of this form and its functions remains a task for future scholars with access to larger Xong corpora.

Nevertheless, instances of *shib* 'it's' in use can be seen in examples (9.187–9.189) below. Many other instances of this form can be found in the text *Oub Meinl Yaos Geud* included near the end of this grammar.

(9.187) ***Shib*** *jix* *raut,* *yaox?*
it's NEG$_1$ good right?
'(The medicine's) no good, right?' (Haili Shi, in *Tooth Conversation*)

(9.188) *Naont* ***shib*** *beul* *baox* *dionb* *Niaox.nhaonl* *monl* *nghauk* *nex.*
thus **it's** 3 father lead PN go visit NEX
'And so it was that (the girls') father took Niao Nhaon to go visiting.' (Xingyu Shi, in *Oub Meinl Yaos Geud*)

(9.189) *Yul* *hnef* ***shib*** *beul* *shaod* *ghaonb.*
again CLF:day **it's** 3 try spy
'One day he decided to spy (on the person cleaning his house for him).' (Xingyu Shi, in *Oub Meinl Yaos Geud*)

9.3 Special clause types

9.3.1 Imperative clauses

Imperative clauses in Xong are relatively straightforward. Such clauses are most commonly formed by simply eliding the argument referring to the entity that the speaker wishes to carry out the action referred to by the clause's predicate (though such argument ellipsis is hardly restricted to imperative clauses in Xong; see Section 9.1.2 above for details). This argument would normally occur in preverbal position, meaning that most such imperative clauses begin with the verb itself. Examples of this can be seen in (9.190–9.193) below, where each individual imperative clause has been enclosed within brackets.

(9.190) [*Jont*]!
[sit]
'Sit!' (Haili Shi, fieldnotes)

(9.191) [*Nbaod* *beul*] *huel.zex* [*zheb* *beul* *sheub*].
[fill.in 3] or.STND [pull.out 3 leave]
'Either get it (i.e. the hole in your tooth) filled in or pull it (i.e. your tooth) out.' (Shixiang Wu, in *Tooth Conversation*)

(9.192) *Zet aoh, zet aoh, [kiak cheid], zet aoh!*
child PART child PART [open gate] child PART
'My children, my children, open the gate, my children!' (Xingyu Shi, in *Oub Meinl Yaos Geud*)

(9.193) *[Qod shonb qod mioul gaons wel nonx], [qod shonb*
[grab shrimp grab fish give 1SG eat] [grab shrimp
qod mioul gaons wel khoud], wel dionb monx ox
grab fish give 1SG consume] 1SG lead 2SG and
monx naond minl monl ah.
2SG ASSOC mother go PART
'Catch some shrimp and catch some fish for me to eat, catch some shrimp and catch some fish for me to consume, and I'll lead you back to your mother.' (Xingyu Shi, in *Oub Meinl Yaos Geud*)

However, the argument in question need not necessarily be elided. In some cases, it occurs overtly in ordinary preverbal position, as in (9.194–9.197) below (in each of these examples, each imperative clause has been enclosed within brackets and each of the arguments in question has been bolded). There appear to be few if any semantic or pragmatic differences between imperative clauses in which the argument in question is elided and imperative clauses in which it appears overtly, and the overt inclusion of said argument appears to be done mainly when its ellipsis might result in ambiguity. Such inclusion is thus particularly common when the argument in question has a first-person plural referent, as in examples (9.196) and (9.197).

(9.194) [***Monx*** *shaont monl heut kiak cheid*].
[**2SG** fast go help open gate]
'Quickly go and open the gate for (our father).' (Xingyu Shi, in *Oub Meinl Yaos Geud*)

(9.195) *Wel lis bionl monl aod-tit-deb ghat*
1SG want exit go one-CLF:time$_3$-DIM go.to
geud-zheit, [***manx oub-leb*** *jont bioud*].
place$_1$-outside [**2PL two-CLF** live home]
'I need to leave home for a little while, (but) you two stay here.' (Xingyu Shi, in *Oub Meinl Yaos Geud*)

(9.196) [***Boub-leb*** *nheis reib-nbat*], *Nhaonl.*
[**1PL-DU** gather greens-pig] PN
'Let's the two of us go gather some pig-feed, Nhaon.' (Xingyu Shi, in *Oub Meinl Yaos Geud*)

(9.197) [*Naonb.naont* ***boub-leb*** *nbanx* *leb* *banb.faox*
[thus **1PL-DU** think CLF solution
geud *beul* *daot* *id-daos* *diex*].
hold 3 kill DID-die finish]
'Then let's the two of us think of a way to kill her instead.' (Xingyu Shi, in *Oub Meinl Yaos Geud*)

Note that any of examples (9.190–9.197) above could also have a non-imperative interpretation given an appropriate context. For instance, example (9.190) could just as easily mean '(I'll) sit' as 'Sit!', and the imperative clause in example (9.195) could just as easily mean 'You two are staying here' as 'You two stay here'. This means that the imperative force in any given (affirmative) imperative clause arises simply from context, rather than from any sort of overt marking or imperative-specific argument ellipsis.[182]

In contrast, negative imperative clauses in Xong do bear an overt negative imperative marker, which is *ghad(.maons)* 'NEG.IMP' for speakers from Yankan Village and *ghaod (.maons)* 'NEG.IMP' for speakers from other parts of Fenghuang County. This marker appears following the argument referring to the entity that the speaker wishes to forbid from carrying out the action referred to by the clause's predicate (if that argument is overtly expressed, which it need not be) and preceding the clause's predicate itself. In examples (9.198–9.201) below, each negative imperative clause has been enclosed within brackets and each instance of *ghad(.maons)/ghaod(.maons)* 'NEG.IMP' has been bolded.

(9.198) [***Ghad*** *ndaot*]!
[**NEG.IMP** curse]
'Stop arguing!' (Haili Shi, fieldnotes)

(9.199) [*Mx* ***ghaod.maons*** *xeud* *ninb* *wel* *naond* *geud-neul*].
[2SG **NEG.IMP** stand at 1SG ASSOC place$_1$-front]
'Don't stand in front of me.' (Shixiang Wu, fieldnotes)

(9.200) [*Monx* ***ghad.maons*** *beux* *monx* *daut-leb* *lah*]!
[2SG **NEG.IMP** hit 2SG REFL-CLF PRF]
'Don't hit yourself!' (Haili Shi, fieldnotes)

182 Given the lack of any overt marking or imperative-specific argument ellipsis in Xong's affirmative imperative clauses, one could reasonably argue that there is no reason to reify these so-called "imperative clauses" as a distinct type of clause in Xong; rather, it is simply the case that some affirmative Xong clauses occur with imperative force (due solely to context) while others do not (again, due solely to context). The author would not necessarily disagree with this view, but affirmative imperative clauses (or at least affirmative clauses with imperative force) are still discussed separately in this Section 9.3.1 for convenience's sake. Note, though, that these claims would not apply to Xong's negative imperative clauses, which always do feature an overt negative imperative marker.

(9.201) *Monx naond jed leh, hnant monx chauk naonb*
2SG ASSOC older.sister LEH call 2SG do what
[*monx at* ***ghad*** *monl*]. *Hnant monx raons*
[2SG SAT **NEG.IMP** go] call 2SG cut.firewood
deul, [*monx at* ***ghad*** *monl*]. *Hnant monx nheis*
firewood [2SG SAT **NEG.IMP** go] call 2SG gather
reib-nbat [*monx at* ***ghad*** *monl*]. *Beul saud*
greens-pig [2SG SAT **NEG.IMP** go] 3 invite
monx chauk naonb [*monx* ***ghad*** *monl*], *jont bioud zaod.*
2SG do what [2SG **NEG.IMP** go] sit home just
Whatever your older sister tells you to do, don’t do it. If she tells you to cut firewood, don’t do it. If she tells you to gather pig-feed, don’t do it. Whatever she tells you to do, don’t do it, just stay at home.’ (Xingyu Shi, in *Oub Meinl Yaos Geud*)

9.3.2 Interrogative clauses

Xong speakers use a variety of methods to signal that a particular clause is intended to have interrogative force. Content questions are signaled through the use of ignorative forms (see Section 9.3.2.1 below), while polar questions are typically signaled through the use of either the [C NEG C] construction (Section 9.3.2.2) or one of several clause-final interrogative markers (Section 9.3.2.3). In addition, it appears that certain interrogative clauses which are overtly marked as such through one of these methods may also have distinct intonational properties compared to non-interrogative clauses, and in a minority of cases it appears that interrogative force may in fact be signaled solely via intonation. Unfortunately, the author’s data on interrogative intonation in Xong is still insufficient to allow for any serious comments on this topic, but see Section 3.6 for some discussion of Xong intonation in general.

9.3.2.1 Interrogative clauses with ignorative forms

Content questions (as opposed to polar questions) in Xong are formed through the use of ignorative forms. These forms, which constitute a small, closed set in Xong, serve functions similar to those of both interrogative and indefinite pronouns in (for example) European languages, with the interpretation of a given ignorative form as interrogative versus indefinite depending largely on context. When serving in an interrogative capacity, Xong’s ignorative forms always occur in situ rather than in any displaced position.

The interrogative and indefinite functions of each ignorative form in Xong are described most thoroughly in Section 7.3 of this grammar. This Section 9.3.2.1 merely provides two examples of each ignorative form occurring in an interrogative context in order to facilitate comparison with the other interrogative clause types described in Sections 9.3.2.2 and 9.3.2.3 further below. The specific ignorative forms exemplified in this section include the ignorative nouns *naonb* 'what, something' and *(dib.)leb/(jud.)leb* 'who, someone', the ignorative demonstrative *dib/dof* 'which, some(thing/one)', and the ignorative quantifiers *mins* 'how many, a few' and *haut/hot* 'how much, so much'. Note that each example in this section is taken from Section 7.3, where, again, Xong's ignorative forms and their interrogative functions are discussed in much more detail.

(9.202) *Monx npof nonx* ***naonb****?*
2SG desire eat **what**
'What do you feel like eating?' (Haili Shi, fieldnotes)

(9.203) *Nins* ***naonb*** *nggaob?*
COP **what** medicine
'What kind of medicine was it?' (Shixiang Wu, in *Tooth Conversation*)

(9.204) *Nins* ***dib.leb*** *chauk naond?*
COP **who** do ASSOC
'Who did this?' (Haili Shi, fieldnotes)

(9.205) *Monx aod-ngonl daob-guk, monx at lis nes*
2SG one-CLF:animate AN-frog 2SG SAT want find.a.wife
npaok, ***jud.leb*** *lol kint ninb monx raut leh?*
woman **who** come willing marry 2SG good LEH
'You're (just) a frog, and you want to find a wife, but who would be willing to marry you?' (Xingyu Shi, in *Deb Guk Ronf*)

(9.206) *Naont mx geud gians* ***dib*** *zhaut?*
thus 2SG hold CLF:kind$_1$ **which** cure
'So which (folk remedy) did you use to fix (your tooth)?' (Shixiang Wu, in *Tooth Conversation*)

(9.207) *Ob-ras ninb* ***dof****? Monx tout wel naond bat* ***dof****?*
NOM-comb at **which** 2SG pick.up 1SG ASSOC put **which**
'Where is the comb? Where did you put (that comb) of mine?' (Xingyu Shi, in *Oub Meinl Yaos Geud*)

(9.208) *Monx naond deb mex* ***mins****-jut?*
2SG ASSOC child exist **how.many**-CLF:year
'How old is your child?' (Haili Shi, fieldnotes)

(9.209) *Aod-hant* *niax* *neind* *lis* ***mins**-shauk* *daont*
one-CLF:PL meat this want **how.many**-CLF:yuan money
aod-gaonb?
one-CLF:catty
'How many *yuan* (unit of currency) is this meat per catty (unit of mass)?' (Shixiang Wu, fieldnotes)

(9.210) *Monx* *mex* ***hot*** *shanb?*
2SG exist **how.much** tall
'How tall are you?' (Haili Shi, fieldnotes)

(9.211) *Monx* *heut* *beul* *diex* ***hot*** *loux* *ah?*
2SG help 3 finish **how.much** long.time PART
'How long were you working for him?' (Qiusheng Long, in *Ngel.kanx*)

Xong also contains two polymorphemic ignorative forms that are derived from its monomorphemic ignoratives. The first of these is *chauk-naonb* 'why' (lit. [do-what]), which is sometimes realized as *hauk-naonb* in fast or casual speech. As examples (9.212–9.214) suggest, *chauk-naonb* 'why' can occur in a variety of positions within a Xong clause, though there do not appear to be any clear semantic, pragmatic, or information-structural differences among these various positions. Note that examples (9.212–9.214) below, like examples (9.202–9.211) above, have been repeated from Section 7.3.

(9.212) ***Chauk-naonb*** *monx* *lis* *hneind* *aod-xeub* *ob-deud-guk?*
do-what 2SG want wear one-CLF:body NOM-skin-frog
'Why would you want to wear a frog skin?' (Xingyu Shi, in *Deb Guk Ronf*)

(9.213) *Mx* ***chauk-naonb*** *xaont* *xox* *puk* *Xonb?*
2SG **do-what** wish study speak Xong
'Why do you want to learn Xong?' (Shixiang Wu, fieldnotes)

(9.214) *Monx* *dand* *neind* ***hauk-naonb,*** *Nhaonl?*
2SG arrive this **do-what** PN
'What did you come here for, Nhaon?' (Xingyu Shi, in *Oub Meinl Yaos Geud*)

The second such form is *chauk-dib/chauk-dof* 'how' (lit. [do-which]), which is sometimes realized as *hauk-dib/hauk-dof* in fast or casual speech. This form is exemplified in (9.215) and (9.216) below, which have also been copied from Section 7.3.

(9.215) *Aod-leb* *reib-yeus* *neind* ***chauk-dib*** *giab?*
one-CLF vegetable-cooked.meat this **do-which** stir.fry
'How do you cook this dish?' (Shixiang Wu, fieldnotes)

(9.216)	*Wel*	*lis*	***chauk-dib***	*chauk?*
	1SG	want	**do-which**	do

'How should I do it?' (unknown Xong consultant, fieldnotes)

9.3.2.2 Interrogative clauses with the [C NEG C] construction

One of the more common ways of forming polar questions (never content questions) in Xong is through the use of the [C NEG C] construction (here 'C' stands for 'clause'). In this construction, a clause is copied, with any preverbal material in the second instance of the copied clause being elided and the negative marker *(j)ix* 'NEG_1' (see Section 9.2.2.1) being inserted in clause-initial position within that second instance of the copied clause. Examples of this can be seen in (9.217) and (9.218) below, where each instance of the [C NEG C] construction has been enclosed within brackets.

(9.217)	*Naont*	*[raut*	*jix*	*raut]?*
	thus	[good	NEG_1	good]

'So did (the ginger) work (to cure your toothache)?' (Shixiang Wu, in *Tooth Conversation*)

(9.218)	"*[Nins*	*monx*	*naond*	*jix*	*nins]?*"	"*Nins.*"
	[COP	2SG	ASSOC	NEG_1	COP]	COP

'(The landlord asked the girl:) "Are (these shoes) yours?" (She answered:) "They are."' (Xingyu Shi, in *Oub Meinl Yaos Geud*)

In example (9.218) above, note that the postverbal argument *monx naond* [2SG ASSOC] 'yours' has been elided from the second instance of the copied clause. Such elision of postverbal material is in fact the norm in the [C NEG C] construction. In this construction, typically either (i) all postverbal material will be elided from the second instance of the copied clause, but will not be elided from the first, or (ii) all postverbal material will be elided from the first instance of the copied clause, but will not be elided from the second (this is in addition to the obligatory elision of any preverbal material in the second instance of the copied clause). An example of a [C NEG C] construction in which all postverbal material has been elided from the first (but not the second) instance of the copied clause is shown in (9.219) below.

(9.219)	*Monx*	*[lis*	*jix*	*lis*	*hauk*	*jeud]?*
	2SG	[want	NEG_1	want	drink	alcohol]

'Do you want to drink some alcohol?' (unknown Xong consultant, fieldnotes)

However, while this elision of postverbal material is quite common in the [C NEG C] construction, it is not obligatory. This can be seen by comparing the two pairs of synonymous examples below, in which the relevant postverbal material has been bolded wherever it occurs (i.e. wherever it has not been elided).

(9.220) *Monx* [*dand* ***neind*** *jix* *dand*], *Nhaonl?*
2SG [arrive **this** NEG_1 arrive] PN
'Have you been here before, Nhaon?' (Xingyu Shi, in *Oub Meinl Yaos Geud*)

(9.221) *Monx* [*dand* ***neind*** *jix* *dand* ***neind***], *Nhaonl?*
2SG [arrive **this** NEG_1 arrive **this**] PN
'Have you been here before, Nhaon?' (Xingyu Shi, in *Oub Meinl Yaos Geud*) (same as (9.220) above)

(9.222) *Tat-hneb* *mx* [*laut* *jix* *laut* ***Zhes***]?
this-CLF:day 2SG [descend NEG_1 descend **Fenghuang**]
'Are you going to Fenghuang today?' (Shixiang Wu, fieldnotes)

(9.223) *Tat-hneb* *mx* [*laut* ***Zhes*** *jix* *laut*
this-CLF:day 2SG [descend **Fenghuang** NEG_1 descend
Zhes]?
Fenghuang]
'Are you going to Fenghuang today?' (Shixiang Wu, fieldnotes) (same as (9.222) above)

This [C NEG C] construction is also the standard way of expressing indirect polar interrogatives in Xong, as is shown in example (9.224) below.

(9.224) *Jud* *nianl* [*nins* *daob-ginb* *jix* *nins*].
NEG_2 know [COP AN-bug NEG_1 COP]
'(We) don't know if it's bugs or not.' (Shixiang Wu, fieldnotes)

There are no forms equivalent to English *yes* or *no* in Xong. Instead, a response to a [C NEG C] question will feature the verb that occurs immediately after the negative marker *(j)ix* 'NEG_1' within the question itself. An affirmative response to a univerbal [C NEG C] question will consist solely of that verb, while a negative response to such a question will consist of that verb preceded by *(j)ix* 'NEG_1'. Examples of [C NEG C] questions and affirmative and negative responses to them are given in (9.225–9.230) below.

(9.225) *Beul-god* [*nonx* *jix* *nonx* *niax-guoud*]?
3-PL [eat NEG_1 eat meat-dog]
'Do they (i.e. Americans) eat dog meat?' (unknown Xong consultant, fieldnotes)

(9.226) *Nonx.*
eat
'Yes, (they do eat dog meat).' (unknown Xong consultant, fieldnotes)

(9.227) *Jix* *nonx.*
NEG_1 eat
'No, (they don't eat dog meat).' (unknown Xong consultant, fieldnotes)

(9.228) *Tat-hnef* *monx* [*nieus* *jix* *nieus*]?
this-CLF:day 2SG [buy NEG_1 buy]
'Will you buy (vegetables at the market) today?' (Chenghua Long, fieldnotes)

(9.229) *Nieus.*
buy
'Yes, (I will buy them).' (Haili Shi, fieldnotes)

(9.230) *Jix* *nieus.*
NEG_1 buy
'No, (I won't buy them).' (Haili Shi, fieldnotes)

Similar responses are also used for polar questions formed via other means in Xong, including those formed via clause-final interrogative markers (see Section 9.3.2.3 below).

9.3.2.3 Interrogative clauses with clause-final interrogative markers

Several clause-final interrogative markers can be used to form polar questions (never content questions) in Xong. One of these (*yoh/yah* 'QP.NTRL') appears to belong to the class of particles (see Section 9.2.1 above) based on its phonological form and syntactic positioning possibilities, but the other clause-final interrogative markers discussed in this section (*yaox* 'right?' and *xaond* 'not yet') do not, appearing instead to be idiosyncratic forms that do not easily fit into any larger lexical category. The forms discussed in this Section 9.3.2.3 are thus more of a loose set grouped together on the basis of certain functional similarities than any sort of strictly defined lexical category. Note that this section is intended merely to provide a non-exhaustive look at some of Xong's more frequent clause-final interrogative markers and the specific sorts of interrogative notions that they signal, and there may well be other clause-final interrogative markers in the language that the author has not yet encountered.

The particle *yoh/yah* 'QP.NTRL' (from 'question particle – neutral') is so glossed because it is the most pragmatically neutral clause-final interrogative marker in Xong, in the sense that an interrogative clause marked with this form does not imply any expectation of either an affirmative or a negative answer. There are no noticeable semantic or pragmatic differences between an interrogative clause marked with *yoh/yah* 'QP.NTRL' and one formed through the use of the [C NEG C] construction described in Section 9.3.2.2 above.

This form occurs in two phonological variants, *yoh* and *yah*. The former variant is more common in the speech of the author's primary consultants, but the two variants are apparently in free variation and both are used by each primary consultant. Examples of this form in use can be seen in (9.231–9.234) below. While the form in question occurs as *yoh* in examples (9.231–9.233) and as *yah* in example (9.234), consultants report that either variant could occur in any of these examples without affecting the meaning or pragmatic import of the example as a whole.

(9.231) *Nins nchaot* ***yoh?***
COP stick.in **QP.NTRL**
'Did (the chicken foot) get stuck (in the hole in your tooth)?' (Chenghua Long, in *Tooth Conversation*)

(9.232) *Mx lis nhaons wel ml* ***yoh?***
2SG want with 1SG go **QP.NTRL**
'Do you want to go with me?' (Shixiang Wu, fieldnotes)

(9.233) *Zhut gil nanx lis zhut aod-nzaut-deb yut yut,*
reach tea only want reach one-CLF:pinch-DIM few few
nins naont ***yoh?***
COP thus **QP.NTRL**
'When (you're) adding tea leaves, (you) only want to add a single pinch, is that right?' (Chenghua Long, fieldnotes)

(9.234) *Tat-hneb mx laut Zhes* ***yah?***
this-CLF:day 2SG descend Fenghuang **QP.NTRL**
'Are you going to Fenghuang today?' (Shixiang Wu, fieldnotes)

The form *yaox* 'right?' is like Xong's particles (see Section 9.2.1 as well as earlier in this section) in that it always appears in clause-final position, but it is unlike those particles in that it bears a tone. This form marks a polar interrogative clause to which the speaker strongly expects an affirmative response, and it thus serves a very similar purpose in Xong as the tag question ... *right?* does in English.

(9.235) *Beul nes: "Niaox.meib, nins monx geud* ***yaox?"***
3 ask PN COP 2SG sweep **right?**
'He asked: "Niao Mei, it's you who's been doing the sweeping, right?"' (Xingyu Shi, in *Oub Meinl Yaos Geud*)

(9.236) *Monx dand neind jix dand neind, Nhaonl? Dut*
2SG arrive this NEG$_1$ arrive this PN obtain
dand neind ***yaox****?*
arrive this **right?**
'Have you been here before, Nhaon? You've been here before, right?' (Xingyu Shi, in *Oub Meinl Yaos Geud*)

(9.237) *Aod-banb neind nins zeib jex.bieb,*
one-CLF:some this COP most simple.and.convenient
zeib jex.jef naond ***yaox****?*
most quick.and.easy ASSOC **right?**
'These (folk remedies) are the simplest, the easiest, right?' (Haili Shi, in *Tooth Conversation*) (repeated from (9.32) above)

(9.238) *Naont hant daob-ginb doub zhaok bionl* ***yaox****?*
thus CLF:PL AN-bug then$_1$ fall exit **right**?
'So then the bugs just fall out, right?' (Shixiang Wu, in *Tooth Conversation*)

Finally, the negative marker *xaond* 'not yet' can also serve as a clause-final interrogative marker. Even when doing so, *xaond* is unlike Xong's particles in that it still bears a tone. When serving as a clause-final interrogative marker, *xaond* entails (or at least very strongly implies) that the speaker has reason to believe that the action (or event, or state, etc.) about which the interrogative clause is inquiring should have (or at least may well have) already occurred (see also Section 9.2.2.3).

(9.239) *Monx nonx hlit* ***xaond****?*
2SG eat cooked.rice **not.yet**
'Have you eaten yet?' (Yan Long, fieldnotes)

(9.240) *Tat-hneb mx laut Zhes* ***xaond****?*
this-CLF:day 2SG descend Fenghuang **not.yet**
'Did you go to Fenghuang today (as you told me you were planning to)?' (Shixiang Wu, fieldnotes)

(9.241) *"Monx xaond tad bioud leh, naont monx chauk*
2SG not.yet establish home LEH thus 2SG do
wel naond nheinx. Monx tad bioud
1SG ASSOC daughter.in.law 2SG establish home
xaond*?" "Wel xaond tad."*
not.yet 1SG not.yet establish
'(The landlord asked:) "If you haven't married yet, then you can be my daughter-in-law. Have you married yet?" (The girl answered:) "I haven't."' (Xingyu Shi, in *Oub Meinl Yaos Geud*)

For information on responses to polar interrogative clauses in Xong, see Section 9.3.2.2 above.

9.3.3 Comparative clauses

Fenghuang Xong features two primary ways of expressing comparison. The first of these involves a clause featuring either the non-verbal comparative marker *ghaod* 'more' or a complement phrase (for details on the latter, see further below in this section), while the second involves a clause featuring the verb *bit/bix* 'to compare' (with *ghaod* 'more' optionally appearing in the same clause as well). This section discusses both of these constructions in detail, and it also provides briefer discussions of Xong's negative comparative, equative, and superlative constructions.

The first type of comparative clause to be discussed here can be either univerbal or multiverbal, but it will obligatorily feature either the non-verbal comparative marker *ghaod* 'more' or a complement phrase, with said complement phrase serving to express the degree or amount of difference between the subject of comparison and the standard of comparison. In either case, the subject of comparison occurs initially, where it is followed first by the verb (or verb and following argument, or multiverbal construction) expressing the quality or property that is being compared, and then by the standard of comparison. If the clause contains *ghaod* 'more', that form will occur between the subject of comparison and the following verb (see examples (9.242) and (9.244)). If the clause instead contains a complement phrase, that complement phrase will occur after the standard of comparison (see examples (9.243) and (9.245)). In the four examples below, each instance of *ghaod* 'more' and each complement phrase has been bolded.

(9.242) *Wel* ***ghaod*** *liox beul.*
1SG **more** big 3
'I'm older than him.' (Chenghua Long, fieldnotes)

(9.243) *Wel liox beul* ***bub-jut.***
1SG big 3 **three-CLF:year**
'I'm three years older than him.' (Chenghua Long, fieldnotes)

(9.244) *Beul* ***ghaod*** *nonx hliob wel.*
3 **more** eat many 1SG
'He ate more than me.' (Shixiang Wu, fieldnotes)

(9.245) *Beul nonx hliob wel* ***aod-zhet.***
3 eat many 1SG **one-CLF:bowl**
'He ate one more bowl (of rice) than me.' (Shixiang Wu, fieldnotes)

Attempts to construct similar comparative clauses that feature neither *ghaod* 'more' nor a complement phrase are judged ungrammatical by consultants, as examples (9.246) and (9.247) show.

(9.246) **Wel liox beul.*
1SG big 3
(intended: 'I'm older than him.')

(9.247) **Beul nonx hliob wel.*
3 eat many 1SG
(intended: 'He ate more than me.')

The complement phrase that expresses the degree or amount of difference between the subject of comparison and the standard of comparison is typically either a numeral-classifier phrase, as in examples (9.243) and (9.245) above, or a phrase containing the verb *hliof/hliob* 'many', as in examples (9.248) and (9.249) below.

(9.248) *Wel liox beul* ***hliof hint****.*
1SG big 3 **many very**
'I'm much older than him.' (Chenghua Long, fieldnotes)

(9.249) *Beul ngaod wel* ***hliof guaot****.*
3 short 1SG **many pass**
'She's much shorter than me.' (Haili Shi, fieldnotes)

A variety of additional comparative clauses of the same type (i.e. with either *ghaod* 'more' or a complement phrase) are given in (9.250–9.254) below. Note that in examples (9.252–9.254) in particular, the argument referring to the standard of comparison has been elided. The author strongly suspects that the argument referring to the subject of comparison in such a comparative clause could be elided as well given an appropriate enough discourse context, but no clear examples of such clauses occur in his corpus.

(9.250) *Beul* ***ghaod*** *faob xonx hliof wel.*
3 **more** draw attractive many 1SG
'She draws much better than me.' (Chenghua Long, fieldnotes)

(9.251) *Aod-ngonl neind* ***ghaod*** *nqat ninx aod-ngonl dox.*
one-CLF:animate this **more** fear NEX one-CLF:animate that
'This (dog) is even more afraid of people than that one.' (Haili Shi, fieldnotes)

(9.252) *Wel naond deb* ***ghaod*** *yanb ninb bioud nkhed ndeud.*
1SG ASSOC child **more** like at home look writing
'My child likes reading at home more (than at school).' (Chenghua Long, fieldnotes)

(9.253) *Shand* ***ghaod*** *raut deb.*
ginger **more** good DIM
'The ginger was a little better (at stopping the pain in my tooth).' (Haili Shi, in *Tooth Conversation*)

(9.254) *Niaox.nhaonl, deb-geud, Niaox.nhaonl leh,* ***ghaod***
PN DIM-younger.sibling PN LEH **more**
lox.shif, ***ghaod*** *zhonk.cheinf, liaos baox naond guaot.*
honest **more** devoted miss father ASSOC pass
'But Niao Nhaon, the younger sister, as for her, she was more honest (than her older sister), more devoted (than her older sister), and she missed her father greatly.' (Xingyu Shi, in *Oub Meinl Yaos Geud*)

A second type of comparative clause in Xong obligatorily involves a multiverbal construction (see Chapter 12) featuring the verb *bit/bix* 'to compare' (this form is *bix* for speakers from Shanjiang Town and *bit* for speakers from other parts of Fenghuang County), with the comparative marker *ghaod* 'more' optionally appearing in the same clause as well. Note that the form *bit/bix* is almost certainly a borrowing of the Standard Mandarin form *bǐ* (比), which can also function as either a verb meaning 'to compare' or as a comparative marker, or of a cognate form from another Sinitic variety. Constituent ordering in comparative clauses featuring *bit/bix* 'to compare' is as follows: (i) an argument expressing the subject of comparison, (ii) the verb *bit/bix*, (iii) an argument expressing the standard of comparison, (iv) the comparative marker *ghaod* 'more' (optional), and finally (v) the verb (or verb and following argument, or multiverbal construction) that expresses the quality or property that is being compared. Examples of such comparative clauses can be seen in (9.255–9.261) below, where each instance of the verb *bit/bix* 'to compare' has been bolded.[183]

183 In examples (9.255–9.261), the comparative marker *ghaod* 'more' occasionally appears within parentheses, reflecting the fact that it can optionally be inserted into the example in question without affecting meaning or grammaticality. However, in examples (9.256), (9.257), and (9.261), the absence of *ghaod* should not be interpreted as implying that it cannot be inserted into the example in question; instead, it reflects the fact that the author did not have the opportunity to test *ghaod*-insertability in these examples while in the field.

(9.255) *Wel* ***bix*** *beul (ghaod) liox.*
1SG **compare** 3 (more) big
'I'm older than him.' (Chenghua Long, fieldnotes) (cf. example (9.242) above)

(9.256) *Wel* ***bix*** *beul liox bub-jut.*
1SG **compare** 3 big three-CLF:year
'I'm three years older than him.' (Chenghua Long, fieldnotes) (cf. example (9.243) above)

(9.257) *Deb-nint* ***bit*** *deb-npaok ngaod aod-bieid.*
DIM-man **compare** DIM-woman short one-CLF:head
'The boy is a head shorter than the girl.' (Shixiang Wu, fieldnotes)

(9.258) *Beul* ***bix*** *wel (ghaod) huaob xonx hliof.*
3 **compare** 1SG (more) draw attractive many
'She draws much better than me.' (Chenghua Long, fieldnotes) (cf. example (9.250) above)

(9.259) *Aod-ngonl neind* ***bit*** *aod-ngonl dox*
one-CLF:animate this **compare** one-CLF:animate that
(ghaod) nqat ninx.
(more) fear NEX
'This (dog) is even more afraid of people than that one.' (Haili Shi, fieldnotes) (cf. example (9.251) above)

(9.260) *Beut nggueb* ***bit*** *sheit zok.nief (ghaod) raut*
lie.down sleep **compare** write homework (more) good
nghauk.zaol.
play
'Sleeping is more fun than doing homework.' (unknown Xong consultant, fieldnotes)

(9.261) *Wel npaok* ***bit*** *beul npaok xonx guaot.*
1SG woman **compare** 3 woman attractive pass
'My wife is much prettier than his.' (unknown Xong consultant, fieldnotes)

There are no obvious functional differences between comparative clauses featuring *ghaod* 'more' or a complement phrase on the one hand and comparative clauses featuring *bit/bix* 'to compare' on the other, but the former are much more common in the author's corpus of naturalistic Xong speech than the latter. For instance, in the two texts included near the end of this grammar, the non-verbal comparative marker *ghaod* 'more' appears eighteen times while the verb *bit/bix* 'to compare' does not even appear once.

Negative comparative notions are expressed using a multiverbal construction that involves (i) the negative marker *(j)ix* 'NEG$_1$', (ii) the verb *diaos* 'to catch up to', (iii) an argument expressing the standard of comparison, and (iv) another verb expressing the quality or property that is being compared, in that order. Examples of this can be seen in (9.262–9.264) below, in which each instance of the verb *diaos* 'to catch up to' has been bolded.

(9.262) *It,* *at* *jix* ***diaos*** *shand* *raut.*
SPRS SAT NEG$_1$ **catch.up.to** ginger good
'Huh, (the medicine) isn't as good as ginger.' (Shixiang Wu, in *Tooth Conversation*)

(9.263) *Nianl-seinb* *eit* *jix* ***diaos*** *toux.faonk.faol*
know-live still NEG$_1$ **catch.up.to** traditional.method
raut *yaox?*
good right?
'(Now you've) learned that (modern medicine) still isn't as good as the old folk remedies, huh?' (Shixiang Wu, in *Tooth Conversation*)

(9.264) *Nek-deb-nek-giad* *chauk* *naonb* *nanx* *ix*
mother-child-mother-grandchild do what only NEG$_1$
diaos *nex* *shaont.*
catch.up.to NEX fast
'Mothers with (young) children can't do anything as fast as other people.' (Chenghua Long, fieldnotes)

To express equative notions (that is to say, notions like *X is as good as Y*, *X runs as fast as Y*, etc.), Xong speakers use the form *aod.sheit* 'the same'.[184] If the standard of comparison is overtly expressed (and in naturalistic speech, it frequently is not), that standard occurs immediately following either the verb *ox/ux* 'and' or the verb *nhaons* 'with' (see Section 8.3), with the entire [*ox/ux* STANDARD] or [*nhaons* STANDARD] constituent preceding *aod.sheit* 'the same'. Examples of clauses expressing equative notions are given in (9.265–9.268) below.

184 The author suspects that *aod.sheit* 'the same' was originally a numeral-classifier phrase (see Section 6.1.2) that has since become lexicalized, possibly due to influence from Sinitic. Note that the form meaning 'the same' in Standard Mandarin is *yīyàng* (一样), which is morphologically [one-CLF:kind], and note also that the first syllable of Xong *aod.sheit* 'the same' is homophonous with *aod* 'one'. However, consultants report that the syllable *sheit* cannot be productively used as a classifier in Xong. In isolation, *sheit* can only mean 'to write', which is perhaps nothing more than accidental homophony.

(9.265) *Wel giab reib-yeus* ***ux/nhaons*** *monx*
1SG stir.fry vegetable-cooked.meat **and/with** 2SG
aod.sheit *raut nonx.*
the.same good eat
'My cooking's just as good as yours.' (Chenghua Long, fieldnotes)

(9.266) *Beul* ***ox/nhaons*** *wel* ***aod.sheit*** *zhaons.*
3 **and/with** 1SG **the.same** fat
'She's as fat as I am.' (unknown Xong consultant, fieldnotes)

(9.267) *Nex niab geud nhex sheub yol dions*
NEX say hold pull.out leave again plant
del manx xanb nins ***aod.sheit*** *raut.*
CLF:rigid.length REL new COP **the.same** good
'They say you can have (your old tooth) pulled out and then put a new (tooth) in, and the new tooth will be just as good as your old one.' (Chenghua Long, in *Tooth Conversation*)

(9.268) *Nins* ***aod.sheit,*** *yaox?*
COP **the.same** right?
'(The new tooth) will be just as good, huh?' (Shixiang Wu, in *Tooth Conversation*)

Finally, superlative notions are expressed through the use of the non-verbal superlative marker *zeib* 'most', which is presumably a borrowing of Standard Mandarin *zuì* (最) 'most' or of a cognate form from another Sinitic variety. Examples of this form in use can be seen in (9.269–9.272) below.

(9.269) *Beul* ***zeib*** *shanb.*
3 **most** tall
'He's the tallest.' (Haili Shi, fieldnotes)

(9.270) *Wel* ***zeib*** *nonx hliof.*
1SG **most** eat many
'I eat the most.' (Chenghua Long, fieldnotes)

(9.271) *Mx* ***zeib*** *huaob xonx.*
2SG **most** draw attractive
'You draw the best.' (Shixiang Wu, fieldnotes)

(9.272) *Aod-banb* *neind* *nins* ***zeib*** *jex.bieb,*
one-CLF:some this COP **most** simple.and.convenient
zeib *jex.jef* *naond* *yaox?*
most quick.and.easy ASSOC right?
'These (folk remedies) are the simplest, the easiest, right?' (Haili Shi, in *Tooth Conversation*) (repeated from (9.32) above)

9.3.4 "Passive" clauses

Yu (2011: 328–337) discusses a so-called "passive marker" /ʈo^{22}/ in Aizhai Xong, which at first glance appears to have grammaticalized from a verb meaning 'to suffer'. A cognate form is found in Fenghuang Xong (as well as in many other Xong varieties), and this Fenghuang cognate is phonologically *zhus* for speakers from Yankan Village or Shanjiang Town and *zhaus* for speakers from La'ershan Town and its surrounding villages (with the exception of Yankan).

This form does indeed often appear to function as a fairly canonical passive (i.e. valency-decreasing) marker, in that it occurs in semantically transitive clauses in which (i) the more patient-like argument occurs preceding any verbs in the clause, (ii) *zhus/zhaus* 'to suffer' occurs following that more patient-like argument, (iii) the more agent-like argument is either not expressed at all or is expressed immediately following *zhus/zhaus* in an apparently oblique-like fashion, and (iv) the verb that appears to express the main predication of the clause occurs following that more agent-like argument (or simply following *zhus/zhaus* itself, if no agent-like argument occurs in the clause).[185] Examples of this can be seen in (9.273–9.277) below. Note that the constituent ordering in these examples differs from that in a typical pragmatically neutral, univerbal, semantically transitive clause, where the more agent-like argument would precede the verb and the more patient-like argument would follow it (see Section 9.1.1).

(9.273) *Beul* ***zhus*** *hnant* *monl* *lah.*
3 **suffer** call go PRF
'He was told to go.' (Haili Shi, fieldnotes)

(9.274) *Miant* *bioud* ***zhaus*** *zheinb.fux* *faol.kuanx.*
3PL home **suffer** government be.fined
'Their family was fined by the government (for having too many children).' (unknown Xong consultant, fieldnotes) (repeated from (9.101) above)

185 Since the behavior of grammaticalized syntactic roles like SUBJECT and AGENT (see Section 9.1.1) with respect to multiverbal constructions in general and complement-taking verbs in particular is still not entirely understood, this section frames its discussion in terms of purely semantic roles like "agent" and "patient".

(9.275) *Dand yes.web naond bioud, ghad* ***zhus***
arrive landlord ASSOC home then$_2$ **suffer**
yes.web tauk dut leh.
landlord pick.up obtain LEH
'(The shoe was blown by the wind) to the landlord's home, where it was picked up by the landlord.' (Xingyu Shi, in *Oub Meinl Yaos Geud*)

(9.276) *Shaod zhut beul deb-geud naond, ghad*
try reach 3 DIM-younger.sibling ASSOC then$_2$
zhus *beul jed id-lias,* ***zhus*** *Niaox.meib lias.*
suffer 3 older.sister DID-switch **suffer** PN switch
'(So the father) examined the younger sister's (length of bamboo), the one that had been switched by her older sister, switched by Niao Mei.' (Xingyu Shi, in *Oub Meinl Yaos Geud*)

(9.277) *Seink.cheinf beul deit nins* ***zhus*** *daob-ginb konk,*
naturally 3 still COP **suffer** AN-bug burrow
ix konk beul hauk-dib dut daont?
NEG$_1$ burrow 3 do-which obtain pass.through
'Well, logically, it must be that there's a bug (in your tooth), otherwise how would there be a hole there?' (Chenghua Long, in *Tooth Conversation*)

From these and other similar examples it can be seen that Xong clauses containing *zhus/zhaus* 'to suffer' are often best translated into passive clauses in other languages (e.g. English), and also that *zhus/zhaus* shows a great deal of functional overlap with unambiguous passive markers in other languages. Nevertheless, there are at least four pieces of evidence that suggest that *zhus/zhaus* is in fact better analyzed as a complement-taking verb meaning 'to suffer, to be adversely affected by' than as a grammaticalized passive marker (cf. Enfield's [2007: 438–441] analysis of the Lao verb *thùùk5* 'to strike, to come into contact with'). The author will here argue that Fenghuang Xong actually lacks a canonical passive marker, with passive-like notions instead being expressed through the use of said complement-taking verb (or through the use of a syntactic frame in which the agent-like argument is elided and the patient-like argument appears in preverbal position; see Section 9.1.3.1 for details).

First, several examples have been found in which the argument preceding *zhus/zhaus* 'to suffer' is not itself the most patient-like argument in the clause, but is rather the possessor of the most patient-like argument. This can be seen in examples (9.278–9.280) below. In example (9.278), the argument *beul* '3' precedes *zhus/zhaus* and serves as the possessor of the argument *aod-del xand* [one-CLF:rigid.length tooth] 'a tooth', which is itself the most patient-like argument in the clause.

(9.278) *Beul* ***zhaus*** *nex* *beux* *det* *aod-del* *xand.*
3 **suffer** NEX hit break one-CLF:rigid.length tooth
'He had a tooth knocked out by someone.' (Shixiang Wu, fieldnotes)

Similarly, in example (9.279), the argument *beul* '3' precedes *zhus/zhaus* and serves as the possessor of the argument *beul naond did.daont* [3 ASSOC money] 'his money', which is itself the most patient-like argument in the clause.

(9.279) *Beul* ***zhaus*** *giox.dauk* *nians* *beul* *naond* *did.daont.*
3 **suffer** thief steal 3 ASSOC money
'He had his money stolen by a thief.' (Lijun Wu, fieldnotes)

In example (9.280), the argument *wel* '1SG' precedes *zhus/zhaus* and serves as the possessor of the argument *beub* 'quilt', which is itself the most patient-like argument in the clause.

(9.280) *Wel* ***zhus*** *teif* *beub!*
1SG **suffer** steal quilt
'My quilt's been stolen!' (Chenghua Long, fieldnotes)

What the arguments preceding *zhus/zhaus* in examples (9.278–9.280) above – and indeed, in examples (9.273–9.277) further above as well – all have in common is not that they serve as semantic patients, but rather that their referents are all adversely affected by the verb that occurs after *zhus/zhaus*. This semantic effect is more similar to what one would expect from a complement-taking verb meaning 'to suffer' than the purely grammatical effect one would expect from a canonical passive marker.

Second, other examples have been attested in which two roughly equally patient-like arguments occur in a clause with *zhus/zhaus* 'to suffer', with one of those arguments preceding *zhus/zhaus* and the other occurring later in the clause following another verb. This can be seen in (9.281) and (9.282) below, where each patient-like argument in each example has been enclosed within brackets. Note that such clauses can optionally feature a third, more agent-like argument as well, like *daob-maonl* [AN-small.flying.insect] 'mosquitos' in (9.282).

(9.281) [*Pil.jeux*] ***zhaus*** *jaont* [*nggaob*]*!*
[beer] **suffer** put [medicine]
'The beer's been drugged!' (Shixiang Wu, fieldnotes)

(9.282) [*Wel*] ***zhus*** *daob-maonl* *ghab* *aont*
[1SG] **suffer** AN-small.flying.insect bite swell

[*ghaob-mins-diaond*].
[NOM-how.many-CLF:lump]
'I've been bitten by a whole bunch of mosquitos.' (Haili Shi, fieldnotes)

This ability to occur in clauses with two highly patient-like arguments would be rather unusual for a canonical passive marker, but it would not be at all unusual for a complement-taking verb meaning 'to suffer' (since one patient-like argument could occur in the matrix clause and the other in the subordinate clause, as in examples (9.281) and (9.282) above).

Third, the formation of [C NEG C] polar questions (see Section 9.3.2.2) with *zhus/zhaus* 'to suffer' and the responses to such questions both suggest that *zhus/zhaus* is closer to an ordinary complement-taking verb than a grammaticalized passive marker. When *zhus/zhaus* 'to suffer' occurs in such a question, it is *zhus/zhaus* itself (rather than any other verb following it) that obligatorily appears twice with *(j)ix* 'NEG$_1$' immediately preceding its second instance (see examples (9.283–9.285) below). This is similar to the behavior of other complement-taking verbs like *niel/nianl* 'to know' or *saud* 'to invite' (see Section 12.4), but it is quite different from that of Xong's non-verbal grammatical markers like *ghaod* 'more' or *hint* 'very'.

(9.283) *Beul* ***zhaus*** *jix* ***zhaus*** *nex* *beux?*
3 **suffer** NEG$_1$ **suffer** NEX hit
'Was he beaten by them?' (Shixiang Wu, fieldnotes)

(9.284) *Beul* ***zhaus*** *nex* *beux* *jix* ***zhaus****?*
3 **suffer** NEX hit NEG$_1$ **suffer**
'Was he beaten by them?' (Shixiang Wu, fieldnotes) (same as (9.283) above)

(9.285) **Beul* ***zhaus*** *nex* *beux* *jix* *beux?*
3 **suffer** NEX hit NEG$_1$ hit
(intended: 'Was he beaten by them?')

Unsurprisingly, only *zhus/zhaus* 'to suffer' can be used in a response to such a question, not any other verb following it. Examples (9.286–9.289) show four possible responses to examples (9.283) and (9.284) above, with the first two being completely grammatical and the last two being completely ungrammatical.

(9.286) *Zhaus.*
suffer
'Yes, (he was beaten by them).' (Shixiang Wu, fieldnotes)

(9.287) *Jix* ***zhaus.***
NEG$_1$ **suffer**
'No, (he wasn't beaten by them).' (Shixiang Wu, fieldnotes)

(9.288) **Beux.*
hit
(intended: 'Yes, [he was beaten by them].')

(9.289) **Jix* *beux.*
NEG$_1$ hit
(intended: 'No, [he wasn't beaten by them].')

Similar statements also apply to examples (9.290–9.294) below, which show a [C NEG C] polar question in which *zhus/zhaus* 'to suffer' appears preceding the verb *ndaot* 'to curse, to scold' and four possible responses to that question (only two of which are grammatical).

(9.290) *Mx* ***zhaus*** *jix* ***zhaus*** *ndaot?*
2SG **suffer** NEG$_1$ **suffer** curse
'Were you scolded?' (Shixiang Wu, fieldnotes)

(9.291) *Zhaus.*
suffer
'Yes, (I was scolded).' (Shixiang Wu, fieldnotes)

(9.292) *Jix* ***zhaus.***
NEG$_1$ **suffer**
'No, (I wasn't scolded).' (Shixiang Wu, fieldnotes)

(9.293) **Ndaot.*
curse
(intended: 'Yes, [I was scolded].')

(9.294) **Jix* *ndaot.*
NEG$_1$ curse
(intended: 'No, [I wasn't scolded].')

Finally, *zhus/zhaus* 'to suffer' can appear as the sole verb in a clause in which it is followed by a noun-phrase argument, in which case it means 'to suffer from' or 'to have (something) suffer'. Examples can be seen in (9.295–9.298) below. Again, this sort of behavior would not be unexpected for a verb meaning ‘to suffer’, but it would be unusual for a passive marker.

(9.295) *Wel* ***zhus*** *nons lah.*
1SG **suffer** rain PRF
‘I’ve gotten wet (from the rain).’ (Haili Shi, fieldnotes)

(9.296) *Wel* ***zhaus*** *put lah!*
1SG **suffer** gun PRF
‘I’ve been shot (with a gun)!’ (Shixiang Wu, fieldnotes)

(9.297) *Wel* ***zhus*** *sed lah!*
1SG **suffer** sword PRF
‘I’ve been stabbed (with a sword)!’ (Haili Shi, fieldnotes)

(9.298) *Wel* ***zhaus*** *ghaob-doul.*
1SG **suffer** NOM-hand
‘My hand has been injured.’ (Shixiang Wu, fieldnotes)

All of the data presented above in this section suggests to the author that *zhus/zhaus* ‘to suffer’ is better analyzed as a complement-taking verb than as a grammaticalized passive marker, although again the form in question certainly does show a fair amount of functional overlap with canonical passive markers in other languages.

For the sake of completeness, it is also worth mentioning here that *zhus/zhaus* ‘to suffer’ occasionally appears in multiverbal clauses following the verb that expresses the main predication of the clause, rather than preceding it as in most of the earlier examples in this section. The verb *zhus/zhaus* can then optionally be followed in turn by a noun phrase, with the entire [VERB *zhus/zhaus* (NP)] structure serving to express ‘to suffer from VERB’ or ‘to suffer from NP by means of VERB’. Examples of this can be seen in (9.299–9.301) below.

(9.299) *Niax-naus wel biat box.nhol manh, nonx* ***zhus***
meat-bird 1SG pour throw.away PART eat **suffer**
aod-houd ah, jaok wel ghaod.lot, biat
one-CLF:mouthful PART prick 1SG mouth pour
box.nhol.
throw.away
‘I threw the bird meat away. I had a bite and it pricked my mouth, so I threw it away.’ (Xingyu Shi, in *Oub Meinl Yaos Geud*)

(9.300) *Naont wel danx.daul jix mb, nins*
thus 1SG always NEG$_1$ hurt COP
*hmaont dox giaot **zhus**.*
CLF:evening that chew **suffer**
'But (my tooth) never hurt before, it was just that night that (I) bit into (a chicken foot).' (Haili Shi, in *Tooth Conversation*)

(9.301) *Nonx **zhaus** naonb?*
eat **suffer** what
'What did you eat (that made your tooth hurt so badly)?' (Shixiang Wu, in *Tooth Conversation*)

10 Verbs

10.1 Introduction

Verbs are one of the major open lexical categories in Fenghuang Xong. Just as was the case with Xong nouns (see Chapter 5), Xong verbs express many of the same concepts as verbs in major European languages such as English, including natural phenomena (e.g. *daox* 'to precipitate', *deuk* 'to thunder', and *piaf* 'to blow'), physical actions, events, and processes both voluntary and involuntary (e.g. *monl* 'to go', *puk* 'to speak', and *daos* 'to die'), mental and emotional states and processes (e.g. *ndiot* 'to recognize', *nbanx* 'to think', and *liaos* 'to miss [a person or place]'), and various abstract concepts (e.g. *nins* 'COP', *mex* 'to exist', and *nbut* 'to be named'). The primary functions of verbs in Xong include serving as heads of clauses (see Section 9.1.1), as predicates of arguments (again, see Section 9.1.1), and as constituents of multiverbal constructions (see Chapter 12).

However, the set of Xong verbs as a whole differs sharply from similar sets in most major European languages in that it includes a wide variety of property-denoting forms (e.g. *nqint* 'red', *ngaod* 'short', and *raut* 'good') in addition to those forms that denote actions, events, or processes (note that here the author is using terms like "action", "event", and "process" in an informal sense rather than to refer to strictly defined Aktionsart classes). These property-denoting forms (or "semantic adjectives", as they are sometimes referred to in the typological literature; see, e.g., Dryer 2013b) are fully canonical members of the verb class in Xong, and note further that Xong does not possess a separate class of adjectives (i.e. a lexical category whose members primarily denote properties). In this respect Xong verbs are much more similar to verbs in many isolating languages of East and Southeast Asia than to verbs in European languages, although Xong goes further than certain other East and Southeast Asian languages in that there does not appear to be *any* way to grammatically distinguish its property-denoting verbs from its other verbs (cf. Enfield [2007: 248–250], where it is argued that Lao's adjectival verbs can still be distinguished from the language's other verbs in certain grammatical respects, and cf. also Arcodia 2014, where similar arguments are advanced for Mandarin's adjectival verbs).

The fact that they include numerous property-denoting forms among their number is not the only way in which Xong's verbs resemble those of other isolating East and Southeast Asian languages. Xong verbs are overwhelmingly monosyllabic, although some apparently native (or, perhaps more accurately, not obviously non-native) Xong verbs are disyllabic (e.g. *box.nhol* 'to throw away', *minx.xaond* 'dirty'), as are a number of verbs recently borrowed from Sinitic languages (e.g. *faos.zof* 'to flare up', *zheinx.bif* 'to prepare').[186] Xong verbs also participate in relatively few morphological constructions,

186 The verb *faos.zof* 'to flare up' is a borrowing of Mandarin *fāzuò* (发作) or of a cognate form from another Sinitic variety, and the verb *zheinx.bif* 'to prepare' is a borrowing of Mandarin *zhǔnbèi* (准备) or of a cognate form from another Sinitic variety.

and in particular they never display any morphological marking of person, number, tense, aspect, or modality (though see Section 10.5 for discussion of the morphological constructions in which they do participate). Finally, multiverbal constructions (see Chapter 12) are just as common and diverse in Xong as they are in other isolating East and Southeast Asian languages, and they bear just as high a functional load.

The remainder of this chapter is divided into four sections, which cover in turn (i) the diagnostic criteria used to distinguish Xong verbs from other Xong forms, (ii) the issue of whether it is possible to distinguish verbal Aktionsart classes in Xong, (iii) semantically intransitive verbs that can occur with two arguments, and (iv) morphologically complex constructions with verbal heads. Certain verb-related topics that more properly fall under the purview of other chapters are not covered here, including ideophonic forms that modify verbs (see Section 11.1) and multiverbal constructions (Chapter 12). Naturally, cross-references to these and other relevant sections are included below wherever appropriate.

10.2 Properties of verbs

The two major distinguishing properties of Xong verbs are (i) their ability to be directly negated and (ii) their ability to undergo relativization through the use of *manx* 'REL' (see Section 8.1.4 for more on this form).[187] Neither of these properties is shared with any of Xong's other major lexical categories, including nouns (see Chapter 5), classifiers (Section 6.1), and ideophones (Section 11.1), and so in theory either one alone would be sufficient to distinguish Xong verbs from other Xong forms. However, using two objective, testable, language-specific criteria rather than one provides stronger evidence that Xong verbs do in fact constitute an independent lexical category. Furthermore, while it is true that only verbs can undergo relativization through the use of *manx* 'REL', there are several other forms homophonous with *manx* 'REL' that can co-occur with non-verbal forms (e.g. *manx* '2PL', *manx* 'um ... '), and so using this criterion alone could potentially result in some ambiguous cases.

Example (10.1) below shows that verbs can readily be negated with *(j)ix* 'NEG_1', while examples (10.2), (10.3), and (10.4) show that it is impossible for nouns, classifiers, and ideophones (respectively) to be similarly negated.

(10.1) *jix* *monl/* *jix* *nonx/* *jix* *nins/* *jix* *nqint*
NEG_1 go/ NEG_1 eat/ NEG_1 COP/ NEG_1 red
'to not go/to not eat/to not be/to not be red' (Shixiang Wu, fieldnotes)

187 Of course, no Xong verb can ever be *directly* relativized by *manx* 'REL'; instead, a verb serves as the head of a clause, and that clause is then relativized by *manx* 'REL'. However, it would be rather awkward to have to repeatedly refer to "the ability to serve as the head of a clause which is relativized by *manx* 'REL'" as a defining characteristic of Xong verbs, and so the author uses a simpler phrasing (i.e. "the ability to undergo relativization through the use of *manx* 'REL'") in this grammar.

(10.2) **jix* *(daob-)mioul/* **jix* *(ghaob-)ndaut/* **jix* *deb-npaok*
NEG$_1$ (AN-)fish/ NEG$_1$ (NOM-)tree/ NEG$_1$ DIM-woman
(intended: 'to not be a fish/to not be a tree [or to not be wooden]/to not be a girl')

(10.3) **jix* *leb/* **jix* *ngonl/* **jix* *zheinb*
NEG$_1$ CLF/ NEG$_1$ CLF:animate/ NEG$_1$ CLF:tool
(intended: 'to not be a thing/to not be an animate being/to not be a tool')

(10.4) **jix* *jel.jel/* **jix* *biaol.biaol*
NEG$_1$ IDEO:A:shiningly/ NEG$_1$ IDEO:A:sour
(intended: 'not shiningly/not sour')

Similarly, example (10.5) below shows that verbs can readily undergo relativization through the use of *manx* 'REL', while examples (10.6), (10.7), and (10.8) show that this is impossible for nouns, classifiers, and ideophones (respectively).

(10.5) *deb-deb manx liox/ deb-deb manx nghauk.zaol/*
child-RED REL big/ child-RED REL play/
deb-deb manx nonx (hlit)
child-RED REL eat (cooked.rice)
'a big child/a child who's playing/a child who's eating' (Haili Shi, fieldnotes)

(10.6) **ghaob-zhous* *manx* *hlod/* **ghaob-zhous* *manx* *hliat*
NOM-chopstick REL bamboo/ NOM-chopstick REL tin
(intended: 'bamboo chopsticks/tin chopsticks')

(10.7) **deb-npaok* *manx* *leb/* **ghaob-hlod* *manx* *del*
DIM-woman REL CLF/ NOM-bamboo REL CLF:rigid.length
(intended: 'a single girl/a single bamboo plant')

(10.8) **gheb-hlaot* *manx* *jel.jel/* **bid-guax* *manx* *biaol.biaol*
???-moon REL IDEO:A:shiningly/ FRT-peach REL IDEO:A:sour
(intended: 'a shining star/a sour peach')

There are several other potential diagnostic criteria that at first appear as though they could be used to reliably distinguish Xong verbs from other Xong forms, including (i) the ability to serve as a nominal modifier by appearing in an unflagged relative clause, (ii) the ability to undergo relativization through the use of *naond* 'ASSOC', (iii) the ability to take aspectual-modal marking, and (iv) the ability to occur in various morphological constructions. However, in each case closer investigation reveals that the potential criterion in question is deficient (either in theory or in practice) in one or more respects.

First, it is certainly true that every unflagged relative clause (meaning every relative clause that does not bear any overt relative clause markers; see Sections 8.1.3 and 8.1.5) will contain at least one verb, and many such relative clauses do not contain any non-verbal forms. However, the ability to serve as a nominal modifier by appearing in one of these relative clauses is not an ideal diagnostic criterion for verbhood because Xong nouns can also occur in a formally similar construction. Compare (10.9) and (10.10) below, with the first example featuring an unflagged relative clause consisting solely of a verb (namely *gueub* 'white') and the second featuring an attributive noun compound (see Section 5.3.1). Note that the hyphen in example (10.10) is merely an orthographic convention.

(10.9) *ndeud gueub*
paper white
'white paper' (Shixiang Wu, fieldnotes)

(10.10) *neus-naus*
egg-duck
'duck egg' (Haili Shi, fieldnotes)

Both example (10.9) and example (10.10) involve the semantic head of a noun phrase occurring noun-phrase–initially, with a modifying form following it. The formal similarities between the two constructions thus make the ability to serve as a nominal modifier by appearing in an unflagged relative clause a poor test for distinguishing Xong verbs from Xong nouns.[188]

Second, similar problems arise if one attempts to use the ability to undergo relativization through the use of *naond* 'ASSOC' as a defining criterion for verbs. The associative marker *naond* 'ASSOC' is used in Xong to mark both certain relative clauses (see Section 8.1.2) and certain possessive constructions (Section 8.2.1), and in both cases *naond* occurs following the construction in question. For instance, example (10.11) shows a *naond* relative clause (in brackets) featuring the verb *nghauk.zaol* 'to play' (bolded), while example (10.12) shows a *naond* possessive construction (in brackets) featuring the noun *khauk-lieux* [hole-well] 'well' (bolded).

(10.11) [***nghauk.zaol*** *naond*] *deb-deb*
[**play** ASSOC] child-RED
'a child who's playing' (Haili Shi, fieldnotes)

188 At first glance, it appears reasonable to suggest that examples (10.9) and (10.10) are in fact instances of the same sort of construction, with *ndeud gueub* [paper white] 'white paper' perhaps better analyzed as a noun compound (i.e. *ndeud-gueub* [paper-white]) just like *neus-naus* [egg-duck] 'duck egg'. See Section 8.1.5 for arguments against this alternate hypothesis.

(10.12) [***khauk-lieux*** *naond*] *aub*
[**hole-well** ASSOC] water
'water from the well' (Xingyu Shi, in *Oub Meinl Yaos Geud*)

The formal similarities between the two examples are obvious: each features a noun phrase containing a modifier that is marked with a final *naond* 'ASSOC' (this modifier is clausal in the first example, nominal in the second), with the semantic head of the noun phrase as a whole following that modifier. Thus, in practice, the ability to undergo relativization through the use of *naond* 'ASSOC' is no more useful a test for verbhood in Xong than the ability to serve as a nominal modifier by appearing in an unflagged relative clause.

Third, while Xong verbs never take any morphological marking of aspect or modality (or, for that matter, of person, number, or tense), verbal predicates can still undergo a wide variety of aspectual and modal modifications, primarily through the use of multiverbal constructions (see Section 12.3). However, the ability to undergo such aspectual-modal modification is not an entirely satisfactory defining characteristic of Xong verbs because not all verbs are equally amenable to it. The ability of a verb to be modified by other aspectual-modal–marking verbs depends a great deal on whether that verb is semantically and pragmatically compatible with the aspectual-modal marking in question. For instance, the various verbs in (10.13) and (10.15) below are readily compatible with certain aspectual-modal–marking verbs due to their semantics, while the verbs in (10.14) and (10.16) are much less compatible for the same reason (the aspectual-modal–marking verbs in all these examples have been bolded).[189]

(10.13) *Wel* ***ninb*** *sheit/chauk/nonx/nhob.*
1SG **at** write/do/eat/walk
'I'm writing (it)/doing (it)/eating (it)/walking.' (Haili Shi, fieldnotes)

(10.14) ??*Wel* ***ninb*** *nins/mex/lis/shanb.*
1SG **at** COP/exist/want/tall
(intended: 'I'm being [it]/having [it]/wanting [it]/being tall.')

(10.15) *Beul* *sheit/chauk/nonx/nhob* ***dut.***
3 write/do/eat/walk **obtain**
'She can write (it)/can do (it)/can eat (it)/can walk.' (Haili Shi, fieldnotes)

189 Aspectual-modal–marking verbs in Xong often have additional, non–aspectual-modal functions as well, and so these forms are typically given relatively lexical glosses, like 'at' for *ninb* in examples (10.13) and (10.14) or 'obtain' for *dut* in examples (10.15) and (10.16). Again, see Section 12.3 for discussion.

(10.16) ??*Beul* *nins/mex/lis/shanb* ***dut.***
3 COP/exist/want/tall **obtain**
(intended: 'She can be [it]/can have [it]/can want [it]/can be tall.')

Similar examples could be provided for any of Xong's other aspectual-modal–marking verbs. While some of the examples of questionable grammaticality above (i.e. (10.14) and (10.16)) might be acceptable to at least some Xong speakers given a suitably unusual discourse context, the reluctance of consultants to allow them under normal circumstances means that this potential diagnostic criterion is not a very useful one in practice. Still, since all forms that can undergo aspectual-modal modification are verbs, this ability does serve as a sufficient, if not necessary, criterion for verbhood in Xong.

Finally, the ability to occur in the various morphological constructions discussed in Section 10.5 below is also unsatisfactory as a diagnostic criterion because there is no such construction in which every verb can appear, and there are some verbs which never appear in any of them. However, it is at least true that no non-verbal forms can ever appear in any of these constructions, making this another sufficient, though not necessary, criterion for verbhood.

This section has so far focused on the grammatical properties of Xong verbs, but there are a few comments worth making about the functional properties of these forms as well. Most significantly (at least from the perspective of a speaker of a European language), Xong verbs are not obligatorily marked for any grammatical categories, including tense, aspect, mode, person, number, or finiteness. Any particular instance of a Xong verb will thus often have a number of possible English translations depending on the discourse context. This can be seen in examples (10.17–10.20) below, where any number of different translations are possible for a given Xong clause.

(10.17) *Nex* ***puk.***
NEX **speak**
'She's speaking/she was speaking/she spoke/she'll speak/she'll be speaking/she'd have spoken/etc.' (Shixiang Wu, fieldnotes)

(10.18) *Wel* ***nhob*** *geud.*
1SG **walk** road
'I'm walking/I was walking/I walked/I'll walk/I'll be walking/I'd have walked/etc.' (Chenghua Long, fieldnotes)

(10.19) *Beul* ***nonx*** *hlit.*
3 **eat** cooked.rice
'He's eating/he was eating/he ate/he'll eat/he'll be eating/he'd have eaten/etc.' (Shixiang Wu, fieldnotes)

(10.20)

Boub	***monl***	***nheis***	*reib.*
1PL	**go**	**gather**	vegetable

'We're going to gather vegetables/we were going to gather vegetables/we went to gather vegetables/we'll go to gather vegetables/we'll be going to gather vegetables/we'd have gone to gather vegetables/etc.' (Xingyu Shi, fieldnotes)

In some cases the discourse context at the time of utterance might make one or another of the various translations given in each example above more accurate than the others. Still, in many other cases multiple translations would be equally accurate, with the Xong verb(s) in question simply being unspecified with respect to tense, aspect, and other distinctions that are often obligatorily specified on verbs in English and other European languages (cf. the discussion of referential properties of Xong nouns in Section 5.2.2, in particular their non-specification with respect to number and definiteness).

Still, when the aspectual-modal properties of a particular verb are important and not obvious from context, Xong speakers have access to a wide variety of optional syntactic (rather than morphological) aspectual-modal markers. (Note, though, that verbs in Xong are never marked – either morphologically or syntactically – for certain grammatical categories, like person, number, tense, or finiteness.) Many of these aspectual-modal markers (which are often verbal in nature themselves) are discussed in more detail in Section 12.3, but several examples of them are given (bolded) in (10.21–10.24) below.

(10.21)

Mx	***lis***	*jont*	*id-raut.*
2SG	**want**	sit	DID-good

'Sit up straight.' (Shixiang Wu, fieldnotes)

(10.22)

Meib-Nhaonl,	*monx*	***dut***	*dand*	*neind,*	*Nhaonl?*
younger.sister-PN	2SG	**obtain**	arrive	this	PN

'Little sister Nhaon, have you been here before, Nhaon?' (Xingyu Shi, in *Oub Meinl Yaos Geud*)

(10.23)

Kox.ix	*raut*	*dut*	*aod-gul-yaonl-hnef,*	*danb.shib*	*beul*
can	good	obtain	one-ten-more-CLF:day	but	3

sheib	***yol***	*faos.zof.*
able.to	**again**	flare.up

'(If you use this treatment method, your tooth) will be good for two weeks or so. But (the pain) will eventually flare up again.' (Chenghua Long, in *Tooth Conversation*)

(10.24) *Aod-hmaont* *dox* ***deit*** *raut* *deb,* *fanx.zheinb*
one-CLF:evening that **still** good DIM anyway
deit *taf* ***dut.***
still endure **obtain**
'By the evening (my tooth) was a little better, at least (I) was able to bear (the pain).' (Haili Shi, in *Tooth Conversation*)

While it is clear from the evidence presented so far that verbs constitute a distinct lexical category in Xong, there is still some degree of overlap between certain verbs and nouns and between certain verbs and classifiers. (There is not, however, any apparent overlap between verbs and Xong's fourth major lexical category, ideophones.) There are a few forms that can serve as either verbs or nouns, including *ghot* 'old; old person', *mb* 'to hurt (intrans.), to be sick; illness', *nbut* 'to be named; name', *gied/giand* 'icy, to freeze; ice', and *ntiot* 'smoky; smoke'. There are also some forms (primarily those referring to physical actions) that can serve as either verbs or classifiers (see Section 6.1.4.9). One such form, *zhox* 'to kick; CLF:kick', is exemplified in both its verbal and classifier functions in example (10.25) below.

(10.25) *Wel* ***zhox*** *monx* *aod-**zhox**.*
1SG **kick** 2SG one-**CLF:kick**
'I'll give you a kick.' (Chenghua Long, fieldnotes)

See also Section 1.2.2 for more discussion of overlap among Xong lexical categories in general.

10.3 Verbs and Aktionsart

Perhaps in part because verbs in the isolating languages of East and Southeast Asia tend to lack the morphology (and thus the morphological classes) of verbs from other parts of the world, a number of attempts to define verbal classes in these languages have focused primarily on Aktionsart, or lexical aspect (see Vendler 1957). Such attempts propose classes of verbs defined by various features of the inherent temporal structure of the verbs themselves (e.g. telicity, duration, punctualness), rather than of the temporal structure of entire verb phrases or clauses.

Of course, scholars do not typically rely on mere intuition to determine the Aktionsart properties of particular verbs. Instead, they use various grammatical and semantic tests, such as (among many others) the possibility of applying progressive marking to a verb or the possibility of a verb co-occurring with duration expressions. Enfield, for instance, divides Lao verbs into five different Aktionsart classes based on a number of different criteria, including the ability (or lack thereof) of verbs to undergo reduplication and the ability (or lack thereof) of verbs to co-occur with progressive marking (2007: 241, 242). Similarly, Fehri and Vinet divide Mandarin verbs into four different Aktionsart classes based on criteria like the ability (or lack thereof) of verbs to co-occur with certain verbal classifiers and the semantic effects that perfective marking on verbs entails (2008).

While the author would certainly not go so far as to argue that such verbal classification schemes are never useful, they do not appear to be particularly applicable to Xong. Working with three of his most semantically sensitive consultants (Mrs. Chenghua Long, Mrs. Haili Shi, and Mrs. Shixiang Wu), the author applied a variety of grammatical and semantic tests (generally adopted from similar tests used in sources that focus on languages typologically similar to Xong) to a set of verbs with widely differing meanings. If well defined Aktionsart classes did exist in Xong, one would expect to find groups of verbs that pattern together in terms of which tests they pass and which tests they fail. However, as is discussed in more detail further below, no such groups of verbs were found, despite the fact that the grammatical and semantic judgments of the three consultants who assisted with this work were generally quite consistent. This seems to suggest that Aktionsart features are not a particularly useful tool for classifying Xong verbs. Of course, the author is not claiming here that Xong verbs do not possess any Aktionsart-related properties at all. For instance, some Xong verbs do imply a durative event while others do not, and some are telic while others are not, and facts like these may naturally be of some interest to semantic typologists. The author would argue, though, that classifying Xong verbs according to their Aktionsart properties reveals relatively little about the grammatical and semantic structure of the Xong language itself (cf. Section 5.2.2 on the apparent lack of a count/mass distinction in Xong nouns).

In total, the author applied a series of ten grammatical and semantic tests to sixteen different verbs, with those verbs having been chosen to provide as wide a semantic range as possible. The sixteen verbs in question are listed below. Note that many of these verbs have additional secondary (or at least less frequent) meanings or functions in addition to their primary (or at least most frequent) meaning or function. These secondary meanings or functions are described in parentheses following each verb's primary meaning or function in the list below. Also note that whenever multiple pronunciations of a single verb are given separated by a slash (</>) in this chapter, the pronunciation before the slash is the one used in Yankan Village (see Sections 2.7.1 and 3.1) while the one after the slash is an alternate pronunciation used elsewhere in Fenghuang County.

1. *mex* 'to exist' (also 'to have'; also 'wealthy')
2. *nins* 'COP' (also 'true, real')
3. *ninb* 'at' (also 'to live [at]'; also functions as a progressive marker)
4. *lis* 'to want' (also functions as a marker of deontic modality, intention, or expected action)
5. *diex/dianx* 'to finish' (also 'to bear fruit'; also functions as a completive marker)
6. *guaot* 'to pass' (also 'very'; also functions as an experiential marker)
7. *nqint* 'red'
8. *kod* 'poor (not wealthy)'

9. *raut* 'good'
10. *nkied/nkiand* 'happy'
11. *niel/nianl* 'to know'
12. *gid* 'to run'
13. *sheit* 'to write'
14. *daos* 'to die'
15. *ndiet/ndit* 'hot'
16. *gied/giand* 'icy, to freeze' (also functions as a noun meaning 'ice')

The reader will note that the list above includes several property-denoting verbs like *nqint* 'red', *kod* 'poor', *raut* 'good', and others. These property-denoting forms are fully canonical members of the verb class in Xong, as they pass all of the verb-defining tests given in Section 10.2. There is thus no a priori reason not to include these property-denoting verbs in this section's discussion. While properties (as distinct from states) may not typically be considered a distinct Aktionsart class, some authors (see, e.g., Enfield [2007: 241–247]) do include property-denoting verbs (i.e. verbal semantic adjectives) as a distinct class in verbal classificatory schemes based primarily on Aktionsart features. However, it will be shown below that there is very little Aktionsart-related evidence (or indeed any evidence at all) for grouping Xong's property-denoting verbs together as a class distinct from Xong's other, non–property-denoting verbs.

The ten different grammatical and semantic tests applied to each verb have been listed below. Note that tests 1 through 7 involve aspectual-modal marking possibilities, test 8 involves a semantic entailment property, test 9 involves a morphological property, and test 10 involves what is arguably a syntactic property (but see Section 10.5.4).

1. The ability (or lack thereof) of the verb to co-occur with the preverbal progressive marker *ninb* 'at'
2. The ability (or lack thereof) of the verb to co-occur with the preverbal experiential marker *dut/daut* 'obtain'
3. The ability (or lack thereof) of the verb to co-occur with the postverbal experiential marker *guaot* 'pass'
4. The ability (or lack thereof) of the verb to co-occur with the circumverbal experiential marker *dut/daut...guaot* 'obtain...pass'
5. The ability (or lack thereof) of the verb to co-occur with the postverbal potential marker *dut/daut* 'obtain'
6. The ability (or lack thereof) of the verb to co-occur with the postverbal completive marker *diex/dianx* 'finish'
7. The ability (or lack thereof) of the verb to co-occur with the postverbal completive marker *ncaos/ncaok* 'be done'
8. Whether or not [VERB PRF] entails that 'VERB is the case now'
9. The ability (or lack thereof) of the verb to occur in the [VERB-*lib*-VERB-*daod*] construction (see Section 10.5.3 for more on this construction)

10. The ability (or lack thereof) of the verb to occur in the [*nak* VERB VERB] (with *nak* 'extremely') reduplicative construction (see Section 10.5.4 for more on verbal reduplication in Xong in general)

Note that when a particular verb had multiple potentially related meanings or functions (e.g. *ninb*, which can mean 'at' or 'to live [at]' and which can also function as a progressive marker), those multiple meanings or functions were all considered together when applying the ten tests listed above. In other words, as long as the verb could pass the test in question while occurring with any of its meanings or in any of its functions, it was considered to have passed the test for the purposes of this section. This was done primarily for practical reasons, since in many cases it is not immediately obvious whether a particular verb with multiple meanings or functions should be considered ambiguous, monosemous, or polysemous (see Gil 2004). Still, the author ignored other verbs that appear to be nothing more than accidentally homophonous with one of the sixteen verbs discussed in this section, like *ninb* 'to marry' (cf. *ninb* 'at') or *niel* 'lazy' (cf. *niel/nianl* 'to know').

The ten different grammatical and semantic tests applied to each verb are discussed in turn below. Of course, providing a unique example sentence to demonstrate whether each particular verb passes or fails each particular semantic or grammatical test would quickly become quite repetitive, and it would likely double the overall length of this chapter. Thus, the author has instead provided two example sentences for each test, with the first showing one verb that passes the test and the second showing one that fails it. Nevertheless, a table showing the results of all sixteen verbs combined with all ten tests (Table 10.1) has been provided following these example sentences.

The first test to be discussed here involves seeing whether the verb in question can co-occur with the progressive marker *ninb* 'at' (see Section 12.3.2 for more information on the various functions that this form serves). Non–property-denoting verbs that can co-occur with this marker are generally dynamic (rather than stative) and durative (rather than instantaneous). For instance, *gid* 'to run' and *guaot* 'to pass' can both co-occur with this marker, while *mex* 'to exist' and *daos* 'to die' cannot. Most property-denoting verbs (e.g. *kod* 'poor', *raut* 'good') cannot co-occur with *ninb* 'at' in its progressive function, but, somewhat unexpectedly, certain fairly prototypical property-denoting verbs can co-occur with it (e.g. *nqint* 'red', *nkied/nkiand* 'happy').

Examples (10.26) and (10.27) below show one verb that can co-occur with this marker and one verb that cannot (respectively). In these and similar examples below, both the verb undergoing the test and the aspectual-modal marker(s) (in this case *ninb* 'at') have been bolded.

(10.26) *Lox.web* ***ninb*** ***sheit*** *ndeud.*
white.foreigner **at** **write** writing
'The (white) foreigner is writing.' (Haili Shi, fieldnotes)

(10.27) **Daob-yul dox* ***ninb daos.***
AN-cow that **at die**
(intended: 'That cow is dying.')

Fenghuang Xong has three different experiential constructions, the first of which involves the preverbal experiential marker *dut/daut* 'to obtain', the second of which involves the postverbal experiential marker *guaot* 'to pass', and the third of which involves both of these markers occurring on either side of the verb (see also Section 12.3.3). The second through fourth tests discussed in this section involve seeing whether the verb in question can occur in each of these three constructions. Most of the sixteen verbs can occur in all three, though *niel/nianl* 'to know' cannot occur in any (which is hardly surprising given the meaning of the verb), and there are three other verbs examined in this section that can occur in only one or two of these constructions, not all of them (these are *nins* 'COP', *daos* 'to die', and *ndiet/ndit* 'hot').

Examples (10.28) and (10.29) below show one verb that can co-occur with the preverbal experiential marker *dut/daut* 'to obtain' and one verb that cannot (respectively).

(10.28) *Beul* ***dut nqint.***
3 **obtain red**
'It (i.e. a lamp whose bulb cycles through various colors) has been red before.' (Chenghua Long, fieldnotes)

(10.29) ****Dut ndit.***
obtain hot
(intended: '[The weather's] been hot before.')

Examples (10.30) and (10.31) below show one verb that can co-occur with the postverbal experiential marker *guaot* 'to pass' and one verb that cannot (respectively).

(10.30) *Wel* ***nins guaot*** *lox.sid.*
1SG **COP pass** teacher
'I've been a teacher before.' (Chenghua Long, fieldnotes)

(10.31) **Wel* ***nianl guaot.***
1SG **know pass**
(intended: 'I've known [this] before.')

Examples (10.32) and (10.33) below show one verb that can co-occur with the circumverbal experiential marker *dut/daut ... guaot* 'obtain ... pass' and one verb that cannot (respectively).

(10.32) *Boub* ***daut kod guaot.***
1PL **obtain poor pass**
'We've been poor before.' (Shixiang Wu, fieldnotes)

(10.33) **Beul* ***daut daos guaot.***
3 **obtain die pass**
(intended: 'He's died before [e.g. a deity who was killed and then returned to life].')

The fifth test involves seeing whether the verb in question can co-occur with the postverbal potential marker *dut/daut* 'to obtain' (again, see Section 12.3.3). As with the progressive marker *ninb* 'at', the non–property-denoting verbs which can co-occur with this marker are typically dynamic and durative (e.g. *gid* 'to run', *sheit* 'to write', and *ninb* 'at' – though here the latter is only acceptable in the sense of 'to live [at]'). Also as with the progressive marker *ninb*, some property-denoting verbs can co-occur with this potential marker *dut/daut* (e.g. *nqint* 'red'), while others cannot (e.g. *kod* 'poor'). Note, though, that there are some property-denoting verbs which can take progressive *ninb* 'at' but not potential *dut/daut* 'to obtain' (e.g. *nkied/nkiand* 'happy'), and there are others which can take potential *dut/daut* 'to obtain' but not progressive *ninb* 'at' (e.g. *raut* 'good').

Examples (10.34) and (10.35) below show one verb that can co-occur with the potential marker *dut/daut* 'to obtain' and one verb that cannot (respectively).

(10.34) *Aod-zhons ndaut dox* ***diex dut.***
one-CLF:vertical.plant tree that **finish obtain**
'That tree is able to bear fruit.' (Haili Shi, fieldnotes)

(10.35) **Beul* ***nins dut.***
3 **COP obtain**
(intended: 'He can be [a teacher].')

The sixth and seventh tests involve seeing whether the verb in question can co-occur with two postverbal completive markers, *diex/dianx* 'to finish' and *ncaos/ncaok* 'to be done' (see Section 12.3.4 for discussion of Xong's completive constructions in general). As an examination of Table 10.1 further below in this section will show, it is difficult to make any sort of generalization at all about which sorts of verbs can co-occur with both of these completive markers (e.g. *guaot* 'to pass'), which can co-occur with *ncaos/ncaok* but not *diex/dianx* (e.g. *niel/nianl* 'to know'), which can co-occur with *diex/dianx* but not *ncaos/ncaok* (e.g. *gied/giand* 'icy, to freeze'), and which cannot co-occur with either (e.g. *mex* 'to exist').

Nevertheless, examples (10.36) and (10.37) show one verb that can co-occur with the completive marker *diex/dianx* 'to finish' and one verb that cannot (respectively).

(10.36) *Miaux-ndaut* ***nqint*** ***dianx*** *lah.*
leaf-tree **red** **finish** PRF
'The leaves have turned red.' (Shixiang Wu, fieldnotes)

(10.37) **Boub* ***kod*** ***dianx*** *lah.*
1PL **poor** **finish** PRF
(intended: 'Now we've become poor.')

Examples (10.38) and (10.39) show one verb that can co-occur with the completive marker *ncaos/ncaok* 'to be done' and one verb that cannot (respectively).

(10.38) *Wel* ***nins*** *zhaol-ginb* ***ncaok.***
1SG **COP** non.Miao-soldier **be.done**
'I'm a soldier now.' (Chenghua Long, fieldnotes)

(10.39) **Wel* ***mex*** ***ncaok.***
1SG **exist** **be.done**
(intended: 'I have [it] now.' *or* 'I'm wealthy now.')

The eighth test discussed here involves seeing whether perfect marking (with clause-final *lah* 'PRF') on the verb in question entails that 'VERB is the case now' (see Section 9.2.1.4 for more information on the form *lah*). It does not appear possible to generalize about this particular entailment property in terms of verbal dynamicity or a stative/active distinction, since *nkied/nkiand* 'happy' (a presumably non-dynamic, stative verb) has this entailment property, while *nqint* 'red' (another presumably non-dynamic, stative verb) does not. Neither does it seem possible to generalize in terms of verbal durativity or telicity, since *ninb* 'at, to live (at)' (a presumably durative, atelic verb, at least in the sense of 'to live [at]') has this entailment property, while *gid* 'to run' (another presumably durative, atelic verb) does not.

Example (10.40) below shows one verb for which perfect marking with clause-final *lah* 'PRF' does entail that 'VERB is the case now', and example (10.41) shows one verb for which the same perfect marking does not carry any such entailment.

(10.40) *Wel* ***ninb*** *xol.taonx* ***lah.***
1SG **at** school **PRF**
'I live at the school now.' (Shixiang Wu, fieldnotes)

(10.41) *Miaux-ndaut* ***nqint*** ***lah.***
leaf-tree **red** **PRF**
'The leaves turned red (though they are not necessarily still red now).' (Shixiang Wu, fieldnotes)

The ninth test involves seeing whether the verb in question can participate in the [VERB-*lib*-VERB-*daod*] construction (see Section 10.5.3). This construction has an attenuating semantic effect, and it occurs with both certain property-denoting verbs and certain non–property-denoting verbs. However, it does not appear possible to predict which particular verbs (whether property-denoting or not) will be able to occur in this construction. For instance, *sheit* 'to write' and *gid* 'to run' both refer to atelic, dynamic, durative actions. However, as examples (10.42) and (10.43) show, *sheit* 'to write' can occur in the construction while *gid* 'to run' cannot.

(10.42) *Aod-bas* *ndeud* *neind* *wel* ***sheit-lib-sheit-daod.***
one-CLF:page paper this 1SG **write-LIB-write-DAOD**
'I've written a little bit on this page.' (Haili Shi, fieldnotes)

(10.43) **Tat-hnef* *wel* ***gid-lib-gid-daod.***
this-CLF:day 1SG **run-LIB-run-DAOD**
(intended: 'I've run a little bit today.')

The tenth and final test discussed here involves seeing whether the verb in question can participate in the [*nak* VERB VERB] (with *nak* 'extremely') reduplicative construction (see Section 10.5.4 for more on verbal reduplication in Xong in general). This construction signals 'extremely VERB', and unlike most of the tests discussed above, in most cases one can predict whether or not a particular verb will be able to occur in this construction. All property-denoting verbs examined in this section can participate, while nearly all non–property-denoting verbs cannot. Only a single exception is found: the non–property-denoting verb *diex/dianx* 'to finish' can also occur in this construction, though only when it occurs with the meaning 'to bear fruit'.

Examples (10.44) and (10.45) below show one verb that can participate in the [*nak* VERB VERB] construction and one verb that cannot (respectively).

(10.44) *Aod-njaod* *ndeinb* *neind* ***nak*** ***nqint*** ***nqint.***
one-CLF:piece cloth this **extremely** **red** **red**
'This piece of cloth is such a bright red.' (Haili Shi, fieldnotes)

(10.45) **Aod-leb* *deb-deb* *dox* ***nak*** ***lis*** ***lis.***
one-CLF child-RED that **extremely** **want** **want**
(intended: 'That child really wants [it].' *or* 'That child is really greedy.')

Table 10.1 below summarizes which of the sixteen Xong verbs listed earlier in this section pass which of the ten grammatical and semantic tests exemplified immediately above (note that these tests were also presented in list format near the beginning of this section). The verbs in question are arranged vertically along the table's left edge, and the grammatical and semantic tests they underwent are arranged horizontally along its top edge. Note that certain verbs' glosses have been simplified in the table due to space concerns, and the tests are referred to only by number for the same reason. The symbol <√> indicates that a particular verb passes a particular grammatical or semantic test, <X> indicates that it does not, and <?> indicates that the author's data for a particular verb–test combination is unclear or inconclusive.

Table 10.1: Ten grammatical and semantic tests applied to sixteen Xong verbs.

	1	2	3	4	5	6	7	8	9	10
mex 'exist'	X	√	√	√	X	X	X	?	√	√
ninb 'at'	X	√	√	√	√	X	X	√	X	X
nins 'COP'	X	X	√	√	X	X	√	√	X	X
lis 'want'	X	√	√	√	X	X	X	√	X	X
diex/ dianx 'finish'	√	√	√	√	√	X	X	X	√	√
guaot 'pass'	√	√	√	√	√	√	√	X	X	X
nqint 'red'	√	√	√	√	√	√	√	X	√	√
kod 'poor'	X	√	√	√	X	X	X	√	X	√
raut 'good'	X	√	√	√	√	X	X	√	√	√
nkied/ nkiand 'happy'	√	√	√	√	X	X	X	√	√	√
niel/ *nianl* 'know'	X	X	X	X	X	X	√	?	√	X
gid 'run'	√	√	√	√	√	√	√	X	X	X
sheit 'write'	√	√	√	√	√	√	√	X	√	X
daos 'die'	X	X	√	X	X	X	√	X	X	X

Table 10.1 (continued)

	1	2	3	4	5	6	7	8	9	10
ndiet/ ndit 'hot'	X	X	√	√	X	X	X	√	√	√
gied/giand 'icy, freeze'	√	√	√	√	X	√	X	√	√	√

As Table 10.1 shows, the sixteen verbs examined in this section do not appear to contain any obvious groups that pattern together in terms of the grammatical and semantic tests they pass and fail. Even verbs which would at first glance appear to have very similar Aktionsart characteristics often pass and fail different tests. For instance, *nqint* 'red' and *nkied/nkiand* 'happy' can both take progressive marking while *kod* 'poor' and *raut* 'good' cannot, despite the fact that all four would seem to be fairly prototypical semantic adjectives (see Dryer 2013b). Similarly, *sheit* 'to write' and *gid* 'to run' are alike in that they both presumably refer to atelic, dynamic, durative actions, but only the former verb can occur in the [VERB-*lib*-VERB-*daod*] construction (see Section 10.5.3 below). Other similar examples can be found throughout Table 10.1 and the discussion preceding it.

This seems to the author to suggest that it would be quite difficult to reliably divide Xong verbs into neatly delimited, clearly distinct Aktionsart classes. Of course, Xong verbs still do appear to have Aktionsart-related properties: consultants report that some verbs refer to punctual events while others do not, some refer to dynamic activities while others refer to states, and so on. Still, on the basis of the evidence currently available, it seems impossible – or at least unproductive – to divide up Xong verbs in an Aktionsart classification scheme similar to those used by other authors working on typologically similar languages (see, e.g., Enfield [2007: 241, 242] on Lao or Fehri and Vinet 2008 on Mandarin).

To be fair, it is not difficult to imagine counterarguments to some of the claims advanced in this section. It is possible that selecting different grammatical and semantic tests, or applying them to different Xong verbs, might have produced different results. The author has no evidence that this is not the case, but it should be kept in mind that the sixteen verbs in this section were selected to provide as high a degree of semantic variety as possible. Similarly, the ten tests applied to those verbs were quite varied, as they included several that involve aspectual-modal marking possibilities, one that involves a semantic entailment property, one that involves a morphological property, and one that involves what is arguably a syntactic property. Given that such a wide variety of tests applied to such a wide variety of verbs has not identified any obvious Aktionsart classes, the author suggests that at the very least, the burden of proof should be on those who would argue that such Aktionsart classes are in fact relevant to the grammatical or semantic structure of the Xong language.[190]

Finally, it is worth stressing the fact that there does not appear to be any clear way of distinguishing Xong's property-denoting verbs (or verbal semantic adjectives) from its non–property-denoting verbs, or at least not on the basis of objective, language-internal, grammatical criteria. Some of Xong's property-denoting verbs (*nqint* 'red', *nkied/nkiand* 'happy') can take progressive marking while others (*kod* 'poor', *raut* 'good') cannot, some (*nqint* 'red') can take completive marking while others (*kod* 'poor') cannot, and some (*kod* 'poor') entail that 'VERB is the case now' when accompanied by perfect marking while others (*nqint* 'red') do not. It is admittedly true that all property-denoting verbs discussed in this section can occur in the [*nak* VERB VERB] reduplicative construction. However, one non–property-denoting verb discussed in this section can occur in this construction as well (this is *diex/dianx* 'to finish, to bear fruit'), and in any case it would be difficult to defend a proposed grammatical distinction between property-denoting and non–property-denoting verbs on the basis of a single grammatical feature.

Of course, the tests used in this section are not exhaustive, and it is certainly possible that there exist some other, fairly subtle grammatical or entailment tests that could be used to clearly distinguish property-denoting and non–property-denoting verbs in Xong. Still, just as was the case with the existence (or lack thereof) of Aktionsart classes in general, the evidence presented in this section seems sufficient to place the burden of proof on those scholars who would argue for the existence of such a distinction.

10.4 Semantically intransitive verbs with two arguments

As is discussed in much more detail in Section 9.1.1, each particular instance of a Xong verb (here referring to verb tokens, not verb types) will occur with zero to three arguments. However, verbs in Fenghuang Xong display a notable amount of valency-related flexibility. In particular, a great number of verbs referring to concepts that would be expressed with strictly intransitive verbs in European languages (including English) can occur with either one or two arguments in Xong. For instance, the verbs *daos* 'to die', *gint* 'to rot', and *ghaus* 'to fall over, to fall down' can each occur with either one or two arguments. The same is even true (in fact, it is especially true) of property-denoting verbs like *gueinx* 'yellow', *ngaod* 'short', and *ghot* 'old', which can also each

---

190 One might also criticize the author's methodology for focusing on a wide variety of grammatical and semantic tests rather than on a smaller number of more significant such tests. However, given the lack of any previously established Aktionsart verb classes in Xong, it is not obvious (to the author, at least) how such a smaller number of tests could be chosen without resorting to either arbitrary decisions or Anglocentric (or Sinocentric, etc.) biases.

occur with either one or two arguments (as was discussed in Section 10.3 above, such property-denoting verbs are fully canonical members of the verb class in Xong).

When a semantically intransitive verb such as these has only a single argument, that single argument can have any one of a number of semantic roles depending on the argument's referent, the verb's meaning, and the discourse context, including such roles as agent, theme, experiencer, patient, instrument, location, and so on (see Section 9.1.1 for definitions of "semantically intransitive verb", "semantically transitive verb", and "semantically ditransitive verb" as the terms are used in this description). However, when a semantically intransitive verb occurs with two arguments, typically one of four specific semantic relationships will hold between those arguments.[191] These are referred to as the *possessive, identifying, rightward causative*, and *leftward causative* relationships in this grammar, and the remainder of this section will discuss each of these in turn.[192]

The most frequent type of semantic relationship that can hold between the two arguments of a semantically intransitive verb in Xong is a *possessive* one, in which the argument preceding the verb functions as the possessor of the argument following the verb. The verb itself then serves to make a predication about the argument following it, with that argument having any one of a number of semantic roles (agent, experiencer, theme, patient, etc.) depending on its own referent, the verb's meaning, and the discourse context.

There do not appear to be any hard restrictions on which semantically intransitive verbs can occur with this sort of relationship holding between their two arguments, as stative and dynamic verbs, property-denoting and non–property-denoting verbs, and telic and atelic verbs have all been attested occurring with it. Both alienably and inalienably possessed noun phrases can occur as the second argument in clauses of this sort. Note, though, that when the second argument is an inalienably possessed noun phrase, that noun phrase must consist of only a single noun; it cannot contain other noun-phrase–internal constituents like numeral-classifier phrases, demonstratives, and so on.

191 This section frames its description simply in terms of "arguments" and semantic roles (e.g. agent, patient, experiencer) rather than in terms of grammaticalized syntactic roles like SUBJECT, AGENT, or PATIENT (see Section 9.1.1). This was done because it is not yet entirely clear which grammaticalized syntactic roles are involved in any given clause that features a semantically intransitive verb with two arguments, though of course the author expects that further research will eventually shed more light on the issue.

192 Semantically intransitive verbs with two arguments can also indicate a comparative relationship between those two arguments, as in *Wel liox beul bub-jut* [1SG big 3 three-CLF:year] 'I'm three years older than him'. However, clauses of this sort arguably represent a distinct type of grammatical construction compared to the other univerbal clause types discussed in this section, rather than just a distinct semantic relationship. This is because unlike all those other clause types, comparative clauses of this sort always require some additional material (either the comparative marker *ghaod* 'more' or a complement phrase) besides the verb itself and its two arguments. Such comparative clauses are thus discussed in Section 9.3.3 rather than here.

Evidence for all these claims can be seen in examples (10.46–10.54) below. Note in particular that the second, possessed arguments in examples (10.46–10.49) are all alienably possessed, and so the more complex versions of those arguments shown in examples (10.47) and (10.49) are just as acceptable as the simpler versions shown in examples (10.46) and (10.48). However, the second, possessed arguments in examples (10.50–10.53) are all inalienably possessed, and so examples (10.51) and (10.53), which contain more complex versions of those arguments, are not accepted by consultants. Finally, only a single version of example (10.54) is given, as the author did not have the opportunity to check additional versions of this example while in the field.

(10.46) [*Beul bioud*] ***daos*** [*daob-nbat*] *lah.*
[3 home] **die** [AN-pig] PRF
'A pig of his family's has died.' (Chenghua Long, fieldnotes)

(10.47) [*Beul bioud*] ***daos*** [*oub-ngonl nbat*] *lah.*
[3 home] **die** [two-CLF:animate pig] PRF
'Two pigs of his family's have died.' (Chenghua Long, fieldnotes)

(10.48) [*Boub*] ***gint*** [*reib*] *lah.*
[1PL] **rot** [vegetable] PRF
'Our vegetables have rotted.' (Chenghua Long, fieldnotes)

(10.49) [*Boub*] ***gint*** [*bub-doud reib*] *lah.*
[1PL] **rot** [three-CLF:dou vegetable] PRF
'Three *dou* (unit of volume) of our vegetables have rotted.' (Chenghua Long, fieldnotes)

(10.50) [*Wel*] ***mos*** [*doul*] *lah.*
[1SG] **tired** [hand] PRF
'My hands are tired (from grading all these exams).' (Shixiang Wu, fieldnotes)

(10.51) *[*Wel*] ***mos*** [*aod-nqad doul neind*] *lah.*
[1SG] **tired** [one-CLF:half.of.pair hand this] PRF
(intended: 'This hand of mine is tired [from grading all these exams].')

(10.52) [*Beul*] *deit* ***xub*** [*deb*] *hint.*
[3] still **small** [child] very
'Her child is still very young.' (Haili Shi, fieldnotes) (note that this utterance can also mean 'She's still a very young child'; cf. example (10.66) below)

(10.53) *[*Beul*] *deit* ***xub*** [*aod-ngonl deb*] *hint.*
[3] still **small** [one-CLF:animate child] very
(intended: 'One of her children is still very young.')

(10.54) [*Beul*] ***ghaus*** [*deb*] *lah.*
[3] **fall.over** [child] PRF
'His child fell over.' (Chenghua Long, fieldnotes) (note that this utterance can also mean 'He made his child fall over'; cf. example (10.73) below)

Of course, this is hardly the only way of making predications about possessed noun phrases in Xong. Two other methods are shown in examples (10.55) and (10.56) below, with the first of these examples containing an instance of the *naond* possessive construction and the second containing an instance of the unflagged possessive construction (see Section 8.2 for thorough discussion of these and other ways of marking possession). The author and his consultants have not yet been able to identify any clear semantic or pragmatic differences between these sentences and their equivalent versions above.

(10.55) [*Beul bioud naond daob-nbat*] ***daos*** *lah.*
[3 home ASSOC AN-pig] **die** PRF
'A pig of his family's has died.' (Chenghua Long, fieldnotes) (cf. example (10.46) above)

(10.56) [*Wel doul*] ***mos*** *lah.*
[1SG hand] **tired** PRF
'My hands are tired (from grading all these exams).' (Shixiang Wu, fieldnotes) (cf. example (10.50) above)

The second and third types of semantic relationship that can hold between the two arguments of a semantically intransitive verb are roughly equal in frequency, but both are significantly less frequent than the possessive one discussed above. In some cases, the relationship between the two arguments of a semantically intransitive verb is an *identifying* one, in a sense very similar to the relationship found between the two arguments of a copular clause. In these cases, the verb is nearly always a property-denoting one, and the sequence [NP_1 VERB NP_2] essentially means 'NP_1 is a VERB NP_2' (so, for example, *Beul raut miex* [3 good person] would mean 'He's a good person'). Only a single example of a non–property-denoting verb has been attested in a clause of this sort; see example (10.65) and the discussion immediately preceding it below.

There appears to be a requirement that the second argument in a clause involving such an identifying relationship must consist of a single noun, rather than consisting of a more complex noun phrase (this is similar to the requirement involving inalienably possessed second arguments in the possessive relationship described above). Evidence of this requirement can be seen in examples (10.57–10.64) below.

(10.57) [*Beul*] ***shanb*** [*miex*] *hint.*
[3] **tall** [person] very
'He's a really tall person.' (Yan Long, fieldnotes)

(10.58) *[*Beul*] ***shanb*** [*aod-meinl miex*] *hint.*
[3] **tall** [one-CLF:person person] very
(intended: 'He's a really tall person.')

(10.59) [*Monx*] ***raut*** [*deb*] *jix raut?*
[2SG] **good** [child] NEG_1 good
'Are you a good kid or not?' (Yan Long, fieldnotes)

(10.60) *[*Monx*] ***raut*** [*wel naond deb*] *jix raut?*
[2SG] **good** [1SG ASSOC child] NEG_1 good
(intended: 'Are you my good kid or not?')

(10.61) [*Beul*] ***jaod*** [*guoud*] *hint.*
[3] **bad** [dog] very
'He's a really bad dog.' (Chenghua Long, fieldnotes)

(10.62) *[*Beul*] ***jaod*** [*ngonl guoud*] *hint.*
[3] **bad** [CLF:animate dog] very
(intended: 'He's a really bad dog.')

(10.63) [*Aod-leb bioud dox*] ***raut*** [*bioud*] *guaot.*
[one-CLF home that] **good** [home] pass
'That's a nice house.' (Shixiang Wu, fieldnotes)

(10.64) *[*Aod-leb bioud dox*] ***raut*** [*aod-bioud*] *guaot.*
[one-CLF home that] **good** [one-CLF:home] pass
(intended: 'That's a nice house.')

Examples (10.65–10.68) show additional instances of this identifying relationship. Example (10.65) in particular is noteworthy in that it features the non–property-denoting verb *daos* 'to die'. This is so far the only attested instance of a non–property-denoting, semantically intransitive verb occurring in a clause in which there exists an identifying relationship between the two arguments of that verb. Nevertheless, the existence of example (10.65) means that the ability to occur in such a clause cannot be used as a test to distinguish property-denoting verbs from non–property-denoting verbs in Xong (see also Section 10.3 above).[193]

(10.65) [*Niaox.meib*] ***daos*** [*miex*] *ah...*
[PN] **die** [person] PART
'Niao Mei died...' (or perhaps 'Niao Mei was/became dead...'?) (Xingyu Shi, in *Oub Meinl Yaos Geud*)

(10.66) [*Beul*] *deit* ***xub*** [*deb*] *hint.*
[3] still **small** [child] very
'She's still a very young child.' (Haili Shi, fieldnotes) (note that this utterance can also mean 'Her child is still very young'; cf. example (10.52) above)

(10.67) [*Manx oub-leb*] ***liox*** [*miex*] *lah, sat mex*
[2PL two-CLF] **big** [person] PRF SAT exist
aod-gul-jons-il-jut lah.
one-ten-seven-eight-CLF:year PRF
'You two are all grown up, you're now seventeen or eighteen years old.' (Xingyu Shi, in *Oub Meinl Yaos Geud*)

(10.68) *Ob-naont, beul baox nbanx-gieb deit nins* [*Niaox.meib*]
NOM-thus 3 father think-??? still COP [PN]
ghaod ***raut*** [*deb*], [*Niaox.nhaonl*] ***jaod*** [*deb*].
more **good** [child] [PN] **bad** [child]
'And so, their father thought that Niao Mei was the better child, Niao Nhaon the worse child.' (Xingyu Shi, in *Oub Meinl Yaos Geud*)

The same concept (i.e. 'NP_1 is a VERB $NP_{2'}$') can alternately be expressed through the use of the copular verb *nins* 'COP' along with a relative clause, as examples (10.69) and (10.70) below demonstrate. Again, the author has yet to identify any semantic or

193 This of course assumes that *daos* is not a property-denoting verb in Xong, and that it is better translated into English as 'to die' (non–property-denoting) than as 'dead' (property-denoting). The author has no independent evidence that *daos* is a non–property-denoting verb, but neither does he have any independent evidence that it is a property-denoting verb. The same is in fact true for every other attested Xong verb. For instance, it was assumed in Section 10.3 that *nkied/nkiand* was a property-denoting verb best translated as 'happy', but the author has no independent evidence that it is not in fact a non–property-denoting verb that would be better translated as 'to rejoice'. The optimal solution to this would have been to simply avoid any reference to "property-denoting" vs. "non–property-denoting" verbs in this description, since such a distinction appears to be completely irrelevant to Xong grammar. However, for purposes of crosslinguistic comparison such reference is still occasionally useful.

pragmatic differences between these sentences and their equivalents above, though there may be some subtle ones that have simply so far escaped notice.

(10.69) *Beul nins (aod-leb) manx* ***shanb*** *(naond) miex.*
3 COP (one-CLF) REL **tall** (ASSOC) person
'He's a really tall person.' (Yan Long, fieldnotes) (cf. example (10.57) above)

(10.70) *Beul deit nins (aod-leb) manx* ***xub*** *(naond) deb.*
3 still COP (one-CLF) REL **small** (ASSOC) child
'She's still a very young child.' (Haili Shi, fieldnotes) (cf. example (10.66) above)

In other cases, the relationship between the two arguments of a semantically intransitive verb is a *rightward causative* one. This relationship is somewhat similar to the possessive relationship discussed above, as in this case the verb again serves to make a predication about the argument following it. However, this rightward causative relationship differs in that here the argument preceding the verb causes the argument following the verb to acquire the property (or undergo the action, etc.) referred to by the verb in question. There appear to be fewer restrictions on the structure of the postverbal noun-phrase argument in this rightward causative relationship than there are in the possessive and identifying relationships discussed above, since consultants readily accept examples of this sort in which that postverbal noun-phrase argument contains a possessive phrase or a numeral-classifier phrase. See, for instance, examples (10.74–10.76) below.

(10.71) [*Niax zhaons*] ***zhaons*** [*mianx*].
[meat fat] **fat** [person]
'(Eating) fatty meat makes one fat.' (Chenghua Long, fieldnotes)

(10.72) [*Banb geud.donb neind*] ***mos*** [*mianx*] *hint.*
[CLF:some work this] **tired** [person] very
'This sort of work really makes one tired.' (Chenghua Long, fieldnotes)

(10.73) [*Beul*] ***ghaus*** [*deb*] *lah.*
[3] **fall.over** [child] PRF
'He made his child fall over.' (Chenghua Long, fieldnotes) (note that this utterance can also mean 'His child fell over'; cf. example (10.54) above)

(10.74) [*Aod-banb nggaob neind*] ***nqint*** [*nex laod.gheb*] *hint.*
[one-CLF:some medicine this] **red** [NEX eye] very
'This medicine really makes one's eyes red.' (Haili Shi, fieldnotes)

(10.75) [*Aod-ngonl* *guk* *dox*] ***minx.xaond*** [*wel* *naond*
[one-CLF:animate frog that] **dirty** [1SG ASSOC
aod-tont *aub*].
one-CLF:bucket water]
'That frog got my bucket of water all dirty (by jumping into it).' (Shixiang Wu, fieldnotes)

(10.76) [*Monx*] ***ndeb*** [*wel* *naond* *aod-nqad* *xux.npeif*
[2SG] **wet** [1SG ASSOC one-CLF:half.of.pair shoe
neind] *lah!*
this] PRF
'You got this shoe of mine all wet!' (Chenghua Long, fieldnotes)

Finally, in a few attested cases involving a semantically intransitive verb with two noun-phrase arguments, the relationship between those two arguments is again one of causation, but with the order reversed. In this *leftward causative* relationship, the postverbal argument causes the preverbal argument to acquire the property referred to by the verb that intervenes between them (so far all attested instances of this leftward causative relationship have involved prototypically property-denoting verbs). Due to a paucity of relevant examples in the author's corpus, it is difficult to say much about restrictions on the postverbal (i.e. causer) noun-phrase argument in clauses that display this particular semantic relationship. However, at least two tentative observations can be made. First, there do not appear to be any significant restrictions on the noun phrase structure of that postverbal argument. See, for instance, example (10.80) below, where the postverbal argument in question contains both a numeral-classifier phrase and a demonstrative. Second, unlike in clauses involving the rightward causative relationship discussed above, it appears that the causer in clauses involving this leftward causative relationship must be an inanimate entity; compare examples (10.80) and (10.81) below. Still, it must be stressed that more data will be needed before either of these observations can be confirmed.

(10.77) [*Beul*] ***saub*** [*jeud*] *lah.*
[3] **drunk** [alcohol] PRF
'He's drunk (lit. because of the alcohol).' (Chenghua Long, fieldnotes)

(10.78) [*Aod-zhet* *reib* *neind*] ***anb*** [*njeud*].
[one-CLF:bowl vegetable this] **bitter** [salt]
'This dish is too salty (lit. because of the salt).' (Shixiang Wu, fieldnotes)[194]

194 The same verb, *anb*, is used to mean both 'bitter' and 'salty' in Xong. The author's consultants are nevertheless quite conscious of a distinction between the two concepts, as there are different

(10.79) [*Monx* *xut.npeif*] ***ndeb*** [*aub*] *lah!*
[2SG shoe] **wet** [water] PRF
'Your shoes are getting wet (lit. because of the water)!' (Haili Shi, fieldnotes)

(10.80) [*Wel* *naond* *eud*] ***lous*** [*aod-hant* *ghaod.laox* *neind*].
[1SG ASSOC clothing] **dirty** [one-CLF:PL mud this]
'My clothes have gotten dirty (lit. because of this mud).' (Haili Shi, fieldnotes)

(10.81) *[*Wel* *naond* *eud*] ***lous*** [*daob-guoud*] *lah.*
[1SG ASSOC clothing] **dirty** [AN-dog] PRF
(intended: 'My clothes have gotten dirty [lit. because of the dog].')

Note that in some cases the semantic relationship that holds between the two arguments of a semantically intransitive verb may be ambiguous, with only context and real-world knowledge allowing the listener to determine which meaning was intended. Examples of this can be seen in (10.82) and (10.83) below.

(10.82) [*Beul*] *deit* ***xub*** [*deb*] *hint.*
[3] still **small** [child] very
'Her child is still very young.' *or* 'She's still a very young child.' (Haili Shi, fieldnotes)

(10.83) [*Beul*] ***ghaus*** [*deb*] *lah.*
[3] **fall.over** [child] PRF
'His child fell over.' *or* 'He made his child fall over.' (Chenghua Long, fieldnotes)

However, when precision is necessary, there are a variety of ways to explicitly indicate which of these meanings is intended by using additional linguistic material; see, for instance, examples (10.55), (10.56), (10.69), and (10.70) above.

10.5 Verbal morphology

Sections 10.5.1 through 10.5.3 below each discuss one particular morphological phenomenon in Xong that operates on a verbal root. For convenience's sake, verbal

---

terms for 'bitter' and 'salty' in the Sinitic varieties spoken by these consultants. When it is necessary to specify 'salty' rather than 'bitter', consultants will typically add a noun-phrase argument *njeud* 'salt' following the verb *anb*, as in example (10.78) here. There does not appear to be any way of specifying 'bitter' rather than 'salty', though when it occurs without a following *njeud* 'salt' consultants report that *anb* is more likely to be interpreted as 'bitter' than as 'salty'.

reduplication is also discussed below in Section 10.5.4, despite the fact that such reduplication is arguably more syntactic in nature than morphological.

10.5.1 The verbal prefix *(d)id-* 'DID'

Many Fenghuang Xong verbs can occur bearing a prefix *(d)id-* 'DID', which is generally realized as *did-* in slow or careful speech and as *id-* in faster or more casual speech. Another phonological variant, *jeud-*, occurs much less often than either *did-* or *id-*, but all three variants appear to be in free variation and all three are used by all of the author's primary consultants.

This prefix is cognate with the form /tɕi^{44}/ in Aizhai Xong (Yu 2011: 63–71) and Jiwei Xong (Xiang 1980), as well as with similar forms in many other Xong varieties. Interestingly, Taguchi (2012a) also describes a purposive/resultative prefix /sz̩^{55}/ in the Miao language Hmyo. This prefix /sz̩^{55}/ shows some amount of functional overlap with *(d)id-* in Xong, despite the fact that (i) Xong and Hmyo are not particularly close in either geographic or genealogical terms and (ii) the forms *(d)id-* and /sz̩^{55}/ are not obviously cognate.[195] Of course, unless otherwise noted, all claims about *(d)id-* advanced in this section should be assumed to apply to Fenghuang Xong only.

The prefix *(d)id-* 'DID' is a fairly high-frequency form; note, for instance, that it occurs over thirty times in the two transcribed texts included in this grammar. It has three main functions in Xong, namely serving as a purposive marker, as a durative marker, and as a reciprocal marker.[196] As with certain other high-frequency forms with relatively abstract meanings (e.g. *nex/ninx* 'NEX', discussed in Section 7.1.4, or *naond* 'ASSOC', discussed in Section 9.2.3.2), it is unclear to what extent the various functions of *(d)id-* should be considered an example of monosemy, polysemy, or ambiguity (see Gil 2004). The remainder of this section discusses the various functions of *(d)id-* separately (and in descending order of frequency), but this is done primarily for presentational convenience and should not be interpreted as a strong claim that these distinctions have any reality in the minds of Xong speakers.

First, the prefix *(d)id-* 'DID' most frequently serves as something like a purposive marker. In such cases *(d)id-* occurs on the second of two verbs to signal that the action or state referred to by the first verb was carried out in order to bring about the action or state referred to by the second verb. In other words, [VERB$_1$ *did*-VERB$_2$] means more or less 'VERB$_1$ in order to VERB$_2$'. In this function *(d)id-* is generally optional, and it can usually be removed without any clear effects on meaning or pragmatics (consultants

195 See Section 8.1.6 for more information on Hmyo and its occasional (though quite striking) grammatical similarities to Xong.

196 The prefix *(d)id-* 'DID' also occurs in a few lexicalized expressions with idiomatic meanings, like *did-nkied/nkiand* [DID-happy] 'to welcome' or *did-liox* [DID-big] 'to over-praise, to over-compliment', as well as in the [*did-lib-did*-VERB] tetrasyllabic morphological construction discussed in Section 10.5.2.

do report that the prefix is obligatory in a handful of cases, but such cases are so few that it is impossible to generalize about them at present). This is quite similar to the function of the prefix /sz^{55}/ in Hmyo as described in Taguchi (2012a), though there are still a number of minor differences between the two forms.[197]

In each of examples (10.84–10.96) below, the entire [VERB$_1$ *did*-VERB$_2$] complex has been enclosed within brackets, while *(d)id-* itself has been bolded.

(10.84) *Monx* [*puk* ***did****-zhax/liox/xub*] *shob.*
2SG [speak **DID**-strong/big/small] sound
'Speak a little louder/louder/softer.' (Chenghua Long, fieldnotes)

(10.85) *Boub* [*nonx* ***did****-diul*] *aod-zhet* *neind.*
1PL [eat **DID**-complete] one-CLF:bowl this
'Let's finish this bowl (of rice).' (Chenghua Long, fieldnotes)

(10.86) *Wel* *geud* *beul* [*peuf* ***did****-ghok*].
1SG hold 3 [crash.into **DID**-fall.over]
'I'm going to knock him over.' (Haili Shi, fieldnotes)

(10.87) *Beul* [*raok* ***id****-qaod*].
3 [hide.oneself **DID**-conceal]
'He hid himself.' (Xingyu Shi, in *Oub Meinl Yaos Geud*)

(10.88) [*Ghab* ***id****-nchot*] *tit-deb* *ghad* *raut* *lah.*
[bite **DID**-tight] CLF:time$_3$-DIM then$_2$ good PRF
'After I'd bitten down tight (on the ginger) for a little while I started to feel better.' (Haili Shi, in *Tooth Conversation*)

(10.89) *Monx* [*lol* ***did****-mieins*] *wel.*
2SG [come **DID**-bright] 1SG
'Come shine a light on me (with your flashlight).' (Chenghua Long, fieldnotes)

197 In particular, the author has observed at least three such differences. First, the second verb in a construction involving /sz^{55}/ in Hmyo must be "non-controllable" (i.e. it cannot have the ability to constitute a directive utterance by itself; see Taguchi 2012a), while there is no such restriction in Xong's purposive [VERB$_1$ *did*-VERB$_2$] construction. Second, a clause containing /sz^{55}/ in Hmyo cannot take perfect marking, while again there is no such restriction on clauses containing *(d)id-* in Xong. Third, /sz^{55}/ is also unlike *(d)id-* in that it only functions as a purposive/resultative marker in Hmyo, never as a durative or reciprocal marker.

(10.90) *Ih, chauk-dib monx at lis [daud **id**-det]*
DSMY$_1$ do-which 2SG SAT want [cut **DID**-break]
lah, dand ghoub hlod raut baod raut,
PRF grow CLF:flexible.length bamboo good quite good
*monx lis [daud **id**-det].*
2SG want [cut **DID**-break]
'Oh no, how could you cut it down? That bamboo plant was just fine, and still you had to cut it down.' (Xingyu Shi, in *Oub Meinl Yaos Geud*)

(10.91) *Dand hnef dox shib yaod.yaod [lol **id**-reinb]*
arrive CLF:day that it's all [come **DID**-determine]
nqad xut.npeif dox nins leb naond.
CLF:half.of.pair shoe that COP who ASSOC
'When the day arrived, everyone came to determine who the shoe belonged to.' (Xingyu Shi, in *Oub Meinl Yaos Geud*)

(10.92) *Aod-ngonl xut.npeif neind lis [chauk **did**-liox/xub] deb.*
one-CLF:pair$_1$ shoe this want [do **DID**-big/small] DIM
'(You) need to make this pair of shoes a little bigger/smaller.' (Haili Shi, fieldnotes)

Examples (10.93–10.96) show that a noun-phrase argument can occur between the two verbs in a [VERB$_1$ *did*-VERB$_2$] complex.

(10.93) *Beul lis [gaons monx **did**-nkiand].*
3 want [give 2SG **DID**-happy]
'He wants to make you happy.' (Chenghua Long, fieldnotes)

(10.94) *Wel npaok xaont [gaons wel **jeud**-nzeit] deb.*
1SG woman wish [give 1SG **DID**-skinny] DIM
'My wife wants me to lose some weight.' (unknown Xong consultant, fieldnotes)

(10.95) *Beul [ceik wel **jeud**-shaont] deb.*
3 [urge 1SG **DID**-fast] DIM
'He's telling me to hurry up.' (Chenghua Long, fieldnotes)

(10.96) *"Boub jed deit nins, yul hnef deit nins*
1PL older.sister still COP again CLF:day still COP
*[hat wel **id**-daos] naond." Mh, beul naond*
[harm 1SG **DID**-die] ASSOC INTJ 3 ASSOC

bod *niab* *deux:* *"Naonb.naont* *boub-leb* *nbanx* *leb*
husband say QUOT thus 1PL-DU think CLF
banb.faox *geud* *beul* [*daot* ***id****-daos*] *diex."*
solution hold 3 [kill **DID**-die] finish
'"My older sister would still – one of these days she'd still try to kill me."
Then her husband said: "Then let's the two of us think of a way to kill her
instead."' (Xingyu Shi, in *Oub Meinl Yaos Geud*)

Second, *(d)id-* 'DID' can serve as a durative marker, signaling that the action referred to by the verb on which it occurs is unusually long in duration and/or is repeated many times. Examples of this are shown in (10.97–10.100) below. Note that in some cases (e.g. in examples (10.98) and (10.99)), the duration or repetition in question is arguably doubly marked by both the prefix *(d)id-* and by verbal reduplication (see Section 10.5.4). Note also that when *(d)id-* occurs on a verb as a durative marker, that verb can also take additional aspectual-modal markers, like the progressive marker *ninb* 'at' in example (10.97) below.

(10.97) *Monx* *ninb* ***did****-nkhed* *ghaob-naonb?*
2SG at **DID**-look NOM-what
'What are you staring at?' (Haili Shi, fieldnotes)

(10.98) *Beul* *monl* *ghat* *khauk* *deul* ***did****-fand* ***did****-fand.*
3 go go.to CLF:place$_2$ fire **DID**-turn.over **DID**-turn.over
'He went to the fire-pit and poked through it.' (Xingyu Shi, in *Oub Meinl Yaos Geud*)

(10.99) *Beul* *bod* *yab...* *kheut* *leb* *baod-god-hlod.*
3 husband also get CLF BUG-stump-bamboo
Did*-saonb* ***id****-saonb,* ***id****-xaok* ***id****-xaok,* *diex* *leb* *deb-ras.*
DID-carve **DID**-carve **DID**-peel **DID**-peel finish CLF DIM-comb
'Her husband then took the bamboo stump, and he carved it and carved it, he pared it and pared it. He made a little comb (out of it).' (Xingyu Shi, in *Oub Meinl Yaos Geud*)

(10.100) *Beul* *hnef-hnef* *jont* *ninb* *dox* ***did****-nbanx.*
3 CLF:day-CLF:day sit at that **DID**-think
'Every day he sits there deep in thought.' (Haili Shi, fieldnotes)

Third, *(d)id-* 'DID' serves as the primary way of explicitly marking reciprocal actions and states in Xong, as in examples (10.101–10.105) below. In each of these examples, *(d)id-* is obligatory if the utterance is to have a reciprocal interpretation.

(10.101) *Manx oub-leb jont bioud, ghad.maons* ***id****-beux* ***id****-ndaot.*
2PL two-CLF live home NEG.IMP **DID**-hit **DID**-curse
'You two stay here at home, not fighting and not arguing.' (Xingyu Shi, in *Oub Meinl Yaos Geud*)

(10.102) *Wel nhaons beul* ***jeud****-heut chauk geud.donb.*
1SG with 3 **DID**-help do work
'He and I will help each other out with the work.' (Haili Shi, fieldnotes)

(10.103) *Oub-leb bod-oud dox hnef-hnef* ***did****-ndaot.*
two-CLF husband-wife that CLF:day-CLF:day **DID**-curse
'That husband and wife argue every day.' (Haili Shi, fieldnotes)

(10.104) *Oub-meinl deb-deb dox* ***did****-raut hint.*
two-CLF:person child-RED that **DID**-good very
'Those two children really get along with each other well.' (Chenghua Long, fieldnotes)

(10.105) *Oub-nqad* ***did****-buk ghad nins aod-ngonl.*
two-CLF:half.of.pair **DID**-combine then$_2$ COP one-CLF:pair$_1$
Did*-buk, hox* ***id****-buk, gaons beul zhut.*
DID-combine put.together **DID**-combine give 3 wear.shoes
Hox raut guaot leh, peif raut guaot leh.
fit good pass LEH match good pass LEH
'When put together, the two shoes were clearly a pair. (The landlord) put the two shoes together and gave them to her to wear. They fit perfectly, they were just the right size.' (Xingyu Shi, in *Oub Meinl Yaos Geud*)

The constructed examples in (10.106) and (10.107) below demonstrate that *(d)id-* can also be used to mark reciprocal actions and states involving more than two participants.

(10.106) *Beul-god bub-meinl* ***did****-beux/****did****-yeb/****did****-nhaons/****did****-ndaot/*
3-PL three-CLF:person **DID**-hit/**DID**-like/**DID**-with/**DID**-curse/
did*-heut.*
DID-help
'Those three people are fighting each other/like each other/are together/ are arguing with each other/are helping each other.' (Haili Shi, fieldnotes)

(10.107) *Aod-god* *deb-deb* *dox* ***did**-beux/**did**-yeb/**did**-nhaons/*
one-CLF:human.group child-RED that **DID**-hit/**DID**-like/**DID**-with/
***did**-ndaot/**did**-heut.*
DID-curse/**DID**-help
'All those children are fighting each other/like each other/are together/are arguing with each other/are helping each other.' (Haili Shi, fieldnotes)

While *(d)id-* 'DID' is the most common method of marking reciprocal actions and states in Xong, other methods do exist. In particular, another common reciprocal construction involves a single classifier occurring twice, once on each side of an intervening verb. The first (i.e. preverbal) classifier is obligatorily preceded by *aod* 'one', and the second (i.e. postverbal) classifier is either preceded by *aod* 'one' or occurs bare (see Section 6.1.3.1). The construction as a whole is then typically preceded by a noun phrase with a semantically plural referent. This can be seen in examples (10.108–10.111) below, in which each instance of the construction in question has been enclosed within brackets.

(10.108) *Beul-god* [*aod-meinl* *daot/niab/beux/ndaot* *(aod-)meinl*].
3-PL [one-CLF:person kill/say/hit/curse (one-)CLF:person]
'Those people are all killing/mocking/hitting/cursing each other.'
(Shixiang Wu, fieldnotes)

(10.109) *Aod-ncaod* *daob-guoud* *dox* [*aod-ngonl* *ghab*
one-CLF:animate.group AN-dog that [one-CLF:animate bite
(aod-)ngonl].
(one-)CLF:animate]
'Those dogs are all biting each other.' (Shixiang Wu, fieldnotes)

(10.110) *Aod-hant* *ob-ndaut* *dox* [*aod-zhons* *giant*
one-CLF:PL NOM-tree that [one-CLF:vertical.plant stick.to
(aod-)zhons].
(one-)CLF:vertical.plant]
'Those trees are all standing close together.' (Haili Shi, fieldnotes)

(10.111) *Beul-gud* [*aod-meinl* *nkhed/ghans* *(aod-)meinl*].
3-PL [one-CLF:person look/see (one-)CLF:person]
'Those people are looking at/see each other.' (Chenghua Long, fieldnotes)

The author has not been able to identify any clear differences in semantics, pragmatics, or productivity between this reciprocal construction and the reciprocal construction involving *(d)id-* described earlier in this section. However, there does appear to be a general preference to use the *(d)id-* reciprocal construction when only two (or at least a relatively small number of) entities are involved, and to use the other reciprocal construction involving classifiers when a larger number of entities are involved. As examples (10.106) and (10.107) above show, though, this is not a strict grammatical rule.

Finally, there are a few attested cases which do not fit into any of the categories discussed so far in this section. Examples of these are given in (10.112–10.115) below. In these cases, consultants report that *(d)id-* 'DID' is completely optional and does not contribute anything to the overall meaning of the utterance, though of course further research may reveal some subtle semantic or pragmatic difference resulting from the presence versus absence of *(d)id-*.

(10.112) *Monx* ***(did****-)shaont* *monl.*
2SG (**DID**-)fast go
'Go faster.' (Chenghua Long, fieldnotes)

(10.113) *Monx* ***(did****-)jont* *ghoub* *deb.*
2SG (**DID**-)sit far DIM
'Sit a little further away.' (Chenghua Long, fieldnotes)

(10.114) *Beul* ***(did****-)beinl* *wel.*
3 (**DID**-)frighten 1SG
'He frightens me.' (Chenghua Long, fieldnotes)

(10.115) *Monx* ***(did****-)choud* *wel* *nzhaod,* *wel* *eint* *ghat*
2SG (**DID**-)follow 1SG return 1SG fly go.to
dib *monx* *nhob* *ghat* *dib.*
which 2SG walk go.to which
'Follow me back. Wherever I fly, you walk.' (Xingyu Shi, in *Oub Meinl Yaos Geud*)

10.5.2 The [*did-lib-did*-VERB] construction

Many Xong verbs can appear in an obligatorily tetrasyllabic construction in which the first and third syllables are each an instance of the verbal prefix *(d)id-* 'DID' (see Section 10.5.1 above) and the fourth syllable is the verb itself. When speaking quickly or casually, the second instance of the prefix in this construction can be realized as *id-*, but this never happens for the first instance of it. Furthermore, both instances of the prefix can optionally be realized as *jeud-*, as in example (10.135) below. The second syllable in this construction is either *-lib-* or is phonologically derived from the verb itself. In the latter case, this second syllable will have the same initial consonant as the verb itself, while it will have /ɤj/ (orthographic <ei>) as its vowel and *-b* as its tone. For example, from the verb *ncod* 'messy' one can derive the morphologically complex construction *did-nceib-did-ncod* 'a bit messy, kind of messy', or, alternately and with the same meaning, *did-lib-did-ncod*. Similarly, from the verb *kuad* 'to stir' one can derive the morphologically complex construction *did-kueib-did-kuad* 'to stir gradually or steadily', or, alternately and with the same meaning, *did-lib-did-kuad*.

As these glosses suggest, this construction has one of two different semantic effects on verbs that appear in it. When this construction features a verb with a stative meaning, it has an attenuative semantic effect, but when it features a verb with a dynamic meaning, it instead adds the meaning of 'gradually, steadily' to the meaning of the verb. This can be seen by comparing examples (10.116–10.118), which feature verbs with stative meanings, with examples (10.119) and (10.120), which feature verbs with dynamic meanings.[198]

(10.116) *Beul zhanx aod-nqof niub neind*
3 tie one-CLF:bundle rice.straw this
did-lib-did-sonk, *aod-dieud leh doub nkhoud lah.*
DID-LIB-DID-loose one-CLF:time$_2$ LEH then$_1$ fall.out PRF
'He tied up this bundle of rice straw kind of loosely, it fell apart in just a moment.' (Haili Shi, fieldnotes) (also acceptable: *did-**seib**-did-sonk*)

(10.117) *Mx lis jont id-raut, ghaod.maons* ***did-gheib-did-ghax.***
2SG want sit DID-good NEG.IMP **DID-LIB-DID-crooked**
'Sit up straight, don't sit there kind of hunched over like that.' (Shixiang Wu, fieldnotes) (also acceptable: *did-**lib**-did-ghax*)

(10.118) *jeud-mieib-jeud-miot*
DID-LIB-DID-moist
'kind of moist, a little moist' (Chenghua Long, fieldnotes) (also acceptable: *jeud-**lib**-jeud-miot*)

(10.119) *Aod-leb gieux dox ik.zhil* ***did-nggueib-did-ngguaot.***
one-CLF bridge that always **DID-LIB-DID-collapse**
'That bridge has always been falling apart.' (Chenghua Long, fieldnotes) (also acceptable: *did-**lib**-did-ngguaot*)

198 These and most other instances of the [*did-lib-did*-VERB] construction in this section were re-elicited from Yu (2011: 489, 490). Note, though, that the example utterances in which each such instance occurs were produced freely by this author's own consultants, since Yu only gives examples of this construction in isolation.

(10.120) *Miant oub-meinl deib dox* ***did-ndeib-did-ndaot,*** *jud*
3PL two-CLF:person at that **DID-LIB-DID-curse** NEG_2
nianl ndaot beint ndaot ghaob-naonb.
know curse ??? curse NOM-what
'Those two people over there just keep arguing and arguing, (and I) don't even know what they're arguing about.' (Shixiang Wu, fieldnotes) (also acceptable: *did-**lib**-did-ndaot*)

The meaning of any particular instance of this construction is thus a product of the meaning of the construction itself and the meaning of the verb occurring in it.[199] So far there do not appear to be any semantic or pragmatic differences between the two variants of this construction (i.e. the one in which the second syllable is *-lib-* and the one in which the second syllable is phonologically derived from the verb itself), although a handful of cases have been attested in which (for unknown reasons) a consultant will only accept one of these variants for a particular verb. Two such cases are shown in (10.121) and (10.122) below, although at present it is unclear whether or not this is an idiolectal idiosyncrasy restricted to the consultant in question.

(10.121) *Mx ghaod.maons chauk hant gaons nex*
2SG NEG.IMP do CLF:PL give NEX
did-lib-did-beinl *naond sib.*
DID-LIB-DID-frighten ASSOC matter
'Don't do those sorts of things that are always scaring other people.' (Shixiang Wu, fieldnotes) (not acceptable: **did-**beib**-did-beinl*)

(10.122) *Wel beut ninb daod.doub* ***did-gieib-did-giaond.***
1SG lie.down at earth **DID-LIB-DID-roll**
'I kept rolling back and forth as I slept on the ground.' (Shixiang Wu, fieldnotes) (not acceptable: **did-**lib**-did-giaond*)

Because no pragmatic or semantic differences are apparent between the two variants of this construction, the author uses a single gloss for both: [DID-LIB-DID-VERB], where the gloss for 'VERB' naturally varies depending on the meaning of the verb itself. Hyphens are used to connect all four component syllables of this construction for two reasons. First, hyphens rather than spaces are used because no other material (verbal, nominal, or otherwise) can occur between any two adjacent syllables of this construction. Second, hyphens rather than periods (as are used to connect, e.g., the component syllables

199 This is somewhat similar to the way in which the meaning of any particular ideophone will be a product of the meaning of the ideophone template and the meaning of the ideophone root itself. See Section 11.1.2 for details.

of polysyllabic monomorphemic forms) are used because three of the four component syllables in any instance of this construction have specific, readily identifiable meanings, with only the second syllable (glossed 'LIB') having no specific meaning apart from the meaning of the construction as a whole. Nevertheless, despite this glossing convention, it is still true that the meaning of any particular instance of this construction is a product of the meaning of the construction itself and the meaning of the verb occurring in it, rather than being the sum of the meanings of all four component syllables.

Finally, there does not appear to be any obvious way to characterize which Xong verbs can appear in this [*did-lib-did*-VERB] construction and which cannot. Several dozen examples of this construction (each featuring a different verb) are listed in Yu (2011: 489, 490), and this author's own consultants have produced about a dozen examples of it, although they do report that certain verbs cannot appear in it. Examples of such verbs found so far include *nins* 'COP', *daos* 'to die', and *box.nhol* 'to throw away'.[200]

10.5.3 The [VERB-*lib*-VERB-*daod*] construction

This is another obligatorily tetrasyllabic construction in which many Xong verbs can appear. In this construction, the first and third syllables are two identical instances of the verb itself, while the second syllable is *-lib-* and the fourth syllable is *-daod*. A syllable *-lib-* is also found in the [*did-lib-did*-VERB] construction described in Section 10.5.2 above, and a syllable *daod* is found in ideophone template B (see Section 11.1.2), although there are no obvious semantic connections among any of these constructions. While the meaning of the [*did-lib-did*-VERB] construction varies depending on the particular verb that occurs in it, and while ideophone template B is used to refer to single, sudden actions or events, this [VERB-*lib*-VERB-*daod*] construction always has an attenuating semantic effect. For instance, *nqint-lib-nqint-daod* (with the verb *nqint* 'red') means 'a little bit red, reddish', while *liaos-lib-liaos-daod* (with the verb *liaos* 'to miss') means 'to miss (a person or place) a little bit'. All four syllables in any particular instance of this construction are connected by hyphens and are given individual glosses for much the same reasons as with the [*did-lib-did*-VERB] construction discussed in Section 10.5.2.

Several examples of this construction are shown in (10.123–10.132) below.

(10.123)	*Boub*	*bioud*	*deid*	*deul,*	***ntiot-lib-ntiot-daod.***
	1PL	home	burn	firewood	**smoky-LIB-smoky-DAOD**

'We're burning firewood in our home, (so it's) a little bit smoky.'
(Chenghua Long, fieldnotes)

200 While the disyllabic verb *box.nhol* 'to throw away' cannot occur in this construction, certain other disyllabic verbs (like *minx.xaond* 'dirty') can. In such cases, the second syllable of the construction must be *-lib-* rather than being phonologically derived from the verb itself.

(10.124) *Zheit-zhauf* ***giand-lib-giand-daod.***
outside-door **icy-LIB-icy-DAOD**
'It's a little bit icy outside.' (Chenghua Long, fieldnotes)

(10.125) *Tat-hnef* ***ndit-lib-ndit-daod.***
this-CLF:day **hot-LIB-hot-DAOD**
'It's a little bit hot out today.' (Chenghua Long, fieldnotes)

(10.126) *Beul bioud jix sanb liot, deit* ***mex-lib-mex-daod.***
3 home NEG_1 count.as wealthy still **exist-LIB-exist-DAOD**
'His family can't be considered wealthy, but they've got a bit of money.' (Shixiang Wu, fieldnotes)

(10.127) *Aod-janb sib neind wel sat* ***nianl-lib-nianl-daod*** *leh.*
one-CLF:matter matter this 1SG SAT **know-LIB-know-DAOD** LEH
'I just know a little bit about this.' (Chenghua Long, fieldnotes)

(10.128) *Jix nanb raut nonx, wel nanx nins* ***ncheut-lib-ncheut-daod.***
NEG_1 really good eat 1SG only COP **full-LIB-full-DAOD**
'(The food) wasn't really good, (so now after eating it) I'm only a little bit full.' (Shixiang Wu, fieldnotes)

(10.129) *Aod-leb pinf.gox neind* ***gint-lib-gint-daod,*** *deit nonx ix dut.*
one-CLF apple this **rot-LIB-rot-DAOD** still eat NEG_1 obtain
'This apple is (only) a little bit rotten, (but you) still shouldn't eat it.' (Chenghua Long, fieldnotes)

(10.130) ***Dianx-lib-dianx-daod,*** *doul aod-nqad donl.*
finish-LIB-finish-DAOD remain one-CLF:half.of.pair sleeve
'(I'm) almost done (sewing this article of clothing, I just) have one sleeve left (to do).' (Chenghua Long, fieldnotes)

(10.131) *Beul* ***qont-lib-qont-daod,*** *nhob geud sat wanx*
3 **arrogant-LIB-arrogant-DAOD** walk road SAT shake
biuk wanx ghaod.
buttocks shake feces
'She's a bit arrogant, she even wiggles her butt when she's walking down the street.' (Shixiang Wu, fieldnotes)

(10.132) *Aod-bas ndeud neind wel* ***sheit-lib-sheit-daod.***
one-CLF:page paper this 1SG **write-LIB-write-DAOD**
'I've written a little bit on this page.' (Haili Shi, fieldnotes)

It is quite difficult to characterize the set of verbs that can appear in this construction. Most property-denoting verbs can readily do so, but some (like *kod* 'poor' and *kueif* 'expensive') cannot. Some non–property-denoting stative verbs (like *niel/nianl* 'to know' and *mex* 'to exist', the latter here in the sense of 'wealthy') can appear in this construction, but others (like *lis* 'to want' and *ninb* 'at, to live [at]') cannot. Finally, most dynamic (i.e. non-stative) verbs cannot appear in this construction, but a few (like *diex/dianx* 'to finish' and *sheit* 'to write') can.

10.5.4 Verbal reduplication

Xong verbs can undergo reduplication to indicate intensity (for property- and state-denoting verbs) or repetitive actions or events (for other verbs). Any given verb can be reduplicated any number of times, with a greater number of reduplications signaling a greater intensity or greater number of repetitions in an iconic fashion.

(10.133) *Daob-guk nins aod-ngonl deb-nceik manx* ***xonx***
AN-frog COP one-CLF:animate DIM-young.man REL **attractive**
xonx *dox.*
attractive that
'The frog was (actually) that handsome young man.' (Xingyu Shi, in *Deb Guk Ronf*)

(10.134) *Baox jix kiak.* ***Hnant hnant*** *deit jix kiak.*
father NEG$_1$ open **call call** still NEG$_1$ open
'(Her) father didn't open (the gate). She called and called, but he still didn't open it.' (Xingyu Shi, in *Oub Meinl Yaos Geud*)

(10.135) *Wel meh, liaos monx naond guaot, daonl jix*
1SG BCKG miss 2SG ASSOC pass wait NEG$_1$
niaons monx nzhaod, hnef-hnef ***nied nied nied.***
ABIL 2SG return CLF:day-CLF:day **cry cry cry**
'But I missed you greatly, I couldn't wait for you to come back. Every day I wept and wept and wept.' (Xingyu Shi, in *Oub Meinl Yaos Geud*)

(10.136) ***Cod cod cod,*** *cod diex aod-tit-deb cod*
sew sew sew sew finish one-CLF:time$_3$-DIM sew
diex ngonl xut.npeif.
finish CLF:pair$_1$ shoe
'(She) sewed and sewed and sewed, and after a little while she'd finished a pair of shoes.' (Xingyu Shi, in *Oub Meinl Yaos Geud*)

(10.137) *Yab* ***nhob nhob nhob nhob nhob nhob****.* *At nhob*
also **walk walk walk walk walk walk** SAT walk
gid.daud ghoub.
extremely far
'So again (they) walked, and walked, and walked, and walked. They walked very, very far.' (Xingyu Shi, in *Oub Meinl Yaos Geud*)

(10.138) *Hant minl-aob-baont aob-ndaut sat ix dand, aob-ncoud*
CLF:PL AUG-NOM-slope NOM-tree SAT NEG$_1$ grow NOM-grass
khaonl khaonl, yab ***jind jind jind jind****!*
nothing.but nothing.but also **steep steep steep steep**
'On those slopes not a single tree grows, there's nothing but grasses, and it's so, so steep!' (Chenghua Long, in *Conversation in La'ershan*)

(10.139) *Yab yul nhob, nhob* ***ghoub ghoub ghoub ghoub ghoub ghoub****.*
also again walk walk **far far far far far far**
'Again they walked, they walked very, very, very far.' (Xingyu Shi, in *Oub Meinl Yaos Geud*)

Verbs that bear the prefix *(d)id-* 'DID' (see Section 10.5.1 above) can also be reduplicated. Typically each instance of the reduplicated verb will bear the prefix, but in some cases (as in example (10.140) below) the prefix will only occur on the first instance of the reduplicated verb.

(10.140) *Wel nanx dionb beul monl* ***id-ghoub ghoub ghoub****.*
1SG only lead 3 go **DID-far far far**
'So I'll just lead her far, far away.' (Xingyu Shi, in *Oub Meinl Yaos Geud*)

(10.141) *Aod-leb soub.xob.tif neind nanx guaot,* ***dib-nbanx***
one-CLF math.problem this difficult pass **DID-think**
did-nbanx *haut-yut loux deit nbanx jud dut bionl.*
DID-think how.much-few long.time still think NEG$_2$ obtain exit
'This math problem is really hard, I've been thinking forever and I still can't get it.' (Haili Shi, fieldnotes)

(10.142) *Beul chot aod-zhet hlit ninb dox* ***did-kuad***
3 take one-CLF:bowl cooked.rice at that **DID-stir**
did-kuad*, aod-hnef deit nonx jix dut diul.*
DID-stir one-CLF:day still eat NEG$_1$ obtain complete
'He kept poking at the bowl of food, never finishing it.' (Haili Shi, fieldnotes)

(10.143) *Aod-ngonl* *deb-deb* *ninb* *dox* ***did-nied*** ***did-nied.***
one-CLF:animate child-RED at that **DID-cry** **DID-cry**
'The child over there just keeps crying and crying.' (Haili Shi, fieldnotes)

(10.144) *Beul* *chot* *aod-del* *gond* ***did-baond*** ***did-baond***
3 take one-CLF:rigid.length bow **DID-shoot** **DID-shoot**
laot-ndaut *naond* *daob-naus.*
top-tree ASSOC AN-bird
'He took a bow and kept shooting and shooting at the birds in the tree.' (Haili Shi, fieldnotes)

Though the author has no decisive evidence one way or the other, verbal reduplication in Xong seems to be rather more of a syntactic phenomenon than a morphological one. For example, Xong verbs can be reduplicated any number of times instead of only once, and each instance of a reduplicated verb can individually bear the verbal prefix *(d)id-* 'DID'. Because of this, reduplicated instances of Xong verbs are not connected by hyphens in this or other sections of this grammar.

11 Expressive forms

In much the same vein as Chapters 7 (on deictic forms) and 8 (on complex nominal constructions), this chapter discusses three formally and functionally distinct phenomena in Xong that nevertheless share certain properties which justify describing them together. The phenomena covered in this chapter in particular are ideophones (see Section 11.1), onomatopoeic forms (Section 11.2), and interjections (Section 11.3).[201] These three phenomena are most saliently similar in that they are often used to describe vivid sensory impressions or to express vivid emotion on the part of the speaker. They are also similar in that they are fairly "inert" in syntactic terms (though not necessarily in phonological or morphological ones), as they participate in relatively few syntactic constructions and display few noteworthy syntactic properties. Still, despite these similarities, there are very real formal and functional differences among ideophones, onomatopoeic forms, and interjections in Xong, and they cannot in any sense be considered to constitute a single lexical category.

11.1 Ideophones

11.1.1 Introduction

Along with nouns (see Chapter 5), classifiers (Section 6.1), and verbs (Chapter 10), *ideophones* constitute one of the major lexical categories in Fenghuang Xong. (For general crosslinguistic surveys of ideophones, see Voeltz and Kilian-Hatz 2001 and Dingemanse 2012.) Approximately 90 ideophones have so far been attested, although the author has no reason to expect that more ideophones will not be found in the future. Ideophones in Xong serve an essentially adverbial function, as they typically express the manner in which an action or event denoted by a non–property-denoting verb occurs, or the manner in which or degree to which a property denoted by a property-denoting verb holds. A wide variety of adverbial notions can be expressed by ideophones in Xong, including relatively general notions like intensity, speed, frequency, duration, and suddenness as well as more specific notions like 'loudly', 'happily', and 'shiningly'. Examples (11.1) and (11.2) below show ideophones modifying a non–property-denoting verb and a property-denoting verb, respectively. For

201 Both the title of this chapter and the grouping of ideophones, onomatopoeic forms, and interjections together in it were inspired by Enfield's 2007 grammar of the Tai-Kadai language Lao. Enfield's grammar also has a chapter titled "Expressive forms" that covers many of the same topics as this chapter (Enfield 2007: 299–315), and the reasons Enfield gives for discussing those topics together apply just as well to Xong as they do to Lao.

discussion of the glossing conventions used with these and other ideophones in this grammar, see Section 11.1.2.

(11.1) *Beul* *zhok* ***reis.reis.***
3 smile **IDEO:A:happily**
'He's grinning happily.' (Chenghua Long, fieldnotes)

(11.2) *Aod-ngonl* *deb-deb* *neind* *xub* ***zeik.zeik.***
one-CLF:animate child-RED this small **IDEO:A:small**
'This child is so tiny.' (Shixiang Wu, fieldnotes)

Ideophones differ from Xong's other major lexical categories in several important ways. First, ideophones are extremely uncommon in the author's collected texts and utterances. For example, in the two transcribed texts included with this grammar, only a single ideophone is attested, although it does at least occur twice in succession. This is shown in (11.3) below.

(11.3) *Beul* *hnef-hnef* *nzhaod,* *hnef-hnef* *chauk-dib*
3 CLF:day-CLF:day return CLF:day-CLF:day do-which
leb *bix.giab* *nqif* ***jel.jel,*** *nhaons-bioud* *nqif*
CLF yard clean **IDEO:A:shiningly** inside-home clean
jel.jel.
IDEO:A:shiningly
'Every day she came back, and every day, no matter what, she'd make the house and yard sparkling clean.' (Xingyu Shi, in *Oub Meinl Yaos Geud*)

This rarity holds regardless of genre, the speaker's age, the speaker's hometown, or any other obvious factors, and it stands in sharp contrast to the omnipresence of nouns, verbs, and classifiers in most Xong texts and utterances. It is unclear whether the very low frequency of ideophones is an unusual feature of Fenghuang Xong compared to other Xong varieties, or whether other sources have exaggerated the importance of these forms to some degree. Certainly, if it were not for previously published descriptions of Xong ideophones in other sources (especially Hong 2011) and the detailed elicitations that those descriptions allowed this author to perform, this grammar would not contain nearly as lengthy an account of ideophones as the one given in this chapter. A description of Fenghuang Xong which neglected to discuss nouns, classifiers, or verbs could hardly be considered a description at all, but it appears that one which neglected to discuss ideophones could still be considered reasonably complete.[202]

202 Of course, this then raises the question of why the author bothers to discuss Xong's ideophones at all, or at least why he bothers to discuss them in such detail. The answer to this is quite simple:

Second, ideophones differ from Xong's other major lexical categories in that the boundaries of the ideophone class as a whole are much more sharply defined. As is discussed in more detail in Section 1.2.2, there is a significant amount of overlap among nouns, classifiers, and verbs in Xong. However, there does not appear to be any overlap whatsoever between nouns and ideophones, between classifiers and ideophones, or between verbs and ideophones. No ideophonic form will ever occur as a noun, a classifier, or a verb, and vice versa. There is, however, some degree of overlap between ideophones and certain other minor lexical categories, in particular onomatopoeic forms (see Section 11.2).

Third, ideophones appear to be a closed class in Xong, albeit a fairly large one. Consultants often produce new nouns, classifiers, and verbs, with the new forms typically being borrowed from another lexical category (e.g. nouns being used as classifiers), being borrowed from another language (usually Fenghuang Chinese or Standard Mandarin), or being produced through processes of compounding or derivation (e.g. creating a noun compound from multiple noun roots, or adding a nominal prefix to a noun root). In contrast, consultants are unable to come up with new ideophones to modify new verbs or to describe unusual situations in which existing ideophones do not apply, and they do not produce new ideophones either through borrowing from other lexical categories or borrowing from other languages.[203]

Fourth and finally, ideophones display a number of unusual morphological, phonological, and syntactic properties not shared by any of Xong's other major lexical categories. These include (i) the fact that Xong ideophones never appear as monosyllabic forms, but instead appear in one of several polysyllabic morphological templates derived from monosyllabic ideophone roots (see Section 11.1.2), (ii) the fact that most ideophones display several unusual phonological properties relating to the relative frequency of certain vowels and tones and to tonal ordering (Section 11.1.3), and (iii) the fact that nearly every ideophone obligatorily co-occurs with a verb, which the ideophone serves to modify (the few attested exceptions to this are described in Section 11.1.4). The first and third properties just mentioned are in fact sufficient to define ideophones as a lexical category distinct from nouns, classifiers, and verbs (the second is not, since it is far from exceptionless), although again there is still some overlap between ideophones and certain onomatopoeic forms.

Before moving on to detailed discussions of the morphological, phonological, syntactic, and semantic properties of Xong ideophones, some comments about Hong (2011) are in order. Hong (2011) is a master's thesis devoted to ideophones in Jiwei Xong (see Sections 2.4 and 2.5.2.1 of this grammar for more on this variety), and it

despite their rarity, ideophones are extremely interesting forms in terms of their phonological, morphological, and semantic properties, which differ quite sharply from the phonological, morphological, and semantic properties displayed by forms belonging to Xong's other major lexical categories.

203 This last point is true despite the fact that ideophones are attested in many other languages of the greater mainland Southeast Asian linguistic area, including many Sinitic ones (see, e.g., Meng 2012).

is by far the most comprehensive description of Xong ideophones published to date. Hong identifies 125 distinct ideophone roots and six distinct ideophone templates (cf. Section 11.1.2 below). There are many formal and semantic differences between the roots and templates identified by Hong and those identified by the author of this grammar, although it is not clear whether these are primarily due to differences in methodology and analysis or due to the fact that Hong and this author worked on different Xong varieties.[204] In any case, while Hong (2011) will not be reviewed in detail here, as an elicitation tool it was invaluable to the author of this grammar in the course of his own fieldwork, and for readers literate in Chinese it is certainly worth consulting for an alternate account of these unusual Xong forms. (Note, though, that unless otherwise specified all references to "Xong" in the remainder of this Section 11.1 are intended to refer to Fenghuang Xong only, and not to the Jiwei variety of Xong on which Hong worked.)

11.1.2 Morphological structure

Ideophones are unique among the major lexical categories of Xong in that they never appear as bare monosyllabic forms; instead, each ideophone root will obligatorily occur in one of several polysyllabic morphological *templates*. When an ideophone root occurs in the morphologically simplest template (this is template A, discussed in more detail further below in this section), the resulting surface form is obligatorily disyllabic, and in more complex templates it will also have at least two syllables, if not more. This obligatory polysyllabicity can be seen in examples (11.4–11.7) below.

(11.4) *Aod-leb* *tont* *neind* *xab* ***nkond.nkond***.
one-CLF bucket this light **IDEO:A:light**
'This bucket is really light.' (Shixiang Wu, fieldnotes)

(11.5) **Aod-leb* *tont* *neind* *xab* ***nkond***.
one-CLF bucket this light **???**
(intended: 'This bucket is really light.')

204 In particular, note that Hong's fieldwork on Xong was done in Beijing, and her sole consultant was a Xong-speaking university professor who had previously published academic articles on Xong in linguistic journals (Hong 2011: 21). In contrast, this author's own fieldwork was done in rural Xong-speaking communities in western Hunan, and his own consultants had not had any formal linguistic training.

(11.6) *Hex.lib* *aod-roul* *ngaonf* *gueub* ***npeif.npeif.***
PN one-CLF:time$_1$ time white **IDEO:A:white**
'He Li is really nice and pale now (after spending so much time in the hospital following the birth of her child).' (Chenghua Long, fieldnotes)[205]

(11.7) **Hex.lib* *aod-roul* *ngaonf* *gueub* ***npeif.***
PN one-CLF:time$_1$ time white **???**
(intended: 'He Li is really nice and pale now.')

Five distinct ideophone templates have so far been attested in the speech of the author's consultants, and these vary in complexity from the basic, contiguous, disyllabic template seen in examples (11.4) and (11.6) above (i.e. template A) to much more complex tetrasyllabic ones. The final syllable of any ideophone is referred to as the ideophone's *root* in this grammar, since (i) many of Xong's more complex ideophone templates involve the insertion of additional syllables that are phonologically derived from the root, and (ii) when a given root can appear in multiple templates, the final syllable in each of those templates (i.e. the root itself) will always be identical across all templates. It is important to note that many of Xong's ideophone templates are themselves associated with some semantic content, so that the meaning of a particular ideophone depends both on the meaning of the root itself and on the meaning of the template in which it occurs.[206]

Nevertheless, the great majority of attested ideophone roots (approximately 85%) only occur in the simplest morphological template (template A), and many of the more complex templates discussed below only allow a handful of ideophone roots to occur in them. Of course, it is possible that ideophonic morphology in Fenghuang Xong has become "fossilized", or less productive than it was at some point in the past, and that the more complex templates discussed below were once much more productive than they currently are. A serious investigation of this hypothesis lies outside the scope of this grammar. Still, it must be mentioned that if fossilization of this sort did indeed occur, it does not appear to have occurred very recently, since the more complex morphological templates do not appear to be notably more common in the speech of the author's elderly consultants than in the speech of his younger ones.

---

205 Just as is the case with China's majority Han culture, pale skin is seen as highly desirable (especially for women) among the Miao people of Fenghuang County.

206 Xong's ideophonic morphology is thus (in a certain very broad sense) somewhat similar to the well known nonconcatenative morphology of the Semitic languages (see, e.g., Simpson 2009), with the monosyllabic roots of Xong ideophones corresponding to the consonantal roots of Semitic languages and the morphological templates in which those Xong roots can occur corresponding to the morphological templates in which Semitic roots can occur. Note, though, that Xong's ideophonic morphology is vastly less productive than nonconcatenative morphology is in many Semitic languages, and also that most of Xong's morphological templates carry much less of a semantic (to say nothing of grammatical) functional load than do the morphological templates of Semitic languages.

Before moving on to detailed discussions of each invidual ideophone template, Table 11.1 summarizes some basic properties of all five templates.[207]

Table 11.1: Summary of Xong ideophone templates.

TEMPLATE	FORMULA	SEMANTICS	PRODUCTIVITY	EXAMPLE
A	A → A.A, A → A′.A	Intensifying	Very high (can occur with every root)	*npeif.npeif* [IDEO:A:white]
B	A → *daod*.A	Single, sudden action or event	Medium (can occur with ~10% of roots)	*daod.gueinl* [IDEO:B:brightly]
C	A → V-C*id*-V-A	Attenuating	Very low (3 attested examples)	*gueb-mid-gueb-miaod* [black-IDEO-black-IDEO:C:black]
D	A → A′.A′.A.A	Strongly intensifying	Very low (3 attested examples)	*zaol.zaol.zous.zous* [IDEO:D:quickly]
E	n/a	'slowly, quietly, lightly'	Very low (4 attested examples)	*shad.shont.shad.shont* [IDEO:E:deeply]

As mentioned above, the morphologically simplest template in Xong is a disyllabic one, with both syllables always having the same consonant and vowel and usually (specifically, in approximately two-thirds of cases) the same tone. This is referred to as template A in this grammar. The derivation of this template from an ideophone root can be represented abstractly with [A → A.A] or [A → A′.A], where *A* represents the ideophone root and *A′* represents a phonologically altered version of that root (in this case, one that bears a different tone). Note that when the two syllables of a template A ideophone bear different tones, the tone on the first syllable is not predictable from the tone on the second (i.e. the root), though there do appear to be certain restrictions on which tones can precede which in this template (see Section 11.1.3 below for details). All attested Xong ideophone roots can occur in this template, and the template itself typically has an intensifying semantic effect on such roots.

Examples of ideophones occurring in template A are given in (11.8–11.13) below.

(11.8) *xob* ***biaol.biaol***
sour **IDEO:A:sour**
'very sour' (Haili Shi, fieldnotes)

207 In both Table 11.1 and the discussion following it, the five ideophone templates of Fenghuang Xong have first been arranged in descending order of productivity, so that template A occurs first, followed by template B, followed in turn by templates C, D, and E. However, templates C, D, and E are all more or less equally unproductive, and so they have been further arranged in descending order of morphological and phonological regularity. See the discussions of each individual template below in this section for details.

(11.9) *Beul khauk-mes gueb* ***miaod.miaod.***
3 hole-face black **IDEO:A:black**
'His face is very dirty/dark.' (Chenghua Long, fieldnotes)

(11.10) *Piaf git* ***louk.louk,*** *lis daox nons.*
blow wind **IDEO:A:breezily** want precipitate rain
'It's a little bit breezy, (so it looks like) it's going to rain.' (Shixiang Wu, fieldnotes)

(11.11) *Beul jont ninb dox giaol* ***npud.npud*** *naond,*
3 sit at that stupid **IDEO:A:stupid** ASSOC
jud niel nbanx hant naonb.
NEG_2 know think CLF:PL what
'He's sitting over there spacing out like an idiot, who knows what he's thinking about.' (Haili Shi, fieldnotes)

(11.12) *nzeit* ***khaod.khaot***
skinny **IDEO:A:skinny**
'very skinny' (Chenghua Long, fieldnotes)

(11.13) *zhaons* ***biaond.biaont***
fat **IDEO:A:chubby**
'very chubby (said of, e.g., a baby)' (Shixiang Wu, fieldnotes)

As can be seen in examples (11.8–11.13) (as well as in earlier examples in this section), ideophones are glossed in this grammar using the formula 'IDEO:X:Y', where *X* is the particular template in which the ideophone root is occurring (e.g. 'A', 'B', 'C', etc.) and *Y* is the meaning of the root itself. The component syllables of a particular instance of an ideophone are generally connected with periods rather than hyphens, since the meaning of an ideophone is more a product of the meaning of the ideophone's root and the meaning of its (occasionally nonconcatenative) template than it is a product of the meanings of its individual syllables. However, hyphens are used to connect the component syllables of template C ideophones, as is discussed further below in this section.

Much less productive than template A (though still much more productive than the other templates discussed further below) is template B, which is an obligatorily disyllabic template in which the ideophone's root is preceded by the syllable *daod*. This template can thus be represented abstractly as [A → *daod*.A]. Approximately 10% of attested ideophone roots can occur in this template, making it the second most productive template encountered so far. Like template A, template B has a fairly clear semantic effect on ideophone roots appearing in it. While a template A ideophone will simply have a general intensifying meaning (with the actual meaning in any particular case depending on the meaning of the ideophone's root), a template B ideophone can only be used to refer to a single, sudden action or event. For example, while *ghab nggont.nggont* [bite IDEO:A:crunching] means 'to chew with loud crunching noises', *ghab daod.nggont* [bite IDEO:B:crunching] means 'to bite down (once) with a loud crunch'.

Examples of template B ideophones are given in (11.14–11.18) below.

(11.14) *Wel ghab aob-sond* ***daod.nggont*** *jeub det lah.*
1SG bite NOM-bone **IDEO:B:crunching** then$_3$ break PRF
'I crunched down on that (chicken) bone (once), and it just snapped.' (Chenghua Long, fieldnotes) (cf. *nggont.nggont* [IDEO:A:crunching])

(11.15) *Beul naond aob-doul shoub* ***daod.zous.***
3 ASSOC NOM-hand tremble **IDEO:B:quickly**
'His hands suddenly shook (once).' (Chenghua Long, fieldnotes) (cf. *zous.zous* [IDEO:A:quickly])

(11.16) *Beul naond cheind.jil ndieut* ***daod.saod.***
3 ASSOC grade ascend **IDEO:B:quick.vertical.movement**
'His grades (on his homework and exams) suddenly went up.' (Shixiang Wu, fieldnotes) (cf. *saod.saod* [IDEO:A:quick.vertical.movement])

(11.17) *Beul nteut* ***daod.cout.***
3 nod **IDEO:B:COUT**
'He suddenly nodded his head (a single time).' (Haili Shi, fieldnotes) (cf. *cout.cout* [IDEO:A:COUT])[208]

(11.18) *Aod-leb dianb.deins dox mians* ***daod.gueinl,*** *yab*
one-CLF electric.lamp that bright **IDEO:B:brightly** also
biok lah.
extinguish PRF
'That (electric) lamp suddenly flickered (i.e. quickly went out and then came back on again), then went out (indefinitely).' (Shixiang Wu, fieldnotes) (cf. *gueinl.gueinl* [IDEO:A:brightly])

208 The primary meaning of the ideophone root *-cout* is difficult to pin down, since it occurs with a wide variety of verbs (including property-denoting verbs like *zanl* 'cold, quiet' and *xab* 'light' as well as non–property-denoting verbs like *daox* 'to precipitate', *nteut* 'to nod', and *raul* 'to sew') with a similarly wide variety of apparent meanings (including 'quickly', 'repeatedly', 'quietly', 'lightly', and 'desolately'). Thus, ideophones that have *-cout* as their root are glossed 'IDEO:X:COUT', where *X* is the particular template in which the root is occurring (e.g. 'A', 'B', etc.).

Template C ideophones differ from template A and template B ideophones in a number of respects: they are obligatorily tetrasyllabic, they involve non-contiguous reduplication of the verb which the ideophone serves to modify, and they feature two ideophonic syllables occurring non-contiguously. In template C, the first syllable is the verb which the ideophone serves to modify (no examples of disyllabic verbs like *box.nhol* 'to throw away' or *minx.xaond* 'dirty' have been attested in this template), the third syllable is that same verb repeated, and the fourth syllable is the ideophone's root. The second syllable of a template C ideophone will always have the same initial consonant as the root, but it will always have /i/ as its vowel and *-d* as its tone. For instance, from the verb *giaol* 'stupid' and the ideophone root *-npud* 'stupid', one can derive the template C ideophone *giaol-npid-giaol-npud* [stupid-IDEO-stupid-IDEO:C:stupid], meaning 'a little bit stupid, kind of stupid'. Template C can thus be represented abstractly with [A → V-C*id*-V-A], where *V* represents the verb that the ideophone serves to modify, *A* represents the ideophone's root, and *C*id represents a syllable with the same initial consonant as the root, but with /i/ as its vowel and *-d* as its tone.

As can be seen from the example just given, template C has an attenuating semantic effect on ideophone roots that occur in it: when an ideophone root with a meaning 'X' occurs in this template, the meaning of the resulting derived ideophone is 'slightly X, Xish'. The semantics associated with this template C would seem to be compatible with a wide variety of ideophone roots (or at least a wide variety of those that refer to states or properties rather than actions or events), but template C is surprisingly unproductive. In fact, it has so far only been attested with three ideophone roots, each of which is shown in (11.19–11.21) below.

(11.19) *gueb-mid-gueb-miaod*
black-IDEO-black-IDEO:C:black
'a little bit black, blackish' (Chenghua Long, fieldnotes) (cf. *miaod.miaod* [IDEO:A:black])

(11.20) *giaol-npid-giaol-npud*
stupid-IDEO-stupid-IDEO:C:stupid
'a little bit stupid, kind of stupid' (Chenghua Long, fieldnotes) (cf. *npud.npud* [IDEO:A:stupid])

(11.21) *xob-bid-xob-biaol*
sour-IDEO-sour-IDEO:C:sour
'a little bit sour, sourish' (Shixiang Wu, fieldnotes) (cf. *biaol.biaol* [IDEO:A:sour])

The glossing conventions for template C differ slightly from those used for other ideophone templates, since hyphens rather than periods are used to connect all four syllables of the ideophone, including both verbal syllables and both ideophonic syllables.

As the use of these hyphens suggests, no other material (verbal, ideophonic, or otherwise) can occur between any two adjacent syllables of a template C ideophone.

Template D is also tetrasyllabic, and it is formed by reduplicating the ideophone root and then inserting two additional syllables in front of that reduplicated root. These two additional syllables are always homophonous with each other, and while they always have the same initial consonant as the root itself, their vowel and tone are non-predictable. This ideophone template can thus be represented abstractly with [A → A′.A′.A.A], where *A* represents the ideophone root and *A′* represents a syllable phonologically derived from that root. For example, from the ideophone root *-zous* 'quickly', one can derive *zaol.zaol.zous.zous* [IDEO:D:quickly] 'wildly, frantically'. Here the third and fourth syllables of the ideophone are phonologically identical to the root itself, while the first and second syllables have the same initial consonant but a different, non-predictable vowel and a different, non-predictable tone.

However, the vowel and tone on the first and second syllables of a template D ideophone are not entirely random. The vowel on these syllables will always be either /ɤj/ or /ɑ/ (orthographic <ei> or <ao>), though it is impossible to predict which of these two will occur in any particular case, and the tone on these syllables will obey certain ordering restrictions relative to the tone on the root (see Section 11.1.3 below for discussion). However, it should be noted that only three ideophone roots have been encountered occurring in this template, and so all of these claims must be considered rather tentative.

Template D has an intensifying semantic effect on ideophone roots that occur in it. In an arguably iconic fashion, template D (which is tetrasyllabic) appears to have a more strongly intensifying effect on ideophone roots than template A (which is disyllabic): compare *bos.bos* [IDEO:A:loudly] 'loudly' with *beis.beis.bos.bos* [IDEO:D:loudly] 'cacophonously'. Just as with template C, the very low productivity of this template is somewhat surprising given its relatively general semantics.

Each of the three attested examples of template D can be seen in (11.22–11.24) below.

(11.22) *beux* ***beis.beis.bos.bos***
hit **IDEO:D:loudly**
'to smash many objects with a terrible crashing sound (e.g. to break many plates and glasses and tables and the like)' (Haili Shi, fieldnotes) (cf. *bos.bos* [IDEO:A:loudly])

(11.23) *Beul naond ghaob-doul shoub* ***zaol.zaol.zous.zous***.
3 ASSOC NOM-hand tremble **IDEO:D:quickly**
'His hands were trembling wildly.' (Shixiang Wu, fieldnotes) (cf. *zous.zous* [IDEO:A:quickly])

(11.24) *Beul-god deib dox did-gaond* ***daod.daod.dol.dol.***
3-PL at that DID-noisy **IDEO:D:noisily**
'They're making a ton of noise over there.' (Shixiang Wu, fieldnotes) (cf. *dol.dol* [IDEO:A:noisily])

Finally, template E displays more phonological and morphological variation than any other ideophone template, to the extent that it is impossible to give a single abstract formula that represents the derivation of a template E ideophone from an ideophone root. This is true despite the fact that only four instances of this template have been attested so far, each of which can be seen in examples (11.25–11.28) below.

(11.25) *nied* ***shad.shont.shad.shont***
cry **IDEO:E:deeply**
'to cry deeply but quietly, as if trying to keep others from hearing' (Haili Shi, fieldnotes) (cf. *shont.shont* [IDEO:A:deeply])

(11.26) *Beul raul eud* ***ghaod.zaol.ghaod.zous.***
3 sew clothing **IDEO:E:quickly**
'He sews clothing very slowly, like a beginner.' (Shixiang Wu, fieldnotes) (cf. *zous.zous* [IDEO:A:quickly])

(11.27) *Beul raul eud* ***baod.caod.bout.cout.***
3 sew clothing **IDEO:E:COUT**
'He's sewing clothing quietly and slowly.' (Chenghua Long, fieldnotes) (cf. *cout.cout* [IDEO:A:COUT])

(11.28) *daox nons* ***baod.ceid.baod.cout***
precipitate rain **IDEO:E:COUT**
'to rain lightly' (Chenghua Long, fieldnotes) (cf. *cout.cout* [IDEO:A:COUT])

Nevertheless, the template E ideophones shown in these four examples all display certain phonological, morphological, and semantic similarities that justify analyzing them as instances of a single ideophone template. With respect to phonology and morphology, all four are tetrasyllabic, and all four feature one or more syllables that (i) are phonologically derived from their respective ideophone roots and (ii) obey certain tonal ordering constraints with respect to those roots (see Section 11.1.3 for details). All four display similar semantics as well: in each case, template E appears to add the meaning of 'slowly, quietly, lightly' to the base meaning of the ideophone root in question.[209]

209 Two additional comments about the semantics of template E are in order here. First, the reader may have noted that the ideophone root *-cout* occurs in the template E ideophone shown in example

Thus, despite the high degree of variation it displays, template E is treated as a single template in this grammar, and template E ideophones are simply glossed as 'IDEO:E:X' (where *X* is the meaning of the ideophone root) whenever they occur.

It is tempting to try to come up with some additional generalizations about template E, despite the low number of attested examples. For instance, in most cases each of the first, second, and third syllables in a template E ideophone will have either /ɤj/ or /ɑ/ (orthographic <ei> or <ao>) as its vowel. This is true for the ideophones shown in examples (11.26) and (11.28), but it is only partially true for the one shown in example (11.27), and it is not true at all for the one in example (11.25). Furthermore, in most cases the first and third syllables of a template E ideophone will have the same initial consonant, as will the second and fourth syllables, but the initial consonant on the former two syllables will differ from the one on the latter two syllables. This is true for the ideophones in (11.26–11.28), but not for the one in (11.25). Overall, though, in terms of structural regularity, template E in Fenghuang Xong is perhaps at best roughly equivalent to a phonestheme in English (e.g. the /gl/ in words like *glitter*, *glisten*, and *glow*, or the /æʃ/ in words like *smash*, *bash*, and *crash*). While the phonological and morphological structures of the various attested instances of template E are not entirely random, they are still far from being perfectly systematic.

11.1.3 Noteworthy phonological characteristics

Unlike ideophones (or at least ideophone-like forms) that have been reported in many other languages from other parts of the world (see, e.g., Ameka [2001: 30], Schultz-Berndt [2001: 356, 357], and Nuckolls [2001: 272], among many others), ideophones in Xong do not display any unique segmental or phonotactic properties.[210] In other words, every phoneme or tone that has been attested in a Xong ideophone has also been attested in forms belonging to other major lexical categories (e.g. nouns, classifiers, and verbs), and ideophonic syllables obey the same phonotactic constraints as other Xong syllables. No particular consonants appear to be especially rare or common in Xong ideophones,

(11.27) as well as in the one shown in example (11.28). The meaning of this root is rather difficult to describe (see the preceding footnote earlier in this section), and from the data currently available to the author it is impossible to say whether the two attested template E ideophones derived from this root differ semantically in any appreciable way.

Second, note that the template E ideophone *ghaod.zaol.ghaod.zous* in example (11.26) appears to mean something like 'very slowly', despite the fact that the ideophone root *-zous* itself usually means 'quickly' (see, e.g., examples (11.15) and (11.23) above). This discrepancy is at present still inexplicable, though when further data is obtained it may turn out that the meaning of the root *-zous* is closer to something like 'with unusual speed (whether fast or slow)' than 'quickly'.

210 Watson (2001: 386, 387) argues that this absence of unique phonological characteristics is in fact a common feature of ideophones in Southeast Asian languages, one that distinguishes them from ideophones in languages spoken in other parts of the world (in particular, Africa).

or at least no more so than in any other major lexical category. However, with respect to vowels, it is worth pointing out that all phonologically derived syllables in attested instances of template D and most (though not all) phonologically derived syllables in attested instances of template E obligatorily have /ɤj/ or /ɑ/ (orthographic <ei> or <ao>) as their vowel, and the syllable *daod* in template B has the vowel /ɑ/ as well (see Section 11.1.2 above for more on Xong's ideophone templates in general). This is not true, though, of the phonologically derived syllables in template C, and the issue is irrelevant for template A (in which both syllables are always segmentally homophonous).

There are also at least two tone-related observations that can be made about ideophones in Xong (this is in addition to the fact that approximately two-thirds of all attested template A ideophones bear the same tone on both of their syllables). First, tone *-d* is by far the most common tone in Xong ideophones. Nearly half of all attested template A ideophones either bear tone *-d* on both syllables or bear tone *-d* on the first syllable and another tone on the second syllable (interestingly, though, template A ideophones with *-d* on their second syllable and some other tone on their first syllable are quite rare, with only two examples having been attested so far). Furthermore, the syllable *daod* in template B and the phonologically derived second syllable in template C (which has the same initial consonant as the ideophone's root, but which has /i/ as its vowel) also bear tone *-d* as well (see Section 11.1.2).

Second, with only a few exceptions (less than 10%), ideophones in Fenghuang Xong obey the same tonal ordering restrictions that sequences of consecutive numerals do (see Section 6.2.2, as well as Section 5.3.3.2).[211] Specifically, the tone on any given syllable in any given ideophone (regardless of template) will almost always either "precede" or be identical to the tone on any following syllable in terms of the eight historical tones of Miao-Yao (see Section 3.5.2.1). Thus, for instance, if the tone on the second syllable of an ideophone is a reflex of historical tone 1, then the tone on the first syllable will almost always be a reflex of historical tone 1 as well; if the tone on the second syllable is a reflex of historical tone 2, then the tone on the first syllable will almost always be a reflex of either historical tone 1 or historical tone 2; if the tone on the second syllable is a reflex of historical tone 3, then the tone on the first syllable will almost always be a reflex of historical tone 1, 2, or 3; and so on up to ideophones whose second syllables bear a tone that is a reflex of historical tone 8, in which case the preceding first syllable can readily bear any tone. Similarly, for those ideophones that have four syllables, the tone on the second syllable will almost always precede or be identical to the tone on the third syllable, and the tone on the third syllable will almost always precede or be identical to the tone on the fourth syllable.

---

211 To the best of the author's knowledge, the first scholar to describe tonal ordering restrictions of this sort in any Xong variety was Jinzhi Yu (see, for instance, Yu [2011: 69, 70, 327–329]), although Yu's work focuses on Aizhai Xong rather than Fenghuang Xong. See also Mortensen (2006: 174–270) for more information on tonal ordering restrictions in the languages of greater mainland Southeast Asia in general.

11.1.4 Syntactic properties

Although ideophones are arguably some of the most interesting forms in Xong in morphological (and to a lesser extent phonological) terms, their syntactic properties are not particularly remarkable. The vast majority of attested ideophones can only occur in one of a handful of syntactic environments: either immediately following a verb (to produce a structure [VERB IDEO]) or immediately following a noun-phrase argument which itself immediately follows a verb (to produce a structure [VERB NP IDEO]). In the latter case, the verb can optionally be reduplicated before the ideophone (to produce a structure [VERB_{A} NP VERB_{A} IDEO]). In general, consultants are extremely reluctant to allow any additional linguistic material to occur between adjacent elements in any of these syntactic environments (e.g. between a verb and a following ideophone, between a noun phrase and a following ideophone, between a verb and a following noun phrase when that noun phrase is itself followed by an ideophone, etc.).

Examples of ideophones occurring in the [VERB IDEO] syntactic environment are given in (11.29–11.31).

(11.29) *Oub-meinl* *miex* *deib* *dox* ***did-ndaot*** ***bos.bos.***
two-CLF:person person at that **DID-curse** **IDEO:A:loudly**
'There are two people there arguing loudly.' (Haili Shi, fieldnotes)

(11.30) *Hneind* *aod-hnanb* *eud* *leh,* *ghaob-dieud* ***ceind***
wear one-CLF:clothing clothing LEH NOM-body **cool**
rous.rous.
IDEO:A:cool
'Just wear one layer of clothing, (you'll) be nice and cool (that way).' (Shixiang Wu, fieldnotes)

(11.31) *Beul* *khauk-mes* ***nqint*** ***gians.gians.***
3 hole-face **red** **IDEO:A:very**
'His face is bright red.' (Chenghua Long, fieldnotes)

Examples of ideophones occurring in the [VERB NP IDEO] syntactic environment are given in (11.32–11.34). The relevant noun phrases have been enclosed within brackets.

(11.32) *Beul* ***zox*** *[**zhet**]* ***beis.beis.bos.bos.***
3 **smash** **[bowl]** **IDEO:D:loudly**
'He's smashing (all those) bowls and making a terrible racket.' (Haili Shi, fieldnotes)

(11.33) ***Piaf*** ***[git]*** ***louk.louk,*** *lis* *daox* *nons.*
blow **[wind]** **IDEO:A:breezily** want precipitate rain
'It's a little bit breezy, (so it looks like) it's going to rain.' (Shixiang Wu, fieldnotes)

(11.34) *Beul* ***baond*** ***[beul*** ***naond*** ***put]*** ***nzhaot.nzhaot.***
3 **shoot** **[3** **ASSOC** **gun]** **IDEO:A:noisily**
'He fired his gun with a great big bang.' (Chenghua Long, fieldnotes)

Examples of ideophones occurring in the [VERB$_A$ NP VERB$_A$ IDEO] syntactic environment are given in (11.35–11.37). Again, the relevant noun phrases have been enclosed within brackets.

(11.35) *Beul* ***baond*** ***[beul*** ***naond*** ***put]*** ***baond*** ***nzhaot.nzhaot.***
3 **shoot** **[3** **ASSOC** **gun]** **shoot** **IDEO:A:noisily**
'He fired his gun with a great big bang.' (Chenghua Long, fieldnotes) (cf. example (11.34) above)

(11.36) *Beul* ***ndieut*** ***[aod-zhaus*** ***ndaut*** ***dox]*** ***ndieut***
3 **ascend** **[one-CLF:vertical.plant** **tree** **that]** **ascend**
saod.saod.
IDEO:A:quick.vertical.movement
'She climbed that tree really quickly.' (Shixiang Wu, fieldnotes)

(11.37) *Beul* ***sheit*** ***[ndeud-Xonb]*** ***sheit*** ***gaot.gaot.***
3 **write** **[writing-Xong]** **write** **IDEO:A:quickly**
'He writes Xong really quickly.' (Haili Shi, fieldnotes)

Many ideophones can occur in more than one of these syntactic environments, and it appears that the primary factor determining which environments a particular ideophone can occur in is whether the verb that the ideophone serves to modify is semantically compatible with an immediately postverbal argument or not. An ideophone modifying a verb that is not compatible with such an argument will naturally only occur in the [VERB IDEO] environment, while an ideophone modifying a verb that is compatible with such an argument will typically be able to occur in all three environments. This means that virtually all ideophones that can occur in the [VERB NP IDEO] environment can also occur in the [VERB$_A$ NP VERB$_A$ IDEO] environment, and the reverse is true as well. (In a handful of cases consultants report that an ideophone can only occur in one of these two environments and not the other, but such cases are so few and vary so much among consultants in terms of acceptability that it is impossible to characterize them at present.) Note that there do not appear to be any distinct semantic or pragmatic effects associated with any of these three syntactic environments vis-à-vis the others.

While the claims put forward in this section so far are true for the great majority of ideophones, particular ideophone templates occasionally display slightly different syntactic properties. Template C, for example, involves two ideophonic syllables and two verbal syllables occurring in a fixed tetrasyllabic sequence, though both the two ideophonic syllables and the two verbal syllables occur discontiguously (see Section 11.1.2 above for more details). This can be seen in examples (11.38) and (11.39) below, where the first and third syllables in each case are verbal and the second and fourth are ideophonic.

(11.38) *gueb-mid-gueb-miaod*
black-IDEO-black-IDEO:C:black
'a little bit black, blackish' (Chenghua Long, fieldnotes)

(11.39) *xob-bid-xob-biaol*
sour-IDEO-sour-IDEO:C:sour
'a little bit sour, sourish' (Shixiang Wu, fieldnotes)

No other material – whether verbal, ideophonic, or otherwise – can occur between any two adjacent syllables of a template C ideophone, and the entire tetrasyllabic [VERB-IDEO-VERB-IDEO] construction itself serves as a predicate. With this template, it does not make sense to speak of the ideophone and the verb that it serves to modify as distinct syntactic constituents; instead, the two occur together as a single, morphologically complex constituent.

In a handful of cases, consultants have produced utterances in which an ideophone precedes rather than follows the verb that it modifies. In such cases, the associative marker *naond* 'ASSOC' (but no other linguistic material) may optionally appear between the preceding ideophone and the following verb, apparently functioning as something like an adverbial marker (see Section 9.3.3.2 for more on *naond* 'ASSOC'). Instances of this can be seen in examples (11.40) and (11.41) below, and note that both of these examples are equally grammatical regardless of whether they contain *naond* 'ASSOC' or not.

(11.40) *shad.shont.shad.shont* *(naond)* *nggueb*
IDEO:E:deeply (ASSOC) sleep
'to sleep deeply or heavily' (Chenghua Long, fieldnotes)

(11.41)

Beul	***saod.saod***	***(naond)***	***ndieut***
3	**IDEO:A:quick.vertical.movement**	**(ASSOC)**	**ascend**

aod-zhaus	*ndaut*	*dox.*
one-CLF:vertical.plant	tree	that

'She climbed that tree really quickly.' (Shixiang Wu, fieldnotes) (cf. example (11.36) above)

All ideophones attested in this preverbal syntactic environment can also occur in the much more common postverbal syntactic environments described earlier in this section, and whether an ideophone occurs preverbally vs. postverbally in any particular clause does not appear to have any effect on the meaning of the clause as a whole. However, it must be emphasized that preverbal ideophones of the sort seen in examples (11.40) and (11.41) above are quite uncommon, and the author's consultants generally reject constructed examples containing such ideophones. Unfortunately, due to the rarity of such preverbal ideophones in general, it is not yet possible to describe what factors determine whether a particular ideophone can occur in preverbal position or not.

Finally, while template C ideophones (which are obligatorily tetrasyllabic, and which are composed of both verbal and ideophonic material) always serve as predicates in their own right, one of the author's consultants (Mrs. Chenghua Long, from Shanjiang Town) occasionally allows template D and E ideophones to do so as well. Examples of this can be seen in (11.42) and (11.43) below.

(11.42)

Beul	*oub-leb*	***beis.beis.bos.bos,***	*nianl*	*nins*	*chauk*	*naonb.*
3	two-CLF	**IDEO:D:loudly**	know	COP	do	what

'Those two are making a ton of noise, (who) knows what they're doing.' (Chenghua Long, fieldnotes)

(11.43)

Beul	*chauk*	*naonb*	*nanx*	***ghaod.zaol.ghaod.zous.***
3	do	what	only	**IDEO:E:quickly**

'He does everything so slowly.' (Chenghua Long, fieldnotes)

However, examples such as these are only marginally grammatical for the author's other consultants, and no consultant (including Mrs. Long) ever allows template A or B ideophones to serve as predicates in their own right.

11.1.5 Semantics and selectional restrictions

Roughly half of all attested ideophones (and the ideophone roots from which they are derived) have extremely strict selectional restrictions, in that they can only co-occur with a single verb. Examples of this are shown in (11.44–11.52) below.

(11.44) *anb* ***ghant.ghant***
bitter **IDEO:A:bitter**
'very bitter' (Haili Shi, fieldnotes)

(11.45) **xob* ***ghant.ghant***
sour **IDEO:A:bitter**
(intended: 'very sour')

(11.46) **mieil* ***ghant.ghant***
spicy **IDEO:A:bitter**
(intended: 'very spicy')

(11.47) *gueinx* ***roud.roud***
yellow **IDEO:A:yellow**
'very yellow, bright yellow' (Chenghua Long, fieldnotes)

(11.48) **nqint* ***roud.roud***
red **IDEO:A:yellow**
(intended: 'very red, bright red')

(11.49) **gueub* ***roud.roud***
white **IDEO:A:yellow**
(intended: 'very white, bright white')

(11.50) *zhok* ***ghat.ghat***
laugh **IDEO:A:loudly**
'to laugh loudly' (Shixiang Wu, fieldnotes)

(11.51) **puk* ***ghat.ghat***
speak **IDEO:A:loudly**
(intended: 'to speak loudly')

(11.52) **niand* ***ghat.ghat***
cry **IDEO:A:loudly**
(intended: 'to cry loudly')

In many cases consultants insist that an ideophone simply signals an intensification or exaggeration of the meaning of the verb that it serves to modify, and not any more specific adverbial notion. This is especially (but not solely) true for (i) ideophones that can only co-occur with a single verb, (ii) ideophones that modify property-denoting verbs, and (iii) template A ideophones (see Section 11.1.2). Nevertheless, there does at least appear to be some sort of pragmatic or registral difference between a verb modified by such an intensity-signaling ideophone and one modified by a non-ideophonic degree marker like *heint/hint* 'very' or *guaot* 'to pass'. This difference is difficult to describe in specific terms, but such intensity-marking ideophones seem to convey an additional sense of vividness or drama (cf. the author's comments on the pragmatic properties of generic noun compounds in Section 5.3.3.4 and of verbal tetrasyllabic expressions in Section 12.2.2).

Other ideophones (and the ideophone roots from which they are derived) can similarly only co-occur with a single verb, but in doing so they convey a more specific adverbial meaning than simple intensity. This is particularly common for the more complex ideophone templates, since those templates often convey rather specific semantic information themselves, but it is true for some template A ideophones as well (again, for more on Xong's ideophone templates, see Section 11.1.2). Meanings signaled by such ideophones include ones related to speed, frequency, duration, and suddenness, as well as even more specific adverbial notions like 'breezily' or 'happily'.

This can be seen in examples (11.53–11.56) below, each of which contains an ideophone expressing an adverbial notion other than mere degree or intensity. Examples (11.53) and (11.54) feature template B and C ideophones (respectively), and the meaning of each ideophone as a whole is a product of the meaning of its template and the meaning of its root. In example (11.53), the ideophone *daod.ghos* [IDEO:B:loudly] expresses both loudness (with this meaning contributed by the root *-ghos* itself) and suddenness (with this meaning contributed by the B template in which the root appears).

(11.53) *Beul* *nied* ***daod.ghos.***
3 cry **IDEO:B:loudly**
'He suddenly started sobbing.' (Haili Shi, fieldnotes)

In example (11.54), the ideophone *gueb-mid-gueb-miaod* [black-IDEO-black-IDEO:C:black] expresses an attenuated or diminished degree of blackness, with the meaning of "blackness" itself contributed by the ideophone root *-miaod* 'black' and the attenuated or diminished degree contributed by the C template in which the root appears.

(11.54) *gueb-mid-gueb-miaod*
black-IDEO-black-IDEO:C:black
'a little bit black, blackish' (Chenghua Long, fieldnotes)

In contrast, examples (11.55) and (11.56) feature template A ideophones, which typically merely signal intensity, but nevertheless these particular ideophones convey relatively specific meanings (in these cases, meanings of 'breezily' and 'happily').

(11.55) *Piaf* *git* ***louk.louk,*** *lis* *daox* *nons.*
blow wind **IDEO:A:breezily** want precipitate rain
'It's a little bit breezy, (so it looks like) it's going to rain.' (Shixiang Wu, fieldnotes)

(11.56) *Beul* *zhok* ***reis.reis.***
3 smile **IDEO:A:happily**
'He's grinning happily.' (Chenghua Long, fieldnotes)

Rather more interesting are those ideophones that can co-occur with multiple verbs. In the simplest cases, a given ideophone can co-occur with several verbs that have roughly similar meanings. For instance, ideophones derived from the root *-saod* 'quick vertical movement' can co-occur with both *ndieut* 'to ascend' and *lot* 'to descend', as examples (11.57) and (11.58) below demonstrate.

(11.57) *ndieut* ***saod.saod***
ascend **IDEO:A:quick.vertical.movement**
'to ascend quickly' (Chenghua Long, fieldnotes)

(11.58) *lot* ***saod.saod***
descend **IDEO:A:quick.vertical.movement**
'to descend quickly' (Chenghua Long, fieldnotes)

Ideophones derived from the root *-jel/-janl* 'shiningly' are even more productive, as they can co-occur with nearly half a dozen verbs referring to concepts like 'bright', 'white', 'shiny', and 'clean'.

(11.59) *mians* ***janl.janl***
bright **IDEO:A:shiningly**
'brightly lit (e.g. a room)' (Shixiang Wu, fieldnotes)

(11.60) *gueub* ***janl.janl***
white **IDEO:A:shiningly**
'very white, bright white' (Chenghua Long, fieldnotes)

(11.61) *tob* ***janl.janl***
shiny **IDEO:A:shiningly**
'very shiny (e.g. gold, silver, jewels)' (Shixiang Wu, fieldnotes)

(11.62) *nqif* ***jel.jel***
clean **IDEO:A:shiningly**
'sparkling clean' (Xingyu Shi, in *Oub Meinl Yaos Geud*)

(11.63) *liaol* *sob* ***jel.jel***
flash lightning **IDEO:A:shiningly**
'for there to be a very bright lightning strike' (Haili Shi, fieldnotes)

Conversely, there are some verbs which can co-occur with multiple distinct ideophones (and note that there are also some verbs which never co-occur with any ideophones at all, particularly verbs with abstract meanings like *lis* 'to want' or *nins* 'COP'). In many cases a handful of intensity-indicating ideophones can co-occur with the same verb, and consultants generally report that these ideophones all mean more or less the same thing. Examples of this can be seen in (11.64–11.66) and (11.67–11.69) below. The author's consultants report that the first three of these examples all have essentially the same meaning, as do the last three.

(11.64) *Beul* *khauk-mes* *nqint* ***shaud.shaud.***
3 hole-face red **IDEO:A:red**
'His face is bright red.' (Chenghua Long, fieldnotes)

(11.65) *Beul* *khauk-mes* *nqint* ***ghaos.ghaos.***
3 hole-face red **IDEO:A:red**
'His face is bright red.' (Chenghua Long, fieldnotes)

(11.66) *Beul* *khauk-mes* *nqint* ***gians.gians.***
3 hole-face red **IDEO:A:very**
'His face is bright red.' (Chenghua Long, fieldnotes)

(11.67) *Beul* *khauk-mes* *gueb* ***miaod.miaod.***
3 hole-face black **IDEO:A:black**
'His face is very dirty/dark.' (Shixiang Wu, fieldnotes)

(11.68) *Beul* *khauk-mes* *gueb* ***zeid.zeib.***
3 hole-face black **IDEO:A:black**
'His face is very dirty/dark.' (Shixiang Wu, fieldnotes)

(11.69) *Beul* *khauk-mes* *gueb* ***gians.gians.***
3 hole-face black **IDEO:A:very**
'His face is very dirty/dark.' (Shixiang Wu, fieldnotes)

Finally, there are some ideophones with fairly generic meanings that can co-occur with a wide variety of verbs. These include *gians.gians* [IDEO:A:very] 'very', which can co-occur with a wide variety of property-denoting verbs like *nzeit* 'skinny', *shanb* 'tall', *ngaod* 'short', *ngox* 'fierce', *gueb* 'black', and *nqint* 'red' (see examples (11.66) and (11.69) above). Other ideophones with similarly loose selectional restrictions include *zheis.zheif* [IDEO:A:very] 'very', *fut.fut* [IDEO:A:quickly] 'quickly', and *gaot.gaot* [IDEO:A:quickly] 'quickly', as is shown in examples (11.70–11.72) below. If there are any semantic or pragmatic differences between *gians.gians* 'very' and *zheis.zheif* 'very', or between *fut.fut* 'quickly' and *gaot.gaot* 'quickly', they are slight enough that the author has not yet been able to identify them.

(11.70) *gueind/shanb/nqint/liox/ngaod/liot/mos/zhax/sonx/yeb* ***zheis.zheif***
broad/tall/red/big/short/wealthy/tired/strong/weak/like **IDEO:A:very**
'very broad/tall/red/big/short/wealthy/tired/strong/weak/to like very much'
(Haili Shi, fieldnotes)

(11.71) *kek/nhob/eint/monl/lol/nonx/sheit/piaf* ***fut.fut***
drive/walk/fly/go/come/eat/write/blow **IDEO:A:quickly**
'to drive/walk/fly/go/come/eat/write/blow quickly' (Shixiang Wu, fieldnotes)

(11.72) *nhob/eint/monl/lol/sheit/raul/hod/deuk* ***gaot.gaot***
walk/fly/go/come/write/sew/sharpen/thunder **IDEO:A:quickly**
'to walk/fly/go/come/write/sew/sharpen/thunder quickly' (Haili Shi, fieldnotes)

Although this section has laid out all the noteworthy semantic attributes and selectional restrictions related to Xong ideophones that the author has been able to discern so far, it is likely still far from constituting a comprehensive description of the meanings of these forms. Many more ideophones likely remain to be elicited, and it is possible that further work with other Xong consultants would reveal additional patterns.[212] Still, based on the data currently available to the author, it does appear that Xong ideophones in general tend to have significantly less specific meanings than ideophones in certain other well described languages of mainland Southeast Asia, including the Austroasiatic language Semelai (Kruspe 2004: 397–399) and the Tai-Kadai language Lao (Enfield 2007: 299–303), and they also appear much less frequently in Xong (for both younger and older speakers) than in those languages.

212 The Xong consultants who worked on ideophones with the author were normally quite sensitive to minor semantic differences, and so it was somewhat surprising when they reported that most ideophones simply expressed something like "intensification" or "exaggeration" of the meanings of the relevant verbs, especially given the rather specific ideophone meanings reported in Hong (2011). While these consultants were relatively young, attempts to elicit ideophones from older speakers were not productive, and ideophones were neither more common nor (apparently) any more specific in meaning in naturalistic texts produced by those older speakers than in those produced by younger ones.

11.2 Onomatopoeic forms

Although Hong (2011: 71) argues that there is a clear distinction between ideophones and onomatopoeic forms in Jiwei Xong, the line between the two is significantly murkier in Fenghuang Xong. When all the evidence currently available to the author is taken together, it is not clear whether onomatopoeic forms should be considered a non-canonical (or "defective") subset of ideophones, a distinct lexical category that merely happens to overlap with ideophones in some respects, or even just a heterogenous set of idiosyncratic forms that happen to display certain functional similarities with each other and with certain ideophones. This section thus describes the semantic, phonological, morphological, and syntactic properties of Xong's onomatopoeic forms with a particular eye toward comparing them to ideophones. Note, though, that only about a dozen examples of clearly onomatopoeic forms have been attested so far (although the author has no reason to suspect that more onomatopoeic forms will not be found in the future), and so the discussion in this section will be much briefer than the discussion of ideophones in Section 11.1 above.

At first glance there appears to be a clear semantic difference between onomatopoeic forms and ideophones, since the former serve only to iconically represent or imitate real-world aural phenomena. This can be seen in examples (11.73) and (11.74) below, in which the onomatopoeic forms have been highlighted.

(11.73) *Daob-maonb* ***miauk.miauk.***
AN-cat **ONOM:miau.miau**
'The cat goes *miau miau.*' (Haili Shi, fieldnotes)

(11.74) *Bux aub* ***guk.lod.guk.lod.***
boil water **ONOM:gu.lo.gu.lo**
'The water's boiling *gu lo gu lo.*' (Chenghua Long, fieldnotes)

In contrast, ideophones are used to signal a variety of adverbial notions, including intensity, speed, frequency, duration, and suddenness. Significantly, ideophones do not appear to be noticeably more iconic than members of Xong's other major lexical categories (i.e. nouns, classifiers, and verbs). Examples of this can be seen in (11.75) and (11.76), where the phonological form of each ideophone has no obvious iconic relation to the ideophone's meaning.

(11.75) *Aod-zheinb saok.faol neind nes* ***hlout.hlout!***
one-CLF:tool sofa this soft **IDEO:A:soft**
'This sofa is really soft!' (Shixiang Wu, fieldnotes)

(11.76) *Mx nonx hlit ghaod.maons taox jaol*
2SG eat cooked.rice NEG.IMP smash chin

njaot.njaot.
IDEO:A:noisily
'Don't smack your lips while you're eating.' (Shixiang Wu, fieldnotes)

However, there are a few ideophones that arguably do serve to iconically represent real-world sounds, or at least to iconically represent such sounds and some additional adverbial notion as well. Examples of this are given in (11.77) and (11.78) below. Consultants report that the ideophone *nggont.nggont* [IDEO:A:crunching] iconically represents the *nggon nggon* sound of someone chewing, and similarly the ideophone *kit.kit* [IDEO:A:giggling] iconically represents the *ki ki* sound of a young woman giggling. Nevertheless, these two forms satisfy all other ideophone criteria. They are obligatorily polysyllabic, they cannot occur without an accompanying verb, and they occur in one of the five ideophone templates described in Section 11.1.2 (in these particular cases, in template A, though the ideophone roots *-nggont* 'crunching' and *-kit* 'giggling' have also been attested occurring in template B). This means that the apparent semantic difference between onomatopoeic forms and ideophones just discussed cannot be used to reliably distinguish the two sets of forms (and of course, even if it could, it would be difficult to defend a proposed distinction between two lexical categories that was based solely on semantic evidence).

(11.77) *Boub naond deb nonx daonx giaot nbot*
1PL ASSOC child eat candy chew make.noise
nggont.nggont.
IDEO:A:crunching
'Our kid is really chowing down on that candy (with a *nggon nggon* sound).' (Chenghua Long, fieldnotes)

(11.78) *Beul zhok* ***kit.kit*** *sheub lah.*
3 laugh **IDEO:A:giggling** leave PRF
'She walked off giggling (with a *ki ki* sound).' (Shixiang Wu, fieldnotes)

In terms of phonology, onomatopoeic forms in Xong again display some level of overlap with ideophones, though not a particularly high one. Like ideophones, onomatopoeic forms (or at least all attested such forms) are obligatorily polysyllabic. Also like ideophones, they do not show any unique segmental or phonotactic properties: they feature the same phonemes and tones as other lexical categories, and their syllables have the same phonotactic structure as other Xong syllables. Onomatopoeic forms further resemble ideophones (and Xong's other major lexical categories as well, for that matter) in that no particular consonants are especially common or rare among them, though of course the small number of onomatopoeic forms attested so far should be kept in mind here. However, these forms differ from ideophones in that no vowels or tones are particularly common or rare among them. In contrast, the vowels

/ɤj/ and /ɑ/ (orthographic <ei> and <ao>) are unusually common in ideophones (or at least in certain ideophone templates; see Section 11.1.3 above for details), as is tone *-d*. The component syllables of onomatopoeic forms do appear to obey the same tonal ordering restrictions as ideophones (again, see Section 11.1.3), but this may simply be accidental given how few onomatopoeic forms have so far been encountered.

However, onomatopoeic forms do differ from ideophones quite sharply in that they universally appear to be monomorphemic forms. While ideophones always consist of a root that appears in one of five morphologically complex templates (see Section 11.1.2), onomatopoeic forms are invariant and cannot be broken down into smaller units (or into nonconcatenative morphological templates) that still possess distinct meanings. Thus, for example, the disyllabic, trisyllabic, and tetrasyllabic onomatopoeic forms shown in examples (11.79–11.81) are all fixed – they cannot be broken down into smaller units, and they cannot appear in any other morphological variants.

(11.79)	*Daob-guoud*	***nkuaont.nkuaont.***
	AN-dog	**ONOM:nkuaon.nkuaon**

'The dog goes *nkuaon nkuaon*.' (Haili Shi, fieldnotes)

(11.80)	*Nek-ghab*	***ghod.ghod.daok.***
	FM-chicken	**ONOM:gho.gho.dao**

'The hen goes *gho gho dao*.' (Shixiang Wu, fieldnotes)

(11.81)	*Puk*	***ghad.lad.ghad.lad,***	*jix*	*det*	*daut,*	*dont*	*jix*
	speak	**ONOM:gha.la.gha.la**	NEG$_1$	break	speech	listen	NEG$_1$
	minx.						
	understand						

'(Those foreigners on TV are) speaking *gha la gha la* without pausing, (I) can't understand (what they're saying).' (Haili Shi, fieldnotes)

However, one could argue that this apparent distinction is less significant than it first appears, since there are some cases in which it arguably does not apply. Ideophone roots that can appear in multiple morphological templates do clearly differ from onomatopoeic forms (which cannot do so), and some onomatopoeic forms (like *ghod.ghod.daok* in example (11.80) above) are clearly not occurring in any of the five attested ideophone templates. But it must be kept in mind that most ideophone roots only occur in template A, which simply involves two adjacent syllables that are always segmentally identical and usually tonally identical (see Section 11.1.2). Since several onomatopoeic forms themselves simply consist of two adjacent, homophonous syllables, it is sometimes unclear whether one is dealing with a template A ideophone or with an onomatopoeic form that just happens to formally resemble a template A ideophone. This makes the apparent morphological distinction between the two sets of forms more useful in theory than in practice.

Finally, onomatopoeic forms appear to be somewhat more syntactically versatile than ideophones, in the sense that they can occur in a larger number of syntactic positions. Like ideophones, they can occur immediately following a verb, and they can also occur immediately following a noun-phrase argument which itself immediately follows a verb. An example of the former can be seen in (11.81) above, and examples of the latter in (11.82) and (11.83) below.

(11.82) *Beul zheb ghaod.lons* ***ghok.ghok.***
3 snore throat **ONOM:gho.gho**
'He's snoring *gho gho.*' (Haili Shi, fieldnotes)

(11.83) *Deuk sob* ***lonl.lonl.***
thunder thunder **ONOM:lon.lon**
'It thundered *lon lon.*' (Shixiang Wu, fieldnotes)[213]

When an onomatopoeic form occurs in the latter environment – that is, immediately following a noun-phrase argument that itself immediately follows a verb – the verb preceding that noun-phrase argument cannot be reduplicated after the argument and before the onomatopoeic form. Compare (11.84) and (11.85) below, in which the newly inserted, reduplicated verbs have been bolded, with (11.82) and (11.83) above.

(11.84) **Beul zheb ghaod.lons* ***zheb*** *ghok.ghok.*
3 snore throat **snore** ONOM:gho.gho
(intended: 'He's snoring *gho gho.*')

(11.85) **Deuk sob* ***deuk*** *lonl.lonl.*
thunder thunder **thunder** ONOM:lon.lon
(intended: 'It thundered *lon lon.*')

This is one apparent syntactic distinction between onomatopoeic forms and ideophones, since ideophones readily allow such reduplication of the verbs that they modify. This is shown in example (11.86) below, in which the optional, reduplicated verb has been bolded (see also Section 11.1.4 above for further discussion).

213 While both forms are glossed as 'thunder' here, the form *deuk* is a verb meaning 'to thunder', while the form *sob* is a noun meaning 'thunder, lightning' (cf. example (11.63)).

(11.86) *Beul baond beul naond put* ***(baond)*** *nzhaot.nzhaot.*
3 shoot 3 ASSOC gun **(shoot)** IDEO:A:noisily
'He fired his gun with a great big bang.' (Chenghua Long, fieldnotes) (cf. examples (11.34) and (11.35) above)

Also unlike most ideophones, many onomatopoeic forms can readily serve as predicates in their own right, with no accompanying verb (see example (11.87) below, as well as examples (11.73), (11.79), and (11.80) above).[214] They can also readily appear in preverbal position, with *naond* 'ASSOC' optionally appearing between the onomatopoeic form and the following verb (see example (11.88) below).

(11.87) *Daob-nbat* ***onk.onk.***
AN-pig **ONOM:on.on**
'The pig goes *on on.*' (Shixiang Wu, fieldnotes)

(11.88) *Beul* ***ghok.ghok (naond) zheb*** *ghaod.lons.*
3 **ONOM:gho.gho (ASSOC) snore** throat
'He's snoring *gho gho.*' (Haili Shi, fieldnotes) (cf. example (11.82) above)

While it is true that a few cases have been attested of ideophones serving as predicates in their own right with no accompanying verb (see Section 11.1.4 above), this ability is much more common among onomatopoeic forms. The same is true of onomatopoeic forms and ideophones that appear in preverbal position with *naond* 'ASSOC' optionally occurring between them and the following verb. Only a handful of ideophones can appear in this preverbal position (and as was discussed in Section 11.1.4, the factors determining whether a particular ideophone can appear in this position are not yet clear), but nearly all attested onomatopoeic forms can do so. Nevertheless, as these observations suggest, it is impossible to draw a sharp line between onomatopoeic forms and ideophones even in terms of syntactic behavior. It is simply the case that certain syntactic behaviors are relatively more common among onomatopoeic forms than among ideophones, and vice versa.

In conclusion, at least some onomatopoeic forms display some level of semantic, phonological, and syntactic overlap with at least some ideophones – enough that it is impossible to draw a clear boundary between the two (purported) lexical categories, but not enough for one to definitively say that the two sets of forms constitute only a single lexical category, or that one constitutes a subcategory of the other. The morphological differences between onomatopoeic forms and ideophones at first seem

214 The four onomatopoeic forms appearing in these examples – *miauk.miauk* in example (11.73), *nkuaont.nkuaont* in (11.79), *ghod.ghod.daok* in (11.80), and *onk.onk* in (11.87) – all refer to animal noises. Given the small number of attested onomatopoeic forms in the author's corpus, it is impossible to say whether or not this is mere coincidence.

more stark, since there are some onomatopoeic forms that clearly are not occurring in any of the five attested ideophone templates, and no onomatopoeic form ever occurs in multiple morphological variants. But it is questionable how significant this apparent difference really is when many onomatopoeic forms simply involve two identical, adjacent syllables (e.g. *miauk.miauk* [ONOM:miau.miau], representing the sound of a cat meowing) and many ideophone roots only ever appear in template A, which itself usually involves two identical, adjacent syllables (e.g. *zeik.zeik* [IDEO:A:small] 'tiny'). Identifying the precise nature of the distinction between ideophones and onomatopoeic forms in Fenghuang Xong remains a task for future scholars, although given how uncommon both sets of forms are, and how marginal to the grammatical system of the language as a whole, it is perhaps not the most pressing one.

11.3 Interjections

In addition to the forms already described in this chapter, Xong also possesses a class of *interjections*. These are forms which are in a sense "outside" Xong's grammatical system, as they do not occur as components of noun phrases, clauses, or other syntactic structures. Instead, an interjection will typically occur as an utterance in its own right, and even when one occurs as part of a larger utterance it will typically be produced in an independent intonational phrase. Interjections in Xong display a high level of interspeaker and interdialectal variation, along with a general lack of internal structure (though there are some minor exceptions to that latter claim, like the form *aod-minl(-nek)* 'mother' discussed in Section 11.3.5). However, it is difficult to generalize about Xong's interjections in functional terms. While many of them serve to express vivid emotion on the part of the speaker (e.g. surprise, dismay, etc.), others serve merely to indicate agreement (e.g. *hos* 'okay', discussed in Section 11.3.2) or to indicate that the speaker is listening or paying attention to another discourse participant (e.g. *nh* 'uh-huh', discussed in Section 11.3.1). Nevertheless, interjections are still easily distinguished from ideophones (which differ from interjections in that they are derived from bound roots and only occur in conjunction with an accompanying verb) and onomatopoeic forms (which differ from interjections in that their primary purpose is to iconically represent a particular real-world sound).

A comprehensive description of Xong interjections lies outside the scope of this grammar, and so no such description is attempted in this section. Instead, each of Sections 11.3.1 to 11.3.5 below describes one or two high-frequency interjections that have fairly clear meanings and discourse functions and display relatively little interspeaker variation. The purpose here is merely to give some idea of the functional range covered by some of Xong's more common interjections – or at least some of the ones more commonly used by the author's own consultants. Interjections that occur less frequently and/or have meanings that are still relatively unclear to the author are not explicitly discussed here, but note that such forms are uniformly glossed as 'INTJ' (from 'interjection') whenever they occur in this grammar.

11.3.1 The interjection *nh* 'uh-huh'

This extremely common form is generally used to indicate agreement with another discourse participant's suggestion or observation, although in some cases it seems to merely signal that the speaker is listening or paying attention. So far it appears that in most cases *nh* can be accurately glossed and translated as English 'uh-huh'.

Examples (11.89) and (11.90) below show two consecutive utterances from a naturalistic Xong conversation. In the second of these examples, the speaker begins her utterance by using *nh* 'uh-huh' to acknowledge the previous speaker's tag question.

(11.89) *Aod-banb neind nins zeib jex.bieb,*
one-CLF:some this COP most simple.and.convenient
zeib jex.jef naond yaox?
most quick.and.easy ASSOC right?
'These (folk remedies) are the simplest, the easiest, right?' (Haili Shi, in *Tooth Conversation*)

(11.90) ***Nh,*** *mx shaod shaod, mx geud chauk-dib naont shaod?*
uh.huh 2SG try try 2SG hold do-which thus try
'Uh-huh, so you tried (using these folk remedies), so how did you try?' (Shixiang Wu, in *Tooth Conversation*)

The same is true of the two consecutive utterances shown in examples (11.91) and (11.92) below, which are taken from the same naturalistic conversation as examples (11.89) and (11.90) above.

(11.91) *Ranf.houb tit-deb naont yab geud aub yeil, yaox?*
afterward CLF:time$_3$-DIM thus also hold water rinse right?
'A little while later (after taking the medicine) I rinsed my mouth with water, right?' (Haili Shi, in *Tooth Conversation*)

(11.92) ***Nh.*** *Nins naonb nggaob?*
uh.huh COP what medicine
'Uh-huh. What kind of medicine was it?' (Shixiang Wu, in *Tooth Conversation*)

The form *nh* 'uh-huh' is unique among all the interjections discussed in this Section 11.3 in that it violates Xong's lexical phonotactics. While this form occurs in a number of different phonological variants (see below), it is most often realized as either a toneless syllabic alveolar nasal [n̩] or as a toneless nasalized mid back unrounded vowel [ɤ̃] (see Section 3.6 for more on toneless syllables). No other Fenghuang Xong form features a syllabic alveolar nasal or a nasalized mid back unrounded vowel, though some do feature certain phonetically similar sounds, including a syllabic bilabial nasal /m̩/ (see Section 3.3.4), a non-nasalized mid back unrounded vowel /ɤ/ (Section 3.3.1.6), and a nasalized diphthong /ɤ̃j/ (Section 3.3.3.4).

The interjection in question is transcribed as *nh* when it occurs in either of its two most common phonological variants (i.e. [n̩] or [ɤ̃]), with the orthographic <n> representing the form's segmental material and the orthographic <h> representing its tonelessness (see Section 4.4.2). Other variants are transcribed differently as their phonological form warrants, as in (11.93) (in which the variant in question is a disyllabic one that bears tone *-d* on each syllable) and (11.94) below. Note that these other variants are still glossed and translated as 'uh-huh'.

(11.93) ***And.hand.*** *Manx ... zhix.tonb.pianb.*
uh.huh um... painkiller
'Uh-huh. It's a, um...painkiller.' (Chenghua Long, in *Tooth Conversation*)

(11.94) ***Anh.*** *Zhaok zhut aob-beinf, wel dut ghans nex*
uh.huh fall reach NOM-basin 1SG obtain see NEX
chauk. Chanf daos.
do gross die
'Uh-huh. They fall into a basin, I've seen them do it before. It's so gross.' (Chenghua Long, in *Tooth Conversation*)

11.3.2 The interjection *hos* 'okay'

This form generally serves to indicate the speaker's agreement with some proposal or suggestion, as in examples (11.95–11.97) below. It is thus glossed as 'okay', and it can usually be quite accurately translated into English as 'okay' as well. It appears likely that the Xong form *hos* is a borrowing of Standard Mandarin *hǎo* (好) 'good, okay' (or of a cognate form from another Sinitic variety), which often serves a similar discourse function.

(11.95) *Niaox.nhaonl danx hint: "**Hos,** wel monl nheis*
PN honest very **okay** 1SG go gather
reib, naont monx dieud hlit aoh."
vegetable thus 2SG boil.rice cooked.rice PART
'Niao Nhaon was very honest, (and she said:) "Okay, I'll go gather some vegetables, and you stay here and boil the rice."' (Xingyu Shi, in *Oub Meinl Yaos Geud*)

(11.96) *"Nhaons wel monl aoh, Nhaonl?"* ***"Hos,*** *monx*
with 1SG go PART PN **okay** 2SG
dionb wel monl wel nhaons monx monl."
lead 1SG go 1SG with 2SG go
'(Nhaon's father asked her:) "Won't you come with me, Nhaon?" (Nhaon answered:) "Okay, if you take me then I'll go with you."' (Xingyu Shi, in *Oub Meinl Yaos Geud*)

(11.97) *Beul baox niab: "Meib-Nhaonl, wel nkheik aub*
3 father say younger.sister-PN 1SG thirsty water
guaot, monx heut wel teuf aod-tit aub gaons
pass 2SG help 1SG scoop one-CLF:time$_3$ water give
wel hauk." ***"Hos."*** *"Wel jont neind daonl monx."* ***"Hos."***
1SG drink **okay** 1SG sit this wait 2SG **okay**
'(Nhaon's) father said: "Little sister Nhaon, I'm very thirsty. Go get some water for me to drink." (Nhaon said:) "Okay." (Her father said:) "I'll sit here and wait for you." (Nhaon said:) "Okay."' (Xingyu Shi, in *Oub Meinl Yaos Geud*)

In some cases, *hos* does not serve to indicate the speaker's agreement, but rather it occurs between two utterances to indicate something like a causal relationship between them. Even in these cases, though, *hos* can still be accurately translated as 'okay' (or perhaps 'so'). For instance, example (11.98) below describes a father in a folktale who had instructed his two daughters to collect their tears in hollow lengths of bamboo while he was away so that he could determine which of the two was the more loyal (his thinking being that the more loyal daughter would shed more tears in his absence). In this example, he checks one of his daughters' bamboo lengths, finds that the liquid in it is tasteless, and thus realizes that the "tears" he is examining are actually fake. The interjection *hos* 'okay' is here used to connect the father's realization about the fake tears with his reasons for that realization.

(11.98) *Ob-naonb weib.dob at jix mex, doub nins aub,*
NOM-what flavor SAT NEG$_1$ exist then$_1$ COP water
hos, *beul niel lah, aod-leb neind nins manx*
okay 3 know PRF one-CLF this COP REL
giaox naond, jix nins aub-gheb.
fake ASSOC NEG$_1$ COP water-eye
'(The tears) didn't have any flavor at all, they were just water. Okay, so he knew, this (length of bamboo) was fake, it didn't contain tears at all.' (Xingyu Shi, in *Oub Meinl Yaos Geud*)

While *hos* 'okay' is regularly used by all of the author's primary consultants in casual conversation, the only consultant to actually use the form in a transcribed text so far is Xingyu Shi, the narrator of this grammar's Text 1 (*Oub Meinl Yaos Geud*).

11.3.3 The interjection *it* 'SPRS'

The form *it* is used to express surprise on the part of the speaker, and so it is glossed as 'SPRS'. This form is widespread among the author's primary consultants in both casual conversation and transcribed texts. As examples (11.99–11.101) below demonstrate, *it* 'SPRS' is generally used in reaction to relatively minor, benign surprises or unexpected information, meaning that it can often be translated into English as merely 'huh'. For more severe, unpleasant surprises, one of the forms discussed in Section 11.3.4 below is usually used instead.

(11.99) ***It,*** *at* *jix* *diaos* *shand* *raut.*
SPRS SAT NEG_1 catch.up.to ginger good
'Huh, (the medicine) isn't as good as ginger.' (Shixiang Wu, in *Tooth Conversation*)

(11.100) *Nhob* *nhob* *nhob,* ***it,*** *aod-leb* *zhonx-hlod* *jix*
walk walk walk **SPRS** one-CLF length-bamboo NEG_1
doul *aub.*
remain water
'(The girl) walked and walked and walked, but then, huh, all of a sudden there was no water left in the length of bamboo.' (Xingyu Shi, in *Oub Meinl Yaos Geud*)

(11.101) ***It,*** *tat-hnef* *beul* *yab* *cif.dob* *lah.*
SPRS this-CLF:day 3 also be.late PRF
'Huh, he's late again today.' (Haili Shi, fieldnotes)

11.3.4 The interjections *ih* '$DSMY_1$' and *aos.il* '$DSMY_2$'

To express exasperation or to react to rather severe, unpleasant surprises, Xong speakers frequently use either *ih* '$DSMY_1$' or *aos.il* '$DSMY_2$' (both glosses are derived from 'dismay'). Both of these forms are used by all of the author's primary consultants and they appear to be largely interchangeable, although – as the examples below and the two texts included with this grammar show – some consultants tend to favor the use of one form over the other.

In examples (11.102) and (11.103), the speaker is a husband who is complaining to his wife that she keeps destroying things that he enjoys. In both cases the speaker uses *ih* 'DSMY$_1$' to express his frustration.

(11.102) ***Ih,*** *zhet niax-naus doud.doub raut nonx, monx*
DSMY$_1$ CLF:bowl meat-bird extremely good eat 2SG
lis biat box.nhol, zod.guaod lah. Zod.guaod!
want pour throw.away what.a.pity PRF what.a.pity
'Oh no, that bowl of bird meat was so delicious, and you had to go and throw it away. What a pity. What a pity!' (Xingyu Shi, in *Oub Meinl Yaos Geud*)

(11.103) ***Ih,*** *chauk-dib monx lis ob lah, wel dut*
DSMY$_1$ do-which 2SG want burn PRF 1SG obtain
naonb monx at baol wel naond.
what 2SG SAT break.down 1SG ASSOC
'Oh no, how could you burn (that comb)? Whatever I get you destroy.' (Xingyu Shi, in *Oub Meinl Yaos Geud*)

In examples (11.104) and (11.105), the speaker uses *aos.il* 'DSMY$_2$' to signal how badly her tooth hurt.

(11.104) ***Aos.il,*** *daob.bieid nanx npof nzheub baont.jaonx.*
DSMY$_2$ head only desire pound wall
'My God, (my tooth hurt so bad that I) just wanted to bang my head against the wall.' (Haili Shi, in *Tooth Conversation*)

(11.105) *Naont sox.ix aod-hmaont dox taf jix dut,* ***aos.il,***
thus so one-CLF:evening that endure NEG$_1$ obtain **DSMY$_2$**
beut naont ngeinb.shib npof nggueb guaot.
lie.down thus no.matter.what desire sleep pass
'So, that evening (I) couldn't bear (the pain). God, (I) was lying there and (I) wanted to fall asleep so badly.' (Haili Shi, in *Tooth Conversation*)

As the examples just given suggest, *ih* and *aos.il* can be translated as any one of a number of English interjections depending on context (e.g. 'oh no', '[my] God', etc.). Nevertheless, they are consistently glossed as 'DSMY$_1$' and 'DSMY$_2$' whenever they appear.

11.3.5 The interjection *aod-minl(-nek)* 'mother'

The form *aod-minl* (or sometimes *aod-minl-nek*) literally means 'mother', but it functions as an interjection expressing shock or dismay. It could be translated into English equally well as 'man!', 'oh, brother!', 'Jesus!', '(my) God!', or '(my) heavens!'. It is important to note, though, that the Xong form in question has none of the religious connotations associated with some of these English translations.

The initial *aod-* in *aod-minl(-nek)* appears to be a nominal prefix that regularly occurs on nouns referring to kin members in Xong varieties spoken outside of Fenghuang County (and so it is glossed as 'KIN' here), although as far as the author has been able to determine this prefix is no longer used productively by Xong speakers within Fenghuang County (see Section 5.4.1 for more information). The forms *minl* and *nek* each simply mean 'mother' (see Section 5.3.2). This interjection is most often realized as simply *aod-minl* [KIN-mother], though occasionally it is realized as *aod-minl-nek* [KIN-mother-mother] instead. Although it is glossed consistently in this grammar, *aod-minl(-nek)* is given any one of a variety of translations depending on the context in which it occurs.

Note that while *aod-minl(-nek)* literally means 'mother', the form functions only as an interjection – in other words, it is never used as a noun to refer to an actual mother. For that latter purpose Xong speakers will simply use *minl* 'mother' (or much more rarely *nek* 'mother') instead.

(11.106) *Ix* *mex* *naonb,* *aod-hnef* *dox* *wel* *aod*
NEG$_1$ exist what one-CLF:day that 1SG as.soon.as
ghab *ghad,* ***aod-minl*** *aoh,* *zhaux* *xed* *naont.*
bite then$_2$ **KIN-mother** PART be.in.agony tooth thus
'I never had any problems (with that tooth before), but then that day, as soon as I bit down, man, my tooth was in agony.' (Haili Shi, in *Tooth Conversation*)

(11.107) ***Aod-minl-nek,*** *wel* *naond* *deb* *gheil* *ghaod* *zhut*
KIN-mother-mother 1SG ASSOC child excrete feces reach
manx *bioud* *lah!*
2PL home PRF
'Oh no, my kid's pooped (on the floor) in your house!' (unknown Xong consultant, fieldnotes)

In example (11.108), the speaker is reacting to her friend's description of a traditional method for dealing with infected teeth, one that involves a traditional doctor blowing smoke into the patient's mouth until the "bugs" inside the teeth have fallen out.

(11.108) *Aod-minl-nek.*
KIN-mother-mother
'My God.' (Haili Shi, in *Tooth Conversation*)

12 Multiverbal constructions

12.1 Introduction

In this grammar, a *multiverbal construction* is defined as any construction that involves at least two verbs and does not feature any markers of subordination or coordination among those verbs. Even a cursory examination of any naturalistic Xong text will quickly show that such constructions are extremely common, carry a very high functional load, and display a great deal of structural variety in the language. Examples (12.1) and (12.2), for instance, give some idea of the degree of size and complexity that these constructions can reach in Xong.

(12.1) *Aod-ngonl* *naus* ***beux*** ***daos*** ***geud*** ***giab*** ***nonx***.
one-CLF:animate bird **hit** **die** **hold** **stir.fry** **eat**
'(I) killed the bird and cooked it (to eat).' (Xingyu Shi, in *Oub Meinl Yaos Geud*)

(12.2) *Beul* *dad.kit* ***monl*** ***ncot*** ***nqif*** ***meb*** ***shok*** *zhel*.
3 not.until **go** **wash.clothing** **clean** **take** **dry.in.sun** sun
'She took (the shoes), washed (them) clean, and put (them outside) to dry in the sun.' (Xingyu Shi, in *Oub Meinl Yaos Geud*)

The author wishes to make it clear that this chapter provides only a brief sketch of some of the more common types of multiverbal construction attested in his Xong corpus. A comprehensive description of all of the language's multiverbal constructions would likely require several additional chapters, and the author did not have sufficient time in the field to acquire the data necessary for such a description. The specific constructions covered in this chapter include coordinating multiverbal constructions, in which the component verbs or clauses appear to be of roughly equal syntactic and semantic rank (see Section 12.2), aspectual-modal–marking multiverbal constructions, in which one or more verbs serve to express some aspect- or modality-related feature of another verb (Section 12.3), and multiverbal constructions involving complement-taking verbs, in which a verb takes a clause (which itself will naturally contain at least one verb, at least in the vast majority of cases) as an argument (Section 12.4). Several additional types of multiverbal construction – including ones that express direction and/or complex motion, ones that express degree, ones that express result, and ones that introduce oblique-like arguments – are briefly exemplified in Section 12.5. As these descriptions suggest, all multiverbal constructions discussed in this chapter have been organized along rough structural and functional lines. A more thorough account would ideally organize all of Xong's multiverbal constructions using a set of objective syntactic and semantic tests, but, again, more research is needed before this will be possible.

For the sake of completeness, Section 12.6 in this chapter also discusses some overtly marked clausal coordination constructions, though the presence of overt marking in these means that they are not actually multiverbal constructions according to the definition used in this grammar. Incidentally, although the high frequency and wide variety of multiverbal constructions in Xong constitute some of the most striking and immediately obvious ways in which the language's grammar differs from that of English and other European languages, the author is not entirely convinced that these constructions actually form a viable natural class in Xong. The fact that they involve multiple verbs without any overt markers of coordination or subordination might be rather incidental, and the author suspects that in at least some cases there might well be more semantic and grammatical similarities between a particular type of multiverbal construction and a particular overtly marked coordinative or subordinative construction than there are between two different types of multiverbal construction. Thus, while multiverbal constructions are still discussed more or less as a group in this chapter, a more in-depth description of the language might well end up using a very different organizational scheme.

12.2 Coordinating multiverbal constructions

12.2.1 Verb chains

It is quite common in Xong for multiple verbs to occur in sequence with no overt markers of coordination or subordination and with a single, relatively agent-like argument appearing only once (if at all) before the entire sequence of verbs rather than appearing before each verb individually, although more patient-like arguments may still appear following any of the verbs.[215] A wide variety of semantic relations can hold among the verbs in such a *verb chain*, including simple coordination ('V_1 and V_2'), simultaneity ('V_1 and V_2 at the same time'), sequential action ('V_1 then V_2'), and purpose ('V_1 in order to V_2'). By definition, none of these semantic relations are overtly

215 While the author frames his discussion in this section in terms of "verbs" for convenience's sake, he remains agnostic as to whether the linked constituents in a verb chain would more properly be analyzed as verbs or as clauses. Furthermore, as was mentioned earlier in Section 9.3.4 (see also Section 12.4.2 below), the behavior of grammaticalized syntactic roles like AGENT and PATIENT (discussed in Section 9.1.1) with respect to multiverbal constructions is still not entirely understood. The author thus takes a conservative approach in this Section 12.2.1 and makes reference only to semantically defined "agent-like" and "patient-like" arguments, not to any of those syntactic roles.

indicated in a verb chain, though of course any of them could be so indicated through the addition of non-verbal coordinative or subordinative markers (see Section 12.6).

Examples of verb chains are given in (12.3–12.8) below, in which each constituent verb and its following patient-like argument (if present) has been enclosed within brackets and each verb-chain–initial agent-like argument has been bolded. Note that each of these examples is taken from the narrative text *Oub Meinl Yaos Geud* (included in its entirety near the end of this grammar). This is not accidental, as verb chains appear to be rather more common in single-speaker narratives than in elicited sentences or multi-speaker conversations. Note also that any number of verbs can be linked in a single verb chain, though naturally the author has more examples of verb chains involving smaller numbers of linked verbs than ones involving larger numbers of them.

(12.3) ***Wel*** [*jont* *neind*] [*daonl* *monx*].
1SG [sit this] [wait 2SG]
'I'll sit here and wait for you.' (Xingyu Shi, in *Oub Meinl Yaos Geud*)

(12.4) ***Wel*** [*dand* *neind*] [*nheis* *reib-nbat*].
1SG [arrive this] [gather greens-pig]
'I came here to gather pig-feed.' (Xingyu Shi, in *Oub Meinl Yaos Geud*)

(12.5) ***Niaox.nhaonl*** [*zhaok* *aub*] [*daos*] *manh*.
PN [fall water] [die] PART
'Niao Nhaon had fallen into the water and drowned.' (Xingyu Shi, in *Oub Meinl Yaos Geud*)

(12.6) *Hnef-hnef* [*monl* *chaut*] [*chauk* *geud.donb*].
CLF:day-CLF:day [go wilderness] [do work]
'Every day (the child) went out into the wilderness to work.' (Xingyu Shi, in *Oub Meinl Yaos Geud*)

(12.7) [*Keuf* *zhut* *ob-raonf-naus*], [*gaons* *deb* *hlit*],
[shut reach NOM-cage-bird] [give DIM cooked.rice]
[*gaons* *deb* *aub*].
[give DIM water]
'(He) shut (the bird) in a birdcage and gave (it) a little bit of rice and a little bit of water.' (Xingyu Shi, in *Oub Meinl Yaos Geud*)

(12.8) *Sat* *lous* *ghaod-nbat* *ndeb* *meh,* **beul** *dad.kit*
SAT dirty feces-pig wet BCKG **3** not.until
[*monl*] [*ncot* *nqif*] [*meb*] [*shok* *zhel*].
[go] [wash.clothing clean] [take] [dry.in.sun sun]
'(When the girl's shoes) were filthy with pig droppings, and wet, she took (the shoes), washed (them) clean, and put (them outside) to dry in the sun.' (Xingyu Shi, in *Oub Meinl Yaos Geud*)

Consultants report that most attested verb chains allow for multiple interpretations. The verb chain in example (12.3), for instance, could be interpreted as expressing simple coordination, simultaneity, sequential action, purpose, or any combination thereof. The author suspects that this is more a case of underspecification than of ambiguity, in the sense that the appearance of two or more verbs in a verb chain simply indicates that there is some sort of semantic relationship between the verbs in question without specifying what particular semantic relationship that is (with that information instead being supplied by context and real-world knowledge). Still, at present this is only a hypothesis, and more research will be needed before it can be confirmed.

12.2.2 Verbal tetrasyllabic expressions

Xong features a rich inventory of *verbal tetrasyllabic expressions*, which are tetrasyllabic idiom-like expressions in which the first and third syllables are both instances of the same monosyllabic verb and the second and fourth syllables are either two different monosyllabic verbs or two different monosyllabic nouns. These expressions are fairly "inert" in grammatical terms, in the sense that their constituent verbs are not particularly amenable to aspectual-modal marking or negation (consultants sometimes allow aspectual-modal marking or negation of the constituent verbs in particular verbal tetrasyllabic expressions in particular contexts, but not in any obviously systematic way) and in the sense that the order of the second and fourth syllables cannot be reversed. Verbal tetrasyllabic expressions tend to have somewhat noncompositional meanings, though the exact degree of noncompositionality varies from expression to expression. Xong's verbal tetrasyllabic expressions have already attracted a great deal of attention from previous scholars of the language; see, e.g., Xiang (1983), Yang (2004: 136–138), Luo (2005: 133–147), and Yu (2004; 2006; 2011: 325–338). Note, though, that these scholars generally consider these verbal expressions to be a subtype of a larger set of tetrasyllabic expressions that includes nominal and other subtypes as well (see Section 5.3.3.1 for more information).

Arguably, there is little need to examine Xong's verbal tetrasyllabic expressions in a descriptive grammar, since they appear to be largely idiomatic constructions with relatively few unusual grammatical properties. However, these expressions are still discussed here because Xong speakers have a high degree of metalinguistic awareness of them. The author is not aware of any native Xong term for these expressions, and his consultants instead refer to them with the Standard Mandarin term *chéngyǔ* (成语), which is typically used to refer to certain tetrasyllabic idioms in Sinitic varieties. These consultants universally report that the use of verbal tetrasyllabic expressions is particularly common for skilled (rather than merely fluent) Xong speakers, and that they are generally associated with particularly poetic or dramatic speech registers. In all of these semantic and pragmatic respects, verbal tetrasyllabic expressions greatly resemble generic compounds, which are obligatorily tetrasyllabic nominal constructions that also have a high degree of metalinguistic salience for Xong speakers (see Section 5.3.3, and especially Section 5.3.3.4).

There are a large number of distinct tetrasyllabic verbal expressions in Xong: Yu (2010: 468–502), for instance, lists at least several dozen. Furthermore, it is not entirely clear to what extent speakers can create novel verbal tetrasyllabic expressions, meaning that the set of these expressions may in fact be an open one. Thus, naturally, the author does not attempt to exhaustively list all verbal tetrasyllabic expressions in this section. Instead, only a few representative examples are provided in order to give the reader some idea of the semantic variety that these expressions display.

Although other classification schemes are possible, the author here divides Xong's verbal tetrasyllabic expressions into two subtypes based on their internal constituent structures. In the first subtype, the first and third syllables are both instances of the same monosyllabic verb, while the second and fourth syllables are two different monosyllabic nouns (see examples (12.9–12.13) below). These expressions are noncompositional in the sense that the truth of any such expression as a whole does not entail the truth of each of its constituent halves. For example, the truth of the verbal tetrasyllabic expression *uk ndeinb uk dut* [dance knife dance axe] in example (12.9) does not entail that one both waved around a knife and waved around an axe, but rather merely that one waved around some sort of bladed implement. In example (12.10), the truth of the expression *beut doub beut roub* [lie.down earth lie.down stone] does not entail that one both slept on earth and slept on stone, but rather merely that one is willing or able to sleep anywhere. Similar claims hold for examples (12.11–12.13).

(12.9) *Beul ninb dox* ***uk ndeinb uk dut,*** *manx seid*
3 at that **dance knife dance axe** 2PL away
beul jeud-rout deb.
3 DID-far DIM
'He's swinging (his axe) around over there, you guys stay away from him.' (Chenghua Long, fieldnotes)

(12.10) *Aod-meinl deb-deb neind* ***beut doub beut roub.***
one-CLF:person child-RED this **lie.down earth lie.down stone**
'This child just sleeps anywhere.' (Chenghua Long, fieldnotes)

(12.11) *Aod-god miex daox.gonk jeub nins*
one-CLF:human.group person perform.migrant.labor then$_3$ COP
heut nex ***chauk guoud chauk nbat.***
help NEX **do dog do pig**
'Those people who go out to do migrant labor, they're just going out to work like slaves for other people.' (Haili Shi, fieldnotes)

(12.12) *Giaok-bioud aod-meinl mianx dox* ***gint tib gint***
side-home one-CLF:person person that **rot stomach rot**
xed.
intestine
'(Our) neighbor over there is a really bad guy.' (Chenghua Long, fieldnotes)

(12.13) *Shib.taond giab naond reib-yeus* ***diaonl xeb***
cafeteria stir.fry ASSOC vegetable-cooked.meat **sweet oil**
diaonl njeud.
sweet salt
'The food in the cafeteria is delicious.' (Haili Shi, fieldnotes)

In the second subtype, the first and third syllables are both instances of the same monosyllabic verb, while the second and fourth syllables are two different monosyllabic verbs (see examples (12.14–12.17) below). Expressions of this subtype are also noncompositional in the same way as the first subtype discussed above, namely in that the truth of such an expression as a whole does not entail the truth of each of its constituent halves.

(12.14) *Manx-eib aod-zeid ghot yaod.yaod* ***nas xib***
AT-yon one-CLF:generation old all **endure hungry**
nas nkheik *guaot lol.*
endure thirsty pass come
'Members of the older generation have all gone hungry before.' (Chenghua Long, fieldnotes)

(12.15) *Aod-gud deb-deb yaod.yaod nins* ***nonx liox***
one-CLF:human.group child-RED all COP **eat big**
nonx zhaonl.
eat grow
'The children are all growing up big and strong.' (Chenghua Long, fieldnotes)

(12.16) *Beul-gud* ***khad*** ***nzod*** ***khad*** ***mieins*** *doub* *lis* *lol*
3-PL **dry** **early** **dry** **bright** then$_1$ want come
dand *xox.ndaonb.*
arrive school
'They have to be at school at the crack of dawn.' (Chenghua Long, fieldnotes)

(12.17) *Aod-meinl* *miex* *dox* *zhank.meinf* *yeb* ***puk*** ***xaob***
one-CLF:person person that always like **speak** **scrape**
puk ***kuad*** *nex* *leh.*
speak **stir** NEX LEH
'That person is always criticizing other people.' (Haili Shi, fieldnotes)

12.3 Aspectual-modal–marking multiverbal constructions

12.3.1 Introduction

This section examines several verbs that function both as canonical lexical verbs and as markers of various aspectual-modal notions (in the latter case these verbs obligatorily co-occur with other verbs within the same clause, which justifies their inclusion in this chapter). With some of these verbs there is a relatively clear distinction between the verb's lexical meaning and its aspectual-modal meaning, so that it is usually obvious whether any given instance of the verb is functioning as a canonical lexical verb or as an aspectual-modal marker. With other verbs, though, it is difficult or even impossible to draw a clear line between the two functions, so that many attested instances of the verb could be equally well interpreted as serving a canonical lexical function, as serving an aspectual-modal–marking function, or as serving both simultaneously. To reflect this, each verb discussed in this section is given a uniform gloss regardless of the specific function it is serving in any particular case. Thus, for instance, the verb *lis* (see Section 12.3.2) is glossed as 'want' in all cases, including those where it is clearly serving as a canonical lexical verb, those where it is clearly serving as an aspectual-modal marker, and those where it is arguably serving both functions at the same time.

This section does not discuss every attested aspectual-modal–marking verb in Xong; instead, it looks at only a few of the most commonly used ones. In particular, Section 12.3.2 covers two of the most common preverbal aspectual-modal–marking verbs, namely *ninb* 'at' and *lis* 'to want', Section 12.3.3 covers two verbs which can each serve to (among other things) indicate experiential aspect, namely *guaot* 'to pass' and *dut/daut* 'to obtain', and Section 12.3.4 covers three postverbal completive-marking verbs, namely *diex/dianx* 'to finish', *diul* 'to complete', and *ncaos/ncaok* 'to be done'.

Note, though, that not every aspectual-modal–marking form in Xong is a verb. The non-verbal form *niaons* 'ABIL', for instance, is discussed in Section 12.3.3, the perfect marker *lah* 'PRF' is discussed in Section 9.2.1.4, and various morphological processes that signal (among other things) certain aspectual-modal distinctions are discussed in Section 10.5. Other non-verbal forms with arguably aspectual-modal meanings, including most prominently certain grammatical operators (see Section 9.1.1), are not explicitly discussed in this grammar at all. However, this omission is due solely to the time- and data-related constraints under which the author was working, and it does not in any way mean that these non-verbal forms are insignificant or marginal within the context of Xong's grammatical system as a whole.

12.3.2 Constructions with *ninb* 'at' and *lis* 'to want'

The verb *ninb* 'at' appears to serve three major functions in Xong, though it is unclear whether these should be considered an instance of monosemy, polysemy, or ambiguity (see Gil 2004). First, it can be used to indicate simple spatial location, including the location of an entity (in which case *ninb* may be the sole verb in its clause, as in (12.18)) or the location where a particular event or activity takes place (in which case *ninb* will be accompanied by another verb expressing that event or activity, as in (12.19)). In either of these cases, the most appropriate English translation for the form is simply '(be) at'.

(12.18) *Ob-ras* ***ninb*** *dof?*
NOM-comb **at** which
'Where is the comb?' (Xingyu Shi, in *Oub Meinl Yaos Geud*)

(12.19) *Wel* ***ninb*** *bioud dieud hlit*
1SG **at** home boil.rice cooked.rice
'I'll boil the rice here at home.' (Xingyu Shi, in *Oub Meinl Yaos Geud*)

Second, it can mean 'to live (at)', as in example (12.20).

(12.20) *Wel* ***ninb*** *xol.taonx lah.*
1SG **at** school PRF
'I live at the school now.' (Shixiang Wu, fieldnotes)

Third, and most relevantly for this section, *ninb* can also serve as a marker of progressive aspect (i.e. it can signal that a particular event, activity, state, or property is or was ongoing at the time of reference). In such cases it always occurs preceding the verb that it marks for progressive aspect, as in examples (12.21–12.23) below.

(12.21) *Wel* ***ninb*** *nonx* *hlit* *nzod.*
1SG **at** eat cooked.rice early
'I'm eating breakfast.' (Yan Long, fieldnotes)

(12.22) *Lox.web* ***ninb*** *sheit* *ndeud.*
white.foreigner **at** write writing
'The (white) foreigner is writing.' (Haili Shi, fieldnotes)

(12.23) *Beul* ***ninb*** *chauk* *geud.donb.*
3 **at** do work
'He's working.' (unknown Xong consultant, fieldnotes)

Note that the use of *ninb* 'at' as a progressive marker forces a progressive reading of the clause in which it appears, but such a reading is still possible without *ninb*. For instance, example (12.21) above could only be interpreted as meaning 'I'm eating breakfast', but it could also be interpreted the same way if *ninb* were removed. In that case, though, a number of other readings would also be possible (e.g. 'I ate breakfast', 'I will eat breakfast', 'I had been eating breakfast', etc.; see Section 10.2), with only context and real-world knowledge making one of those readings more likely than the others. The same applies to examples (12.22) and (12.23), as well as to other utterances in which *ninb* serves as a progressive marker.

Just like *ninb* 'at', the verb *lis* 'to want' can of course function as a canonical lexical verb with the meaning that its gloss suggests. In such cases the "wanted" argument can be either a noun phrase, as in example (12.24), or a clause, as in (12.25) (see also Section 12.4 below).

(12.24) *Wel* ***lis*** *aod-leb* *neind.*
1SG **want** one-CLF this
'I want this one.' (Haili Shi, fieldnotes)

(12.25) *Wel* *naond* *geub.bul* ***lis*** *wel* *dionb* *beul* *monl*
1SG ASSOC friend **want** 1SG lead 3 go
nieus *reib.*
buy vegetable
'My friend wants me to take him (to the market) to buy food.' (Chenghua Long, fieldnotes)

In addition, *lis* 'to want' very often functions as a marker of a wide variety of deontic notions, including obligation, necessity, recommendation, and directives.[216]

216 In addition to functioning as a canonical lexical verb and as an aspectual-modal marker, the verb *lis* may also serve to make certain argument types more amenable to relativization, though more research will be needed before this can be confirmed. See Section 8.1.4 for details.

A representative sample of utterances in which *lis* serves this deontic function is given in (12.26–12.34) below.

(12.26) *Aod-ngonl xut.npeif neind* ***lis*** *chauk did-liox deb.*
one-CLF:pair$_1$ shoe this **want** do DID-big DIM
'(You) need to make this pair of shoes a little bigger.' (Haili Shi, fieldnotes)

(12.27) *At jix* ***lis*** *kiak dieb.nox, at giet.xeb*
SAT NEG$_1$ **want** open computer SAT convenient
geud shoux.jik.
hold cell.phone
'(I) didn't even need to turn on the computer, (I) could just use my cell phone.' (Haili Shi, in *Tooth Conversation*)

(12.28) *Zhut gil nanx* ***lis*** *zhut aod-nzaut-deb yut yut,*
reach tea only **want** reach one-CLF:pinch-DIM few few
nins naont yoh?
COP thus QP.NTRL
'When (you're) adding tea leaves, (you) only want to add a single pinch, is that right?' (Chenghua Long, fieldnotes)

(12.29) *Mx* ***lis*** *jont id-raut.*
2SG **want** sit DID-good
'Sit up straight.' (Shixiang Wu, fieldnotes)

(12.30) *Nbaod beinx nhaons raul eud aod.sheit* ***lis***
embroider flower with sew clothing the.same **want**
aod-jub aod-jub naond lol.
one-CLF:needle one-CLF:needle ASSOC come
'Whether (you're) embroidering or sewing, (you) need to take it one stitch at a time.' (Chenghua Long, fieldnotes)

(12.31) *Beul naond bod jix bod niab deux*
3 ASSOC husband NEG$_1$ tell say QUOT
nghauk aub jix ***lis*** *monl.*
bathe water NEG$_1$ **want** go
'Her husband hadn't told her not to go bathing.' (Xingyu Shi, in *Oub Meinl Yaos Geud*)

(12.32) *Tat-hnef monx aod-bix dib at jix* ***lis*** *monl.*
this-CLF:day 2SG one-CLF:place$_1$ which SAT NEG$_1$ **want** go
'Don't go anywhere today.' (Haili Shi, fieldnotes)

(12.33) *Ghaob-deb-ghaob-maot* *jix* ***lis*** *did-ndaot*
NOM-child-NOM-father NEG$_1$ **want** DID-curse
'Fathers and children shouldn't argue with each other.' (Chenghua Long, fieldnotes)

(12.34) *Wel* ***lis*** *bionl* *monl* *aod-tit-deb* *ghat* *geud-zheit.*
1SG **want** exit go one-CLF:time$_3$-DIM go.to place$_1$-outside
'I need to leave home for a little while.' (Xingyu Shi, in *Oub Meinl Yaos Geud*)

As examples (12.26–12.34) suggest, the form *lis* appears to cover a much wider semantic territory than many deontic expressions in English (e.g. *should, must, need to, want to*, etc.). This means that a single Xong utterance featuring *lis* can often have multiple possible English translations. For instance, example (12.26) above could be translated equally well as 'You need to make this pair of shoes a little bigger', 'You should make this pair of shoes a little bigger', 'You want to make this pair of shoes a little bigger', 'Make this pair of shoes a little bigger', and so on.

In addition to signaling various deontic notions, *lis* 'to want' can also signal intention (when referring to the speaker himself) or expected action (when referring to someone other than the speaker). In such cases *lis* shows more semantic overlap with future tense markers in other languages than with deontic expressions. Examples of this are given in (12.35–12.38).

(12.35) *Wel* ***lis*** *geud* *mx* *tat-hnef* *ndaot* *lox.sik*
1SG **want** hold 2SG this-CLF:day curse teacher
naond *sib* *bod* *boub* *baox!*
ASSOC matter tell 1PL father
'I'm going to tell our father about how you swore at the teacher today!' (unknown Xong consultant, fieldnotes)

(12.36) *Beul* ***lis*** *yol* *roul-deb* *shaod* *lol.*
3 **want** again CLF:time$_1$-DIM not.until come
'It'll be a little while before he comes.' (Shixiang Wu, fieldnotes)

(12.37) *Bof.tok* *bud* *beul* *xeub-hnef* ***lis*** *lol* *lah.*
PN tell 3 tomorrow-CLF:day **want** come PRF
'Bo To told (me) that he (i.e. Bo To) will come tomorrow.' (Haili Shi, fieldnotes)

(12.38) *Wel* *beux* *monx* *aod-ted* **lis** *gaons* *monx* *hnant*
1SG hit 2SG one-CLF:beating **want** give 2SG call
pouf *hnant* *niaox.*
paternal.grandfather call paternal.grandmother
'I'm going to beat you (so badly that) you cry for your (paternal) grandparents.' (Haili Shi, fieldnotes)

Unsurprisingly, there is some degree of overlap between *lis* as a marker of deontic modality and *lis* as a marker of intention or expected action. For instance, consultants report that example (12.34) above could be equally well translated as 'I'll leave home for a little while' or 'I'm going to leave home for a little while' as 'I need to leave home for a little while', and the same is true of many other examples given in this section.

Finally, when the form *lis* precedes another, more canonically lexical verb within a single clause, it is often unclear whether *lis* should be interpreted as more of an aspectual-modal marker or as more of a complement-taking verb (see Section 12.4). For instance, in example (12.39) below (repeated from (12.37) above), it is unclear which verb expresses the main predication in the subordinate clause, *lis* 'to want' (in which case a literal translation would be 'Bo To told [me] that he wants to come tomorrow') or *lol* 'to come' (in which case a literal translation would be 'Bo To told [me] that he'll come tomorrow').

(12.39) *Bof.tok* *bud* *beul* *xeub-hnef* **lis** **lol** *lah.*
PN tell 3 tomorrow-CLF:day **want** **come** PRF
'Bo To told (me) that he (i.e. Bo To) will come tomorrow.' (Haili Shi, fieldnotes) (repeated from (12.37) above)

Of course, this may be something of a false dilemma, and it might be most accurate to simply say that *lis* 'to want' displays some properties that are canonically associated with aspectual-modal–marking verbs and some that are canonically associated with complement-taking verbs. In some cases *lis* appears to be serving as a relatively clear aspectual-modal marker and in some it appears to be serving as a relatively clear complement-taking verb, but in many other cases it appears to be serving as something in between the two – or, alternately, it appears to be serving both functions simultaneously.

12.3.3 Constructions with *guaot* 'to pass' and *dut/daut* 'to obtain'

The verbs *guaot* 'to pass' and *dut/daut* 'to obtain' each serve multiple functions in Xong. For instance, the verb *guaot* can serve as a canonical lexical verb meaning 'to pass' or 'to cross', as in example (12.40) below.

(12.40)

Tat-hnef	*wel*	***guaot***	*oub-taonb*	*aub.*
this-CLF:day	1SG	**pass**	two-CLF:trip	water

'I crossed the river twice today.' (Haili Shi, fieldnotes)

The same verb can also appear following a state- or property-denoting verb, in which case it can serve as a degree marker meaning roughly 'very'.

(12.41)

Niaox.nhaonl	*danx*	***guaot***	*meh...*
PN	honest	**pass**	BCKG

'Niao Nhaon was very honest...' (Xingyu Shi, in *Oub Meinl Yaos Geud*)

The verb *dut/daut* 'to obtain' can, of course, serve as a canonical lexical verb with that meaning, as in example (12.42). Note that this form is pronounced *dut* by speakers from Shanjiang Town and Yankan Village, but it is pronounced *daut* by speakers from La'ershan Town and most of the surrounding villages (with the exception of Yankan).

(12.42)

Giat	*nkhed*	*diul*	*jud.leb*	*ghaod*	***dut***	*hliof*	*aub-gheb.*
share	look	complete	who	more	**obtain**	many	water-eye

'Let (me) see which of (you) has gotten more tears.' (Xingyu Shi, in *Oub Meinl Yaos Geud*)

This form can also serve as the second verb in a multiverbal construction indicating potential or ability. In such cases *dut/daut* follows the verb that expresses the main predication of the clause, with the entire [VERB *dut/daut*] construction meaning 'can VERB' or 'able to VERB'.[217] Examples of this are given in (12.43–12.48) below, in which each instance of the [VERB *dut/daut*] construction has been enclosed within brackets and each instance of *dut/daut* itself has been bolded. Note that while in the author's corpus there are no instances of this construction being preceded by the negative marker *(j)ix* 'NEG$_1$' (see Section 9.2.2.1), that negative marker does frequently occur *within* the construction in question (see examples (12.46) and (12.47) below). In such cases it occurs between *dut/daut* and the preceding verb, with the entire [VERB *(j)ix dut/daut*] construction then meaning 'cannot VERB' or 'unable to VERB'.

217 In the author's corpus this construction is only ever used to express natural ability, not permission, but the author has not had the chance to specifically check whether it can be used to express permission as well.

(12.43) *Tit-deb* *wel* *doub* *geud* *shand* *giaot* *naont*
CLF:time$_3$-DIM 1SG then$_1$ hold ginger chew thus
wel *doub* [*nggueb* ***dut***].
1SG then$_1$ [sleep **obtain**]
'So after a while I chewed some ginger (to help with my toothache), and then I was finally able to fall asleep. (Haili Shi, in *Tooth Conversation*)

(12.44) *Fanx.zheinb* *deit* [*taf* ***dut***].
anyway still [endure **obtain**]
'At least (I) was able to bear (the pain in my tooth).' (Haili Shi, in *Tooth Conversation*)

(12.45) *Jud.leb* [*deib* ***dut***] *aod-nqad* *neind,* *doul*
who [match **obtain**] one-CLF:half.of.pair this remain
nqad, *jud.leb* *doub* *chauk* *beul* *naond*
CLF:half.of.pair who then$_1$ do 3 ASSOC
nheinx.
daughter.in.law
'Whoever could match this shoe, whoever had the other half of the pair, she would become the landlord's daughter-in-law.' (Xingyu Shi, in *Oub Meinl Yaos Geud*)

(12.46) *Beul* [*nzhaod* *jix* ***dut***].
3 [return NEG$_1$ **obtain**]
'She won't be able to come back.' (Xingyu Shi, in *Oub Meinl Yaos Geud*)

(12.47) [*Teuf* *jix* ***dut***] *aub* *nzhaod* *lol.*
[scoop NEG$_1$ **obtain**] water return come
'(She) wouldn't be able to bring any water back.' (Xingyu Shi, in *Oub Meinl Yaos Geud*)

It is worth mentioning here the non-verbal form *niaons* 'ABIL' (from 'abilitative'), which shows a fair amount of functional and semantic overlap with *dut/daut* 'to obtain', at least in that latter form's potential- or ability-indicating capacity. The form *niaons* is clearly not a verb, as it cannot be directly negated by a preceding *(j) ix* 'NEG$_1$' nor can it undergo relativization through the use of *manx* 'REL' (see Section 10.2). This form only ever appears following a verb, though the negative marker *(j)ix* 'NEG$_1$' can appear between that verb and the following *niaons*. The whole [VERB *niaons*] construction means 'can VERB' or 'able to VERB', or, if the form *(j)ix* appears within it, 'cannot VERB' or 'unable to VERB'. Examples of this are given in (12.48–12.50) below.

(12.48) *Monx* [*gheint* ***niaons***] *yaox?*
2SG [carry.on.shoulder.pole **ABIL**] right?
'You can carry that (on a shoulder-pole), right?' (Shixiang Wu, fieldnotes)

(12.49) *Wel* [*hauk* *ix* ***niaons***].
1SG [drink NEG_1 **ABIL**]
'I can't drink (this alcohol because it's too expensive).' (unknown Xong consultant, fieldnotes)

(12.50) *Wel* *meh,* *liaos* *monx* *naond* *guaot,* [*daonl* *jix*
1SG BCKG miss 2SG ASSOC Pass [wait NEG_1
niaons] *monx* *nzhaod.*
ABIL] 2SG return
'But I missed you greatly, I couldn't wait for you to come back.' (Xingyu Shi, in *Oub Meinl Yaos Geud*)

There does appear to be some slight semantic difference between the [VERB *dut/daut*] and [VERB *niaons*] constructions, but it is not yet possible to characterize this difference in any specific way.

Returning to the main topic of this section, the verbs *guaot* 'to pass' and *dut/daut* 'to obtain' can each also function as an aspectual-modal marker, more specifically as a marker of experiential aspect. This aspectual marking carries a meaning of roughly 'to have ever VERBed', and it can be expressed in three different ways. First, the verb expressing the main predication of the clause can be preceded by *dut/daut* 'to obtain', as in examples (12.51–12.53).

(12.51) *Meib-Nhaonl,* *monx* [***dut*** *dand*] *neind,* *Nhaonl?*
younger.sister-PN 2SG [**obtain** arrive] this PN
'Little sister Nhaon, have you been here before, Nhaon?' (Xingyu Shi, in *Oub Meinl Yaos Geud*)

(12.52) *Naont* *loux* *lol* *at* *xaond* [***dut*** *nzhaod*]
thus long.time come SAT not.yet [**obtain** return]
nkhed *deb-ghot.*
look DIM-old
'It's been such a long time and (you) still haven't gone back to visit your father.' (Xingyu Shi, in *Oub Meinl Yaos Geud*)

(12.53) *Ranf.houb* *bid-ghaond* *wel* *ix* [***dut*** *shaod*].
afterward FRT-garlic 1SG NEG_1 [**obtain** try]
'Afterward I didn't try the garlic.' (Haili Shi, in *Tooth Conversation*)

Second, the verb expressing the main predication of the clause can be followed by *guaot* 'to pass', as in examples (12.54) and (12.55).[218]

(12.54) *Wel* [*nins* ***guaot***] *lox.sid.*
1SG [COP **pass**] teacher
'I've been a teacher before.' (Chenghua Long, fieldnotes)

(12.55) *Beul* [*nqint* ***guaot***].
3 [red **pass**]
'It (i.e. a lamp whose bulb cycles through various colors) has been red before.' (Chenghua Long, fieldnotes)

Third, the verb expressing the main predication of the clause can be both preceded by *dut/daut* and followed by *guaot*, as in examples (12.56) and (12.57).

(12.56) [***Dut*** *dand* ***guaot***] *meh, ghad deit ndiot geud nzhaod.*
[**obtain** arrive **pass**] BCKG then$_2$ still recognize road return
'Well, if (she's) been here before, then (she'll) know the way back.' (Xingyu Shi, in *Oub Meinl Yaos Geud*)

(12.57) *Wel* [***daut*** *bit* ***guaot***] *lah.*
1SG [**obtain** compare **pass**] PRF
'I've (already) compared them.' (Shixiang Wu, fieldnotes)

These three experiential constructions can all be negated, but in such cases the negative marker always precedes the construction as a whole (as in examples (12.52) and (12.53) above) rather than occurring within it.

Finally, much as with the [VERB *dut/daut*] and [VERB *niaons*] constructions examined earlier in this section, there do appear to be some subtle semantic differences among the three experiential constructions just discussed, but further research will be needed before these differences can be described in any meaningful way.

---

218 Postverbal *guaot* 'to pass' can also serve as a degree marker (see example (12.41) above), which can sometimes result in ambiguous cases with state- or property-denoting verbs. Example (12.55), for instance, is equally interpretable as either 'It has been red before' or 'It's very red', with only context and real-world knowledge allowing listeners to determine which meaning was intended.

12.3.4 Constructions with *diex/dianx* 'to finish', *diul* 'to complete', and *ncaos/ncaok* 'to be done'

Xong features three verbs that each function both as a canonical lexical verb and as some sort of completive marker: *diex/dianx* 'to finish', *diul* 'to complete', and *ncaos/ncaok* 'to be done'. The first of these verbs is realized as *diex* for speakers from Yankan Village and as *dianx* for speakers from other parts of Fenghuang County, and it can occur as a canonical lexical verb meaning either 'to bear fruit' (as in example (12.58)) or 'to become' (as in example (12.59)).

(12.58)

aod-zhaus	*ndaut*	*manx*	*xaond*	***dianx***	*bid*
one-CLF:vertical.plant	tree	REL	not.yet	**finish**	fruit

'the tree that hasn't yet borne fruit' (Chenghua Long, fieldnotes)

(12.59)

Beul	***diex***	*lox.sid*	*lah.*
3	**finish**	teacher	PRF

'He's become a teacher now.' (Haili Shi, fieldnotes)

The form *diex/dianx* can also occur in clause-final position (though it may then still be followed by one of the clause-final forms discussed in Section 9.1.1) to mean something like 'and be done with it' or 'and that'll be that'. Examples of this are given in (12.60) and (12.61) below. In this capacity *diex/dianx* appears to have semantic scope over the entire clause, and it is not amenable to negation or aspectual-modal marking (except by clause-final *lah* 'PRF').

(12.60)

Meib-Nhaonl	*jaod*	*deb*	*hint,*	*boub*	*ghad*	*lis*
younger.sister-PN	bad	child	very	1PL	NEG.IMP	want
beul	***diex.***					
3	**finish**					

'Little sister Nhaon is such a bad child, let's just get rid of her and be done with it.' (Xingyu Shi, in *Oub Meinl Yaos Geud*)

(12.61)

Xaond	*tad*	*naont*	*monx*	*chauk*	*wel*	*naond*
not.yet	establish	thus	2SG	do	1SG	ASSOC
nheinx	***diex***	*lah.*				
daughter.in.law	**finish**	PRF				

'Since (you) haven't married yet, you can be my daughter-in-law, and that'll be that.' (Xingyu Shi, in *Oub Meinl Yaos Geud*)

The second and third verbs, *diul* 'to complete' and *ncaos/ncaok* 'to be done', can each occur as a canonical lexical verb meaning 'to complete/finish (some task or activity), to be done'. The task or activity in question is often identifiable only from context, as in examples (12.62) and (12.63). Note that the verb glossed as 'to be done' is realized as *ncaos* for speakers from Yankan Village and as *ncaok* for speakers from other parts of Fenghuang County.

(12.62)

Diul	*leh*	*beul*	*naond*	*jed,*	*Niaox.meib,*
complete	LEH	3	ASSOC	older.sister	PN

Niaox.meib	*leh,*	*jaod*	*deb*	*hint,*	*Jix*	*liaos*	*baox*	*naond.*
PN	LEH	bad	child	very	NEG_1	miss	father	ASSOC

'After (the sisters' father had left), the older sister, Niao Mei, as for her, (she) was a very bad child. (She) didn't miss her father.' (Xingyu Shi, in *Oub Meinl Yaos Geud*)

(12.63)

Ncaok	*lah.*
be.done	PRF

'(The auditing) is already done.' (Chenghua Long, fieldnotes)

As was mentioned above, these three verbs can also function as completive markers, in that they can indicate that a particular event (or activity, or state, or property, etc.) has been completed or has finished coming into effect, without indicating anything about the current relevance (or lack thereof) of that completion (cf. the discussion of the perfect marker *lah* 'PRF' in Section 9.2.1.4). In such cases they obligatorily follow the verb that expresses the main predication of the clause, as in examples (12.64–12.73). The fact that the two examples containing *ncaos/ncaok* 'to be done', namely examples (12.68) and (12.69), are taken from elicitation sessions rather than from naturalistic texts is a reflection of the fact that *ncaos/ncaok* occurs much less frequently in the author's Xong corpus than either *diex/dianx* 'to finish' or *diul* 'to complete'.

(12.64)

Beul	*puk*	***diex***	*naond,*	*aod-meinl*	*gaons*	*aod-leb*
3	speak	**finish**	ASSOC	one-CLF:person	give	one-CLF

bid-zhonx-hlod,	*beul*	*monl*	*lah.*
FRT-length-bamboo	3	go	PRF

'He finished speaking, gave each (sister) a length of bamboo, and then he left.' (Xingyu Shi, fieldnotes)

(12.65)

Deit	*doul*	*ndeib,*	*xaond*	*ndok*	***diex.***
still	remain	cloth	not.yet	weave	**finish**

'(She'd) left some cloth behind, (cloth that she) hadn't finished weaving.' (Xingyu Shi, in *Oub Meinl Yaos Geud*)

(12.66) *Nieux.ghoub* *wel* *xaond* *nonx* ***diul.***
just.now 1SG not.yet eat **complete**
'I hadn't finished eating (the bird meat) just now.' (Xingyu Shi, in *Oub Meinl Yaos Geud*)

(12.67) *"Gieb* ***diul*** *loh?"* *"Gieb* ***diul*** *lah."*
burnt **complete** PART burnt **complete** PRF
'(The husband asked:) "Did (you) burn the whole (comb)?" (The wife answered:) "(I) did."' (Xingyu Shi, in *Oub Meinl Yaos Geud*)

(12.68) *Beul* *sheit* ***ncaok.***
3 write **be.done**
'She finished (her homework).' (Chenghua Long, fieldnotes)

(12.69) *Beul* *xaond* *gid* ***ncaok.***
3 not.yet run **be.done**
'He hasn't finished running (laps) yet.' (Shixiang Wu, fieldnotes)

The semantic distinctions among *diex/dianx* 'to finish', *diul* 'to complete', and *ncaos/ncaok* 'to be done' in their capacities as completive markers are subtle and still require further investigation, but some impressionistic notes can be given here. The verb *diex/dianx* appears to be the most semantically general completive marker, as it seems to simply entail that the event (or activity, etc.) in question was carried out to completion. The verb *diul*, in contrast, often seems to emphasize that the event (or activity, etc.) in question was carried out "thoroughly" or "all the way", such that it would not be possible to continue carrying out the event any further (see, e.g., examples (12.66) and (12.67) above). In many cases, though, consultants report that *diul* is freely interchangeable with *diex/dianx*. Finally, *ncaos/ncaok* differs from the other two completive markers discussed here in that it tends to occur with relatively durative predicates, including those referring to durative activities (e.g. *sheit* 'to write', *gid* 'to run'), those referring to states (e.g. *nins* 'COP', *niel/nianl* 'to know'), and those referring to properties (e.g. *nqint* 'red', *gueinx* 'yellow'). The other two completive markers, *diex/dianx* and *diul*, do not show any apparent preferences with respect to durative vs. non-durative predicates. However, it should be kept in mind that *ncaos/ncaok* 'to be done' does in some cases occur with non-durative predicates as well, and also that relatively few instances of the form occur in the author's corpus overall.

12.4 Multiverbal constructions involving complement-taking verbs

12.4.1 Introduction

Xong possesses a wide variety of verbs that take clausal complements, including verbs like *xaont* 'to wish', *saud* 'to invite', and *zhus/zhaus* 'to suffer'. The complement of such a verb will follow the verb itself, as in example (12.70) below. In this example, the complement-taking verb has been bolded and its complement has been enclosed within brackets.

(12.70)	*Wel*	***xaont***	[*beul*	*xib-hneb*	*jix*	*sheib*	*lol*].
	1SG	**wish**	[3	tomorrow-CLF:day	NEG_1	able.to	come]

'I hope he won't be able to come tomorrow.' (Shixiang Wu, fieldnotes)

In Sections 12.4.2 and 12.4.3 below, the author refers to thirteen particular complement-taking verbs which were examined with respect to a variety of grammatical and semantic properties. The verbs in question are *nbanx* 'to think', *puk* 'to speak', *niab* 'to say', *bod/bud* 'to tell', *niel/nianl* 'to know', *ghans* 'to see', *hnaond* 'to hear', *zhus/zhaus* 'to suffer', *lis* 'to want', *xaont* 'to wish', *hnant* 'to call, to ask (someone to do something)', *saud* 'to invite', and *gaons* 'to give, to let/make (someone do something)', which were selected to provide as much semantic variety as possible. Section 12.4.2 discusses coreference restrictions between certain arguments in matrix and subordinate clauses in complement constructions involving these verbs, while Section 12.4.3 describes complementation markers which can co-occur with some (but not all) of the verbs. The thirteen verbs in question were also examined with respect to several other grammatical and semantic properties, including their possible argument structure alternations, their behavior in the [C NEG C] interrogative construction (see Section 9.3.2.2), and the insertion possibilities of the particle *leh* 'LEH' in complement constructions featuring each verb (see Section 9.2.1.1). However, the author's results for those latter three properties are fairly "messy" and moreover rather less interesting than his results regarding coreference restrictions and complementation-marker insertion, so they are not discussed in detail here (though see Section 12.4.3 below for some very brief discussion of *leh*-insertion possibilities in complement constructions).

12.4.2 Coreference restrictions

It appears that complement-taking verbs in Xong can be divided into three classes based on coreference restrictions between each verb's matrix and subordinate clauses: *non-control complementation*, *optional control complementation*, and *anti-control complementation*.[219] Of the thirteen verbs listed in Section 12.4.1 above, eight fall into the non-control complementation class, two fall into the optional control complementation class, and three fall into the anti-control complementation class. Additional work on complement-taking verbs may reveal that every such verb in Xong falls into one of these three classes, or it may reveal the existence of additional classes beyond these three.

In non-control complementation, there are no coreference restrictions whatsoever between the preverbal arguments of the matrix and subordinate clauses.[220] These arguments may or may not be coreferential, and in either case either argument can be overtly expressed or elided. The eight verbs that fall into this class are *nbanx* 'to think', *puk* 'to speak', *niab* 'to say', *bod/bud* 'to tell', *niel/nianl* 'to know', *ghans* 'to see', *hnaond* 'to hear', and *zhus/zhaus* 'to suffer', which (as their glosses suggest) mostly refer to forms of speech, cognition, or sensation.

The lack of coreference restrictions in non-control complementation is demonstrated in examples (12.71–12.74) below. In examples (12.71) and (12.73), the preverbal argument in each subordinate clause is overtly expressed, and this argument may – but need not – be coreferential with the preverbal argument in the matrix clause. In examples (12.72) and (12.74), the preverbal argument in each subordinate clause is elided, and each such elided argument may again be interpreted equally well as being coreferential or non-coreferential with the preverbal argument in the matrix clause. Note that in these and subsequent examples in this section, each matrix and subordinate clause has been enclosed within brackets, each relevant complement-taking verb has been bolded, each overtly expressed preverbal argument has also been bolded, and each elided preverbal argument has been represented with a null symbol <Ø>.

(12.71) [***Wel*** ***nbanx*** [***wel/beul*** *xib-hneb* *kox.ix* *nzhaond*]].
[**1SG** **think** [**1SG/3** tomorrow-CLF:day can return]]
'I think I'll/he'll be able to return tomorrow.' (Shixiang Wu, fieldnotes)

(12.72) [***Wel*** ***nbanx*** [Ø *xib-hneb* *kox.ix* *nzhaond*]].
[**1SG** **think** [tomorrow-CLF:day can return]]
'I think (I'll/he'll) be able to return tomorrow.' (Shixiang Wu, fieldnotes) (same as (12.71) above)

219 For information on how the coreference restrictions of complement-taking verbs interact with reflexive forms, see Section 7.1.3.

220 As was mentioned previously in Sections 9.3.4 and 12.2.1, the behavior of grammaticalized syntactic roles like SUBJECT and AGENT (see Section 9.1.1) with respect to multiverbal constructions in general and complement-taking verbs in particular is still not entirely understood. This section thus frames its discussion solely in terms of "preverbal arguments" rather than in terms of those syntactic roles. Furthermore, the author here largely ignores clauses featuring multiple preverbal arguments (see Section 9.1.3.1) due to a lack of relevant data.

(12.73) [***Bol.toc*** ***puk*** [***beul*** *xeub-hneb* *lol* *ix* *dut*]].
[**PN** **speak** [**3** tomorrow-CLF:day come NEG_1 obtain]]
'Bo To$_i$ says he$_i$ can't come tomorrow.' *or* 'Bo To$_i$ says he$_j$ can't come tomorrow.' (Chenghua Long, fieldnotes)[221]

(12.74) [***Bol.toc*** ***puk*** [Ø *xeub-hneb* *lol* *ix* *dut*]].
[**PN** **speak** [tomorrow-CLF:day come NEG_1 obtain]]
'Bo To$_i$ says he$_i$ can't come tomorrow.' *or* 'Bo To$_i$ says he$_j$ can't come tomorrow.' (Chenghua Long, fieldnotes) (same as (12.73) above)

In optional control complementation, the preverbal arguments of the matrix and subordinate clauses may again be either coreferential or non-coreferential. However, if they are coreferential, then the preverbal argument in the subordinate clause must be elided rather than overtly expressed, and if they are non-coreferential, then the preverbal argument in the subordinate clause must be overtly expressed rather than elided. Only two complement-taking verbs in this class have been attested so far, namely *lis* 'to want' and *xaont* 'to wish' (which naturally have fairly similar semantics), though there may well be other such verbs in Xong that the author has simply not yet encountered.

Example (12.75) below shows that a construction involving an optional control complement-taking verb (here *xaont* 'to wish') is perfectly grammatical when the preverbal arguments in the matrix and subordinate clauses are both overtly expressed and non-coreferential.

(12.75) [***Wel*** ***xaont*** [***beul*** *xib-hneb* *jix* *sheib* *lol*]].
[**1SG** **wish** [**3** tomorrow-CLF:day NEG_1 able.to come]]
'I hope he won't be able to come tomorrow.' (Shixiang Wu, fieldnotes) (repeated from (12.70) above)

Example (12.76) shows that the same utterance becomes ungrammatical when the preverbal arguments in the matrix and subordinate clauses are both overtly expressed and coreferential. Note that consultants report that the inclusion of a reflexive pronoun (see Section 7.1.3) in the subordinate clause of this example (either in place of or in addition to the personal pronoun *wel* '1SG') would not affect the ungrammaticality of the utterance in any way.

(12.76) *[***Wel*** ***xaont*** [***wel*** *xib-hneb* *jix* *sheib* *lol*]].
[**1SG** **wish** [**1SG** tomorrow-CLF:day NEG_1 able.to come]]
(intended: 'I hope I won't be able to come tomorrow.') (Shixiang Wu, fieldnotes)

221 For information on Mrs. Chenghua Long's tone *-c* (which appears on the second syllable of the personal name *Bol.**toc*** 'Bo To' in examples (12.73) and (12.74)), see Section 3.5.3.1

Finally, example (12.77) shows that when the preverbal argument in the subordinate clause is elided, it can only be interpreted as being coreferential with the preverbal argument in the matrix clause.

(12.77) [***Wel*** ***xaont*** [Ø *xib-hneb* *Jix* *sheib* *lol*]].
[**1SG** **wish** [tomorrow-CLF:day NEG_1 able.to come]]
'I hope I won't be able to come tomorrow.' (*not* *'I hope [somebody else] won't be able to come tomorrow') (Shixiang Wu, fieldnotes)

In anti-control complementation, the preverbal argument in the matrix clause and the preverbal argument in the subordinate clause are obligatorily non-coreferential, though either or both of these arguments can be elided rather than occur overtly. The three complement-taking verbs attested in this class so far are *hnant* 'to call, to ask (someone to do something)', *saud* 'to invite', and *gaons* 'to give, to let/make (someone do something)', all of which have rather causative-like semantics.

The coreference restrictions operative in this anti-control complementation class are illustrated in examples (12.78–12.83) below. In each of examples (12.78) and (12.79), the preverbal argument in the matrix clause and the preverbal argument in the subordinate clause are both overtly expressed, and the two are obviously non-coreferential in each case.

(12.78) [***Beul*** ***hnant*** [***mx*** *ghaod.maons* *chauk*]] *mx* *ghad-doub* *ghaod.maons* *chauk*.
[**3** **call** [**2SG** NEG.IMP do]] 2SG $then_2$-$then_1$ NEG.IMP do
'If he told you not to do it, then just don't do it.' (Shixiang Wu, fieldnotes)

(12.79) [***Wel*** ***saud*** [***beul*** *tat-hneb* *nhaons* *wel* *ml* *kiad* *njaonx*]].
[**1SG** **invite** [**3** this-CLF:day with 1SG go attend weekly.market]]
'I invited him to go to the weekly market with me today.' (Shixiang Wu, fieldnotes)

In example (12.80), the most immediately preverbal argument in the matrix clause, *beul baox* [3 father] 'her father', is non-coreferential with the elided preverbal argument in the subordinate clause, *leb zhonx-hlod* [CLF length-bamboo] 'the bamboo-length'. Note, though, that that elided argument is overtly expressed in fronted position (see Section 9.1.3.1) in the matrix clause.

(12.80) [*Leb* *zhonx-hlod* ***beul*** ***baox*** *ghad* *zaox* *leb* *khauk*
[CLF length-bamboo **3** **father** then$_2$ drill CLF hole
gaons [Ø *roub* *aub*]].
give [leak.out water]]
'Her father had drilled a hole in the bamboo-length so that it would leak.' (Xingyu Shi, in *Oub Meinl Yaos Geud*)

However, consultants do not accept constructions involving complement-taking verbs from this class in which the preverbal arguments in the matrix and subordinate clauses are coreferential. This is demonstrated in examples (12.81–12.83) below. In particular, example (12.81) shows that when the preverbal argument in the subordinate clause is elided, it can only be interpreted as being non-coreferential with the preverbal argument in the matrix clause.

(12.81) [***Beul*** ***hnant*** [Ø *lol*]].
[**3** **call** [come]]
'He asked (someone else) to come.' (*not* *'He asked himself to come' *or* *'He was asked to come') (Chenghua Long, fieldnotes)

Examples (12.82) and (12.83) show that constructions involving anti-control complementation verbs are simply impossible when the matrix and subordinate clauses contain overt, coreferential preverbal arguments. Note that consultants report that the inclusion of a reflexive pronoun (see Section 7.1.3) in the subordinate clause of either example (either in place of or in addition to the personal pronouns *beul* '3' and *wel* '1SG') would not affect the grammaticality or possible meanings of these utterances in any way.

(12.82) [***Beul*** ***hnant*** [***beul*** *lol*]].
[**3** **call** [**3** come]]
'He$_i$ asked him$_j$ to come.' (*not* *'He asked himself to come') (Chenghua Long, fieldnotes)

(12.83) *[***Wel*** ***hnant*** [***wel*** *lol*]].
[**1SG** **call** [**1SG** come]]
(intended: 'I asked myself to come.') (Chenghua Long, fieldnotes)

12.4.3 Insertability of complementation markers

Two overt markers of complementation have been attested in Xong: the verbal complementation marker *niab* 'to say' (this form serves as both a canonical verb meaning 'to say' and as a complementation marker, and it is glossed as 'say' in both cases) and the non-verbal complementation marker *deux* 'QUOT' (this form's gloss is derived from 'quote', though note that *deux* is not solely used when quoting speech). These forms occur following a complement-taking verb and preceding that verb's complement clause. In addition, the two forms in question can occur together in sequence between a preceding complement-taking verb and a following complement clause, though in such cases they always occur in the order *niab deux* [say QUOT], never **deux niab* [QUOT say]. As the examples in this section show (see in particular examples (12.84–12.86)), there are no apparent semantic or pragmatic differences among (i) a complement construction with no overt complementation marker, (ii) a complement construction marked with *niab* 'to say' alone, (iii) a complement construction marked with *deux* 'QUOT' alone, and (iv) a complement construction marked with both *niab* and *deux*.

Five of the thirteen complement-taking verbs examined in this Section 12.4 (namely *nbanx* 'to think', *xaont* 'to wish', *puk* 'to speak', *bod/bud* 'to tell', and *niel/nianl* 'to know') allow the insertion of any of these complementation markers between the complement-taking verb itself and the following complement clause. Examples of some of these verbs occurring with complementation markers are given in (12.84–12.86) below, where each complement-taking verb and each complementation marker has been bolded. A sixth complement-taking verb, *niab* 'to say', can only be followed by the complementizer *deux* 'QUOT', not by *niab* or *niab deux*.

(12.84) *Tat-hnef* *nex* ***bud*** ***(niab/deux/niab*** ***deux)*** *tat.shib*
this-CLF:day NEX **tell** **(say/QUOT/say** **QUOT**) everybody
ghaod.maons *bionl.*
NEG.IMP exit
'They told everyone to stay inside today.' (Chenghua Long, fieldnotes)

(12.85) *Wel* ***nbanx*** ***(niab/deux/niab*** ***deux)*** *nex* *noul* *zheid* *nins*
1SG **think** **(say/QUOT/say** **QUOT**) NEX catch crab COP
manx *raut* *nghauk.zaol* *naond.*
REL good play ASSOC
'I think it must be a lot of fun when people go crab-catching.' (Chenghua Long, fieldnotes)

(12.86) *Wel* ***nianl*** ***(niab/deux/niab*** ***deux)*** *beul* *tat-hneb*
1SG **know** **(say/QUOT/say** **QUOT**) 3 this-CLF:day
jix *mex* *konb* *nhaons* *boub* *nghauk.zaol.*
NEG$_1$ exist free.time with 1PL play
'I know he doesn't have time to hang out with us today.' (Shixiang Wu, fieldnotes)

However, six other complement-taking verbs out of the thirteen under discussion (namely *lis* 'to want', *hnaond* 'to hear', *gaons* 'to give, to let/make [someone do something]', *saud* 'to invite', *ghans* 'to see', and *zhus/zhaus* 'to suffer') do not allow the insertion of any of these complementation markers. Examples of these latter verbs are given in (12.87) and (12.88). These two examples show that if any complementation markers are inserted after the verbs in question, the resulting utterance will be ungrammatical.

(12.87) **Wel* *nieux.ghoub* ***ghans*** ***niab/deux/niab*** ***deux*** *beul* *ninb*
1SG just.now **see** **say/QUOT/say** **QUOT** 3 at
dib-laos *chauk* *geud.donb.*
LOC-field do work
(intended: 'I just saw him working in the fields.')

(12.88) **Xib-hneb* *lot* *Zhes* *wel* ***lis***
tomorrow-CLF:day descend Fenghuang 1SG **want**
niab/deux/niab ***deux*** *mx* *nhaons* *wel* *ml* *nieus*
say/QUOT/say **QUOT** 2SG with 1SG go buy
aod-ngonl *xut.npeib.*
one-CLF:pair$_1$ shoe
(intended: 'Tomorrow when we go to Fenghuang I want you to go buy a pair of shoes with me.')

Finally, among the thirteen verbs that the author examined there is one which is exceptional with respect to its ability to co-occur with complementation markers. This is *hnant* 'to call, to ask (someone to do something)'. Like several other complement-taking verbs in Xong (e.g. *nbanx* 'to think', *xaont* 'to wish', *puk* 'to speak', etc.), *hnant* can co-occur with the complementation marker *niab* 'to say', with the complementation marker *deux* 'QUOT', or with both together (i.e. *niab deux* [say QUOT]). However, *hnant* is quite distinct from those other verbs in that in its case, these complementation markers must occur following the preverbal argument in the complement clause rather than preceding it. This is exemplifed in (12.89) and (12.90) below. In particular, example (12.89) shows that when *hnant* is used in a complement construction, any of the complementation markers *niab*, *deux*, or *niab deux* can optionally occur immediately after the preverbal argument in the complement clause.

(12.89) *Wel* ***hnant*** *beul* ***(niab/deux/niab*** ***deux)*** *heut* *meb*
1SG **call** 3 **(say/QUOT/say** **QUOT**) help take
aod-leb *xeud-ghaod* *lol.*
one-CLF ???-feces come
'I asked him to get me a diaper (for the baby).' (Haili Shi, fieldnotes)

In contrast, example (12.90) shows that if any of these complementation markers are inserted immediately following *hnant* itself, the resulting utterance will be ungrammatical.

(12.90) **Wel* ***hnant*** ***niab/deux/niab*** ***deux*** *beul* *heut* *meb*
1SG **call** **say/QUOT/say** **QUOT** 3 help take
aod-leb *xeud-ghaod* *lol.*
one-CLF ???-feces come
(intended: 'I asked him to get me a diaper [for the baby].')

From the data available to the author, there appears to be a tendency for verbs of speech (*puk* 'to speak', *bod/bud* 'to tell', *niab* 'to say', *hnant* 'to call, to ask [someone to do something]') and cognition (*nbanx* 'to think', *xaont* 'to wish', *niel/nianl* 'to know') to have the ability to co-occur with the complementation markers discussed in this section, while other complement-taking verbs (*lis* 'to want', *hnaond* 'to hear', *gaons* 'to give, to let/make [someone do something]', *saud* 'to invite', *ghans* 'to see', *zhus/zhaus* 'to suffer') generally lack this ability.[222] Still, further research is needed to determine whether there is any reliable way to predict which, if any, complementation markers a particular complement-taking verb can co-occur with.

12.5 Other multiverbal constructions

This section briefly exemplifies several other apparent types of multiverbal construction in Xong. Note that this is done solely to give the reader some further idea of the functional and structural variety that these constructions display in the language, and more work will be needed before any of these purported multiverbal construction types can be properly defined or described.

Examples (12.91–12.93) each feature a multiverbal construction expressing direction and/or complex motion. In each of these examples, the multiverbal construction in question has been enclosed within brackets and each of its constituent verbs has been bolded.

---

222 The particle *leh* 'LEH' (see Section 9.2.1.1) can also be inserted following certain complement-taking verbs but not others. However, there are no obvious correlations between the possibility of a complement-taking verb being followed by *leh* and the possibility of it being followed by *niab* 'to say' and *deux* 'QUOT' or between the possibility of such a verb being followed by *leh* and the coreference restrictions of the verb in question, and so *leh*-insertion in complement constructions is not discussed in detail here.

(12.91) *Yul hnef monx jaont monx ghad* [***dionb nzhaod lol***].
again CLF:day 2SG herd 2SG then$_2$ [**lead return come**]
'Next time when you go herding, lead the bird back here with you.' (Xingyu Shi, in *Oub Meinl Yaos Geud*)

(12.92) *Meib-Nhaonl at* [***zhaok lot*** *aub* ***monl***] *oh.*
younger.sister-PN SAT [**fall descend** water **go**] PART
'Little sister Nhaon fell into the water.' (Xingyu Shi, in *Oub Meinl Yaos Geud*)

(12.93) *Wel lis* [***bionl monl*** *aod-tit-deb* ***ghat*** *geud-zheit*].
1SG want [**exit go** one-CLF:time$_3$-DIM **go.to** place$_1$-outside]
'I need to leave home for a little while.' (Xingyu Shi, in *Oub Meinl Yaos Geud*)

Examples (12.94) and (12.95) each feature a multiverbal construction expressing degree. In each case, the verb expressing degree (either *daos* 'to die' or *guaot* 'to pass') follows the verb(s) expressing the main predication of the clause. In each of these examples, too, the relevant multiverbal construction has been enclosed within brackets and each of its constituent verbs has been bolded.

(12.94) [***Chanf daos***].
[**gross die**]
'(The traditional method for curing a toothache) is so gross.' (Chenghua Long, in *Tooth Conversation*)

(12.95) *Aos.il, beut naont ngeinb.shib* [***npof nggueb guaot***]...
DSMY$_2$ lie.down thus no.matter.what [**desire sleep pass**]
'God, (I) was lying there and (I) wanted to fall asleep so badly...' (Haili Shi, in *Tooth Conversation*)

Examples (12.96–12.98) each feature a resultative multiverbal construction, in which the second verb expresses the result of the action or event referred to by the first verb. These examples again follow the same bracketing and bolding conventions as the ones given above.

(12.96) *Wel* [***nonx ncheut***] *wel ghad dionb monx nzhaod.*
1SG [**eat full**] 1SG then$_2$ lead 2SG return
'Once I'm full I'll lead you back.' (Xingyu Shi, in *Oub Meinl Yaos Geud*)

(12.97) *Chauk-dib monx lis* [***beux daos***]*?*
do-which 2SG want [**hit die**]
'How could you kill (that bird)?' (Xingyu Shi, in *Oub Meinl Yaos Geud*)

(12.98) *Beul* *dad.kit* *monl* [***ncot*** ***nqif***] *meb* *shok*
3 not.until go [**wash.clothing** **clean**] take dry.in.sun
zhel.
sun
'She took (the shoes), washed (them) clean, and put (them outside) to dry in the sun.' (Xingyu Shi, in *Oub Meinl Yaos Geud*) (repeated from (12.2) above)

Finally, examples (12.99–12.102) each feature a multiverbal construction that serves to add an oblique-like argument to a clause. More precisely, example (12.99) involves a locative-like argument (see also Section 12.3.2), example (12.100) involves an instrumental-like argument, example (12.101) involves a comitative-like argument (see also Section 8.3), and example (12.102) involves a benefactive-like argument. Note that in these examples each oblique-like argument and each verb introducing such an argument have simply been bolded.

(12.99) *Wel* ***ninb*** ***bioud*** *dieud* *hlit.*
1SG **at** **home** boil.rice cooked.rice
'I'll boil the rice here at home.' (Xingyu Shi, in *Oub Meinl Yaos Geud*)

(12.100) *Gank.ceib* ***geud*** ***shoux.jik*** *deib* *Bes.doub* *caof* *dieud.*
simply **hold** **cell.phone** at Baidu search CLF:time$_2$
'(I) just used my cell phone to search on (the popular Chinese search engine) Baidu for a while.' (Haili Shi, in *Tooth Conversation*)[223]

(12.101) *Hnef-hnef* ***nhaons*** ***nex*** *nghauk.zaol.*
CLF:day-CLF:day **with** **NEX** play
'Every day (she) was out playing with people.' (Xingyu Shi, in *Oub Meinl Yaos Geud*)

(12.102) *Ranf.houb,* *nieux-hnef,* *nex* *ab* ***heut*** ***wel*** *nieus*
afterward yester-CLF:day NEX also **help** **1SG** buy
dut *aod-zhit* *nggaob.*
obtain one-CLF:tube medicine
'Afterward, yesterday, he bought some medicine for me, too.' (Haili Shi, in *Tooth Conversation*)

223 The Xong verb *geud* 'to hold, to use' shows a significant amount of distributional and functional overlap with certain forms used to mark affectedness in other isolating East and Southeast Asian languages, with the most well known of these probably being the form *bǎ* (把) in Standard Mandarin (see, e.g., Bender 2000). Nevertheless, the Xong and Standard Mandarin forms in question naturally differ in many of the particulars of their semantic and grammatical properties.

As examples (12.99–12.102) above suggest, oblique-like arguments in Xong tend to occur before the verb expressing the main predication of the clause, with the most patient-like argument within the clause then occurring following that verb. In the typological classification scheme presented in Dryer and Gensler (2013), then, Xong would be classified as a predominantly XVO language. Dryer and Gensler report that this word order feature value is extremely rare among the languages of the world, with the only attested examples of it being found within the Sinitic branch of Sino-Tibetan. However, XVO order is in fact the norm within Miao-Yao (Sposato 2014). Thus, while this particular aspect of Xong constituent order may be quite rare in worldwide terms, it is hardly unusual for a member of the Miao-Yao family.

12.6 Overtly marked clausal coordination

Although multiverbal constructions with no overt markers of coordination are extremely common in Xong speech of all genres, the language features a number of overtly marked coordination constructions as well. This section provides a representative overview of some of the more common of these constructions, most of which appear to operate at the level of the clause rather than at the level of the individual verb. Note that several of these constructions involve grammatical operators (see Section 9.1.1), including *biank* 'SIMUL' and *deit* 'SIMUL' (Section 12.6.1), *aod* 'as soon as' (Section 12.6.2), and *(y)ab* 'also' (Section 12.6.3). Several other grammatical operators can arguably serve as markers of clausal coordination as well, including various forms meaning 'then', various forms meaning 'still', and various forms meaning 'not until, only then' (see the introduction to Section 9.2). These latter forms are not discussed in detail in this grammar (except when they occur together with another grammatical operator in a particular coordination construction, as in Sections 12.6.1 and 12.6.2 below), and a thorough description of their meanings and grammatical properties when serving as clausal coordination markers remains a task for future scholars.

12.6.1 Expressing simultaneous action with *biank* 'SIMUL' and *deit* 'SIMUL'

To express simultaneous action, Xong speakers often make use of a verb chain (Section 12.2.1) or a verbal tetrasyllabic expression (Section 12.2.2), neither of which bears any overt marker of coordination and both of which can be used to express non-simultaneous actions as well. However, speakers also have the option of overtly signaling simultaneous action through the use of either *biank* 'SIMUL' or *deit* 'SIMUL'. Note that the first of these forms is homophonous with *biank* 'side' (Section 5.5.2.5) and the second is homophonous with *deit* 'still', but both are glossed as 'SIMUL' when serving as markers of simultaneous action.

The forms *biank* 'SIMUL' and *deit* 'SIMUL' always occur twice when used as coordinators, with the first instance of the form occurring in the grammatical operator slot (see Section 9.1.1) of the first coordinated clause and the second instance occurring in the same slot of the second coordinated clause. While *biank* and *deit* are apparently completely interchangeable when used as coordinators, the two forms never occur "mixed". In other words, any given example of this simultaneous action construction will contain either two instances of *biank* or two instances of *deit*, but never one instance of *biank* and one of *deit*. This can be seen in examples (12.103–12.105) below, where each instance of *biank* 'SIMUL' and *deit* 'SIMUL' has been bolded.

(12.103)	***Deit***	*nied*	***deit***	*hnant,*	***deit***	*nied*	***deit***	*hnant*	*leh.*
	SIMUL	cry	**SIMUL**	call	**SIMUL**	cry	**SIMUL**	call	LEH

'(She) called out as she wept.' (Xingyu Shi, in *Oub Meinl Yaos Geud*)

(12.104)	*Wel*	*naond*	*deb*	***biank***	*nhob*	*geud*	***biank***	*yanb*	*xib.*
	1SG	ASSOC	child	**SIMUL**	walk	road	**SIMUL**	act	play

'My child is dancing as she walks.' (Chenghua Long, fieldnotes)

(12.105)	*Wel*	***deit***	*puk*	*daut,*	*beul*	***Deit***	*gaond*	*wel.*
	1SG	**SIMUL**	speak	speech	3	**SIMUL**	bother	1SG

'He's bothering me while I'm trying to speak.' (Shixiang Wu, fieldnotes)

This simultaneous action construction is most often used when a single entity is performing both of the simultaneous actions in question, as in examples (12.103) and (12.104). However, it can still be used when two distinct entities are each performing a single activity at the same time as the other, as in example (12.105).

12.6.2 Expressing immediately subsequent action with *aod* 'as soon as'

To explicitly indicate that one action follows immediately after another, Xong speakers use a construction that obligatorily features the grammatical operator *aod* 'as soon as' in one clause and optionally features one of the apparently interchangeable grammatical operators *doub* 'then$_1$', *ghad* 'then$_2$', or *jeub* 'then$_3$' in the following clause (see Section 9.1.1 for more on grammatical operators in general).[224] In elicitation sessions,

224 The Xong form *aod* 'as soon as' is homophonous with the numeral *aod* 'one'. Standard Mandarin also features a marker of immediately subsequent action *yī* (一) which is homophonous (and homographic) with the numeral *yī* (一) 'one'. This, along with the structural similarities between Standard Mandarin's immediately subsequent action construction and the equivalent Xong construction, suggests that the Xong construction in question is a calque from either Standard Mandarin or from another Sinitic variety in which the same facts apply.

consultants insist that the second coordinated clause must feature one of the three forms *doub*, *ghad*, or *jeub*, and indeed in slow, careful speech one of these will always occur. However, in more casual, naturalistic speech, it is quite common for *aod* 'as soon as' to occcur as the sole marker of immediately subsequent action, with none of the forms *doub*, *ghad*, or *jeub* occurring in the second coordinated clause.

Examples of this construction are given in (12.106–12.109) below, where each instance of *aod* 'as soon as', *doub* 'then$_1$', *ghad* 'then$_2$', and *jeub* 'then$_3$' has been bolded.

(12.106) *Boub* ***aod*** *nonx* *ncheut* *hlit,* *wel* *naond* *deb*
1PL **as.soon.as** eat full cooked.rice 1SG ASSOC child
jeub *cox* *monl* *nghauk* *aub.*
then$_3$ make.noise go bathe water
'As soon as we finished eating, my child started making a fuss (because she wanted to) go swimming.' (Chenghua Long, fieldnotes)

In example (12.107), a verbless clause composed of the interjection *aod-minl* [KIN-mother] 'man!' (see Section 11.3.5) followed by the particle *aoh* 'PART' (Section 9.2.1) interrupts the second coordinated clause.

(12.107) *Aod-hnef* *dox* *wel* ***aod*** *ghab* ***ghad,***
one-CLF:day that 1SG **as.soon.as** bite **then$_2$**
aod-minl *aoh,* *zhaux* *xed* *naont.*
KIN-mother PART be.in.agony tooth thus
'(But then) that day, as soon as I bit down, man, my tooth was in agony.' (Haili Shi, in *Tooth Conversation*)

Example (12.108) contains two consecutive (and rather synonymous) clauses each featuring *aod* 'as soon as' followed by a single clause featuring *doub* 'then$_1$', but such minor deviations are hardly unexpected in naturalistic conversation.

(12.108) *Beul* *doub* *nins* ***aod*** *naont,* ***aod*** *ghab* *beul*
3 then$_1$ COP **as.soon.as** thus **as.soon.as** bite 3
doub *naonb.nex* *zhut* *aod-ghoub* *sheinf.jind*
then$_1$ seem reach one-CLF:flexible.length nerve
dox *lah.*
that PRF
'It was just that as soon as (I) did it, as soon as I bit down it was like I'd hit the nerve (in my tooth).' (Haili Shi, in *Tooth Conversation*)

Finally, in example (12.109), note that the second coordinated clause (or rather series of coordinated clauses) does not contain any of the forms *doub* 'then$_1$', *ghad* 'then$_2$', or *jeub* 'then$_3$'.

(12.109) ***Aod*** *caof,* *ab* *kox.ix* *geud* *shand,* *ab* *kox.ix*
as.soon.as search also can hold ginger also can
geud *bid-ghaond,* *ab* *kox.ix* *geud* *weib.jink,* *yaox?*
hold FRT-garlic also can hold MSG right?
'As soon as I searched (on the internet for information on curing a toothache), I found out you could use ginger, you could use garlic, you could use MSG (i.e. monosodium glutamate).' (Haili Shi, in *Tooth Conversation*)

Just as with the simultaneous action construction described in Section 12.6.1 above, this immediately subsequent action construction is most often used when a single entity is performing both of the actions in question (see, e.g., example (12.107)), but it can also be used when one entity is performing the initial action and another entity is performing the immediately subsequent action (see, e.g., example (12.106)).

12.6.3 Coordinative constructions with *(y)ab* 'also'

The grammatical operator *(y)ab* 'also' (generally realized as *yab*, but sometimes realized as *ab* in fast or casual speech) occurs in two different coordinative constructions. In the simpler of these two, *(y)ab* occurs in the grammatical operator slot (see Section 9.1.1) of each coordinated clause, with the resulting construction meaning essentially '(both) CLAUSE$_1$ and CLAUSE$_2$'. Unlike with the simultaneous action and immediately subsequent action constructions described in Sections 12.6.1 and 12.6.2, consultants show a very strong dispreference for inserting a preverbal argument in the second coordinated clause in this *(y)ab* coordinative construction.

Examples of this construction are given in (12.110–12.113) below, where each instance of *(y)ab* has been bolded.

(12.110) *Beul* ***yab*** *raos* ***yab*** *xonx* *npaok.*
3 **also** clever **also** attractive woman
'She's both smart and pretty.' (Shixiang Wu, fieldnotes)

(12.111) *Beul* ***yab*** *shanb* ***yab*** *xonx* ***yab*** *liot.*
3 **also** tall **also** attractive **also** wealthy
'He's tall, handsome, and wealthy.' (unknown Xong consultant, fieldnotes)

(12.112) *Beul* ***yab*** *sheib* *giab* *reib-yeus* ***yab*** *sheib*
3 **also** able.to stir.fry vegetable-cooked.meat **also** able.to
chauk *geud.donb.*
do work
'She knows how to cook and how to farm.' (Chenghua Long, fieldnotes)

(12.113)

Beul	***yab***	*nieus*	*ix*	*niaons*	*bioud*	***yab***	*nieus*	*ix*
3	**also**	buy	NEG_1	ABIL	home	**also**	buy	NEG_1

niaons	*chek.*
ABIL	vehicle

'He can't afford a house or a car.' (Chenghua Long, fieldnotes)

The second coordinative construction in which *(y)ab* 'also' occurs has a more specific meaning, namely 'the more CLAUSE$_1$, the more CLAUSE$_2$'. This construction involves two coordinated clauses that each feature *(y)ab* in the grammatical operator slot and *cauf* 'to add' in clause-final position, as can be seen in examples (12.114) and (12.115). Note that, as its gloss suggests, the form *cauf* is a verb, not a non-verbal coordination marker like most of the other forms discussed in this Section 12.6.

(12.114)

Yab	*lis*	*xaont*	*id-shaont*	***cauf,***	***yab***	*lieul*	***cauf.***
also	want	wish	DID-fast	**add**	**also**	wrong	**add**

'The faster (you) go, the more mistakes (you) make.' (Chenghua Long, fieldnotes)

(12.115)

Wel	***yab***	*puk*	***cauf,***	*beul*	***yab***	*kif*	***cauf.***
1SG	**also**	speak	**add**	3	**also**	angry	**add**

'The more I spoke, the angrier he got.' (Chenghua Long, fieldnotes)

As with the simultaneous action and immediately subsequent action constructions described in Sections 12.6.1 and 12.6.2 (but unlike with the first *[y]ab* coordinative construction discussed earlier in this Section 12.6.3), consultants readily allow the occurrence of different preverbal arguments in each of the two coordinated clauses in this 'the more ... the more ... ' construction, as in example (12.115) above.

Finally, note that not every use of *(y)ab* 'also' involves coordination. In addition to occurring as a coordinative marker in the constructions described above, this same form also frequently occurs in non-coordinated clauses with the meaning 'again', as in example (12.116) below.

(12.116)

It,	*aod-leb*	*zhonx-hlod*	*jix*	*doul*	*aub.*	*Jix*
SPRS	one-CLF	length-bamboo	NEG_1	remain	water	NEG_1

doul	*aub*	***yab***	*nzhaod*	*monl*	*teuf.*	***Yab***	*nhob*
remain	water	**also**	return	go	scoop	**also**	walk

nhob	***yab***	*jix*	*doul*	*aub.*
walk	**also**	NEG_1	remain	water

'Huh, all of a sudden there was no water left in the length of bamboo. There was no water left, and so (she) went back again to get more. Again (she) walked and walked, and again there was no water left (in the length of bamboo).' (Xingyu Shi, in *Oub Meinl Yaos Geud*)

12.6.4 Clausal disjunction

In the author's Xong corpus, disjunction of clauses is much less common, displays much less structural variety, and is much more likely to be overtly signaled than conjunction of clauses (for examples of the latter, see Sections 8.3, 12.6.1, 12.6.2, and 12.6.3). In the most basic type of clausal disjunction, any one of four distinct forms meaning 'or' is used between the two disjoined clauses. Two of these forms, *huel.zex* 'or.STND' and *haf.shib/hes.shib/hel.shib* 'or.INT', are clearly recent borrowings from Sinitic and display a distinction between standard and interrogative disjunction (see discussion further below in this section). The other two forms, *bid.deux* 'or' and *doub.nins* 'or', are not obviously borrowings, and both can be used for either standard or interrogative disjunction. Examples of all four forms can be seen in (12.117–12.124) below, where each form meaning 'or' has been bolded and each disjoined clause has been enclosed within brackets.

(12.117) *[Nbaod beul]* ***huel.zex*** *[zheb beul sheub].*
[fill.in 3] **or.STND** [pull.out 3 leave]
'Either get it filled in or pull it out.' (Shixiang Wu, in *Tooth Conversation*)

(12.118) *[Nonx niax-nbat]* ***huel.zex*** *[nonx niax-yul] sat kox.ix.*
[eat meat-pig] **or.STND** [eat meat-cow] SAT can
'It's okay to eat pork or beef.' (Haili Shi, fieldnotes)

(12.119) *Jud niel [nins ink.qib teb zhonb]*
NEG_2 know [COP cold.and.wet.weather too heavy]
haf.shib *[nins hauk-naonb], yaox?*
or.INT [COP do-what] right?
'(I) don't know if it's because the weather's been so cold and wet lately or what, right?' (Haili Shi, in *Tooth Conversation*)

(12.120) *[Monx lis manx sheib eint naond aod-leb dox]*
[2SG want REL able.to fly ASSOC one-CLF that]
hes.shib *[lis manx bianb tanx.kef naond]?*
or.INT [want REL change.into tank ASSOC]
'Do you want the (toy robot) that can fly or the one that can change into a tank?' (Chenghua Long, fieldnotes)

(12.121) *Monx lis [hauk aub]* ***bid.deux*** *[hauk kox.los]?*
2SG want [drink water] **or** [drink soda]
'Do you want to drink water or soda?' (Chenghua Long, fieldnotes)

(12.122)

Nanb	*liax*	*nins*	...	*[ub*	*shut]*	***bid.deux***
really	resemble	COP		[burn	sesame]	**or**
[ub	*naonb],*	*yaox?*				
[burn	what]	right?				

'It was just like (he) was...burning sesame or something, right?' (Chenghua Long, in *Tooth Conversation*)

(12.123)

Mx	*lis*	*[nonx*	*hlit]*	***doub.nins***	*[nonx*	*mianb]?*
2SG	want	[eat	cooked.rice]	**or**	[eat	noodles]

'Do you want to eat rice or noodles?' (Shixiang Wu, fieldnotes)

(12.124)

[Mx	*yanb*	*manx*	*gueinx]*	***doub.nins***	*[yanb*	*manx*	*nqint]?*
[2SG	like	REL	yellow]	**or**	[like	REL	red]

'Do you like the yellow one or the red one?' (Shixiang Wu, fieldnotes)

A few notes about these four forms meaning 'or' are in order here. First, the form glossed as 'or.INT' shows a fair deal of phonological variation among the author's consultants, as it is pronounced *haf.shib* by his primary consultant from Yankan Village (Mrs. Haili Shi), *hes.shib* by his primary consultant from Shanjiang Town (Mrs. Chenghua Long), and *hel.shib* by his primary consultant from Zhuigaolai Village (Mrs. Shixiang Wu). Second, the forms *huel.zex* 'or.STND' and *haf.shib/hes.shib/hel.shib* 'or.INT' are clearly recent borrowings of Standard Mandarin *huòzhě* (或者) 'or.STND' and *háishì* (还是) 'or.INT' or of cognate forms from another Sinitic variety, and they are considered as such by consultants. Third and finally, the author's consultants from Shanjiang Town and Yankan Village use only the form *bid.deux* 'or', not the form *doub.nins* 'or', while his consultants from La'ershan Town and its surrounding villages (aside from Yankan) do the opposite.

Just like the Sinitic forms from which they were borrowed, the Xong forms *huel.zex* 'or.STND' and *haf.shib/hes.shib/hel.shib* 'or.INT' display a distinction between standard disjunction and interrogative disjunction (see Haspelmath [2007: 3, 4, 25, 26]). This distinction is most obvious in interrogative clauses. In such clauses, the use of the form *huel.zex* 'or.STND' (from 'or – standard') signals that the addressee can simply give an affirmative or negative response, while the use of *haf.shib/hes.shib/hel.shib* 'or.INT' (from 'or – interrogative') signals that the addressee must specify one of the disjuncts in his or her response.

For instance, the two most felicitous responses to the question featuring *huel.zex* 'or.STND' in example (12.125) are equivalent to English *yes* and *no*, as examples (12.126) and (12.127) show.

(12.125)

Monx	*lis*	*nonx*	*hlit*	***huel.zex***	*nonx*	*mieb?*
2SG	want	eat	cooked.rice	**or.STND**	eat	noodles

'Do you want to eat rice or noodles?' (Haili Shi, fieldnotes)

(12.126) *Lis.*
want
'Yes.' (Haili Shi, fieldnotes)

(12.127) *Jix lis.*
NEG_1 want
'No.' (Haili Shi, fieldnotes)

However, a felicitous response to the question featuring *haf.shib* 'or.INT' in example (12.128) will contain either *hlit* 'cooked rice' or *mieb* 'noodles', as examples (12.129) and (12.130) show.

(12.128) *Monx lis nonx hlit* ***haf.shib*** *nonx mieb?*
2SG want eat cooked.rice **or.INT** eat noodles
'Do you want to eat rice or noodles?' (Haili Shi, fieldnotes)

(12.129) *Nonx hlit.*
eat cooked.rice
'Rice.' (Haili Shi, fieldnotes)

(12.130) *Nonx mieb.*
eat noodles
'Noodles.' (Haili Shi, fieldnotes)

Each of the four disjunctive forms discussed so far can be used to disjoin noun phrases as well as clauses (for information on conjunction of noun phrases, see Section 8.3). Examples of this are given in (12.131–12.134) below.

(12.131) [*Niax-nbat*] ***huel.zex*** [*niax-yul*] *sat kox.ix.*
[meat-pig] **or.STND** [meat-cow] SAT can
'It's okay (to eat) pork or beef.' (Haili Shi, fieldnotes) (cf. example (12.118) above)

(12.132) *Monx lis* [*manx sheib eint naond aod-leb dox*]
2SG want [REL able.to fly ASSOC one-CLF that]
hes.shib [*manx bianb tanx.kef naond*]*?*
or.INT [REL change.into tank ASSOC]
'Do you want the (toy robot) that can fly or the one that can change into a tank?' (Chenghua Long, fieldnotes) (cf. example (12.120) above)

(12.133) *Monx lis hauk [aub]* ***bid.deux*** *[kox.los]?*
2SG want drink [water] **or** [soda]
'Do you want to drink water or soda?' (Chenghua Long, fieldnotes) (cf. example (12.121) above)

(12.134) *Mx lis nonx [hlit]* ***doub.nins*** *[mianb]?*
2SG want eat [cooked.rice] **or** [noodles]
'Do you want to eat rice or noodles?' (Shixiang Wu, fieldnotes) (cf. example (12.123) above)

Xong also features an emphatic disjunction construction (see Haspelmath [2007: 15–17]) with a meaning roughly similar to the *either ... or ...* construction in English. This involves the use of the form *jeux.naonb/qaonb.naont* 'either' at the beginning of each of the disjoined clauses, with the pronunciation *jeux.naonb* being used by the author's primary consultant from Shanjiang Town and the pronunciation *qaonb. naont* being used by the author's primary consultant from Zhuigaolai Village. Unfortunately, the author did not have the opportunity to investigate what (if any) pronunciations are used by speakers from other communities or to investigate whether this emphatic disjunction construction can be used to disjoin noun phrases as well as clauses. Nevertheless, examples of the construction are given in (12.135) and (12.136), where each instance of the form *jeux.naonb/qaonb.naont* 'either' has been bolded and each disjoined clause has been enclosed within brackets.

(12.135) [***Jeux.naonb*** *monx touf ndeud*], [***jeux.naonb*** *monx monl daox.gont*].
[**either** 2SG read writing] [**either** 2SG go perform.migrant.labor]
'Either you go to school or you go work as a migrant laborer.' (Chenghua Long, fieldnotes)

(12.136) [***Qaonb.naont*** *mx ml*], [***qaonb.naont*** *wel ml*].
[**either** 2SG go] [**either** 1SG go]
'Either you go or I go.' (Shixiang Wu, fieldnotes)

Text 1 *Oub Meinl Yaos Geud*

The following is a transcription of a twenty-five-minute Xong folktale recorded on October 16th, 2012, with accompanying interlinear glosses and free translations. The narrator of the folktale was Xingyu Shi, who hails from Yankan Village. Xingyu is a male farmer and part-time taxi driver, and he is one of the author's primary Xong-speaking consultants. The folktale was recorded in the room where the author was staying while in La'ershan, which happened to be located in the home of one of Xingyu's distant relatives. Aside from the narrator and the author, no one else was present during the recording. For more information on the narrator and his hometown, see Sections 2.6.2 and 2.7.1.

Unfortunately, Xingyu was only available long enough to help analyze the first quarter or so of this text. Three of the author's other Xong-speaking consultants (Chenghua Long, Haili Shi, and Shixiang Wu) helped analyze the remainder. While this was less than ideal, note that Haili Shi is herself a distant relative of Xingyu and comes from the same village as him, and so she already had a great deal of familiarity with his idiolect.

The title of the folktale is *Oub Meinl Yaos Geud*, which is grammatically *oub-meinl yaos-geud* [two-CLF:person older.sister-younger.sibling] and which means 'the two sisters'. The two sisters in question are the only two named characters in the story, and their names deserve some comment here. The older sister is named *Niaox.meib* and the younger *Niaox.nhaonl*. While the older sister is sometimes referred to as just *Meib* and the younger as just *Nhaonl*, the narrator and the other consultants who helped analyze the text were quite clear that *Niaox* is not the sisters' surname, but is rather just the first half of each of their given names (similar, perhaps, to two brothers in an English folktale named *Edward* and *Edwin*). To avoid confusion, the sisters' names are not glossed as 'PN' (from 'personal name') in this text. Instead, *Niaox.meib* and *Meib* are glossed as 'Mei', and *Niaox.nhaonl* and *Nhaonl* are glossed as 'Nhaon'.

Since this text is a folktale rather than a casual conversation, the author deliberately chose to make the free English translation of each section somewhat more formal and more literal than the free translations given in Text 2 (*Tooth Conversation*). Still, even here it was often necessary to add English forms to the free translations that had no equivalent in the original Xong material. This was especially true for elided arguments (see Section 9.2.2).

In order to accurately transcribe the narrator's speech while still making the English translation of that speech intelligible to the reader, the author was often forced to use differing punctuation in the Xong transcription and the English translation of each utterance. In general, though, a comma represents a short pause, a period a longer pause, an ellipsis (< ... >) an even longer pause or an instance in which the narrator trailed off while considering what to say next, and an em dash (<–>) an instance in which the narrator suddenly stopped speaking or suddenly switched topics (e.g. to make a side comment about some particular issue).

(Begin text.)

Niaox.meib Niaox.nhaonl, manx.eib.manx.ab, mex deib
Mei Nhaon a.long.time.ago exist CLF:pair$_2$

yaos-geud. Yaos nbut Niaox.meib,
older.sister-younger.sibling older.sister name Mei

deb-geud nbut Niaox.nhaonl. Niaox.meib Niaox.nhaonl
DIM-younger.sibling name Nhaon Mei Nhaon

zhaos xub jix doul minl, nanx doul baox.
from small NEG$_1$ remain mother only remain father

Beul baox leh, soud beul aod-deib yaos-geud
3 father LEH raise 3 one-CLF:pair$_2$ older.sister-younger.sibling

liox miex lah. Beul baox niab deux: "Manx oub-leb
big person PRF 3 father say QUOT 2PL two-CLF

liox miex lah, sat mex aod-gul-jons-il-jut lah,
big person PRF SAT exist one-ten-seven-eight-CLF:year PRF

sat kox.ix cheinf.jaok lah, kox.ix tad bioud ah,
SAT can get.married PRF can establish home PART

kox.ix bionl ah. Naont leh, manx liox miex lah, wel
can exit PART thus LEH 2PL big person PRF 1SG

mex deb sib. Wel lis bionl monl aod-tit-deb
exist DIM matter 1SG want exit go one-CLF:time$_3$-DIM

ghat geud-zheit, manx oub-leb jont bioud, ghad.maons
go.to place$_1$-outside 2PL two-CLF live home NEG.IMP

id-beux id-ndaot. Wel monl oub-hnef-deb wel nzhaod
DID-hit DID-curse 1SG go two-CLF:day-DIM 1SG return

lol. Naonb.roul wel gaons manx oub-leb aod-leb
come now 1SG give 2PL two-CLF one-CLF

zhonx-hlod. Aod-leb zhonx-hlod leh, nkhed manx
length-bamboo one-CLF length-bamboo LEH look 2PL

oub-meinl dib ghaod raut deb. Aod-meinl dib ghaod
two-CLF:person which more good child one-CLF:person which more

raut deb, aod-meinl dib ghaod kint nied, ghaod mex
good child one-CLF:person which more often cry more exist

hliof aub-gheb. Wel gaons manx aod-leb zhonx-hlod
many water-eye 1SG give 2PL one-CLF length-bamboo

geud	*dis*	*aub-gheb.*	*Aod-meinl*	*ghaod*	*jaod*	*deb,*	*jix*
hold	catch	water-eye	one-CLF:person	more	bad	child	NEG$_1$

nanb	*nied,*	*jix*	*liaos*	*baox*	*naond,*	*jix*	*nied*	*jix*
really	cry	NEG$_1$	miss	father	ASSOC	NEG$_1$	cry	NEG$_1$

mex	*aub-gheb.*	*Wel*	*lis*	*shaod*	*manx*	*leb*	*dib*	*ghaod*
exist	water-eye	1SG	want	try	2PL	CLF	which	more

raut	*deb.*	*Naonb.naont*	*wel*	*monl."*	*Beul*	*puk*	*diex*	*naond,*
good	child	thus	1SG	go	3	speak	finish	ASSOC

aod-meinl	*gaons*	*aod-leb*	*bid-zhonx-hlod,*	*beul*	*monl*	*lah.*
one-CLF:person	give	one-CLF	FRT-length-bamboo	3	go	PRF

Beul	*baox*	*monl*	*lah.*
3	father	go	PRF

'This is the story of Niao Mei and Niao Nhaon. A long time ago, there were two sisters. The older sister was named Niao Mei, and the younger Niao Nhaon. Their mother passed away when they were very young, leaving only their father. This father, he raised them to adulthood, and then one day he said to them: "You two are all grown up, you're now seventeen or eighteen years old. Now you can get married, you can start families, and you can leave this home. And so, now that you're all grown up, there's something I need to take care of. I need to leave home for a little while. You two stay here, not fighting and not arguing. I'll be gone for a few days before I return. Now I'm going to give each of you a length of bamboo. These lengths of bamboo, they'll show which of you is the better child. Whichever of you is the better child, whichever of you weeps more, she'll have more tears. These lengths of bamboo are for holding your tears. Whichever of you is the worse child, whichever of you doesn't weep, doesn't miss her father, she won't cry and she won't have any tears. I want to see which of you is the better child. And so I leave." He finished speaking, gave each sister a length of bamboo, and then he left. The sisters' father left.'

Monl	*diex*	*aod-tit*	*gid.daud*	*loux*	*leh,*	*sat*	*monl*
go	finish	one-CLF:time$_3$	extremely	long.time	LEH	SAT	go

loux	*hint.*	*Diul*	*leh*	*beul*	*naond*	*jed,*
long.time	very	complete	LEH	3	ASSOC	older.sister[225]

225 The form *jed* 'older sister' is a recent borrowing from Sinitic. The source form is pronounced *jiě* in Standard Mandarin, though the immediate source of Xong *jed* may have been a cognate form in another Sinitic variety. The more "native" Xong term for 'older sister' is *yaos*, although – as with so many other Xong forms – this may itself be an older, less transparent borrowing from Sinitic.

Niaox.meib, Niaox.meib leh, jaod deb hint, jix liaos baox
Mei Mei LEH bad child very NEG$_1$ miss father

naond. Hnef-hnef at npod mel ah, zhox
ASSOC CLF:day-CLF:day SAT toss stone.toss.game PART kick

ghab lah, ndanb sheinb.kiet lah, hnef-hnef nghauk.zaol
shuttlecock PRF jump hopscotch PRF CLF:day-CLF:day play

leh. Niaox.nhaonl, deb-geud, Niaox.nhaonl leh, ghaod
LEH Nhaon DIM-younger.sibling Nhaon LEH more

lox.shif, ghaod zhonk.cheinf, liaos baox naond guaot.
honest more devoted miss father ASSOC pass

Hnef-hnef nied-giaol, nbanx baox daonl jix niaons
CLF:day-CLF:day cry-??? think father wait NEG$_1$ ABIL

beul baox nzhaod. Beul hnef-hnef nied. Deit nied
3 father return 3 CLF:day-CLF:day cry still cry

doub geud aod-leb zhonx-hlod id-lons aub-gheb, nied
then$_1$ hold one-CLF length-bamboo DID-gather water-eye cry

nied nied. Dut aod-zhonx-hlod aub-gheb diex lah,
cry cry obtain one-CLF:[length-bamboo] water-eye finish PRF

diex gid.daud loux beul baox nzhaod lol leh. Beul
finish extremely long.time 3 father return come LEH 3

baox nzhaod, beul baox dand zheit-cheid, hnant cheid:
father return 3 father arrive outside-gate call gate

"Zet aoh, zet aoh, kiak cheid, zet aoh!"
child PART child PART open gate child PART

'Their father was gone for a very long time, a very long time indeed. After he left, the older sister, Niao Mei, as for her, she was a very bad child. She didn't miss her father. Every day she played the stone-tossing game, she played shuttlecock, she played hopscotch, every day she was out playing. But Niao Nhaon, the younger sister, as for her, she was more honest, more devoted, and she missed her father greatly. Every day she wept. She missed her father so much that she couldn't wait for him to return. Every day she wept, and weeping she took her length of bamboo and gathered her tears in it. She wept and wept and wept. After her length of bamboo was filled with tears, after a very long time, their father returned. Their father returned, he arrived at the gate, and he called there: "My children, my children, open the gate, my children!"'

Niaox.meib ghaod raos, Niaox.meib hnaond beul baox nzhaod,
Mei more clever Mei hear 3 father return

Niaox.meib doub hnant Niaox.nhaonl: "Geud, geud,
Mei then$_1$ call Nhaon younger.sibling younger.sibling

boub baox nzhaod. Monx shaont monl heut kiak cheid."
1PL father return 2SG fast go help open gate

Naonb.naont, Niaox.nhaonl danx guaot meh, jix niel,
thus Nhaon honest pass BCKG NEG$_1$ know

nbanx-gieb beul baox nzhaod, beul jix nbanx niab
think-??? 3 father return 3 NEG$_1$ think say

Niaox.meib lis ghaob-kiot zhut beul. Beul gid monl kiak
Mei want NOM-trick reach 3 3 run go open

cheid. Naonb.naont, Niaox.meib leh, doub geud beul naond
gate thus Mei LEH then$_1$ hold 3 ASSOC

aub-gheb doub geud lias Niaox.meib naond leb zhonx-hlod.
water-eye then$_1$ hold switch Mei ASSOC CLF length-bamboo

Beul jix nied-giaol, jix mex aub-gheb, beul ghat
3 NEG$_1$ cry-??? NEG$_1$ exist water-eye 3 go.to

ob-gaond-aub monl guanb aub. Guanb hant aub manx ...
NOM-tank-water go scoop water scoop CLF:PL water REL

hant aub hauk, khauk-lieux naond aub. Beul
CLF:PL water drink hole-well ASSOC water 3

deb-geud naond, doub nins Niaox.nhaonl manh,
DIM-younger.sibling ASSOC then$_1$ COP Nhaon PART

zheinb.zheinb nins aub-gheb. Beul doub lias beul
really COP water-eye 3 then$_1$ switch 3

deb-geud naond teid bat dox. Beul
DIM-younger.sibling ASSOC put.back put that 3

deb-geud naond, beul meb dut sheub. Doul beul
DIM-younger.sibling ASSOC 3 take obtain leave remain 3

naond	*leh,*	*beul*	*doub*	*geud*	*gaons*	*beul*	*deb-geud*	*lah.*
ASSOC	LEH	3	then$_1$	hold	give	3	DIM-younger.sibling	PRF

'Niao Mei was cleverer. She heard their father return, and then she called to Niao Nhaon: "Little sister, little sister, our father has returned. Quickly go and open the gate for him." And so, Niao Nhaon being very honest, she didn't know [what Niao Mei was up to]. She thought it was merely that their father had returned, she didn't think that Niao Mei would trick her. She ran to open the gate. And so, Niao Mei then took her younger sister's tears and switched them into her own length of bamboo. Niao Mei hadn't cried, she had no tears of her own, and so she went to the water tank to get some water. She scooped up some water that ... some drinking water, some water from the well. Her younger sister's, that is to say Niao Nhaon's, really was tears, and so she switched the drinking water into Niao Nhaon's length of bamboo. Niao Mei took her younger sister's tears with her, and gave her own drinking water to her younger sister.'

Beul	*baox*	*nzhaod*	*dand.*	*"Wel*	*monl*	*diex*	*naont*	*loux*
3	father	return	arrive	1SG	go	finish	thus	long.time

lol	*ah,*	*manx*	*deit*	*liaos*	*baox*	*naond*	*jix*	*liaos*
come	PART	2SG	still	miss	father	ASSOC	NEG$_1$	miss

ah?"	*Niaox.meib:*	*"Liaos*	*ah,*	*hnef-hnef*	*nbanx*	*monx."*
PART	Mei	miss	PART	CLF:day-CLF:day	think	2SG

"Deb-geud	*liaos*	*jix*	*liaos?"*	*"Liaos,*	*oub-meinl*	*at*
DIM-younger.sibling	miss	NEG$_1$	miss	miss	two-CLF:person	SAT

liaos."	*"Liaos*	*naont*	*wel*	*gaons*	*manx*	*oub-leb*	*bid-zhonx-hlod*
miss	miss	thus	1SG	give	2PL	two-CLF	FRT-length-bamboo

leh,	*gaons*	*manx*	*geud*	*zhut*	*aub-gheb.*	*Manx*	*meb*	*lol*
LEH	give	2PL	hold	store	water-eye	2PL	take	come

gaons	*wel*	*shaod*	*diul.*	*Giat*	*nkhed*	*diul*	*jud.leb*	*ghaod*
give	1SG	try	complete	share	look	complete	who	more

dut	*hliof*	*aub-gheb.*	*Niaox.nhaonl,*	*geud*	*monx*	*naond*	*gaons*
obtain	many	water-eye	Nhaon	hold	2SG	ASSOC	give

wel	*nkhed,*	*Nhaonl."*	*Niaox.nhaonl,*	*deb-geud,*	*geud*
1SG	look	Nhaon	Nhaon	DIM-younger.sibling	hold

zhonx-hlod-aub-gheb	*gaons*	*beul*	*baox*	*shaod.*	*Beul*	*baox*	*shaod*
length-bamboo-water-eye	give	3	father	try	3	father	try

leh,	*aub-gheb*	*ghad*	*nins*	*manx*	*diaonl,*	*mex*	*deb*	*diaonl*
LEH	water-eye	then$_2$	COP	REL	sweet	exist	DIM	sweet

njeud. Aub nins manx uk.seb uk.weib, houd-deb
salt water COP REL colorless flavorless CLF:mouthful-DIM

weib.dob jix mex, oh. Shaod zhut beul deb-geud
flavor NEG$_1$ exist INTJ try reach 3 DIM-younger.sibling

naond, ghad zhus beul jed id-lias, zhus Niaox.meib
ASSOC then$_2$ suffer 3 older.sister DID-switch suffer Mei

lias, ob-naonb weib.dob at jix mex, doub nins aub,
switch NOM-what flavor SAT NEG$_1$ exist then$_1$ COP water

hos, beul niel lah, aod-leb neind nins manx giaox
okay 3 know PRF one-CLF this COP REL fake

naond, jix nins aub-gheb. Shaod Niaox.meib naond, nins
ASSOC NEG$_1$ COP water-eye try Mei ASSOC COP

aub-gheb. Ob-naont, beul baox nbanx-gieb deit nins Niaox.meib
water-eye NOM-thus 3 father think-??? still COP Mei

ghaod raut deb, Niaox.nhaonl jaod deb, jud niel
more good child Nhaon bad child NEG$_2$ know

Niaox.meib heit bat zhux.ib.
Mei still put scheme

'Their father arrived. [He said:] "I've been gone for a long time, did you two miss me or not?" Niao Mei [said:] "I did, I've been thinking of you every day." [Their father asked:] "And did little sister miss me?" [Niao Nhaon said:] "I did, we both missed you." [Their father said:] "If you missed me, then give me your two lengths of bamboo, the ones I gave you to store your tears with. Bring them to me and let me examine them. Let me see which of you has more tears. Niao Nhaon, let me see yours, Nhaon." Niao Nhaon, the younger sister, gave her bamboo-length of tears to her father to examine. He examined it – [but first remember that] tears are a bit sweet, a bit salty. Water is colorless and tasteless, it doesn't have any flavor at all. So the father examined the younger sister's length of bamboo, the one that had been switched by her older sister, switched by Niao Mei. It didn't have any flavor at all, it was just water. Okay, so he knew, this one was fake, it didn't contain tears at all. Then he examined Niao Mei's, and it did contain tears. And so, their father thought that Niao Mei was the better child, Niao Nhaon the worse child. He didn't know that it was all part of Niao Mei's scheme.'

"Nheis deb reib ah, nheis reib boub-leb dieud
gather DIM vegetable PART gather vegetable 1PL-DU boil.rice

hlit gaons boub baox nonx.” Niaox.nhaonl danx hint:
cooked.rice give 1PL father eat Nhaon honest very

“Hos, wel monl nheis reib, naont monx dieud hlit
okay 1SG go gather vegetable thus 2SG boil.rice cooked.rice

aoh.” “Hos, naont monx shaont monl nheis reib
PART okay thus 2SG fast go gather vegetable

aoh, wel ninb bioud dieud hlit.” Niaox.nhaonl monl
PART 1SG at home boil.rice cooked.rice Nhaon go

nheis reib. Niaox.meib nhaons beul baox puk niab deux:
gather vegetable Mei with 3 father speak say QUOT

“Baox, meib-Nhaonl jaod deb guaot. Monx monl naont
father younger.sister-Nhaon bad child pass 2SG go thus

loux lol, nkhed beul jix liaos monx naond.
long.time come look 3 NEG_1 miss 2SG ASSOC

Hnef-hnef at yeux nghauk.zaol leh, npod mel,
CLF:day-CLF:day SAT stroll play LEH toss stone.toss.game

ndanb sheinb.kiet, hnef-hnef nhaons nex nghauk.zaol, jix
jump hopscotch CLF:day-CLF:day with NEX play NEG_1

liaos monx naond. Wel meh, liaos monx naond guaot,
miss 2SG ASSOC 1SG BCKG miss 2SG ASSOC pass

daonl jix niaons monx nzhaod, hnef-hnef nied nied
wait NEG_1 ABIL 2SG return CLF:day-CLF:day cry cry

nied. Nbanx jix nond. Meib-Nhaonl jaod deb hint,
cry think NEG_1 forget younger.sister-Nhaon bad child very

boub ghad lis beul diex. Meib-Nhaonl jaod
1PL NEG.IMP want 3 finish younger.sister-Nhaon bad

deb hint meh, wel at qiaos.kueis hint manh.”
child very BCKG 1SG SAT suffer very PART

“Soud manx oub-meinl soud ix dut niaons, beul
raise 2PL two-CLF:person raise NEG_1 obtain ABIL 3

at jaod deb hint meh, jix liaos baox naond.
SAT bad child very BCKG NEG_1 miss father ASSOC

Naonb.naont ghad lis at ghad lis. Ghad
thus NEG.IMP want SAT NEG.IMP want NEG.IMP

lis naont ... chauk-dib ghad lis raut?" Naonb.naont
want thus do-which NEG.IMP want good thus

Niaox.meib niab: "Ghad lis, boub ghad ... monx ghad
Mei say NEG.IMP want 1PL then$_2$ 2SG then$_2$

did-ghous beul niab dionb ghat ib-dof monl id-ghoub
DID-trick 3 say lead go.to ???-which go DID-far

ghoub ghoub monl, beul ghad jix ndiot geud nzhaod.
far far go 3 then$_2$ NEG$_1$ recognize road return

Boub dand dox boub ghad box.nhol beul zhut dox.
1PL arrive that 1PL then$_2$ throw.away 3 reach that

Beul nzhaod jix dut, boub ghad del beul lis
3 return NEG$_1$ obtain 1PL then$_2$ let 3 want

chauk-dib beul at chauk, naont boub nzhaod lol. Boub-leb
do-which 3 SAT do thus 1PL return come 1PL-DU

ninb bioud diex." Beul baox niab: "Hos, naont raut. Naont
at home finish 3 father say okay thus good thus

nanx, wel nanx dionb beul monl id-ghoub ghoub ghoub."
only 1SG only lead 3 go DID-far far far

Niaox.nhaonl nzhaod lol, nonx diex hlit, beul baox
Nhaon return come eat finish cooked.rice 3 father

bod meib-Nhaonl: "Nhaonl, wel dionb monx, boub-leb
tell younger.sister-Nhaon Nhaon 1SG lead 2SG 1PL-DU

monl nghauk raonl, nghauk nex monl, nghauk maox.ceins.
go visit friend visit NEX go visit relative

Nhaons wel monl aoh, Nhaonl?" "Hos, monx dionb
with 1SG go PART Nhaon okay 2SG lead

wel monl wel nhaons monx monl." "Niaox.meib ninb
1SG go 1SG with 2SG go Mei at

bioud lieus bioud aoh, boub doub monl." "Hos." Naont
home guard home PART 1PL then$_1$ go okay thus

shib beul baox dionb Niaox.nhaonl monl nghauk nex.
it's 3 father lead Nhaon go visit NEX

'[Niao Mei said to Niao Nhaon:] "Gather some vegetables, gather some vegetables and we'll cook some rice for our father." Niao Nhaon was very honest, [and she said:] "Okay, I'll go gather some vegetables, and you stay here and boil the rice." [Niao Mei said:] "Okay, then hurry and gather the vegetables, I'll boil the rice here at home." Niao Nhaon went off to gather the vegetables. Niao Mei then said to her father: "Father, little sister Nhaon is a very bad child. You were gone for such a long time, but look how she didn't miss you. Every day she went out to play, she played the stone-tossing game, she played hopscotch, every day she was out playing with people, she didn't miss you. But I missed you greatly, I couldn't wait for you to come back. Every day I wept and wept and wept. I couldn't forget you. Little sister Nhaon is such a bad child, let's just get rid of her and be done with it. Little sister Nhaon is such a bad child, I'm suffering so much with her here." [Her father replied:] "I can't afford to continue raising the both of you, and she is a very bad child, she didn't miss her father. So fine, we'll just get rid of her. So to get rid of her ... how should we go about doing it?" Then Niao Mei said: "To get rid of her, let's just ... you trick her and take her to a place far, far away. Then she won't know the way back. When we get there we'll just abandon her there. She won't be able to come back. We'll just let her do whatever she wants to, and we'll come back. It'll be just the two of us at home, and that'll be that." Her father said: "Okay, good. So I'll just lead her far, far away." Niao Nhaon returned. After they finished eating, the father told little sister Nhaon: "Nhaon, I'll take you, the two of us can go visit friends, visit some people, visit relatives. Won't you come with me, Nhaon?" [Nhaon answered:] "Okay, if you take me then I'll go with you." [Her father said:] "Niao Mei will stay at home to watch the house, and we'll go." [Niao Nhaon replied:] "Okay." And so it was that their father took Niao Nhaon to go visiting.'

At nins ghous naond, dionb monl ghoub ghoub ghoub, dionb
SAT COP trick ASSOC lead go far far far lead

nhob hant bid-gheul-ghaob-chaut ah. Dand ghaob-chaut,
walk CLF:PL FRT-mountain-NOM-wilderness PART arrive NOM-wilderness

beul nes: "Nhaonl, monx dand neind jix dand, Nhaonl?
3 ask Nhaon 2SG arrive this NEG$_1$ arrive Nhaon

Monl ghoub guaot." Meib-Nhaonl niab: "Dand." "Monx dand
go far pass younger.sister-Nhaon say arrive 2SG arrive

neind hauk-naonb, Nhaonl?" "Wel dand neind nheis reib-nbat."
this do-what Nhaon 1SG arrive this gather greens-pig

Yab nhob nhob nhob nhob nhob nhob. At nhob
also walk walk walk walk walk walk SAT walk

gid.daud ghoub. "Meib-Nhaonl, monx dut dand neind,
extremely far younger.sister-Nhaon 2SG obtain arrive this

Nhaonl?" "Dand." "Monx dand neind hauk-naonb, Nhaonl?" "Wel
Nhaon arrive 2SG arrive this do-what Nhaon 1SG

dand neind raons deul." "Dut dand guaot meh,
arrive this cut.firewood firewood obtain arrive pass BCKG

ghad deit ndiot geud nzhaod." Yab yul nhob, nhob
then$_2$ still recognize road return also again walk walk

ghoub ghoub ghoub ghoub ghoub ghoub. "Monx dand neind jix
far far far far far far 2SG arrive this NEG$_1$

dand neind, Nhaonl? Dut dand neind yaox?" "Jix dut
arrive this Nhaon obtain arrive this right? NEG$_1$ obtain

dand, sout.gaont wel jix dut dand neind." Beul baox
arrive before 1SG NEG$_1$ obtain arrive this 3 father

niel lah, niel beul jix dut dand neind.
know PRF know 3 NEG$_1$ obtain arrive this

Meib-Nhaonl jix dut dand neind, beul jix doul
younger.sister-Nhaon NEG$_1$ obtain arrive this 3 NEG$_1$ remain

ndiot geud nzhaod.
recognize road return

'It was all a trick. Niao Nhaon's father led her far, far, far away, he led her out into the wilderness. When they got there, he asked: "Nhaon, have you been here before, Nhaon? We've come very far." Little sister Nhaon said: "I have." [Her father asked:] "What did you come here for, Nhaon?" [She answered:] "I came here to gather pig-feed." So again they walked, and walked, and walked, and walked. They walked very, very far. [Her father asked:] "Little sister Nhaon, have you been here before, Nhaon?" [She answered:] "I have." [He asked:] "What did you come here for, Nhaon?" [She answered:] "I came here to gather firewood." [Her father thought to himself:] "Well, if she's been here before, then she'll know the way back." Again they walked, they walked very, very, very far. [Her father asked:] "Have you been here before, Nhaon? You've been here before, right?" [She answered:] "No, I haven't, I've never been here before." Then her father knew, he knew that she had never been there before. And if little sister Nhaon had never been there before, she wouldn't know the way back.'

Dand dox leh, beul baox niab: "Meib-Nhaonl, wel
arrive that LEH 3 father say younger.sister-Nhaon 1SG

nkheik aub guaot, monx heut wel teuf aod-tit aub
thirsty water pass 2SG help 1SG scoop one-CLF:time$_3$ water

gaons wel hauk." "Hos." "Wel jont neind daonl monx." "Hos."
give 1SG drink okay 1SG sit this wait 2SG okay

Beul baox gaons beul aod-leb deb-zhonx-hlod. Gaons beul
3 father give 3 one-CLF DIM-length-bamboo give 3

leb deb-zhonx-hlod monl teuf aub. Beul baox jont
CLF DIM-length-bamboo go scoop water 3 father sit

dox daonl. Beul monl teuf aub, ghat khauk-lieux-aub monl
that wait 3 go scoop water go.to hole-well-water go

teuf aub. Beul teuf dut aub leh, beul chot, chot
scoop water 3 scoop obtain water LEH 3 take take

nhob nzhaod gaons beul baox hauk. Nhob nhob nhob,
walk return give 3 father drink walk walk walk

it, aod-leb zhonx-hlod jix doul aub. Jix doul
SPRS one-CLF length-bamboo NEG$_1$ remain water NEG$_1$ remain

aub yab nzhaod monl teuf. Yab nhob nhob yab
water also return go scoop also walk walk also

jix doul aub. Beul jix niel hauk-dib jix doul
NEG$_1$ remain water 3 NEG$_1$ know do-which NEG$_1$ remain

aub. Dand kheut nek-geud roub diul khad,
water arrive CLF:rigid.segment AUG-road leak.out complete dry

jix doul aub. Mex ngonl deb-naus. Mex ngonl
NEG$_1$ remain water exist CLF:animate DIM-bird exist CLF:animate

deb-naus niab deux: "Leud-Nhaonl, leud-Nhaonl, leud-Nhaonl,
DIM-bird say QUOT FAM-Nhaon FAM-Nhaon FAM-Nhaon

giaol tif heint, jud niel zheb reib, ghaod.laox
stupid stomach very NEG$_2$ know pull.out greens mud

leins." "Aod-ngonl naus at bob wel, niel
fill.in one-CLF:animate bird SAT talk.about 1SG know[226]

226 It is not uncommon for clauses featuring the verb *niel/nianl* 'to know' to be negative in meaning even without containing any overt negative marker. Thus the clause in question here – *niel niab hant naonb* [know say CLF:PL what] – should be translated as '(I) don't know what (the bird) is saying' or '(who) knows what (the bird) is saying', not as '(I) know what (the bird) is saying'. Still, it is even more

niab hant naonb. Jud niel zheb reib, ghaod.laox
say CLF:PL what NEG$_2$ know pull.out greens mud

leins." Oh, aod-leb zhonx-hlod at guoux bol. Leb
fill.in INTJ one-CLF length-bamboo SAT leak underside CLF

zhonx-hlod beul baox ghad zaox leb khauk gaons roub
length-bamboo 3 father then$_2$ drill CLF hole give leak.out

aub. Teuf jix dut aub nzhaod lol. Beul baox
water scoop NEG$_1$ obtain water return come 3 father

ghad, bat beul zhux.ib, gaons beul teuf jix dut
then$_2$ put 3 scheme give 3 scoop NEG$_1$ obtain

aub, daonl beul teuf dut aub nzhaod lol beul
water wait 3 scoop obtain water return come 3

baox ghad sheub gueil. Oh, Nhaonl beul ghans, Nhaonl
father then$_2$ leave go.away INTJ Nhaon 3 see Nhaon

dad.kit geud ghaod.laox geud ghaob-reib ncaut leb khauk
not.until hold mud hold NOM-greens insert CLF hole

dox. Geud leb bid-ndaod ncaut, Nhaonl beul kit yul
that hold CLF FRT-finger insert Nhaon 3 not.until again

monl teuf. Teuf dut aub lah, dut aub jix roub
go scoop scoop obtain water PRF obtain water NEG$_1$ leak.out

lah, nzhaod dand beul baox naond ob-def jont,
PRF return arrive 3 father ASSOC NOM-place sit

jix ghans beul baox leh. Beul baox jud niel ghat
NEG$_1$ see 3 father LEH 3 father NEG$_2$ know go.to

ib-dof leh, dut aub jix ghans beul baox leh,
???-which LEH obtain water NEG$_1$ see 3 father LEH

hnant beul baox, hnant jix doub. Chauk-dib hnant jix
call 3 father call NEG$_1$ answer do-which call NEG$_1$

doub leh, naont shib, beul baox sheub ncaos leh.
answer LEH thus it's 3 father leave be.done LEH

common for clauses featuring *niel/nianl* without any overt negative marker to be affirmative in meaning. So far it appears that only context determines the (semantic) polarity of a clause featuring *niel/nianl*.

'Having arrived there, her father said: "Little sister Nhaon, I'm very thirsty. Go get some water for me to drink." [Nhaon said:] "Okay." [Her father said:] "I'll sit here and wait for you." [Nhaon said:] "Okay." Her father gave her a little length of bamboo. He gave her a little length of bamboo to get water with, then he sat there and waited. She went to get water, she went to a spring to get water. She scooped up some water, and she started taking it back to give to her father to drink. She walked and walked and walked, but then, huh, all of a sudden there was no water left in the length of bamboo. There was no water left, and so she went back to get more. She walked and walked [to get more water and then return], and again there was no water left [in the length of bamboo]. She didn't know how the water kept disappearing. She'd get halfway [back to her father], and the water would have all leaked out.

A little bird appeared. A little bird appeared and said: "Nhaon, Nhaon, Nhaon, so stupid [lit. 'stupid-bellied'], she doesn't know to take some grass and take some mud and fill in the hole." [Niao Nhaon thought to herself:] "This bird's talking about me. Who knows what it's going on about? [What does it mean,] 'she doesn't know to take some grass and take some mud and fill in the hole'?" Oh, it was that the bottom of the bamboo-length was leaking. Her father had drilled a hole in the bamboo-length so that it would leak. She wouldn't be able to bring any water back. Her father, he was tricking her, he was making it so that she couldn't get water. By the time she brought the water back, her father would have run off. Oh, then Nhaon saw the hole, and she finally took some mud and took some grass and stuck it in there. She stuck her finger in, and then she finally went back to get more water. This time she could scoop up the water, she could get it without it leaking out. She went back to the place where her father had been sitting, but she didn't see him. She didn't know where he'd gone, she'd gotten the water but she didn't see him. She called out to him, but he didn't answer. No matter how she called there was no answer. And so it was that her father left.'

Naont	*shib,*	*beul*	*nkhed,*	*jix*	*ndiot*	*geud*	*nzhaod.*
thus	it's	3	look	NEG$_1$	recognize	road	return

Jix	*niel*	*nhob*	*ib-dof*	*raut*	*leh,*
NEG$_1$	know	walk	???-which	good	LEH

bid-gheul-ghaob-chaut	*bob-raud-ndaut.*	*Dob*	*bob*	*guaot,*
FRT-mountain-NOM-wilderness	forest-forest-tree	deep	forest	pass

jix	*dut*	*nek-geud*	*nzhaod.*	*Jud*	*niel*	*nhob*	*nhaux*
NEG$_1$	obtain	AUG-road	return	NEG$_2$	know	walk	CLF:broad.length

dof	*raut,*	*jont*	*nied.*	*Nied-giaol.*	*Nied*	*nied,*	*aod-ngonl*
which	good	sit	cry	cry-???	cry	cry	one-CLF:animate

deb-naus	*yab*	*niab*	*beul,*	*niab*	*deux*	*niab*	*deux,*	*hnant*
DIM-bird	also	say	3	say	QUOT	say	QUOT	call

beul	*niab*	*deux:*	*"Qod*	*shonb*	*qod*	*mioul*	*gaons*	*wel*	*nonx,*
3	say	QUOT	grab	shrimp	grab	fish	give	1SG	eat

qod	*shonb*	*qod*	*mioul*	*gaons*	*wel*	*khoud,*	*wel*	*dionb*
grab	shrimp	grab	fish	give	1SG	consume	1SG	lead

monx	*ox*	*monx*	*naond*	*minl*	*monl*	*ah.*	*Qod*	*shonb*
2SG	and	2SG	ASSOC	mother	go	PART	grab	shrimp

qod	*mioul*	*gaons*	*wel*	*giaot,*	*wel*	*dionb*	*monx*	*ox*	*monx*
grab	fish	give	1SG	chew	1SG	lead	2SG	and	2SG

naond	*maot."*	*It,*	*aod-ngonl*	*deb-naus*	*bod*	*beul*	*yab*
ASSOC	father	SPRS	one-CLF:animate	DIM-bird	tell	3	also

niab:	*"Monx*	*qod*	*shonb*	*qod*	*mioul*	*gaons*	*wel*	*nonx,*
say	2SG	grab	shrimp	grab	fish	give	1SG	eat

wel	*nonx*	*ncheut*	*wel*	*ghad*	*dionb*	*monx*	*nzhaod."*	*Naont*
1SG	eat	full	1SG	then$_2$	lead	2SG	return	thus

beul	*jix*	*doul*	*banb.faox.*	*"Deb-naus*	*at*	*niab*	*qod*	*shonb*
3	NEG$_1$	remain	solution	DIM-bird	SAT	say	grab	shrimp

qod	*mioul*	*gaons*	*beul*	*nonx,*	*beul*	*dionb*	*wel*	*nzhaod,*	*qod*
grab	fish	give	3	eat	3	lead	1SG	return	grab

at	*qod."*	*Qod*	*ghat*	*khauk-yox-aub*	*ghat*	*aod-khauk*	*manx*
SAT	grab	grab	go.to	hole-ditch-water	go.to	one-CLF:place$_2$	REL

teuf	*aub*	*dox*	*geud*	*deb-ob-doul*	*qod*	*deb-daob-shonb,*
scoop	water	that	hold	DIM-NOM-hand	grab	DIM-AN-shrimp

fand	*deb-daob-zheid*	*gaons*	*deb-naus*	*nonx.*	*Beul*	*fand*
turn.over	DIM-AN-crab	give	DIM-bird	eat	3	turn.over

dut	*hliof*	*hint,*	*daob-naus*	*nonx*	*ncheut.*	*"Naont,*	*meib-Nhaonl,*
obtain	many	very	AN-bird	eat	full	thus	younger.sister-Nhaon

wel	*nonx*	*ncheut,*	*monx*	*did-choud*	*wel*	*nzhaod,*	*wel*	*eint*
1SG	eat	full	2SG	DID-follow	1SG	return	1SG	fly

ghat	*dib*	*monx*	*nhob*	*ghat*	*dib,*	*dionb*	*monx*	*nzhaod*	*ox*
go.to	which	2SG	walk	go.to	which	lead	2SG	return	and

monx	*naond*	*baox*	*monl*	*ah."*	*Daob-naus*	*eint*	*aod-deik*
2SG	ASSOC	father	go	PART	AN-bird	fly	one-CLF:wing

zos	*aod-deik,*	*eint*	*jix*	*dut*	*hot*	*ghoub*	*yab*
land	one-CLF:wing	fly	NEG$_1$	obtain	how.much	far	also

zos aod-dieud daonl, dionb dionb dionb dionb dionb shib
land one-CLF:time$_2$ wait lead lead lead lead lead it's

nzhaod leh, nzhaod dand beul naond bioud, keuf zhauf
return LEH return arrive 3 ASSOC home shut door

keuf cheid.
shut gate

'And so, she looked, but she didn't know the way back. She didn't know where she should go, [everywhere around her was] wilderness, deep forest. The forest was so deep, she couldn't find the way back. She didn't know which path she should take, and so she sat and wept. She wept and wept, and then the little bird again spoke to her, it called to her saying: "Catch some shrimp and catch some fish for me to eat, catch some shrimp and catch some fish for me to consume, and I'll lead you back to your mother. Catch some shrimp and catch some fish for me to chew, and I'll lead you back to your father." Huh, and then the little bird also told her: "Catch some shrimp and catch some fish for me to eat, once I'm full I'll lead you back." And so there was nothing else she could do. [Niao Nhaon thought:] "The little bird said it would lead me back if I caught some shrimp and caught some fish for it to eat, so catch them I will." She went to the little stream, to the place where she'd been getting water, and she used her hands to catch some shrimp and flip [over rocks to find] some crabs for the bird to eat. She caught a great many of them, and the bird ate his fill. [The bird said:] "So, little sister Nhaon, I've eaten my fill. Follow me back. Wherever I fly, you walk, and I'll lead you back to your father." The bird would fly for a bit and then land for a bit. Before it flew too far, it would stop and wait for a while. It led Niao Nhaon on, and on, and on, until she'd returned, returned to her home. But the door and the gate were shut.'

Beul baox leh, Niaox.meib leh, baod-zhauf at keuf
3 father LEH Mei LEH BUG-door SAT shut

baod-cheid at keuf. Nhaonl beul hnant cheid, hnant: "Baox
BUG-gate SAT shut Nhaon 3 call gate call father

ah, baox ah, kiak cheid!" Baox jix kiak. Hnant hnant
PART father PART open gate father NEG$_1$ open call call

deit jix kiak. Deit jix kiak leh, beul baox nex
still NEG$_1$ open still NEG$_1$ open LEH 3 father NEX

ninb bioud, beul baox nex hnaond. It, meib-Nhaonl
at home 3 father NEX hear SPRS younger.sister-Nhaon

nzhaod dand. Nzhaod dand jix heut kiak, deit jix
return arrive return arrive NEG$_1$ help open still NEG$_1$

heut kiak. Beul deib geud-zheit nied leh. Nied nied

help open 3 at place$_1$-outside cry LEH cry cry

nied nied, deit nied deit hnant, deit nied deit hnant

cry cry SIMUL cry SIMUL call SIMUL cry SIMUL call

leh. Beul baox niab deux: "Zok.nief hint, kox.lief beul

LEH 3 father say QUOT pitiful very pity 3

hint, nank.hauf.ix.dut, deit heut kiak." Naont shib, heut

very there.is.nothing.to.be.done still help open thus it's help

beul kiak cheid, kiak cheid nzhaod lol. Beul baox leh,

3 open gate open gate return come 3 father LEH

beul baox ox beul jed, gaons beul jont zhonx-nbat.

3 father and 3 older.sister give 3 live pen-pig

Jix gaons beul jont bioud. Gaons beul jont zhonx-nbat.

NEG$_1$ give 3 live home give 3 live pen-pig

Jix gaons beul jont ninb bioud, gaons beul jont

NEG$_1$ give 3 live at home give 3 live

zhonx-nbat, jont zhonx-nbat, niab beul jaod deb hint. Jaod

pen-pig live pen-pig say 3 bad child very bad

deb hint, jix gaons beul jont ninb bioud, gaons beul

child very NEG$_1$ give 3 live at home give 3

jont zhonx-nbat, jont zhonx-nbat. Jont zhonx-nbat, jix mex

live pen-pig live pen-pig live pen-pig NEG$_1$ exist

naonb sib chauk, beul ghad cod deb-xut.npeif.

what matter do 3 then$_2$ sew DIM-shoe

Cod cod cod, cod diex aod-tit-deb cod diex

sew sew sew sew finish one-CLF:time$_3$-DIM sew finish

ngonl xut.npeif. Cod diex ngonl xut.npeif beul sat

CLF:pair$_1$ shoe sew finish CLF:pair$_1$ shoe 3 SAT

zhaok box.nhol ghat zhonx-nbat meh. Zhaok zhut daob-nbat

fall throw.away go.to pen-pig BCKG fall reach AN-pig

naond ob-def gheil ghaod. Sat lous ghaod-nbat

ASSOC NOM-place excrete feces SAT dirty feces-pig

ndeb meh, beul dad.kit monl ncot nqif meb

wet BCKG 3 not.until go wash.clothing clean take

shok zhel, ghat geud-zheit monl shok. Mex
dry.in.sun sun go.to place$_1$-outside go dry.in.sun exist

hnef beul ghad shok, ghad zhax git guaot meh,
CLF:day 3 then$_2$ dry.in.sun then$_2$ strong wind pass BCKG

piaf raol git meh, dut beul naond xut.npeif
blow CLF:weather wind BCKG obtain 3 ASSOC shoe

sat piaf sheub monl. Mex nqad piaf sheub, doul
SAT blow leave go exist CLF:half.of.pair blow leave remain

nqad. Dand hmaont-dius beul xeub xut.npeif, jix
CLF:half.of.pair arrive evening-??? 3 retrieve shoe NEG$_1$

ghans xut.npeif. Doul nqad leh, daod dib eit
see shoe remain CLF:half.of.pair LEH place$_3$ which still

id-ngual chaot. Jix dut def chaot, nes nex
DID-circle look.for NEG$_1$ obtain place look.for ask NEX

jud.leb at jix ghans. Leb-leb at nes, leb-leb at
who SAT NEG$_1$ see CLF-CLF SAT ask CLF-CLF SAT

niab jix ghans. Giaok-bioud-giaok-deul yaod.yaod nes bans
say NEG$_1$ see side-home-side-firewood all ask everywhere

jix ghans, jix dut def chaot. Shib beul ngonl
NEG$_1$ see NEG$_1$ obtain place look.for it's 3 CLF:pair$_1$[227]

xut.npeif – ghad zhax git guaot – piaf ghat nex
shoe then$_2$ strong wind pass blow go.to NEX

link.web bioud monl, miex liot naond bioud,
another home go person wealthy ASSOC home

yes.web naond bioud.
landlord ASSOC home

'Her father, and Niao Mei, they'd shut the door, and shut the gate. Nhaon called at the gate, she called: "Father, father, open the gate!" But her father didn't open it. She called and she called, but he still didn't open it. He still didn't open it, but her father and sister were at home, her father and sister must have heard her. Huh, little sister

227 The use of *ngonl* 'CLF:pair$_1$' here appears to simply be an error on the part of the narrator. Both context and the author's other consultants make it clear that only one shoe was blown away, not both, and so *nqad* 'CLF:half.of.pair' should have been used instead. The same error occurs in the third line of the following section, although there the narrator corrects himself in the next line.

Nhaon had come home, she'd come home but they wouldn't open the gate for her, they still wouldn't open it. She wept outside. She wept and wept and wept, and she called out as she wept. Her father said: "So pitiful, I pity her so much. There's nothing else we can do, let's just open the gate for her." And so, he opened the gate for her, he opened the gate so she could return. But her father, her father and her older sister, they made her live in the pig-pen. They didn't let her live in the house, they only let her live in the pig-pen. They said she was a very bad child, and so they didn't let her live in the house, only in the pig-pen.

In the pig-pen there was nothing to do, so she started to sew some shoes. She sewed and sewed and sewed, and after a little while she'd finished a pair. But once she finished them, they fell into the pig-pen, into the place where the pig defecated. The shoes were filthy with pig droppings, and wet. She took the shoes, washed them clean, and put them outside to dry in the sun. Then one day, as they were drying, a great wind blew through, a gust of wind blew through, and it blew a shoe away. It blew away one shoe, leaving the other. That evening she went to retrieve the shoes, but she saw that one was missing, and only one was left. She went around everywhere looking, everywhere she could, but everyone she asked said they hadn't seen the missing shoe. She asked everyone, but everyone said they hadn't seen it. She asked every one of her neighbors, but none of them had seen it. She had nowhere else to look. But it turned out that her shoe – when the great wind blew through – it had been blown to another person's home, a wealthy person's home, a landlord's home.'

Dand	*yes.web*	*naond*	*bioud,*	*ghad*	*zhus*	*yes.web*
arrive	landlord	ASSOC	home	then$_2$	suffer	landlord

tauk	*dut*	*leh.*	*Yes.web:*	*"It,*	*zhaos*	*dib*	*ah?*
pick.up	obtain	LEH	landlord	SPRS	from	which	PART

Piaf	*eint*	*aod-ngonl*	*xut.npeif*	*dand*	*neind*	*lol,*
blow	fly	one-CLF:pair$_1$	shoe	arrive	this	come

aod-nqad	*xut.npeif,*	*xonx*	*ngonl,*	*raut,*	*aod-ngonl*
one-CLF:half.of.pair	shoe	attractive	CLF:pair$_1$	good	one-CLF:animate

manx	*chauk*	*xut.npeif*	*neind*	*at*	*neub."*	*Yes.web*	*sat*
REL	do	shoe	this	SAT	skilled	landlord	SAT

niab	*deux:*	*"Aod-ngonl*	*xut.npeif,*	*xut.npeif,*	*deb-npaok*	*naond*
say	QUOT	one-CLF:pair$_1$	shoe	shoe	DIM-woman	ASSOC

xut.npeif."	*Yes.web*	*at*	*niab*	*deux:*	*"Naonb.naont,*	*gaons*	*wel*
shoe	landlord	SAT	say	QUOT	thus	give	1SG

hnant,	*hnant*	*aod-gheul*	*miex*	*naond*	*deb-ngueif,*
call	call	one-CLF:village	person	ASSOC	DIM-unmarried.woman

deb-npaok yaod.yaod hnant lol reinb nqad
DIM-woman all call come determine CLF:half.of.pair

xut.npeif nins leb naond xut.npeif. Manx nins
shoe COP who ASSOC shoe REL COP

deb-ngueif nins deb-npaok leh, xaond tad
DIM-unmarried.woman COP DIM-woman LEH not.yet establish

bioud naond jeub chauk wel naond nheinx."
home ASSOC $then_3$ do 1SG ASSOC daughter.in.law

Bioud yes.web mex ngonl deb-nint sat liox
CLF:home landlord exist CLF:animate DIM-man SAT big

miex, sat oub-gul-kiak-jut xaond mex npaok. Aod-ngonl
person SAT two-ten-more-CLF:year not.yet exist woman one-CLF:animate

yes.web bod leh, bod seinb, jaont seinb
landlord tell LEH tell message release message

ngual leh, leb-leb hnaond seinb leh. Dand
circle LEH CLF-CLF hear message LEH arrive

hnef dox leh, dand hnef dox shib yaod.yaod
CLF:day that LEH arrive CLF:day that it's all

lol id-reinb nqad xut.npeif dox nins leb
come DID-determine CLF:half.of.pair shoe that COP who

naond. Leb-leb at lol, leb-leb at shaod, jix
ASSOC CLF-CLF SAT come CLF-CLF SAT try NEG_1

nins, nins leb zhut hox? Jud.leb deib dut
COP COP who wear.shoes fit who match obtain

aod-nqad neind, doul nqad, jud.leb doub
one-CLF:half.of.pair this remain CLF:half.of.pair who $then_1$

chauk beul naond nheinx.
do 3 ASSOC daughter.in.law

'The shoe arrived at the landlord's home, where it was picked up by the landlord. The landlord [said]: "Hey, where did this come from? A shoe has blown here, and it's a very attractive shoe, a good shoe. Whoever made this must be very skilled." The landlord then said: "A pair of shoes, a young woman's shoes." He then said: "So, call for me all the unmarried women, all the young women in the village. Call them to come and determine who this shoe belongs to. If [the person this shoe belongs to] is an unmarried woman, a young woman, if she hasn't yet started a family, then she can be my daughter-in-law." The landlord had a grown son at home, a son who was already more than twenty years old and still hadn't married. And so the landlord had the message sent out, he had it sent out all over, and everyone heard it. When the day arrived, everyone came to determine who the shoe belonged to. Everyone came, and everyone tried on the shoe, but it didn't fit. Who would the shoe fit? Whoever could match this shoe, whoever had the other half of the pair, she would become the landlord's daughter-in-law.'

Yaod.yaod	*monl*	*shaod,*	*monl*	*zhut,*	*zhut*	*jix*	*yaonx,*
all	go	try	go	wear.shoes	wear.shoes	NEG$_1$	fit.into

zhut	*jix*	*hox.*	*Aod-banb*	*liox,*	*aob-banb*	*xub.*
wear.shoes	NEG$_1$	fit	one-CLF:some	big	one-CLF:some	small

Dand	*beul*	*naond*	*jed,*	*dand*	*Niaox.meib*	*lol*
arrive	3	ASSOC	older.sister	arrive	Mei	come

shaod.	*Niaox.meib*	*zhut*	*at*	*xub,*	*zhut,*	*chauk-dib*
try	Mei	wear.shoes	SAT	small	wear.shoes	do-which

zhut	*deit*	*jix*	*hox.*	*At*	*xub.*	*Jix*	*mex*
wear.shoes	still	NEG$_1$	fit	SAT	small	NEG$_1$	exist

aod-ngonl	*manx*	*hox*	*leh.*	*Leb-leb*	*zhut*	*at*
one-CLF:animate	REL	fit	LEH	CLF-CLF	wear.shoes	SAT

jix	*peif,*	*zeib.houf*	*meinl*	*dand*	*Niaox.nhaonl.*
NEG$_1$	match	last	CLF:person	arrive	Nhaon

Niaox.nhaonl	*lol*	*shaod*	*zhut,*	*it,*	*peif*	*raut*	*guaot,*
Nhaon	come	try	wear.shoes	SPRS	match	good	pass

jix	*liox*	*jix*	*xub.*	*"Deit*	*doul*	*nqad?"*
NEG$_1$	big	NEG$_1$	small	still	remain	CLF:half.of.pair

"Doul	*nqad*	*ninb*	*wel*	*neind,*	*wel*	*chot*	*lol."*
remain	CLF:half.of.pair	at	1SG	this	1SG	take	come

Oub-nqad	*meb*	*gaons*	*yes.web*	*nkhed.*	*Oub-nqad*
two-CLF:half.of.pair	take	give	landlord	look	two-CLF:half.of.pair

did-buk	*ghad*	*nins*	*aod-ngonl.*	*Did-buk,*	*hox*
DID-combine	then$_2$	COP	one-CLF:pair$_1$	DID-combine	put.together[228]

228 The glossing of *hox* here as 'put together' and elsewhere in this text as 'fit' is not an error. Consultants insist that *hox* 'put together' and *hox* 'fit' are distinct forms that are merely accidentally homophonous.

id-buk, gaons beul zhut. Hox raut guaot leh,
DID-combine give 3 wear.shoes fit good pass LEH

peif raut guaot leh. "Nins monx naond jix nins?"
match good pass LEH COP 2SG ASSOC NEG$_1$ COP

"Nins." "Nins naont raut guaot lah! Monx ... naonb.naont
COP COP thus good pass PRF 2SG thus

nins monx naond leh, monx xaond tad bioud leh,
COP 2SG ASSOC LEH 2SG not.yet establish home LEH

naont monx chauk wel naond nheinx. Monx tad
thus 2SG do 1SG ASSOC daughter.in.law 2SG establish

bioud xaond?" "Wel xaond tad." "Xaond tad
home not.yet 1SG not.yet establish not.yet establish

naont monx chauk wel naond nheinx diex lah.
thus 2SG do 1SG ASSOC daughter.in.law finish PRF

Wel naond deb sat oub-gul-kiak-jut, at xaond
1SG ASSOC child SAT two-ten-more-CLF:year SAT not.yet

mex npaok, xaond dut quf leh, naont monx
exist woman not.yet obtain take.a.wife LEH thus 2SG

chauk wel naond nheinx." "Naont chauk nheinx."
do 1SG ASSOC daughter.in.law thus do daughter.in.law

Naont meib-Nhaonl beul shib jix nzhaod leh,
thus younger.sister-Nhaon 3 it's NEG$_1$ return LEH

chauk nex naond npaok, chauk nex yes.web naond
do NEX ASSOC woman do NEX landlord ASSOC

nheinx. Niaox.meib meh, nzhaod. Doul god
daughter.in.law Mei BCKG return remain CLF:human.group

manx shaod xut.npeif naond yaod.yaod jix nins,
REL try shoe ASSOC all NEG$_1$ COP

yaod.yaod nzhaod diul khad. Doul Niaox.nhaonl jix
all return complete dry remain Nhaon NEG$_1$

nzhaod. Jix nzhaod shib ... chauk nex bioud
return NEG$_1$ return it's do NEX CLF:home

dox naond nheinx.
that ASSOC daughter.in.law

'Everyone went to try, to try on the shoe, but it didn't fit for any of them, none of them were the right size. For some of them the shoe was too big, and for some of them it was too small. Then it came to be [Niao Nhaon's] older sister's turn, it came to be Niao Mei's turn to try on the shoe. The shoe was too small for Niao Mei, no matter how she tried to put it on it still wasn't the right size. It was too small. No one was the right size. No one who tried on the shoe fit. The final person [to try on the shoe] was Niao Nhaon. She tried it on, and lo and behold – it fit perfectly! It wasn't too big or too small. [The landlord asked her:] "Do you have the other shoe?" [Niao Nhaon answered:] "I have the other shoe right here, I brought it with me." She took both shoes and showed them to the landlord. When put together, the two shoes were clearly a pair. The landlord put the two shoes together and gave them to Niao Nhaon to wear. They fit perfectly, they were just the right size. [The landlord asked:] "Are these shoes yours?" [Niao Nhaon answered:] "They are." [The landlord said:] "In that case, excellent! You ... then if they're yours, if you haven't married yet, then you can be my daughter-in-law. Have you married yet?" [Niao Nhaon answered:] "I haven't." [The landlord said:] "Since you haven't married yet, you can be my daughter-in-law, and that'll be that. My son is over twenty years old and he still doesn't have a wife, he still hasn't married. So you can be my daughter-in-law." [Niao Nhaon said:] "Then I'll be your daughter-in-law."

And so little sister Nhaon didn't go back. She became the landlord's son's wife, she became the landlord's daughter-in-law. But Niao Mei, she went back. All of the others who'd tried on the shoe and had it not fit, they all went back too. Only Niao Nhaon stayed behind. She stayed behind to be the landlord's daughter-in-law.'

Ob-naont	*diex*	...	*oub-bub-jut*	*ix.houf.*	*Oub-bub-jut*
NOM-thus	finish		two-three-CLF:year	later	two-three-CLF:year

ix.houf	*mex*	*leb*	*deb-deb.*	*Mex*	*aod-meinl*	*deb-deb,*
later	exist	CLF	child-RED	exist	one-CLF:person	child-RED

sat	*mex*	*oub-jut.*	*Naont*	*yes.web*	*ghad*	*niab*	*deux,*
SAT	exist	two-CLF:year	thus	landlord	then$_2$	say	QUOT

hnant	*beul*	*naond*	*deb*	*beul*	*naond*	*nheinx*
call	3	ASSOC	child	3	ASSOC	daughter.in.law

niab	*deux:*	*"Monx*	*nzhaod*	*monl*	*nghauk*	*manx*
say	QUOT	2SG	return	go	visit	2PL

deb-ghot	*aod-tit,*	*monx*	*ninb*	*neind*	*naont*	*loux*
DIM-old	one-CLF:time$_3$	2SG	at	this	thus	long.time

lol.	*Naont*	*loux*	*lol*	*at*	*xaond*	*dut*	*nzhaod*
come	thus	long.time	come	SAT	not.yet	obtain	return

nkhed	*deb-ghot.”*	*Naont*	*beul*	*naond*	*deb*	*beul*	*naond*
look	DIM-old	thus	3	ASSOC	child	3	ASSOC

nheinx	*nzhaod*	*monl*	*nkhed*	*Niaox.nhaonl*	*naond*	*baox.*
daughter.in.law	return	go	look	Nhaon	ASSOC	father

Dionb	*meinl*	*deb-deb*	*nzhaod.*	*Nzhaod*	*monl*	*shib*	*...*
lead	CLF:person	child-RED	return	return	go	it’s	

nzhaod	*dand*	*bioud.*	*Nzhaod*	*dand*	*beul*	*naond*	*...*	*nghauk*
return	arrive	home	return	arrive	3	ASSOC		visit

dand	*beul*	*naond*	*baox*	*naond*	*bioud*	*leh.*	*Shaod.kit*
arrive	3	ASSOC	father	ASSOC	home	LEH	not.until

geud	*hant*	*qink.kuaonf*	*ghaob-naonb*	*bod*	*beul*	*baox*
hold	CLF:PL	situation	NOM-what	tell	3	father

diul	*diul.*	*Naont,*	*beul*	*baox*	*jix*	*guant,*	*raut*
complete	complete	thus	3	father	NEG$_1$	care	good

hint,	*Niaox.meib*	*leh,*	*ghans*	*Niaox.nhaonl*	*raut*	*guaot*	*leh,*
very	Mei	LEH	see	Nhaon	good	pass	LEH

ninb	*nex*	*bioud*	*miex*	*liot,*	*mex*	*aod-meinl*	*deb-deb.*
marry	NEX	CLF:home	person	wealthy	exist	one-CLF:person	child-RED

Niaox.meib	*xaond*	*tad*	*bioud,*	*Niaox.meib*	*jaod*	*tif*
Mei	not.yet	establish	home	Mei	bad	stomach

guaot.	*Niaox.meib*	*doub*	*bat*	*zhux.ib*	*lis*	*hat*	*Niaox.nhaonl.*
pass	Mei	then$_1$	put	scheme	want	harm	Nhaon

‘And so ... then it was two or three years later. Two or three years later [Niao Nhaon and her husband] had a child. They had a two-year-old child. And then the landlord said, he told his son and his daughter-in-law [i.e. Niao Nhaon and her husband], he said: “You should go back to visit your [i.e. Niao Nhaon’s] father for a while. You’ve been here for such a long time, it’s been such a long time and you still haven’t gone back to visit your father.” And so his son and his daughter-in-law went back to visit her father. They took their child back with them. They went back, back to [Niao Nhaon’s] home. They went back to visit Niao Nhaon’s father’s home. Only then did they tell her father everything that had happened. Her father didn’t mind, he thought it was wonderful. But Niao Mei, she saw that Niao Nhaon was doing so well, that she’d married into a wealthy family, and that she had a child. Niao Mei hadn’t yet married, and she had an evil heart [lit. ‘stomach’]. She began to plot to hurt Niao Nhaon.’

Naont	*shib*	*...*	*Niaox.nhaonl*	*naond*	*bod*	*leh,*	*yes.web*
thus	it's		Nhaon	ASSOC	husband	LEH	landlord

naond	*meinl*	*deb*	*dox*	*deit*	*bod*	*Niaox.nhaonl*	*niab*
ASSOC	CLF:person	child	that	still	tell	Nhaon	say

deux:	*"Diex*	*monx*	*nghauk*	*dand*	*monx*	*naond*
QUOT	finish	2SG	visit	arrive	2SG	ASSOC

baox	*naond*	*bioud,*	*monx*	*naond*	*jed*	*leh,*
father	ASSOC	home	2SG	ASSOC	older.sister	LEH

hnant	*monx*	*chauk*	*naonb*	*monx*	*at*	*ghad*	*monl.*	*Hnant*
call	2SG	do	what	2SG	SAT	NEG.IMP	go	call

monx	*raons*	*deul,*	*monx*	*at*	*ghad*	*monl.*	*Hnant*
2SG	cut.firewood	firewood	2SG	SAT	NEG.IMP	go	call

monx	*nheis*	*reib-nbat*	*monx*	*at*	*ghad*	*monl.*	*Beul*
2SG	gather	greens-pig	2SG	SAT	NEG.IMP	go	3

saud	*monx*	*chauk*	*naonb*	*monx*	*ghad*	*monl,*	*jont*	*bioud*
invite	2SG	do	what	2SG	NEG.IMP	go	sit	home

zaod."	*"Oh."*	*Beul-god*	*dand*	*dox,*	*shib*	*beul*	*naond*	*...*
just	INTJ	3-PL	arrive	that	it's	3	ASSOC	

beul	*naond*	*baox*	*leh,*	*beul-god*	*naond*	*baox,*	*monl*
3	ASSOC	father	LEH	3-PL	ASSOC	father	go

chauk	*manx*	*...*	*chauk*	*geud.donb*	*manh.*	*Doul*	*Niaox.meib*
do	um...		do	work	PART	remain	Mei

leh,	*Niaox.meib*	*leh*	*Niaox.nhaonl*	*oub-leb*	*ninb*	*bioud.*
LEH	Mei	LEH	Nhaon	two-CLF	at	home

Niaox.meib	*saud*	*Niaox.nhaonl:*	*"Nhaonl,*	*Nhaonl,*	*boub-leb*	*monl*
Mei	invite	Nhaon	Nhaon	Nhaon	1PL-DU	go

raons	*deul,*	*Nhaonl."*	*"Jix*	*monl*	*oh."*	*"Boub-leb*	*nheis*
cut.firewood	firewood	Nhaon	NEG$_1$	go	PART	1PL-DU	gather

reib-nbat,	*Nhaonl."*	*"Jix*	*monl*	*oh."*	*"Naont*	*boub-leb*	*nghauk*
greens-pig	Nhaon	NEG$_1$	go	PART	thus	1PL-DU	bathe

aub	*monl,*	*nias*	*zhel*	*guaot."*	*Niaox.nhaonl*	*niab*
water	go	hot.and.sunny	sun	pass	Nhaon	say

nieux.ghoub	*beul*	*naond*	*bod*	*jix*	*bod*	*niab*	*deux*
just.now	3	ASSOC	husband	NEG$_1$	tell	say	QUOT

nghauk aub jix lis monl. Nanx bod niab deux
bathe water NEG$_1$ want go only tell say QUOT

raons deul at jud lis monl, jix puk niab
cut.firewood firewood SAT NEG$_2$ want go NEG$_1$ speak say

deux nghauk aub jud lis monl. Nghauk aub
QUOT bathe water NEG$_2$ want go bathe water

ox.sheib jud guant monl. Oh, naont monl at monl,
perhaps NEG$_2$ care go INTJ thus go SAT go

naont oub-leb dionb monl nghauk aub.
thus two-CLF lead go bathe water

‘And so, Niao Nhaon’s husband, the landlord’s son, told her: “Once you’ve arrived at your father’s home, whatever your older sister tells you to do, don’t do it. If she tells you to cut firewood, don’t do it. If she tells you to gather pig-feed, don’t do it. Whatever she asks you to do, don’t do it, just stay at home.” [Niao Nhaon replied:] “Okay.” They arrived there, but her father, their father, was out working. Niao Mei was left at home, so then Niao Mei and Niao Nhaon were there at the house together. Niao Mei told Niao Nhaon: “Nhaon, Nhaon, let’s the two of us go cut some firewood, Nhaon.” [Niao Nhaon replied:] “No.” [Niao Mei said:] “Let’s the two of us go gather some pig-feed, Nhaon.” [Niao Nhaon replied:] “No.” [Niao Mei said:] “Then let’s the two of us go bathing, it’s so hot and sunny.” Niao Nhaon thought, just now her husband hadn’t told her not to go bathing. He’d only told her not to go cut firewood, he hadn’t told her not to go bathing. Perhaps he wouldn’t care if she went bathing. All right, she’d just go. And so the two of them went to go bathing together.’

Dand def nghauk aub leh, beul dand def nghauk aub
arrive place bathe water LEH 3 arrive place bathe water

shib beul hnant leud-Nhaonl nghauk aub. “Naont monx
it’s 3 call FAM-Nhaon bathe water thus 2SG

nghauk aub, wel heut monx juk deb. Monx
bathe water 1SG help 2SG hold.in.arms child 2SG

nghauk diex, diex wel eit nghauk.” Hos, naont
bathe finish finish 1SG still bathe okay thus

leud-Nhaonl zheinx.bif nghauk aub, dand ob-zheud-aub, dand
FAM-Nhaon prepare bathe water arrive NOM-edge-water arrive

ob-zheud-jet. Beul ndat monx aod-qonf, paf qonf
NOM-edge-pool 3 push 2SG[229] one-CLF:shove strike shove

leh, yeut, zhaok nhaons-aub meh. Zhaok nhaons-aub
LEH INTJ fall inside-water BCKG fall inside-water

shib beul yab tauk ob-roub choud zox, oh, ndieut
it's 3 also pick.up NOM-stone follow smash INTJ ascend

ix dut ob-zheud, daos lah. Daos nhaons-aub, doul
NEG$_1$ obtain NOM-edge die PRF die inside-water remain

beul daut-leb dionb deb nzhaod. Dionb deb nzhaod,
3 REFL-CLF lead child return lead child return

nzhaod shib ... naont beul naond ... beul naond ...
return it's thus 3 ASSOC 3 ASSOC

Niaox.nhaonl naond bod nhaons beul baox ninb
Nhaon ASSOC husband with 3 father at

bioud. Doul meib-Nhaonl jix nzhaod. "Meib-Nhaonl
home remain younger.sister-Nhaon NEG$_1$ return younger.sister-Nhaon

at zhaok lot aub monl oh, monl nghauk
SAT fall descend water go PART go bathe

aub at zhaok lot aub ah, at daos
water SAT fall descend water PART SAT die

lol oh." Naont shib ... meib-Nhaonl naond bod
come PART thus it's younger.sister-Nhaon ASSOC husband

kif. Kif deit nank.hauf.ix.dut. "Chauk-dib lah,
angry angry still there.is.nothing.to.be.done do-which PRF

chauk-dib monx lis gaons beul zhaok aub?" "Naont
do-which 2SG want give 3 fall water thus

beul nghauk aub ghad zhaok aub. Naont beul at
3 bathe water then$_2$ fall water thus 3 SAT

229 Note that in this line the narrator suddenly uses the second-person pronoun *monx* '2SG' to refer to the younger sister Niao Nhaon, while he still uses the third-person pronoun *beul* '3' to refer to the older sister Niao Mei. This sort of rapid switching of narrative viewpoint is quite common in texts produced by Xingyu Shi (the narrator of this folktale), but much less so in texts produced by other speakers.

daos monl diul aoh, daos naont bix.quf, naont
die go complete PART die thus sister's.husband thus

deb-geud daos meh, naont jix doul leb heut
DIM-younger.sibling die BCKG thus NEG$_1$ remain who help

monx khauf deb meh, naont wel heut monx khauf
2SG take.care.of child BCKG thus 1SG help 2SG take.care.of

deb diex. Monx leb dauk, monx dionb ix dut
child finish 2SG CLF REFL 2SG lead[230] NEG$_1$ obtain

deb-deb, deb-deb xub miex, naont wel heut monx
child-RED child-RED small person thus 1SG help 2SG

dionb." Naont shib ... yes.web naond deb shib jix dut
lead thus it's landlord ASSOC child it's NEG$_1$ obtain

ob-ped chauk. Dionb at dionb, jix dionb meh ...
NOM-matter do lead SAT lead NEG$_1$ lead BCKG

beul at dionb jix dut deb. Ob-naont dionb at
3 SAT lead NEG$_1$ obtain child NOM-thus lead SAT

dionb. Naont beul at chauk. Niaox.nhaonl ... Niaox.nhaonl
lead thus 3 SAT do Nhaon Nhaon

zhaok aub daos manh, Niaox.meib yab chauk beul naond
fall water die PART Mei also do 3 ASSOC

npaok. Chauk beul naond npaok leh, nhaons beul
woman do 3 ASSOC woman LEH with 3

chauk aod-bioud.
do one-CLF:home

'They arrived at the bathing spot, they arrived there and Niao Mei told Niao Nhaon to go bathe. [Niao Mei said:] "So go bathe, I'll hold your child for you. I'll bathe once you've finished." And so Niao Nhaon got ready to bathe. She went to the edge of the water, to the edge of the pool, and then Niao Mei pushed her. Niao Mei shoved her, and then – oh no! – Niao Nhaon fell into the water. Once she fell in, Niao Mei picked up a rock and threw it at Niao Nhaon, striking her. Niao Nhaon couldn't climb back up, and so she drowned. She drowned in the water, leaving only Niao Mei to bring her

---

230 The verb *dionb*, which occurs several dozen times in this text, can mean either 'to lead/guide/bring (someone to someplace)' or 'to raise/take care of (a child)' (cf. the Mandarin verb *dài* [带], which has a similar range of meaning). Still, *dionb* is consistently glossed as 'lead' when it occurs in this grammar.

[i.e. Niao Nhaon's] child back. She brought the child back, and then her ... her ... Niao Nhaon's husband and father were at home. They saw that little sister Nhaon hadn't returned. [Niao Mei said:] "Little sister Nhaon fell into the water, we went bathing and she fell into the water. She drowned." Then little sister Nhaon's husband was angry. He was angry, but there was nothing he could do. [He asked:] "How? How could you have let her fall into the water?" [Niao Mei answered:] "She was bathing and she just fell into the water. Now she's dead, she's dead, my sister's husband, my younger sister's dead. Now there's no one left to help you care for your child. I'll just help you care for the child, and that'll be that. You can't care for the child on your own, he's too young, so I'll help you care for him."[231] And so there was nothing else the landlord's son could do. He'd just let Niao Mei help him care for his child. If she didn't help him, he wouldn't be able to care for the child on his own. And so he'd just let Niao Mei help care for him. And so she did. Niao Nhaon had fallen into the water and drowned, so now Niao Mei would be his wife. She became his wife, and they became a family.'

Naont chauk bioud, Niaox.meib shib jaod miex guaot.
thus do CLF:home Mei it's bad person pass

Hnef-hnef choud nex naond deb monl jaont
CLF:day-CLF:day send NEX ASSOC child go herd

yul, hnef-hnef monl chaut chauk geud.donb. Beul
cow CLF:day-CLF:day go wilderness do work 3

leh, hnef-hnef ninb bioud jont konf. Deb-deb
LEH CLF:day-CLF:day at home sit free.time child-RED

nzhaod nonx hlit leh, zhaob hlit nanx
return eat cooked.rice LEH scoop.rice cooked.rice only

zhaob aod-naons-zhet. At jix heut nex zhaob
scoop.rice one-half.full-CLF:bowl SAT NEG$_1$ help NEX scoop.rice

bed zhet. Reib-yeus at gaons houd-deb
full bowl vegetable-cooked.meat SAT give CLF:mouthful-DIM

yut yut, heut daok houd-deb yut yut leh.
few few help take.food CLF:mouthful-DIM few few LEH

Jix nonx cauf lah. Deb-deb jix ncheut hlit, hnant
NEG$_1$ eat add PRF child-RED NEG$_1$ full cooked.rice call

231 While the gender of Niao Nhaon's child is not explicitly specified in this text itself, the narrator (Xingyu Shi) reported that the child is in fact male, and so references to the child in the author's free translations will use male pronouns.

yab yul cauf. Jix gaons cauf. Hnef-hnef choud
also again add NEG$_1$ give add CLF:day-CLF:day send

jaont yul, oh, jaod miex guaot. Minl xeb jaod miex
herd cow INTJ bad person pass mother new bad person

guaot. Naont shib ... deb-deb hnef-hnef jaont yul,
pass thus it's child-RED CLF:day-CLF:day herd cow

jaont dand leb ob-deind-aub manh, aod-tit beul
herd arrive CLF NOM-edge-water PART one-CLF:time$_3$ 3

minl zhaok aub leb ob-deind-aub dox. Jaont dand
mother fall water CLF NOM-edge-water that herd arrive

dox shib ... hnef-hnef jaont dand dox shib mex
that it's CLF:day-CLF:day herd arrive that it's exist

ngonl deb-naus. Ngonl deb-naus ... mex ngonl
CLF:animate DIM-bird CLF:animate DIM-bird exist CLF:animate

deb-naus shib ... zos ninb beul jaont daob-yul naond
DIM-bird it's land at 3 herd AN-cow ASSOC

sond-guaod-yul laot-gheul. Ngheub sad gaons beul dont.
bone-back-cow top-place$_2$ sing Xong.song give 3 listen

Ngheub sad gaons beul dont, yab yab hnant beul
sing Xong.song give 3 listen also also call 3

naond nbut, deb-deb naond nbut. Ngonl deb
ASSOC name child-RED ASSOC name CLF:animate child

shib mox.faob guaot: "Chauk-naonb naus at sheib ngheub
it's confused pass do-what bird SAT able.to sing

sad, ndiot wel nbut leb, at niab wel nbut?"
Xong.song recognize 1SG name who SAT say 1SG name

Deb-naus, hnef-hnef jont dox, hnef-hnef at
DIM-bird CLF:day-CLF:day sit that CLF:day-CLF:day SAT

ngheub hnef-hnef at lol, hnef-hnef niab
sing CLF:day-CLF:day SAT come CLF:day-CLF:day say

beul naond nbut.
3 ASSOC name

'So they became a family, but Niao Mei was a very wicked person. Every day she sent her husband's child out to herd the cows, every day she sent him out into the wilderness to work. But she, every day she stayed at home and relaxed. The child would return home to eat, but he would only be given a half-bowl of rice. She wouldn't even give him a full bowl. He would only receive a tiny little bit of meat and vegetables, she would only give him a tiny little bit. He wouldn't be given any more. The child wouldn't be able to eat his fill, and he would ask for more food, but he wouldn't be given any. Every day she would send him out to herd the cows – what a wicked person! [The child's] new mother was a very wicked person. And so ... every day the child would herd the cows, he would herd them to the water's edge, to the water's edge where his mother had fallen in. Every day he would herd them there, [and then one day] there was a little bird there. There was a little bird that landed on the back of a cow he was herding. It sang a Xong song for the child. It sang a Xong song for him, and it also called his name, the child's name. The child was confused, [and he thought to himself:] "How is the bird able to sing Xong songs? How does it know my name, and how is it even able to say my name?" Every day the little bird would sit there, every day it would come and sing, every day it would say his name.'

Beul nzhaod beul bod beul baox: "Baox! Aod-ngonl
3 return 3 tell 3 father father one-CLF:animate

deb-naus, wel jaont yul ninb dox mex ngonl
DIM-bird 1SG herd cow at that exist CLF:animate

naus hnef-hnef ngheub sad, hnef-hnef
bird CLF:day-CLF:day sing Xong.song CLF:day-CLF:day

at niab wel naond nbut. Jud niel chauk-naonb
SAT say 1SG ASSOC name NEG$_2$ know do-what

hnef-hnef at niab wel naond nbut." Naont beul
CLF:day-CLF:day SAT say 1SG ASSOC name thus 3

baox niab: "Yul hnef monx jaont monx ghad dionb
father say again CLF:day 2SG herd 2SG then$_2$ lead

nzhaod lol." Yul hnef wel jaont, aod-ngonl deb-naus
return come again CLF:day 1SG herd one-CLF:animate DIM-bird

yab ninb dox, deit ninb dox. Naont beul ah,
also at that still at that thus 3 PART

aod-ngonl naus zos ninb sond-guaod-yul beul jix
one-CLF:animate bird land at bone-back-cow 3 NEG$_1$

beinl ngonl deb-naus, jix eint sheub. Jix
frighten CLF:animate DIM-bird NEG$_1$ fly leave NEG$_1$

jit beul, dionb ngonl naus nzhaod. Dionb
chase.off 3 lead CLF:animate bird return lead

ngonl naus nzhaod, nzhaod dand bioud, beul baox
CLF:animate bird return return arrive home 3 father

noul keuf zhut ob-raonf. Keuf zhut ob-raonf-naus, gaons
catch shut reach NOM-cage shut reach NOM-cage-bird give

deb hlit, gaons deb aub. Soud, beul baox soud.
DIM cooked.rice give DIM water raise 3 father raise

Soud, keuf zhut nhaons-bioud, beul baox monl chauk. Doul
raise shut reach inside-home 3 father go do remain

Niaox.meib daut-leb ninb bioud, Niaox.meib ... manx.eib.manx.ab
Mei REFL-CLF at home Mei a.long.time.ago

ghad ndok ndeib. Niaox.meib ghad ndok ndeib, ndok
then$_2$ weave cloth Mei then$_2$ weave cloth weave

Niaox.nhaonl naond ndeib. Sout.gaont Niaox.nhaonl deit ndok
Nhaon ASSOC cloth before Nhaon still weave

ndeib xaond ndok diex. Deit doul ndeib, xaond ndok diex,
cloth not.yet weave finish still remain cloth not.yet weave finish

beul monl ndok saod.gud. Beul ndok, beul ghad jud
3 go weave finish.up 3 weave 3 then$_2$ NEG$_2$

sheib ndok, ndok dut ninx naond baol diul
able.to weave weave obtain NEX ASSOC break.down complete

khad yaod.yaod. Hant ob-zeif yaod det cef det
dry all CLF:PL NOM-thread all break ??? break

diul. Aod-ngonl deb-naus niab beul:
complete one-CLF:animate DIM-bird say 3

"Aod.ngonl.det.jox.shaond." Beul kif guaot leh, gox gox
???[232] 3 angry pass LEH do do

232 As was mentioned above, the narrator of this text (Xingyu Shi) was only able to assist with the analysis of its first quarter or so. None of the other three consultants who assisted with the analysis

at ndok ix dut cauf, at lis kif cauf.
SAT weave NEG$_1$ obtain add SAT want angry add

Aod-ngonl naus yab lis niab beul, beul kif guaot.
one-CLF:animate bird also want say 3 3 angry pass

Beul mex ob-biaod, beul beux ngonl naus, geud
3 exist NOM-club 3 hit CLF:animate bird hold

ngonl naus beux daos. Beux daos giab nonx.
CLF:animate bird hit die hit die stir.fry eat

"Pik.shid. Wel ndok, ndok ix dut. Kif daos
little.bastard 1SG weave weave NEG$_1$ obtain angry die

kif seinb, yab lis niab wel cauf, giab monx
angry live also want say 1SG add stir.fry 2SG

nonx. Puk hliof giab monx nonx."
eat speak many stir.fry 2SG eat

'The child returned home and told his father: "Father! There's a little bird, I was herding cows out there and there was a bird that sings Xong songs every day, that says my name every day. I don't know why it says my name every day." And so his father said: "Next time when you go herding, lead the bird back here with you." The next time the child went herding, the little bird was there again, it was still there. And so, when the bird landed on the back of a cow, the child didn't frighten it, and it didn't fly away. The child didn't chase the bird off, he led it back, back to his home. His father caught the bird and shut it in a cage. He shut it in a birdcage, and [every day] he would give it a little bit of rice and a little bit of water. He raised the bird [as a pet]. [One day] he left the bird in the house, and he went out to work. Only Niao Mei was left at home, and Niao Mei ... she used to be able to weave cloth. She used to be able to weave cloth, so she [tried to] weave Niao Nhaon's cloth. Before, Niao Nhaon had started weaving some cloth, but she hadn't finished. She'd left some cloth behind, some unfinished cloth, so Niao Mei went to finish weaving it.

She started weaving, and then all of a sudden she wasn't able to weave. In trying to weave it, she managed to ruin all of Niao Nhaon's cloth. The threads were all snapped and broken. The little bird said to her: "*Ao ngon de jo shaon.*" Niao Mei became very angry. No matter how she tried, she couldn't weave the cloth, and now she was very angry. And now the bird was mocking her, too. She was enraged. She took a club and

of the remainder were able to understand the meaning of the phrase *aod.ngonl.det.jox.shaond* here, though based on context they all agreed that it was intended as mockery or criticism of Niao Mei by the bird.

struck the bird with it, she killed the bird with it. She killed the bird and cooked it. [She said:] "You little bastard. I couldn't weave the cloth. I was so angry, and you had to mock me, too. I'll cook you and eat you. If you're going to talk so much I'll cook you and eat you."'

Giab nonx leh, beul naond bod leh, deb-deb
stir.fry eat LEH 3 ASSOC husband LEH child-RED

naond baox nzhaod lol leh, nonx hlit nzod,
ASSOC father return come LEH eat cooked.rice early

nonx niax-naus. "It, monx gaons banb nins naonb
eat meat-bird SPRS 2SG give CLF:some COP what

yeus oh?" "Niax-naus." "Monx zhaos dib dut
cooked.meat PART meat-bird 2SG from which obtain

niax-naus?" "Aod-ngonl naus beux daos geud giab nonx."
meat-bird one-CLF:animate bird hit die hold stir.fry eat

"Chauk-dib monx lis beux daos? Aod-ngonl naus
do-which 2SG want hit die one-CLF:animate bird

raut baod raut, wel soud raut baod raut, monx
good quite good 1SG raise good quite good 2SG

lis beux daos." "Nh. Wel ndok ndeib, ndok ix
want hit die uh.huh 1SG weave cloth weave NEG$_1$

dut, beul at lis niab wel cauf, wel beux beul
obtain 3 SAT want say 1SG add 1SG hit 3

nonx." Beul naond ngonl nint, nank.hauf.ix.dut,
eat 3 ASSOC CLF:animate man there.is.nothing.to.be.done

beul naond ngonl nint, beul nonx. "Raut nonx
3 ASSOC CLF:animate man 3 eat good eat

guaot leh! Heif, raut nonx guaot." "Raut nonx, raut nonx
pass LEH INTJ good eat pass good eat good eat

hint ah, raut nonx gaons wel giat shaod leh."
very PART good eat give 1SG share try LEH

Niaox.meib ghad shaod leh. Shaod leh, sat jaok beul
Mei then$_2$ try LEH try LEH SAT prick 3

ghaod.lot, jaok beul ghaod.lot, giaot zhut aod-houd
mouth prick 3 mouth chew reach one-CLF:mouthful

meh.	*At*	*deink*	*git,*	*beul*	*at*	*faox*	*kif.*
BCKG	SAT	fill.up.with	anger	3	SAT	become	angry

“Wel	*biat*	*box.nhol.”*	*Beul*	*naond*	*ngonl,*	*hmaont-dius,*
1SG	pour	throw.away	3	ASSOC	CLF:animate	evening-???

beul	*naond*	*ngonl*	*nint*	*nzhaod,*	*beul*	*naond*
3	ASSOC	CLF:animate	man	return	3	ASSOC

bod	*nzhaod.*	*Yab*	*nes*	*beul:*	*“Zhet*	*niax-naus*
husband	return	also	ask	3	CLF:bowl	meat-bird

leh?	*Nieux.ghoub*	*wel*	*xaond*	*nonx*	*diul.”*	*“Niax-naus*	*wel*
LEH	just.now	1SG	not.yet	eat	complete	meat-bird	1SG

biat	*box.nhol*	*manh,*	*nonx*	*zhus*	*aod-houd*	*ah,*
pour	throw.away	PART	eat	suffer	one-CLF:mouthful	PART

jaok	*wel*	*ghaod.lot,*	*biat*	*box.nhol.”*	*“Ih,*	*zhet*
prick	1SG	mouth	pour	throw.away	DSMY$_1$	CLF:bowl

niax-naus	*doud.doub*	*raut*	*nonx,*	*monx*	*lis*	*biat*	*box.nhol,*
meat-bird	extremely	good	eat	2SG	want	pour	throw.away

zod.guaod	*lah.*	*Zod.guaod!”*	*“Wel*	*nonx*	*jaok*	*wel*	*ghaod.lot,*
what.a.pity	PRF	what.a.pity	1SG	eat	prick	1SG	mouth

biat	*box.nhol.”*	*“Monx*	*biat*	*dib?”*	*“Wel*	*biat*	*geud-neul*
pour	throw.away	2SG	pour	which	1SG	pour	place$_1$-front

dox,	*biat*	*zheit-zhauf*	*dox.”*
that	pour	outside-door	that

‘She cooked the bird, and then her husband, the child’s father, came home. He ate some of the bird meat for breakfast. [He said:] “Hey, what’s this dish that you gave me?” [Niao Mei answered:] “It’s bird meat.” [Her husband asked:] “Where did you get bird meat from?” [She answered:] “I killed that bird [of yours] and cooked it.” [Her husband said:] “How could you kill it? That bird was fine, I was raising it quite well, and you had to kill it.” [She replied:] “Uh-huh. I tried to weave some cloth, but I couldn’t do it, and the bird was mocking me. I killed it so we could eat it.” There was nothing her husband could do, so he ate the bird. [He said:] “Delicious! Mmm, this is delicious.” [Niao Mei said:] “If it’s delicious, if it’s that delicious, then let me try it.” And so she tried it. She tried it, and [the bird’s bones] pricked her mouth, they pricked her mouth as she had a bite. She became enraged, she became very angry. [She said:] “I’m throwing it away.” In the evening, her husband came home [again]. He asked her: “Where did that bowl of bird meat go? I hadn’t finished eating it before.” [She replied:] “I threw the bird meat away. I had a bite and it pricked my mouth, so I threw it away." [Her husband said:] "Oh no, that bowl of bird meat was so delicious, and you had to go and throw it away. What a pity. What a pity!" [Niao Mei said:] "It pricked my mouth when I ate it, so I threw it away." [Her husband asked:] "Where did you throw it away?" [She answered:] "I threw it out in front there, outside the door there."'

Oh,	*beul*	*monl*	*nkhed,*	*biat*	*zhut*	*khauk*	*dox*	*dand*
INTJ	3	go	look	pour	reach	CLF:place$_2$	that	grow

del	*hlod.*	*Dand*	*del*	*hlod,*	*beul*
CLF:rigid.length	bamboo	grow	CLF:rigid.length	bamboo	3

monl	*ntous.*	*Mok*	*mok*	*mok*	*mok,*	*aod-del*	*hlod*
go	touch	touch	touch	touch	touch	one-CLF:rigid.length	bamboo

liox	*hint*	*leh.*	*Niaox.meib,*	*sat*	*lol*	*ntous.*	*Sat*	*lol*
big	very	LEH	Mei	SAT	come	touch	SAT	come

pieut	*aod-del*	*hlod.*	*Pieut*	*aod-doul,*	*sat*
stroke	one-CLF:rigid.length	bamboo	stroke	one-CLF:hand	SAT

jaok	*beul*	*ob-doul.*	*Beul*	*yab*	*kif,*	*beul*	*yab*	*mex*
prick	3	NOM-hand	3	also	angry	3	also	exist

ob-mok,	*beul*	*yab*	*daud*	*id-det.*	*Daud*	*id-det*
NOM-sickle	3	also	cut	DID-break	cut	DID-break

shib,	*beul*	*naond*	*bod*	*yab:*	*"Ih,*	*chauk-dib*	*monx*
it's	3	ASSOC	husband	also	DSMY$_1$	do-which	2SG

at	*lis*	*daud*	*id-det*	*lah,*	*dand*	*ghoub*	*hlod*
SAT	want	cut	DID-break	PRF	grow	CLF:flexible.length	bamboo

raut	*baod*	*raut,*	*monx*	*lis*	*daud*	*id-det."*	*"Ntous*
good	quite	good	2SG	want	cut	DID-break	touch

aod-doul	*jaok*	*aod-doul,*	*jaok*	*wel*	*ob-doul.*	*Jix*
one-CLF:hand	prick	one-CLF:hand	prick	1SG	NOM-hand	NEG$_1$

daud	*id-det?*	*Daud*	*beul*	*id-det*	*diex."*	*Daud*	*id-det,*
cut	DID-break	cut	3	DID-break	finish	cut	DID-break

beul	*bod*	*shib*	*xeut*	*daos*	*guaot.*	*Beul*	*bod*
3	husband	it's	mournful	die	pass	3	husband

yab	*...*	*kheut*	*leb*	*baod-god-hlod.*	*Did-saonb*	*id-saonb,*
also		get	CLF	BUG-stump-bamboo	DID-carve	DID-carve

id-xaok	*id-xaok,*	*diex*	*leb*	*deb-ras.*	*Diex*	*leb*	*ras*
DID-peel	DID-peel	finish	CLF	DIM-comb	finish	CLF	comb

beul	*geud*	*njis*	*bieid.*	*Naonb.naont*	*raut*	*njis*	*hint,*
3	hold	comb[233]	head	thus	good	comb	very

beul	*niab:*	*"Raut*	*njis*	*hint*	*leh."*	*Niaox.meib*	*niab:*	*"Raut*
3	say	good	comb	very	LEH	Mei	say	good

njis	*hint*	*aoh,*	*raut*	*njis*	*gaons*	*wel*	*giat*	*shaod*
comb	very	PART	good	comb	give	1SG	share	try

dieud."	*Niaox.meib*	*at*	*lol*	*shaod*	*aod-doul,*	*at*
CLF:time$_2$	Mei	SAT	come	try	one-CLF:hand	SAT

gheud	*nkhoud*	*beul*	*naond*	*bib,*	*det*	*beul*	*naond*
get.stuck	fall.out	3	ASSOC	hair	break	3	ASSOC

bib.	*Yab*	*kif*	*guaot*	*meh,*	*beul*	*yab*	*meb*	*monx*	*naond*
hair	also	angry	pass	BCKG	3	also	take	2SG	ASSOC

geud	*ob*	*monl*	*aoh.*
hold	burn	go	PART

'So, he went to look, and where the bird meat had been thrown out there had grown a bamboo plant. There had grown a bamboo plant, and he went to feel it. He touched it over and over and over again. It was quite a large bamboo plant. Niao Mei came to feel the bamboo plant too. She felt it, and it pricked her hand. She became angry. She took a sickle and cut the bamboo plant down. She cut it down, and her husband said: "Oh no, how could you cut it down? That bamboo plant was just fine, and still you had to cut it down." [Niao Mei replied:] "As soon as I felt it, it pricked me, it pricked my hand. [How could I] not cut it down? I cut it down, and that's that." After she cut it down, her husband was very depressed. He then took the bamboo stump, and he carved it and carved it, he pared it and pared it. He made a little comb [out of it]. He made a comb and then combed his hair with it. The comb was great, and so he said: "This is a great comb."[234] Niao Mei said: "If it's a great comb, if it's such a great comb, then let me try it for a bit." So she tried it for a bit, but it got tangled in her hair, it pulled her hair out. She became enraged again, and she took the comb to go burn it.'

233 To avoid confusion in this and subsequent sections, the reader should note that while *njis* and *ras* are both glossed as 'comb', *njis* is a verb meaning 'to comb', while *ras* (sometimes preceded by one of several nominal prefixes) is a noun meaning '(a) comb'.

234 A more literal, if more awkward, translation of the sequence *raut njis hint* [good comb very] would be '(this comb) is very good for combing'. See also the previous footnote immediately above.

Yab ob leh, beul naond bod yab niab lis
also burn LEH 3 ASSOC husband also say want

chaot ras njis bieid. "Ob-ras ninb dof? Monx
look.for comb comb head NOM-comb at which 2SG

tout wel naond bat dof? Nieux.ghoub monx njis
pick.up 1SG ASSOC put which just.now 2SG comb

monl diul." "Bat ninb dof? Monx leb minl-ras njis
go complete put at which 2SG CLF AUG-comb comb

dut wel bib at gheud res. Wel ob manh."
obtain 1SG hair SAT get.stuck remove 1SG burn PART

"Ih, chauk-dib monx lis ob lah, wel dut naonb
DSMY$_1$ do-which 2SG want burn PRF 1SG obtain what

monx at baol wel naond, dut naonb at
2SG SAT break.down 1SG ASSOC obtain what SAT

baol." "Wel njis at gheud nkhoud wel naond
break.down 1SG comb SAT get.stuck fall.out 1SG ASSOC

bib, wel ghad ob ah. Jaod daos jaod seinb."
hair 1SG then$_2$ burn PART bad die bad live

"Monx ob ninb dib?" "Ob khauk ib-deul dox."
2SG burn at which burn CLF:place$_2$ LOC-fire that

"Gieb diul loh?" "Gieb diul lah." Beul monl ghat
burnt complete PART burnt complete PRF 3 go go.to

khauk deul did-fand did-fand. Fand fand,
CLF:place$_2$ fire DID-turn.over DID-turn.over turn.over turn.over

deit doul del ob-xed-ras. Kox.kob doul
still remain CLF:rigid.length NOM-tooth-comb only remain

del ob-xed-ras, doul hant gieb
CLF:rigid.length NOM-tooth-comb remain CLF:PL burnt

diul khad. Tout diet ob-xed-ras, beul geud
complete dry pick.up hide NOM-tooth-comb 3 hold

diet lah. Beul nchaok zhut khauk-roub, diet. Diet
hide PRF 3 insert reach hole-stone hide hide

monl shib ... diet zhut dox, yul dob
go it's hide reach that again CLF:occurrence

aod-del ob-xed-ras dox ghad doub nins
one-CLF:rigid.length NOM-tooth-comb that then$_2$ then$_1$ COP

Niaox.nhaonl.
Nhaon

'She burned it, and then her husband said he was looking for the comb. [He asked:] "Where is the comb? Where did you put it? Just now you went to comb your hair." [Niao Mei replied:] "Where is it? That wonderful comb of yours was tearing my hair out. I burned it." [Her husband said:] "Oh no, how could you burn it? Whatever I get you destroy, whatever I get you destroy." [Niao Mei said:] "It tore my hair out when I was combing with it, so I just burned it. It was an awful, awful [comb]." [Her husband asked:] "Where did you burn it?" [She answered:] "In the fire-pit." [He asked:] "Did you burn the whole thing?" [She answered:] "I did." Her husband went to the fire-pit and poked through it. He poked through it, and [he found that] only a single tooth of the comb remained. There was only a single tooth of the comb left, the rest of it had all burned away. He picked up the comb-tooth and hid it. He stuck it into a hole in the stone [walls of their home], hiding it. He hid it and ... he hid it there, and then soon the comb-tooth [turned into] Niao Nhaon.'

Niaox.nhaonl ah, zhaos del ob-xed-ras dox
Nhaon PART from CLF:rigid.length NOM-tooth-comb that

bianb diex Niaox.nhaonl leh, heut beul geud bioud
change.into finish Nhaon LEH help 3 sweep home

ah, geud bix.giab. Mh, beul hnef-hnef nzhaod,
PART sweep yard INTJ 3 CLF:day-CLF:day return

hnef-hnef chauk-dib leb bix.giab nqif jel.jel,
CLF:day-CLF:day do-which CLF yard clean IDEO:A:shiningly

nhaons-bioud nqif jel.jel. Beul nes: "Niaox.meib,
inside-home clean IDEO:A:shiningly 3 ask Mei

nins monx geud yaox?" "Jix nins." Jix nins naont shib
COP 2SG sweep right? NEG$_1$ COP NEG$_1$ COP thus it's

mox.faob, hnef-hnef heut geud, hnef-hnef heut
confused CLF:day-CLF:day help sweep CLF:day-CLF:day help

geud nqif. Yul hnef shib beul shaod ghaonb. Beul
sweep clean again CLF:day it's 3 try spy 3

zhaonb monl chauk, beul jix monl, beul raok
pretend go do 3 NEG$_1$ go 3 hide.oneself

id-qaod, beul ghaonb. Oh, zhaos leb ob-def
DID-conceal 3 spy INTJ from CLF NOM-place

manx diet leb ob-xed-ras dox bionl ngonl
REL hide CLF NOM-tooth-comb that exit CLF:animate

deb-npaok, nins Niaox.nhaonl bionl lol heut beul geud
DIM-woman COP Nhaon exit come help 3 sweep

bioud, geud bix.giab, naont beul ghans, ghans nins
home sweep yard thus 3 see see COP

beul Niaox.nhaonl. Naont beul doub kaot leh, jix gaons
3 Nhaon thus 3 then$_1$ stop LEH NEG$_1$ give

sheub, jix gaons nzhaod ghat leb khauk-roub dox.
leave NEG$_1$ give return go.to CLF hole-stone that

'Niao Nhaon changed from the comb-tooth back into herself, and she swept the house and yard for them. Every day she came back, and every day, no matter what, she'd make the house and yard sparkling clean. The husband asked: "Niao Mei, it's you who's been doing the sweeping, right?" [She replied:] "No, it's not." Since it wasn't her, the husband was confused. Every day someone was sweeping for them, they were sweeping the place clean for them. One day the husband decided to spy [on the person doing the sweeping]. He pretended to go out to work, but he didn't really go. He hid himself and spied. From the place where he'd hidden the comb-tooth there appeared a young woman, it was Niao Nhaon coming out to sweep the house and yard for them. And so he saw, he saw that it was his Niao Nhaon. And so he stopped her, he didn't let her leave. He didn't let her go back to the hole in the stone [wall].'

Jix gaons nzhaod shib ... leud-Nhaonl shib jix nzhaod.
NEG$_1$ give return it's FAM-Nhaon it's NEG$_1$ return

Niab: "Ih, gaons wel nbanx monx tit naont
say DSMY$_1$ give 1SG think 2SG CLF:time$_3$ thus

loux leh, wel liaos monx. Wel nbanx-gieb monx
long.time LEH 1SG miss 2SG 1SG think-??? 2SG

daos. Monx manh, jix daos. Jix daos naont monx ghad
die 2SG PART NEG$_1$ die NEG$_1$ die thus 2SG then$_2$

yul nzhaod. Monx jont diex." "Wel jont chauk-dib
again return 2SG live finish 1SG live do-which

jont dut ah? Boub jed at ninb, wel at
live obtain PART 1PL older.sister SAT at 1SG SAT

ninb. Boub jed deit nins, yul hnef deit nins
at 1PL older.sister still COP again CLF:day still COP

hat wel id-daos naond." Mh, beul naond bod
harm 1SG DID-die ASSOC INTJ 3 ASSOC husband

niab deux: "Naonb.naont boub-leb nbanx leb banb.faox
say QUOT thus 1PL-DU think CLF solution

geud beul daot id-daos diex." "Monx nbanx naonb
hold 3 kill DID-die finish 2SG think what

banb.faox raut lah?" "Nbanx leb banb.faox, boub ghad
solution good PRF think CLF solution 1PL then$_2$

xaont leb banb.faox, jeub laus beul."
think CLF solution then$_3$ trick 3

'He didn't let her go back and so ... Niao Nhaon didn't go back. [Her husband] said: "Oh, you made me miss you for such a long time. I've missed you. I thought you were dead. But you, you're not dead. And since you're not dead, then just come back. You'll live [here], and that'll be that." [Niao Nhaon replied:] "How can I live here? My older sister would be here, and I'd be here too. My older sister would still – one of these days she'd still try to kill me." Then her husband said: "Then let's the two of us think of a way to kill her instead." [Niao Nhaon asked:] "What way do you think is best?" [Her husband replied:] "[Hmm,] think of a way, we need to think of a way, to trick her ... "'

Oh, naont beul naond, Niaox.nhaonl naond, beul
INTJ thus 3 ASSOC Nhaon ASSOC 3

bod laus beul jed. Nggut leh oh, aod-leb
husband trick 3 older.sister enter LEH PART one-CLF

deb-ob-raonf-naus, bid.deux nins ob-naonb. Chauk guab
DIM-NOM-cage-bird or COP NOM-what do pretend

niab: "Monx nggut neind, boub ndax monx." Oh, beul
say 2SG enter this 1PL lift.up 2SG INTJ 3

nggut nggut nggut ghat nhaons. "Wel doub ntet."
enter enter enter go.to inside 1SG then$_1$ put.lid.on

Ntet doub keuf lah, keuf oub-meinl doub ndax
put.lid.on then$_1$ shut PRF shut two-CLF:person then$_1$ lift.up

beul, wanx lot, wanx lot nhaons, wanx lot
3 throw descend throw descend inside throw descend

aub	*oh.*	*Beul,*	*Niaox.meib*	*daos*	*miex*	*ah,*	*doul*
water	PART	3	Mei	die	person	PART	remain

Niaox.nhaonl	*leh,*	*Niaox.nhaonl*	*leh,*	*nzhaod*	*lol*	*lah,*	*ox*
Nhaon	LEH	Nhaon	LEH	return	come	PRF	and

beul	*naond*	*bod*	*lah,*	*ox*	*deb-deb.*	*Ob-naont*
3	ASSOC	husband	PRF	and	child-RED	NOM-thus

Niaox.meib	*daos.*	*Geud-zheit*	*doul*	*Niaox.nhaonl*	*ox*	*beul*
Mei	die	place$_1$-back	remain	Nhaon	and	3

naond	*bod,*	*geud-zheit*	*doub*	*doul*	*manx*	*raut*
ASSOC	husband	place$_1$-back	then$_1$	remain	REL	good

lex	*lah.*	*Diul*	*khad*	*lah.*
only	PRF	complete	dry	PRF

‘And so her – Niao Nhaon’s – her husband would trick the older sister. [He would have the older sister] climb into a little bird cage, or something like that. He tricked her by saying: “Climb in here, we’ll carry you around.” So she climbed inside. [The husband said:] “Now I’ll put on the lid.” He put on the lid and shut it. Once it was shut, the two of them [i.e. Niao Nhaon and her husband] lifted the older sister up and then threw her down, they threw her down into the water. Niao Mei died, leaving Niao Nhaon behind. And as for Niao Nhaon, she came back to live with her husband and child. And so it was that Niao Mei died. From then on it was just Niao Nhaon and her husband, from then on there were only good things [for them].

The end.’

Text 2 *Tooth conversation*

The following is a transcription of a six-minute casual Xong conversation recorded on November 4th, 2013, with accompanying interlinear glosses and free translations. There were three participants in the conversation: Chenghua Long from Shanjiang Town, Haili Shi from Yankan Village, and Shixiang Wu from Zhuigaolai Village. All three participants are female teachers at the primary school in La'ershan, and all three are among the author's primary Xong-speaking consultants. The conversation was recorded with all three participants sitting around a small table in Chenghua Long's home, which is located on the campus of the primary school where the participants teach. All three participants are close friends and regularly spend time with each other outside of the elicitation sessions conducted by the author. For more information on these three participants and their hometowns, see Sections 2.6.2 and 2.7.1.

The reader will quickly see that the free translation of each utterance has been made as informal and natural-sounding as possible. This is in contrast to the approach taken in Text 1 (*Oub Meinl Yaos Geud*), where slightly more formal, more literal translations were deliberately used, but it seemed appropriate given the casual register of the conversation and the close personal relationships among its three participants. In order to make these free translations sound sufficiently natural, it was often necessary to translate certain Xong forms (especially those that primarily serve discourse-pragmatic functions) differently in different utterances, though these forms were still always given consistent glosses. It was also often necessary to add in certain English forms that had no equivalents in the original Xong material, in particular for elided arguments (see Section 9.2.2).

Explanatory comments have been kept to a minimum, though when unavoidable they are given in square brackets from the speaker's point of view (e.g. "[my husband]" rather than "[the speaker's husband]"). The punctuation used in the Xong transcription and the English translation of each utterance often differ from each other (for the same reasons described in the previous paragraph), but in general a comma represents a short pause, a period a longer pause, an ellipsis (< ... >) an even longer pause or an instance in which the speaker trailed off while considering what to say next, and an em dash (<–>) an instance in which the speaker stopped speaking suddenly, either of her own volition or because she was cut off by another speaker.

(Begin text.)

Haili: *Wel kit, aoh? ... Aod-roul neind yab*
1SG begin PART one-CLF:time$_1$ this also

jud dut def puk.
NEG$_2$ obtain place speak
'So I guess I'll begin?...I don't know what to talk about this time either.'

Chenghua:	*Nieux-hmaont*	*lah.*
	yester-CLF:evening	PRF

'Talk about last night.'

Haili:	*Wel*	*at*	*jix*	*nins*	*nieux-hmaont,*	*at*
	1SG	SAT	NEG$_1$	COP	yester-CLF:evening	SAT

loux	*ob-hmaont*	*daos*	*lah,*	*diex*
long.time	NOM-evening	die	PRF	finish

bub-bieib-hmaont.
three-four-CLF:evening

'It's not just last night, it's been a whole bunch of nights now, three or four whole nights.'

Chenghua:	*Mb*	*dianx*	*bub-bieib-hmaont*	*lah?*
	hurt	finish	three-four-CLF:evening	PRF

'It's been hurting for three or four nights now?'

Haili:	*Mb*	*diex*	*bub-bieib-hmaont.*
	hurt	finish	three-four-CLF:evening

Noub-hmaont	*wel*	*roul-roul,*	*wel*
day.before.yesterday-CLF:evening	1SG	CLF:time$_1$-CLF:time$_1$	1SG

beut,	*beut,*	*beut*	*jix*	*nggueb.*	*Wel,*	*wel*
lie.down	lie.down	lie.down	NEG$_1$	sleep	1SG	1SG

puk,	*wel*	*niab,*	*yab*	*jix*	*dut*	*lot*	*haond*
speak	1SG	say	also	NEG$_1$	obtain	descend	bottom

monl	*nieus*	*nggaob.*	*Gank.ceib*	*geud*	*shoux.jik*	*deib*
go	buy	medicine	simply	hold	cell.phone	at

Bes.doub	*caof*	*dieud.*	*At*	*jix*	*lis*	*kiak*
Baidu	search	CLF:time$_2$	SAT	NEG$_1$	want	open

dieb.nox,	*at*	*giet.xeb*	*geud*	*shoux.jik,*	*aod*
computer	SAT	convenient	hold	cell.phone	as.soon.as

caof	*doub*	*bank.yeb*	*naond*	*lah,*	*aod-died.zhonk.*
search	then$_1$	midnight	ASSOC	PRF	one-CLF:o'clock

Aod-died.zhonk,	*chad,*	*chad*	*geud*	*shoux.jik*	*caof,*
one-CLF:o'clock	not.until	not.until	hold	cell.phone	search

aod	*caof,*	*ab*	*kox.ix*	*geud*	*shand,*	*ab*	*kox.ix*
as.soon.as	search	also	can	hold	ginger	also	can

geud bid-ghaond, ab kox.ix geud weib.jink, yaox?
hold FRT-garlic also can hold MSG right?

Aod-banb neind yaod.yaod zhix tonb naond.
one-CLF:some this all cure pain ASSOC

Aod-banb neind nins zeib jex.bieb,
one-CLF:some this COP most simple.and.convenient

zeib jex.jef naond yaox?
most quick.and.easy ASSOC right?
'It's been hurting for three or four nights. The night before last I just couldn't get to sleep. I say – I'm telling you, I didn't have the chance to go down [to the main street in La'ershan, downhill from where I live] to buy medicine. I just used my cell phone to search on [the popular Chinese search engine] Baidu for a while. I didn't even need to turn on the computer, it was easy enough to just search on my cell phone. I started searching and then all of a sudden it was the middle of the night, one o'clock. So it was already one o'clock by the time I started searching. As soon as I searched I found out you could use ginger, you could use garlic, you could use MSG [i.e. monosodium glutamate], all of these things can be used as painkillers. These things are the simplest, the easiest, right?'

Shixiang: *Nh, mx shaod shaod, mx geud chauk-dib naont*
uh.huh 2SG try try 2SG hold do-which thus

shaod?
try
'Uh-huh, so you tried it, so how did you try?'

Haili: *Kox.ix, kox.ix jeub.dib.qix.cef ih.*
can can use.materials.at.hand EMPH
'You can – you can just make use of what you've already got.'[235]

Shixiang: *Nh.*
uh.huh
'Uh-huh.'

235 The tetrasyllabic form *jeub.dib.qix.cef* in this line is a borrowing of a Chinese idiom meaning 'to use materials one already has at hand, to draw on local resources'. The idiom in question is *jiùdìqǔcái* (就地取材) in Standard Mandarin.

Chenghua: *Aob-naonb ghaod raut?*
NOM-what more good
'What works best?'

Shixiang: *Naont mx geud gians dib zhaut?*
thus 2SG hold CLF:kind$_1$ which cure
'So which one did you use to fix your tooth?'

Haili: *Naont wel doub geud shand, shand doub kox.ix*
thus 1SG then$_1$ hold ginger ginger then$_1$ can

geud ghaod.lot, aod giaot aos.il, ...
hold mouth as.soon.as chew DSMY$_2$

sout-cif hant, nonx shand nqat,
past.few-CLF:occurrence CLF:PL eat ginger fear

aod-hmaont dox wel heit giaot shand at
one-CLF:evening that 1SG still chew ginger SAT

mieil, wel eit taf, wel deit raut taf.
spicy 1SG still endure 1SG still good endure
'So I took the ginger – you can put it in your mouth – and as soon as I chewed it...man, the past few times, when I ate ginger I'd be afraid [that it would be too spicy]. That evening when I ate the ginger it was still spicy, but I just toughed it out, and actually I toughed it out pretty well.'

Shixiang: *Naont raut jix raut?*
thus good NEG$_1$ good
'So did it work?'

Haili: *Naont wel doub, wel khauk neind ob-xed*
thus 1SG then$_1$ 1SG CLF:place$_2$ this NOM-tooth

tonk leb khauk-khauk, wel aod giaot
pass.through CLF hole-RED 1SG as.soon.as chew

leux deb naont wel doub geud, geud hant
shatter DIM thus 1SG then$_1$ hold hold CLF:PL

shand doub gox ghat leb khauk-khauk doub,
ginger then$_1$ do go.to CLF hole-RED then$_1$

ghab id-nchot lah. Ghab id-nchot tit-deb
bite DID-tight PRF bite DID-tight CLF:time$_3$-DIM

ghad raut lah.
then$_2$ good PRF
'So I – my tooth here had gotten a little hole in it, and as soon as I chewed the ginger the tooth cracked a little bit, so I just took the ginger and stuck it into the hole. Then I bit down tight on it. After I'd bitten down tight on it for a little while I started to feel better.'

Shixiang: *Nh.*
uh.huh
'Uh-huh.'

Haili: *Ghab id-nchot naont wel, aod-dieud-deb doub*
bite DID-tight thus 1SG one-CLF:time$_2$-DIM then$_1$

hnaond ghaod raut. Wel kox.ix, wel doub
feel more good 1SG can 1SG then$_1$

beut lah. Ranf.houb, nieux-hnef, nex ab
lie.down PRF afterward yester-CLF:day NEX also

heut wel nieus dut aod-zhit nggaob.
help 1SG buy obtain one-CLF:tube medicine

Sat nins geud maond zhut leb
SAT COP hold hold.in.mouth reach CLF

khauk-khauk dox. Ranf.houb tit-deb naont
hole-RED that afterward CLF:time$_3$-DIM thus

yab geud aub yeil, yaox?
also hold water rinse right?
'So I bit down tight, and after a little while I started to feel better. I was able to go to sleep. Afterward, yesterday, he [i.e. my husband] bought some medicine for me, too. I put it in my mouth where the hole in my tooth was. A little while later I rinsed my mouth with water, right?'

Shixiang: *Nh. Nins naonb nggaob?*
uh.huh COP what medicine
'Uh-huh. What kind of medicine was it?'

Haili: *Danb.shib jix qix.zob.yonb.*
but NEG$_1$ effective
'But it didn't work.'

Chenghua: *Monx naond aob-xand daont khauk nins*
2SG ASSOC NOM-tooth pass.through hole COP

zhus daob-ginb konk aoh?
suffer AN-bug burrow PART
'Maybe it was a bug that made that hole in your tooth?'

Haili: *Jix nins zhus daob-ginb konk.*
NEG$_1$ COP suffer AN-bug burrow
'It's not a bug.'

Chenghua: *Nins aob-naonb?*
COP NOM-what
'Then what is it?'

Haili: *Nins, nqat nins manx, yaof.inf mex deb*
COP fear COP um... gums exist DIM

baol.
break.down
'It's – I'm afraid it's, um...that there's a problem with my gums.'

Chenghua: *Seink.cheinf beul deit nins zhus daob-ginb konk,*
naturally 3 still COP suffer AN-bug burrow

ix konk beul hauk-dib dut daont?
NEG$_1$ burrow 3 do-which obtain pass.through
'Well, logically, it must be that there's a bug in your tooth, otherwise how would there be a hole there?'

Haili: *Hant niel nins daob-ginb konk ix nins.*
CLF:PL know COP AN-bug burrow NEG$_1$ COP

Fanx.zheinb aod-leb khauk-khauk dox loux
anyway one-CLF hole-RED that long.time

hint, wel ghad nanx.gaond hnant nex
very 1SG then$_2$ can't.be.bothered.to call NEX

Shif.jek nex lol heut gox.
PN NEX come help do
'Who knows if it's a bug or not. Anyway that hole's been there for a long time, I couldn't be bothered to ask Shi Je [the dentist] to take care of it.'

Shixiang: *Nbaod beul huel.zex zheb beul sheub.*
fill.in 3 or.STND pull.out 3 leave
'Either get it filled in or pull it out.'

Chenghua: *Monx ix gaons nex zheb ghaod nieud?*
2SG NEG$_1$ give NEX pull.out more simple
'Wouldn't it be easier to just have someone pull it out?'

Haili:	*Wel*	*jix*	*zheb.*	*Wel*	*sout-hnef*	*wel*
	1SG	NEG$_1$	pull.out	1SG	past.few-CLF:day	1SG

jix	*mb*	*lah.*
NEG$_1$	hurt	PRF

'I'm not going to get it pulled out. The past few days it hasn't hurt.'

Shixiang:	*Nonx*	*zhaus*	*naonb?*
	eat	suffer	what

'What did you eat?'

Haili:	*Wel*	*doub*	*nins*	*aod-hnef*	*dox,*	*wel*
	1SG	then$_1$	COP	one-CLF:day	that	1SG

nonx	*leb*	*jik.zaox.zaod,*	*sout-cif*	*wel*
eat	CLF	chicken.claw	past.few-CLF:occurrence	1SG

danx.daul	*aod-biank*	*neind*	*nonx.*	*Ix*	*mex*
always	one-CLF:side	this	eat	NEG$_1$	exist

naonb,	*aod-hnef*	*dox*	*wel*	*aod*	*ghab*	*ghad,*
what	one-CLF:day	that	1SG	as.soon.as	bite	then$_2$

aod-minl	*aoh,*	*zhaux*	*xed*	*naont.*	*Aos.il,*
KIN-mother	PART	be.in.agony	tooth	thus	DSMY$_2$

daob.bieid	*nanx*	*npof*	*nzheub*	*baont.jaonx.*
head	only	desire	pound	wall

'That day I just ate a chicken foot, and the past few times I've always used this side of my mouth [i.e. the one with the problematic tooth] to eat. I never had any problems, but then that day, as soon as I bit down, man, my tooth was in agony. My God, it hurt so bad that I just wanted to bang my head against the wall.'

Chenghua:	*Nins*	*nchaot*	*yoh?*
	COP	stick.in	QP.NTRL

'Did the chicken foot get stuck in the hole?'

Haili:	*Ix*	*nins*	*nchaot,*	*beul*	*doub*	*nins*	*aod*
	NEG$_1$	COP	stick.in	3	then$_1$	COP	as.soon.as

naont,	*aod*	*ghab*	*beul*	*doub*	*naonb.nex*
thus	as.soon.as	bite	3	then$_1$	seem

zhut	*aod-ghoub*	*sheinf.jind*	*dox*	*lah.*
reach	one-CLF:flexible.length	nerve	that	PRF

'It didn't get stuck in, it was just that as soon as I bit down it was like I'd hit the nerve in my tooth.'

Shixiang: *Nh.*
uh.huh
'Uh-huh.'

Haili: *Naont beul mb guaot, naont doub aod-hmaont*
thus 3 hurt pass thus then$_1$ one-CLF:evening

dox deit raut deb, fanx.zheinb deit taf
that still good DIM anyway still endure

dut, yul aod-hmaont leh, mb guaot.
obtain again one-CLF:evening LEH hurt pass

Mb, fanx.zheinb beul yab jix nanb mb
hurt anyway 3 also NEG$_1$ really hurt

zhax, beul mb njut mb njut, aod-gaol
strong 3 hurt throb hurt throb one-CLF:thick.sheet

bieid naont njut, njut njut njut.
head thus throb throb throb throb
'So it really hurt, but by the evening it was a little better, at least I was able to bear it. But the evening after that, it really hurt. Well, it hurt, but anyway it didn't hurt all *that* bad. It was a throbbing pain, that whole side of my head was just throbbing and throbbing.'

Shixiang: *Qaonb.naont nex kox.ix bux donb, nex kox.ix*
in.that.case NEX can fill.in hole NEX can

heut nbaod.
help fill.in
'In that case you could have someone fill in the hole, have someone fill it in for you.'[236]

236 The forms *bux* 'to fill in' and *donb* 'hole' are simply the Xong pronunciations of Sinitic forms with the same meanings (these forms are pronounced *bǔ* and *dòng* in Standard Mandarin). The more "native" Xong equivalents (which also occur frequently in this text) are *nbaod* 'to fill in' and *khauk* 'hole', though these forms may themselves merely be older, less transparent borrowings from Sinitic. Similar alternations between more "native" Xong forms and the Xong pronunciations of synonymous Sinitic forms can be found throughout this text.

Haili: *Bux donb wel niel. Wel ghad jix monl*
fill.in hole 1SG know 1SG then$_2$ NEG$_1$ go

nbaod. Wel at niab del beul gint diul
fill.in 1SG SAT say let 3 rot complete

khad, wel nhex sheub.
dry 1SG pull.out leave
'I know that I could get it filled in. But I'm not going to do it. I say just let it rot, and then I'll have it pulled out.'

Chenghua: *Nex niab geud nhex sheub yol dions*
NEX say hold pull.out leave again plant

del manx xanb nins aod.sheit raut.
CLF:rigid.length REL new COP the.same good
'They say you can have it pulled out and then put a new tooth in, and the new tooth will be just as good as your old one.'

Haili: *Nins aod.sheit, yaox?*
COP the.same right?
'It'll be just as good, huh?'

Chenghua: *Yab ix mb. Dand geud-zheit aod-del*
also NEG$_1$ hurt arrive place$_1$-back one-CLF:rigid.length

reux manh, dions aod-del,
lifetime PART plant one-CLF:rigid.length

aod-del reux manh.
one-CLF:rigid.length lifetime PART
'And it doesn't hurt, either. Afterward it'd last your whole life, if you put in a new tooth, for your whole life.'

Haili: *Naont wel ghad del beul niab, del baol*
thus 1SG then$_2$ let 3 say let break.down

diul khad. Naont sox.ix aod-hmaont dox taf
complete dry thus so one-CLF:evening that endure

jix dut, aos.il, beut naont ngeinb.shib
NEG$_1$ obtain DSMY$_2$ lie.down thus no.matter.what

npof nggueb guaot. Beut, beut jix dut.
desire sleep pass lie.down lie.down NEG$_1$ obtain

Tit-deb wel doub geud shand giaot naont
CLF:time$_3$-DIM 1SG then$_1$ hold ginger chew thus

wel doub nggueb dut. Ranf.houb nieux-hnef
1SG then$_1$ sleep obtain afterward yester-CLF:day

nex heut wel nieus banb nggaob, yab
NEX help 1SG buy CLF:some medicine also

nins … yab nins aod-zhonx faonk.faof dox.
COP also COP one-CLF:kind$_3$ method that

Shib jix raut, yaox?
it's NEG$_1$ good right?
'Then I'll just let it rot. So, that evening I couldn't bear the pain. God, I was lying there and I wanted to fall asleep so badly, but I just couldn't. So after a while I chewed some ginger, and then I was finally able to fall asleep. And then, yesterday he [i.e. my husband] bought some medicine for me. It was…it was the same kind as before. It's no good, right?'

Shixiang: *Nh.*
uh.huh
'Uh-huh.'

Haili: *Shif.jek gaons banb nggaob. Hmaont-dius wel*
PN give CLF:some medicine evening-??? 1SG

at gox oub-cif deit jix raut,
SAT do two-CLF:occurrence still NEG$_1$ good

tit-deb wel eit hnant boub bioud ngonl
CLF:time$_3$-DIM 1SG still call 1PL home CLF:animate

heut wel guaox deb shand, wel geud giaot
help 1SG peel DIM ginger 1SG hold chew

zhut dox. Diex aod-hmaont at jix mb.
reach that finish one-CLF:evening SAT NEG$_1$ hurt
'It was medicine from Shi Je [the dentist]. That evening I used the medicine twice but it still wasn't working, so after a while I asked my husband to peel some ginger for me. I chewed it near my bad tooth, and then it didn't hurt for the whole evening.'

Shixiang: *It, at jix diaos shand raut.*
SPRS SAT NEG$_1$ catch.up.to ginger good
'Huh, the medicine isn't as good as ginger.'

Haili: *Aod-hmaont at jix mb, ranf.houb wel*
one-CLF:evening SAT NEG$_1$ hurt afterward 1SG

doub wel hanf khauk shand dox,
then$_1$ 1SG hold.in.mouth CLF:place$_2$ ginger that

hanf dand mieins, naont aod tout
hold.in.mouth arrive bright thus as.soon.as pick.up

sheub leh, tit-deb yab hnaond
leave LEH CLF:time$_3$-DIM also feel

houd-houd-deb diul.
CLF:mouthful-CLF:mouthful-DIM complete
'It didn't hurt the whole evening, since after that I just held the ginger in my mouth until dawn. But as soon as I took the ginger out, after a little while it started to hurt a little again.'

Chenghua: *Naont monx at sheib, yol hnef*
thus 2SG SAT able.to again CLF:day

monx at sheib nggaob, monx at
2SG SAT able.to medicine 2SG SAT

daut-leb zhut beul, lis nieus nggaob
REFL-CLF cure 3 want buy medicine

hauk-naonb?
do-what
'So now you can – from now on you know how to treat it, you can just treat it yourself. So what do you need to buy medicine for?'

Shixiang: *Daut-leb zhaut yaox?*
REFL-CLF cure right?
'Just treat it yourself, right?'

Haili: *Wel niab at ... wel nbanx niab nieus nex*
1SG say SAT 1SG think say buy NEX

naond manx ... ghaod kueb.souf deb lah.
ASSOC um... more fast DIM PRF
'I'd say...I think that buying their, um...it might be a little bit quicker.'

Chenghua: *Tief.xok.yok haf deit nins baod-dauk-leb*
high.quality.medicine still still COP BUG-REFL-CLF

naond aod-banb dox, ux Hex yaox?
ASSOC one-CLF:some that and PN right?
'The best medicine is still that stuff of your own, isn't that right, He [i.e. Haili]?'

Shixiang: *Nianl-seinb eit jix diaos toux.faonk.faol*
know-live still NEG$_1$ catch.up.to traditional.method

raut yaox?
good right?
'Now you've learned that [modern medicine] still isn't as good as the old folk remedies, huh?'

Haili: *Ranf.houb bid-ghaond wel ix dut shaod.*
afterward FRT-garlic 1SG NEG$_1$ obtain try

Doub nins shand leh. Shand ghaod
then$_1$ COP ginger LEH ginger more

raut deb. Dib-hnef fanx.zheinb beul ... jud
good DIM LOC-day anyway 3 NEG$_2$

niel nins ink.qib teb zhonb
know COP cold.and.wet.weather too heavy

haf.shib nins hauk-naonb, yaox? Hmaont-dius
or.INT COP do-what right? evening-???

doub ngeinb.shib lis ghaod mb,
then$_1$ no.matter.what want more hurt

dib-hnef beul jix anb mb.
LOC-day 3 NEG$_1$ really hurt
'Afterward I didn't try the garlic, I just stuck with ginger. The ginger was a little better. Anyway, during the day it...I don't know if it's because the weather's been so cold and wet lately or what, right? It always hurts more in the evening. During the day it doesn't hurt all that much.'

Shixiang: *Nh.*
uh.huh
'Uh-huh.'

Haili: *Yab nins mex deb hox.qib leh. Geud-neul*
also COP exist DIM internal.heat LEH place$_1$-front

aod-hmaont manx Meik.jinb nex nonx
one-CLF:evening REL PN NEX eat

niax-guoud wel ix lot haond monl
meat-dog 1SG NEG$_1$ descend bottom go

giat nex nonx manx mieil. Wel deib
share NEX eat REL spicy 1SG at

Huaonf.yef.lib	*nex*	*giat*	*nex*	*shaod*	*deb*
PN	NEX	share	NEX	try	DIM

manx	*ix*	*mieil*	*naond.*
REL	NEG_1	spicy	ASSOC

'Also, I tend to have a bit too much internal heat. The night before my tooth started hurting, when Mei Jin's family was having dog meat, I didn't go down [from the school where I live] to her home to eat spicy food [as I knew the dog meat would be]. I went to Huaon Ye Li's home instead to eat some non-spicy food.' [237]

Shixiang: *Nh.*
uh.huh
'Uh-huh.'

Haili:

Shaod	*zhus*	*tit-deb,*	*beinx.lef*	*bix*	*neind*
try	suffer	CLF:$time_3$-DIM	originally	CLF:$place_1$	this

at	*jef.baok*	*at*	*raut,*	*shaod*	*zhus*
SAT	scab.over	SAT	good	try	suffer

tit-deb	*yab*	*mb*	*lah.*
CLF:$time_3$-DIM	also	hurt	PRF

'A little while after – originally this spot here [at the corner of my mouth] had already scabbed over and was doing ok, but a little while after I ate it was hurting again.'

Shixiang:

Yab	*mb.*
also	hurt

'So it was hurting again.'

Haili:

At	*nins*	*hox.qib.*
SAT	COP	internal.heat

'It's all because of this internal heat of mine.'

Shixiang:

Naont	*keinx.dinb*	*nins*	*shaonb.hox,*	*yaox?*
thus	definitely	COP	have.one's.internal.heat.flare.up	right?

'So it must have been that your internal heat flared up, right?'

Haili: *Nh.*
uh.huh
'Uh-huh.'

---

237 The *hox.qib*, or 'internal heat', mentioned in this utterance is a concept from traditional Chinese medicine. Excessive internal heat is said to be the cause of a very wide variety of ailments, including in some cases dental problems. The Standard Mandarin term for the concept is *huǒqì* (火气), and the Xong term *hox.qib* is a borrowing of either this Mandarin form or a cognate form from another Sinitic variety.

Chenghua: *Hat doul leb zeib raut naond faonk.faob.*
still remain CLF most good ASSOC method
'There's still an even better way.'

Haili: *Hat doul nins naonb?*
still remain COP what
'What's that?'

Chenghua: *Geud ngank.nex.jinb jis jeud.*
hold metamizole soak alcohol
'Soak some metamizole [a painkilling/fever-reducing drug] in alcohol.'

Shixiang: *Jis jeud?*
soak alcohol
'Soak it in alcohol?'

Chenghua: *And.hand. Manx ... zhix.tonb.pianb.*
uh.huh um... painkiller
'Uh-huh. It's a, um...painkiller.'

Haili: *Nex kox.ix geud couf, geud couf, yab*
NEX can hold vinegar hold vinegar also

yul gox naonb dat, kox.ix.
again do what truly can
'They can take vinegar, take vinegar and then mix it with some other thing, really.'

Chenghua: *Geud zhix.tonb.pianb jis jeud, naont doub*
hold painkiller soak alcohol thus then$_1$

aod nbaod, nbaod leb khauk-khauk dox
as.soon.as fill.in fill.in CLF hole-RED that

aod nbaod, naonb.naont, beul sat raut,
as.soon.as fill.in thus 3 SAT good

kox.ix raut dut aod-gul-yaonl-hnef, danb.shib beul
can good obtain one-ten-more-CLF:day but 3

sheib yol faos.zof. Ix det chot.
able.to again flare.up NEG$_1$ break root.of.problem
'Take a painkiller soaked in alcohol, then as soon as you stick it in, as soon as you stick it into that hole in your tooth, then, it'll feel fine, it'll be good for two weeks or so. But the pain will eventually flare up again. You won't have dealt with the root of the problem.'

Haili:

Naont	*banb*	*neind*	*nins*	*monx*	*ob-xed*	*chauk.*
thus	CLF:some	this	COP	2SG	NOM-tooth	do

'So the problem is with your tooth itself.'[238]

Chenghua:

Monx	*at*	*konk*	*ginb.*	*Monx*	*gaons*	*nex*	*geud*
2SG	SAT	burrow	bug	2SG	give	NEX	hold

naonb	*ah?*	*Nex*	*yux.sid-Xonb,*	*nex*	*mex*
what	PART	NEX	traditional.doctor-Miao	NEX	exist

aod-zhonx	*manx*	*niab*	*nggaob*	*chauk*	*naont,*
one-CLF:kind$_3$	REL	say	medicine	do	thus

geud	*ub,*	*ub,*	*nianl*	*nins*	*ub*	*aob-naonb,*
hold	burn	burn	know	COP	burn	NOM-what

ub	*id-jeut-jeut.mos,*	*naont*	*doub,*	*hot*	*sut,*
burn	DID-RED-fragrant[239]	thus	then$_1$	rapidly	smoke

naont	*hant*	*daob-ginb*	*doub*	*zhaok*	–
thus	CLF:PL	AN-bug	then$_1$	fall	

'You've got bugs in your teeth. So what do you have them use to treat it? The traditional doctors, they have a kind of medicine that works like this. They take it and they burn it, they burn it, who knows what they burn it with, but they burn it until it's nice and fragrant. Then they quickly smoke [the patient's mouth with it], and it makes the bugs fall –'

Shixiang:

Naont	*hant*	*daob-ginb*	*doub*	*zhaok*	*bionl*	*yaox?*
thus	CLF:PL	AN-bug	then$_1$	fall	exit	right?

'So then the bugs just fall out, right?'

Chenghua:

Anh.	*Zhaok*	*zhut*	*aob-beinf,*	*wel*	*dut*	*ghans*
uh.huh	fall	reach	NOM-basin	1SG	obtain	see

nex	*chauk.*	*Chanf*	*daos.*
NEX	do	gross	die

'Uh-huh. They fall into a basin, I've seen them do it before. It's so gross.'

---

238 The speaker (Haili) is here using *monx* '2SG' in a generic sense; it is not the case that the topic of conversation has suddenly switched to the addressee's (Chenghua's) teeth.

239 Note the unusual reduplication of the first syllable of the verb *jeut.mos* 'fragrant' here. While it is quite common for monosyllabic Xong verbs to undergo reduplication (see Section 10.5.4), this reduplication of the first syllable of a disyllabic verb is otherwise unattested in the author's corpus. The author suspects that the unusual reduplication here is an indication that *jeut.mos* 'fragrant' is actually (or at least was originally) a dimorphemic form, though the meaning of each of the form's component syllables is currently completely opaque to both the author and his consultants.

Haili:

Mex	*daob-ginb*	*dat,*	*aoh?*
exist	AN-bug	truly	PART

'There were really bugs, huh?'

Chenghua:

Nh.
uh.huh

'Uh-huh.'

Haili:

Wel	*nbanx*	*niab*	*jix*	*mex*	*daob-ginb.*
1SG	think	say	NEG$_1$	exist	AN-bug

'I don't think there are really bugs in people's teeth.'

Chenghua:

Daont	*khauk*	*keinx.dinb*	*nins*	*mex*
pass.through	hole	definitely	COP	exist

daob-ginb.
AN-bug

'If there's a hole in your tooth, then you've definitely got a bug.'

Haili:

Naont	*aoh?*
thus	PART

'That's how it is?'

Chenghua:

Ix	*daont*	*khauk*	*ghad*	*ix*	*mex.*
NEG$_1$	pass.through	hole	then$_2$	NEG$_1$	exist

Wel	*mex*	*del*	*at*	*daont.*
1SG	exist	CLF:rigid.length	SAT	pass.through

'If there's no hole, then there's no bug. I've got a tooth that's got a hole in it too.'

Haili:

Daont	*khauk*	*wel*	*nbanx*	*niab*	*nins*
pass.through	hole	1SG	think	say	COP

manx ...	*ob-xed*	*jaod*	*chauk,*	*baod-dauk-leb*	–
um...	NOM-tooth	bad	do	BUG-REFL-CLF	

beul	*hant*	*yaof-zhif*	*jix*	*raut,*	*aod*
3	CLF:PL	tooth-quality	NEG$_1$	good	one

yaof	*manx*	*zhif,*	*ghaob-xed*	*naond*	*hant*
tooth	???	quality	NOM-tooth	ASSOC	CLF:PL

naond yaof-zhif jix diaos nex ghaod
ASSOC tooth-quality NEG$_1$ catch.up.to NEX more

ngeinb.
hard
'If there's a hole in my tooth, I think it's because, um...because the tooth was just bad, itself. These teeth of mine aren't very good, my – um – my tooth quality, the quality of my teeth, they're just not as sturdy as other people's.'[240]

Shixiang: *Nqat deit nins mex daob-ginb.*
fear still COP exist AN-bug
'I'm afraid it still might be that you've got a bug.'

Haili: *Naont nex, wel hnaond nex puk niab*
thus NEX 1SG hear NEX speak say

ghaob-xed jix nins ... puk daob-ginb,
NOM-tooth NEG$_1$ COP speak AN-bug

shif.jib.shaonb nins monx daut-leb ob-xed
in.reality COP 2SG REFL-CLF NOM-tooth

zhif.liaonb jaod.
quality bad
'So I've heard people say that teeth aren't...when you're talking about bugs, in reality it's just that your teeth themselves are bad.'

Chenghua: *Ix.*
NEG$_1$
'No.'

Haili: *Shif.jib.shaonb daod dib yab mex daob-ginb?*
in.reality place$_3$ which also exist AN-bug
'Seriously, how could you possibly have bugs in your teeth?'

240 This particular utterance contains several unusual grammatical structures, including a numeral directly preceding a noun with no intervening classifier (*aod yaof* [one tooth]), a form *manx* (homophonous, at least, with *manx* 'REL') apparently functioning as something like a possessive marker (*yaof manx zhif* [tooth ??? quality] 'quality of teeth'), and two instances of *naond* 'ASSOC' occurring within a single possessive construction (*ghaob-xed naond hant naond yaof-zhif* [NOM-tooth ASSOC CLF:PL ASSOC tooth-quality] 'quality of teeth'). However, the significance of these unusual structures should not be overestimated. The speaker (Haili) appeared to the author to be somewhat stumbling over her words here, and she later reported that she misspoke at several points in the utterance in question. Furthermore, every time the utterance was replayed for Haili and the other two participants in the conversation (Chenghua and Shixiang) for purposes of analysis, all three consultants would invariably burst into laughter at Haili's (self-admittedly) awkward phrasing.

Chenghua: *Boub dut ghans nex, sut, nanb liax*
1PL obtain see NEX smoke really resemble

nins nex, nanb liax nins ... ub
COP NEX really resemble COP burn

shut bid.deux ub naonb, yaox? Bionl –
sesame or burn what right? exit

geud aob-beinf-aub dis, naont ghans liaob
hold NOM-basin-water catch thus see drip.out

zhut aub nhaons-ndaub, nanb ghans ghans hliof.
reach water inside-place$_4$ really see see many
'We've seen him, smoke – it was just like he was – just like he was... burning sesame or something, right? And out they came – and he caught them in a basin full of water. So out they dripped into the water. We saw a ton of them.'

Shixiang: *Saut nex niab bionl ginb dant yaox?*
smoke NEX say exit bug truly right?
'He said that you can really smoke the bugs out, huh?'

Haili: *Sut ghaod.lot aoh?*
smoke mouth PART
'So they smoke your mouth out?'

Chenghua: *Sut aob-ntiot nex nins ub aob-naonb*
smoke NOM-smoke NEX COP burn NOM-what

gaons sut ntiot.
give smoke smoke
'When he's making the smoke, who knows what he's burning to do it.'[241]

Haili: *Naont shib sut ghat ghaod.lot nhaons-ndaub?*
thus it's smoke go.to mouth inside-place$_4$
'So they blow the smoke into your mouth?'

Chenghua: *Nanb, deit.naonb nex ub ninb daox.doub*
INTJ like.this NEX burn at earth

naont yaox? Monx jeub geud deib ghaod.lot,
thus right? 2SG then$_3$ hold facing mouth

241 The form *ntiot* can function as a noun meaning 'smoke' or as a verb meaning 'smoky' (see Section 1.2.2 for more on porous lexical category boundaries in Xong). The form *sut* (or *saut* for certain consultants) is a verb meaning 'to smoke out, to blow smoke into/against'.

ghaod.lot doub zhaok monl. Dis
mouth then$_1$ fall go catch

aob-kaok, yaox? Aob-kaok nggut nhaons-ndaub.
NOM-scent right? NOM-scent enter inside-place$_4$

Naont doub hot zhaok hot zhaok
thus then$_1$ rapidly fall rapidly fall

hot zhaok.
rapidly fall
'Okay, look – so he's burning the stuff on the ground like this, right? Then you put your mouth up against the smoke, and then open it. So you can catch the smoke, right? The smoke goes into your mouth. And then the bugs just come pouring and pouring and pouring out.'

Shixiang: *Zhaok hant ub-niub naont doub choud zhaok.*
fall CLF:PL water-lip thus then$_1$ follow fall
'So the saliva drips out of your mouth, and the bugs drip out with it.'

Chenghua: *Hant aub-niub zhaok daob-ginb lot*
CLF:PL water-lip fall AN-bug descend

aob-beinf nhaons-ndaub.
NOM-basin inside-place$_4$
'The saliva drops the bugs into the basin.'

Haili: *Aod-minl-nek.*
KIN-mother-mother
'My God.'[242]

Chenghua: *Anb chanf chanf.*
really gross gross
'It's super gross.'

Haili: *Monx sheib hant dox aoh?*
2SG able.to CLF:PL that PART
'Can't you do it yourself?'

242 See Section 5.3.2 for information on the differences between *minl* 'mother' and *nek* 'mother', and see Section 11.3.5 for more information on the interjection *aod-minl-nek* in general.

Chenghua: *Wel ix sheib. Nex dut bud wel. Wel*
1SG NEG$_1$ able.to NEX obtain tell 1SG 1SG

ix mex sheib.
NEG$_1$ exist able.to
'I can't. They just told me about it. I can't do it myself.'

Haili: *Naont wel danx.daul jix mb, nins*
thus 1SG always NEG$_1$ hurt COP

hmaont dox giaot zhus.
CLF:evening that chew suffer
'But my tooth never hurt before, it was just that night that I bit into a chicken foot.'

Shixiang: *Naont nqat deit jix nins, jix nins*
thus fear still NEG$_1$ COP NEG$_1$ COP

daob-ginb, yaox? Jud nianl nins daob-ginb jix
AN-bug right? NEG$_2$ know COP AN-bug NEG$_1$

nins.
COP
'Then maybe it's not that, it's not bugs after all, right? We don't know if it's bugs or not.'

Haili: *Jaox.ruf nins daob-ginb naont inb.gek ...*
if COP AN-bug thus should
'If it really was bugs, then it should...'

Shixiang: *Nins daob-ginb at inb.gek jink.chaond mb,*
COP AN-bug SAT should often hurt

yaox?
right?
'If it really was bugs, then your tooth should often hurt, right?'

Haili: *Wel aod-khauk dox wel baol, doul leb*
1SG one-CLF:place$_2$ that 1SG break.down remain CLF

baod-jonx-jonx, yul hnef zheinx.bif niab lis
BUG-root-RED again CLF:day prepare say want

nex sheub.
NEX leave
'That tooth of mine is broken, there's only a little bit of the root left. One of these days I'm going to have them take it out.'

Shixiang:	*Mx*	*zheb*	*beul*	*sheub,*	*at*	*doul*	*leb*
	2SG	pull.out	3	leave	SAT	remain	CLF

baod-jonx-jonx,	*zheb*	*beul*	*sheub*	*ghad*
BUG-root-RED	pull.out	3	leave	$then_2$

dianx,	*yaox?*
finish	right?

'You should just get it taken out. If there's only a little bit of the root left, just get it taken out and then you'll be done with it, right?'

References

Ameka, Felix K. 2001. "Ideophones and the nature of the adjective word class in Ewe." In *Ideophones*, F. K. Erhard Voeltz and Christa Kilian-Hatz (eds.), 25–48. Amsterdam: John Benjamins Publishing Company.

Arcodia, Giorgia Francesco. 2014. "The Chinese adjective as a word class." In *Word Classes*, Raffaele Simone and Francesca Massini (eds.), 1–29. Amsterdam: John Benjamins Publishing Company.

Atkinson, Quentin D. 2011. "Phonemic diversity supports a serial founder effect model of language expansion from Africa." *Science* 332 (6027): 346–349.

Author unknown. 1985. *Xiangxi Miaoyu Wenxuan [Selected Xiangxi Miao Texts]*. Beijing: Department of Minority Languages and Literature, Minzu University of China.

Bender, Emily. 2000. "The syntax of Mandarin *bǎ*: Reconsidering the verbal analysis." *Journal of East Asian Linguistics* 9 (2): 105–145.

Bisang, Walter. 1999. "Classifiers in East and Southeast Asian languages: Counting and beyond." In *Numeral Types and Changes Worldwide*, Jadranka Gvozdanović (ed.), 113–185. Berlin: De Gruyter Mouton.

Boeckx, Cedric. 2003. *Linguistic Minimalism: Origins, Concepts, Methods, and Aims.* Oxford: Oxford University Press.

Bowern, Claire. 2008. *Linguistic Fieldwork: A Practical Guide*. New York: Palgrave Macmillan.

Bradley, David. 1980. "Phonological convergence between languages in contact: Mon-Khmer structural borrowing in Burmese." In *Proceedings of the Sixth Annual Meeting of the Berkeley Linguistics Society*, Bruce R. Caron (ed.), 259–267. Berkeley: Berkeley Linguistics Society.

Bradley, David. 2005. "Language policy and language endangerment in China." *International Journal of the Sociology of Language* 173: 1–21.

Bradley, David. 2006. "Endangered languages of China and South-East Asia." In *Language Diversity in the Pacific: Endangerment and Survival*, Denis Cunningham, David E. Ingram, and Kenneth Sumbuk (eds.), 112–120. Clevedon, UK: Multilingual Matters.

Brown, Lea, and Matthew S. Dryer. 2008. "The verbs for 'and' in Walman, a Torricelli language of Papua New Guinea." *Language* 84 (3): 528–565.

Bulag, Uradyn E. 2003. "Mongolian ethnicity and linguistic anxiety in China." *American Anthropologist* 105 (4): 753–764.

Chafe, Wallace (ed.). 1980. *The Pear Stories: Cognitive, Cultural, and Linguistic Aspects of Narrative Production*. Norwood, NJ: Ablex.

Chao, Yuen Ren. 1930. "A system of tone-letters." *Le Maître Phonétique* 45: 24–27.

Chappell, Hilary. 2006. "From Eurocentrism to Sinocentrism: The case of disposal constructions in Sinitic languages." In *Catching Language: The Standing Challenge of Grammar Writing*, Felix Ameka, Alan Dench, and Nicholas Evans (eds.), 441–486. Berlin: De Gruyter Mouton.

Chen, Hong. 2009. "Guizhou Songtao Daxing Zhen Miaoyu yanjiu [A study of the Miao variety spoken in Daxing Town, Songtao County, Guizhou Province]." Ph.D. dissertation, Department of Literature, Nankai University.

Chen, Qiguang. 1993. "Miao-Yaoyu qianzhui [Prefixes in Miao-Yao]." *Minzu Yuwen* 1993 (1): 1–7.

Chen, Qiguang. 1998. "Miao-Yao yuzu yuyan yanjiu [Research on the languages of the Miao-Yao branch]." In *Ershi Shiji de Zhongguo Shaoshu Minzu Yuyan Yanjiu [Research on China's Minority Languages in the Twentieth Century]*, Qingxia Dai (ed.), 99–165. Shanghai: Shanghai Chubanshe.

Chen, Qiguang. 2001. "Banayu gaikuang [A sketch of Bana]." *Minzu Yuwen* 2001 (2): 69–81.

Chen, Qiguang. 2013. *Miao-Yao Yuwen [Miao and Yao Language* [sic]]. Beijing: Zhongyang Minzu Daxue Chubanshe.

Comrie, Bernard. 1998. "Rethinking the typology of relative clauses." *Language Design* 1: 59–86.
Corbett, Greville G. 2013. "Number of genders." In *The World Atlas of Language Structures Online*, Matthew S. Dryer and Martin Haspelmath (eds.), Chapter 30. Munich: Max Planck Digital Library. Available online at http://wals.info/chapter/30.
Court, Christopher. 1985. "Fundamentals of Iu Mien (Yao) grammar." Ph.D. dissertation, Department of Linguistics, University of California, Berkeley.
Culas, Christian, and Jean Michaud. 1997. "A contribution to the study of Hmong (Miao) migrations and history." *Bijdragen tot de Taal-, Land- en Volkenkunde* 153 (2): 211–243.
Dai, Qingxia, Zaibiao Yang, and Jinzhi Yu. 2005. "Yuyan jiechu yu yuyan yanbian: Xiaopoliu Miaoyu weili [Language contact and language change: Language contact & variation of Xiaopoliu Miao language [sic]]." *Yuyan Kexue* 4 (4): 3–10.
Dai, Qingxia, Jinzhi Yu, and Zaibiao Yang. 2005. "Xiaopoliu Miaoyu gaikuang [A sketch of Xiaopoliu Miao]." *Minzu Yuwen* 2005 (3): 68–81.
Daniel, Michael, and Edith Moravcsik. 2013. "The associative plural." In *The World Atlas of Language Structures Online*, Matthew S. Dryer and Martin Haspelmath (eds.), Chapter 36 Munich: Max Planck Digital Library. Available online at http://wals.info/chapter/36.
Diamond, Norma. 1995. "Defining the Miao: Ming, Qing, and contemporary views." In *Cultural Encounters on China's Ethnic Frontiers*, Stevan Harrell (ed.), 92–116. Seattle: University of Washington Press.
Dingemanse, Mark. 2012. "Advances in the cross-linguistic study of ideophones." *Language and Linguistics Compass* 6 (10): 654–672.
Dixon, R. M. W. 1972. *The Dyirbal Language of North Queensland*. Cambridge: Cambridge University Press.
Dixon, R. M. W. 2010a. *Basic Linguistic Theory, Vol. 1: Methodology*. Oxford: Oxford University Press.
Dixon, R. M. W. 2010b. *Basic Linguistic Theory, Vol. 2: Grammatical Topics*. Oxford: Oxford University Press.
Dixon, R. M. W. 2012. *Basic Linguistic Theory, Vol. 3: Further Grammatical Topics*. Oxford: Oxford University Press.
Dong, Hongqin (comp.). 1907. *Guzhangping Ting Zhi* [*Gazetteer of Guzhangping Sub-Prefecture*]. Other publication data unknown.
van Driem, George. 2005. "Sino-Austronesian vs. Sino-Caucasian, Sino-Bodic vs. Sino-Tibetan, and Tibeto-Burman as default theory." In *Contemporary Issues in Nepalese Linguistics*, Yogendra Prasada Yadava, Govinda Bhattarai, Ram Raj Lohani, Balaram Prasain, and Krishna Parajuli (eds.), 285–338. Kathmandu: Linguistic Society of Nepal.
Dryer, Matthew S. 2006. "Descriptive theories, explanatory theories, and basic linguistic theory." In *Catching Language: The Standing Challenge of Grammar Writing*, Felix Ameka, Alan Dench, and Nicholas Evans (eds.), 207–234. Berlin: De Gruyter Mouton.
Dryer, Matthew S. 2013a. "Coding of nominal plurality." In *The World Atlas of Language Structures Online*, Matthew S. Dryer and Martin Haspelmath (eds.), Chapter 33. Munich: Max Planck Digital Library. Available online at http://wals.info/chapter/33.
Dryer, Matthew S. 2013b. "Order of adjective and noun." In *The World Atlas of Language Structures Online*, Matthew S. Dryer and Martin Haspelmath (eds.), Chapter 87. Munich: Max Planck Digital Library. Available online at http://wals.info/chapter/87.
Dryer, Matthew S. 2013c. "Order of relative clause and noun." In *The World Atlas of Language Structures Online*, Matthew S. Dryer and Martin Haspelmath (eds.), Chapter 90. Munich: Max Planck Digital Library. Available online at http://wals.info/chapter/90.
Dryer, Matthew S. 2013d. "Determining dominant word order." In *The World Atlas of Language Structures Online*, Matthew S. Dryer and Martin Haspelmath (eds.), Chapter S6. Munich: Max Planck Digital Library. Available online at http://wals.info/chapter/s6.

Dryer, Matthew S., and Orin D. Gensler. 2013. "Order of object, oblique, and verb." In *The World Atlas of Language Structures Online*, Matthew S. Dryer and Martin Haspelmath (eds.), Chapter 84. Munich: Max Planck Digital Library. Available online at http://wals.info/chapter/84.

Eberhard, David M., Gary F. Simons, and Charles D. Fennig (eds.). 2019. *Ethnologue: Languages of Asia*. 22nd ed. Dallas: SIL International.

Enfield, N. J. 2005. "Areal linguistics and mainland Southeast Asia." *Annual Review of Anthropology* 34: 181–206.

Enfield, N. J. 2007. *A Grammar of Lao*. Berlin: De Gruyter Mouton.

Evans, Nicholas D. 1995. *A Grammar of Kayardild: With Historical-Comparative Notes on Tangkic*. Berlin: De Gruyter Mouton.

Fehri, Abdelkader Fassi, and Marie-Thérèse Vinet. 2008. "Verbal and nominal classes in Arabic and Chinese." *Recherches linguistiques de Vincennes* 37: 55–83.

Feng, Xianghong. 2008. "Economic and socio-cultural impacts of tourism development in Fenghuang County, China." Ph.D. dissertation, Department of Anthropology, Washington State University.

Gerner, Matthias. 2003. "Demonstratives, articles, and topic markers in the Yi group." *Journal of Pragmatics* 35: 947–998.

Gerner, Matthias. 2009. "Deictic features of demonstratives: A typological survey with special reference to the Miao group." *Canadian Journal of Linguistics* 54 (1): 43–90.

Gerner, Matthias, and Walter Bisang. 2010. "Classifier declinations in an isolating language: On a rarity in Weining Ahmao." *Language and Linguistics* 11 (3): 579–623.

Gil, David. 2004. "Riau Indonesian *sama*: Explorations in macrofunctionality." In *Coordinating Constructions*, Martin Haspelmath (ed.), 371–424. Amsterdam: John Benjamins Publishing Company.

Gil, David. 2013. "Numeral classifiers." In *The World Atlas of Language Structures Online*, Matthew S. Dryer and Martin Haspelmath (eds.), Chapter 55. Munich: Max Planck Digital Library. Available online at http://wals.info/chapter/55.

Groves, Julie M. 2008. "Language or dialect – or topolect?: A comparison of the attitudes of Hong Kongers and mainland Chinese towards the status of Cantonese." *Sino-Platonic Papers* 179.

Guan, Xinqiu. 2006. "Xiangxi Miaoyu de *qo*^{35} [*qo*^{35} in Miao language of western Hunan [sic]]." *Zhongnan Minzu Daxue Xuebao (Renwen Shehui Kexue Ban)* 26 (3): 41–45.

Gumperz, John J., and Robert Wilson. 1971. "Convergence and creolization: A case from the Indo-Aryan/Dravidian border in India." In *Pidginization and Creolization of Languages*, Dell Hymes (ed.), 151–167. Cambridge: Cambridge University Press.

Haspelmath, Martin. 1993. *A Grammar of Lezgian*. Berlin: De Gruyter Mouton.

Haspelmath, Martin. 2006. "Against markedness (and what to replace it with)." *Journal of Linguistics* 42: 25–70.

Haspelmath, Martin. 2007. "Coordination." In *Language Typology and Syntactic Description (2nd Ed.), Vol. II: Complex Constructions*, Timothy Shopen (ed.), 1–51. Cambridge: Cambridge University Press.

Hay, Jennifer, and Laurie Bauer. 2007. "Phoneme inventory size and population size." *Language* 83 (2): 388–400.

He, Fuling. 2009. *Hunan Sheng Fenghuang Xian Hanyu Fangyan yu Miaoyu de Diaocha he Bijiao* [*A Survey and Comparison of the Chinese Dialect and Miao Language of Fenghuang County, Hunan Province*]. Changsha: Hunan Shifan Daxue Chubanshe.

Himmelmann, Nikolaus P., and D. Robert Ladd. 2008. "Prosodic description: An introduction for fieldworkers." *Language Documentation & Conservation* 2 (2): 244–274.

Hong, Yuqian. 2011. "Xiangxi Miaoyu zhuangmaoci yanjiu [A study of ideophones in Xiangxi Miao]." Master's thesis, National Taiwan Normal University.

Hu, Xiaodong. 2009. "Miao-Yaoyu de zaoqi laiyuan jiqi xishu [The early source of Miao and Yao languages and their families [sic]]." *Guizhou Minzu Xueyuan Xuebao (Zhexue Shehui Kexue Ban)* 2009 (5): 109–113.

Iggesen, Oliver A. 2013. "Number of cases." In *The World Atlas of Language Structures Online*, Matthew S. Dryer and Martin Haspelmath (eds.), Chapter 49. Munich: Max Planck Digital Library. Available online at http://wals.info/chapter/49.

Kaup, Katherine P. 2002. "Regionalism versus ethnicnationalism [sic] in the People's Republic of China." *The China Quarterly* 172: 863–884.

Keenan, Edward L., and Bernard Comrie. 1977. "Noun phrase accessibility and universal grammar." *Linguistic Inquiry* 8 (1): 63–99.

Kruspe, Nicole. 2004. *A Grammar of Semelai*. Cambridge: Cambridge University Press.

Ladefoged, Peter, and Ian Maddieson. 1996. *The Sounds of the World's Languages*. Oxford: Blackwell Publishing.

Lemoine, Jacques. 2005. "What is the actual number of the (H)mong in the world?" *Hmong Studies Journal* 6: 1–8.

Li, Charles N., and Sandra A. Thompson. 1976. "Subject and topic: A new typology of language." In *Subject and Topic*, Charles N. Li (ed.), 457–489. New York: Academic Press.

Li, Rong, Zhenghui Xiong, and Zhenxing Zhang (eds.). 1987. *Zhongguo Yuyan Ditu Ji* [*Linguistic Atlas of China*]. Hong Kong: Xianggang Langwen Chuban Youxian Gongsi.

Li, Yunbing. 2002. "Lun Miaoyu mingci qianzhui de gongneng [On the functions of nominal prefixes in Miao]." *Minzu Yuwen* 2002 (3): 32–42.

Li, Yunbing. 2003. "Miaoyu de xingtai jiqi yuyi yufa fanchou [Morphology in Miao and its semantic and grammatical scope]." *Minzu Yuwen* 2003 (3): 19–28.

Li, Yunbing. 2006. "Miao-Yaoyu de feifenxi xingtai jiqi leixingxue yiyi [Non-analytic morphology in Miao-Yao and its typological significance]." *Minzu Yuwen* 2006 (2): 31–41.

Li, Yunbing. 2007. "Lun Miao-Yaoyu mingci fanchouhua shouduan de leixing [On a typology of nominal classification methods in Miao-Yao]." *Minzu Yuwen* 2007 (1): 18–30.

Li, Yunbing. 2008. *Zhongguo Nanfang Minzu Yuyan Yuxu Leixing Yanjiu* [*A Cross-Linguistic Typology on Word Orders of Minority Languages in Southern China* [sic]]. Beijing: Beijing Daxue Chubanshe.

Liang, Feng. 2012. "Hunan Fenghuang Xian Shanjiang Miaoyu shengdiao shiyan [An experiment on the tones of the Miao variety spoken in Shanjiang Town, Fenghuang County, Hunan Province]." *Xiandai Yuwen* 2012 (3): 19, 20.

Ling, Chunsheng, and Yifu Rui. 2003. Reprint. *Xiangxi Miaozu Diaocha Baogao* [*An Ethnographic Report on the Miao People in the Xiangxi Area* [sic]]. 2nd ed. Beijing: Minzu Chubanshe. Original edition, Beijing: Shangwu Yinshuguan, 1947.

Liu, Chen-Sheng Luther. 2001. "Antilogophoricity, sympathy, and the antilogophor *renjia*." *Journal of East Asian Linguistics* 10 (4): 307–336.

Liu, Ziqi. 1982. "Miaozu gesheng Shi Bantang [The Miao poet Bantang Shi]." *Guizhou Minzu Yanjiu* 1982 (2): 142–148.

Long, Bingwen, and Xiuxiang Long. 1990. *Gulaohua: Dut Ghot Dut Yos* [*The Ancient Words: Dut Ghot Dut Yos*]. Changsha: Yuelu Shushe.

Long, Jie, and Zaibiao Yang. 2012. "Hunan Luxi Xiaozhang Miaoyu shengdiao shiyan [An experiment on the tones of the Miao variety spoken in Xiaozhang Township, Luxi County, Hunan Province]." *Yuwen Xuekan* 2012 (10): 13–15.

Long, Mingchun. 2011. "Fenghuang Xian Yangguang Cun Miaoyu yuyin kaocha [A phonological study of the Miao variety spoken in Yangguang Village, Fenghuang County]." *Sanxia Luntan* 2011 (6): 94, 95.

Long, Xiuhai. 2006a. *Songtao Miaozu Qingge Xuan (Shang)* [*Selected Love Songs of the Songtao Miao (Volume 1)*]. Beijing: Zuojia Chubanshe.

Long, Xiuhai. 2006b. *Songtao Miaozu Qingge Xuan (Xia)* [*Selected Love Songs of the Songtao Miao (Volume 2)*]. Beijing: Zuojia Chubanshe.

Long, Zhenghai. 2011. "Qianlun Xiangxi Gouliang Miaoyu de Hanyu jieci [On Chinese borrowing words of Miao language in Xiangxi Gouliang [sic]]." In *Xuexingtang Yuyan Wenzi Luncong (Di-Yi Juan)* [*Xuexingtang Linguistics Series (Vol. 1)*], Zhangying Deng (ed.). Chengdu: Sichuan Daxue Chubanshe.

Luo, Anyuan. 1980. "Guizhou Songtao Miaohua de guanci [Articles in the Miao variety spoken in Songtao County, Guizhou Province]." *Minzu Yuwen* 1980 (4): 28–35.

Luo, Anyuan. 1990. *Xiandai Xiangxi Miaoyu Yufa* [*Modern Xiangxi Miao Grammar*]. Beijing: Zhongyang Minzu Xueyuan Chubanshe.

Luo, Anyuan. 2002. "Cong liangci kan Miao-Han liang zhong yuyan de guanxi [Looking at the relation of Miao language and Han language from the classifier [sic]]." *Zhongyang Minzu Daxue Xuebao (Zhexue Shehui Kexue Ban)* 29 (5): 117–224.

Luo, Anyuan. 2005. *Songtao Miaohua Miaoxie Yufaxue* [*A Descriptive Grammar of Songtao Miao*]. Beijing: Zhongyang Minzu Daxue Chubanshe.

Lyman, Thomas A. 1979. *Grammar of Mong Njua (Green Miao): A Descriptive Linguistic Study.* Sattley, CA: The Blue Oak Press.

Maddieson, Ian. 2013a. "Consonant inventories." In *The World Atlas of Language Structures Online*, Matthew S. Dryer and Martin Haspelmath (eds.), Chapter 1. Munich: Max Planck Digital Library. Available online at http://wals.info/chapter/1.

Maddieson, Ian. 2013b. "Vowel quality inventories." In *The World Atlas of Language Structures Online*, Matthew S. Dryer and Martin Haspelmath (eds.), Chapter 2. Munich: Max Planck Digital Library. Available online at http://wals.info/chapter/2.

Mair, Victor H. 1991. "What is a Chinese 'dialect/topolect'?: Reflections on some key Sino-English linguistic terms." *Sino-Platonic Papers* 29.

Mao, Zongwu. 2004. *Yaozu Mianyu Fangyan Yanjiu* [*A Study of the Mian Dialects of the Yao People*]. Beijing: Minzu Chubanshe.

Mao, Zongwu, and Yunbing Li. 1997. *Bahengyu Yanjiu* [*A Study of Baheng*]. Shanghai: Shanghai Yuandong Chubanshe.

Mao, Zongwu, and Yunbing Li. 2007. *Younuoyu Yanjiu* [*A Study of Younuo*]. Beijing: Minzu Chubanshe.

Matisoff, James. 1973. *The Grammar of Lahu.* Berkeley: University of California Press.

Matsumoto, Yoshiko, Bernard Comrie, and Peter Sells. 2017. "Noun-modifying clause constructions in languages of Eurasia: Rethinking theoretical and geographical boundaries." In *Noun-Modifying Clause Constructions in Languages of Eurasia: Rethinking Theoretical and Geographical Boundaries*, Yoshiko Matsumoto, Bernard Comrie, and Peter Sells (eds.), 3–21. Amsterdam: John Benjamins Publishing Company.

Mayer, Mercer. 1981. *Frog, Where Are You?* New York: Dial Press.

Meng, Chenxi. 2012. "A description of ideophonic words in Mandarin Chinese." Master's thesis, Leiden University.

Michaud, Jean. 1997. "From southwest China into upper Indochina: An overview of Hmong (Miao) migrations." *Asia Pacific Viewpoint* 38 (2): 119–130.

Mortensen, David. 2003. "Hmong elaborate expressions are coordinate compounds." Unpublished ms. Available online at http://www.davidmortensen.org/papers/elaborate_expressions.pdf.

Mortensen, David. 2004. "The development of tone sandhi in Western Hmongic: A new hypothesis." Unpublished ms. Available online at http://www.davidmortensen.org/papers/development_whmongic_tone_sandhi.pdf.

Mortensen, David. 2006. "Logical and substantive scales in phonology." Ph.D. dissertation, Department of Linguistics, University of California, Berkeley.

Mosel, Ulrike. 2006. "Fieldwork and community language work." In *Essentials of Language Documentation*, Jost Gippert, Nikolaus P. Himmelmann, and Ulrike Mosel (eds.), 67–85. Berlin: De Gruyter Mouton.

Niederer, Barbara. 1998. *Les langues Hmong-Mjen (Miao-Yao): Phonologie historique* [*The Hmong-Mien (Miao-Yao) Languages: Historical Phonology*]. Munich: Lincom Europa.

Nuckolls, Janis B. 2001. "Ideophones in Pastaza Quechua." In *Ideophones*, F. K. Erhard Voeltz and Christa Kilian-Hatz (eds.), 271–285. Amsterdam: John Benjamins Publishing Company.

Peng, Feng. 2007. "Miaoyu xianzhuang yanjiu: Songtao Miaoyu shuxie gaige [Study on the current situation of Miao language: The reform in writing of Songtao Miao language [sic]]." *Tongren Xueyuan Xuebao* 2007 (1): 29–32.

Pollard, Carl, and Ivan A. Sag. 1994. *Head-Driven Phrase Structure Grammar.* Chicago: University of Chicago Press.

Poser, William J. 1992. "Blocking of phrasal constructions by lexical items." In *Lexical Matters*, Ivan Sag and Anna Szabolcsi (eds.), 111–130. Stanford: Center for the Study of Language and Information.

Prince, Alan, and Paul Smolensky. 2004. *Optimality Theory: Constraint Interaction in Generative Grammar.* Oxford: Blackwell Publishing.

Purnell, Herbert. 1970. "Toward a reconstruction of Proto-Miao-Yao." Ph.D. dissertation, Department of Linguistics, Cornell University.

Ratliff, Martha. 1998. "Ho Ne (She) is Hmongic: One final argument." *Linguistics of the Tibeto-Burman Area* 21 (2): 97–109.

Ratliff, Martha. 2006. "Prefix variation and reconstruction." In *Variation and Reconstruction*, Thomas D. Cravens (ed.), 165–178. Amsterdam: John Benjamins Publishing Company.

Ratliff, Martha. 2010. *Hmong-Mien Language History.* Canberra: Pacific Linguistics.

Ross, Malcolm. 1996. "Contact-induced change and the comparative method: Cases from Papua New Guinea." In *The Comparative Method Reviewed: Regularity and Irregularity in Language Change*, Mark Durie and Malcolm Ross (eds.), 180–217. Oxford: Oxford University Press.

Ross, Malcolm. 2001. "Contact-induced change in Oceanic languages in North-West Melanesia." In *Areal Diffusion and Genetic Inheritance: Problems in Comparative Linguistics*, Alexandra Y. Aikhenvald and R. M. W. Dixon (eds.), 134–166. Oxford: Oxford University Press.

Ross, Malcolm. 2007. "Calquing and metatypy." *Journal of Language Contact* 1 (1): 116–143.

Sagart, Laurent, Roger Blench, and Alicia Sanchez-Mazas. 2005. "Introduction." In *The Peopling of East Asia: Putting Together Archaeology, Linguistics, and Genetics*, Laurent Sagart, Roger Blench, and Alicia Sanchez-Mazas (eds.), 1–14. London: RoutledgeCurzon.

Schultz-Berndt, Eva. 2001. "Ideophone-like characteristics of uninflected predicates in Jaminjung (Australia)." In *Ideophones*, F. K. Erhard Voeltz and Christa Kilian-Hatz (eds.), 355–373. Amsterdam: John Benjamins Publishing Company.

Shi, Defu. 2004. "Miao-Yao minzu de zicheng jiqi yanbian [Autonyms of the Miao-Yao peoples and their evolution]." *Minzu Yuwen* 2004 (6): 22–28.

Shi, Dingxu. 2000. "Topic and topic-comment constructions in Mandarin Chinese." *Language* 76 (2): 383–408.

Shi, Qigui. 2002. Reprint. *Xiangxi Miaozu Shidi Diaocha Baogao* [*Report on a Field Survey of the Miao People of Xiangxi*]. 2nd ed. Changsha: Hunan Renmin Chubanshe. Original edition, Changsha: Hunan Renmin Chubanshe, 1986.

Shi, Rujin (comp.). 1997. *Miao-Han/Han-Miao Cidian: Xiangxi Fangyan* [*Miao-Chinese/Chinese-Miao Dictionary: Xiangxi Dialect*]. Changsha: Yuelu Shushe.

Simpson, Andrew Kingsbury. 2009. "The origin and development of nonconcatenative morphology." Ph.D. dissertation, Department of Linguistics, University of California, Berkeley.

Sposato, Adam. 2012. "Relative clauses in Xong (Xiangxi Miao)." *Journal of the Southeast Asian Linguistic Society (JSEALS)* 5: 49–66.

Sposato, Adam. 2014. "Word order in Miao-Yao (Hmong-Mien)." *Linguistic Typology* 18 (1): 83–140.
Stalin, Joseph. 1913. "Marxism and the national question." *Prosveshcheniye* 3–5.
Sumbuk, Kenneth M. 2002. "Morphosyntax of Sare." Ph.D. dissertation, Department of Linguistics, University of Waikato.
Taguchi, Yoshihisa. 2012a. "On the irrealis marker *sz*[55] in Hmyo." Handout from a presentation given at the 45th International Conference on Sino-Tibetan Languages and Linguistics. Nanyang Technological University, Singapore, October 2012.
Taguchi, Yoshihisa. 2012b. "On the phylogeny of the Hmong-Mien languages." Handout from a presentation given at the Conference in Evolutionary Linguistics 2012. Peking University, Beijing, November 2012.
Taguchi, Yoshihisa. 2013. "On the phylogeny of Hmongic languages." Handout from a presentation given at the 23rd Annual Meeting of the Southeast Asian Linguistics Society. Chulalongkorn University, Bangkok, May 2013.
Taguchi, Yoshihisa. 2015. "Myao-go no keetoo ni tsuite [On the phylogeny of Hmongic languages]." Handout from a presentation given at the 37th Meeting of the Tibeto-Burman Linguistics Study Group. Kobe Academic Park Association for the Promotion of Inter-University Research and Exchange, Kobe, December 2015.
Thompson, Laurence C. 1965. *A Vietnamese Grammar.* Seattle: University of Washington Press.
Tosco, Mauro. 1998. "A parsing view on inconsistent word order: Articles in Tigre and its relatives." *Linguistic Typology* 2: 355–380.
Trudgill, Peter. 2011. "Social structure and phoneme inventories." *Linguistic Typology* 15: 155–160.
Vendler, Zeno. 1957. "Verbs and times." *The Philosophical Review* 66 (2): 143–160.
Voeltz, F. K. Erhard, and Christa Kilian-Hatz (eds.). 2001. *Ideophones*. Amsterdam: John Benjamins Publishing Company.
Wang, Fushi (ed.). 1985. *Miaoyu Jianzhi [A Sketch of Miao]*. Beijing: Minzu Chubanshe.
Wang, Fushi, and Zongwu Mao. 1995. *Miao-Yaoyu Guyin Gouni [A Reconstruction of Proto-Miao-Yao]*. Beijing: Zhongguo Shehui Kexue Chubanshe.
Wang, Wei (comp.). 1739. *Qianzhou Zhi [Qianzhou Gazetteer]*. Other publication data unknown.
Wang, William Shiyuan, and Xiaohua Deng. 2003. "Miao-Yao yuzu yuyan de qinyuan guanxi de jiliang yanjiu: Ciyuan tongji fenxi fangfa [A quantitative study on the genetic relationship of Miao-Yao languages: The lexicostatistics approach [sic]]." *Zhongguo Yuwen* 2003 (3): 253–263.
Watson, Richard L. 2001. "A comparison of some Southeast Asian ideophones with some African ideophones." In *Ideophones*, F. K. Erhard Voeltz and Christa Kilian-Hatz (eds.), 385–405. Amsterdam: John Benjamins Publishing Company.
Wierzbicka, Anna. 1980. *Lingua Mentalis: The Semantics of Natural Language.* Sydney: Academic Press.
Wu, Bihui. 2007. "Hunan Sheng Fenghuang Xian Luochaojing Xiang Gouliang Cun Miaoyu yusu de chengci nengli yanjiu [A study of the word-formation abilities of morphemes in the Miao variety spoken in Gouliang Village, Luochaojing Township, Fenghuang County, Hunan Province]." Master's thesis, Hunan Normal University.
Wu, Xiuju. 2011. "Fenghuang Gouliang Miaoyu guanxi congju yanjiu [A study of relative clauses in the Miao variety spoken in Gouliang Village, Fenghuang County]." Master's thesis, Hunan University.
Wu, Zhengbiao, and Guangying Yang. 2010. "Mashan cifangyan qu Miaowen fang'an de sheji yu shiyong: Jiantan Miaozu yingxiong shishi *Yaluwang* de jiyi zhengli wenti [The design and implementation of a Miao orthography program for the Mashan sub-dialect area: With comments on issues in the transcription and translation of the Miao epic poem *Yaluwang*]." *Minzu Fanyi* 76: 58–65.
Xiang, Rizheng. 1980. "Miaoyu Xiangxi fangyan de citou *tɕi*[44] [The prefix *tɕi*[44] in Xiangxi Miao]." Minzu Yuwen 1980 (3): 29–31.

Xiang, Rizheng. 1983. "Xiangxi Miaoyu de sizi binglie jiegou [Tetrasyllabic coordinate constructions in Xiangxi Miao]." *Minzu Yuwen* 1983 (3): 26–32.

Xiang, Rizheng. 1992. "Xiangxi Miaowen [The Xiangxi Miao orthography]." In *Zhongguo Shaoshu Minzu Wenzi* [*Writing Systems of China's Ethnic Minorities*], The Ethnic Research Center of the Chinese Academy of Social Sciences and the Cultural Promotion Department of the National Committee on Ethnic Affairs (eds.), 165–169. Beijing: Zhongguo Zangxue Chubanshe.

Xiang, Rizheng. 1999. *Jiwei Miaoyu Yanjiu* [*A Study of Jiwei Miao*]. Chengdu: Sichuan Minzu Chubanshe.

Xiang, Rizheng (comp.). 1992. *Han-Miao Cidian: Xiangxi Fangyan* [*Chinese-Miao Dictionary: Xiangxi Dialect*]. Chengdu: Sichuan Minzu Chubanshe.

Yan, Ruyu. 1820. *Miao Fangbei Lan* [*On Repelling the Miao*]. Other publication data unknown.

Yang, Zaibiao. 2004. *Miaoyu Dongbu Fangyan Tuyu Bijiao* [*Comparative Dialectology of Eastern Miao*]. Beijing: Zhongyang Minzu Daxue Chubanshe.

Yang, Zaibiao. 2011. *Hunan Xibu Si Zhong Binwei Yuyan Diaocha* [*A Survey of Four Endangered Languages of Western Hunan*]. Beijing: Minzu Chubanshe.

Yang, Zaibiao, and Hongyuan Luo. 2008. "Xiangxi Miaozu minjian Miaowen zaozi tixi [On the folk coinage of characters of the Miao people in Xiangxi area [sic]]." *Jishou Daxue Xuebao (Shehui Kexue Ban)* 29 (6): 130–134.

Yang, Zaibiao, Xiaoling Bi, Xuemei Wu, and Jie Long. 2004. "Xiaomaopoying Miaoyu yinxi yu Dongmaku, Jiwei Miaoyu de bijiao [A phonological and phonetical comparison between Miao language in Xiao Maopo Village and Dong Maku, Ji Wei [sic]]." *Hubei Minzu Xueyuan Xuebao (Zhexue Shehui Kexue Ban)* 22 (1): 5–10.

Yu, Jinzhi. 2004. "Jishou Aizhai Miaoyu binglie fuhe mingci de jiegou he shengdiao tezheng [The structural and tonal characteristics of coordinate compound nouns in the Miao variety spoken in Aizhai Town, Jishou City]." *Minzu Yuwen* 2004 (1): 26–29.

Yu, Jinzhi. 2006. "Xiangxi Aizhai Miaoyu siyin geci yanjiu [Four-syllables structured words in Aizhai Miao language in West Hunan region [sic]]." *Zhongyang Minzu Daxue Xuebao (Zhexue Shehui Kexue Ban)* 2006 (3): 104–111.

Yu, Jinzhi. 2010. "Aizhai Miaoyu cankao yufa [A reference grammar of Aizhai Miao]." Ph.D. dissertation, Department of Minority Languages and Literature, Minzu University of China.

Yu, Jinzhi. 2011. *Xiangxi Aizhai Miaoyu Cankao Yufa* [*A Reference Grammar of Xiangxi Aizhai Miao Language* [sic]]. Beijing: Zhongguo Shehui Kexue Chubanshe.

Zhang, Yinghe, and Rongde Peng. 1987. *Miaozu Hunyin Lici: Ghob Xongb Dut Qub Dut Lanl* [*Wedding Songs of the Miao People: Ghob Xongb Dut Qub Dut Lanl*]. Changsha: Yuelu Shushe.

Zhao, Liming, and Ziqi Liu. 1990. "Xiangxi fangkuai Miaowen [Sinographic Xiangxi Miao scripts]." *Minzu Yuwen* 1990 (1): 44–49.

Zhao, Liming, and Ziqi Liu (comps., trans.). 1992. *Bantang Miaoge Xuan* [*Selected Bantang Miao Songs*]. Changsha: Yuelu Shushe.

Zhao, Yang. 2005. "Xiaomaopoying Cun Miaoyu xianzhuang yu bianqian touxi [An analysis on the current situation and change of Miao langnage in Xiaomaopoying Village [sic]]." *Hubei Minzu Xueyuan Xuebao (Zhexue Shehui Kexue Ban)* 23 (2): 18–22.

Zhou, Minglang. 2000. "Language policy and illiteracy in ethnic minority communities in China." *Journal of Multilingual and Multicultural Development* 21 (2): 129–148.

Zhou, Youguang. 1998. *Bijiao Wenzixue Chutan* [*An Introduction to Comparative Philology*]. Beijing: Yuwen Chubanshe.

Index

www.ingramcontent.com/pod-product-compliance
Lightning Source LLC
Chambersburg PA
CBHW060256240426
43661CB00060B/2802

* 9 7 8 3 1 1 1 0 8 7 6 2 7 *